D1561608

CLINICAL BIOFEEDBACK: EFFICACY AND MECHANISMS

CLINICAL BIOFEEDBACK: EFFICACY AND MECHANISMS

Edited by

LEONARD WHITE

Long Island Research Institute
Department of Psychiatry and Behavioral Science
State University of New York at Stony Brook

and

BERNARD TURSKY

Laboratory for Behavioral Research
Department of Political Science
State University of New York at Stony Brook

THE GUILFORD PRESS
New York, London

A Division of Guilford Publications, Inc.
200 Park Avenue South, New York, N.Y. 10003

Printed in the United States of America

LIBRARY OF CONGRESS CATALOGING IN PUBLICATION DATA

Main entry under title:

Clinical biofeedback.

Papers from the proceedings of an invitational research symposium held May 15–18, 1980, at the Health Sciences Center of the State University of New York at Stony Brook, sponsored jointly by the Dept. of Psychiatry and Behavioral Science and the Dept. of Political Science.

Includes bibliographies and indexes.

1. Biofeedback training—Congresses. I. White, Leonard. II. Tursky, Bernard. III. State University of New York at Stony Brook. Dept. of Psychiatry and Behavioral Science. IV. State University of New York at Stony Brook. Dept. of Political Science.

[DNLM: 1. Biofeedback—Psychology—Congresses. WL C6415 1980]

RC489.B53C56 615.8′51 81-1048

ISBN 0-89862-619-6 AACR2

CONTRIBUTORS

Henry E. Adams, PhD, Department of Psychology, University of Georgia, Athens, Georgia

Jackson Beatty, PhD, Department of Psychology and Brain Research Institute, The University of California at Los Angeles, Los Angeles, California

Edward B. Blanchard, PhD, Department of Psychology, State University of New York at Albany, Albany, New York

Phillip J. Brantley, PhD, Department of Psychology, Louisiana State University, Baton Rouge, Louisiana

Jasper M. Brener, PhD, Department of Psychology, University of Hull, Hull, England

Joseph Brudny, MD, Department of Rehabilitation Medicine, New York University Medical Center, Bellevue Hospital, New York, New York

Martin D. Cheatle, PhD, Department of Psychiatry, University of Pennsylvania, Philadelphia, Pennsylvania

Daniel J. Cox, PhD, Behavioral Medicine Center and Department of Behavioral Medicine and Psychiatry, University of Virginia Medical Center, Charlottesville, Virginia

John J. Furedy, PhD, Department of Psychology, University of Toronto, Toronto, Ontario, Canada

Robert J. Gatchel, PhD, Department of Psychiatry, University of Texas Health Sciences Center, Dallas, Texas

Iris Balshan Goldstein, PhD, Department of Psychiatry, School of Medicine, The University of California at Los Angeles, Los Angeles, California

Howard Haymes, EdD, Department of Psychiatry and Behavioral Science, School of Medicine, and Long Island Research Institute, State University of New York at Stony Brook, Stony Brook, New York

William Hobbs, MD, Behavioral Medicine Center and Department of Behavioral Medicine and Psychiatry, University of Virginia Medical Center, Charlottesville, Virginia

Beatrice C. Lacey, PhD, Section of Behavioral Physiology, Fels Research Institute, School of Medicine, Wright State University, Yellow Springs, Ohio

John I. Lacey, PhD, Section of Behavioral Physiology, Fels Research Institute, School of Medicine, Wright State University, Yellow Springs, Ohio

Peter J. Lang, PhD, Department of Psychology, University of Wisconsin, Madison, Wisconsin

Joel F. Lubar, PhD, Department of Psychology, University of Tennessee, Knoxville, Tennessee

Neal E. Miller, PhD, DSc, Laboratory of Physiological Psychology, The Rockefeller University, New York, New York

Thomas B. Mulholland, PhD, Psychophysiology Laboratory, Edith Nourse Rogers Memorial Veterans Administration Hospital, Bedford, Massachusetts

Paul A. Obrist, PhD, Department of Psychiatry, Division of Health Affairs, The School of Medicine, University of North Carolina at Chapel Hill, Chapel Hill, North Carolina

Martin T. Orne, MD, PhD, Department of Psychiatry, University of Pennsylvania, Philadelphia, Pennsylvania; Unit for Experimental Psychiatry, The Institute of Pennsylvania Hospital, Philadelphia, Pennsylvania

Diane M. Riley, PhD, Department of Psychology, University of Toronto, Toronto, Ontario, Canada

Gary E. Schwartz, PhD, Department of Psychology, Yale University, New Haven, Connecticut

David Shapiro, PhD, Department of Psychiatry and Biobehavioral Sciences, The University of California at Los Angeles, Los Angeles, California

M. Barry Sterman, PhD, Research Service, Veterans Administration Medical Center, Sepulveda, California; Departments of Anatomy and Psychiatry, The University of California at Los Angeles, Los Angeles, California

Richard S. Surwit, PhD, Department of Psychiatry, Duke University Medical Center, Durham, North Carolina

Kevin Thompson, PhD, Department of Psychology, University of Georgia, Athens, Georgia

Bernard Tursky, Laboratory for Behavioral Research and Department of Political Science, State University of New York at Stony Brook, Stony Brook, New York

Theodore Weiss, MD, Department of Psychiatry and Biofeedback Unit, University of Pennsylvania, Philadelphia, Pennsylvania

Leonard White, PhD, Long Island Research Institute and Department of Psychiatry and Behavioral Science, School of Medicine, State University of New York at Stony Brook, Stony Brook, New York

Steven L. Wolf, PhD, Departments of Rehabilitation Medicine, Anatomy, Surgery, and Community Health, and Biofeedback Research Programs, Emory University School of Medicine, Atlanta, Georgia

Stanley F. Yolles, MD, MPH, Department of Psychiatry and Behavioral Science, School of Medicine, and Long Island Research Institute, State University of New York at Stony Brook, Stony Brook, New York

PREFACE

The valid transformation of scientific findings into clinical practice is a primary function of the clinical sciences. This transfer of information has proven to be particularly difficult in the area of biofeedback. Interest in the clinical potential of biofeedback was initially stimulated by animal laboratory demonstrations and preliminary clinical trials. These early findings challenged traditional views in anatomy and the behavioral sciences, which sharply differentiated between the structure and function of the voluntary and involuntary portions of the nervous system; the findings stimulated the imaginations of trained researchers, clinical practitioners, and the lay public as have few other developments in the behavioral sciences.

This initial burst of enthusiasm is, however, yielding to a more reasoned evaluation of biofeedback. Theoretical formulations are now more precisely tied to confirmed observations, while, with increasing frequency, clinicians have critically examined the literature on clinical efficacy. Reports now appearing in archival publications indicate that critical studies of clinical efficacy have not been undertaken or that findings are either ambiguous or negative. It would be unfortunate, indeed, if an accompanying phenomenon should be premature discouragement resulting in a failure to exploit the scientific opportunity provided by the emerging theoretical and technological sophistication of biofeedback.

We perceived the need for an intensive examination of the field of biofeedback that would examine the dual issues of the efficacy and the mechanisms of biofeedback. A summary statement of therapeutic efficacy alone is incomplete and problematic. The exploitation of the clinical potential of a method, as well as a determination of its limits, depends upon delineation of the mechanisms of action, as well as upon statements of efficacy. Since biofeedback methods have been attempted as therapy in a wide variety of disorders, and since each application confronts unique psychophysiological constraints, the universal effects initially envisioned are unlikely. It is axiomatic, then, that an examination of the field would not result in a consensus on all issues and that further research would be indicated. It was our hope that critical examination of the literature in which the mechanisms of both successful and ineffective clinical trials were delineated might yield new research approaches to clinical problems.

In order to conduct this kind of intensive examination of the field, and to encourage a lively interchange, we developed the format of a closed, invitational symposium of prominent, active researchers; this format fostered a focused and coordinated interaction not characteristic of the many open biofeedback workshops now held. We were fortunate to be joined in this venture by a number of distinguished researchers.

The following text contains the proceedings of this closed, invitational research symposium, entitled "Clinical Biofeedback: Efficacy and Mechanisms," and held May 15–18, 1980, at the Health Sciences Center of the State University of New York at Stony Brook. The papers are presented here in their entirety, as are the formal observations of expert discussants. In order to maximize the opportunity for an open interchange of ideas, papers were circulated to the participants in advance of the symposium and only summarized during the conference. This format allowed ample time for round-table discussion, and it proved to be extremely practical. The opportunity for discussion was utilized to the fullest and resulted in many stimulating and useful exchanges.

In the preparation of this publication, we decided to include many of the transcripts of these unique exchanges as they occurred, retaining the conversational style. We felt that this would reflect the spontaneity of, as well as the broader meanings communicated during, the exchanges. Unlike prepared texts, however, round-table discussions are rarely linear sequences of thought; connecting constructions are frequently omitted. We have attempted to compensate for these deficiencies by presenting actual discussions in a more coherent sequence than that in which they actually occurrred, as well as by preceding each section with a guide to the issues discussed in that section.

There will no doubt be many readers who will consult these proceedings only for individual papers of particular interest. We particularly recommend that they also read the exceptional summary papers by Martin Orne and John Lacey, who served as scholarly critics throughout the symposium. These papers clarify the complementary relationship between the search for specific treatments and the understanding of mechanisms of action, which were the central themes of the meeting.

We gratefully acknowledge a grant from the van Ameringen Foundation of New York, which funded this meeting.

The meeting was sponsored jointly by the Department of Psychiatry and Behavioral Science and the Department of Political Science, State University of New York at Stony Brook, Stony Brook, New York. We express our appreciation to Howard Haymes for his assistance in managing the logistics of the meeting and to Rose Brown for her assistance in preparation of the text.

Leonard White
Bernard Tursky

Stony Brook, New York

CONTENTS

CLINICAL BIOFEEDBACK: EFFICACY AND MECHANISMS

I

KEYNOTE ADDRESS

1 SOME DIRECTIONS FOR CLINICAL AND EXPERIMENTAL RESEARCH ON BIOFEEDBACK

NEAL E. MILLER

A QUICK OVERVIEW OF THERAPEUTIC STATUS

A few general conclusions can be drawn from extensive reviews of the current status of therapeutic uses of biofeedback (e.g., Miller, 1978; Ray, Raczynski, Rogers, & Kimball, 1979; Stoyva, 1978; Yates, 1980). (1) Biofeedback is being widely used to treat a variety of ailments. (2) For a number of these uses, uncontrolled case studies report that many patients appear to have benefited, in some cases quite impressively. (3) The relatively few better-controlled studies that are beginning to accumulate report mixed results, some of which support the specific effectiveness of certain applications of biofeedback; more of which indicate that it is no more effective than other, simpler techniques such as progressive relaxation; and a few of which indicate that certain applications may be no more effective than placebo procedures. (4) In those of the better-controlled studies that raise questions about the efficacy of biofeedback, these questions tend to be raised not by a failure to find any therapeutic effect of biofeedback, but by equally positive results from patients in comparison or control groups. (5) None of the better-controlled studies have been conducted rigorously enough on a large enough number of patients to yield completely definitive results. The papers that follow add important qualifications to the application of the foregoing general conclusions to uses of specific types of biofeedback to treat specific conditions.

Neal E. Miller. Laboratory of Physiological Psychology, The Rockefeller University, New York, New York.

NEED FOR COOPERATIVE STUDIES TO EVALUATE THERAPEUTIC EFFECTS

The state of affairs just described clearly calls for studies using larger samples of patients followed up for longer periods of time to evaluate rigorously the therapeutic effectiveness of applications of specific types of biofeedback to specific, well-diagnosed conditions. Where the follow-up procedures in such studies primarily involve subjective reports (e.g., headaches), rather than more objective evidence, they should be conducted by individuals identified as being separate from the original therapeutic group, in order to avoid answers biased to please a therapist who has put forth considerable effort and established a personal relationship with the patient. The difficulties of conducting extensive and rigorous studies indicate the desirability of carefully organizing one or more model cooperative studies. These should be organized first for the applications that are therapeutically most promising and that have well-defined procedures, biomedically plausible rationales, and outcomes that lend themselves to rigorous testing.

In fairness, it should be noted clearly that many of the more traditional forms of medical treatment have not yet been subjected to the rigorous type of evaluation that have just been called for.

With increases in the strength of the consumer protection movement and in the proportion of medical bills paid by insurance companies and by the government, there will be increasing demands for more rigorous evaluation of all therapeutic techniques (e.g., Klerman, 1979). Therefore, therapists will be wise to devote sufficient attention to the complex problems involved in evaluation.

FACTORS CAUSING OVERESTIMATE OF EFFECTIVENESS

A number of factors tend to produce a considerable overestimate of the effectiveness of any therapeutic technique. Two of these are the marvelous ability of the body to recover spontaneously from acute conditions, and the tendency for chronic conditions to fluctuate so that patients seek treatment when they are feeling worse than usual and are discharged when they are feeling better than usual. The foregoing factors produce a strong bias in favor of observing improvement. To the extent that all of the successes of a treatment are due to these factors, there is no need for further research on such a treatment.

A third factor causing overestimates of therapeutic effectiveness is a powerful placebo effect that increases with the enthusiasm of the therapist, the impressiveness and expensiveness of the treatment, and the faith of the patient (Beecher,

1961; Goodman, Greene, & Laskin, 1976; Shapiro, 1960, 1971). From the broader point of view of behavioral medicine, powerful placebo effects show the effectiveness of purely psychological factors, may be therapeutically very useful, and are worthy of being studied to learn more about the factors that determine their strength and about the behavioral and physiological mechanisms involved. For example, to what extent are they related to the reductions in the level of fear and of corticosteroids that are produced by coping responses—for example, by an infant clinging to his or her mother (Miller, 1980)?

If a technique produces therapeutic effects that are solely placebo ones, there is no point in investigating any other aspects of its efficacy. But if it has some genuine effects that are specific to its rationale, even though these effects may be weaker than those of competing types of treatment, it often is worthwhile to investigate the parameters determining the effectiveness of the technique and the mechanisms involved. Such increased understanding can be the basis for changes that greatly improve therapeutic effectiveness.

FROM BIOFEEDBACK TO BEHAVIORAL MEDICINE

Before proceeding to a discussion of the type of experimental work that may improve the effectiveness of biofeedback, I would like to make a few other points about therapy. The first is that biofeedback should be considered within the broader context of behavioral medicine, as illustrated by the chapters in Weiss, Fox, and Herd (1981). It should be used in conjunction with other medical and behavioral techniques. As I have pointed out elsewhere (Miller, 1978; Miller & Dworkin, 1977), if a symptom is being reinforced strongly, it may be necessary to discover how it is being reinforced and to remove these sources of reinforcement by such means as manipulating the environment or teaching patients alternative means of achieving their needs. Furthermore, deep relaxation may elicit feelings of disorientation and lack of control, or frightening images, fantasies, and emotions, which must be dealt with.

A number of the studies summarized here show that, for certain applications, simpler means of achieving relaxation are just as effective as the use of electromyographic (EMG) feedback to achieve it. Other studies show that, in certain cases, the simpler relaxation techniques are just as effective as a specific type of biofeedback—for example, finger-warming techniques in treating Raynaud's disease. From the broader perspective of behavioral medicine, such results should not be considered negative. In many cases they show that a therapeutically important phenomenon exists; the simpler means of achieving it is an advantage. Biofeedback should be given credit for focusing interest on relaxation techniques. Furthermore, where the effects of treatment are shown to disappear after a considerable lapse of time, this result should not necessarily be considered negative, provided there is good reason to believe that a suitable refresher treatment (one that is cost-effective with respect to other alternatives) can restore the therapeutic effect.

In many cases, the choice of techniques may not be clear-cut, either/or one; flexible approaches may be found to be the most desirable. For many patients, simpler relaxation techniques may be used at first, and then, if less than optimal results are secured, the EMG may be used to discover residual areas of muscular tension and to help to train the patients to eliminate them. In other cases, increases in muscular tension, galvanic skin response, and the like may be used to help therapists and patients to discover emotional problems that can be dealt with by psychodynamic or behavior therapies. Finally, as Schwartz (1977) and Stroebel (1979) have emphasized, patients may be taught patterns of skeletal and visceral responses that are incompatible with more centrally organized, undesirable states. In short, biofeedback should be but one part of a far wider therapeutic armamentarium.

In the long run, research on biofeedback may have its greatest medical effects in unexpected ways. It may lead to a better understanding of some of the vital processes of homeostasis (Miller & Dworkin, 1980). To quote an earlier statement,

> As the use of instrumentation to record moment-to-moment changes in visceral responses is developed further, the use of such instrumentation will increase the general public's awareness of the psychosomatic consequences of environmental stress. This same instrumentation can be used to detect those aspects of the physical occupational or social environment that expose people to the greatest stress. This and other increased knowledge may lead to actions to reduce such stress and hence help to produce a healthier environment. (Miller & Dworkin, 1977, p. 156)

IMPROVING CONTRIBUTIONS FROM THE LABORATORY

Laboratory experiments have played a major role in initiating the new types of clinical applications that have come to be called biofeedback. These experiments have shown that instrumental learning (also called "operant conditioning") can affect a wider range of responses—visceral responses, the firing of single motor units, and brain waves—than hitherto had been believed possible. Since the demonstration of the challenging new phenomena in these early experiments, laboratory work has contributed surprisingly little toward discovering principles to help clinicians to improve the learning that would increase the effectiveness of biofeedback. An examination of some of the reasons for this may raise key issues and help point the way to the types of research that will be more fruitful.

One of the reasons for the lack of contributions from the laboratory is purely quantitative. Many laboratory workers have turned their efforts toward the more exciting prospects of clinical applications. Furthermore, of all the experimental research on learning that has been conducted since Ebbinghaus, Thorndike, and

Pavlov, only a tiny fraction has been on visceral learning or on difficult types of learning relevant to neuromuscular rehabilitation. It is to be hoped that more attention will be devoted in the near future to experimental research specifically relevant to the kinds of learning involved in the clinical applications for biofeedback. To make a qualitative as well as a quantitative point, such research should be more analytical and should pay more attention to the mechanisms involved.

TRADITIONAL PARAMETERS OF LEARNING

To start with simple problems, there has been relatively little research on the effects of the traditional parameters of learning on visceral responses or on the type of learning involved in the recovery of function after neuromuscular disorders. Such research has been summarized elsewhere (Miller, 1978). Yet for these difficult types of learning it is entirely possible that the optimal value of a parameter, such as distribution of practice, will be different from the value of that parameter for easier types of learning. My own experience indicates that such learning demands great concentration of attention and is surprisingly tiring, so that at first it is difficult to continue for more than 30 seconds at a time. To take another example, although a number of investigators believe that bidirectional training often is the most effective way of producing an effect in a desired single direction, I know of no systematic experimental research on this obvious but important problem.

PRIMARY VERSUS SECONDARY LEARNING

To continue with the next and more qualitative points, I need to make the distinction between the extremes of a continuum from what might be called a more primary type of learning to a more secondary type. For example, an expert ice skater has already learned skilled voluntary control (which has become virtually automatic) of the various response units involved in executing the standard figures of exhibition skating. It is relatively easy for him or her to learn how to recombine these standard figures into a new sequence for an exhibition performance. Such recombination of overlearned units is a secondary type of learning. To learn a short sequence, the expert skater may need only instructions or a single demonstration of the desired sequence. In contrast, the first wobbling movements of the complete novice, trying to learn to move forward on skates without falling, exemplify a more primary type of learning. Many hours of practice are necessary before the novice can even begin to learn to skate a figure eight.

But even with the novice, there is a tremendous amount of transfer of training from previous forms of locomotion. For speakers of English, learning to pronounce a new English word is a highly secondary type of learning; learning to pronounce unfamiliar phonemes in a foreign language, such as the Italian "u" in "Mussolini" or a tonal inflection in Chinese, is a more primary type of learning. The novice in a language may not even perceive any difference, so obvious to a native speaker, between a mistake and the correct response. Most adult learning is highly secondary; virtually all research on learning is on this type that involves an enormous amount of transfer of training.

We do not know how much of the difficulty of primary learning is due to the low initial probability of a correct response and how much is due to something like the greater difficulty in forming associations between relatively unfamiliar elements, such as a list of nonsense syllables compared with one of English words. Where the elements are still more unfamiliar—for example, a series of paired choices between completely unfamiliar odors—learning is astonishingly difficult.

Learning the direct control of visceral responses and of the responses involved in the rehabilitation of neuromuscular disorders appears to be an example of the more primary kind of learning. On the one hand, studying such learning offers an opportunity to gain a deeper understanding of the primary learning involved in acquiring voluntary control; on the other hand, a deeper understanding should increase therapists' ability to produce such learning.

LONGER TRAINING

To date, most experiments on the roles of various variables in biofeedback have involved relatively little practice—15 or 20 minutes of actual practice per day for 2 to 5 days. This is a minute amount, compared with that required to learn an athletic skill or to play a violin. Typically, such experiments have produced relatively small and clinically insignificant changes. Often there is an initial, almost immediate effect and little or no evidence for any additional improvement during the relatively few subsequent trials.

A few experiments, however, clearly illustrate the value of using much longer periods of training. In the original experiments on nonparalyzed dogs by Miller and Carmona (1967), the difference between the groups rewarded for salivating and for not salivating was small at the end of 10 hours of training, but at the end of 40 hours of training the "increase" group salivated 14 times as much as the "decrease" one. In experiments by Harris, Gilliam, Findley, and Brady (1973), baboons learned in approximately 250 hours of training to produce 30 mm Hg increases in systolic blood pressure sustained for 12 hours.

Figure 1 shows the results on a patient, paralyzed from below the neck (C5) down, who was trained to increase his blood pressure in order to overcome severe

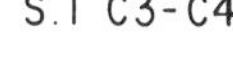

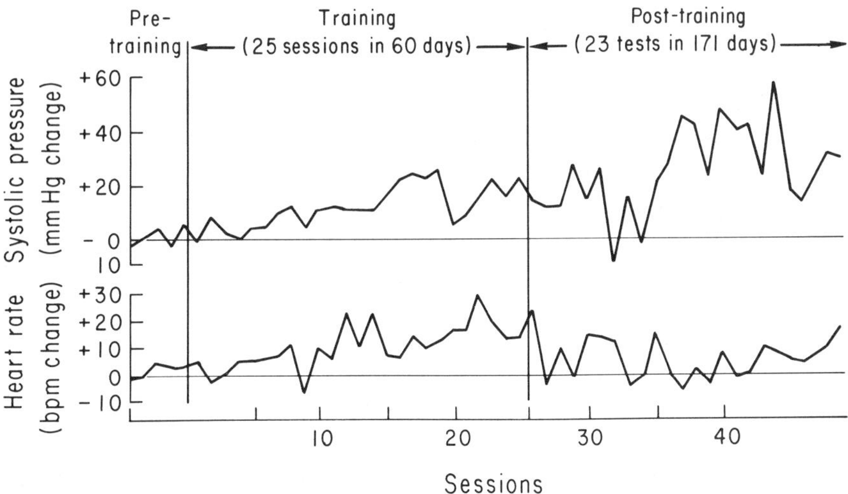

FIG. 1. Gradual learning to make larger and more specific increases in systolic blood pressure by a patient paralyzed from below the neck (C5) down. (From "Biofeedback and Rehabilitation" by B. S. Brucker, in L. P. Ince [Ed.], *Behavioral Psychology in Rehabilitation Medicine: Clinical Applications.* Baltimore: Williams & Wilkins, 1980. Copyright 1980 by B. S. Brucker. Reprinted by permission.)

orthostatic hypotension that had caused him to be confined to a reclining posture. The figure indicates that at the end of five training sessions, he was producing relatively insignificant changes in blood pressure, but from the 16th session on he was producing 20 mm Hg increases. With additional practice, which he gave to himself because he had learned to perceive the increases that were rewarding because they helped him to avoid fainting, he acquired the ability to elicit increases ranging from 40 to 60 mm Hg. His responses also became more specific, often involving increases in blood pressure without increases in heart rate; this effect became still more striking after still further training (Miller & Brucker, 1979). Similarly, progressively larger learned temperature increases, which became more specific with extensive training, have been reported by Taub (1977). Such results indicate that it is worthwhile, indeed essential, to use more training trials in order to get meaningful results on the effects of other parameters on these difficult types of training. Similarly, it may be necessary to use a sufficient amount of training to evaluate the effectiveness of the training as therapy. If Brudny had used only a few hours of training, he would not have achieved the promising results that he reports in Chapter 10 on teaching stroke patients to regain the use of their upper extremities.

ANALYZING THE MECHANISMS INVOLVED

In analyzing a difficult problem, it often is useful to consider an extreme example. Suppose experimenters were monitoring the heart rates of patients seated on an exercise bicycle. If the experimenters were studying the effects of instructions, telling the patients to pump the bicycle as hard as they could would produce a prompt, large increase in their heart rates; whether or not the patients received feedback for heart rate would have relatively little effect. With only instructions to increase the signal indicating an increase in heart rate, many subjects would hit upon the skeletal response of pumping the bicycle and, after that, would show relatively little effect of further training. With ambiguous instructions, those suggesting activity would increase the likelihood of pumping the bicycle and producing increases in heart rate. There would be large individual differences that could not be explained without watching the subjects to see which of them were pumping the bicycle. Experimenters who subtly and perhaps unconsciously encouraged pumping the bicycle would get much better results than experimenters who effectively discouraged it. Finally, the experimenters would find that increases were much easier to learn than were decreases.

With relatively few training trials under the foregoing conditions, it would be much easier for the subjects to show more secondary learning by employing thoroughly learned units of pumping the bicycle than to show the more primary learning of direct control over heart rate.

Studies in the literature show results similar to those in this example, although the conditions are not as extreme. The subjects of the studies have been instructed to remain seated on a chair. They may or may not have been told to remain relaxed. But isometric contractions of their muscles, which Lynch, Schuri, and D'Anna (1976) in my laboratory have shown can produce increases of 5 to 10 beats per minute in heart rate without being readily observed, have usually not been carefully measured. Similarly, breathing, another way of affecting heart rate, has been measured poorly if at all. With relatively few training trials, the results are almost certain to emphasize secondary learning—the use of already available skills of controlling skeletal muscles. And indeed, a study by VanDercar, Feldstein, and Solomon (1977) in my laboratory showed heart rate changes typical of those appearing in the literature. These changes appeared almost immediately; there was no reliable improvement during relatively few additional days of training, and the changes were small, 5% to 10%. When the experimenters exerted rigid control over breathing by respirating subjects through a respirator and face mask to which they had become thoroughly habituated so that their breathing was done for them by the respirator and was rigorously controlled, the changes in heart rate virtually disappeared; most, if not all, of the changes that remained were produced by changes in isometric muscle tension as measured by the EMG. Similarly, Obrist, Galosy, Lawler, Gaebelein, Howard, and Shanks (1975) have found that the more carefully skeletal responses are controlled, the smaller the learned changes in heart rate become.

To summarize certain points made so far, too many of the relatively few experiments in visceral learning have used too few training trials and have failed to control adequately for skeletal responses that are already under skilled control. Therefore, these experiments very probably show the results of a highly secondary type of learning, rather than those of any direct, more primary type of visceral learning that may be possible.

I believe that it will be profitable, and indeed essential, for these experiments to become more analytical and to be concerned with the mechanisms involved. On the one hand, they should investigate the question of what kind of visceral changes can be produced by what kind of skeletal responses; for example, can the pattern of small increases in blood pressure accompanied by small decreases in heart rate (and vice versa) and of independent changes in heart rate and blood pressure, which Schwartz (1977) has studied, be produced by skeletal responses? In this connection, it should be remembered that skeletally mediated visceral changes can have importance in both the etiology and the therapy of visceral symptoms (Miller, 1978). Perhaps research on the effectiveness of various skeletal responses can elucidate etiology and facilitate therapy.

On the other hand, I believe it is highly important theoretically, and probably also clinically, to direct research toward the question of what conditions, if any, can produce the direct learning of specific visceral changes that do not need to be mediated by skeletal ones. Such direct learning would allow visceral responses to play a much greater and more flexible role in normal homeostasis and in the etiology and therapy of visceral disorders (Dworkin, Filewich, Miller, Craigmyle, & Pickering, 1979; Miller, 1978; Miller & Dworkin, 1980).

J. V. Brady (1976) believes that it would be impossible for any skeletal responses to produce the large and long-maintained increases of blood pressure that he and his associates (Harris *et al.*, 1973) have obtained in baboons, but so far he has made no direct measurements to test this opinion. Brucker and I have shown that patients paralyzed by high spinal lesions can, without noticeably changing their breathing as measured by a spirometer, or action of skeletal muscles as measured by the EMG, produce increases in blood pressure that are more than twice as great as those produced by drastic changes of breathing or by a maximal effort to contract *all* muscles, normal or paralyzed. Furthermore, these increases in blood pressure can be maintained for hours and can be produced without increases in heart rate (Miller & Brucker, 1979). The mechanisms involved in the large learned changes in blood pressure by these patients merit further investigation.

GETTING RESPONSES TO OCCUR

One of the problems with difficult learning is to get the desired response to occur so that it can be reinforced. For such learning, various possibilities are as follows:

1. Classical conditioning. Furedy and Riley describe an interesting approach of this type in Chapter 4. It is an approach that needs to be studied further.
2. Reflex elicitation. One of the skills of the physical therapist in the rehabilitation of neuromuscular disorders is the knowledge of how to elicit the desired response by making use of various reflexes. The conditions under which such reflexes aid or possibly interfere with independent learned control could be investigated, either with patients or with animal models.
3. The use of a skeletal response to elicit a visceral change as a part of a larger pattern and, where desirable, trying to phase out the skeletal component. Harris *et al.* (1973) may have done this with their baboons by requiring that blood pressure be held above a certain level for 12 hours, thereby eliciting fatigue to motivate the dropping out of skeletal components and thus producing greater specificity during many days of training. This approach has not yet been thoroughly investigated.
4. The avoidance of skeletal mediation as a bad habit that excludes the possibility for direct learning. The rationale of this opposite approach has been described elsewhere (Miller & Dworkin, 1974).
5. Imitation (renamed "modeling"). One would not expect this approach to work unless the required units for imitatively eliciting the visceral response had already been learned or were innate. These units, learning to discriminate and to respond appropriately to the direction and size of differences, are discussed later. Absence of these units is part of the difficulty in the rehabilitation of patients with neuromuscular disorders.
6. Imagery. This approach is discussed by Brener (1977), Lang (1979), and Miller and Dworkin (1974).
7. Shaping. This is the most commonly used approach, but experimenters may not be shaping the correct responses in the proper way. In shaping a rat to press a bar, it is obvious that the first thing to reward is approaching the bar. The next thing is lifting a paw off the ground. The rat cannot possibly press the bar if it is standing still on all four feet in the opposite corner of the apparatus. Imagine a blind experimenter trying to shape a rat to press a small bar somewhat removed from the place where food is delivered. He or she might make the bar very sensitive so that it would respond to extremely small pressures. But then the rat might be rewarded for responses such as biting and shaking the floor mesh to produce enough vibration to trip the bar; as long as these responses were rewarded, the rat could not be shaped to exert large pressures on

the bar. The blind experimenter might easily conclude that rats could readily be trained to run T mazes, but that their learning anything but the minute pressures on the bar was completely impossible.

In shaping a visceral response such as reduced blood pressure, investigators know virtually nothing about how to proceed. Is there anything short of a slight decrease in blood pressure that is analogous to rewarding the rat for approaching the bar? Perhaps investigators should start by rewarding variability in blood pressure, irrespective of the direction of change. Would it be better to reward a correct change in any one of the components that contribute to blood pressure—peripheral resistance, cardiac output or its components, heart rate, and stroke volume—even though the first small changes in the rewarded component might be canceled out by compensatory changes in some other component? Again, I emphasize the desirability of being more analytical and of studying the mechanisms involved in producing the desired response.

WHAT TO REWARD?

What constitutes a learnable response? Should investigators reward small, frequent changes, or only large, infrequent ones? Are both of these learnable responses, or is one a response while the other is noise? Should investigators reward the downswings of the rhythmic changes in blood pressure that occur with breathing or with the longer Traube–Hering's rhythms, or only deviations below the predicted level of such rhythms? Should the criterion be set at an absolute level, or should any relative change in the desired direction be reinforced? In short, investigators need to discover what aspects of variability are learnable responses and what aspects are either unlearnable responses, innate responses, or random noise (Miller & Dworkin, 1977).

SINGLE "RESPONSES" VERSUS PATTERNS

Two other related questions for research are (1) whether investigators can get larger changes in individual visceral responses by also reinforcing changes in related ones, and (2) if investigators are interested in a central effect such as reducing fear or arousal, whether they can get larger and more consistent results by reinforcing a pattern. Patients can be extremely anxious when their EMG shows deep relaxation or their electroencephalogram (EEG) shows much alpha (Miller, 1978; Orne & Paskewitz, 1974; Raskin, Johnson, & Rondestvedt, 1973); would training a pattern including more elements increase the incompatibility with anxiety? Schwartz (1977), who has been a pioneer in problems of patterning, reports that larger changes, although only approximately 7 mm Hg in blood pressure of 7 beats per minute in heart rate, can be produced if subjects are rewarded for changes in the same direction than can be produced if they are rewarded for changes in opposite directions; he also reports that rewarding both blood pressure and heart rate for reductions produces a verbal report of greater relaxation than does rewarding only one of them. When a pattern is rewarded, will it be more effective to train each component separately and then to combine them, or to use combined training from the beginning?

The work of Patel and North (1975) on combining autogenic training with rewards for higher skin resistance, and of Stroebel (1979) for training patients in a pattern that he calls "the quieting reflex," suggests that further work in analyzing the effects of training patterns, rather than only individual responses, should be fruitful.

MODELS FOR ACTION OF BIOFEEDBACK

I believe that it will be useful to follow out, in more analytical detail, the implications of an instrumental-learning (or, in other words, an operant-conditioning) model for biofeedback. Even if the eventual result is to spotlight the shortcomings of that model, the procedure should be useful.

The fact is that, given exactly the same feedback, subjects who are motivated (usually by instructions) to learn to increase a response, so that signals indicating an increase serve as a reward, learn to do so; correspondingly, subjects motivated to decrease a response learn that opposite response. This fact indicates that, in biofeedback, motivation and reward play an important role of the type that would be expected from an instrumental learning model. According to this model, without *any* motivation, experimenters would not expect mere exposure to feedback to produce the performance of learned control. But the foregoing possibility should be tested.[1] The word "any" is italicized because it is possible that in some situations feedback that makes perspicuous the deviations from, for example, a regular heart beat, will cause those deviations to arouse some anxiety—anxiety that will be reduced by a return to a performance that is perceived as normal.

In this exposition, I deal with the empirical law of effect, but it may be useful for research in this area to consider the implications of various theories of the mechanisms responsible for the empirical law of effect (Estes, 1975).

A motor-skill model has been proposed as an alternative to an instrumental

[1]Some subjects who have been trained by an operant procedure report that remembering the sound of the tone used to signal success helps them to produce the correct response (Miller, 1978). Would actually sounding the tone elicit this response? If so, would mere unmotivated prior exposure to the response—tone contingency cause the tone to acquire the same ability to elicit the response?

learning one. But it seems to me that motor skills are acquired by instrumental learning; rather than there being two separate types of learning, there have for historical reasons developed two relatively separate bodies of literature emphasizing two bodies of knowledge about essentially the same phenomena of learning and performance. A far more fundamental distinction appears to be that between short-term and long-term memory. It might be worthwhile to consider how the transition from short- to long-term memory is involved in the instrumental learning of the motor skills involved in the control of visceral responses and in neuromuscular rehabilitation.

From an instrumental-learning model, investigators would not expect the ability to discriminate the occurrence of a response to be essential for its voluntary control, as tested by the ability of a request to serve as the discriminative stimulus to elicit it. Indeed, Pickering and Miller (1977) report on a patient who, when given feedback by the electrocardiogram (ECG) on an oscilloscope, could learn voluntary control over premature ventricular contractions (PVCs), as indicated by his ability to produce increases in them when these were requested and decreases when those were requested. But this patient could not be taught to discriminate the occurrence of PVCs in the absence of the artificial feedback. From the model, this patient could not be expected to continue to perform in the absence of artificial feedback, because he would have no cues to indicate the success that would serve as a reinforcement for continued performance. And, unfortunately, this prediction from the theory turned out to be all too true. The model predicts that training patients to discriminate the successful performance of the correct response in the absence of artificial feedback should facilitate their ability to continue performing when the artificial feedback is withdrawn. Where fading procedures are not efficient, or where prior training is desired, the anticipation method can be adapted to such training by letting subjects know that the signal indicating a change will be slightly delayed and asking them to try to learn how to anticipate its occurrence (Miller, 1972).

The role of feedback in learning has been discussed. Conversely, the crucial role of learning in the use of certain forms of feedback is illustrated by the first exposure of subjects to the task of mirror drawing. The subjects have perfect visual feedback, but the habitual relationship between the feedback and their responses is reversed. According to an analysis of copying applied also to other forms of behavior (Miller, 1959; Miller & Dollard, 1941), in cases where the process is not innate, the subjects must first learn to discriminate a difference from the correct outcome; then to respond to the direction of the difference with the correct directional response (the problem for mirror drawing); and, finally, to respond to the size of the difference with an appropriately large correctional response. After reducing the size of a discrepancy from the correct outcome has acquired secondary reward value, feedback can shape the learning of further refinements in behavior more effectively than can any artificial arrangement of contingencies that is easy to achieve.

RELEVANT TYPE OF MOTIVATION AND REWARD

In many forms of biofeedback training, the reinforcement is a signal indicating that a subject has achieved success. This is a derived sort of reward that involves the cognitive processes required for recognizing that the feedback signal indicates success. Will a more primitive type of reward, such as avoidance of and escape from pain, be more effective for visceral learning and neuromuscular reeducation?

As Miller and Dworkin (1977) have pointed out, in the light of work such as that by Garcia and Koelling (1966), it is possible that certain types of motivation and reward are more relevant than others are to some types of visceral learning. For example, would mild peripheral ischemia produced by a pressure cuff as the drive, and relief from it as the reward, be especially effective in changing a cardiac function?

ANALYZING ROLE OF LEARNING IN HOMEOSTASIS

Miller (1969) and Miller and Dworkin (1980) have suggested that learning may play an important role in refining some of the autoregulatory processes involved in normal homeostasis. For example, in Fig. 1 (see p. 7), it can be seen that the patient with a high spinal lesion corrected the homeostatic defect of severe orthostatic hypotension by learning to raise his blood pressure. If learning also plays a role in normal homeostasis, discovering and using the types of motivation and reward involved in such learning might be particularly effective in both experiments on and clinical applications of visceral learning. Because of the basic role of homeostasis in maintaining health, any increment in the understanding of it is certain to be important.

Research by Dworkin *et al.* (1979) illustrates the value of paying attention to the behavioral and physiological mechanisms involved in homeostasis. The authors cite considerable physiological evidence that stimulation of the baroreceptors that register increases of blood pressure has an inhibitory effect on the reticular formation and cerebral cortex. Figure 2 dramatically illustrates the power of this effect. Injections of phenylephrine have produced marked increases in the blood pressure of both rats. The central inhibitory effects elicited are indicated by the somnolent posture of the one in the background. For the control rat in the foreground, the stimulation from the baroreceptors has been eliminated by denervating them and interrupting the fibers from the aortic arch. When this influence is removed, the pressor drug (somewhat resembling amphetamine) does not inhibit the reticular formation and cortex, but, if anything, has an excitatory effect.

FIG. 2. Marked inhibitory effect of stimulation of the baroreceptors by elevated blood pressure. The rat in the background shows the inhibitory effect; the one in the foreground has had stimulation from the baroreceptors eliminated by denervation of the carotid sinus and interruption of fibers from the aortic arch. Similar elevations in blood pressure were produced in both rats by injections of phenylephrine. (Photo by B. R. Dworkin.)

The hypothesis of Dworkin is that this inhibition of the reticular formation and cortex reduces the aversive effect of noxious stimulation, which, in turn, may reinforce an increase in blood pressure. Just as some people may learn to cope with aversive situations by learning to take a barbiturate, others may secure the same effect by learning to raise their blood pressure. Thus far, a reduction in the responsiveness of normal, but not of denervated, rats to an aversive situation has been demonstrated. If further confirmed, the hypothesis would provide one explanation for part of the problem of noncompliance with a regime of taking antihypertensive pills; it would also suggest the desirability of training such patients in other ways of coping with aversive situations. This particular hypothesis may turn out to be false, but it illustrates a type of research—paying attention to motivational factors and combining a behavioral with other biomedical approaches—that I believe will be fruitful.

STRENGTH OF MOTIVATION

To continue with problems of motivation, the more primary type of learning—acquiring extensive control over visceral or completely novel skeletal responses—is a difficult, frustrating, boring task. It requires persistent effort and hence persistent motivation; however, at least for lowering blood pressure or relaxing certain types of muscular tension, motivation that is too strong may block the correct responses by eliciting opposing ones. Successful learning may require a paradoxical combination of motivation and passivity. More research is needed in this area.

DIFFERENCES IN EXPERIMENTERS AND SUBJECTS

Taub (1977) reports that while one experimenter was able to train only 2 out of 22 subjects to produce sizable increases in hand temperature, a different experimenter was able to succeed with 19 out of 21. Somewhat similar results have been reported informally by a number of investigators. We need to analyze why some experimenters are more successful than others. Are they better able to maintain the proper level, and perhaps even type, of motivation? Do some experimenters unconsciously suggest the impossibility of the task, thus putting their subjects up against the same sort of barrier that for years prevented the achievement of the 4-minute mile, whereas other experimenters suggest success? Do some experimenters indirectly suggest successful skeletal maneuvers, while others effectively prohibit them? In addition, research must investigate the mechanisms involved in the large individual differences in the success of various subjects in learning to control specific visceral responses (Miller, 1978).

NEURAL PLASTICITY

The success of biofeedback in the treatment of neuromuscular diseases, which is described by Brudny (Chapter 10) and Wolf ("Comments on the Chapter by Brudny"), suggests that it should be profitable to use animal models to perform analytical studies that will teach researchers more about the types of neural plasticity involved. In turn, such knowledge may suggest ways of improving neuromuscular rehabilitation.

For example, Taub (1980) has pointed out that monkeys normally will never use a deafferented forelimb. But if the good one is tied down, they will use the deafferented one. If the restraint is continued for several days, the use of the deafferented limb will continue after the other one is released. He believes that these and other observations point to a learned disuse developed during a transient postoperative phase of actual paralysis and continuing after recovery from this paralysis. The absence of normal afferent return probably contributes to the persistence of learned disuse. He believes that a similar learned disuse could complicate the recovery of function after conditions such as stroke, and that biofeedback could be one way of overcoming it.

Human beings show remarkable neural plasticity. As Stratton (1897) and Kohler (1961) showed, people can adjust to prisms that invert their vision. But such radical reorganization requires time, and, as experiments summarized by Held (1965) have shown, it is greatly facilitated by active motor responses.

There are many problems of neural reorganization to be investigated by a combination of behavioral and neurophysiological techniques.

OPPORTUNITIES FROM ADVANCES IN ELECTRONIC TECHNOLOGY

The increasing availability at more reasonable cost of more sophisticated miniaturized electronic components, such as chips containing integrated circuits and microprocessors, opens up new opportunities for automating biofeedback procedures and for designing portable devices that can be worn inconspicuously by patients. Such devices have the potential for solving the problem of giving a larger number of training trials; by being worn in the life situation, they can obviate the problem of transfer from the clinic to life.

Dworkin and I have designed and are in the process of testing one such device. It is a posture prompter for use in the treatment of scoliosis, an S-shaped curvature of the spine (Miller, 1981). As a possible substitute for a cosmetically disfiguring and physically restraining brace, this inconspicuous device, about the size of a pack of cards, sounds a barely audible tone whenever the patient has been out of a good posture for more than 20 seconds. If the posture has not been corrected in an additional 20 seconds, the device sounds a louder tone. Assuming correct posture immediately turns off either tone. In order to avoid phasic responses, the 20-second grace period has to be earned by a period in good posture.

Preliminary tests show that the posture prompter does work well mechanically and electronically and does cause children to adopt better posture. Preliminary data on effects on X-ray measures of curvature of the spine are quite encouraging, but at this time the device is an illustration of new possibilities, rather than something for which the therapeutic value is definitely proven. To appreciate the economy of this approach—if indeed it proves to be effective—imagine the difficulty of following a preadolescent girl around all day, saying "Straighten up" whenever she slips into a bad posture and "Good" whenever she straightens up. But, as we have discovered, such a device does not necessarily eliminate the need for a trained therapist. To be effective, the device must be properly worn and used. Securing the necessary compliance and choosing the correct rate of shaping involve subtle and complex motivational problems.

If an analogous device can be designed to secure a continuous, noninvasive measure of blood pressure—perhaps an adaptation of the pulse transit time (PTT) procedure—it is conceivable that it could produce much better learned reductions in pressure than are now achieved by the relatively short, intermittent periods of training. At the very least, it could warn patients when their pressure is getting too high, and could help them to identify the situations producing such increases. Then a therapist could help them to devise strategies for coping with such situations; in the extreme case, they could simply avoid or leave the situations.

NEED FOR EXTENSIVE RESEARCH NOT UNIQUE TO BIOFEEDBACK

In conclusion, it should be clear that there is much more work to be done. Current clinical applications of biofeedback have been made on a relatively narrow scientific base. The need for a more extensive scientific foundation for health procedures is not unusual. Two examples, each of which is worthy of being read in the original full text, suffice to prove such a need. In 1935, an early attempt at a vaccine for polio was a tragic failure because scientific understanding had not advanced far enough to show that there were three immunologically distinct types of polio viruses, to allow adequate safety tests to be devised, and to anticipate the hazard of human allergic encephalitis as a reaction to the spinal cords of monkeys used in the preparation. Twenty more years of intensive research, much of it basic, were required before the vaccines that conquered this dreaded disease could be put into general use (Shannon, 1967).

The second example is contained in Lewis Thomas' summary (1976) of one of the outstanding triumphs of biomedical science—antibiotics. Thomas concludes:

> We tend to forget how many generations of talented scientists, beginning with Pasteur, worked out their lives on the problems of infection before the stage was set for the era of antibiotics. (p. 6)

REFERENCES

Beecher, H. K. Surgery as placebo. *Journal of the American Medical Association,* 1961, *176,* 1102–1107.

Brady, J. V. Personal communication, 1976.

Brener, J. Sensory and perceptual determinants of voluntary visceral control. In G. E. Schwartz & J. Beatty (Eds.), *Biofeedback: Theory and research.* New York: Academic Press, 1977.

Brucker, B. S. *Learned voluntary control of systolic blood pressure of spinal cord injury patients.* Unpublished doctoral dissertation, New York University, 1977.

Brucker, B. S. Biofeedback and rehabilitation. In L. P. Ince (Ed.), *Behavioral psychology in rehabilitation medicine: Clinical applications.* Baltimore: Williams & Wilkins, 1980.

Dworkin, B. R., Filewich, R. J., Miller, N. E., Craigmyle, N., & Pickering, T. G. Barorecepter activation reduces reactivity to noxious stimulation: Implications for hypertension. *Science,* 1979, *202,* 1299–1301.

Estes, W. K. (Ed.). *Handbook of learning and cognitive processes* (Vol. 2). Hillsdale, N.J.: Erlbaum, 1975.

Garcia, J., & Koelling, R. A. Relation of cue to consequence in avoidance learning. *Psychonomic Science,* 1966, *4,* 123–124.

Goodman, P., Greene, C. S., & Laskin, D. M. Response of patients with myofascial pain–dysfunction syndrome to mock equilibration. *Journal of the American Dental Association,* 1976, *92,* 755–758.

Harris, A. H., Gilliam, W. J., Findley, J. D., & Brady, J. V. Instrumental conditioning of large-magnitude, daily, 12-hour blood pressure elevations in the baboon. *Science*, 1973, *182*, 175–177.

Held, R. Plasticity in sensory–motor systems. *Scientific American*, 1965, *213*(5), 84–94.

Klerman, G. L. *Treatment assessment and new research directions: Evaluation of psychotherapy.* Address, presented at the annual meeting of the American Psychological Association, New York, 1979.

Kohler, I. On the development and transformation of the perceptual world. *Psychological Issues*, 1961, *2*(8).

Lang, P. J. Emotional imagery: Theory and experiment on instructed somatovisceral control. In N. Birbaumer & H. D. Kimmel (Eds.), *Biofeedback and self-regulation.* Hillsdale, N.J.: Erlbaum, 1979.

Lynch, W. C., Schuri, U., & D'Anna, J. Effects of isometric muscle tension on vasomotor activity and heart rate. *Psychophysiology*, 1976, *13*, 222–230.

Miller, N. E. Liberalization of basic S-R concepts: Extensions to conflict behavior, motivation and social learning. In S. Koch (Ed.), *Psychology: A study of a science* (Study 1, Vol. 2). New York: McGraw-Hill, 1959.

Miller, N. E. Learning of visceral and glandular responses. *Science*, 1969, *163*, 434–445.

Miller, N. E. A psychologist's perspective on neural and psychological mechanisms in cardiovascular disease. In A. Zanchetti (Ed.), *Neural and psychological mechanisms in cardiovascular disease.* Milan: Casa Editrice "Il Ponte," 1972.

Miller, N. E. Biofeedback and visceral learning. *Annual Review of Psychology*, 1978, *29*, 373–404.

Miller, N. E. A perspective on the effects of stress and coping on disease and health. In S. Levine & H. Ursin (Eds.), *Coping and health.* NATO Conference Series. New York: Plenum, 1980.

Miller, N. E. An overview of behavioral medicine: Opportunities and dangers. In S. M. Weiss, B. Fox, & J. A. Herd (Eds.), *Perspectives in behavioral medicine.* New York: Academic Press, 1981.

Miller, N. E., & Brucker, B. S. Learned large increases in blood pressure apparently independent of skeletal responses in patients paralyzed by spinal lesions. In N. Birbaumer & H. D. Kimmel (Eds.), *Biofeedback and self-regulation.* Hillsdale, N.J.: Erlbaum, 1979.

Miller, N. E., & Carmona, A. Modification of a visceral response, salivation in thirsty dogs, by instrumental training with water reward. *Journal of Comparative and Physiological Psychology*, 1967, *63*, 1–6.

Miller, N. E., & Dollard, J. *Social learning and imitation.* New Haven: Yale University Press, 1941.

Miller, N. E., & Dworkin, B. R. Visceral learning: Recent difficulties with curarized rats and significant problems for human research. In P. A. Obrist, A. H. Black, J. Brener, & L. V. DiCara (Eds.), *Cardiovascular psychophysiology.* Chicago: Aldine, 1974.

Miller, N. E., & Dworkin, B. R. Critical issues in therapeutic applications of biofeedback. In G. E. Schwartz & J. Beatty (Eds.), *Biofeedback: Theory and research.* New York: Academic Press, 1977.

Miller, N. E., & Dworkin, B. R. Homeostasis as goal-directed learned behavior. In R. F. Thompson, L. H. Hicks, & V. B. Shvyrkov (Eds.), *Neural mechanisms of goal-directed behavior.* New York: Academic Press, 1980.

Obrist, P. A., Galosy, R. A., Lawler, J. E., Gaebelein, C. J., Howard, J. L., & Shanks, E. M. Operant conditioning of heart rate: Somatic correlation. *Psychophysiology*, 1975, *12*, 445–455.

Orne, M. T., & Paskewitz, D. A. Aversive situational effects on alpha feedback training. *Science*, 1974, *186*, 458–460.

Patel, C., & North, W. R. S. Randomized controlled trial of Yoga and biofeedback in management of hypertension. *Lancet*, 1975, *2*, 93.

Pickering, T. G., & Miller, N. E. Learned voluntary control of heart rate and rhythm in two subjects with premature ventricular contractions. *British Heart Journal*, 1977, *39*, 152–159.

Raskin, M., Johnson, G., and Rondestvedt, J. W. Chronic anxiety treated by feedback-induced muscle relaxation. *Archives of General Psychiatry*, 1973, *28*, 263–267.

Ray, W. J., Raczynski, J. M., Rogers, T., & Kimball, W. H. *Evaluation of clinical biofeedback.* New York: Plenum, 1979.

Schwartz, G. E. Biofeedback and patterning of autonomic and central processes: CNS–cardiovascular interactions. In G. E. Schwartz & J. Beatty (Eds.), *Biofeedback: Theory and research.* New York: Academic Press, 1977.

Shannon, J. A. NIH—Present and potential contribution to application of biomedical knowledge. In *Research in the service of man: Biomedical knowledge, development, and use.* Committee on Government Operations, U.S. Senate. Washington, D.C.: U.S. Government Printing Office, 1967.

Shapiro, A. K. A contribution to a history of the placebo effect. *Behavioral Science,* 1960, *5,* 109–135.

Shapiro, A. K. Placebo effects in medicine, psychotherapy, and psychoanalysis. In A. E. Bergin & S. L. Garfield (Eds.), *Handbook of psychotherapy and behavior change: Empirical analysis.* New York: Wiley, 1971.

Stoyva, J. (Ed.). Task force reports of the Biofeedback Society of America. *Biofeedback and Self-Regulation,* 1978, *3,* 331–455.

Stratton, G. M. Vision without inversion of the retinal image. *Psychological Reviews,* 1897, *4,* 341–360, 463–481.

Stroebel, C. *The quieting reflex.* New York: Guilford, 1979.

Taub, E. Self-regulation of human tissue temperature. In G. E. Schwartz & J. Beatty (Eds.), *Biofeedback: Theory and research.* New York: Academic Press, 1977.

Taub, E. Somatosensory deafferentation research with monkeys: Implications for rehabilitation medicine. In L. P. Ince (Ed.), *Behavioral psychology in rehabilitation medicine: Clinical applications.* Baltimore: Williams & Wilkins, 1980.

Thomas, L. The place of biomedical science in medicine. In *Report of the President's biomedical research panel* (Appendix A, *The place of biomedical science in medicine and the state of the science)* (DHEW Publication No. (05)76-501). Washington, D.C.: U.S. Government Printing Office, 1976.

VanDercar, D. H., Feldstein, M. A., & Solomon, H. Instrumental conditioning of human heart rate during free and controlled respiration. *Biological Psychology,* 1977, *5,* 221–231.

Weiss, S. M., Fox, B., & Herd, J. A. (Eds.). *Perspectives in behavioral medicine.* New York: Academic Press, 1981.

Yates, A. J. *Biofeedback and the modification of behavior.* New York: Plenum, 1980.

II

EFFICACY, MECHANISMS, AND NEW DIRECTIONS

FORMAL PRESENTATIONS

The goal of this section is to examine general models of biofeedback and criteria of clinical efficacy, which may then be useful in evaluating the chapters in the following sections reviewing specific clinical applications.

The primary model used in the biofeedback literature is that of operant conditioning. Presented here in the chapters by Brener, Furedy and Riley, and Tursky are alternative perspectives.

Brener examines the major alternative to an operant paradigm, the hypothesis that response detection precedes response control. He finds that there are a number of apparent difficulties with testing the hypothesis in its present form. Particularly important is the recognition that even in the development of motor-control programs, monitoring of central afferent processes is a major source of information, and therefore the processes of discrimination and control may be mutually interdependent.

Furedy and Riley review the evidence from a unique series of studies involving the sequential use of classical and operant paradigms, which results in an otherwise unobtainable, operantly conditioned phasic heart rate deceleration of large magnitude. These procedures lead to a consideration of methods for eliciting the target response before attempting to teach it. Furedy and Riley stress the particular significance of temporal contiguity between conditional stimulus (CS)/unconditional response (UR) in the classical paradigm, and immediacy of reinforcement in the operant paradigm. The degree of similarity between the afferent inputs of the reinforcing stimulus and unconditional stimulus (US) may be an important and often ignored determinant of the biofeedback effect.

Since the procedures characteristically employed in clinical biofeedback do not conform to the engineering concept of "feedback," Tursky suggests that the term "biofeedback" be dropped. He proposes methodological and technical approaches that would be consistent with the concept of "physiological information processing," which he proposes as an alternative perspective. Tursky emphasizes the importance of the characteristics of the feedback signal in terms of phase, amplitude, and precision of information.

These theoretical chapters, as well as Shapiro's chapter on criteria of clinical efficacy examining the complexities of clinical trials, explicitly accept a "narrow" definition of "biofeedback." In this narrow definition, experimental effects or clinical change in the target response or symptom are solely attributable to the biofeedback procedure.

The broader meaning of "biofeedback" is usually encountered in the context of clinical application and is considered in Schwartz's remarks. In this usage, biofeedback is not the only treatment, but is incorporated as one of several approaches in a "package" treatment approach. Ultimately, clinical effects may be the consequence of changes in life style rather than of direct organ control. According to Schwartz, in this broader view, the assumptions and logic of narrowly defined biofeedback have been developed without adequate consideration of the biological, psychological, and etiological factors in the various disorders being treated. If the therapy is to address these etiological considerations, a broader, biobehavioral approach leading to cognitive reevaluation and changes in life style is rationalized. In this approach, biofeedback may be part of the treatment but is not *the* treatment.

An adequate theory of "biofeedback" is important because of its pragmatic consequences; not only does a theory lend legitimacy to clinical practice, but it also guides the search for more effective clinical procedures and the experimental controls necessary to demonstrate that specific efficacy.

ROUND-TABLE DISCUSSIONS

There are three round-table discussions in this section. The first round table, which follows Schwartz's discussion of Brener and Shapiro, elaborates upon the logic and consequences of adapting either the broad or the narrow clinical application of "biofeedback."

Whether an investigator accepts a broad or a narrow definition of "biofeedback" has important consequences for specification of mechanisms and the controls necessary to establish clinical efficacy. The narrow definition of "biofeedback" is comparable to an operant-conditioning paradigm; with it, a researcher obtains a greater degree of precision and experimental control, providing the possibility of a rigorous test of efficacy. In its broader definition, "biofeedback" includes feedback of information regarding physiological functioning in a multimodal, behaviorally oriented treatment program. In this broader usage, a rigorous evaluation of the therapeutic gains specifically attributable to the addition of biofeedback procedures becomes more difficult. If the emerging rubric of behavioral medicine includes this broader definition of "biofeedback," the sophisticated therapist should not assume that the efficacy and mechanisms of "biofeedback" as narrowly defined have been firmly established. An adequate theory concerning the therapeutic process not only validates clinical practices, but also has pragmatic consequences. Theory guides the establishment of control groups in the study of clinical efficacy and suggests new procedures for enhancing efficacy. Brener offers a further clarification of the processes involved in the generation of motor-control programs and explains why these motor control systems may be an appropriate model for biofeedback-assisted acquired control of autonomic systems. Further studies are needed in order to determine whether the comparisons between development of motor-control processes and autonomic-control processes are valid.

Mulholland, who serves as formal discussant for the Furedy and Riley chapter and the Tursky chapter, could not attend this session of the symposium. The round-table discussions of these papers, therefore, do not have the benefit of his comments; as a result, it was deemed advisable at this session to hold separate discussions for each of these papers.

In the discussion following the presentation by Furedy and Riley, the magnitude of heart rate change is examined within the context of biological mechanisms. The magnitude of change in heart rate must be seen within the context of its physiologically determined dynamic range. Within the full dynamic range of heart rate response, there are a variety of neural dynamics brought into play that may vary at intervals within the range. These differential biological mechanisms are not well understood. Biofeedback methods may achieve effects by altering unknown mechanisms. There is further emphasis on the need for noncontingent controls. It is important to keep in mind the distinction between instructional effects and demonstrated biofeedback effects, which may be confused if experiments do not include noncontingent control groups. The sequential use of classical and operant paradigms as described by Furedy and Riley is useful in altering phasic heart rate responses rather than in altering tonic levels. Although these "response-learning" techniques have clinical potential, clinical populations may be functioning at a different level within the range of heart rate variability and may not respond as normal subjects. A question is raised concerning the precision of the delivery of reinforcement during the operant phase of the procedures. Although the reinforcement procedures used may be comparable to hand methods used to shape an animal's responses using minimal instrumentation, a more precise and prompt method may yield a larger effect. The theoretical issues of the contiguity versus the informational content of the feedback signal raised by the Furedy and Riley chapter are also raised in Tursky's chapter. The issue reappears in the clinical context of motor rehabilitation when Brudny (see Chapter 10) describes a "sensory feedback" technique involving patterned feedback requiring cognitive interpretation, and when Wolf (see "Comments on the Chapter by Brudny") concludes that a simpler feedback signal yields comparable therapeutic effects.

Tursky's presentation notes Brudny's use of sensory feedback techniques for muscle rehabilitation as one of the more successful applications of biofeedback techniques and theorizes that part of this success may be due to the existence of a visual–motor loop within the central nervous system (CNS). In the round-table discussion following Tursky's presentation, Brudny acknowledges the validity of the engineering concept of feedback in understanding the physiology of motor control systems and his retraining techniques. Sensory feedback loops are fundamental and physiologically determined characteristics of the nervous system.

The discussion that follows illustrates the dual function of a model or theory: summarizing data and organizing new experiments. The terminology used for a procedure is not a mere semantic matter; it is important because a term carries with it a specific context that guides the search for reliable phenomena or efficacious treatments through modifications of procedures. Further, theory provides a guide for the development of experimental controls to isolate the specific mechanisms of action. The modality, as well as the phase and amplitude characteristics, of the external sensory feedback signal may be important determinants of the biological meaning of the signal. These properties of the sensory feedback signal may directly affect the stability and phasic responses of physiological systems. In addition, however, these signals are processed cognitively. Motivational processes may serve to direct attention and to make the characteristics of the feedback signal more salient. The response to biofeedback procedures may be determined by an interaction between the biological meaning of the feedback signal and the subject's motivation. The efficacy of alternative systems of feedback incorporating various sensory modalities, information densities, and timing may be tested within an operant-conditioning paradigm, using control groups in which the characteristics of the feedback signal are the independent measure and physiological responses are the dependent measure. Tests of comparative efficacy must also include experimental controls for motivational variables, which may significantly influence clinical results.

2 PSYCHOBIOLOGICAL MECHANISMS IN BIOFEEDBACK

JASPER M. BRENER

INTRODUCTION

I think it will be agreed that biofeedback treatments are a direct by-product of laboratory procedures that purported to generate voluntary control over otherwise involuntary activities. These experiments in turn were performed in an attempt to refine some fundamental theoretical questions. However, it would seem that the issues broached by current clinical biofeedback research are rather remote from those theoretical considerations that gave rise to the development of this treatment method. Such divergence is to be expected, since the criteria employed in assessing the effectiveness of a treatment are generally quite independent of the methods employed to identify how the treatment achieves its effects. It could even be argued that theoretical considerations may introduce biases into the therapeutic assessment procedure that could hinder the objective evaluation of a therapy. On the other hand, it can also be argued that understanding the mode of action of a treatment is an essential precondition to its rational application.

THE ANAYLSIS OF BIOFEEDBACK LEARNING

By virtue of its rate of growth and the size of its following, the study of biofeedback must qualify as a significant expression of some aspect of the intellectual enterprise. Its popularity is scarcely surprising, since biofeedback research makes an almost plausible claim to have begun to uncover the mechanisms of voluntary behavior. Kimmel (1974) has provided an account of the experimental history of this subject

Jasper M. Brener. Department of Psychology, University of Hull, Hull, England.

and more recently has commented on the potential conceptual impact of biofeedback research (Kimmel, 1978). He points out that this research could have been a watershed in psychology's search for a scientific model of man if psychology were still searching for one. However, over the past 30 years or so, psychology has lost the revolutionary zeal imparted to it by behaviorism and has regressed back to its mentalistic roots. Mentalistic interpretations of the mechanisms underlying biofeedback training also form the target of Black, Cott, and Pavlovski's criticism (1977) of the so-called "awareness view." They characterize this view as resting upon the assumption that biofeedback training facilitates voluntary control over activity by making subjects aware of the activity. Black and his colleagues contrast the ambiguous conceptual framework of the awareness view with the rigorous methodology and "rich theoretical potential" of the conditioning approach (Black, 1974; Black & Cott, 1977; Black *et al.*, 1977).

Although it is quite clear that the study of conditioning has generated a very powerful methodology, the "rich theoretical potential" to which Black *et al.* (1977) refer is far from being realized. The "paradigm shift" toward cognitivism or mentalism in current psychology, to which many authors like to refer, may be attributed in some measure at least to the theoretical inadequacy of the operant-conditioning approach. Two of the problems with operant conditioning to which Black *et al.* (1977) refer are its failure to deal with human cognitive processes and its failure to provide a description of behavior that may be transcribed into a neurophysiological model. These two problems may be complementary. Perhaps if learning models were more compatible with biological descriptions of behavioral regulation, the need to deal explicitly with human cognitive processes would recede. In other words, the variance in performance that cannot be accounted for by the concepts of stimulus control and the Law of Effect, and that appears to require recourse to cognitive processes, may be more satisfactorily accounted for by exploiting the vast conceptual repertoire of the biological sciences.

Although the cognitive movement in psychology has cut a broad swath and is fully represented in animal learning (e.g., Mackintosh, 1974), the last decade has also witnessed a more progressive accommodation by psychology to the organizing principles of biology. A good example is Staddon's (Staddon, 1975; Staddon & Simmelhag, 1971) adoption of the evolutionary analogue in the analysis of conditioning. His use of the principles of behavioral variation and selection in analyzing superstitious behavior in the pigeon not only avoids the tautological and teleological overtones of Skinner's adventitious reinforcement analysis but also provides a far more comprehensive description of the process. The work on autoshaping (Hearst & Jenkins, 1974), species-specific defense reactions in avoidance behavior (Bolles, 1970), taste aversion (Garcia & Rusiniak, 1977), and constraints on learning (Hinde & Stevenson-Hinde, 1973) all provide accounts of behavior that are quite compatible with the principles that organize biological sciences. As such, they open the possibility of far more comprehensive understandings of behavior than may be achieved within the narrow and scientifically isolated constraints of a cognitive, or for that matter, an operant-conditioning theoretical framework.[1]

The point is made by Black *et al.* (1977) that when one operationalizes and thereby imparts some literal significance to the terms "awareness" (response discrimination) and "volition" (compliance with instructions), the biofeedback procedure becomes virtually indistinguishable from an operant-conditioning procedure. Furthermore, the primary hypothesis that biofeedback training engenders voluntary control of a target response by making subjects aware of that response is rendered amenable to an experimental test. In operant-conditioning terminology, this hypothesis may be stated as follows: Response-contingent reinforcement leads to discriminative control of response only if the response is itself discriminable or is rendered discriminable by the reinforcement operations. However, they claim that experimental evidence indicates that response discrimination is not necessary for operant conditioning. Hence, if the "awareness view" is to offer any advantage over an operant analysis of biofeedback training, the data should confirm the relationships between response discrimination and response control predicted by this view.

It will be recognized that the issue has shifted from the value of awareness approaches versus operant-conditioning approaches to the validity of the hypothesis that response discrimination is implicated in the development of response control. In view of this, the term "voluntary-control approach" is used in this chapter in place of the term "awareness approach," which seems to carry more superfluous meaning. Although the term "voluntary control" also carries mentalistic connotations, in the experimental literature this process is almost universally operationalized in terms of instructional compliance. The analysis of voluntary control is clearly a central problem in psychology, and its experimental analysis has provided an enduring preoccupation for generations of psychologists (Kimble & Perlmuter, 1970).

Before going on to discuss the evidence related to the response-discrimination/control hypothesis, let us consider the bases, identified by Black *et al.* (1977), on which operant conditioning predicts that response discrimination is not prerequisite to control. There are two sources of evidence cited for this conviction: data indicating operant conditioning of responses in deafferented animals, and data on conditioning without awareness. The work on conditioning without awareness refers to the commonly reported observation that the activity of subjects may be influenced by reinforcement contingencies without their being able to describe the contingencies (e.g., Verplanck, 1962). It is recognized by Black *et al.* (1977) that these data are not directly relevant to the issue at hand, because, as it is employed in this litera-

[1]The point has been made previously (e.g., Brener, 1974a) that the concept of operant conditioning embodies the least satisfactory components of the philosophical concept of volition: Like a voluntary response, an operant arises from unknown sources and is controlled by its consequences.

ture, "awareness" does not refer explicitly to response discrimination. In any case, it will be recognized that since individuals may be taught to discriminate response events without their displaying evidence of awareness of the events being discriminated, the "conditioning without awareness" issue is a red herring. For example, Hefferline and Perera (1963) demonstrated that subjects could be trained to discriminate muscle twitches without having the faintest idea before or after training what they were doing. The view that response discrimination is unnecessary for response conditioning therefore rests exclusively upon the evidence for the conditioning of motor responses in deafferented limbs. This work comes mainly from the laboratories of Taub and his collaborators (e.g., Taub, Bacon, & Berman, 1965; Taub & Berman, 1968; Taub, Ellman, & Berman, 1966) and purports to demonstrate that motor conditioning may occur in the absence of either internal or external response feedback. The experiments are well designed and fully reported, and they appear to offer a strong case in favor of the proposition that quite intricate muscular responses may be conditioned in the absence of neural feedback from the effector. Since these data appear to challenge a viewpoint that is quite firmly entrenched in theories of the development of motor control, they warrant particularly careful scrutiny.

Before interpreting the deafferentation data to indicate that response discrimination is unnecessary for the development of response control, certain reservations must be considered. Firstly, since the deafferentation procedure entails only dorsal rhizotomy, it does not exclude the possibility that information about activity may be gained through afferent fibres traveling in the ventral roots (McCloskey, 1978). It is also possible that the organism may be able to detect its movement through nonspecific feedback—by way of the vestibular system, for example. Central feedback[2] is another source of information through which the nervous system may detect the activation of the motor system. The idea that the nervous system monitors its own motor commands and stores copies of them for comparison with reafferent feedback is accepted on the bases of both behavioral and neurophysiological studies. In fact, Taub's analysis of motor regulation in deafferented animals confers an important role on this process. So it is not altogether clear that complete dorsal rhizotomy deprives the nervous system of all information about the activities of its effectors. Secondly, the experiments on motor conditioning in deafferented animals do not contain tests of the animals' capacity to discriminate responses of the deafferented limbs. In view of the arguments to follow, it is important to recognize here that such a test of response discrimination (where the occurrence of the response serves as a discriminative stimulus (SD) for some

[2]It should be noted that "central efferent monitoring" implies a process that is functionally afferent or sensory. The distinction between it and peripheral feedback is that, in the case of central efferent processes, the feedback arises from a more proximal component of the motor control circuit.

other response) will not ipso facto identify the sensory channels through which the response is detected. In the intact organism, it could be detected through any internal or external feedback pathway or through a central efferent process.

Thus, it would seem that the operant-conditioning approach cannot unequivocally reject the involvement of response discrimination in the development of motor conditioning. In fact, Taub notes that deafferentation severely retards the rate of acquisition of an avoidance response and the rate of its extinction (Taub, Teodoru, Ellman, Bloom, & Berman, 1965, 1966). These investigators also reported that the provision of external feedback produced normal extinction rates in deafferented monkeys. Numerous other learning theorists have attributed an important if not an essential role to response discrimination in the acquisition of behavior (Dinsmoor, 1954; Hull, 1943; Notterman & Mintz, 1965). Therefore, there is no crucial experimental test of whether the voluntary-control approach is more or less effective than the operant-conditioning approach.

The role of response discrimination in response control is also questioned by Black *et al.* (1977), who ask why a response should display discriminative functions before it can be voluntarily controlled. The voluntary-control model argues that this discriminative function of the response is established by the process of calibration during biofeedback training. Calibration, which is assumed to operate by a process like classical conditioning, occurs as a natural consequence of biofeedback. The exteroceptive feedback stimulus is paired with the organism's internal sensory state at the instant of response execution, and an association is thereby conditioned.[3] The model requires that this association between the internal sensory accompaniments of the response and its external consequences must fulfill two functions: (1) the identification of a sensory state that provides the basis for formulating a motor plan for the target response; and (2) the provision of access to the motor plan, thereby permitting its activation by external stimuli such as the instructions that have a conditioned association with the biofeedback stimuli.[4]

[3]From the point of view of Pavlovian conditioning, this learned association is somewhat problematic. This is because it is assumed not only that the internal stimulus state at the time of the response comes to imply the biofeedback stimulus, but also that the biofeedback stimulus acquires control of a central response that is unconditionally elicited by the internal feedback. The latter process could imply backward conditioning. However, since the associative mechanism seems to have evolved so as to maximize the acquisition of biologically adaptive associations (Garcia & Koelling, 1966; Hearst & Jenkins, 1974), it is not impossible that it facilitates backward conditioning where the unconditional stimulus (US) is a movement and the conditional stimulus (CS) is the exteroceptive consequences of that movement. Certainly this would be an efficient means of classifying motor plans in terms of their environmental functions.

[4]The ability of a verbal feedback stimulus to evoke its heart rate referent has been studied by Wright, Carroll, and Newman (1977). These investigators respectively labeled elicited heart rate increases corectly (VF), incorrectly (RF), or not at all (C) in three groups of subjects. A subsequent heart rate control probe partially supported the predictions of the model, with subjects in the VF condition displaying greater heart rate increases than subjects in the RF or C conditions.

Neither of these requirements implies that the response (or its sensory accompaniments) must serve as a discriminative stimulus. However, it can be argued that these functions establish conditions that will permit the response to act as a discriminative stimulus. Thus, tests of response discrimination examine whether the subject can recognize instances of the target response; as such, they provide an indirect means of examining whether the nervous system has formulated a motor plan, which in this case functions as a recognition template. As indicated below, the concept of awareness is quite extraneous to the implementation of such tests and is not required for the interpretation of their results.

In deciding on a theoretical framework the analysis of biofeedback learning, two considerations seem paramount: (1) that the theory should generate testable hypotheses, and (2) that these hypotheses should be compatible with existing physiological knowledge concerning the process of motor control. In other words, the process of the model should be biologically computable. In this regard, the model of voluntary control that I have previously employed to describe the processes of biofeedback learning and that is based upon William James' (1890) ideomotor theory and data from perceptual motor research (Brener, 1974a, 1974b, 1977a, 1977b) is accomodated well by the following description of the mechanisms of learned motor control recently provided by Numan (1978):

> Since the frontal cortical areas receive (and presumably integrate) sensory and motor information derived from primary and secondary cortical areas, I would like to suggest that motor programs are formulated in the prefrontal cortex. Konorski (1967) and Luria (1966) have reached similar conclusions. Recent neurophysiological data also support this point of view (Niki, 1974a, 1974b, 1974c; Niki & Watanabe, 1976). Niki's data will be discussed shortly. The formulation of these motor programs is based on the available sensory information, the motivational and emotional state of the organism (perhaps integrated in orbital cortex), and previous experiential factors which dictate the organism's expectations. We might also add that the area lying in the region of the principal sulcus (middle third?) of the dorsolateral frontal cortex would appear to be of particular importance for the assessment of proprioceptive and/or spatio-vestibular information for incorporation in the motor program. Once a motor program is formulated, it is transmitted to the hippocampus where it is temporarily stored. The hippocampus can thus be considered the memory mechanism of the system, since it stores the trace of the original motor program [after Von Holst (1954), I will call this trace an efference copy]. Initiation of the motor program occurs when the FAC [frontal association cortex] activates motor mechanisms in the precentral gyrus which, in turn, emits an efferent signal. The efferent signal activates the efference copy in hippocampus to be ready for reafferent feedback (reafferent feedback is used loosely to indicate stimulus changes in the environment and the organism that are the result of responding, i.e., response-dependent stimulus changes). The efferent signal also leads to response initiation, which in turn leads to reafference. This reafferent feedback is transmitted to mesencephalic centers. From these midbrain centers, the reafference (both intero- and exteroceptive) is carried to (1) the cerebral cortex, and (2) the medial septum. From these

> points, the reafferent information is transmitted to (1) the frontal cortical areas and (2) hippocampus. In hippocampus reafference is compared with the efference copy. If the consequences of responding are congruent with the expectations written into the motor program, the reafference and efferent copy will match and the response sequence will be terminated. However, if these expected consequences of responding are not attained, reafference and efferent copy will not match and the mechanisms involved in formulating a new motor program are set into motion. Under this condition, the frontocortical areas are signaled as to the inappropriateness of the previous response pattern via septohippocampal-entorhinal pathways (Hjorth-Simonsen, 1971; Votaw, 1959, 1960). Based on the stimulus information available, and especially the reafference which was just transmitted to the frontal cortical areas, a new motor program is written and transmitted to hippocampus, and the process begins anew, and continues until efference copy and reafference match, thus terminating the response sequence. (p. 461)

Models of this sort that attempt to identify function with structure suggest numerous experimental hypotheses, which, when tested, may help to refine our understanding of the mechanism of voluntary control. However, difficulties do arise in trying to analyze the effects of biofeedback training of visceral responses in terms of the sort of model proposed by Numan. One of these is intrinsic to this and most otherwise clearly formulated models of motor control—they do not describe with any precision the processes by which motor programs are generated. It seems to me, however, that one of the great potential benefits of studying the development of visceromotor control is that it may help to clarify the mechanisms underlying the writing of motor programs. The extent to which this potential may be realized must depend heavily on the degree to which the functional organization of the visceromotor control system is comparable to the organization of the somatomotor control system. Researchers may derive some relevant information on this topic by examining whether visceral responses are influenced by environmental contingencies in the same way as somatomotor responses are. Although, with the possible exceptions of Johnston (1977), Lang and Twentyman (1974, 1976), and Williamson and Blanchard (1979), this has not been done very systematically, there is no clear evidence as yet that the two systems obey different programming principles. Nevertheless, the data are marginal. For example, Morley (1979) recently concluded that biofeedback research has not yet confirmed whether or not the partial reinforcement effect applies for visceral learning.

AFFERENT PATHWAYS AND RESPONSE DISCRIMINATION

A traditional distinction that has been drawn between the voluntary somatomotor response system and the involuntary visceral response system relates to their afferent processes. Only fairly recently has it been established that the functions and anatomy of the visceral afferent system are not clearly different from those of the somatosensory or exteroceptive systems (Adam, 1967; Chernigovskiy, 1967; Neil, 1972; Newman, 1974; see Brener, 1977b, for overview). Sherrington (1906) was convinced that the visceral afferent system was different from the somatosensory system on the grounds that individuals could tell what their limbs were doing, whereas they could not tell what their viscera were doing. However, researchers engaged in kinesthetic research are still undecided about whether muscle stretch receptors or the Golgi tendon organs produce discharges that are available to consciousness (McCloskey, 1978). For example, Gelfan and Carter (1967), using human subjects, exposed muscles responsible for moving the fingers and pulled on the tendons, thereby stretching the muscles. On the basis of the verbal responses of their subjects, these investigators proclaimed in no uncertain terms that "there is no muscle sense" (p. 472). This finding conformed to the prevalent point of view. However, Matthews and Simmonds (1974) performed almost exactly the same experiment and came to the opposite conclusion. They reported that in every case when a muscle tendon was pulled, the subject reported movement in the appropriate finger. The reasons underlying this discrepancy are illuminating in relation to the issue of visceral perception to be discussed below. Gelfan and Carter apparently asked their subjects whether they experienced "muscle sensations"; Matthews and Simmonds asked their subjects whether they experienced "finger movement." Just as individuals do not refer auditory and visual sensations to the ears and eyes, they do not refer sensations of changing muscle length to the muscle stretch receptors, but rather to movements of the limbs being served by the muscles. Thus, the use of verbal discriminative responses can be just as misleading in the investigation of proprioception as they have been in visceroception.

A really compelling example of something that might be called cardiac discrimination has been reported by Jammes and Rosenberger (1971). These investigators reported that senile patients often engaged in rocking behavior that was precisely synchronized with their pulse rates. This precise synchrony was not disturbed by pharmacological interventions that produced substantial increases and decreases in pulse rate. Their remarkable data are summarized in Table 1.

TABLE 1. Means and Standard Deviations of Heart Rates and Rocking Frequencies of 96 Senile Patients[a]

		Heart Rate/Rocking Rate Ratio	
		1:1 (N = 80)	1:2 (N = 16)
No medication	Heart rate	77.8 ± 3.7	78.8 ± 6.1
	Rocking frequency	77.9 ± 2.3	38.9 ± 7.8
After epinephrine	Heart rate	107.8 ± 4.9	112.1 ± 5.3
	Rocking frequency	107.2 ± 2.7	52.6 ± 2.9
After ouabain	Heart rate	58.3 ± 5.9	58.9 ± 6.9
	Rocking frequency	51.0 ± 6.3	28.9 ± 5.1

[a]Adapted from Jammes and Rosenberger (1971).

patients were triggered by their cardiac activity. However, like most of the other data on response discrimination, they do not identify the sensory sources of the signals that triggered the rocking movements. These could have arisen from intracardiac receptors, from arterial baroceptors, or from noncardiovascular receptors that were activated by the pulsatile mechanical activity of the pressure pulse wave. Regardless of the signals' sources, this example indicates quite emphatically that the nervous system receives and acts upon information about cardiac activity.

Since the heart beat is initiated peripherally, the one source of response discrimination that may be safely discounted in this example is some central efferent process. However, in the case of responses that are initiated by central neural processes, efferent monitoring cannot be discounted as a factor in response discrimination. Following a comprehensive review of the experimental literature, McCloskey (1978) concludes that "sensations of movement are not generated by centrifugal mechanisms" (p. 794). However, he does concede that the activation of motor plans may be perceived by subjects and that central efferent monitoring provides the primary source for judging force or heaviness. Thus, he concludes that "almost all normal subjects appear to neglect any alternative signals in favor of the centrifugal commands in their judgments of force and heaviness, even when this choice leads to error" (p. 803). The capacity of individuals to sense the initiation of an act through these central feedback pathways has been advanced to account for the acquisition of response control in subjects with deafferented limbs. It also accounts for the performance of subjects with functional deafferentation of the thumb who were able to move the digit accurately on instruction but did not know that they had not complied when movement was physically prevented (Merton, 1972). Hence, the capacity of the CNS to monitor its own outflow may enable the discrimination of motor acts independently of their peripheral consequences.

MOTOR PROCESSES IN PERCEPTION

A consideration that complicates the study of response discrimination is that the perceptual process itself has a strong motoric component. For example, Metzger (1974) lists the following 12 ways in which the activity of the subject may be implicated in perception.

> 1. Receptors are exposed to stimulation by certain objects (as looking about, bending to a key-hole, grasping something etc.)
>
> 2. The area accessible to receptors is enlarged (as wandering about in order to survey, groping in the dark, etc.)
>
> 3. Stimulus configurations are shifted to the most sensitive parts of a receptor (fixation reaction that shifts stimuli to the fovea centralis, bringing objects to the fingertips or to the tip of tongue)

> 4. State of receptors is optimized (as in accommodation, convergence, retinal adaptation, modification of width of pupil etc.)
>
> 5. Outer conditions of perception are improved (as in moving the watch toward the ear, putting on or taking off eyeglasses, turning on a light, twinkling, snuffing, sucking, moistening and lifting up a finger in order to feel the direction of subliminal air draught, leaving and reentering a room in order to recognize a smell, stopping one's breath in order to hear faint noise, shutting the window in order to understand one's partner, etc.)
>
> 6. Local adaptation and fading are slowed down (cf. above, Section IV, C, ¶ 3)
>
> 7. Exploratory movements in the strict sense of the word (as touching and scanning, including tracing; but cf. above, Section IV, C, ¶ 4)
>
> 8. Voluntary movements that are intended to be observed themselves as a means of building up or restoring visual–kinesthetic coordination (Held, 1966; and Smith & Smith, 1966)
>
> 9. Accompanying music by abortive conducting or dancing movements
>
> 10. Active performance of music or recitation of poetry; active reproduction of handwriting in order to facilitate empathy
>
> 11. Operations with objects which serve the purpose of knowing them better (as matching, arranging, copying, memorizing, building up out of given parts; cf. Zaporozhets & Gibson, 1966, passim)
>
> 12. Searching for principles of organization of a given material (Katona, 1940). As this survey shows, subject's action in perception above all supports the "receiving" function of receptors, and does by no means serve the purpose of "creating" anything, as some of us believe. This is the task of poets and artists. By the way, we ought to be content with this. For should freedom of subjective creation of the perceptive world surpass a very limited range, incessant paranoid misunderstandings between all of us would be the unavoidable consequence, and communication and cooperation would be impossible. (pp. 119–120)

In most of these cases, perception involves an active behavioral process. Motor processes that are more subtle but no less important are implicated in perception by Festinger, Ono, Burnham, and Bamber's account (1967) of perception as the experience of efference. Their view, which is another expression of the motor theory of perception, is more or less that the perceptual experience of an object is determined by the efferent patterns activated by that object. As a classic example of this process, they describe Gibson's experiment (1933) in which subjects wore prisms that made straight lines look curved. When subjects were asked to run their hands along the straight edges, they reported no disparity between visual input and kinesthetic input. In other words, the edges felt curved. Festinger *et al.* (1967) explain Gibson's observation as follows:

> Let us imagine that the conscious perception of the path of movement of a limb is not the organization of informational input from the receptors in that limb, but is rather the organization of the efferent signals issued from the central nervous system to that limb. The arm would be felt to move in a curved path if the efferent signals issued through the motor pathways directed the arm to move in a

> curve. The fact that the arm and hand, because they are maintaining pressure on the straight edge, actually move in a straight line would then be irrelevant to the conscious experience of path of movement. The arm is felt to move as it has been directed to move (p. 4)

By "efferent monitoring" Festinger and his colleagues do not mean the monitoring of motor output. They mean something more akin to monitoring a central state of motor preparation in which "[preprogrammed] sets of efferent instructions are brought into a state of immediate readiness for use" (1967, p. 12).[5] This does not, of course, preclude the full activation of efferent instructions. The general implication of their argument is that, to perceive an object, an individual must have formulated a way of behaving in relation to that object.

Within the context of this understanding of perception, in order to perceive, say, a heart rate increase, the subject must prepare for activities that are appropriate to sensing what he or she has labeled "heart rate increases." Even if such activities did result in heart rate variation, this would not distinguish heart rate perception from other perceptions. In perceptual tasks, it is to be expected that the subject will prepare for and engage in appropriate information-gathering behaviors.

The point of this discussion has been to emphasize the conceptual problems inherent in distinguishing between the mechanisms of response discrimination and response control. As Powers (1973) points out, "sensory inputs affect and are affected by behavior" (p. 54). Because of the physiological functions of these inputs and outputs, when researchers ask subjects to discriminate a response, it is likely that the same circuits will be activated that would be activated if the subjects were instructed to control that response. With this in mind, I now examine the literature on the relationship between response discrimination and response control in biofeedback experiments.

RESPONSE DISCRIMINATION AND RESPONSE CONTROL

The bases on which investigators might expect response discrimination to be implicated in the development of visceromotor control have been outlined. The view that has been presented makes two predictions: (1) As individuals acquire control of a response, they should also manifest an improved capacity to detect instances of that response. (2) If individuals are trained to detect instances of a response, they should show an improved capacity to control that response.

Testing these hypotheses would seem to be a necessary first step in examining the effectiveness of the model from which they stem. Since a number of review ar-

[5]It will be recognized that this concept of perceptual experience is closely related to Sechenov's (1863/1965) view of consciousness as the first two-thirds of a reflex. It is also clear that Festinger and his colleagues' use of "sets of efferent instructions" is equivalent to "motor plans."

ticles on this subject have been published (Brener, 1977b; Brener, Ross, Baker, & Clemens, 1980; Carroll, 1977; Gannon, 1977; Roberts, 1977; Roberts & Marlin, 1979; Whitehead, Drescher, Heiman, & Blackwell, 1977), the experimental literature will not be described in any detail here. Most of the early studies of the relationship between visceral response discrimination and visceral response control employed Mandler's Autonomic Perception Questionnaire (APQ) (Mandler, Mandler, & Uviller, 1958). It has been pointed out previously (Brener, 1977b) that this test, which was not intended to measure the accuracy of visceral perception, does not provide a valid index of visceral response discrimination. This point is made most clearly by the failure to find correlations between APQ scores and performance on direct tests of visceral discrimination (Donelson, 1966; McFarland, 1975; Whitehead, Drescher, & Blackwell, 1976). Hence, this discussion will not consider the results of experiments in which the APQ was employed to index visceral perception.

Even when the results of these experiments are discounted, the picture that emerges is far from clear. Some experimental results indicate that response discrimination and control are related in a manner predicted by the voluntary control model (Kamiya, 1969; Kleinman, 1970; Lacroix, 1977; McFarland & Campbell, 1975; Stern, 1972). Other results (Black *et al.*, 1977; Whitehead *et al.*, 1977; Whitehead & Drescher, 1979) show no relationship between discrimination and control. And yet others provide some evidence that favors and other evidence that does not favor the predictions of the model (Clemens, 1976; Clemens & MacDonald, 1976; McFarland, 1975). The failure of these experiments to provide clear tests of the model's predictions may be traced to several interrelated conceptual and methodological problems.

In this discussion, the view is taken that the definitions of the processes under investigation are tied to the experimental operations that are employed to evidence them. This is mentioned here because one of the recurrent problems in the published research related to this topic is that although experimenters generally commence an experiment employing rigorous operational definitions of voluntary control and response discrimination, additional criteria for inclusion in these classes seem to intrude as the discussion of results progresses. It is clear that before experimenters can have any consensus on the nature of the relationship between response discrimination and response control, they must have a consensus on what response discrimination and response control are.

DEFINING VOLUNTARY CONTROL AND RESPONSE DISCRIMINATION

What researchers mean by "voluntary control" in the scientific sense is identified by the operations they employ to evidence its occurrence in the experimental setting. A reading of the literature indicates that when experimenters use the term "voluntary" to describe a behavior (rather than an anatomical structure) of a human, they are referring to a response that is controlled by verbal instructions. However, compliance with instructions is not considered by everyone to be an adequate criterion for classifying visceral responses as voluntary. For example, Katkin and Murray (1968) suggest that the way in which the response is produced or mediated should be included in the criteria for classification. So, if a verbally controlled change in visceral performance is accompanied by somatomotor or cognitive activities, then it does not constitute evidence of voluntary control. These additional criteria are not applied in the voluntary / nonvoluntary classification of somatomotor responses. It is not required that before an instructionally controlled limb movement is classified as a voluntary response, it should not be accompanied by cognitive activities or visceral correlates. If experimenters knew how "true voluntary" responses were mediated, then adopting evidence of the operation of such mechanisms as criteria for classifying voluntary and nonvoluntary activities would have some organizing function. However, since the mechanisms of voluntary behavior have not been adequately described, it is not possible to employ mechanistic criteria rationally in this context.

The same general arguments may be advanced in favor of distinguishing the methods for identifying instances of response discrimination from questions regarding the mechanisms of response perception. McCloskey's review of kinesthetic processes (1978) provides an excellent conceptual and methodological guide to the study of response discrimination. As the contents of his review indicate, despite a far longer history and much greater volume of research, fundamental questions regarding the sources of kinesthetic sensibility and the functions of the various afferent and efferent processes involved have yet to be resolved. Nevertheless, this work does offer an extremely valuable basis for developing the study of visceral perception and its relationship to visceral control.

The theoretical importance of an efferent monitoring process is underlined by the research on motor learning following deafferentation and in accounting for sensations of muscular force.[6] This work adds credibility to the motor theory of perception, which, in any case, is not significantly compromised by the available data on perception. In fact, the relevant data suggest that it would be foolhardy to exclude as evidence of response perception those cases that were accompanied by observing

[6]In this context, it should be noted that in biofeedback studies, although fairly precise measures of response discrimination are employed, the measures of response control are generally very gross and are often confined to magnitude measurements. If the magnitude or intensity of visceral response is sensed in the same way that the force of somatomuscular activity is sensed, it would imply that central efferent processes are a more important source of information about voluntary visceral responses than is afferent feedback from the target organ.

responses. However, researchers studying the perception of visceral activities have tried to apply this stricture rigorously. For example, in criticizing a test of cardiac discrimination, Carroll (1977) says, "active respiratory and cognitive maneuvers rather than cardiac events could have controlled discriminative responding. . . ." (p. 359). Whitehead *et al.* (1977), in describing the merits of an alternative discriminative procedure, comment that "it was impossible for subjects to detect bogus heart rate information by manipulating their heart rate. . . ." (p. 388). Similarly, Black *et al.* (1977) make this point in relation to sources of artifact in their EEG discrimination procedure: "subjects often reported that they tested 'hypotheses' about the two EEG patterns by actively putting themselves into a particular state and then determining on the basis of the outcome of their responses which EEG pattern corresponded to that state. The manipulations involved ranged from eye movements and visual imagery to problem solving and highly emotional thoughts" (p. 112). Each of these statements implies that data clearly indicating that a subject was able to distinguish reliably between the presence and absence of a response should not be accepted as evidence of response discrimination, on the grounds that the subject may have been detecting central efferent processes associated with the response rather than detecting peripheral afferent processes. This presupposes without justification that efferent monitoring is not involved in response discrimination processes generally.

On these grounds, it is suggested that in order to generate clear evidence on the hypotheses mentioned at the beginning of this section, it is necessary for experimenters to agree upon the operations employed for evidencing instances of voluntary visceral control and visceral response discrimination. It has been argued that since there are a number of viable proposals regarding the mechanisms of visceral control and visceral discrimination, such definitions should initially be relatively unrestrictive with regard to mechanism. In other words, the definitions should not arbitrarily restrict the investigation of the processes of visceral response control or discrimination.

However, even when strict operational criteria are employed in identifying instances of response discrimination and control, the investigation of the relationship between these two processes can go awry because the operations are not adequately matched. In particular, it is essential that the operations probe the discrimination and control of the same response. For example, Whitehead *et al.* (1977) have presented data that indicate fairly persuasively that cardiac discrimination and cardiac control are unrelated. Following tests of heart beat discrimination, subjects were tested on compliance with instructions to modify their heart rates and were trained to regulate their heart rates under conditions of biofeedback. The cardiac discrimination procedure devised by Whitehead *et al.* (1976) and employed in this series of studies would seem to provide a valid test of the discrimination of peripheral sensory events associated with the beating of the heart, and it thereby rules out the possibility of subjects employing efferent processes in solving the discrimination problem. The results revealed no differences between subjects who performed very well and very poorly on this test, either in voluntary control of heart rate or in heart rate learning under conditions of biofeedback. This study may be criticized on the grounds that the event being discriminated (the heart beat) is different from the response being controlled (changes in heart rate). In terms of the requirements of the voluntary-control model, the heart beat, which is propagated peripherally and is not dependent upon the brain for its occurrence, does not constitute a response. In order to conclude that heart rate control is independent of cardiac perception, the discrimination test should have probed the subjects' capacity to detect variations in heart rate, which are initiated centrally. Nevertheless, these data do indicate that the capacity to regulate heart rate is independent of a subject's sensitivity to peripheral sensory events associated with the activity of the target organ, and this would seem to require an accommodation by the model.[7] A broad analogy to these results, but one involving the somatomuscular system, might be that the tactile sensitivity of a limb surface was unrelated to the control of that limb or to motor learning in that limb. As Paillard (1960) indicates, this is not the case; the surfaces of the most controllable effectors are the most sensitive.

One view that is compatible with the experimental literature on motor regulation is that the precision with which an effector is regulated depends upon the proximity to the command center of the source from which the control mechanism derives its error (feedback) signal. The more distal or peripheral the source of error signal tapped by the control process is, the greater the potential precision of the system's controlled response will be. So for very fine-grain motor adjustments, such as manipulating a specimen under a microscope, exteroceptive visual feedback is required; whereas for the production of very gross adjustments, such as the production of ergotrophic or trophotropic response states, centrifugal feedback is sufficient and exteroceptive feedback is redundant. If the motor control process responsible for regulating instructionally controlled heart rate changes cannot tap peripheral cardiac feedback signals as Whitehead *et al.*'s data (1977) suggest, it may be incapable of generating more specific control than has been observed so far. (Lacroix,

[7]In this connection, it may be noted that Ross and Brener (1981) found no relationship between performance on the discrimination procedure employed by Whitehead *et al.* (1976) and another, ostensibly similar cardiac discrimination procedure (Brener & Jones, 1974). Furthermore, initial training on the Brener and Jones procedure predisposed subjects to engage in active testing maneuvers, whereas initial training on the Whitehead procedure did not promote the adoption of such strategies in solving the discrimination problem. Subjects who adopted active solution strategies were found subsequently to produce significantly larger heart rate increases on instruction than were subjects who solved the discrimination problem by more passive means.

in press, has recently presented a well-documented case in favor of the conclusion that efferent processes are more strongly implicated in visceral learning than was previously thought.)

BIOFEEDBACK AND RESPONSE SPECIFICITY

In the history of biofeedback research, questions regarding the precision with which a response may be controlled have frequently been expressed in terms of "the mediation debate". So if instances of voluntary heart rate control were accompanied by correlated changes in respiration, it is likely that the respiration would be viewed as a mediator of the observed heart rate changes. The term "mediation" is employed in this area in a sense that makes it more or less equivalent to "elicitation." In other words, when respiration is said to mediate heart rate changes, it is implied that the mediating part of the respiration process antedates and causes the heart rate change.

The experiments on visceral conditioning in curarized animals (DiCara, 1970; Miller, 1969) addressed the question of response specificity from the mediational point of view. Despite replication difficulties (e.g., Brener, Eissenberg, & Middaugh, 1974; Miller & Dworkin, 1974; Roberts, 1978), there can be little doubt either (1) that the curare data were important in promoting the acceptance of visceral learning as a real phenomenon, albeit for rather obscure reasons, or (2) that, conceptually, they have been very illuminating. Gatchel and Price (1979) assert that it is believed that the curare experiments "convincingly demonstrate that internal visceral events can be instrumentally conducted in a manner analogous to instrumental conditioning of skeletal muscular responses" (p. 8). Presumably, the basis of this belief is the assumption that instrumental conditioning leads to response-specific skeletal muscular control. Although the evidence is rather sparse, most theories of learning do assume that response control becomes more specific with training. This assumption has a plausible biological basis in the principle of least effort (Solomon, 1948).

The greatest source of variance in an organism's overall rate of energy expenditure is its rate of skeletal muscular activity. In the transition from a state of rest to a state of strenuous exercise, the rate of energy expenditure may increase 16-fold, and this increase is almost entirely accounted for by skeletal muscular activity. It may therefore be expected that the elimination of functionally redundant skeletal motor activities may provide a primary purpose for the learning mechanisms that have evolved to promote behavioral adaptation. It is assumed here that the response differentiation that is anticipated during the course of operant conditioning (Notterman & Mintz, 1965) is an expression of this principle. In other words, during training, functionally redundant components of the organism's behavior (those that do not result in reinforcement) recede, resulting eventually in a maximally efficient adaptation.

The elimination of unadaptive activities during the course of motor learning is assumed to depend upon processes that function to refine the specifications of the relevant motor programs. In visceral learning, somatomotor activities that accompany the target visceral response may entail superfluous energy expenditure in terms of the demands of the reinforcement or biofeedback contingencies. However, if they provide the feedback that is necessary for regulating the motor plan that drives the target visceral response, these somatomotor activities may not be considered functionally redundant. It has been suggested previously (Brener, 1974b) that the limiting factor in generating response-specific visceral control is the nervous system's capacity to discriminate the sensory correlates of the target visceral response from the sensory correlates of those other activities that form its normal biological context. Thus, studying the extent to which biofeedback is effective in generating response-specific control may provide investigators with clues about the neural processes governing biofeedback learning. A similar point has been made by Schwartz (1977), who has argued convincingly for the use of patterned feedback in uncovering the neural organization of visceromotor control processes. His work on training integration and differentiation of heart rate and blood pressure patterns (Schwartz, 1972) has uncovered constraints and synergisms between responses that were not revealed by independent training of the component responses. Observations such as these naturally raise questions regarding the mechanisms by which components of the target response state interact. They thereby demand a more precise description of the mechanisms underlying learned visceromotor control.

Where the covariation between particular activities is very strong, feedback of response patterns may be impracticable as a procedure for examining whether the activities are independently controllable. Heart rate and somatomotor activity provide a case in point. It is well established that heart rate and cardiac output vary as a direct function of the organism's rate of energy expenditure (Astrand, Cuddy, Saltin, & Sternberg, 1964). Therefore, when a feedback or reinforcing stimulus is made contingent on a heart rate variation, it will also be contingent on the somatomotor activity through which the accompanying variation in energy expenditure is expressed (Kimmel & Burns, 1977). Thus we (Brener, Phillips, & Connally, 1980) have observed that shock avoidance contingencies give rise to very similar ergotropic behavioral adjustments, regardless of whether increases in heart rate or increases in ambulation serve as the avoidance response. Also, when unrestrained rats are submitted to a heart rate shock avoidance procedure, although very substantial discriminated increases and decreases in heart rate are conditioned, these cardiac responses are accompanied by parallel variations in oxygen consumption and ambulation

(Brener, Phillips, & Connally, 1977).[8] The lack of independence between conditioned cardiac and somatomotor activities has been recorded by many investigators in a variety of species and under a variety of conditions. Do these studies indicate that the nervous system is unable to generate cardiospecific control, and, if so, what are the constraints?

The available physiological evidence indicates that variations in cardiac activity and somatomotor activity are coupled both peripherally and centrally. For example, cardiac output covaries precisely with the rate of energy expenditure, both when the neural connections between the heart and the brain have been severed and when they are intact (Donald & Shepherd, 1963). However, it is also known that when energy expenditure is experimentally regulated or controlled for, the nervous system continues to exert control over the heart (Blix, Stromme, & Ursin, 1974; Langer, Obrist, & McCubbin, 1979; Obrist, 1976; Smith, 1974). Thus, although the linkage between cardiac and somatomotor activities is very strong, it is not immutable. This establishes the biological feasibility of those operant-conditioning and biofeedback experiments that have attempted to demonstrate cardiospecific control. Because of the normally close coupling between the two response systems, these studies have generally approached the problem by restraining or regulating somatomotor activity during training of cardiac control. The curare experiments (DiCara, 1970; Miller, 1969), which employed an extreme form of somatomotor control, indicated that skeletal muscular activities could be eliminated without impairing cardiac conditioning. Because curare acts peripherally, and because it is known that the cardiac and somatomotor control systems may interact centrally, these data do not provide evidence on the specificity of the central neural processes that produced the conditioned heart rate response. In fact, the curare data are quite compatible with the results on unrestrained subjects, which indicate that heart rate training leads to the development of stimulus control over central motor programs that are responsible for the concurrent regulation of functionally related somatomotor and cardiovascular responses. This proposal, in turn, is not inconsistent with the findings by Obrist, Galosy, Lawler, Gaebelein, Howard, and Shanks (1975) that the degree of learned heart rate control is inversely related to the level of somatomotor restraint imposed upon the subject. Taken together, these results seem to imply that when centrally mediated restraints are imposed on the subject's somatomotor activity (e.g., Obrist *et al.*, 1975), heart rate control is impaired, but when the restraints are

[8]It is interesting that reinforcement contingencies that demand an increase in cardiac activity, when applied in a running-wheel situation, give rise to systematic increases in ambulation. On the other hand, when reinforcement contingencies that require an increase in activity to avoid electric shock are applied in an open-field situation, animals do not learn to avoid (Brener & Goesling, 1970). This implies that situational factors (the availability of appropriate releasing stimuli), rather than the reinforcement contingencies, determine the topography of a subject's behavioral adaptation.

imposed peripherally, as in curare, heart rate control is not impaired. Thus, these apparently conflicting results may be accommodated by the suggestions made earlier in this chapter that visceral control is engendered by the calibration or reinforcement of central efferent processes and that internal effector-related feedback is not significantly implicated in visceral learning. As a consequence, the control developed by these procedures is of a relatively gross and undifferentiated nature.

Recently, however, evidence has begun to accumulate that biofeedback may after all provide a method of programming cardiovascular control that is independent of somatomotor activity. For example, Goldstein, Ross, and Brady (1977) have demonstrated that under conditions of biofeedback, individuals learn to reduce the heart rate elevations associated with controlled exercise. This finding has been confirmed by Perski and Engel (1980). A similar observation has also been recorded by Clemens and Shattock (1979), who have presented data showing that individuals may learn both to augment and to attenuate the heart rate increases associated with controlled levels of static muscular effort. Although these data are very impressive, they do not establish that the biofeedback training led to the development of motor programs for the differential and independent regulation of cardiac activity. Because overall energy expenditure was not monitored in any of these studies, the possibility remains open that subjects learned to eliminate superfluous somatomotor activities, resulting in parallel decreases of energy expenditure and heart rate. Thus, although biofeedback procedures are effective in establishing differential response control within either the somatomotor (Basmajian, 1963; Fridlund, Fowler, & Pritchard, 1980) or cardiovascular (Schwartz, 1972; Shapiro, Tursky, & Schwartz, 1970) effector systems, there is no conclusive evidence that the relationships existing between variations in somatomotor and cardiovascular activities may be reprogrammed by biofeedback.

This conclusion would seem to have clinical ramifications. For example, Fridlund *et al.* (1980) have recently reported data supporting Alexander's view (1975) that EMG biofeedback training will result in highly differentiated response-specific control. These investigators showed that frontalis EMG control learned under conditions of biofeedback did not generalize to seven adjunctive muscle groups. As they point out, this implies that the provision of biofeedback for activity in a localized muscle group cannot be expected to foster general relaxation. On the other hand, heart rate biofeedback, which does not lead to differentiated response control, may be quite effective in achieving this result. It has been suggested in this chapter that the specificity of the control generated by biofeedback is related to the point at which the process identified by the biofeedback lies on the central–peripheral control vector. If the biofeedback calibrates a peripheral process, the response control will be relatively specific; if it calibrates a central process, the control will be relatively gross.

CONCLUSIONS

It has been suggested previously that the specificity of visceromotor control is a function of the specificity of response discrimination (Brener, 1974b). If a subject is able to distinguish the sensory correlates of a target response from the sensory correlates of those other activities that normally accompany it, differentiated control of the target response may be expected. Since heart rate control has not been shown to be independent of somatomotor control, it would be inferred from the model that the sensory correlates of heart rate variation have not been discriminated from the sensory correlates of accompanying somatomotor activities. This, in turn, may imply that heart rate control is regulated on the basis of central efferent processes rather than on the basis of peripheral cardiac feedback. A considerable amount of evidence supports this interpretation. However, the response discrimination/control hypothesis seems to conflict with the evidence presented by Whitehead and his colleagues (Whitehead *et al.*, 1976; Whitehead *et al.*, 1977), who showed that the capacity of individuals to detect peripheral signals associated with the beating of the heart was unrelated to their capacity to control heart rate. This conflict could imply that the hypothesis is false or that the test is invalid. A criticism of the test has been presented. In particular, it was suggested that the Whitehead group's cardiac discrimination procedure probed the capacity of individuals to detect sensory events that were associated with cardiac activity but that were unrelated to the controlled response. Research has not established precisely how the nervous system assesses heart rate, but it would seem very unlikely that it does so by counting and timing those peripheral mechanical events associated with the beating of the heart that subjects discriminate in the Whitehead group's procedure. Since the heart beat is propagated peripherally, it is quite unclear how the peripheral sensory consequences of heart beats that subjects are required to detect in the Whitehead group's procedure could be implicated in the formation of central motor plans for the production of heart rate variations. Nevertheless, Whitehead and his colleagues' data do indicate that the sensitivity of individuals to peripheral stimuli associated with cardiac activity is independent of the magnitude of their voluntary heart rate responses. Although interesting, this observation would not seem to demand a modification of the discrimination/control hypothesis. A more direct test of the hypothesis would be provided by an examination of the relationship between performance on a cardiospecific discrimination test and the specificity (rather than the magnitude) of voluntary cardiac control.

Examination of the hypothesis that biofeedback achieves its effects on response control by establishing in subjects the ability to detect instances of the target response reveals a number of apparent difficulties. For example, research on the regulation of striate muscle activity indicates that the detection of a response may rely, not upon peripheral feedback from the effector organ, but instead on central efferent monitoring. In this case, the subject detects the response by monitoring the activation of the response's motor program. Hence, the processes of response discrimination and response control become mutually interdependent: in order to detect the response, the subject must control it, and in order to control the response, the subject must detect it. On the one hand, this indicates that our conceptions of response discrimination and response control are very closely allied. On the other, it suggests that the idea that biofeedback engenders response control by training response discrimination is a simple tautology that carries little explanatory value or predictive power. However, it may be that this tautology is implicit in the structures and functions associated with learned motor control and that the predictive power of the hypothesis may be better tested by examining the relationship between the specificity of response discrimination and the specificity of response control.

REFERENCES

Adam, G. *Interoception and behavior.* Budapest: Akademiai Kiado, 1967.

Alexander, A. B. An experimental test of assumptions relating to the use of electromyographic biofeedback as a general relaxation technique. *Psychophysiology,* 1975, *12,* 656–662.

Astrand, P., Cuddy, T. E., Saltin, B., & Sternberg, J. Cardiac output during submaximal and maximal work. *Journal of Applied Physiology,* 1964, *19,* 268–274.

Basmajian, J. V. Control and training of individual motor units. *Science,* 1963, *20,* 662–664.

Black, A. H. Operant autonomic conditioning: the analysis of response mechanisms. In P. A. Obrist, A. H. Black, J. Brener, & L. V. DiCara (Eds.), *Cardiovascular psychophysiology: Current issues in response mechanisms, biofeedback and methodology.* Chicago: Aldine, 1974.

Black, A. H., & Cott, A. A perspective on biofeedback. In J. Beatty & H. Legewie (Eds.), *Biofeedback and behavior.* New York: Plenum, 1977.

Black, A. H., Cott, A., & Pavlovski, R. The operant learning theory approach to biofeedback training. In G. E. Schwartz & J. Beatty (Eds.), *Biofeedback: Theory and research.* New York: Academic Press, 1977.

Blix, A. S., Stromme, S. B., & Ursin, H. Additional heart rate—An indicator of psychological activation. *Aerospace Medicine,* 1974, *45,* 1219–1222.

Bolles, R. C. Species-specific defense reactions and avoidance learning. *Psychological Review,* 1970, *77,* 32–48.

Brener, J. A general model of voluntary control applied to the phenomena of learned cardiovascular change. In P. A. Obrist, A. H. Black, J. Brener, & L. V. DiCara (Eds.), *Cardiovascular psychophysiology: Current issues in response mechanisms, biofeedback and methodology.* Chicago: Aldine, 1974. (a)

Brener, J. Factors influencing the specificity of voluntary cardiovascular control. In L. V. DiCara (Ed.), *The limbic and autonomic nervous systems: Advances in research.* New York: Plenum, 1974. (b)

Brener, J. Sensory and perceptual determinants of voluntary visceral control. In G. E. Schwartz & J. Beatty (Eds.), *Biofeedback: Theory and research.* New York: Academic Press, 1977. (a)

Brener, J. Visceral perception. In J. Beatty & H. Legewie (Eds.), *Biofeedback and behavior.* New York: Plenum, 1977. (b)

Brener, J., Eissenberg, E., & Middaugh, S. Respiratory and somatomotor factors associated with operant conditioning of cardiovascular responses in curarized rats. In P. A. Obrist, A. H. Black, J. Brener, & L. V. DiCara (Eds.), *Cardiovascular psychophysiology: Current issues in response mechanisms, biofeedback and methodology*. Chicago: Aldine, 1974.

Brener, J., & Goesling, W. J. Avoidance conditioning of activity and immobility in rats. *Journal of Comparative and Physiological Psychology*, 1970, *70*, 276–280.

Brener, J. M., & Jones, J. M. Interoceptive discrimination in intact humans: Detection of cardiac activity. *Physiology and Behavior*, 1974, *13*, 763–767.

Brener, J., Phillips, K., & Connally, S. Oxygen consumption and ambulation during operant conditioning of heart rate increases and decreases in freely moving rats. *Psychophysiology*, 1977, *14*, 483–491.

Brener, J., Phillips, K., & Connally, S. Energy expenditure heart rate and ambulation during shock-avoidance conditioning of heart rate increases and ambulation in freely moving rats. *Psychophysiology*, 1980, *17*, 64–74.

Brener, J., Ross, A., Baker, J., & Clemens, W. J. On the relationship between cardiac discrimination and control. In N. Birbaumer & H. D. Kimmel (Eds.), *Biofeedback and self-regulation*. Hillsdale, N.J.: Erlbaum, 1980.

Carroll, D. Cardiac perception and cardiac control: A review. *Biofeedback and Self-Regulation*, 1977, *2*, 349–369.

Chernigovskiy, V. N. *Interoceptors*. Washington, D.C.: American Psychological Association, 1967.

Clemens, W. J. *Heart beat discrimination and the learning and transfer of voluntary heart rate control*. Paper presented at the annual meeting of the Southeastern Psychological Association, New Orleans, 1976.

Clemens, W. J., & MacDonald, D. F. Relationship between heart beat discrimination and heart rate control. *Psychophysiology*, 1976, *13*, 176. (Abstract)

Clemens, W. J., & Shattock, R. J. Voluntary heart rate control during static muscular effort. *Psychophysiology*, 1979, *16*, 327–332.

DiCara, L. V. Learning in the autonomic nervous system. *Scientific American*, 1970, *222*, 30–39.

Dinsmoor, J. A. Punishment: I. The avoidance hypothesis. *Psychological Review*, 1954, *61*, 34–46.

Donald, D. E., & Shepherd, J. T. Response to exercise in dogs with cardiac denervation. *American Journal of Physiology*, 1963, *205*, 393–400.

Donelson, F. E. *Discrimination and contol of human heart rate*. Unpublished doctoral dissertation, Cornell University, 1966.

Festinger, L., Ono, H., Burnham, C. A., & Bamber, D. Efference and the conscious experience of perception. *Journal of Experimental Psychology Monograph*, 1967, *74*, (4, P. 2).

Fridlund, A. J., Fowler, S. C., & Pritchard, D. A. Striate muscle tensional patterning in frontalis EMG biofeedback. *Psychophysiology*, 1980, *17*, 47–55.

Gannon, L. The role of interoception in learned visceral control. *Biofeedback and Self-Regulation*, 1977, *2*, 337–347.

Garcia, J., & Koelling, R. A. Relation of cue to consequence in avoidance learning. *Psychonomic Sciecne*, 1966, *4*, 123–124.

Garcia, J., & Rusiniak, K. W. Visceral feedback and the taste signal. In J. Beatty & H. Legewie (Eds.), *Biofeedback and behavior*. New York: Plenum, 1977.

Gatchel, R. J., & Price, K. P. Biofeedback: An introduction and historical overview. In R. J. Gatchel & K. P. Price (Eds.), *Clinical applications of biofeedback: Appraisal and status*. New York: Pergamon, 1979.

Gelfan, S., & Carter, S. Muscle sense in man. *Experimental Neurology*, 1967, *18*, 469–473.

Gibson, J. J. Adaptation, after-effect and contrast in the perception of curved lines. *Journal of Experimental Psychology*, 1933, *16*, 1–31.

Goldstein, D. S., Ross, R. S., & Brady, J. V. Biofeedback heart rate training during exercise. *Biofeedback and Self-Regulation*, 1977, *2*, 107–125.

Hearst, E., & Jenkins, H. M. *Sign-tracking: The stimulus-reinforcer relation and directed action*. Austin, Tex.: The Psychonomic Society, 1974.

Hefferline, R. F., & Perera, T. B. Proprioceptive discrimination of a covert operant without its observation by the subject. *Science,* 1963, *139,* 834–835.

Hinde, R. E., & Stevenson-Hinde, G. *Constraints on learning.* New York: Academic Press, 1973.

Hull, C. L. *Principles of behavior.* New York: Appleton-Century-Crofts, 1943.

James, W. *The principles of psychology.* New York: Holt, 1890.

Jammes, J. L., & Rosenberger, P. B. Rocking behavior and heart rate in the mentally retarded. *Journal of Nervous and Mental Disease,* 1971, *153,* 57–59.

Johnston, D. Biofeedback, verbal instructions and the motor skills analogy. In J. Beatty & H. Legewie (Eds.), *Biofeedback and behavior.* New York: Plenum, 1977.

Kamiya, J. Operant control of EEG alpha rhythm and some of its reported effects on consciousness. In C. Tort (Ed.), *Altered states of consciousness.* New York: Wiley, 1969.

Katkin, E. S., & Murray, E. N. Instrumental conditioning of autonomically mediated behavior: Theoretical and methodological issues. *Psychological Bulletin,* 1968, *70,* 52–68.

Kimble, G. A., & Perlmuter, L. C. The problem of volition. *Psychological Review,* 1970, *77,* 361–384.

Kimmel, H. D. Instrumental conditioning of autonomically mediated responses in human beings. *American Psychologist,* 1974, *29,* 325–335.

Kimmel, H. D. Making involuntary behavior voluntary: What does this do to the distinction? *The Southern Journal of Philosophy,* 1978, *16,* 213–226.

Kimmel, H. D., & Burns, R. A. Inter-effector influences in operant autonomic control. In J. Beatty & H. Legewie (Eds.), *Biofeedback and behavior.* New York: Plenum, 1977.

Kleinman, R. A. *The development of voluntary cardiovascular control.* Unpublished doctoral dissertation, University of Tennessee, 1970.

Lacroix, J. M. Effects of biofeedback on the discrimination of electrodermal activity. *Biofeedback and Self-Regulation,* 1977, *2,* 239–406.

Lacroix, J. M. The acquisition of autonomic control through biofeedback: The case against an afferent process and a two process alternative. *Psychophysiology,* in press.

Lang, P. J., & Twentyman, C. T. Learning to control heart rate: Binary vs. analogue feedback. *Psychophysiology,* 1974, *11,* 616–629.

Lang, P. J., & Twentyman, C. T. Learning to control heart rate: Effects of varying incentive and criterion of success. *Psychophysiology,* 1976, *13,* 378–385.

Langer, A. W., Obrist, P. A., & McCubbin, J. A. Hemodynamic and metabolic adjustments during exercise and shock avoidance in dogs. *American Journal of Physiology,* 1979, *236,* H225–H230.

Mackintosh, N. J. *The psychology of animal learning.* New York: Academic Press, 1974.

McCloskey, D. I. Kinesthetic sensibility. *Physiological Review,* 1978, *58,* 763–820.

McFarland, R. A. Heart rate perception and heart rate control. *Psychophysiology,* 1975, *12,* 402–405.

McFarland, R. A., & Campbell, C. Precise heart rate control and heart rate perception. *Perceptual and Motor Skills,* 1975, *41,* 730.

Mandler, G., Mandler, J. M., & Uviller, E. T. Autonomic feedback: The perception of autonomic activity. *Journal of Abnormal and Social Psychology,* 1958, *56,* 367–373.

Matthews, P. B. C., & Simmonds, A. Sensations of finger movement elicited by pulling upon flexor tendons in man. *Journal of Physiology, London,* 1974, *239,* 27–28.

Merton, P. A. How we control the contraction of our muscles. *Scientific American,* 1972, *226,* 30–37.

Metzger, W. Consciousness, perception, and action. In E. C. Carterette & M. P. Friedman (Eds.), *Handbook of perception* (Vol. 1). New York: Academic Press, 1974.

Miller, N. E. Learning of visceral and glandular responses. *Science,* 1969, *163,* 434–445.

Miller, N. E. General discussion and a review of recent results with paralysed patients. In R. J. Gatchel & K. P. Price (Eds.), *Clinical applications of biofeedback: Appraisal and status.* New York: Pergamon, 1979.

Miller, N. E., & Dworkin, B. Visceral learning: Recent difficulties with curarized rats and significant problems for human research. In P. A. Obrist, A. H. Black, J. Brener, & L. V. DiCara (Eds.), *Cardiovascular psychophysiology: Current issues in response mechanisms, biofeedback and methodology.* Chicago: Aldine, 1974.

Morley, S. Partial reinforcement in human biofeedback learning. *Biofeedback and Self-Regulation,* 1979, *4,* 221–227.

Neil, E. *Enteroceptors.* Berlin: Springer-Verlag, 1972.

Newman, P. P. *Visceral afferent functions of the nervous system.* London: Edward Arnold, 1974.

Notterman, J. M., & Mintz, D. E. *Dynamics of response.* New York: Wiley, 1965.

Numan, R. Cortical–limbic mechanisms and response control: A theoretical review. *Physiological Psychology,* 1978, *6,* 445–470.

Obrist, P. A. The cardiovascular–behavioral interaction: As it appears today. *Psychophysiology,* 1976, *13,* 95–107.

Obrist, P. A., Galosy, R. A., Lawler, J. E., Gaebelein, C. J., Howard, J. L., & Shanks, E. M. Operant conditioning of heart rate: Somatic correlation. *Psychophysiology,* 1975, *12,* 445–455.

Paillard, J. The patterning of skilled movement. In J. Field, H. W. Magoun, & V. E. Hall (Eds.), *Handbook of physiology* (Section 1, Neurophysiology; Vol. 2). Washington, D.C.: American Physiological Society, 1960.

Perski, A., & Engel, B. T. The role of behavioral conditioning in the cardiovascular adjustment to exercise. *Biofeedback and Self-Regulation,* 1980, *5,* 91–104.

Powers, W. T. *Behavior: The control of perception.* Chicago: Aldine, 1973.

Roberts, L. E. The role of exteroceptive feedback in learned electrodermal and cardiac control: Some attractions of and problems with discrimination theory. In J. Beatty & H. Legewie (Eds.), *Biofeedback and behavior.* New York: Plenum, 1977.

Roberts, L. E. Operant conditioning of autonomic responses: One perspective on the curare experiments. In G. E. Schwartz & D. Shapiro (Eds.), *Consciousness and self-regulation: Advances in research* (Vol. 2). New York: Plenum, 1978.

Roberts, L. E., & Marlin, R. G. Some comments on the self-description and discrimination of visceral response states. In N. Birbaumer & H. D. Kimmel (Eds.), *Biofeedback and self-regulation.* Hillsdale, N.J.: Erlbaum, 1979.

Ross, A., & Brener, J. Two procedures for training cardiac discrimination: A comparison of solution strategies and their relation to heart rate control. *Psychophysiology,* 1981, *18,* 62–70.

Schwartz, G. E. Voluntary control of human cardiovascular integration and differentiation through feedback and reward. *Science,* 1972, *175,* 90–93.

Schwartz, G. E. Biofeedback and patterning of autonomic and central processes: CNS and cardiovascular interactions. In G. E. Schwartz & J. Beatty (Eds.), *Biofeedback: Theory and research.* New York: Academic Press, 1977.

Sechenov, I. M. *Reflexes of the brain.* Cambridge, Mass.: MIT Press, 1965. (Originally published in Russian, 1863.)

Shapiro, D., Tursky, B., & Schwartz, G. E. Differentiation of heart rate and blood pressure in man by operant conditioning. *Psychosomatic Medicine,* 1970, *32,* 417–423.

Sherrington, C. S. *The integrative action of the nervous system.* New Haven: Yale University Press, 1906.

Smith, O. A. Reflex and central mechanisms involved in the control of the heart and circulation. *Annual Review of Physiology,* 1974, *36,* 93–123.

Solomon, R. L. The influence of work on behavior. *Psychological Bulletin,* 1948, *45,* 1–40.

Staddon, J. E. R. Learning as adaptation. In W. K. Estes (Ed.), *Handbook of learning and cognitive processes* (Vol. 2). Hillsdale, N.J.: Erlbaum, 1975.

Staddon, J. E. R., & Simmelhag, V. L. The "Superstition" experiment: A re-examination of its implications for the principles of adaptive behavior. *Psychological Review,* 1971, *78,* 3–16.

Stern, R. M. Detection of one's own spontaneous GSRs. *Psychonomic Science,* 1972, *29,* 354–356.

Taub, E., Bacon, R., & Berman, A. J. The acquisition of a trace-conditioned avoidance response after deafferentation of the responding limb. *Journal of Comparative and Physiological Psychology,* 1965, *58,* 275–279.

Taub, E., & Berman, A. J. Movement and learning in the absence of sensory feedback. In S. J. Freeman (Ed.), *The neuropsychology of spatially oriented behavior.* Homewood, Ill.: Dorsey Press, 1968.

Taub, E., Ellman, S. J., & Berman, A. J. Deafferentation in monkeys: Effect on conditioned grasp response. *Science,* 1966, *151,* 593–594.

Taub, E., Teodoru, D., Ellman, S. J., Bloom, R. F., & Berman, A. J. *Deafferentation in monkeys: The function of proprioception in extinction.* Paper presented at the meeting of the Psychonomic Society, Chicago, October 1965.

Taub, E., Teodoru, D., Ellman, S. J., Bloom, R. F., & Berman, A. J. Deafferentation in monkeys: Extinction of avoidance responses, discrimination and discrimination reversal. *Psychonomic Science,* 1966, *4,* 323–324.

Verplanck, W. S. Unaware of where's awareness: Some verbal operants. In C. W. Erikson (Ed.), *Behavior and awareness.* Durham, N.C.: Duke University Press, 1962.

Whitehead, W. E., & Drescher, V. M. *Perception of stomach contractions.* Paper presented at the annual meeting of the Society of Psychophysiological Research, Cincinnati, 1979.

Whitehead, W. E., Drescher, V. M., & Blackwell, B. Lack of relationship between autonomic perception questionnaire scores and actual sensitivity for perceiving one's heart beat. *Psychophysiology,* 1976, *13,* 177. (Abstract)

Whitehead, W. E., Drescher, V. M., Heiman, P., & Blackwell, B. Relation of heart rate control to heart beat perception. *Biofeedback and Self-Regulation,* 1977, *2,* 371–392.

Williamson, D. A., & Blanchard, E. B. Effect of feedback delay upon learned heart rate control. *Psychophysiology,* 1979, *16,* 108–115.

Wright, A., Carroll, D., & Newman, C. V. The effects of verbal feedback of elicited heart rate changes on subsequent voluntary control of heart rate. *Bulletin of the Psychonomic Society,* 1977, *10,* 209–210.

3 RESEARCH DESIGN AND ASSESSMENT IN CLINICAL BIOFEEDBACK

DAVID SHAPIRO

In recent times, there has been a continuing and growing concern about the safety and effectiveness of treatments in various fields of medicine, including psychiatry. Medical practice is being challenged because of unnecessary and harmful surgery, excessive use of diagnostic procedures, uncovering and treatment of problems not requiring attention, overmedication, illnesses and deaths caused by side effects of drugs, overreliance on drugs, underemphasis on prevention, and so on. These issues, along with the rising cost of health services, have led to additional questions about the accountability of medical practices and have raised concerns about treatment in general—to justify treatments, to guarantee their safety, and to assess their outcomes and cost more precisely than has been done before.

In psychiatry, recent debate has centered around the most commonly employed

David Shapiro. Department of Psychiatry and Biobehavioral Sciences, The University of California at Los Angeles, Los Angeles, California.

treatment approach—psychotherapy. Is it safe? Does it work? In the debate, psychiatry as a profession seems to be on the defensive in this challenge to its core technique. Extensive and expensive studies are being planned to try to deal with these questions, but there appears to be little consensus on how best to proceed. Is there a commonly accepted form (or forms) of psychotherapy to select for study? What types of disorders and what types of patients are to be selected? What criteria are to be used in assessing the outcomes of psychotherapy? Broadly speaking, psychological therapies are diversified, psychologists say, so why pick out this or that procedure? In addition, they feel that psychologists are more apt to be selective, choosing techniques appropriate to a particular patient, the patient's complaint and its history, and the social context in which the complaint is embedded. In addition, they point to evidence suggesting that psychotherapy and probably other psychologically and behaviorally oriented treatments may work for some therapists (or for some patients) but not for all, and that the important problem is to identify those characteristics that make for a "good" therapist (or a "good" patient).

Many scientists and clinicians would add a further caution. Since little is known about the nature of the psychological disorders or problems for which psychotherapy is used as a treatment, or about the mechanisms of psychotherapy, and since the variables involved are so complex and uncontrolled, it is simplest to consider psychotherapy as an art; and it is inappropriate to take the results of any one large-scale study as definitive. Basic knowledge and experience are the ingredients of the art. The failure to have clear-cut answers to questions of safety and effectiveness has not greatly affected the practice of psychotherapy, however defined. Clients are willing to pay for it, although third-party payers have been reluctant.

Compared to psychotherapy and its long history, biofeedback as a treatment modality is relatively new—it is little more than 10 to 15 years old—yet similar debates and parallel issues have quickly arisen. Biofeedback treatment appears to be practiced widely, without research in the field having dealt in depth with the many issues of safety and effectiveness. Basic knowledge and systematic clinical evidence have not been clearly defined as requirements for practical applications of a method such as biofeedback. Although there have been attempts at social and legal regulation, an "accepted" medical or psychological therapy is that which is commonly practiced.

Questions of the safety of biofeedback are not addressed at length in this chapter. There are few, if any, documented cases of harm or serious side effects of biofeedback treatment. As commonly applied, the treatments do not seem powerful enough to cause any harm. However, generally, the clinical benefits of biofeedback (or other behavioral) treatments of physical disorders take time to develop. There does not seem to be any simple way to give a "big dose" of biofeedback to achieve an immediate and dramatic effect. This is not to say that biofeedback treatments cannot be inappropriately or unwisely utilized. And, as with drugs, there may be contraindications. Perhaps the most serious complication is that a patient with a serious disorder may be sidetracked from other appropriate and available remedies.

As to effectiveness, the very concrete nature of biofeedback seems to suggest that research on the assessment of treatment outcomes should be very straightforward. The techniques are deceptively simple. The physiological measurements are objective, and the biofeedback displays are quite easy to specify precisely. In addition, unlike psychotherapy, biofeedback treatments are typically applied to physical or psychophysiological disorders that have more well-defined and objectified symptoms and etiologies than most psychological disorders do. Yet, with the possible exception of certain neuromuscular disorders, there is persistent doubt about the efficacy of clinical biofeedback, as evidenced by the decision to put together this volume. Is clarifying this doubt simply a matter of time, effort, and money? Or are there inherent problems, as in the case of psychotherapy, that will inevitably frustrate the quest for definitive evaluations of clinical biofeedback?

In 1976, Surwit and I concluded a review paper as follows: "there is *not one* well controlled scientific study of the effectiveness of biofeedback and operant conditioning in treating a particular physiological disorder" (Shapiro & Surwit, 1976, p. 113). This conclusion has been cited several times since then. Yet, as a colleague wrote me later on, "What are the requirements of a *well controlled* study?" The approach to design of treatment studies and assessment of treatment outcomes involves a number of considerations: (1) the investigator's model of the nature of the disorder; (2) the investigator's model of clinical research; (3) the biological and behavioral variables affecting the predisposition, development, maintenance, and rehabilitation of the disorder; (4) the complexity of symptomatology; (5) the assumptions about, and evidence available to the investigator regarding, the association between the targeted biofeedback measure and the symptoms; (6) the investigator's assumptions about mechanisms of biofeedback and the behavioral regulation of physiological responses; (7) the role of intervening factors, such as change in habit patterns, life stress, risk factors, and so on. This chapter considers some of these questions under the two general headings of treatment models and design and of criteria of assessment. The issues raised relate to clinical biofeedback and to other behavioral interventions as well. Examples are mainly taken from treatment research on essential hypertension.

TREATMENT MODELS AND DESIGN

Many clinicians and investigators consider a "medical" model most germane. A diagnosis is made, which presumably determines the course of treatment. Biofeedback is then given as a treatment, whether or not it has a well-defined relation to the diagnosis or to the particular symptoms involved. As an example, it can be argued that blood pressure biofeedback is inherently appropriate as a treatment for essential hypertension, inasmuch as the target biofeedback variable is closely correlated with a physiological measure primary to the diagnosis of the disorder. Of course, the decision should be made as to whether systolic or diastolic feedback would be most appropriate. Moreover, the particular characteristics and history of a patient with hypertension might argue for some form of feedback other than that for blood pressure: feedback for cardiac output, heart rate, peripheral resistance, muscle or skin blood flow, muscle activities, and electrodermal activity or some other function of the sympathetic nervous system. Decisions about drug treatment for essential hypertension proceed along similar lines—to assess particular processes related to blood pressure in a patient and to utilize a drug or a combination of drugs to reduce blood pressure to a target level and without excessive side effects. In many, if not most, instances, the process of drug treatment is one of trial and error. Medical treatments are often applied without any firm knowledge about the fundamental mechanisms of their action.

In designing studies on the effectiveness of biofeedback, one approach is to compare the treatment (whatever its rationale) with the "best available forms for specific conditions and types of patients" (Miller, 1978). The assessment then involves making multiple comparisons between the biofeedback treatment and the alternative—in this case, some standard, commonly utilized medical treatment—using a number of salient dependent measures for evaluation. In such designs, no-treatment conditions (if ethical) should be employed, unless knowledge about the effects of no treatment is already available. In addition, placebo treatments may also be compared. These would involve an attempt to control for nonspecific and adventitious influences on the outcome of any treatment: for example, the fact that the patient is involved in a treatment at all and the various changes that may ensue because of such participation (changes not specifically related to active treatment ingredients, which are beneficial to the disorder); the positive role of attention and involvement of therapists; patient participation in the measurement process, particularly self-monitoring, and its implications for increased awareness of bodily and cognitive processes; perception on the part of the patient and reinforced by the therapist that the disorder or symptom can be controlled; spontaneous recovery ro remission; regression to the mean; and so on (see Miller & Dworkin, 1977).

As an example of a study employing a medical–behavioral model, we (Shapiro & Goldstein, research in progress) are currently completing research in which patients with mild to moderate essential hypertension are withdrawn from drugs and assigned at random to the best available treatment employing antihypertensive medications or to one of two behavioral treatments (blood pressure biofeedback, relaxation response). That is, we are comparing a currently standard treatment using drugs against treatment without drugs. In choosing criteria of assessment, we looked to the medical, psychological, and psychophysiological literature. The dependent variables include laboratory blood pressure, clinic blood pressure, home blood pressure, life stress, psychological factors (anxiety), psychophysiological reactivity (loud noise, mental arithmetic, cold pressor), medical examination variables, physiological variables (plasma renin activity), and changes in patient habits and behaviors. Although the dependent variables studied are chosen for specific reasons, the major concern in the medical model is whether each patient improves, does not change, or gets worse. The several blood pressure measurements typically employed in the diagnosis of essential hypertension are considered primary in the assessment procedure. Such use of multiple assessment criteria are discussed further below.

Parenthetically, in the design of this study of behavioral approaches to essential hypertension, no "placebo" control was included in the original study. The comparisons involved of drug versus behavioral treatments are of interest in and of themselves, but the interpretation of outcomes may leave open some additional questions. For example, we have noted what appears to be a better drug effect in our drug group (mainly patients on diuretics) than would be normally observed in medicated patients who are seen in a clinic or private practice. Our drug patients may be taking their drugs more consistently. Their blood pressure may be decreasing more because the patients are involved in a program; taking their own blood pressure; having very close and repeated contacts with our laboratory and staff; and perhaps being more careful about their diet, exposure to stress, other risk factors, and so on. A no-research program drug group (no frequent contacts with the lab, no self-monitoring, etc.) would answer this question. Such data may be otherwise available. Secondly, the observed change in blood pressure in our behaviorally treated unmedicated patients would be good to compare either with changes in unmedicated patients having no program involvement at all (not an ethically acceptable alternative in patients with diagnosed essential hypertension) or with changes in unmedicated patients who are in a minimal treatment process but receiving attention, getting measured, and so on. This last control procedure is of greatest interest to us and is currently under way. Should this group show an increase in blood pressure, for example, it may suggest that those unmedicated patients who are not showing any reduction but who are also not showing an increase in pressure are responding in some positive degree to the behavioral interventions.

With regard to specific controls vis-à-vis biofeedback itself, various forms of false or random biofeedback stimuli may be appropriate. As Katkin and Goldband (1979) and others have pointed out, such false feedback may be readily detected and may reduce the credibility of the procedure. Feedback for an irrelevant but controllable target variable—for example, increasing some band of EEG activity (such as 12–16 Hz in the central area)—would be a possibility. Feedback for changes in the direction opposite to that considered desirable is another alternative (see Reeves, Shapiro, & Cobb, 1979). These false feedback techniques have suggested that double-blind procedures may also be useful in effectively controlling for placebo effects (Cohen, Graham, Fotopoulos, & Cook, 1977). Double-blind procedures that inherently eliminate or play down the role of attention and motivation in the process of biofeedback training are unsatisfactory. That is, a biofeedback technique is administered in a context of beliefs, expectations, clear and effective instructions, and so on, and any attempt to sanitize them in a double-blind design must take account of these factors.

Yates (1980) has challenged the "medical" model in biofeedback, pointing out that behavioral therapies (biofeedback is one of them) emerged out of a critique of the medical model, and that the major assessment of a therapeutic behavioral procedure should revolve only around specific changes in the patient's target behavior predicted by the very concepts and techniques used to generate the treatment. That is, the treatment should not follow solely from a diagnosis, but from a clear specification of the critical behaviors or physiological responses to be modified. The problem for many applications of biofeedback is that the target physiological response does not always have a well-defined relationship to the disorder. It does have such a relationship, more or less, in the case of blood pressure biofeedback for essential hypertension or of motor activities for neuromuscular disorders, but it is less clear in the case of skin temperature feedback for migraine or EMG feedback for chronic anxiety. Or the relationship between the feedback and the disorder may be ambiguous, as in sensorimotor rhythm EEG feedback for epilepsy or heart rate feedback for certain cardiac abnormalities, but a complex rationale has been formulated in these instances to link the target variable with the problem. Experimenters need to be more precise about the behavioral rationale in applying biofeedback treatment to a particular disorder (or person), and particularly about the choice of relevant variables for assessment. Following the lines of the Yates critique, a proper evaluation would ask in depth how the biofeedback target variable has changed. That is, what were the changes shown in this variable during the treatment sessions themselves? How did these changes relate to symptom reduction or control? Did the changes persist after treatment was terminated? Did the treatment effects generalize to situations outside the treatment situation? If other changes have been brought about by participation in the treatment process, how did they relate to changes in the target biofeedback variable?

Behavioral concepts and techniques are probably not sufficient by themselves to generate specific treatments for psychophysiological or other disorders without adequate consideration of biological concepts and techniques. Biobehavioral models and approaches are needed to generate suitable treatments or sets of treatments and to provide a basis for systematic assessment of treatment effects. In the case of essential hypertension, complex interactions are likely to occur between such biological factors as sodium and cholesterol intake, body weight, and use of stimulants and alcohol on the one hand, and various life stresses, emotional reactions, and the like on the other. Greater attention to these interactions should be paid in the design and assessment of biofeedback treatment studies. In a similar vein, interactions between drug and behavioral treatments need to be examined more closely. Drugs may be utilized to enhance or potentiate the effects of biofeedback, or vice versa. Then again, drugs may block neural pathways necessary in the voluntary control achieved by biofeedback.

Still another viewpoint on design and assessment is that it is not profitable to attempt large-scale treatment studies, given the huge complications that arise in clinical research. There may be (and usually are) unanticipated changes in a patient's life circumstances or changes in patient motivation, life style, and habits (related or unrelated to participation in a program); complicated effects related to use or withdrawal from medication; changes in various beliefs and attitudes of the patient (and therapist); and so on. Moreover, each patient has a peculiar life history, particular biological and psychological predispositions, and modes of adaptation to the disorder, so that a treatment should ideally be fashioned according to these factors. Moreover, in typical group outcome studies, the effects of single-treatment variables are usually compared. However, most patients would probably benefit from some combination of treatments, given the combination of factors likely to be involved in their disorders. It can be argued that an "engineering" orientation is required to apply whatever basic knowledge is appropriate to the problem and the person in question, and to assess the effects of each application in direct relation to the specifics involved. Single-case designs provide a systematic means of research on the processes and mechanisms involved. Given our present state of knowledge about the effectiveness of single treatments or combinations of treatments, such systematic case studies may help provide the necessary body of critical clinical evidence and provide a basis for group outcome studies and extensive clinical trials. For example, if experimenters can rank treatments (biofeedback *and* other behaivoral treatments) in terms of presumed effectiveness, cost, and ease of administration, then a "stepped care" approach to treatment may proceed accordingly (Shapiro, 1979). Each additional treatment can be added to the previous one in turn. In this way, estimates can be made of the increasing benefit (or lack thereof) of combining treatments in succession, and of the costs and effort involved at each step.

One final note is in order concerning clinical research design and also the analysis of outcomes. Typically, investigators report their results in terms of means and related statistical analyses. This has led to debates about statistical versus clinical versus therapeutic significance. A proper course of action may be to define as clearly as possible a target goal of the therapy. In the case of mild essential hypertension, for example, a goal would be to reduce absolute diastolic blood pressure to a level below 90 mm Hg. A secondary goal would be to reduce diastolic pressure by 10 mm Hg, regardless of the starting level. A more limited goal of 5 mm Hg reduction might define a partial "cure." This assumes, of course, that a stable average and reliable measure of each individual's pressure is obtained under well-defined and standardized conditions, as outlined in the next section. Then, a simple percentage of successes and failures (variably defined) would be a clear way of summarizing the effects of the various treatment procedures. Analyses of mean effects have their place, so long as some expected mean difference is hypothesized and then evaluated precisely.

CRITERIA OF ASSESSMENT

It is important to utilize multiple criteria in assessing treatment outcomes in biofeedback studies. This issue relates to a fair degree of uncertainty about what measures collected under what conditions are appropriate to the disorder. For example, in the case of essential hypertension, evidence is available that the level of blood pressure measured in nonmedical contexts may be more relevant to the severity and complications of the disorder (Sokolow, Werdegar, Kain, & Hinman, 1966). The use of electronic sphygmomanometers to record pressures at home, at work, or in other situations would greatly add to our knowledge about the value of treatments (e.g., Kleinman, Goldman, Snow, & Korol, 1977; Kristt & Engel, 1975). Portable devices that provide frequent (every 15 minutes) measures around the clock, particularly if information about corresponding events were also avialable, would greatly add to such evaluations. Such data could be collected at periodic intervals before, during, and after treatment.

A related issue is that of whether the learned changes are general across different situations or stimuli. To the extent that the abnormal physiological responses are elicited by specific environmental events, how will the training affect such reactions? Will a patient who has learned in the laboratory to reduce muscular contractions related to headaches be able to keep such contractions to a minimum when confronted with stress conditions that tend to elicit such reactions? This last example points up an important distinction. In certain disorders, the symptom is quite variable from time to time and from situation to situation, while in others the symptom is maintained consistently. This is comparable to the concept of "state versus trait" in research on personality dimensions.

Examples of trait symptoms are found in neurological or neuromuscular disorders. In these instances, biofeedback treatments are conceived to alter basic neuronal or muscular characteristics so as to achieve structural changes through the actions of neural pathways or the exercise of particular collections of motor units. If a particular muscle or set of muscles is strengthened through biofeedback training, enabling a stroke patient to walk without a brace, and if the more effective use of the affected muscles in the person's leg leads to continued strengthening of the muscles, then the treatment has more or less facilitated a permanent and easily documented change. Conceivably, there may be some regression in the patient's condition, which can be ameliorated by additional practice and exercise. In the biofeedback treatment of epilepsy, EEG biofeedback treatment serves to increase certain rhythmic activities of the brain and to decrease others, and as a result there are multiple changes in the patient. The frequency of epileptic seizures is reduced, but, more importantly, the total abnormal EEG appears to be normalized during waking as well as sleeping conditions (Sterman, 1977). Again, booster treatments can help restore treatment benefits if there is regression in the condition.

The state-type symptoms are more characteristic of the psychophysiological symptoms for which biofeedback treatments are often considered appropriate. High blood pressure is a good case in point. Blood pressure varies widely according to the time of day and the situations in which it is measured, whether in individuals with normal blood pressure or in patients with essential hypertension. In the latter, theis variability appears to be greater in what is variably called borderline or labile hypertension, but the variability also occurs in more typically fixed moderate levels of hypertension (with diastolic blood pressure ranging from 105 to 120 mm Hg). Understanding this variability is particularly critical to the issues of generalization and maintenance of biofeedback treatments.

In tracing through research in my laboratory on biofeedback and other behavioral treatments for essential hypertension, my colleagues and I did not recognize the importance of this variability at first. In our first study (Benson, Shapiro, Tursky, & Schwartz, 1971), significant and in several patients large reductions (30 mm Hg systolic) were obtained over the course of sessions. The reasons for the effects were unclear; we could not be certain whether they were due to the training itself or to some other, nonspecific effect. Moreover, no systematic effort was made to determine whether the lowered pressures occurred outside the clinical situation. If, in fact, these patients learned to reduce their blood pressure, was it possible that this reduction occurred only in the clinical setting and not elsewhere? The reduction could simply represent successive habituation to the clinical measurement situation, a possibility that could have been discounted by adequate baseline measurements in this same situation. Miller and Dworkin (1977) point out that if the reduction in blood pressure is specific *only* to the treatment situation and not to situations outside it, the therapist may be misled to take the patient off medication. As indicated above, more recent research has moved in this direction of more indices of blood pressure under different conditions.

A recent patient of mine illustrates this issue very clearly. The patient was referred to me shortly after his father had died of heart disease. Concerned about his own health, the patient took his pressure in a supermarket and found it to be elevated. His physician measured his pressure at 160/110 mm Hg, and the patient was put on triple drug therapy. It seemed to me that the patient's blood pressure was excessive primarily in medical examinations. He associated the measurements of pressure with early negative experiences with doctors. His father's death led to financial concerns, complex issues about wills and probate, and so on. I asked the patient to record his blood pressure at home and at work several times a day, using an electronic sphygmomanometer. The values at home ranged from 140/90 to 110/60. This evidence collected over a few months led eventually to a complete cessation of drug treatment. Recently, I asked the patient to measure his own blood pressure in my office, and it was 160/110 mm Hg. Subsequent readings over a 5-minute period showed a steady decrease to 135/85 mm Hg. Interestingly, this blood pressure variability had occurred at our first session and helped suggest to the patient that his own reactions had a bearing on his pressure (and his health), and that he might do something about it by being less apprehensive, by coping more effectively with everyday stress and strain, and by being more realistic about current and future life difficulties. In subsequent weeks, home- and office-recorded pressures appeared to have lowered still further, again with the patient under no medication. The patient appeared reassured by his progress; he now felt that he could achieve some control himself and that he did not necessarily have any physical derangements. This brief case history suggests the importance, where possible, of examining the physiological symptom under different (and nonmedical) situations, such as at home or at work, and of utilizing home monitoring as a means of reinforcing the clinic treatment procedure as well as of gathering important data on evaluation. It also suggests the possible value for some additional stress-reduction or stress-inoculation procedures facilitated by biofeedback or other means. In the past few years, my colleagues and I have been examining the usefulness of biofeedback in modifying heart rate and blood pressure changes (using a beat-to-beat tracking-cuff system) elicited by stressful stimuli, particularly the cold pressor test (Victor, Mainardi, & Shapiro, 1978; Reeves *et al.*, 1979; Shapiro & Goldstein, research in progress; Shapiro, Greenstadt, Lane, & Rubinstein, 1981). These techniques may be a means of increasing the relevance of the treatment condition to situations typically eliciting symptoms of interest.

As to the maintenance of treatment effects after treatment has terminated, it is obvious that continuous follow-up measures are needed. Again, multiple indices are desirable—for example, clinic and home blood pressures in the case of hypertension. Greater effort should be paid to means of fostering maintained changes.

It is also important to examine individual variables related to treatment outcomes. For example, in our current hypertension clinical research, my colleagues and I have observed success in a subsample of patients undergoing blood pressure biofeedback. What determines success and failure? There are many individual difference measures that need to be appraised, both biological and psychological. Is there a subclass of patients who can be categorized as "neurogenic" along a number of biological and psychological criteria, and are these patients more susceptible to biofeedback or to other behavioral treatments? Are there ways of differentiating who is more suitable for biofeedback and who is more suitable for relaxation, counseling, autogenic, or other techniques? Experimenters need to be more imaginative in designing means of assessing individual reactions, particularly as they may be pertinent to the disorder in question. Such individual differences are useful, not only as means of predicting treatment successes and failures, but as additional means of evaluating the outcomes themselves. Various other psychophysiological and performance tests may be useful here: tests of ability to detect or discriminate the target physiological response; tests of response to warned or unwarned noxious stimuli; tests of habituation to simple stimuli; tests of reaction time and other kinds of motor performance tests; tests of cognitive functions; tests of response to suggested or progressive relaxation; and so on. Obviously, there are many choices, and it is best to be guided by specific hypotheses about the particular "deficits" involved in the disorder. For example, if essential hypertension involves some process of particular reaction to pain or threat, as has been suggested (Miller & Dworkin, 1977), then procedures assessing this process should be employed. Or if unexpressed anger is associated with neurogenic hypertension (Esler, Julius, Zweifler, Randall, Harburg, Gardiner, & DeQuattro, 1977), then paper-and-pencil tests or stress interview situations designed to examine such processes would be required.

CONCLUDING REMARKS

The variety of issues discussed in this chapter concerning the design of clinical biofeedback studies and the assessment of treatment outcomes suggests that there are no simple prescriptions to guarantee the health and prosperity of research in this area. Investigators' understanding of fundamental processes varies greatly from disorder to disorder and from person to person. The selection of appropriate criteria of assessment in determining the efficacy of treatments requires a thorough consideration of biological and behavioral factors as they may be related to the disorder. Such knowledge either does not exist or is not definitive in many, if not most, cases. Criteria can be selected on the basis of what is known or what has been suggested in previous research. It seems likely that comprehensive clinical biofeedback research in and of itself will involve the collection of data relevant to questions about the basic biological and behavioral processes in the disorders being studied.

Unlike basic psychophysiological research in the laboratory, clinical biofeedback research is difficult and time-consuming. External factors affecting patient motivation and cooperation greatly complicate the effective execution of such research. Yet, despite such frustrations and complications, effective clinical biofeedback research is both possible and necessary. If biofeedback is a useful tool in treating various disorders, how useful is it? How does it compare with other behavioral treatments, standard medical treatments, no treatment, or placebo treatments? Rather than orient our question in an either/or fashion (does it work or not?), we need to be able to estimate more precisely for what percentage of selected patients with a specified disorder the method works, and how it works under different conditions. Estimates of expected effectiveness made in advance will also help guide us in designing appropriate designs, selecting adequate samples for comparison, and so on.

There is a different strategy, however—that is, to back up a bit in the wholesale application of biofeedback techniques to everything imaginable, and to apply biofeedback as a *tool*, along with other appropriate tools, in treating problems. Then the burden is not placed entirely on biofeedback as a panacea for everything. Yates (1980) has brought out this viewpoint and summarized it nicely:

> Where it [biofeedback] has been used as a precision instrument it has achieved outstanding success, as in the training in voluntary control of single motor unit activity and the careful clinical investigations of the rehabilitation of physical function. It has, however, suffered the fate of so many new approaches in psychology during the course of this century: overenthusiastic adoption by clinicians eager to add a new technique to their clinical armamentarium long before the experimental foundations and theory have been adequately developed to enable its use as a precision instrument rather than a crude new weapon. (p. 499)

It seems likely, however, that the quest for rapid and dramatic solutions to problems will continue to press biofeedback into service before it is ready. It is to be hoped that some of the considerations of design and criteria for determining efficacy discussed in this chapter will facilitate a more comprehensive and appropriate evaluation of clinical biofeedback. To the extent that this process incorporates both biological and behavioral knowledge and approaches, and a consequent fostering of multidisciplinary communication, then the process will probably result in reasonable answers, improved methods of treatment, and new knowledge.

ACKNOWLEDGMENT

Preparation of this paper was supported by Research Grant HL 19568, National Institutes of Health.

REFERENCES

Benson, H., Shapiro, D., Tursky, B., & Schwartz, G. E. Decreased systolic blood pressure through operant conditioning techniques in patients with essential hypertension. *Science,* 1971, *173,* 740–742.

Cohen, H. D., Graham, C., Fotopoulos, S. S., & Cook, M. R. A double-blind methodology for biofeedback research. *Psychophysiology,* 1977, *14,* 603–608.

Esler, M., Julius, S., Zweifler, A., Randall, O., Harburg, E., Gardiner, H., & DeQuattro, V. Mild high-renin essential hypertension: Neurogenic human hypertension? *New England Journal of Medicine,* 1977, *296,* 405–411.

Katkin, E. S., & Goldband, S. The placebo effect and biofeedback. In R. J. Gatchel & K. P. Price (Eds.), *Clinical applications of biofeedback: Appraisal and status*. New York: Plenum, 1979.

Kleinman, K. M., Goldman, H., Snow, M. Y., & Korol, B. Relationship between essential hypertension and cognitive functioning: II. Effects of biofeedback training generalize to non-laboratory environment. *Psychophysiology*, 1977, *14*, 192–197.

Kristt, D. A., & Engel, B. T. Learned control of blood pressure in patients with high blood pressure. *Circulation*, 1975, *51*, 370–378.

Miller, N. E. Biofeedback and visceral learning. *Annual Review of Psychology*, 1978, *29*, 373–404.

Miller, N. E., & Dworkin, B. R. Critical issues in therapeutic applications of biofeedback. In G. E. Schwartz & J. Beatty (Eds.), *Biofeedback: Theory and research*. New York: Academic Press, 1977.

Reeves, J. L., Shapiro, D., & Cobb, L. F. Relative influences of heart rate biofeedback and instructional set in the perception of cold pressor pain. In N. Birbaumer & H. D. Kimmel (Eds.), *Biofeedback and self-regulation*. Hillsdale, N.J.: Erlbaum, 1979.

Shaprio, D. Biofeedback and behavioral medicine in perspective. *Biofeedback and Self-Regulation*, 1979, *4*, 371–374.

Shaprio, D., & Goldstein, I. B. Research in progress.

Shaprio, D., Greenstadt, L., Lane, J. D., & Rubinstein, E. Tracking-cuff system for beat-to-beat recording of blood pressure. *Psychophysiology*, 1981, *18*, 129–136.

Shapiro, D., & Surwit, R. S. Learned control of physiological function and disease. In H. Leitenberg (Ed.), *Handbook of behavior modification and behavior therapy*. Englewood Cliffs, N.J.: Prentice-Hall, 1976.

Sokolow, M., Werdegar, D., Kain, H. K., & Hinman, A. T. Relationship between level of blood pressure measured casually and by portable recorders and severity of complications in essential hypertension. *Circulation*, 1966, *34*, 279–288.

Sterman, M. B. Effects of sensorimotor EEG feedback training on sleep and clinical manifestations of epilepsy. In J. Beatty & H. Legewie (Eds.), *Biofeedback and behavior*. New York: Plenum, 1977.

Victor, R., Mainardi, J. A., & Shapiro, D. Effect of biofeedback and voluntary control procedures and perception of pain during the cold pressor test. *Psychosomatic Medicine*, 1978, *40*, 216–225.

Yates, A. J. *Biofeedback and the modification of behavior*. New York: Plenum, 1980.

COMMENTS ON THE CHAPTERS BY BRENER AND BY SHAPIRO

GARY E. SCHWARTZ

COMMENTS ON THE CHAPTER BY BRENER

Brener has provided a stimulating and important analysis of some possible psychobiological mechanisms underlying biofeedback. He has modified the main conclusion of his earlier theoretical writing regarding the role of peripheral afferent feedback in learned voluntary control by stressing here the potential importance of central efferent feedback in learned voluntary control. This is a

Gary E. Schwartz. Department of Psychology, Yale University, New Haven, Connecticut.

curious and significant shift in emphasis. It is a curious shift because it provides a psychobiological rationale for conceptualizing how cognitive and affective "mediators" may contribute to the mechanisms underlying learned voluntary control. The role of cognitive and affective mechanisms in biofeedback has been debated since the very beginning. And Brener's shift is significant, because it places emphasis on developing feedback connections within the brain per se as being fundamental to an organism's ability to learn to self-regulate its peripheral physiology, and thereby to control its overt behavior.

Brener's chapter is so rich that a brief commentary can only skim some of the highlights. I will raise a few issues that might be considered in future research and clinical applications. Brener notes that "the issues broached by current clinical biofeedback research are rather remote from those theoretical considerations that gave rise to the development of this treatment method" (p. 24). I agree with Brener that the models that gave rise to the use of biofeedback in therapy were too narrow and simplistic. The actual uses of biofeedback in clinical practice are more varied and complex than those originally envisioned, as most of the current clinical research indicates.

Importantly, the emerging psychobiological theories of biofeedback are themselves becoming more complex and more directly relevant to the ways in which biofeedback is actually used in clinical practice. For example, the use of biofeedback in helping patients to discover what cognitive, emotional, and somatic processes influence a given target organ, and the use of biofeedback in helping patients alter these cognitive, emotional, and somatic processes so as to promote the health of the target organ, can be reconceptualized in psychobiological terms using Brener's current theory. It is reassuring to see that this basic clinical issue, which was emphasized early in biofeedback's history (but was not embraced by clinical researchers because of the lack of a suitable psychobiological model—e.g., Schwartz, 1973), is now finding support in more advanced theory.

Unfortunately, in his effort to develop a psychobiological model that can successfully avoid the need to use psychological language, Brener has inadvertently misinterpreted the specific conditions under which psychological terms are helpful in, if not essential to, describing and predicting human behavior. There are numerous instances in Brener's chapter where concepts such as "expectance" and "awareness" are used to describe certain phenomena relevant to biofeedback. Unfortunately, Brener erroneously equates "mentalism" with "cognitive" psychology. Modern cognitive psychology draws heavily on information-processing theory. Information-processing theory is a component of general systems theory, which was first developed in the physical and biological sciences. Hence, modern cognitive psychology generally presumes that cognitive processes (involving sensation, perception, imagery, attention, learning, memory, and decision making) have a biological substrate. Furthermore, modern cognitive psychology presumes that processes at a psychological level necessarily involve processes at the biological level. Issues of "mentalism" only come up when the question of consciousness is raised. The question of consciousness is as much a quagmire for cognitive psychology as it is for psychobiology, especially since many theories in cognitive psychology assume that cognitive processes per se occur out of awareness! In fact, a major theory proposes that humans never have direct awareness of their cognitive processes per se, but rather become aware only of the central *consequences* of these processes (in Brener's terms, "central efferent responses") (Nisbett & Wilson, 1977).

The direct parallel between modern cognitive psychology and Brener's approach to psychobiology becomes apparent when a living systems perspective is applied to both (see Miller, 1978; Schwartz, 1979). For example, a basic tenet of systems theory is that *at some level*, a complex system must be able to discriminate and react to feedback of its own behavior in order to self-regulate that component of its behavior (here the term "behavior" is used in the general systems sense—e.g., a cell, an organ, or an organism can "eat," that is, ingest nutrients to meet some internal needs; the "eating" is a behavior of the living system). Brener proposes that the organism must be able to discriminate a response in order to self-regulate it, even if the subject is not "aware" of the response (i.e., is not able to report it verbally). This implies that the brain has the ability to sense, perceive, and label its own behavior as being relevant to self-control processes that include regulation of peripheral organs. As Powers (1973) beautifully illustrates, higher-level cognitive–biological information processing involves the integration of information obtained in a hierarchical fashion from lower levels. In fact, Powers implies that end organ control by the brain is a side effect of the direct control of higher-order central processes themselves.

These seemingly abstract notions can be translated directly into research and clinical practice. For example, as cited by Brener, Gelfan and Carter (1967) found that subjects who were asked if they experienced "muscle sensations" did not report feeling their tendons being moved, whereas Matthews and Simmonds (1974) found that subjects who were asked if they experienced "finger movement" did report feeling the consequences of their tendons being moved. Brener suggests, "Just as individuals do not refer auditory and visual sensations to the ears and eyes, they do not refer sensations of changing muscle length to the muscle stretch receptors, but rather to movements of the limbs being served by the muscles" (p. 31).

The fundamental question is, why is this so? Maybe attention can be focused at various *levels* organized hierarchically within the system, and awareness as reflected by self-report only appears for certain processes occurring at certain levels in the nervous system and under certain conditions. Maybe organisms are biologically designed to be aware of certain higher-order consequences of specific centrally organized actions. (For example, when subjects are instructed to attend to finger movement, they may also process specific skin sensations that are generated when the muscles are moved, and they may perceptually organize these sensations as changes taking place over time.) The theory and data clearly indicate that certain instructions to subjects may be important, and that seemingly subtle differences in wording may have a significant impact on subjects' awareness and on subjects' ability to self-regulate different psychobiological processes.

The work by Adam (1967) illustrates that it may be necessary to use physiological recording of brain activity (e.g., alpha blocking or evoked potentials) to determine whether the brain is processing central and/or peripheral feedback differently as a function of learned voluntary control. Simply asking a subject to report his or her experiences may be insufficient, since conscious awareness may not have direct access to these underlying processes. I have proposed that attention focused on particular peripheral processes may alter the homeostatic (self-regulatory) control of these processes, even though the subject is not "trying" to alter the processes (Schwartz, 1979). Furthermore, such unconscious cybernetic effects may be influenced consciously, even though the subject may not be aware that these discriminative processes are actually playing a role in the voluntary control (London & Schwartz, 1980). The critical issue here is that these kinds of examples can be potentially explained by Brener's insightful analysis if this analysis is extended to conceptualize consciously reportable processes as centrally controlled psychobiological processes that can modulate lower-level central and peripheral control mechanisms.

COMMENTS ON THE CHAPTER BY SHAPIRO

The chapter by Shapiro provides a sober and insightful analysis of research design and assessment in clinical biofeedback. This excellent chapter includes many essential suggestions for effective and responsible clinical evaluation of biofeedback. It is curious that as clinical biofeedback research has matured, conceptions of clinical research in general have matured. It is my opinion that the problems and issues outlined by Shapiro can be viewed as general systems problems applicable broadly to any type of clinical evaluation research (e.g., see Schwartz, Shapiro, Redmond, Ferguson, Ragland, & Weiss, 1979).

I would like to highlight some specific points made by Shapiro that have not received much attention to date and deserve to do so in the future. Shapiro notes that because biofeedback per se is not an especially powerful clinical tool, its direct side effects (be they negative or positive) appear to be minimal. However, Shapiro comments that patients may be sidetracked by seeking biofeedback at the expense of other, more effective, and even necessary, biomedical modalities. It behooves clinical researchers and practicing clinicians to make sure that patients do not inadvertently seek biofeedback (or other behavioral modalities) at the expense of responsible medical care.

Biofeedback may have a positive side effect in changing patients' attitudes regarding both the role that psychosocial stress plays in triggering physiological responses, and the role that perceptions, emotions, and cognitions (as well as health behavior) play in modulating their physiological responses to stress. However, this change in attitude can be carried to an extreme, at the expense of a person's health. Some patients may become overconfident. They may think that they have more voluntary control over their health than they actually do. On the other hand, the issue of the ways in which biofeedback can be used constructively to alter attitudes about the role of self-care in health, with the goal of enhancing short-term and long-term health behavior, deserves to be evaluated in future research.

Shapiro notes that patients participating in research studies may take their drugs more consistently than patients not participating in such studies may do. Also, specific aspects of self-monitoring and other psychological variables inherently involved in the process of being a subject in clinical research may alter the patients' psychophysiological response to the medication itself. These "nonspecific" variables (or, more appropriately, these specific psychological variables that were heretofore not specified in the situation) may play an important role in modulation of the effectiveness of medical treatments. If biofeedback research inadvertently leads us to specify better these potentially "active" behavioral (placebo) variables, this would be a significant beneficial side effect of clinical biofeedback research.

There is a major problem in conceptualizing the ways in which multiple variables interact in treatment (including variables of genetic makeup, diet, psychosocial stress history, personality, etc.). Researchers and clinicians need a general biobehavioral theory that can make it possible for them to translate from one level of analysis to another (e.g., from the relative microlevels of analysis of biology to the relative macrolevels of analysis of psychology and sociology). The translation process is not easy. However, steps are being taken to facilitate cross-level, interdisciplinary thinking and communication (e.g., see Schwartz, 1979). Shapiro illustrates the ways in which understanding mechanisms at one level (e.g., drugs) may have a significant bearing on making predictions about variables operating at higher levels (e.g., biofeedback). Certain drugs may potentiate biofeedback effects by simply adding to the total effect, producing effects that operate by different mechanisms. For example, diuretics can act to reduce the total volume of blood, whereas biofeedback for blood pressure may decrease peripheral resistance by reducing sympathetic outflow to the heart and/or vasculature. The total effect of both treatments on blood pressure may be greater than either treatment alone. On the other hand, drugs (e.g., beta blockers) may actually interfere with biofeedback by attenuating (if not eliminating) the very neural and/or humoral pathways essential to learned voluntary control. A better understanding of the peripheral and central mechanisms involved in biofeedback may make it possible for researchers to improve the possibilities of coupling biofeedback with specific drug treatments (whose mechanisms are somewhat understood).

A related problem in conducting multilevel research is that it requires close attention to the timing of different treatments and the use of complex statistical procedures for evaluating multivariate effects, both within and between subjects. The concept of "rational" stepped care is a good one, especially if the stepped procedure makes psychobiological sense and can be effectively evaluated. Clearly, the decision as to when to use biofeedback as a component of stepped biobehavioral care is one that needs to be conceptualized and evaluated. It seems quite likely that the choice of timing will vary as a function of the nature of the disorder, as well as of the status and needs of the individual patient.

Defining clinical goals turns out to be more complex than had been originally recognized. As Shapiro points out, part of the reason for this is that a "modest" clinical effect for a single treatment (e.g., a decrease of 10 mm Hg using biofeedback in essential hypertension) may be of marginal clinical importance by itself. However, when this same decrease is combined with drug therapy, the importance of the decrease may become substantial if not critical. For example, a 10 mm Hg decrease in blood pressure with biofeedback may make it possible to lower the dosage of drugs taken. This could reduce or even eliminate the side effects of certain drugs, and thereby enhance long-term drug adherence. Clinical pharmacologists are experienced in dealing with interactive effects (both positive and negative) of different medications. The conceptual model developed in pharmacology can be translated into a more general model of drug and behavioral therapy interaction, which has important implications for theory, research, and practice in biofeedback and behavioral medicine (see Schwartz *et al.*, 1979). A more general model of interactive effects that can be applied to all living systems has been described by Miller (1978).

Shapiro emphasizes the need to measure multiple variables across different situations in order to determine appropriately what treatments are needed, and to evaluate appropriately the total effectiveness of the treatment package. An extension of this general recommendation is that the full set of effects of each treatment should be evaluated in order to determine true cost/benefit ratios. For example, biofeedback-assisted relaxation may produce a 10 mm Hg decrease in blood pressure in a subset of hypertensive patients. However, the total impact of the relaxation training may be substantially greater than the 10 mm Hg drop in blood pressure per se. Relaxation can have a wide set of psychological and physiological effects, of which decreased blood pressure is but one effect. The relaxation training may reduce other psychophysiological symptoms (e.g., tension headaches) that are not modified by the more selective actions of drugs such as diuretics. Also, if relaxation becomes part of the patients' life styles, it is possible that the patients will gain multiple psychosocial as well as physiological benefits that extend far beyond the target symptom or disease that initially led them to seek treatment. If researchers can develop more comprehensive models describing the complete set of effects (across multiple levels) that accompany different treatments (both behavioral and biological), they will be better able to evaluate the true cost/benefit ratios of specific treatments.

Parenthetically, the definition of a "main" effect as opposed to a "side" effect depends upon the purpose of the therapist, rather than upon something intrinsic about the nature of the treatment itself. For the therapist who recommends relaxation training for hypertension, decreases in blood pressure may be seen as a main effect, while decreases in frontalis muscle tension may be seen as a side effect. However, for the therapist who recommends relaxation training for tension headache, decreases in frontalis muscle tension may be seen as the main effect, whereas decreases in blood pressure may be seen as a side effect. Similarly, certain effects may be viewed as "negative" in one context, but may be seen as "positive" effects in other clinical contexts. It therefore becomes critical to distinguish between the intent of the treatment as determined by the therapist and the full set of effects elicited by the treatment itself.

As Shapiro points out, numerous practical issues dictate the number of variables that can be measured in any one patient or outcome study. Consequently, researchers must select variables wisely; it is to be hoped that this selection will be guided by hypotheses implying a specific model of the disorder and the treatment(s). In the case of biofeedback treatment, this requires that researchers clarify what they mean by biofeedback, how they plan to use it, and what they would consider to be a comprehensive set of independent and dependent variables. As Shapiro illustrates with his case example, biofeedback is often used clinically for purposes other than specific skill training per se. Biofeedback is used for self-monitoring to promote increased patient awareness of problems that must be solved, and to alter patients' attitudes regarding the role that their thoughts, feelings, and actions play in causing or maintaining disease and in promoting health. Early in the development of biofeedback, it was recognized that biofeedback served more purposes (and had more effects, both cognitive and affective) than basic skill training for enhancing voluntary control (e.g., Schwartz, 1973). Although specific skill training has its appropriate place, especially in muscular rehabilitation, specific skill training with biofeedback proves to be unnecessary (if not ineffective) for many multidetermined disorders involving the autonomic nervous system. Does this mean that investigators should stop doing research on biofeedback for these disorders? I believe that if they do so, they may end up inadvertently "throwing the baby out with the bath water." It is my opinion that past models of the ways in which biological feedback were used in clinical practice were clinically naive and theoretically too restricted. Future clinical research on biofeedback may profit not only from improving the precision and scope of clinical assessment per se, but also from improving conceptualizations of the multiple uses that biofeedback can play in a comprehensive self-regulation approach to treatment, in which the patient is viewed as an active participant in the therapeutic process along with appropriately trained health professionals.

REFERENCES

Adam, G. *Interoception and behavior.* Budapest: Akademiai Kiado, 1967.

Gelfan, S., & Carter, S. Muscle sense in man. *Experimental Neurology,* 1967, *18,* 469–473.

London, M. D., & Schwartz, G. E. The interaction of instruction components with cybernetic feedback effects in the voluntary control of human heart rate. *Psychophysiology,* 1980, *17,* 437–443.

Matthews, P. B. C., & Simmonds, A. Sensations of finger movement elicited by pulling upon flexor tendons in man. *Journal of Physiology, London,* 1974, *239,* 27–28.

Miller, J. G. *Living systems.* New York: McGraw-Hill, 1978.

Nisbett, R. E., & Wilson, T. D. Telling more than we can know: Verbal reports on mental processes. *Psychological Review,* 1977, *84,* 231–259.

Powers, W. T. *Behavior: The control of perception*. Chicago: Aldine, 1973.

Schwartz, G. E. Biofeedback as therapy: Some theoretical and practical issues. *American Psychologist,* 1973, *28,* 666–673.

Schwartz, G. E. Research and feedback in clinical practice: A commentary on responsible biofeedback therapy. In J. V. Basmajian (Ed.), *Biofeedback: Principles and practice for clinicians*. Baltimore: Williams & Wilkins, 1978.

Schwartz, G. E. Disregulation and systems theory: A biobehavioral framework for biofeedback and behavioral medicine. In N. Birbaumer & H. D. Kimmel (Eds.), *Biofeedback and self-regulation*. Hillsdale, N.J.: Erlbaum, 1979.

Schwartz, G. E. Behavioral medicine and systems theory: A new synthesis and paradigm. *National Forum,* Winter 1980, pp. 25–30.

Schwartz, G. E., Shapiro, A. P., Redmond, D. P., Ferguson, D. C. E., Ragland, D. R., & Weiss, S. M. Behavioral medicine approaches to hypertension: An integrative analysis of theory and research. *Journal of Behavioral Medicine,* 1979,*2,* 311–363.

ROUND-TABLE DISCUSSION OF BRENER, SHAPIRO, AND SCHWARTZ

Neal Miller: I think Gary [Schwartz]'s point is consistent with statements made in my introductory remarks [see Chapter 1]. What we may be seeing, and certainly shouldn't be concerned about, is that biofeedback may gradually fade out into the broader area of behavioral medicine. I think, also, there are two ways that awareness or perception can come in. One way, the way Jasper [Brener] has been talking about, is the ideomotor idea that it gives you control. Another way, a simpler and more obvious way, is the knowledge of whether you've succeeded or failed. Then you can substitute your own awareness for the biofeedback equipment, and thus greatly facilitate the transfer to the life situation.

Peter Lang: When Gary [Schwartz] was talking about the way biofeedback is used in the clinic, I kept wanting to substitute "physiological information" for the word "biofeedback." I think the best thing about the biofeedback movement is that it moved physiological recording apparatus into the clinician's environment. He doesn't know how to use these instruments much yet, because he hasn't been routinely trained in psychophysiology (and he surely needs that), but at least the physiological recording is in the clinical setting. Physiological information certainly should be available to the therapist; whether patients need it or not, I think, is still to be determined. To a great extent, high-density feedback, or organ feedback, is not terribly useful to patients. Whether patients need knowledge of results and information about their performance, and how that should be done, is another issue; but I certainly would second Gary [Schwartz] as far as the clinical issues are concerned.

Another point: I think we're having trouble with the the word "biofeedback" when imprecisely defined. It was a word I came to very reluctantly. It was used in a lot of papers before I used the word, and then only because it was forced on me; and now it's giving us trouble. In terms of Jasper [Brener]'s chapter, specifically, there are different things being discussed here with this issue of information. There is the exact information on organ functioning, which I think is what Jasper [Brener] is talking about; and we could project it as possible that such information can be utilized to control the particular organ from which that information comes. It's also possible that that's not true, that the mechanism of control is completely different. Another thing involved in what we call "biofeedback studies" is performance, or what used to be called, in motor-skills learning, "knowledge of results." It may have nothing to do with any exact knowledge of how the organ is functioning that we're trying to control. We confuse those things. Very often in a clinical procedure, and even in a laboratory procedure, performance and knowledge are confounded; and we make very little effort to separate them out. Another thing that we're interested in is the extent to which somebody controls his physiology because he becomes aware of cues in the environment that are coincident with an alteration in a specified function—let's say, high blood pressure. He didn't know that when he talked to the boss, his blood pressure went up. But now, maybe because his clinician monitors this function, he can come to use that information. He still doesn't have any organ feedback. He doesn't know a damn thing about what his blood pressure is doing, but he has learned that there's this relationship, so he can avoid the stimulus.

Richard Surwit: I'd like to make one other point, and that is that I think we need to think about which disorders will respond best to our treatment from a *behavioral* point of view. I've made this point repeatedly in my written work—that hypertension, I think, presents a particularly poor target for behavioral treatments because it makes a poor target for medical treatments as well. It's an asymptomatic condition. The patients are not motivated to comply with even a simple medical regimen. It's been my experience clinically that we do best when we focus our attention on patients who are in distress, number one, and number two, on disorders which respond fairly immediately to the behavioral dimension in question. From a very simple-minded behavioral point of view, we can see why this would be efficacious. I think that in order to make a general statement about the efficacy of behavioral techniques —biofeedback being one of them—in the treatment of any disease, we need to take into account the underlying basic and intrinsic behavioral mechanisms which the topography of the disease will allow to occur.

Barry Sterman: I disagree to some extent, understandably, with Gary [Schwartz]'s emphasis on the more holistic approach, but I kind of call myself an evolutionary empiricist. Not only what you see is what you got, but it's there for a reason. Biology is a wonderful teacher in that respect. If you look at the application of clinical medicine today, you see a few places like Lourdes and a lot of Kaiser–Permanente.[1] We deal with this problem all the time. The reason that the medical model has been so effective is because it's simple. If someone has a broken leg, you give him a splint or something simple like a pill, and the patient readily accepts it. You try and set up a life style change, and it's a lot of problems. The point is that *efficacy*, at this stage in the evolution of this field, is the issue.

Gary Schwartz: If we define "efficacy" only in terms of removing the final damage, yes, the best thing for everyone is just repair. Any way that you could possibly repair or get rid of the problem, no matter what it costs, is going to make lots of money, and most people are going to flock to it. But that doesn't mean that it's adaptive from an evolutionary perspective, or from a self-regulation, balance, or systems perspective. Let's think about the biology of feedback, using something for which the individual does have some con-

[1]Editors' note: Kaiser–Permanente is a medical center and medical care program in Oakland, California. "Kaiser–Permanente" is used here to represent the achievements of scientific medicine and is contrasted with Lourdes, a symbol of faith healing. Orne's position is that, from the point of view of the patient, faith is aroused in both settings.

scious awareness, like headaches or backaches, where part of that information is related to problems of life style and problems of environment. If you have a broken arm, you have pain; and what it tells you to do is not to move that limb and to seek help. It has some adaptive function for gaining repair. I want to suggest it is possible that there may be some wisdom to what the feedback is providing with regard to making alterations in the environment and in people's perception of the environment, as well as simply removing that information at all costs. And to the extent that we listen to the biological functioning of those signals, it may direct us toward directing our approach toward intervention, which justifies things like life style modification, environmental modification, diet change, or whatever.

Robert Gatchel: I think one word of caution should be noted concerning the use of biofeedback in the clinical setting, where you're taking a multimodal approach. One of the potential dangers is that if this viewpoint is accepted, many clinicians will assume, since we have already used biofeedback as one part of the treatment process, that biofeedback has been shown to be effective and that we have all the parameters hammered out. And I think that's one real danger in using it as one part of the treatment package. I think people will start abandoning future research looking at ways of increasing effectiveness. In biofeedback, not enough is known about some of the parameters.

John Furedy: I feel very strongly about this. I agree with Gary [Schwartz] that it's very important to think about these processes in a systematic and, perhaps, new way. And I also agree with Jasper [Brener] that the mechanism issues are extremely important, and it's only by getting down to the mechanisms that we're likely to achieve any significant improvement and know what's going on. I also agree with Dave Shapiro that control groups under the various control conditions are very important. It's very important to find out whether a given individual is going to benefit from a given treatment. But I don't think any of this is going to go anywhere until we take a step back and remember to use adequate definitions of what it is that we're talking about. The first adequate definition is that "biofeedback," the phenomenon, occurs if, and only if, you can show that giving the subject information about some biological function has increased control. This narrow definition of "biofeedback" is quite defensible, and I won't go through all the details. It does not mean that you don't get into other areas; and, in particular, I think it's very important for clinical applications. This is not a research laboratory question; it's a clinical application question. The issue for the clinician is, does the addition of the biofeedback as narrowly defind increase the potency of the clinical treatment? The only way to assess whether the addition of biofeedback, narrowly defined, increases the potency of the treatment is to compare it to a controlled condition, where you have the clinical treatment without the biofeedback treatment; but, in terms of the perception of the subject, the patient, the two treatments are equivalent. And this, of course, is done with a noncontingent control group with the safeguards that are necessary to maintain equivalence of subject perception. This has to be done for every response. It's only after you've established that this is better than that, in a given situation, that you can get down to the physiological mechanisms issues and the various other clinical issues.

Richard Surwit: I do think that most medical treatments are not based on basic research but actually evolve as practice through consensus. We need to be able to make a distinction, or make a decision perhaps, as a group of people who are working in the clinical and research area, as to whether or not we want to hold ourselves to a more rigid standard than the medical community does. Very often we shoot ourselves down with brilliant, articulate arguments. Very often, too, and I've been one of the greatest offenders here, we destroy the possibilities of some of our techniques which, for reasons that Gary [Schwartz] has outlines, may in fact have some efficacy, even though they do not show up under the scrutiny of the careful research study. I think we need to be able to make a distinction as to the two kinds of evidence, the clinical evidence and the research evidence.

Martin Orne: At the risk of taking away most of what I have to say on Sunday [see Chapter 17], I really can't let one thing go by. That is the notion of what makes medical treatments acceptable. And there's a very common misconception, namely, that it's related to effectiveness. Effectiveness really isn't the main criterion. And I am quite serious about this. The homeopaths were considerably more effective than the allopaths around the turn of the century because they had good nursing care and they had various other good things, and they didn't use treatments that made people sicker. As a result, their results were excellent. That didn't mean they were therefore accepted by medicine, because they lacked a reasonable theory to explain their treatments. Contrary to what you may believe, medicine, establishment medicine, has always felt that it had to be a rational treatment, which translates into having an acceptable theory. Not a proven theory—that is something which may take time—but an acceptable theory. I think that we tend to forget that, number one.

Now, lest we be quite as snooty as most of us are vis-à-vis some of our medical confreres (and let me put on that hat for a moment), I'd like to point out that the physician does not have the privilege of finding a convenient illness to treat, saying that he will do his research on that illness, and then saying, "Ah, you guys don't know what you're doing!" He has to treat them as they come. And he does it with what seems to be rational therapy. Obviously, scientific medicine would like to document things in depth. If you look at the scientific medical field, academic medicine at its best, it will hold its head up with academia in other areas very nicely. Now, indeed, I should also say I used to always have a profound inferiority feeling about the low state of knowledge in psychiatry until I developed a bad back; and then suddenly I learned that psychiatry is an exact science. So all things are relative.

Let me now go back to the point that Dave [Shapiro] made and that others have also addressed. I'd like to just suggest that if we go ahead and expand the notion of "biofeedback" to include all physiological informations, this has a merit to it. It has a merit that we borrow the pseudolegitimacy from the laboratory studies of biofeedback, which tend to be reasonably tight studies. We can then say we're doing "biofeedback." That is why biofeedback has kept its name in the clinical field. It is, of course, a fraud. And I think that this is what we are also saying, namely, that these are not studies. There are no data to support the hypotheses; what is done in the clinic is nothing more than using the name of "biofeedback" to lend the necessary legitimacy so that we can muck around and try to find out what's going on. But I do think that, in this group at least, we ought not to fall into the trap of a public relations measure as some of the clinical people have done in this regard. And we ought to make a clear distinction. I think that this kind of statement, or the fact that rigorous documentation is a necessity, has got to be made; because, contrary to what Barry [Sterman] says, there are far more Lourdes than any of us know. We just think they're Kaiser–Permanentes.

Joseph Brudny: It seems to me I'm the only practicing and pragmatic physician in this group, so I have to respond to Martin [Orne]'s statement. I must say I feel like the man who sees his mother-in-law going over the cliff in his brand-new Cadillac. I have mixed feelings on this matter. Things are not that bad. I feel that the concepts of bypass and substitution that are apparently the leading concepts in medicine over the past 10 years may give us a much firmer ground to stand on and say we do good medicine. If you look at things like coronary bypass, total joint replacement, and kidney dialysis—there's a host of them—I think you will find these are sound scientific procedures. I feel that a model of clinical treatment and feedback versus clinical treatment without feedback has an ideal area for all of you to get involved in—the area of the neurologically disabled patient. After all, we have a model where conventional therapy has been rendered with diminishing returns; you can document very easily the degree of deficit. Studies are abundant where, seemingly, recovery won't take place on its own after a certain amount of time. An introduction of feedback of information that is related to motor control seems to help many of these people.

Richard Surwit: I just wanted to make one point that essentially everybody else has said from a clinical perspective. I think that it's clear that biofeedback in its holistic and clinical application, as Martin [Orne] said, provided a scientific rationale to the notion that we can teach people to control autonomic dysfunction. Now I think we have to be careful when talking about biofeedback and its utility as opposed to more general relaxation procedures. We need to differentiate the disorders that are autonomically based from those that are central nervous system dysfunctions, or dysfunctions for which central nervous system control is clearly applicable, as in the case of seizure disorders and neuromuscular rehabilitation. My clinical experience has been that when dealing with autonomic dysfunction, we're dealing with a very gross system, which can be manipulated with a variety of nonspecific techniques; and I've never seen any advantage to specific techniques. My academic knowledge of the literature on the CNS dysfunctions leads me to think that there may be an entirely different model operating there, and I'd just like to call our attention to the fact that we shouldn't be talking about them in the same breath when we're approaching them from a clinical perspective.

Paul Obrist: Just one point. I'm disturbed that we've focused this whole discussion on clinical problems. Jasper [Brener] presented a very fundamental paper, and it invokes little discussion. Aren't we interested in mechanisms and processes? This is disturbing to me.

Joel Lubar: I think that the issue that Jasper Brener raised and that Black [Black, Cott, & Pavlovski, 1977] has raised in the past, this whole concept of to what extent awareness is necessary, is very important. It may be true to some extent that many of our epileptics who become surprisingly improved cannot begin to tell you of any state of awareness that they generate in order to do this [see Chapter 11]. They can't conceptualize it. But I think in many other areas—particularly, let's say, in headache, perhaps in hypertension, and certainly in neuromuscular disorders—I would feel that if you hadn't developed some awareness of the response as a result of the conditioning procedure, learning would be almost impossible. One way to increase awareness that works very well in a clinical setting is to have patients, for example, chart the headache's duration and intensity and gather that information in conjunction with the feedback. One of the things I try to do that works very well is to have the patient try to develop an awareness or an explanation for why he has developed a particular headache or a particular symptom. We will look at the chart on a day that the individual has developed a very severe headache and examine all the antecedent events that may have occurred, life style problems that may have occurred, or interoceptive things that he may become aware of, or has been aware of, that may explain why he has that headache. I find that when people learn to do that, and many of them do, they become very successful at avoiding headaches in the future. The point I'm trying to make is that you can develop this kind of internal awareness, and this may be even more powerful than the use of specific feedback in terms of controlling the problem.

John Furedy: I think that Jasper Brener, like most other psychologists in the last ten years, has become a closet cognitivist. There's an assumption, a ready assumption, that the CNS information is readily translated into action by the autonomic nervous system. I think these two hypotheses—that as individuals acquire control of a response they should also manifest an improved capacity to detect instances of that response, and then the obverse, if individuals are trying to detect instances of a response, they should show an improved capacity to control that response—are questionable. The idea that information about a particular function is going to help you control that function is a very seductive one in the current paradigm. But it is precisely that idea which first has to be tested in any specific biofeedback preparation. And I think Jasper Brener, like most of us, is assuming that to be the case. Now when Jasper [Brener] talks about the Lang and Twentyman [1974], the Johnston [1977], and the Williamson and Blanchard [1979] studies, he suggests that these studies suggest that the two systems, the motor-skill system and the ANS [autonomic nervous system], seem to obey similar programming principles. I don't know the Williamson and Blanchard study, but I do know that Dave Johnston, in that paper, was trying to make the point very strongly that heart rate deceleration is not like a motor skill because it does not improve as a function of amount of feedback; it doesn't improve over sessions. And I think that's one instance where Jasper [Brener]'s taking the notion of informational control for granted and then going on to other mechanisms. I think he should step back along with the rest of us and just see where informational control really works.

Jasper Brener: The question of mechanism, it seems to me, is a difficult one because one has to start off with a framework or a model for the mechanism. There are a variety of different models that one might propose to account for the observations made under conditions of biofeedback, and it seems to me that the area in which the effects of exteroceptive feedback or performance are best understood and have been most clearly formulated is in the case of striate muscular control, in the case of motor control. The mechanisms have been fairly precisely specified. The neuroprocesses and their anatomy have been plotted. And there is a sort of cogent outline of how the provision of exteroceptive feedback operates in the development of response control. The point is independent of the clinical implications of biofeedback. Studies of how the provision of feedback in the development of visceral motor control operates help us to generate a more precise understanding of motor-control processes generally. In other words, we have to choose a model from somewhere. If we go to neuromuscular control, the system has been precisely specified, and the mechanisms that operate it are available. The rational approach would be to see whether, in the provision of biofeedback for visceral motor control, similar processes operate.

This business about awareness and control, I think, is a restatement in much more flaccid terms of the calibration notions that come out of motor control. And I think that when one starts speaking about awareness and implying some sort of conscious processing of information, that one is almost in a different ball game. That sort of approach engenders an understanding of how biofeedback operates that is essentially abiological and diverts us from a true understanding of the mechanisms. I don't know whether that point is clear.

Paul Obrist: Are you backing off of your calibration notion because maybe afferent feedback isn't all that important? You seem to be implying that when you talk about the studies of the deafferented limbs, and I didn't follow you.

Jasper Brener: I think that what Peter [Lang] has just said is what I am concerned about. Biofeedback is used in a variety of ways and for a variety of different processes. My own interest in it is the interest in the process of calibration. That is to say, how information is encoded, and in particular, how motor programs are generated by the nervous system for the production of particular motor processes. Barry Sterman and others have raised the point or the question of the functional significance of these structures that exist in the nervous system and in the body. And an important issue is, what is the function of afferent feedback? This is a topic the Laceys have commented on at great length and great lucidity. It seems to me that a central concept in our understanding of how afferent feedback participates in the processes of motor control stems from the reafference principle described and experimentally demonstrated by Von Holst [Von Holst, 1954]. His experiment suggested that feedback from the periphery provides a central comparator mechanism with information on the basis of which peripheral compliance with central motor commands may be evaluated. This is a specific notion that was confirmed with a single experiment, and a lot of our ideas about the functions of feedback in the regulation of motor control derive from that. When one looks at the deafferentation stage, it is clear that you can not only regulate motor responses without afferent effect, or apparently without afferent effect, but that you can also recalibrate central efferent processes—for example, by putting displacement prisms on monkeys that are deafferented. So, what I have done is to retract my emphasis on afference and to speak about response discrimination, because I think that responses can be discriminated, not only on the basis of peripheral feedback from the effector, but also on the basis of commands sent from the central nervous system to the effector; and there is a lot of evidence that supports that notion.

Paul Obrist: Let me comment concretely. John Lacey, 22 years ago, in 1958, informed us and made us aware of the fact that we have a tremendous wealth of visceral afferent feedback. Now Jasper [Brener], and I don't know whether John [Lacey] influenced him or not, in the sense of this calibration model, has spoken the same way. Here we have something very concretely biological that's going on. Can we use that visceral afferent feedback? Do you get my point? Jasper [Brener]'s is the only model that ever appealed to me in terms of any of the biofeedback work, because it is anchored in biology and is a potential, anyhow. To me, talking about biofeedback in terms of learning alone or the black box model is limiting. If it works, it's fine. But here we have tied down into some potential biological mechanisms, and I think we tend just to ignore this. We don't see the tremendous value of it. I teach 6 hours every spring. It's an introductory graduate level course in psychobiology, and the one thing when I get to biofeedback that I talk about very concretely is just this sort of thing. We have the Russian literature on interoceptive conditioning [Adam, 1967; Chernigovskiy, 1967], regardless of what it's worth (I notice that some disagree with that), in terms of is it so? But I think we need to get away from concepts like awareness—that's just a boogeyman—and talk about [this:] can we use this wealth of visceral information that we have?

Joel Lubar: I was just going to say one thing. I would like to see, and I think it would help a lot in terms of this business of efficacy, some trials run in which we try to ferret out specific additions that biofeedback makes for specific disorders. We need experiments or clinical studies where we're looking at a specific disorder, whether it be gastrointestinal or hypertension or headache, and also where we compare matched groups—relaxation training; autogenic training; imagery; therapist variables, which nobody deals with and we know are critical; and specific biofeedback—to try to answer the question, "Does the biofeedback add anything above and beyond, let's say, what autogenic training does?" Autogenic training can be used with just about every disorder we're going to discuss in the next three days; and it works just about as well for most of them, with the exception of very specific neuromuscular disorders. I agree, there it doesn't. But for headaches, hypertension, and gastrointestinal problems, it seems to do very well. I think if we do these kinds of things, then we can begin to ferret out not only the question of to what extent awareness comes in, but also, what does the feedback specifically add? There have been some studies along this line, but they've been confused; and usually they come out showing that biofeedback plus relaxation is about as effective as relaxation alone, or biofeedback plus autogenic training is about as good as biofeedback alone, and we don't have a clear picture of what the feedback really adds.

Bernard Tursky: We've been talking about biofeedback as if we really had a handle on the procedure and the method and the way that this information is brought back to the individual. That is, we talk about it in terms of "Let's use it and compare it"; and if Jasper [Brener] has worked out mechanisms, we have not yet worked out the actual procedures that insure us that we are able to transmit this inforamtion. So, before we get into the discussion of comparisons, we must also be able to say that for a particular physiological function, we know what the track of the information is and whether, indeed, it follows the model of feedback. We are continuously using that word "feedback." It's been used a thousand times already this morning, and it will be used ten thousand times before we get through; but we have to be very careful that when we use it, we don't make this global assumption that there is this feedback loop. Joseph Brudny's work certainly indicates a loop [see Chapter 10]. There is the brain, the muscle, and the environment; and this indicates that the loop is only formed because there is a patterning effect that the patient can use. In all our other cases, we don't have that patterning effect. We don't have a patterning effect for blood pressure; we don't have a patterning effect for heart rate, in terms of what we can perceive. If we can demonstrate awareness, then maybe we can say there is a patterning effect that we can use; but until we can demonstrate awareness, I don't think we do have that patterning effect. I think we have to be very careful that before we go ahead and expound these ideas about comparisons, we do have that kind of information for each individual function.

Neal Miller: It seems to me there are two different purposes of clinical evaluation. One of them is to see whether there's anything more than a placebo effect on various selection errors involved in the apparent success of the treatments, and then to see whether we have a problem for research to improve upon. If it's just a placebo effect and doesn't involve the rationale that we think it does at all, then we shouldn't attempt to improve upon it by that rationale. That's sort of a guide to ourselves. The other function is to see whether it's good for the patients. It's my impression that with the growth of third-party payments, plus the consumer movement, plust the sort of general raising of standards in the medical profession, we are eventually going to be called to accountability to show if the thing is worth anything. It would be quite worthwhile to have some positive evidence for some applications.

REFERENCES

Adam, G. *Interoception and behavior.* Budappest: Akademiai Kiado, 1967.

Black, A. H., Cott, A., & Pavlovski, R. The operant learning theory approach to biofeedback training. In G. E. Schwartz & J. Beatty (Eds.), *Biofeedback: Theory and research.* New York: Academic Press, 1977.

Chernigovskiy, V. N. *Interoceptors.* Washington, D.C.: American Psychological Association, 1967.

Johnston, D. Biofeedback, verbal instructions and motor skills analogy. In J. Beatty & H. Legewie (Eds.), *Biofeedback and behavior.* New York: Plenum, 1977.

Lang, P. J., & Twentyman, C. T. Learning to control heart rate: Binary vs. analogue feedback. *Psychophysiology,* 1974, *11,* 616–629.

Von Holst, E. Relations between the central nervous system and peripheral organs. *British Journal of Animal Behaviour,* 1954, *2,* 89–94.

Williamson, D. A., & Blanchard, E. B. Effect of feedback delay upon learned heart rate control. *Psychophysiology,* 1979, *16,* 108–115.

4 CLASSICAL AND OPERANT CONDITIONING IN THE ENHANCEMENT OF BIOFEEDBACK: SPECIFICS AND SPECULATIONS

JOHN J. FUREDY AND DIANE M. RILEY

More general formulations of the approach to biofeedback enhancement that is employed in the University of Toronto laboratory have been provided previously (Furedy, 1977, 1979). In this chapter we first describe this approach in a detailed way, wherein we provide "specifics." In the first section, we lay out the ways in which our approach differs from conventional biofeedback approaches, and then provide some testable hypotheses derived from this approach, together with brief descriptions of the methods of testing those hypotheses. In the second major section we move beyond such empirical considerations to more theoretical and historical ones. These considerations are necessarily more speculative and subjective than are the empirical, essentially descriptive, considerations raised in the first section. Nevertheless, such speculations are important, if only because they often form a powerful influence on the manner in which a research program is carried out. In such contexts as those of grant proposals or papers directed at a large group of generalists, these

John J. Furedy and Diane M. Riley. Department of Psychology, University of Toronto, Toronto, Ontario, Canada.

speculative aspects are seldom laid out systematically, the result being that they are not subjected to adequate critical examination. A specialized group of contributors such as that represented in this volume can provide the detailed criticism that will allow for improvement of these formulations, particularly with respect to their explicitness and clarity.

SPECIFICS: A RESPONSE-LEARNING APPROACH TO THE CONTROL OF STRESS-ELICITED PHASIC AUTONOMIC CHANGES[1]

BACKGROUND AND THE RESPONSE-LEARNING APPROACH

Modern life is full of stressful events that produce the "fight or flight" reflex in humans. Components of this reflex are short-term or phasic autonomic changes, such as heart rate acceleration. In some cases, even "normal" responses to stress can be undesirable. One strategy for eliminating such reactions is that of eliminating the stressors themselves. However, this strategy is impractical because people vary so much in what they find stressful. Thus, to take an extreme but illuminating example, consider the coronary patient resting in a quiet ward designed to minimize the occurrence of stressful stimuli. A new doctor comes to visit the patient, and it happens that the doctor's face is similar to the face of another person with whom the patient has had a very emotional disagreement. As a result, the new doctor's face serves as a stressor, and it elicits an undesirable heart rate acceleration (HRA), which can itself percipitate another debilitating cardiovascular episode. It will be noted that the strategy of eliminating such stressors from the environment is unlikely to work, because there is no way of predicting what, for a given patient, will be stressful.

An alternative to the strategy of external environmental control is that of internal *behavioral* control. In this strategy, persons are taught to control their reactions to whatever events happen to be stressful to them. So, to control stress-induced HRA, a patient might learn to produce the opposing heart rate deceleration (HRD) at the time that the HRA-inducing stressor appears. The particular tactic for such behavioral control that has been most generally used adopts the approach of providing information about the autonomic nervous system's functioning through biofeedback. For example, in applying this "informational-biofeedback" approach to the teaching of HRD, the procedure is to have the person informed (using expensive computerized polygraphic equipment) about the rate of his or her beating heart, on the assumption that this information will enable the person to learn to decelerate his or her heart rate.

[1]For some of the ideas formulated in this section, we are indebted to J. Arabian, R. Heslegrave, and E. Tulving.

Recent research has indicated that this assumption is largely a "hope" that is "unfulfilled" (Blanchard & Young, 1973), at least with regards to the control of such autonomically mediated changes as HRD. To draw this pessimistic conclusion is not to deny the few successes that some workers have had in producing large HRDs and control of cardiac arrhythmias (e.g., Engel, 1972). What has continued to fail to emerge is statistically significant evidence (1) that such control is indeed attributable to the provision of information, and (2) that it varies as a function of the adequacy of that information. Recent strong support for this pessimistic conclusion is the fact that one of the most influential and thorough investigators of the informational-biofeedback approach to HRD has counseled clinicians to use the less expensive relaxation methods to control anxiety, in preference to the more expensive computerized polygraphic biofeedback arrangements (Lang, 1977). The basis of this advice includes evidence from Lang's own studies where, for example, a group given precise information about their heart rate produced less HRD than did a group of subjects who were simply told to repeat a "mantra" on a regular (and presumably relaxing) basis.

The alternative tactic or approach that we have adopted in our studies of HRD learning is based on the assumption that the desired response should be elicited first, before any attempt is made to teach it. This "response-learning" approach (Furedy, 1979) begins with events such as an instructed breath hold (e.g., Furedy & Poulos, 1975, Exp. I) or a negative body tilt (e.g., Furedy & Poulos, 1976, Exp. I). These events reliably elicit a short-term or phasic HRD response of large magnitude (over 30 beats per minute). In terms of Pavlovian conditioning, the events are unconditional stimuli (USs) that elicit the HRD response as the unconditional response (UR). Moreover, at least on the face of it, this sort of UR appears to be a good candidate for controlling the phasic HRA responses elicited by stressors. That is, if the subject can learn to produce a significant portion of the HRD UR in the absence of the US but in the presence of the stressor, then this response-learning tactic may be an effective way of learning behavioral control over stress.

Accordingly, the next step is to determine whether pairing a relatively neutral stimulus (such as a tone) as the conditional stimulus (CS) with the US will produce some HRD response learning to the CS alone in a Pavlovian-conditioning paradigm. This has in fact been shown to occur both with the instructed breath-hold US (Furedy & Poulos, 1975, Exp. II) and the negative-tilt US (Furedy & Poulos, 1976, Exp. II). Moreover, it appears that the most promising form of this Pavlovian paradigm is the "imaginational" one (Furedy, 1977), wherein part of the CS is an instruction to the subject to imagine the US. This imaginational paradigm, which has produced the largest HRD responses, is still Pavlovian inasmuch as the target anticipatory HRD response does not affect the tilt US. The procedure, however, is quite complex (for details, see Furedy & Klajner, 1978), with the role of imagery in particular being apparently important but very difficult to specify.

We have also extended this complex but still Pavlovian paradigm to an operant-conditioning procedure with discrete trials. In this arrangement (see Furedy, 1979, pp. 210–211), the HRD response elicited by the CS through Pavlovian conditioning is now shaped or contingently reinforced by verbal praise ("good," "very good," or "excellent"); the larger the HRD response in the presence of the CS (now a discriminative stimulus in an operant-conditioning procedure with discrete trials), the more praise the subject gets. This Pavlovian–operant procedure has produced some encouraging results (e.g., Furedy, 1977, 1979) both in terms of HRD and in terms of probable sympathetic withdrawal as indexed by the T-wave component of the electrocardiogram (see Fig. 14.1 in Furedy, 1979).

The two approaches that we have characterized respectively as "informational-biofeedback" and "response-learning," are not completely incompatible. For example, it will be noted that the operant-conditioning paradigm described above, which has stemmed from our response-learning approach, is a form of biofeedback. Nevertheless, the response-learning approach does differ from the conventional biofeedback approach in ways that have been indicated elsewhere (Furedy, 1979) and are summarized in an injunction to "remember the response." Among the important differentiating characteristics (elaborated in the cited study) of the response-learning approach are (1) the focus on phasic rather than tonic changes; (2) initial elicitation of the target response before attempting to teach it, and (3) the relative deemphasis of such purely informational aspects of learning as the exact stage of the target behavior (e.g., the precise heart rate) and the predictive or sign-significant relationship (in Pavlovian conditioning) between the CS and the US. What the Furedy study (1979) does not provide, however, are a number of *testable* hypotheses that can be generated from the response-learning approach, and that are not derivable from or even compatible with the informational-biofeedback approach. We now present four such hypotheses.

HYPOTHESES TO BE INVESTIGATED

Hypothesis 1 (H1)

The Pavlovian HRD conditioning preparations that we have developed through the response-learning approach are premised on a stimulus-substitution or response-transfer account of the process. For example, on this account, the HRD response initially elicited as a UR by the tilt US comes through stimulus substitution to be elicited to a lesser extent by the CS as a result of CS-US pairings; the HRD response, that is, is partially "transferred" from the US to the CS. It follows from this account that an important factor determining the strength of conditioning is the temporal *contiguity* or closeness between the CS (the future elicitor of the HRD response) and the UR (elicited by the US). Because the UR is closely time-locked to the US, this CS-UR contiguity is closely related to the temporal interval between the onsets of the CS and the US, which is commonly termed the "interstimulus interval" (ISI).

Accordingly, H1 is as follows: *It is the ISI that is important, rather than information given to the subject about the relationship between the CS and UR or about his or her heart rate following CS presentation.* It will be noted that this ISI (H1) hypothesis denies significance to informational "cognitive" factors that are statable in terms of *propositional* information, either about the CS-US relationship or about the state of some autonomic function. (For further elaboration of the distinction between propositional and response processes, see Furedy, 1979, pp. 211–212.)

Hypothesis 2 (H2)

There is, as we have noted previously (Furedy & Poulos, 1976, p. 95), another aspect of the tilt-conditioning procedure that makes this form of human cardiac conditioning more consistent with a stimulus-substitution, response-transfer view than are the other, more conventional procedures, which use noxious stimuli (such as shocks and loud noises) as USs. This aspect is the topographical similarity of the CR and UR, both being decelerative. In contrast, the conventional cardiac conditioning procedures produce an acceleratory UR, but a CR that has been variously identified as multiphasic (Hendrick & Graham, 1969; Zeaman, Deane, & Wegner, 1954), decelerative (Wood & Obrist, 1964) or accelerative (Zeaman & Smith, 1965). Indeed, it is from this human cardiac conditioning area, with its failure to yield clear evidence for UR-CR topographical similarity, that much of the support has come for the currently dominant cognitive view of Pavlovian conditioning. On this cognitive view, the mechanism involved is the learning of (propositional information about) CS-US relationships and not the transfer of responses from US to CS. For the present purposes, our interest is not in Pavlovian conditioning in general (for which issue the distinction between propositional and response processes offered by Furedy, 1979, may turn out to be relevant), but in the more circumscribed question of what mechanism of learning is involved in the tilt-conditioning preparation. The clear decelerative CR-UR similarity found in that preparation tends to support a response-learning view; however, a more compelling source of support for this view would be obtained if the following, more "daring" hypothesis (H2) were confirmed: *Reversing the direction of the UR in the tilt-conditioning preparation will reverse the direction of the CR.*[2]

Hypothesis 3 (H3)

The next two hypotheses concern the operant-conditioning extensions that we have developed for HRD response learning. Although, as indicated above, biofeedback terminology is applicable to these operant-conditioning procedures with dis-

[2]This hypothesis was recently formulated by T. Matyas, and its test will, we hope, be carried out in collaboration with him.

crete trials, the emphasis on response learning or response shaping yields a view that is different from the conventional, informational-biofeedback approach. That approach emphasizes the *quality* of the propositional information given to subjects about their target behaviors (here, HRD). From a quality-of-information point of view, the emphasis is on such aspects as the degree to which the feedback is continuous and hence contains accurate information about the target behavior, in contrast to the cruder information transmitted by "binary" feedback (i.e., presence vs. absence of some contingent reinforcer). On the other hand, in operant response-conditioning terms, what is being shaped is a response. From this vantage, the important factor is not the amount of information contained in the reinforcement, but its temporal *contiguity* or closeness to the target response that it is meant to reinforce. In other, more Hullian, words, it is the minimization of the delay-of-reinforcement gradient that would be emphasized by a response-learning approach.

Accordingly, H3 is as follows: *In the operant decelerative paradigm, what is important is the immediacy of reinforcement* (i.e., the continguity between the instrumental or target response and the reinforcer), *rather than the amount of information provided in the reinforcement about the target responses.*

Hypothesis 4 (H4)

The final hypothesis is also focused on the response–reinforcement link rather than on information *about* the response, but the aspect of the link in this case is not temporal contiguity but the degree of similarity of afferent inputs associated with the two (response and reinforcement) elements. The possible importance of this aspect was first noted by Tursky (see Furedy, 1979, p. 215). We have been able to demonstrate that the tilt can be used as an effective reinforcer (see Furedy, 1979, pp. 215–216). However, H4 is as follows: *In the operant decelerative paradigm, a reinforcer that shares afferent pathways with the target response will be* more *effective in an operant procedure than one that does not.*

PROPOSED HYPOTHESIS-TESTING EXPERIMENTS

We regard the testing of the above hypotheses as a way of evaluating the fruitfulness of the response-learning approach. Here, we outline the proposed experimental tests that we have devised in the University of Toronto laboratory. Methodological criticisms of these tests are especially welcome at a time when these tests have not actually been carried out.

To test the ISI aspects of H1, levels of HRD performance will be compared between groups of subjects conditioned with ISIs of 1, 5, and 10 seconds, respectively. It is predicted that conditioning will be a negative function of ISI, with little or no conditioning shown in the 10-seconds ISI group. As a control for conditioning, a fourth group will be run in which the CS and US are presented in a random relationship (Rescorla, 1967). Then, to test the aspect of H1 that relates to information about the relationship of the CS to the US, a fifth and a sixth group will be run under the random CS and US arrangements, but instructed, respectively, that the CS is an imperfect predictor of US presence (excitatorily instructed) or absence (inhibitorily instructed). A postexperimental continuous measure of subjective CS-US contingency (e.g., Furedy & Schiffmann, 1971) will be used to assess the subjects' beliefs about the CS-US relationship in the three physically random groups. If, as expected on the basis of past evidence, this measure indicates the instructional manipulation to have been effective, then the question will be whether the three physically random groups differ appropriately with respect to their HRD responding to the CS; according to H1, they will not, nor will there be a correlation between degrees of belief in the CS-US relationship and magnitude of HRD responses. Finally, to test the aspect of H1 relating to information about heart rate, all six of the above groups (the three ISI and the three random groups) will each be divided into two equal subgroups. The "informed" subgroups will be given accurate information about their HRD response to the CS, whereas the "misinformed" subgroups will be given inaccurate information. Past evidence suggests that in this phasic HRD situation subjects cannot tell that they are in a "false" feedback condition. If this is confirmed in the study, then the question will be whether the accuracy of feedback affects HRD performance; according to H1, it will not.

To test H2, the "reversal" hypothesis, we shall contrast conditioning between head-up (positive-tilt) and head-down (negative-tilt) USs. The negative tilt will be 45°, rather than the 90° tilt used in our previously published studies, and will commence from a horizontal plane. Earlier studies have indicated that this negative-half-tilt procedure does produce a reliable HRD UR (about half the magnitude of the UR elicited by the "full" tilt), as well as learned HRD conditioning. Completely uninvestigated, however, is the effect of using the positive-tilt US. This will also begin from a horizontal starting point, and will be a 45° head-up change in body position with the same speed as that used for the negative half tilt—that is a duration of about 1.2 seconds. The initial studies will explore the URs elicited by these positive- and negative-tilt USs, with the expectation that the USs will produce changes in heart rate that are topographically similar *except* for direction; the negative- and positive-tilt USs are expected, respectively, to produce deceleration and acceleration. Topographical analyses of the UR will follow the method used by Furedy and Poulos (1976, Exp. I). These initial steps will aim at developing negative- and positive-tilt USs that produce opposite but otherwise equivalent topographical heart rate changes. Tone stimuli will then be paired with each US in a Pavlovian-conditioning paradigm. If conditioning is demonstrated in the positive-tilt as well as in the negative-tilt groups, then the question will be whether the CR under the former (acceleratory-inducing US) condition is itself acceleratory, as required by H2.

To test H3, we shall employ an HRD-response paradigm, the Pavlovian–operant tilt arrangement described in Furedy (1979). In this method, a previously trained

CS is now a discriminative stimulus in an operant arrangement with discrete trials. Delay of reinforcement will be varied between groups by contingent verbal reinforcement delivered either as immediately as possible after the response (in fact this is a delay of about 2 seconds), or at least 20 seconds following the response. Amount of information about the target (HRD) response will also be varied. Half the subjects in each of the above groups will be given either simple binary information ("good" or no comment) or more accurate quasicontinuous information (i.e., number of beats decelerated). According to H3, the immediacy-of-reinforcement factor, but not the amount-of-information factor, should affect the amount of operant HRD responding.

The testing of H4 will also employ the tilt-operant paradigm, because it is this paradigm that uniquely permits focusing on the variable of communality of afferent pathways between the target response and the reinforcer. This communality is achieved, as indicated in Furedy (1979, pp. 215–216), by using the tilt as an operant reinforcer contingent on the target HRD response. In addition to the noncontingent control conditions that are necessary for assessing true operant conditioning effects (see Furedy & Riley, 1979), the main experimental contrast will be between two groups. Both groups will receive contingent verbal reinforcement, but, in addition, the "tilt" group will receive contingent tilt reinforcement, while a "light" group will receive contingent light reinforcement. As with the "tilt" group described in Furedy (1979, p. 216), members of both groups will receive instructions that the tilt (or light) means that they have done well on that trial. In other words, the presence versus absence of the tilt or light is used as a binary (i.e., informationally "crude") but contingent reinforcer. The prediction from H4 is that the tilt group will perform better than the light group will in production of the operant HRD response. If this result is obtained, another experiment will be performed to verify that the obtained difference is due to the communality-of-afferent-pathways factor rather than some "amount-of-reinforcement" difference between the tilt and light *qua* stimuli. In this experiment the target response to be operantly conditioned will be performance on a visual discrimination threshold task, rather than the HRD response. Otherwise, the design (including verbal reinforcement and instructions that the tilt and light, respectively, are indicative of good performance) will be the same. If H4 is correct, then the superiority of the tilt over the light group should disappear or even reverse with this change of the target response.

SIGNIFICANCE

One relevant aspect of the proposed research is its implications for models of Pavlovian and operant conditioning (see also Furedy, 1977). In general, current models have tended not to concentrate on the response-acquisition features of conditioning paradigms. Rather, the tendency has been to focus on the more cognitive, informational aspects, such as the learning of the sign-significate relationship between CS and US in Pavlovian conditioning. Our explorations of Pavlovian and operant conditioning, with HRD as the main target response and with our response-learning-oriented approach, are likely to increase understanding of the processes involved in conditioning.

Of broader interest is the problem of autonomic control. As indicated at the outset, this represents an internal–behavioral rather than an external–environmental strategy for coping with potentially harmful, stressful events. However, most investigators have adopted the informational-biofeedback approach as the dominant tactic for achieving autonomic control, and the results, especially with HRD as the target behavior, have not been very impressive. The response-learning approach used in our laboratory has, as indicated above, already produced some promising results. The hypothesis-testing studies proposed here should provide more information as to the relative fruitfulness of the response-learning approach for solving the problem of autonomic control.

SPECULATIONS: TERMINOLOGY, THEORY, AND SOME HISTORICAL INTERPRETATIONS

TERMINOLOGICAL AND METHODOLOGICAL CONSIDERATIONS

To begin with a point of terminology, we have elsewhere indicated that we favor a "contingency" definition of the term "biofeedback" (Furedy & Riley, 1979). According to this definition, and stating the matter in terms of operant conditioning, the biofeedback of, for example, HRD is effective if and only if it is shown that it is the contingency between the target behavior (HRD) and the reinforcement (i.e., information or feedback about HRD) that is responsible for the increase in HRD. It should be noted however, that the terminology of operant conditioning is not an essential part of the argument, it not being necessary to regard biofeedback as merely a case of operant conditioning. What is important, both conceptually and empirically, is to insist on the adequate definition of terms, and in the present instance this means to use what has elsewhere been called a "narrow" definition of the term "biofeedback" (Furedy, 1979, pp. 205–206). Thus, in informational terms, "biofeedback" as a phenomenon has to be stated as occurring if and only if it is the contingent signal ("feedback") from a biological function that has led to the increase of control of that function.

This narrow definition of "biofeedback" in terms of its contingency or informational components is to be preferred over broader, more liberal "biofeedback package" definitions, according to which any increase in control is viewable as part of the biofeedback treatment.[3] There are a number of reasons for this preference. The first reason is an historical one. The excitement over biofeedback in the late 1960s was based, we suggest, on those aspects central to the narrow definition. The idea that captured the imagination of so many people was not that some combination of relaxation training, therapist–patient interactions, and computerized-feedback-based placebo effects would, as a package, provide improved autonomic control. The notion of such a package was itself not particularly innovative. The point of interest was, rather, the more precise idea that if information or feedback were provided concerning biological functions of which the subject was not normally aware, then this information would itself enhance control.

There are also scientific reasons for restricting the use of the term "biofeedback" to those phenomena where feedback per se leads to increased control. These reasons are basically taxonomic ones. When a new term such as "biofeedback" becomes popular, there is a natural tendency to broaden its use to include many phenomena. Such broad usage, however, while useful for generating enthusiasm, is of no worth for making distinctions—for developing, that is, a sound taxonomy of the phenomena to be studied. Further, in order to understand the underlying principles of any phenomenon, it is necessary to be able to refer to a sound classification system for the identification of what it is that is being so investigated.

Aside from the above seemingly academic reasons, there are also practical, applied reasons for adhering to a narrow definition of "biofeedback." In this connection, it is important to note that the provision of information to a subject by computerized polygraphic equipment is an extremely expensive process. It is critical, from the practical standpoint of cost-effectiveness, to determine whether the provision of this information is in fact relevant to the success of therapy. Without this determination, it is poor technology to assume that biofeedback has been effective

[3]An alternative to seeking an adequate definition of the term "biofeedback" is that of abandoning the term. This move has been advocated by a number of contributors to this volume as a means of resolving disagreements, as well as of ridding ourselves of certain troublesome evaluative connotations that the term has come to acquire. In our view such a strategy, although it may be attractive in the short run, can only be counterproductive in the long term. Essentially, it is a way of solving a problem by shelving it. Such "outlawed" terms tend to return when the paradigm shifts again; when that return occurs, what happens is that one finds that because the term was outlawed on emotional grounds rather than closely examined on rational ones, it brings the latent conceptual confusions with its return. On the other hand, to oppose any wholesale abandonment of the term "biofeedback" is not to advocate any wholesale retention of it to apply to any form of behavioral control. This is why we oppose any broad "biofeedback package" definition. It is also why we take Tursky's suggestion that the term be dropped (see the end Chapter 5 in this volume) not to be advocating the emotive abandonment strategy that we have attacked, but rather to be questioning whether the processes involved are, in fact, "biofeedback" or "feed*forward*" ones. From both a scientific and a technological point of view, then, we suggest that in the long run it is far better to continue grappling with the problems of defining difficult terms than it is to take the short-term, superficially attractive path of "solving" these problems simply by shelving them.

when it is not known whether some other component of the package, such as relaxation, would have worked just as well. Indeed, any technological assessment has also to consider the possibility that a specific component of a package is not only useless but actually deleterious. It is possible that in certain instances the computerized polygraphic equipment's signals to subjects (i.e., "biofeedback" in the narrow sense of the term) are actually lessening rather than increasing their control over a behavior, such as HRD, because this feedback increases anxiety and thus leads to HRA. It is also possible that interference with the production of the target behavior occurs because the stimulus properties of the information display, such as density, produce competing responses. Any technological system that does not conceptually separate the biofeedback component of the total treatment package from the package itself will not permit the discovery or the elimination of such problems.

Given that we accept the narrow, contingency-based definition of the biofeedback phenomenon, a methodological question then arises: What are the proper controls for deciding that we have found an instance of the phenomenon? This question can be best discussed by recalling a formally identical problem that arose in the late 1950s, when learning theorists wished to determine whether nonbiological reinforcers such as weak lights were really reinforcing for rats (e.g., Berlyne, 1960). The early proponents of this view thought it sufficient simply to show that the rate of lever pressing ("operant conditioning") in rats would increase if such a light followed each lever press. It will be noted that, just as biofeedback can be formulated in terms of operant conditioning or in terms of voluntary control, so the lever-pressing example could have been formulated as either operant lever-press conditioning with light as reinforcement or as the rats' voluntarily "emitting" lever presses "in order to get" the light.

The methodological control issue, however, was not the distinction between "mere" operant conditioning and true "voluntary" control, but whether, *in fact*, the light was serving as a contingent reinforcer for lever pressing, or whether lever pressing had increased simply because of certain properties of the light *qua* stimulus. For example, the light may have energized the animals, raised their overall responsiveness, and hence raised their lever-pressing rate; or it may have calmed the animals, lowered their overall responsiveness, and hence increased their level pressing with which their overall responsiveness competed. Viewed in these terms, it is clear that what was needed in this instance in order to determine whether the lever pressing was an instance of operant conditioning (or of biofeedback) was a noncontingent control, wherein identical reinforcing stimuli are provided but where the contingency between the target response (TR) and the reinforcer is removed.

It is also apparent from these considerations that the only appropriate control in both this example and the present situation regarding biofeedback is the noncontingent one; other forms of control are not adequate because, while they may control for some factors that may be related to contingency, they do not control for the contingency factor itself. In this connection, it is important to note that, while we can make the theoretical distinction clearly, we may not be able to do so in the practical case. While the specification of noncontingency in general, conceptual terms is quite readily made, it is an empirical matter, and hence a matter of potential dispute, whether, under a specific set of conditions, an adequate noncontingent control has actually been attained. For it is possible that some other confounding factor may have an effect that provides *another* source of difference between the contingent and noncontingent conditions.

An analogous situation has recently occurred in arguments about the proper controls for Pavlovian autonomic conditioning. It is generally agreed that the proper control condition has to be equal to the experimental condition except for that which defines Pavlovian conditioning: the increase in responding to the CS attributable to the association of the CS with the US (e.g., see Furedy & Poulos, 1977, p. 352). This clarity of definition does not mean, however, that the attainment of the condition in practice is guaranteed. For example, relatively expert and experienced researchers in two laboratories have an unresolved disagreement over how to produce a CS that is random in relation to the US (see Furedy, Poulos, & Schiffmann, 1975a, 1975b; Prokasy, 1975a, 1975b). Until that disagreement is resolved, there will be difficulties in reaching an agreement in the scientific community that, in a given Pavlovian-conditioning experiment, a nonassociate or noncontingent CS-US arrangement has in fact been attained in the control condition. The fact that such disagreements occur in Pavlovian conditioning is no reason for accepting such grossly inadequate substitutes for control conditions as the CS-alone condition, wherein the control group receives only the CSs and not the USs. Such a control was one that was offered in the early, formative days of Pavlovian conditioning, but it is no longer regarded as an appropriate one. For while the CS-alone treatment controls for the effects of the CS itself, it does not control for the nonassociative (e.g., energizing) effects of the US.

We have fulminated against the CS-alone control in this way because in operant autonomic conditioning the no-feedback control is logically equivalent and has, therefore, the same shortcomings. Yet, at least in the field of heart rate control, the no-feedback condition has been used in a large proportion of studies, and this proportion shows little sign of diminishing in the future.

According to the narrow definition of "biofeedback," it appears that the so-called "bidirectional control" (BC) design is also inadequate, although not as obviously and as seriously as the no-feedback control. The BC design apparently stems from its use by Miller and DiCara (e.g., see Miller, 1969) in their work on animal autonomic conditioning. Their heart rate change results were assessed in the BC arrangement, wherein either accelerative or decelerative responses were contingently reinforced. The problem with this design does not stem from the sort of argument made by Rescorla (1967) against the differential Pavlovian-conditioning design—

namely, that the design does not permit the assessment of the degree to which the difference is due to the two components. In Pavlovian conditioning, a CS + to CS − difference allows the inference that associative learning has occurred, even though it cannot be known how much of the learning is due to excitation and how much to inhibition. Similarly, in the BC design in operant conditioning, an acceleration–deceleration difference is characterizable as contingency-related,[4] *provided that* there are no other potential confounds. The problem with the BC design, rather, is that unless the reinforcement schedules are equated between the two conditions in the operant case, the obtained difference may be due to the stimulus rather than to the informational properties of the reinforcement. Such equation of the reinforcement schedules has not, in general, been done, so that any acceleration–deceleration difference is not necessarily contingency-related.

There are, in fact, aspects of these animal operant studies that render these methodological considerations against the BC design either logically or empirically irrelevant. To the extent that these studies show specificity of responding, the argument against the BC design can be logically ruled out. Further, given the size difference between heart rate increase and heart rate decrease conditions, it is empirically unlikely that all of this difference was attributable to the stimulus rather than to the informational properties of the feedback. However, aside from the fact that problems of replicability have arisen, the main problem is that the BC design, which may have been adequate in these animal studies where effects were powerful, is taken to be valid in the human situation, where the effects are much smaller. Again, there is an analogy between the autonomic biofeedback situation and the earlier animal skeletal operant situation of the 1950s. In the latter case, with an obvious and strong reinforcer like food, it was unnecessary to be overly concerned with running precisely the appropriate control conditions to establish whether or not this reinforcer would contingently support lever pressing. With the weaker reinforcer like light, the reinforcing status of which was open to question and the effects of which were relatively small, it was important to use proper controls (see Berlyne, 1960; Church, 1964) to establish whether, in fact, the light was serving as reinforcement for lever pressing. It should be noted that in the light assessment situation no variation of the BC design, where one group would be reinforced for lever pressing and the other for the suppression of lever pressing, was proposed. Rather, the aim, through the yoked-

[4]Of course, from an applied point of view, differentiating between acceleratory and deceleratory biofeedback (analogous to conditional excitation and inhibition) is probably critical. This is so because clinically only one direction is typically of therapeutic interest (i.e., deceleration), and that direction is also often harder to achieve. It is of interest in this connection that in such directly observed conditional responses as the galvanic skin response (GSR), inhibitory effects of the sort talked of by Rescorla (1967, 1969) seem, in fact, not to exist (e.g., Furedy, Poulos, & Schiffmann, 1975a, p. 102): the autonomic nervous system does not, in its Pavlovian CR form, appear to be sensitive to negative contingency differences.

control design, was to contrast a condition that was equivalent in all respects except for the *absence* of that contingency.

The yoked-control version of the noncontingent control was strongly criticized in an influential paper by Church (1964). His main criticism of the procedure was that, to the extent that there were individual differences in the effectiveness of the stimulus properties of the reinforcement, the master group would be favored over the yoked group. This paper is not, however, as is often supposed, an argument against the noncontingent control; it is only an argument for a *proper* noncontingent control. The problem with yoking is obviated either by ensuring that individual differences are minimal, or by equating the reinforcement schedules not only between but also within groups (e.g., see Riley & Furedy, 1979).

However, practical problems can arise with a simple noncontingent control. The major one of these problems is that the presence of noncontingency can be *detected*, either by the therapist or patient, and such detection can destroy the equivalence of the therapeutic situation across treatment and control conditions. The first step toward resolving this problem is to determine, by rigorous and sensitive methods, whether in a given preparation such detection has in fact occurred. Signal detection methods are recommended for this determination. Evidence suggests that with some preparations, such as phasic HRD (Riley & Furedy, 1979) and EEG changes, no detection of noncontingency occurs. In such cases, the practical problem is solved and the simple noncontingent control remains the proper method for evaluating specific effects.

There are other preparations, however, such as tonic heart rate change or muscle training, where noncontingency is usually detectable. These situations require further conceptual clarification. Specifically, the detection problem arises because patients bring to the therapeutic situation a number of strategies, or mediating behaviors (MBs), which they *know* produce the TR. Insofar as an MB and the TR are related, a simple noncontingent control will involve noncontingent reinforcement of the MB as well as of the TR. Since the patients know that, *having produced MB*, they have produced a TR, they may infer nonreinforcement of the TR. That is, they may detect that they are in a noncontingent condition. Such detection can, as indicated above, destroy perceived equivalence of treatment and control conditions, to the detriment of the latter condition. Detection occurs because of the perceived connection between an MB (which is a strategy for production of the TR) and nonreinforcement (perceived as "unjust"). The *solution* to this problem is, therefore, to arrange the control condition so that the patients do receive reinforcement every time they are reasonably sure that they have produced a TR—that is, every time they perform an MB. This can be done by first establishing the minimum level of the TR (resulting from any MB) that the patients are sure of having produced. That is, researchers must determine the size of the smallest TR that, if it were the result of an MB, would result in detection of noncontingency should it not be given correct reinforcement. Noncontingency can then be introduced for any TR below this level. Thus, the difference between the treatment and the control condition is still one of contingency, but it is a difference of degree rather than a difference between all or none. Contingency is not removed completely in the contol condition, but it is degraded.

If, at the end of training, there is a specific *feedback* effect on the *TR*, as postulated by the biofeedback formulation, then there should be less control over the TR in the control condition than in the treatment condition. If there is no such difference, and yet both conditions increase control over the TR with training, then this is a "feedforward" effect. This feedforward effect is due to the provision of MB-contingent reinforcement, which improves control over the TR by central, superordinate systems rather than by peripheral, autoregulatory ones. In systems where the relevant principles of control involve feedforward, as is the case in an intelligent, hierarchical system, the biofeedback technology may be neither necessary nor even useful for increasing control over the majority of the system's responses. The only means of properly assessing whether, in fact, biofeedback or feedforward is the appropriate methodology for controlling a specific response is through systematic manipulation of response-reinforcement contingencies.

Finally there is the question of the validity of the "best alternative treatment" (BAT) as the control for biofeedback. The BAT is generally advocated over the noncontingent or false-feedback control by clinically oriented researchers. The grounds for this preference are quite apparent. The false-feedback control not only is difficult to institute in an undiscovered form, but also involves deception when it is instituted. Further, in a clinical setting investigators dislike providing nothing "useful" to the patients, preferring to provide the controls with at least some reasonably effective alternative—that is, the BAT control. The arguments against the BAT have been given elsewhere in summary form (Furedy, 1979). Here, we would like to expand on these counterarguments and to suggest, specifically, that the BAT design is especially undesirable from a scientific as well as from a technological point of view. It is especially undesirable because biofeedback is quite frequently used to treat symptoms that are at least partly psychosomatically mediated. For such problems the true BAT is seldom known, and a particular BAT may simply represent a given clinician's individual preference. Moreover, the grounds for this preference cannot be readily operationalized for the purposes of checking by other investigators. In addition, even if the BAT were more precisely specifiable, there would still be the problem that the biofeedback–BAT comparison would include the placebo benefits of biofeedback. These placebo effects are themselves not reliable, but vary over time (as a function of society's awareness of the feelings toward biofeedback) and place. The attitude of the therapist towards the treatments and the therapist–patient relationship are also factors that affect the nature of the placebo effects of biofeedback. It is because of such changeable factors that, in the medical context, the evaluation of drugs is done against a placebo control group that is treated in an identical manner except for the giving of the specific drug under investigation. A good technology does not require artists to practice it, for such a technology works even with minimally competent administrators. To the extent that biofeedback requires skilled and convincing application for a placebo effect to result, it cannot be said that biofeedback is efficient even in terms of the strictly pragmatic criteria of technology.

SOME IMPLICIT THEORETICAL ASSUMPTIONS REEXAMINED

In this section, we attempt to avoid raising esoteric issues that have no applied significance. Nevertheless we are dealing with questions that are seldom raised by researchers concerned with pragmatics, and these questions will probably seem initially to be completely irrelevant to practice. We try in each case to indicate the applied relevance of each issue to the problem of enhancing autonomic control. The more general premise is, however, that the examination of implicit assumptions is not just scientifically interesting, but technologically useful; incorrect theoretical assumptions lead to a technology that is inefficient not only in the sense of having negligible beneficial effects, but also in the sense of having significant detrimental ones.

The Nature of the Response Unit in Biofeedback

Given that it is the operant-conditioning model that has been applied most commonly to biofeedback, it seems important to examine the question of what it is that is being reinforced or shaped in the acquisition of a target behavior such as HRD. In the acquisition of an operant, a cardinal principle is that the reinforcement not only must be contingent, it must also be relatively immediate (i.e., the delay between the TR and reinforcement must be short). That is, to shape a lever press efficiently, with food as the contingent reinforcement, one must reduce the press–food delay to a minimum. The question then arises: With HRD as the target behavior, what is the response that is being immediately and contingently reinforced in that instance of operant conditioning?

In this connection, it should be remembered that the term "response" is a scientific abstraction rather than an ostensively definable property of behavior. Investigators can apply or misapply the concept of "response" to behavior, and it is our contention that such a misapplication has occurred in conventional HRD biofeedback, where feedback is on a beat-by-beat basis and the target behavior to be changed is a tonic mean level of heart rate over a period ("trial") of at least 30 seconds. Consider, by comparison, a phasic HRD response such as that with which we work (e.g., Furedy, 1979; Riley & Furedy, 1979, 1980), where the attempt is to shape a CS-elicited (or emitted-in-the-presence-of-a-discriminative-stimulus) HRD response in an operant-conditioning paradigm with discrete trials. The phasic HRD that we shape with contingent verbal or proprioceptive reinforcement has the normal properties of responses—that is, not only magnitude but also onset latency, full-development latency, recruitment, recovery, and so on. Also, as in the shaping of the lever-press response situation, the TR is identical with the immediately reinforced response, both being the HRD response occurring within about 2 to 5 seconds following the onset of the CS (discriminative stimulus).

Consider, from this point of view, the conventional biofeedback preparation for HRD. The behavior being immediately reinforced is each single interbeat interval (IBI), whereas the target behavior is the *mean* of the IBIs over the trial period. Also, the immediately reinforced behavior—the single IBI—is something to which the concept of "response" is applied only with some difficulty, since this behavior has only one of the usual properties of responses, that is, magnitude (the duration of the IBI), without any of the others. There are grounds, therefore, for suggesting that both the response concept and the operant-*response* conditioning model has been misapplied in the conventional (tonic) HRD preparation, and this may be one reason why biofeedback in fact appears to be quite ineffective (cf. Blanchard & Young, 1973) for producing HRD. The fault, then, may lie not in the instrumental response-conditioning model, but in its misapplication through investigators' wrongly assuming that they are actually shaping a response according to the rules of operant conditioning.[5]

In Human Systems, Is All Information Processing of a Cognitive Form?

We have cast this question as a proposition that is similar in form to one which was denied by Tolman and his students in the 1940s and 1950s, that is, the Hull–Spence claim that all learning was response learning. With the shift in psychology

[5]In oral discussions of this point, some members of other audiences have suggested that the analogy between conventional HRD biofeedback is not to the learning of lever presses, but to the learning of more complex schedules like differential reinforcement of low rates (DRL). However, a schedule manipulation like DRL already assumes (correctly) that the basic indicator response, the lever press, is itself learnable and shapable. With HRD rather than lever pressing as the TR, it is this very assumption that remains in doubt. It is, therefore, possible that biofeedback has not been effective with HRD simply because the shaping technique of operant conditioning has never actually been applied. The empirical difficulty, however, is that because the operant animal literature tells us so little about the principles of shaping (it being commonly described as an "art"), it is not easy to determine whether instances where there is no contingency-of-reinforcement effect are due to the nonexistence of these effects or to ineffective shaping.

from an S-R to a cognitive approach (e.g., see Segal & Lachman, 1972), there has been a corresponding move to attempt to explain all psychological processes in terms of cognitive rather than of response concepts.[6] In this discussion we use "cognitive" to mean "that which can be expressed in propositional terms"—that is, statements to which it makes sense to attribute truth and falsity, and which can be expressed in the form "*X* is *Y*." Tolman's "cognitive maps" were cognitive in this sense, being expressible in propositions of the form "This is a sign of that"—propositions to which the true/false category could be meaningfully applied (cf. also Furedy, 1979, p. 211). Such propositional relationships represent a particular form of relationship between subject and object that is not simply one of contiguity, of temporal association between stimulus and response, but of sign-significate association. The propositional relationship that characterizes the cognitive is, then, of the predicative form, wherein the subject is related to the predicate by the copula, that is, the copular relationship. By comparison, noncognitive processes do not involve such propositional relationships, these processes being characterized by associations that are of a contiguous form. So while learning at the cognitive level can involve propositional information about relationships between stimuli, learning at the noncognitive level can only involve the transfer of responses from one stimulus to another. In the cognitive instance we can thus speak sensibly of "knowing that" a given response is required, but in the noncognitive case we can only sensibly speak of "being able" to produce some response.

It will be noted that this response-production aspect of the issue of propositional versus contiguous association is of particular relevance to practitioners of biofeedback. For example, if an autonomically mediated target behavior such as HRD is required, the question of empirical and practical import is the degree to which centrally processed propositional (i.e., cognitive) information can be translated accurately by the autonomic nervous system (ANS) to produce the desired effect on the target system. To the extent that the answer is affirmative to the question of whether all information processing in the human system is cognitive, such purely cognitive methods will readily result in the enhancement of the target behavior

[6]Another result of a shift in emphasis in recent psychological theorizing has been the replacement of the term "learning" with the term "information processing," especially as applied to human in contrast with animal subjects. Most biofeedback researchers have followed this shift in preferring to think of "biofeedback" as an information-processing rather than as a learning phenomenon. Thus, whereas earlier investigators referred to "operant autonomic conditioning," later workers described their work in more informational terms, that is, as "biofeedback." However, unlike the distinction between cognitions and responses, we suggest that the distinction between information processing and learning represents no more than semantic preference (although like all preferences, this one is not unmotivated). Accordingly, the empirical question is not whether certain processes are learning-like or information-processing-like, but whether these processes, whatever we wish to call them, are all cognitive. This is the reason for the phrasing of the question asked at the beginning of this subsection.

through biofeedback. We, however, wish to argue against an affirmative answer both on general psychological grounds and in more specific, information-theoretic terms, holding that there are important information-processing events of a noncognitive form occurring that need to be considered in relation to human learning.

In terms of the psychological considerations, acceptance of all forms of human information processing as cognitive may be popular, especially amongst writers of textbooks on "cognitive psychology," but it is inconsistent with certain facts. Thus, while it is true that some psychological processes such as thinking, hoping, and believing are propositional or cognitive, others, such as feeling, willing, and acting, are not. Nor are these noncognitive processes unimportant in determining behavior or the way in which other information is processed. While it is the case that in digital computers information can be considered to be processed solely in propositional terms, with only the computational rules for these propositions needing to be considered, this is not so in the human instance. In human beings, there are other, simultaneously occurring noncognitive processes that interactively affect the way in which the organism behaves. Thus, in a biofeedback situation, one cognitive process that may occur is a mental state expressible propositionally as "My heart rate is fast." However, this state is only one aspect of the total complex of states that the organism is presently in and about which information is being transmitted. The person in question may also be *feeling* anxious, *wanting* to calm down, and yet producing the *actions* that lead to further HRA, disrupted breathing, increased muscular tension, and so forth. Although computers have been helpful in allowing us to devise cognitive models of human information processing, human beings differ in many important ways from computers and ideal communication systems, and these differences are fundamental ones for response learning.

The view that only cognitive processes are important in determining the nature of human information processing (or learning) has come to enjoy the same sort of hallowed Platonic status that was once enjoyed among the early Hullians by the view that only response processes were important. For example, Pavlovian conditioning has recently come to be dominated almost solely by cognitive accounts that stress only the learning of contingencies between stimuli. From such relational learning accounts (e.g., Rescorla, 1967), it does indeed follow that specific Pavlovian CRs, such as the conditional galvanic skin response (GSR), should differentiate between control CSs that are negatively and simply not correlated with US occurrence. It also follows from such accounts that the extent of the conditioning of a specific CR should be highly and positively correlated with the extent to which the subject is aware of or believes in the contingency between CS and US (i.e., a cognitive, propositionally expressible relationship). In fact, both these consequences of the cognitive account appear to be obviously false (e.g., see Furedy, Poulos, & Schiffmann, 1975a; Furedy & Schiffmann, 1973). Yet there is little sign that the cognitive accounts have been modified in the light of this contrary evidence against the universality of the "cognitive control" (Furedy, 1973) of human autonomic classical conditioning. It is, of course, a feature of Platonic Forms that ideas about them are not modified by observations of mere particulars, the specification of the nature of the general being regarded as primary. Yet in the realm of particulars, where efforts to produce autonomic learning occur, it would seem important to recall that not all learning is based on cognitive processes, no matter how fruitful or intuitively satisfying the cognitive approach may be.

In information-theoretic terms, the same problem of ineffective communication can be stated as follows. For a system to work effectively in the manner that biofeedback requires, two assumptions must hold concerning the transmission of messages in the human information processor. The first assumption is that the intended message is selected from all the possible messages and is sent to the system to be regulated. The second assumption is that the intended message is acutally understood at the destination so that the desired meaning is in fact conveyed, and so that the target system can be affected in the desired way. These two assumptions can be made to hold in some ideal communication system. With a computer, for example, it could be ensured that the desired message is transmitted and that the symbols of the communication are indeed logically commensurate symbols. With human information processors, however, the two assumptions may not always hold.

Concerning the assumption about the *communication of the intended message*, consider a system comprising many information-transmission channels, such as the human being, with its different afferent and efferent pathways. In such a system, the signals for the target that is to be regulated may be conveyed through a number of different channels before those signals reach their ultimate destination. However, for effective communication to take place in the sense that the received meaning affects the target behavior in the desired way, it is necessary that the communication be dealt with in such a manner by these mediary systems that it can have its intended effect. The accurate conveyance of a message, however, is problematic in those cases where the mediary systems are responding to and transmitting messages other than the intended one. The result of such transmissions may be an effect on the target behavior that is quite different from the one intended by the original regulatory message. In such cases, the communication is not effective. For example, in a subject instructed to decrease heart rate, the intended meaning of the feedback display on a screen is to inform the system that the heart rate is at some level and that this level departs from the target state by some certain amount. Along with the transmission of the intended propositional performance-contingent information, other messages are also conveyed by, for example, the visual system. These messages about such things as the stimulus properties of the feedback display (e.g., density), in turn lead to hypothalamic effects that result in heart rate acceleration, rather than in the desired deceleration. Thus environmental stimuli produce effects that are due to intervention by superordinate control systems, and not to the intended control by feedback from the response system. The superordinate effects that occur in an open-loop, hierarchical system are feed*forward* effects, and not feed*back* effects at all. In an intelligent, hierarchical system such as a human being, many of the effects on responses are due to feedforward control, as exemplified by instructional effects and the use of strategies or MBs by subjects. The application of feedback principles to the control of many of the responses in a hierarchical system can often be inappropriate and therefore ineffective (cf. Tursky, Chapter 5).

It bears emphasis that although subjects can quite rationally perceive that the biofeedback is there to "help" them, although they *know that* the feedback is for the purposes of regulation, this knowledge is not sufficient to guarantee effectiveness. As a multifaceted system, many other aspects of the biofeedback situation have effects upon sensory channels that lead to responses in human subjects that compete with the desired behavior. A human being is not a discrete, logical, binary system operating solely according to rules of computation. Other, nonrational factors also enter into human information-transmission processes. In the biofeedback situation, for example, subjects have many ongoing parallel cognitions that are often more probable and more consequential than the intended, feedback one, because these cognitions are occurring in an anxiety-ridden system. These problems with the transmission of the intended message are multiplied when we consider mediationally produced events that are other than cognitive, that is, nonpropositional. For example, consider subjects instructed to decrease muscle tension who are informed by the feedback that they are in fact increasing EMG activity. These subjects then think that they cannot follow instructions, and this cognition leads to the affect of anxiety, resulting in an increase in general tension, further increases in EMG level, tachycardia, and so forth, rather than in the intended behavior of relaxation.

Concerning the assumption about the *accurate conveyance of the desired meaning*, it is important to note that this assumption may be false even though the prior assumption may be true. Thus, even if the intended message is selected and sent, this message may not be accurately delivered to the destination, and the transmitted symbols may not precisely convey the desired meaning. These sorts of communication problems, moreover, can result in a failure to affect the target behavior in the required way. Communication breakdown such as this is paralleled by instances in verbal language usage where persons are faced with some term for which there is no precise equivalent in their vocabulary. A clearer parallel is shown by a breakdown at the conceptual level, as with the difficulty of trying to translate nondiscursive modes, such as those of music and art, into the verbal, sequential form. In these instances, an adequate verbal representation of the analogue process simply cannot be given, no matter how elaborate the discursive account. It appears that in the case of translating the different forms of information transmitted through the human nervous system, it is this problem with which investigators are faced. As indicated above, for example, it appears that the ANS-based Pavlovian CRs, such as the GSR, do not "understand" even quite fundamental propositional messages concerning negative contingency differences (i.e., the difference between *X* being unrelated to *Y* and *X* being negatively related to *Y*), even though there is good cognitive awareness of these messages (e.g., see Furedy & Schiffmann, 1973). To the extent that the ANS is unable to decode certain propositional information, it has to be recognized that there will be serious limitations to what can be expected from this system in terms of its responding to feedback messages that are propositional in nature. Such propositional, performance-contingent information is an important aspect of the standard biofeedback situation, and it is therefore important for the practitioner to recognize these problems. For example, we can teach the CNS *that* an increase in line length represents an increase in IBI, and therefore a decrease in heart rate, which is the target behavior. However, the important event for the ANS may not be this sort of propositional information. It may rather be information about such response-learning-associated aspects as the stimulus properties of the feedback and the interval between the production of the target behavior and the reinforcement that is of importance for ANS activity.

Indeed, there is evidence that both in biofeedback and other (i.e., Pavlovian) forms of autonomic learning, the translation from CNS-propositional to ANS-responding systems is quite imprecise. One thorough exponent of the cognitive approach to HRD reported recently (Lang, 1977) that the density of the computer-generated oscilloscope display produced HRA in subjects for whom the information was intended to promote HRD learning. Concerning Pavlovian autonomic learning, it is the case that although propositional awareness of the CS-US relationship appears to be necessary for autonomic conditioning (Dawson & Furedy, 1976), such conditioning is hardly an epiphenomenon of or fully controlled by the cognitive, CNS-associated variable. Thus, the extent of electrodermal and vasomotor conditioning is not correlated at all with the extent of CS-US relational learning (e.g., Furedy & Schiffmann, 1973). Nor is the degree to which the declerative heart rate response can be transferred from a tilt US to a CS at all related to the extent of the subject's belief in the propositionally statable CS-tilt contingency (see Furedy, 1977, p. 348).

One means of bypassing some of these problems with communication of the intended meaning to the target behavior is to employ feedback that is provided *directly* through input into the afferent systems controlling the response being regulated (as suggested by Tursky; see Furedy, 1979, pp. 215–216). Thus, by using feedback that operates directly on response systems by way of the natural neural pathways, investigators may avoid the above problems of failure of the intended message to reach the destination and of imprecise translation of propositional information by noncognitive systems. Information can be more effectively transmitted through actual afferent input to the target response system, and if this information is of the form of an interoceptive response, it will not be in need of translation from propositional to nonpropositional language. Such an approach, like the more standard conditioning techniques of response learning, teaches the organism *how* to respond instead of simply providing it with information about the response that it cannot effectively process.

Since an intelligent system works according to principles of higher-order control, using strategies and plans to produce the TR, it would be more efficient to provide information about the success of these MBs in producing the TR than it would be to provide fine-grained information about the TR itself. As we have noted above, the question of whether information regarding the MB or the TR specifically is important for the control of the TR is an empirical one. By systematically manipulating contingencies of reinforcement, it can be ascertained whether the control of the TR is through higher-order systems (i.e., feedforward) or through peripheral, autoregulatory systems (i.e., feedback). In some cases, such as muscle retraining (see Brudny, Chapter 10), a feedback loop may actually be set up. In other cases, which are typical in the biofeedback situation, the increasing of control through a feedforward loop is of concern, since changes in the TR are produced through MBs. This increase in higher-order control can be brought about by providing detailed information to the subjects about the processes that affect the TR and through carefully instructing the subjects as to how they should respond. Simply delivering feedback signals to the subjects is not sufficient for the development of effective strategies. Improvement of control over the TR will thus come through providing subjects with maximal information (propositional and nonpropositional) regarding the effects not only of cognition but also of affect, motivation, and environmental stimuli on their responding.

In brief, then, the limitation of the standard biofeedback approach appears to be that it implicitly accepts the notion that the key to all learning rests on concentrating on cognitive processes and propositional information. The ANS, however, would seem to respond rather than to cognise, and the teaching of control should follow this response-learning approach in conjunction with nonpropositional feedback techniques. To produce autonomic control, the emphasis should be not on teaching the ANS *that* something is the case, but on teaching it *how* to do the response.

The Elicited–Emitted and Involuntary–Voluntary Distinctions

We wish to suggest that both the elicited–emitted and the involuntary–voluntary distinctions are misleading and should be dropped not only on scientific but also on technological grounds. Concerning the elicited–emitted distinction, the work of Kimmel (1974) and of Miller (1969) is commonly regarded as having destroyed the distinction as applied to *types* of responses. That is, the Skinnerian notion that an autonomic (and hence elicited) response like the GSR could not be operantly conditioned was refuted by cases where operant conditioning did, in fact, occur. A somewhat stronger refutation of the Skinnerian notion seems to have been those cases where Pavlovian–operant preparations with elicited HRD as the TR worked better than did preparations, such as that of conventional biofeedback, with emitted HRD as the target behavior (see Furedy, 1977, pp. 350–351). However, the broader claim that we wish to make here is that the elicited–emitted distinction is a false one. What underlies the distinction between Pavlovian and operant conditioning is not the elicited–emitted distinction but the question of whether or not there is in fact a contingency between the delivery of the US and the response to be learned.

While conceptually clear, this distinction is empirically an extremely complicated one. The complications are increased when it is recognized that the "contingency" can be said to operate not only if the CR in apparently Pavlovian autonomic aversive conditioning actually prevents US delivery completely, but also if the CR changes the "perceptual impact" of the US. It is because of these complexities that many researchers consider it impossible ever to get a case of "pure" Pavlovian conditioning. It is clear, for example, that the original Pavlovian instance with salivation as the CR and food as the US was not "pure," because the CR would affect the taste of the US. Nevertheless, while empirically complicated, the distinction is by no means a metaphysical one, for researchers can investigate the conditions under which the different types of response do and do not occur. For example, as in the case of GSR conditioning, where the question of whether "instrumental" components exist has been raised, the matter can become one of experimental, though complicated, debate (e.g., see Furedy & Klajner, 1974; Lykken & Tellegen, 1974; Riley & Champion, 1978).

In contrast to the CR-US contingency-based distinction, the elicited–emitted distinction is simply one of current experimental knowledge or ignorance. All responses are "elicited" by certain stimulus conditions, but in some cases (as in operant conditioning) investigators have not attempted to specify what these elicitors are. Instead, they speak (in our view, unscientifically) of responses being "emitted" in the presence of (but not caused by?) a given discriminative stimulus (SD).

Similarly, we would suggest that the term "voluntary" is unscientific because of its connotation of "free will" and uncaused effects. In this case, as in the classical–operant case, there is a related and specifiable distinction. That empirically complex distinction is one as to whether or not the subject is conscious or aware of a particular behavior (i.e., does he or she know some propositionally formulatable information, such as "My heart is slowing"?). As in the case of whether an apparently Pavlovian-conditioned GSR has, in fact, instrumental components, so in this case the distinction's applications may entail much experimental controversy. Determining what an organism knows is often a knotty empirical problem. However, this is at least an empirical question resoluble, though never with certainty, by controlled observations. The question of whether a behavior is "voluntary" or not, on the other hand, is not so resoluble; it is a metaphysical issue turning on such questions as the freedom of the will. It is not, therefore, a scientific issue, and a fortiori, not a question with which the practicing clinician should be concerned.

If the clinical goal, then, is efficacy in teaching autonomic control, the aim should be to produce the appropriate responses by finding the appropriate stimulus conditions that produce these responses. Aiming for the "emission" of "voluntary" behavior, or trying to make the "involuntary" "voluntary," is best left to metaphysicians. The critical issue, according to a pragmatic stance, is whether or not the TR can be produced, and not whether what has been produced is a "true" operant. Investigators should not fear the operant conditioning of "elicited" responses; what they should fear is deluding themselves into believing that they have operant conditioning when, in fact, there is no evidence for a contingency effect. Similarly, we would suggest that the aim of achieving "truly voluntary" control is a metaphysical and misguided one. If the control is learned as a result of our conditioning procedures, if it is a powerful effect and transfers well across situations and time, then there is no reason why it should not be "elicited" by external and/or internal stimuli.

Thus, the making of conceptually clear distinctions that are not purely metaphysical in nature can be seen to be of considerable importance for both science and technology, in that it allows for the empirical investigation of the nature of events rather than for the apparent establishment of their nature by fiat. This clarity, in turn, leads to the formulation of testable hypotheses and the development of efficient procedures.

The Problem of Mediation

Related to the search of the "voluntary" is another false Holy Grail: the goal of achieving "pure" operant autonomic conditioning. One problem here is the empirical one that mediation possibilities cannot ever be completely ruled out, since the measurement of all potential mediators is an endless and impossible task. More important, in our view, is the theoretical argument that even to attempt to rule out such mediators is to assume that systems in the organism do not interact—an assumption that is patently false and therefore likely to be technologically problematic. To search for cases of, for example, "pure" autonomic HRD learning is analogous to searching for purely skeletal lever-press learning. That sort of learning would have to be a disembodied one in the literal sense of the term, simply because parts of the organism interact rather than exist in purely independent states. Because of a fascination with the notion of "voluntarily" controlling the ANS, there has historically been more interest in searching for pure autonomic than for pure skeletal learning, but this is one case in which history teaches us error. Both goals are unrealistic and have no place in either scientific investigation or sound technological development.

We should stress that, by taking a pragmatic position, we are not advocating a "black box" approach that ignores the mechanisms behind certain learned responses. Such physiological investigation is essential, but it should be directed toward determining the relative importance of the contributions of systems such as the autonomic, the skeletal, the cognitive, and so forth. To establish that a biofeedback-induced heart rate change is mainly autonomically mediated is to provide an important piece of scientific information and a potentially useful contribution to technological development. To attempt to rule out nonautonomic mediators altogether is a metaphysical exercise, the empirical rewards of which are nonexistent. Moreover, if, during these forays into the realms of the purely autonomic, investigators neglect those factors that can and should be ruled out—confounding effects that make them wrongly think that they have a biofeedback phenomenon—the exercise is not only fruitless but also costly.

SOME CONTEMPORARY-HISTORICAL INTERPRETATIVE SPECULATIONS

The interpretation of history is always controversial, but that of contemporary history is even more so, and issues raised in this section will accordingly be subject to much criticism. We propose here that much of the reason for biofeedback's failing to fulfil its early potential can be traced to the rise of the cognitive movement in the psychology of learning and conditioning, and the subsequent failure to "remember the response" (Furedy, 1979). Focusing on the potentially clinically important target behavior of HRD, the argument has elsewhere been made (Furedy, 1979, pp. 207–208) that the current *Zeitgeist* concerning the importance of information led to the uncritical use of the purely informational approach. From a practical point of view, this approach was judged by reviewers such as Blanchard and Young (1973) to have produced little of value. From a more scientific stance, the recent work of Lang (1977) has been particularly significant. Lang, who had taken the purely informational approach to a high level of technical sophistication, has now reported that biofeedback, as narrowly defined, is not a reliable phenomenon, particularly in the production of HRD. While researchers such as Lang have chosen, on this basis, to recommend abandoning biofeedback as a general therapeutic tool in favor of cheaper alternatives such as relaxation training, others have chosen to hold to a broader definition of biofeedback. This broad "biofeedback package" definition of the term, however, renders it, as we have argued above, an essentially useless scientific or technological concept.

The response-learning approach of the University of Toronto laboratory, which started with the Pavlovian method of first eliciting the HRD response and then attempting to condition it by Pavlovian and operant means (e.g., Furedy, 1977), has also been highly variable in terms of its success. We do get some impressive results, but often these results are by no means fully predictable. In brief, with respect to the Pavlovian methods used, given the ideal decelerative UR produced by our tilt US (e.g., see Furedy & Poulos, 1976, Exp. I) it would seem to be a simple matter to teach subjects to reproduce a significant part of this US to a CS through CS-US association. This, however, is not the case (see Furedy, 1977, p. 347, for details of some of the failures), and even when we move to the very complex imaginational form of the preparation (Furedy, 1977; Furedy & Klajner, 1978), the amount of obtained Pavlovian conditioning is still less than impressive in relation to the UR. Nor do we seem to have an adequate understanding of the necessary and sufficient conditions for the emergence of this sort of decelerative learning; the Pavlovian-conditioning literature provides little guidance, for that contemporary literature is dominated by the cognitive emphasis on "relational" learning (i.e., learning the propositional information that the CS is related to the US). While propositional learning appears to be a necessary condition for autonomic conditioning, it is not only not sufficient (Dawson & Furedy, 1976), but also, in the Pavlovian case, not particularly relevant. The advice based on the current Pavlovian literature would be to increase the salience of the CS-US relationship in order to increase the amount of HRD learning, advice that is clearly irrelevant, if only because the CS-tilt relationship is already quite clear to all subjects.

Similarly, when we included an operant component in our decelerative preparation and turned to the operant-conditioning literature for information regarding the principles of response shaping, we found little useful advice. This literature is almost exclusively concerned not with the acquisition of responses, but with "steady state" behavior, which is used to indicate different cognitive and motivational states as a function of complicated variations in schedules of reinforced behavior. We do not question the convenience of the lever press in rats or the peck in pigeons as an index of such states, but this convenience has led to the neglect of the principles of response learning or acquisition. This neglect renders most of the operant literature of little use in the scientific or the technological solution of the problem of under which conditions the response, such as HRD, is, in fact, learned. So, from our perspective, it appears that response learning has been more or less forgotten, in both Pavlovian and operant conditioning, and in some respects we may know less about these processes than we did a couple of decades ago.

In this connection, we do not regard it as accidental that most current Pavlovian conditioners appear to focus on the learning of the CS-US relationship rather than on concern with how the CR is attached to the CS. In poison-avoidance Pavlovian conditioning, indeed, there is no focus at all on the CR in this sense. The main dependent variable is not the CR elicited by the CS, but the preference against (i.e., avoidance of) the CS. That CR, presumably, would include the feeling of nausea, vomiting, and so forth. Sometimes these behaviors are reported, but the main dependent variable is not that CR to which the Pavlovian salivary response is analogous. The main dependent variable is, rather, the preference index; this, in our view, measures not response learning but learning of a proposition about CS-US relationships (see also Furedy, 1979, footnote 3). Similarly, in the CER (conditioned emotional response) paradigm, although there was an initial concern with the CER of emotion, this was never primary; the critical dependent variable in this form of Pavlovian conditioning has been the suppression of food-reinforced lever pressing in the presence of the CS. Indeed, the CER paradigm is now frequently called the "response-suppression" paradigm, which makes explicit the neglect of Pavlovian response-*learning* processes. Finally, even in preparations where the CR is directly measured, as in GSR conditioning, the emphasis on cognitive, relational, CS-US learning is very marked. Papers like that of Dawson and Furedy (1976) are often cited as indicating that GSR conditioning is "cognitively mediated" (Bandura, 1974, p. 859) or simply a consequence of propositional learning, even though that paper in fact summarizes previous literature showing no correlation between the two variables (e.g., Furedy & Schiffmann, 1973). This emphasis on the role of relational learning in GSR conditioning—an emphasis that has been strengthened by the information-processing shift that we have discussed above—has resulted in an exclusive concern with the cognitive aspect of autonomic learning, namely, awareness of the propositional CS-US relationship. However, the data in fact indicate that, while necessary, awareness is certainly not sufficient for such learning to occur.

We also want to suggest that an analogous turning away from response learning occurred in the early development of operant autonomic experiments (i.e., biofeedback) without this change being explicitly stated or justified. The shift in the operant case has been from phasic responses as the target behavior to tonic states. Thus, an early heart rate change study such as Shearn's (1962) reinforced (with shock avoidance) phasic heart rate accelerations of a few seconds. In contrast, until the University of Toronto laboratory's focusing on phasic heart rate change as the TR to be reinforced (Furedy, 1977), all heart rate biofeedback studies subsequent to Shearn's appear to have been concerned with modifying tonic heart rate. In the operant modification of electrodermal functions, which in Kimmel's work (see review in Kimmel, 1974) actually predated the cardiovascular biofeedback work, the situation is somewhat more complex, but a response-to-state and phasic-to-tonic shift can be discerned. For example, an early study such as that of Grings and Carlin (1966) focused on a CS-elicited GSR as an avoidance response, with shock avoidance being contingent on the increase in magnitude of this target behavior. Similarly, with reward rather than negative reinforcement as the contingent event, Helmer and Furedy (1968) carried out a biofeedback experiment with an elicited GSR magnitude increase as the target behavior. Later electrodermal operant experiments run by Kimmel and his associates (e.g., Kimmel, 1974) can be classified as those involving the modification of tonic states, because in these the TR was the increase or the suppression of *spontaneous* GSRs. ''Spontaneous'' GSR frequency over a relatively long (e.g., 60 seconds) period of time is a tonic measure analogous to mean heart rate over a similarly extended period, and increase and decrease in this measure would appear to represent, respectively, an increase and a decrease in the level of arousal. There is no real attempt in these experiments to shape the electrodermal response itself, as was the case in the earlier cited experiments, or has been the case in the phasic heart rate response experiments in the University of Toronto laboratory (e.g., Riley & Furedy, 1979, 1980). Moreover, there seems to be a parallel in this shift to an interest in tonic states in operant autonomic conditioning and the shift away from studying how the lever press is acquired to using it as an index of how states vary as a function of complicated reinforcement schedules.

We suggest also in this connection that this sort of shift will tend to increase still further the emphasis on propositional, relational learning and thereby to lead to a continued neglect of the response per se. Although providing investigators with good understanding of the cognitive, propositional processes, such neglect results in poor understanding of the principles of response learning. While it is the case that a great deal of information is being gathered on the way in which organisms learn *that* something is of some form, there appears to be ignorance about the way in which organisms learn *how* to respond. This ignorance, of course, is of considerable significance for the technology of autonomic control, as well as for the science of behavior.

CONCLUSION

Enhancement of biofeedback, in our view, will occur to the extent that there is a return of research attention to response-learning processes in classical and operant conditioning. Once performance of the desired response actually becomes possible for the subject, then the more cognitive aspects of training can be effective in increasing control over the response in terms of temporal precision, appropriateness to the situation, and generalizability. We suggest that the strategy that apparently assumes that efficacious autonomic control of difficult behaviors (such as HRD) can be readily obtained through the mere provision of propositional information or of feedback should be viewed with caution. Similarly, we suggest that the degree of autonomic control cannot be regarded as a simple function of the amount of information provided. Moreover, we also hope that it is clear that, by advocating an emphasis on conditioning methods (at least to instate the behavior), we are not suggesting that these methods themselves are simple techniques the application of which will necessarily guarantee success. As indicated near the end of this chapter, we know very little about the principles of response learning, particularly in the case of teaching difficult behaviors. The organism is a complex of interacting systems that are not only cognitive but also noncognitive in nature. The principles of operation of all of these systems need to be studied in order to gain not only an adequate scientific understanding but also an efficient technology.

REFERENCES

Bandura, A. Behavior theory and the models of man. *American Psychologist,* 1974, *29,* 859–869.

Berlyne, D. E. *Conflict, arousal and curiosity.* New York: McGraw-Hill, 1960.

Blanchard, E. B., & Young, L. D. Self-control of cardiac functioning: A promise as yet unfulfilled. *Psychological Bulletin,* 1973, *79,* 145–163.

Church, R. M. Systematic effects of random error in the yoked control design. *Psychological Bulletin,* 1964, *62,* 122–131.

Dawson, M. E., & Furedy, J. J. The role of awareness in human differential autonomic classical conditioning: The necessary-gate hypothesis. *Psychophysiology,* 1976, *13,* 50–53.

Engel, B. T. Operant conditioning of cardiac function: A status report. *Psychophysiology,* 1972, *9,* 161–177.

Furedy, J. J. Pavlovian and operant-biofeedback procedures combined produce large-magnitude conditional heart rate decelerations. In J. Beatty & H. Legewie (Eds.), *Biofeedback and behavior.* New York: Plenum, 1977.

Furedy, J. J. Teaching self-regulation of cardiac function through imaginational Pavlovian and biofeedback conditioning: Remember the response. In N. Birbaumer & H. D. Kimmel (Eds.), *Biofeedback and self-regulation.* Hillsdale, N.J.: Erlbaum, 1979.

Furedy, J. J., & Klajner, F. On evaluating autonomic and verbal indices of negative perception. *Psychophysiology,* 1974, *11,* 121–124.

Furedy, J. J., & Klajner, F. Imaginational Pavlovian conditioning of large-magnitude cardiac decelerations with tilt as US. *Psychophysiology,* 1978, *15,* 538–543.

Furedy, J. J., & Poulos, C. X. Human Pavlovian decelerative cardiac conditioning based on a respiratory-induced cardiac deceleration as an unconditional reflex. *Biological Psychology,* 1975, *2,* 165–173.

Furedy, J. J., & Poulos, C. X. Heart rate decelerative Pavlovian conditioning with tilt as US: Towards behavioral control of cardiac dysfunction. *Biological Psychology,* 1976, *4,* 93–106.

Furedy, J. J., & Poulos, C. X. Short-interval classical SCR conditioning and the stimulus-sequence-change-elicited OR: The case of the empirical red herring. *Psychophysiology,* 1977, *14,* 351–359.

Furedy, J. J., Poulos, C. X., & Schiffmann, K. Contingency theory and classical autonomic excitatory and inhibitory conditioning: Some problems of assessment and interpretation. *Psychophysiology,* 1975, *12,* 98–105. (a)

Furedy, J. J., Poulos, C. X., & Schiffmann, K. Logical problems with Prokasy's assessment of contingency relations in classical skin conductance conditioning. *Behavior Research Methods and Instrumentation,* 1975, *7,* 521–523. (b)

Furedy, J. J., & Riley, D. M. Clarifying the biofeedback controversy: Consider the contingency. *Psychophysiology,* 1979, *16,* 191–192. (Abstract)

Furedy, J. J., & Schiffmann, K. Test of the propriety of the traditional discriminative control procedure in Pavlovian electrodermal and plethysmographic conditioning. *Journal of Experimental Psychology,* 1971, *91,* 161–164.

Furedy, J. J., & Schiffmann, K. Concurrent measurement of autonomic and cognitive processes in a test of the traditional discriminative control procedure for Pavlovian electrodermal conditioning. *Journal of Experimental Psychology,* 1973, *100,* 210–217.

Grings, W. W., & Carlin, S. Instrumental modification of autonomic behavior. *Psychological Record,* 1966, *16,* 153–159.

Helmer, J. E., & Furedy, J. J. Operant conditioning of GSR amplitude. *Journal of Experimental Psychology,* 1968, *78,* 463–467.

Hendrick, M. W., & Graham, F. Multiple-component heart rate responses conditioned under paced respiration. *Journal of Experimental Psychology,* 1969, *82,* 396–404.

Heslegrave, R. J., & Furedy, J. J. Sensitivities of HR and *T*-wave amplitude for detecting cognitive and *anticipatory stress. Physiology and Behavior,* 1979, *22,* 17–23.

Hurwitz, B., & Furedy, J. J. The human dive reflex: An experimental, topographical and physiological analysis. *Psychophysiology,* 1979, *16,* 192–193. (Abstract)

Kimmel, H. D. Instrumental conditioning of autonomically mediated responses in human beings. *American Psychologist,* 1974, *29,* 325–335.

Lang, P. J. Research on the specificity of feedback training: Implications for the use of biofeedback in the treatment of anxiety and fear. In J. Beatty & H. Legewie (Eds.), *Biofeedback and behavior.* New York: Plenum, 1977.

Lykken, D. T., & Tellegen, A. On the validity of the perception hypothesis. *Psychophysiology,* 1974, *11,* 125–132.

Matyas, T. A., & King, M. G. Stable *T*-wave effects during improvement of heart rate control with biofeedback. *Physiology and Behavior,* 1976, *16,* 15–20.

Miller, N. E. Learning of visceral and glandular responses. *Science,* 1969, *163,* 434–445.

Morrison, J. W., & Furedy, J. J. A response-topography analysis of the effect of water temperature on cardiovascular components of the dive reflex. *Psychophysiology,* 1980, *17,* 137. (Abstract)

Newlin, D. B. & Levenson, R. W. Pre-ejection period: Measuring beta-adrenergic influences upon the heart. *Psychophysiology,* 1979, *16,* 546–553.

Prokasy, W. F. Random control procedures in classical skin conductance conditioning. *Behavior Research Methods and Instrumentation,* 1975, *7,* 516–520. (a)

Prokasy, W. F. Random controls: A rejoinder. *Behavior Research Methods and Instrumentation,* 1975, *7,* 524–526. (b)

Rescorla, R. A. Pavlovian conditioning and its proper control procedures. *Psychological Review,* 1967, *74,* 71–80.

Rescorla, R. A. Pavlovian conditioned inhibition. *Psychological Bulletin,* 1969, *72,* 77–94.

Riley, D. M., & Champion, R. A. Emergence of electrodermal preparatory response in humans. In *Signalling noxious events: Status of evidence and status of paradigms.* Symposium presented at the meeting of the American Psychological Association, Toronto, September, 1978.

Riley, D. M., & Furedy, J. J. Instructional and contingency manipulations in the conditioning of human phasic heart rate change using a discrete-trials procedure. *Psychophysiology,* 1979, *16,* 193. (Abstract)

Riley, D. M., & Furedy, J. J. Transfer of control of human phasic heart rate change: Instructional and contingency factors. *Psychophysiology,* 1980, *17,* 287. (Abstract)

Segal, E. M., & Lachman, R. Complex behavior or higher mental process: Is there a paradigm shift? *American Psychologist,* 1972, *27,* 46–55.

Shearn, D. W. Operant conditioning of heart rate. *Science,* 1962, *137,* 530–531.

Wood, D. M., & Obrist, P. A. Effects of controlled and uncontrolled respiration on the conditional heart rate response in humans. *Journal of Experimental Psychology,* 1964, *68,* 221–229.

Zeaman, D., Deane, C., & Wegner, N. Amplitude and latency characteristics of the conditioned heart response. *Journal of Experimental Psychology,* 1954, *38,* 235–250.

Zeaman, D., & Smith, R. W. Review of some recent findings in human cardiac conditioning. In W. F. Prokasy (Ed.), *Classical conditioning: A symposium.* New York: Appleton-Century-Crofts, 1965.

ROUND-TABLE DISCUSSION OF FUREDY AND RILEY

Theodore Weiss: I want to make two comments about John [Furedy]'s paper. He alluded, in passing, to the problem of small heart rate decelerations with biofeedback. In preparing our paper about heart rate control and treatment of arrhythmias with biofeedback (see Chapter 7), we commented about this, and I'd like to reiterate it. If you think about the range of heart rate in daily activities, which Bell and Schwartz looked at years ago [1975], heart rate varies from about 55 to maybe 150 between someone who's asleep and someone who's either very agitated or exercising. If you take a well-adapted subject, usually his heart rate will be about 70 in the laboratory; and if you do a biofeedback experiment, typically the results have been that there will be a two- or three-beat deceleration that subjects can learn, while if you have them increase heart rate, there will be an increase of, say, 10 to 15 beats. So, here you have a potential for change of an 80-beat-per-minute increase and a 15-beat-per-minute decrease. You have to consider the potential for change in the physiological system that you're dealing with.

The other point I wanted to make concerns one of the advantages of the procedures John [Furedy] is using. We've commented about the difficulty in terms of clinical transfer of doing biofeedback experiments with resting subjects. It seems to me an advantage of what John [Furedy]'s doing, and what Dave Shapiro is doing with the cold pressor test, is that this is a way of getting a kind of stress situation into the laboratory so that you can deal with this in a biofeedback paradigm. That has very great advantages.

John Lacey: I just want to call your attention to the fact that when we state "Here's the biology of the issue," we are introducing many assumptions. Let me point out, however, that that full dynamic range of heart rate is achieved over widely varying circumstances, and those changes are produced by different integrated central neural mechanisms. For example, the higher levels of heart rate will typically be seen in exercise or during a heavy work load. During these conditions, there's a marked resetting of switches within the central nervous system. For example, the baroreflexes are functionally ablated. That is the only way you could achieve such high levels of heart rate without, for example, simultaneously invoking a counter homeostatic decrease in blood pressure. Now then, the small changes can be produced without invoking such central counter homeostatic regulations. Small changes may be physiologically more useful for dissecting mechanisms than the large changes. As a matter of fact, if you take this out of the biofeedback context, there are many instances now in the cardiovascular literature where the study of small changes, which do not invoke all sorts of other counter integrative mechanisms, becomes extremely useful. I would, again, like to challenge the assumption that we understand some things so well that they can be taken as the biological base. This assumption has already arisen in this conference and would, incidentally, be surprising if I were to enunciate it at the next meeting of the Society for Neuroscience. Take the hyperpnea of exercise, for example. We do not know how that occurs. It has to occur, some of us think, through visceral afferent systems, particularly cutaneous and proprioceptive. The joint receptors and the surface cutaneous receptors participate in the hyperpnea of exercise. We don't know how those things are produced; and it's only now that you're beginning to see some neurophysiological investigations stimulating joint receptors, for example, to see what it does to respiration. This physiologic simplicity really should be corrected. There is a central nervous system in which, by analogy, switches are set and reset and certain neurodynamics become effective or ablated. We must be careful about such statements as this without reference to the central neural dynamics; they are all important. I'd be prepared to state that from a scientific point of view, from the point of view of central neural dynamics, it may be more useful to be studying small changes rather than large changes, because you would be studying a smaller domain, a more stable nervous system, where you're not invoking all kinds of counterregulatory mechanisms involving new areas of the limbic system, the posterior hypothalamus, central grey roots, and so on.

Neal Miller: It seems to me that, clinically, we're not usually interested in having somebody who is at a very *low* resting heart rate and reducing his heart rate a few more beats, but we're usually interested in taking somebody with *tachycardia* and trying to reduce it. That could be quite a different problem. You start out from quite a different baseline, so that the experimental work indicating that you don't lower already low heart rate very much may not be relevant to situations where you have a high heart rate.

Joel Lubar: In a paper last month by Engel [Engel & Perski, 1980], they had subjects on an ergometer and they were lowering the heart rate about 20 beats per minute. They had very good controls for the amount of force they were exerting, and automatically compensated if they tried to slow down in terms of increasing the tension on the legs.

Neal Miller: You mean on the ergometer they were using biofeedback?

Joel Lubar: That's right.

John Furedy: Did they use noncontingent controls, or is that just another instructional effect?

Joel Lubar: They had light feedback, which came on when the heart rate was lowered by a specific amount, and they were able to sustain this.

John Furedy: There's little that's dramatic, but we can, by getting subjects' basal rate up to about 100 by having them pull on something, achieve a six- to seven-beat change, which is better than the one or two beats. The point, however, is that it's an instructional effect. It has nothing to do with biofeedback. The information about the heart rate is irrelevant.

I agree that it's a good idea to use high levels, but the essential problem with the heart rate deceleration studies is not so much that the heart rate deceleration is small, but that biofeedback effects have not yet been clearly demonstrated. For example, there's a study [Riley & Furedy, 1979; Riley & Furedy, 1981] where if you instruct subjects to increase or decrease their heart rates while they're involved in a muscle tension task, so that they are producing a basic increase, the subjects separate very nicely according to that instruction; and most people would call that biofeedback. And they would get enthusiastic about these data if they occurred on a transfer trial. When the subjects are then instructed to decelerate, they are able to show a change of six beats from a baseline, which is very good. But that is not a biofeedback effect because a contingency manipulation did not emerge. There is no difference between the subjects' performance depending upon accurate or inaccurate information about their heart beat deceleration. I would call that an instructional effect. By all means, it's nice to study instructional effects in high and low levels all over the place, but don't confuse that with *biofeedback* effects.

Neal Miller: Really, the very interesting thing about John Furedy's work is the attempt to use a classical-conditioning response to elicit the response you're going to reinforce, thus getting around the problem of how you get the response to occur in the first place. And I would like to see the discussion directed towards that in other ways, rather than go too much further on the up-and-down issue.

John Furedy: I just want to point out that it's a classical-conditioning procedure in an operant-conditioning procedure of phasic responses. This procedure I have been showing you is of no use for lowering general tonic tachycardia. What it is useful for in a clinical analogue is when the patient is told of an event which causes him to accelerate suddenly, we may be able to teach him, through classical conditioning and biofeedback properly defined, to decelerate suddenly.

Barry Sterman: I'm interested in the fact that you, I'm sure, because I know what classical-conditioning people do, have gone to great effort to make the interval between the tilt and the CS precise and well control that aspect of the experiment. Then you say, by saying "good," you've added biofeedback; and I don't understand how you can equate those technologically. That's not biofeedback.

John Furedy: This procedure has been described elsewhere in a little more detail. We don't just sort of stand there and say "good"; we say "good," "very good," "excellent," or nothing. That makes it biofeedback because it is contingent on the target response; and even if you just used "good" or "not good," if that were contingent on the target response, it would be biofeedback. It's crude biofeedback. We're as good as when you're shaping a rat to press a bar by hand. We sometimes make mistakes. Your delay of reinforcement is sometimes as long as 1½ seconds, but it is biofeedback and there is a contingency relationship. Remember that, at least in the heart rate deceleration literature, Peter Lang has shown that just to refine the biofeedback itself often doesn't seem to produce anything [Lang & Twentyman, 1976]. So it seems appropriate to me, especially as it works as a contingency effect.

John Lacey: I wish to make a comment to tie together some physiology and clinical concerns, and it goes back to this issue of the dynamic versus the obtained range of heart rates. Regarding the interest in large changes, I suppose you were referring to paroxysmal tachycardias. Wasn't it Engel and Weiss[1] who did a study on paroxysmal tachycardias that showed that biofeedback was effective in their hands; but direct pharmacological tests led them to the conclusion that while they did, indeed, have an effective clinical procedure for a good therapeutic effect in paroxysmal tachycardias, the mechanisms involved apparently had nothing to do with the small changes in heart rate that were produced by the biofeedback training procedure? Rather, the effects were produced by some arcane, exotic, and well-understood routes. It was a very convincing paper. Somehow, their biofeedback procedures had tapped into some unknown effects on the heart. We must stop talking about such things as are already beginning to creep in—sympathetic control of the heart, parasympathetic control of the heart, and so on. The degree of specificity of the enervation of different parts of the heart, for example, by sympathetic efferents is simply incredible, and no respectable cardiologist today will talk

[1]Editors' note: Engel and Weiss did not do this study.

about *the* sympathetic control of the heart or *the* parasympathetic control of the heart. All those comments get us back to the basic mechanisms; but let me again make the point that the issue is efficacy, not the magnitude of the cardiac change that is produced. We really are only at the beginnings of an understanding of the neural and endocrinological enervation of the heart. We can inadvertently be stumbling on pathways we don't know anything about. It may take decades or more of investigation to fully understand the mechanisms of intervention.

REFERENCES

Bell, I. R., & Schwartz, G. E. Voluntary control and reactivity of human heart rate. *Psychophysiology*, 1975, *12*, 339–348.

Engel, B. T., & Perski, A. The role of behavioral conditioning in the cardiovascular adjustment to exercise. *Biofeedback and Self-Regulation*, 1980, *5*, 91–104.

Lang, P. J., & Twentyman, C. T. Learning to control heart rate: Effects of varying incentive and criterion of success. *Psychophysiology*, 1976, *13*, 378–395.

Riley, D. M., & Furedy, J. J. Instructional and contingency manipulations in the conditioning of human phasic heart rate change using a discrete-trials procedure. *Psychophysiology*, 1979, *16*, 192. (Abstract)

Riley, D. M., & Furedy, J. J. Effects of instructions and contingency reinforcement on the operant conditioning of human phasic heart rate change. *Psychophysiology*, 1981, *18*, 75–81.

5 AN ENGINEERING APPROACH TO BIOFEEDBACK

BERNARD TURSKY

INTRODUCTION

The aim of this chapter is to consider two major areas of contiguity between biofeedback and engineering. One is the relationship of the engineer to psychophysiology and biofeedback in the development of methodology and instrumentation that enables the researcher and the clinician to address themselves to the evaluation of an individual's ability to voluntarily manipulate and control his or her physiological functioning. The second, and perhaps more important, is the comparison between "biofeedback" as it might be defined in engineering terms, and "biofeedback" as it is presently defined and practiced by clinicians throughout the world. A close look at this comparison might help to explain some of the successes and failures of biofeedback as a therapeutic procedure.

Bernard Tursky. Laboratory for Behavioral Research and Department of Political Science, State University of New York at Stony Brook, Stony Brook, New York.

SYMBIOTIC RELATIONSHIP: PSYCHOPHYSIOLOGY AND ENGINEERING

It is not surprising that free associations to the term "biofeedback" produce in many respondents verbal responses that are related to electronic instrumentation. The precedent for such an associative pairing begins with the early days of the psychophysiological research that is the generic source of biofeedback. Psychophysiology has had a lengthy and beneficial symbiotic relationship with electrical engineering. The psychophysiological literature, dating back to the original *Psychophysiology Newsletter*, reported regularly on engineering and instrumentation developments related to psychophysiological research. Many of the early psychophysiology laboratory installations employed a full- or part-time electrical engineer to solve the instrumentation problems raised by the recording and processing of psychophysiological information. In many instances, these engineers became identified with and have contributed to the substantive as well as the technical areas of interest under investigation. Bioengineering miniprograms were initiated in some institutions to familiarize psychophysiologists with the specialized engineering problems of their discipline and to provide engineers with information related to the instrumentation problems faced by the psychophysiologist. In some instances, these miniprograms were amplified into biomedical engineering degree programs, which resulted in the development of a common language that enabled psychophysiologists to express their needs in engineering terms and enabled engineers to translate these needs rapidly into useful instruments and methodology.

RECORDING AND PREPROCESSING INSTRUMENTATION

During these formative years, problems related to the recording and processing of physiological measures of interest to the psychophysiologist were pursued with diligence in a number of laboratories, and the growth in interest by social scientists in involuntary indicators of psychological states increased at a rapid rate as new areas of research interest developed. The need to satisfy this growing demand for improved methodology resulted in the utilization of innovative engineering concepts that accelerated the development of instrumentation for the psychophysiology laboratory. Technical developments moved along several tracks. Existing clinical single- and multichannel special-purpose EEG, EMG, and ECG *AC* recorders were modified by psychophysiology laboratory engineers into stable *DC* recording instruments (Ax, 1958; Tursky, 1958). This development, for the first time, permitted the psychophysiologist to record and process multichannel long-term tonic physiological information, as well as the more transient phasic response measures, accurately.

Special circuitry was also developed in the laboratory to permit the psychophysiologist to record preprocessed physiological information. The development of the cardiotachometer enabled the psychophysiologist to record heart rate on a beat-to-beat basis (Tursky, 1958; Welford, 1962). Integrator circuits were designed for the direct quantification of higher frequency sinusoidal information, such as muscle potentials (Shaw, 1967; Tursky, 1964); averaging circuits were designed to extract stimulus specific responses out of noisy brain wave information; and constant current and constant voltage bridge circuits were designed to record electrodermal levels and response measures.

The growing market for this instrumentation created by the increase in interest in psychophysiology made it feasible for the commercial multichannel recorder manufacturing companies to invest the necessary effort and capital to utilize these laboratory-developed ideas to design and manufacture a new and improved line of multichannel modular multipurpose physiological recording instruments. In fact, the process was so successful that some of the smaller and more specialized instrument companies, such as Offner and Sanborn, were absorbed by Beckman and Hewlett Packard, the giants of the scientific instrument industry.

ELECTRODES AND TRANSDUCERS

This symbiotic relationship between psychophysiology and engineering was not confined to the development of recording instruments; careful consideration was also given in the laboratory to the peripheral factors related to recording artifact free physiological information. Silver–silver chloride sponge electrodes and specific contact electrolytes were developed to reduce the effects of polarization and bias potentials on the recording process (Edelberg & Burch, 1962; Lykken, 1959; O'Connell & Tursky, 1960), thus increasing the possibility of faithful recording of low-level *DC* information from physiological systems that generate electrical signals directly. These electrodes and methods were standardized by the instrument manufacturers and made available to the psychophysiology laboratory as commercial products. For measures that do not directly produce electrical outputs, transducers utilizing resistive, capacitive, or inductive elements were developed to convert available changes in pressure, volume, temperature, or movement into recordable electrical energy (Brown, 1967; Venables & Martin, 1967). Where such transducers were too bulky or incapable of operation in the required environment, such as the sleep laboratory, impedance and ultrasound transduction systems were developed in the laboratory, improved by industry, and added to the arsenal of special-purpose devices and circuits that became commercially available to the psychophysiology laboratory. Highly specialized laboratory needs, such as multichannel telemetry, followed the same development process (Mackay, 1967; Wolf, 1967).

Again, the symbiotic relationship between engineering and psychophysiology is demonstrated. A laboratory involved in an area of highly specialized research, such as sleep and dreaming, human sexuality, or biofeedback, develops specific electrodes, transducers, and circuits to serve its own needs. Demand for these items by investigators engaged in similar research or clinical projects motivates a company engaged in the manufacture of analogous equipment to add these items to its line of products. Additional engineering and packaging results in an improved and standardized product, and the availability of off-the-shelf commercial equipment makes it possible for many laboratories to improve their own scientific approach to the research problem. This process also enhances the possibility of uniformity of methodology across laboratories for better comparison of experimental results. Thus, gains are made by all parties concerned in these transactions.

DATA PROCESSING

The introduction of the central electronic digital computing facility to the university campus added still another factor to the symbiotic relationship between the psychophysiology laboratory and the engineer (Zimmer, 1966). The static analog paper record information generated in the psychophysiology laboratory required many hours of processing for each hour of recording. The use of templates, calipers, and electromechanical devices to automate the data reduction process provided some help in data processing but did not provide a real solution to the problem. A number of laboratories developed two-stage automatic data processing systems. Multichannel analog information was recorded on FM tapes in the laboratory and then converted electronically by analog to digital converters into digital information compatible with the data format of the existing university central computing center Ax, 1967; Tursky, Leiderman, & Shapiro, 1966). Special efforts were made to determine optimal sampling rates, and computer programs were written to quantify tonic and phasic information to meet each physiological and experimental need (Tursky, Shapiro, & Leiderman, 1966).

While these efforts produced some positive results in the computer processing of physiological information, the format used in each laboratory was for the most part appropriate only to that laboratory and computer installation. The most significant advance in physiological automatic data processing was achieved by the development of a dedicated laboratory digital computer with built-in analog to digital conversion capabilities. This development revolutionized the recording, data-processing, and experimental-control procedures in the psychophysiology laboratory.

Again, the symbiotic process becomes evident. The psychophysiology laboratories' need for data processing and dynamic experimental control resulted in the laboratory development of the first dedicated digital laboratory computer with analog input capability. The interest in this development by electrophysiologists and psychophysiologists in all parts of the world provided the incentive for commercial development of the dedicated digital laboratory computer capable of operating directly from an input of analog physiological information. The later development of the microprocessor added the possibility of low cost to this picture.

The symbiotic relationship between psychophysiology and engineering has flourished for more than 25 years. Each new engineering development has been closely linked to a specific major area of research interest. Several examples of this linkage are those of the recording of rapid eye movement with sleep and dream research, the recording of penile and vaginal tumescence with research in human sexuality, and the averaging of cortical evoked potentials with research in cognitive processing.

SYMBIOTIC RELATIONSHIP: BIOFEEDBACK AND ENGINEERING

Biofeedback may have begun as one of the best examples of the symbiotic relationship between engineering and psychophysiology. It was initiated as a research exercise to demonstrate that physiological responses, like behavioral responses, are amenable to alteration by reward and punishment (Kimmel, 1967; Shapiro, Crider, & Tursky, 1964; Shearn, 1961); laboratories interested in investigating this relationship took advantage of their ability to utilize the already well-developed technology in psychophysiology and experimental psychology laboratories to conduct experiments designed to manipulate, reinforce, and record the alteration of ANS and CNS activity by instrumental methods. Reported experimental and clinical success in many areas led to a landslide movement among psychophysiologists to become involved in biofeedback research related to the manipulation of various physiological systems.

Instrumentation developed in various laboratories to reinforce alterations in brain waves, muscle potentials, electrodermal responses, heart rate, blood pressure, blood volume, pulse volume, temperature, gastric motility, sphincter control, and sexual arousal was quickly appropriated by new or established commercial instrumentation companies. Commercial instruments ranging in quality from poor to excellent and ranging in price from a few dollars to thousands were developed to satisfy the growing needs of this new research area. The availability of commercial instrumentation, in turn, amplified the interest in this area of research, and it appeared as if the symbiotic cycle would be repeated. However, there was one major difference in the course of the relationship between engineering and biofeedback from that of the relationship of engineering to other psychophysiological research areas. In this instance, there was a rapid parallel development of clinical applications of biofeedback techniques. The possibility that an individual could learn to control or alter body functions voluntarily, and thus to have an impact on a disease state related to visceral or vascular disregulation, became a major challenge to psychophysiologists, physicians, and clinicians throughout the world. This development moved the major market for biofeedback instrumentation from the laboratory to the clinical practice and resulted in further stimulating the commercial instrumentation manufacturer to design and produce instruments that would suit the less sophisticated needs of this new market.

Most instruments developed for clinical biofeedback purposes are well engineered and, for the most part, accomplish the primary purpose of providing binary, proportional, or continuous visual or auditory information related to criterion changes in the physiological measure of interest to the practitioner. The engineer and the instrument manufacturer apply their skills to the production of instruments to satisfy the growing clinical need. Though new laboratory developments are often incorporated into these instruments, the clinical instrument is primarily designed to meet the necessary criteria of this major market. An esthetically pleasing package, an attractive feedback display, and ease of operation are the three criteria that must be met. Simplicity of operation is of particular importance because treatment in many instances is administered by personnel trained only in the rote administration of the process.

BIOFEEDBACK: IS IT FEEDBACK?

A major question that must be raised when the relationship between engineering and biofeedback is examined is that of the apparent lack of interest by the engineering profession in the basic comparison between "biofeedback" as it might be defined and analyzed in engineering terms and the acceptance of "biofeedback" as it is presently defined and practiced. It seems surprising that engineers engaged in the design and manufacture of biofeedback equipment have not addressed themselves to an analysis of the basic relationship between the input and output characteristics of the biofeedback systems they have designed. Their responsibility seems to end with the ability of the equipment to deliver a contingent response consequence.

Can it be true that physiological feedback instrumentation systems do not have to obey the same rules as electronic or electromechanical feedback systems? The assumption seems to be that an instrument designed to detect accurately a unidirectional alteration in a physiological measure, such as an increase or decrease in heart rate, blood pressure, or temperature, can be used to "feed back" this information to the individual by means of a visual or auditory display, and that this process will automatically result in a desired alteration in the overall function of that physiological process. Such an assumption seems to be untenable and unreasonable if looked at from an engineering approach to feedback systems.

FEEDBACK IN ENGINEERING TERMS

"Feedback," in basic engineering terms, describes a condition in which part of the output of an electronic circuit or an electromechanical control system is returned to the input of that circuit or system to enhance the operation of that system. The application of feedback to any circuit consists essentially of adding elements to the basic circuit to stabilize or reduce distortion in the original system. The components of the feedback network are usually passive electronic elements (resistors and capacitors) that control the magnitude and phase relationship between the arriving input information and the feedback signal. It is important to emphasize that both the magnitude of the feedback signal and the phase relationship between the output, the feedback, and the input signal affect the operation of the circuit. As shown in Fig. 1, if a purely resistive feedback (A) network is used, the feedback signal will be proportional to the ratio of resistors used in the network, and the feedback signal will be in phase with the output signal. The algebraic summation of the input and

FIG. 1. Diagram of basic feedback amplifier circuit. Feedback transfer function is dependent on circuit elements (A) resistive r/r; (B) resistive–capacitive r/c; or (c) capacitive c/c.

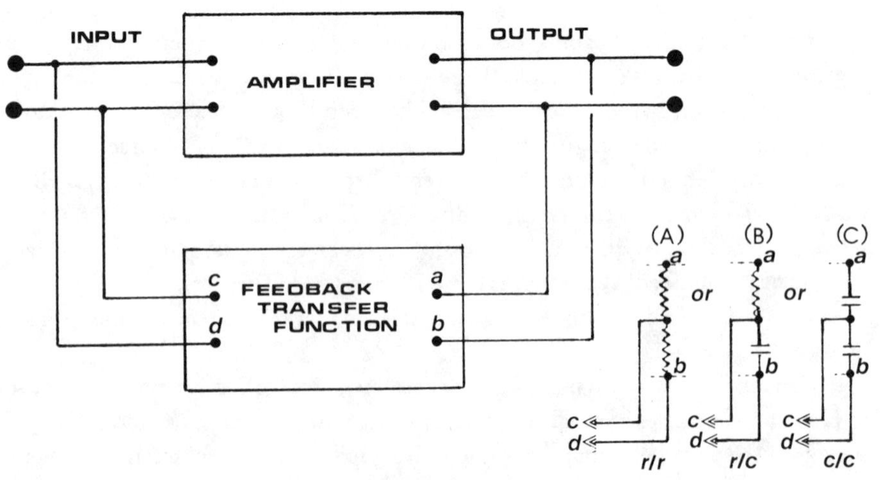

feedback signals will result in positive (regenerative) feedback, which translates into increased gain accompanied by a marked instability in the operation of the circuit. Because of this tendency toward instability, positive feedback is often used in the design of oscillators. If a resistive–capacitive (B) or purely capacitive (C) feedback network is utilized, the feedback signal will be out of phase with the output signal, and the algebraic summation of input and feedback signals will result in negative (degenerative) feedback, which translates into a reduction in gain and an increase in the stability of the output of the circuit.

It can be seen that the phase and magnitude relationships of input, output, and feedback signals are of primary importance in designing electronic feedback circuits and may be of equal importance in the understanding of the biofeedback process; however, the phase and magnitude relationships between input, output, and feedback signals in the biofeedback process are rarely examined, and the consequence of this relationship on the experimental and clinical efficacy of biofeedback has not been clearly assessed in most areas of interest.

A major exception is the work of Mulholland (1977), who has pointed out the importance of understanding engineering feedback systems in order to design more meaningful biofeedback studies. Mulholland and his associates have been able to demonstrate that bilateral EEG alpha activity can be better controlled by the use of a unilateral contingent visual stimulus and that control is found to be greater on the ipsilateral side than it is on the contralateral side. Mulholland suggests that similar analysis techniques can be applied to the understanding and control of any noisy system.

It has been pointed out (Noback, 1967) that most neural control is accomplished by closed-loop systems that utilize negative feedback to maintain homeostasis in the internal physiological systems, such as blood pressure, heart rate, and temperature. Cardiovascular autoregulation is achieved by a number of internal feedback loops involving the ANS and some highly specialized transducers in the walls of blood vessels and the carotid sinus. These autoregulating feedback loops control heart rate, stroke volume, blood volume, and blood pressure. Other regulatory feedback systems control body temperature by maintaining a balance between heat production and heat loss.

THEORIES AND STRATEGIES

In the progression of theories related to biofeedback training, the transition from operant manipulation to voluntary control made assumptions that exposure to biofeedback training could bring a disregulated physiological function back to normal levels of operation. Schwartz (1977), in his theory of disregulation, has suggested that biofeedback training can be used to reregulate affected disregulated physiological systems. The discrepancies between theorized and achieved clinical goals have resulted in the formulation of several explanatory theories.

Schwartz (1972, 1974) raised the question of biological constraints on the system related to the physiological and psychological state of the patient and the range of possible responses in any given organ system. Tursky (1979) has argued that the use of sensory feedback as response reinforcers, plus the necessary cerebral processing of this sensory information, acts as a complex phase-shifting network that must produce negative (degenerative) feedback. When evaluated from an engineering point of view, such a feedback system must produce small but stable changes in the physiological function. This stabilization effect seems to be evident in many laboratory studies, where it has been demonstrated that increased training does not usually produce greater alterations in the physiological function that is being manipulated. Tursky (1979) has further suggested that biofeedback should emulate the inphase (regenerative) feedback model where the response consequence (feedback signal) would impinge as directly as possible on the physiological control mechanisms. Elmore and Tursky (1978) suggest that a further reason for limited therapeutic response may be related to the lack of selective associability (Garcia & Koelling, 1966) between the response and the response consequence. They question whether there can be any natural association of low-level auditory or visual stimuli in the environment with changes in internal regulatory systems implicated in the regulation of temperature, heart rate, or blood pressure, and they suggest that response consequences should be generated that can impinge directly on afferent neural pathways that affect the physiological system under investigation.

The failure of biofeedback training to operate universally with the same effectiveness as that of internal bioregulatory feedback circuits caused researchers and practitioners to formulate a number of experimental and therapeutic strategies to try to improve the clinical effectiveness of the process. These strategies include instructional manipulations (Brener, 1977); manipulations of the type of feedback and reinforcement, binary versus proportional (Colgan, 1977; Lang & Twentyman, 1974; Young & Blanchard, 1974); the reinforcement of patterns of physiological behavior (Schwartz, 1977); and the use of correlative behaviors (Brener, 1974). A major possible contribution to the increased efficacy of the biofeedback treatment process has been proposed and demonstrated by Furedy and his associates (Furedy & Klajner, 1978; Furedy & Poulos, 1976). They have used classical conditioning to give increased signal value to the simple auditory response contingent, and have thus been able to enhance the effectiveness and specificity of the auditory reinforcer.

BIOFEEDBACK: ISSUES INVOLVED IN SUCCESS AND FAILURE

It seems reasonable to believe that a better understanding of the biofeedback process can come from examining the major areas of claimed success and demonstrated failure *in achieving a therapeutic clinical effect*. Review articles (Blanchard &

Young, 1974; Miller & Dworkin, 1974; Shapiro & Surwit, 1978) time and again report neutral or negative results of efficacy in controlled clinical biofeedback studies and advocate further research. Biofeedback practitioners, for the most part, do not question the legitimacy of the process that they have adopted; they are willing to make an assumption of clinical efficacy, even though the reviews of the clinical literature do not support this premise in many areas of investigation.

There have been many reports of success in the use of "biofeedback" training in the treatment of tension and migraine headache, as well as in the reduction of anxiety and tension. The clinical evidence for these therapeutic effects is primarily based on the patients' self-report of effectiveness. This information may be affected by an interaction with natural fluctuations in discomfort, due to exacerbations and remissions of the condition. It has been demonstrated that patients seek treatment when they are experiencing or have experienced a major exacerbation. Thus, any treatment administered at that time may produce a positive self-report based on a natural remission. To avoid this quagmire of confounded evidence, I confine my discussion to the effectiveness of biofeedback in two disease states where clinical effectiveness can be judged by objective criteria: the relearning of muscle function and the treatment of essential hypertension.

The strongest claim of clinical success in the use of biofeedback is in the retraining of lost muscle function due to stroke, head trauma, and other motor disorders Basmajian, Kulkula, Marayan, & Takebe, 1975; Brudny, Korein, Levidow, Grynbaum, Lieberman, & Friedmann, 1974). Physiotherapeutic rehabilitation techniques often fail to accomplish sufficient retraining to effect full recovery, and chronic disability is a common occurrence in victims of these disease states. "Biofeedback" training procedures have been developed that enhance the possibility of retraining lost muscle function. Brudny, Korein, Grynbaum, and Sachs-Frankel (1977) have developed a procedure that is a combination of integrated EMG pattern matching between the normal and afflicted limb, standard physiotherapy manipulation, and auditory reinforcement of successful movement. In several studies, these investigators have demonstrated return of muscle function to about 50% of a population that failed to achieve success using standard retraining techniques. Brudny and his colleagues call their approach "Sensory Feedback Training" (SFT) rather than "biofeedback." They explain the success of this procedure as a *learning process*, wherein the patient learns through the use of EMG pattern matching to reactivate the stored memory related to limb movement. This visual representation eventually becomes internalized and thus becomes the basis for a new neural center for muscle control. The process is not infallible, however, and it has been suggested that motivation and a sufficiently preserved substrate of neural tissue are necessary for success. The proven success of EMG "biofeedback" in the restoration of muscle function may be due to the combination of visual–auditory information in the form of the EMG information pattern, instruction by the therapist, and the fact that muscle potential–brain connection may represent the most direct inphase biofeedback loop possible between the muscles, the brain, and the environment.

The further investigators move from direct cortical involvement, the more complex the idea that a change in a physiological function can be affected by an auditory or visual response consequence in the environment becomes. The cardiovascular system seems particularly segregated from the influence of simple auditory or visual stimuli generated in the environment as a result of an alteration detected in one or more of the cardiovascular measures. A number of internal control systems regulate the cardiovascular system. These operate as negative feedback loops that receive rate, pressure, and volume information from sensitive physiological transducers in various parts of the cardiovascular system and use this information to regulate the internal functioning of the system. It is difficult to believe that a brief flash of light or burst of sound in the environment, initiated by a spontaneous change in systolic or diastolic arterial blood pressure or a momentary acceleration or decleration in heart rate, can influence the complex physiological control systems that regulate these functions. Consider the complicated phase and time relationships between the environmental light or tone response consequence and the internal cardiovascular control systems. The response-congruent stimulus must find its way through the auditory or visual cortex, impinge upon the regulatory centers, and produce an automatic change in a particular cardiovascular function. This scenario does not sound physiologically reasonable, but time and again "biofeedback" researchers have assumed the validity of this relationship without questioning the time and phase relationship between the response and the reinforcer and the cardiovascular system. The majority of the reports of a clinical alteration in arterial blood pressure through biofeedback training are not convincing, but there are exceptions. An examination of two of the more successful clinical blood pressure "biofeedback" studies may indicate whether the procedures used and information generated can provide a reasonable explanation of their success, as well as any additional information that might be useful to an understanding of the biofeedback process.

The reportedly successful studies by Kristt and Engel (1975) and by Kleinman, Goldman, Snow, and Korol (1977) share several common methodological procedures. In both studies, patients were given extensive biofeedback training in a laboratory or hospital setting and then instructed to use a standard auscultatory blood pressure measurement cuff at home to record their systolic and diastolic arterial blood pressure several times a day. They were also instructed to practice their biofeedback routines during this period. Each subject was given instructions about the use of the blood pressure cuff and thus exposed to long periods of extraceptive and proprioceptive information generated by the auscultatory blood pressure measurement. Though not mentioned by these investigators, the cuff pressure, the Korotkoff sounds, and the gradient of oscillometric oscillations felt under the cuff between the systolic and diastolic pressure levels are all possible proprioceptive cues related to level of and change in arterial blood pressure. It is feasible to hypothesize that these proprioceptive cues provide enough cognitive information to enable the subjects to evolve a strategy for altering these proprioceptions, and thus to reduce their arterial blood pressure. Once achieved, the duration of alteration should be related to the accuracy of the subjects' perceptions and the amount of training given the subjects, rather than to the specific pairing of the auditory or visual response consequence to the minor spontaneous alteration in the measure.

PHYSIOLOGICAL INFORMATION AND PROCESSING SYSTEM (PIPS)

This line of reasoning suggests that there may be no direct feedback connection between the auditory or visual response consequence and the alteration in physiological functioning. Instead, the system may operate as shown in Fig. 2. The internal physiological systems are controlled by the autoregulatory negative feedback loops that continuously regulate the cardiovascular, temperature, and visceral functions. The solid black lines represent the "biofeedback" training pathways. A criterion change in a designated physiological system is detected by the electronic physiological monitor and processor. The visual or auditory representation of this information is displayed by the information display unit. The auditory or visual information is registered at the auditory or visual input and cognitively processed on the basis of initial instructions, motivation, or any preconceived notion of the demands of the situation. This processing results in the evolving of a behavioral strategy that may involve physical action, relaxation, or additional cortical manipulation. The effectiveness of this behavioral strategy is demonstrated by another indication of detection of a criterion physiological response by the physiological monitor. The detection of the new response and the display of the response consequence result in a repetition of the whole process. Failure of the behavioral strategy to produce a criterion physiological response results in no appropriate information display and eventually in an alteration of the behavioral strategy. The broken black lines represent the effect of environmental information on the internal system. The same physiological regulatory mechanisms are involved in the simultaneous processing of environmental stimuli that are not related to the biofeedback training program. Various stimuli—some strongly activating and some relaxing, some calling for rapid and drastic action and others requiring no response—are perceived by the same auditory, visual, and tactile input systems, cognitively processed, and consciously acted upon. These environmental stimuli may simultaneously impinge on the physiological regulatory systems, causing an alteration in function based on the cognitions and affect aroused by the stimulus. The two processes are similar, except that the biofeedback training interactions are based on physiological responses that are presumably de-

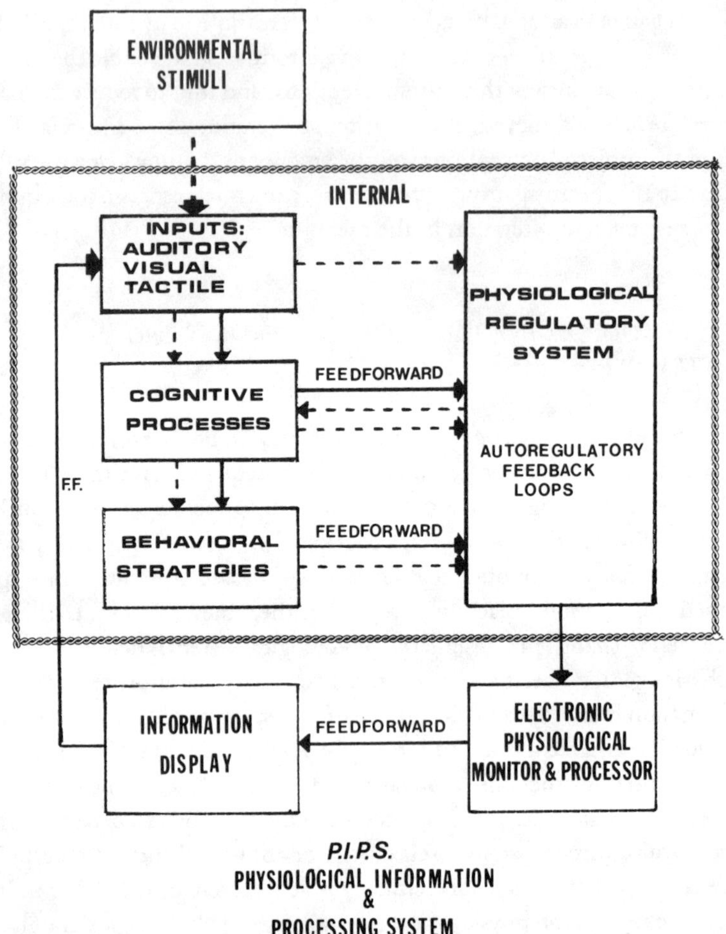

FIG. 2. Block diagram of physiological information and processing system (PIPS). Solid arrows represent "biofeedback"-training pathways. Broken arrows represent environmental-stimuli-processing pathways.

tectable only by the sensitive electronic monitor. The external environmental stimuli are detected, interpreted, and acted upon directly. Neither system fits the model of the electronic feedback circuit, and their interactions are not separable. This complicated interactive system cannot be easily analyzed as a feedback circuit. Schwartz (1980) suggests that a better understanding of the basic conceptual and mathematical properties of biofeedback and behavioral medicine could be achieved by the use of a general systems theory approach. Though he uses a broad brush to outline these ideas, the complexity of the interactions between the biofeedback training pathways and the pathways utilized by environmental stimuli seems to indicate that only a general systems analysis procedure could unravel these complex interactions.

Such an approach must be left to people qualified in this area. Mine must be a much simpler line of reasoning. The system as outlined in Fig. 2 can be classified as a physiological information and processing system (PIPS) that uses a series of feedforward linkages to effect a change in the physiological regulatory systems. If this analysis of the process is reasonable, the task of the psychophysiologist and the engineer is to address themselves to the problem of optimizing the processing procedure. What methods can be developed to maximize the information intake and improve the behavioral strategies based on cognitive processing? One is to provide patients or subjects with maximum and continuous information about their individual success or failure in producing a criterion response. This procedure may result in a more rapid development of successful behavioral strategies to improve performance.

FREQUENCY AND GAIN CHARACTERISTICS

Though some of the questions related to response manipulation have been investigated within the framework of the operant-conditioning paradigm by the manipulation of reinforcement schedules (Shapiro & Crider, 1967), these variables have not been critically examined from the engineer's point of view. If the system under investigation can be compared to an electronic amplification or control system, then it should be useful to look at the frequency and gain characteristics of the system.

The input–output frequency characteristics of the system in this instance might be described as the maximum rate at which outside influences can be integrated into the physiological system and the maximum rate at which information can be usefully extracted from the system. Of the familiar natural physiological rhythms (respiration, brain waves, or heart action), the heart cycle seems to provide the most appropriate frequency unit for information input or output. The heart cycle is sensitive to the environment and defines the maximum rate of measurement of cardiovascular functions such as blood pressure and pulse volume. It also provides a natural clock for sampling slower measures such as temperature, skin conductance, or blood volume.

INFORMATION DISPLAY

In several recent studies (Elmore & Tursky, 1978; Kluger, Jamner, & Tursky, 1980), my colleagues and I have reported the development of a computer-controlled physiological information system that delivers both binary and continuous information related to a change in any physiological measure of interest at each heart cycle. Figure 3 is a representation of the computer monitor display that is viewed by each subject during each laboratory session. Bar (a) represents the averaged response of the measure of interest for 20 heart cycles. On each beat of the subject's heart for the

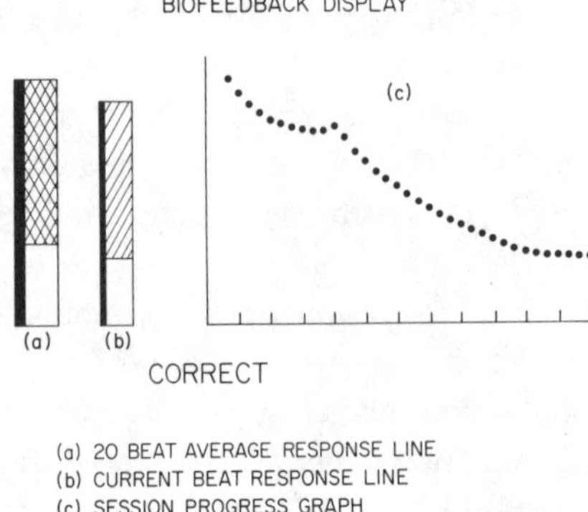

FIG. 3. Computer-controlled binary and continuous physiological information system. Bar (a) represents any averaged physiological response measure for preceding 20 heart cycles. Bar (b) represents the amplitude of that physiological response measure for the current heart cycle. Graph (c) is a continuous record of the individual's progress.

next 20 heart cycles, the amplitude of the measure of interest is displayed by the height bar (b). The height of the two bars is compared in the computer, and a criterion difference in the right direction is rewarded by the word "CORRECT" appearing on the screen. An auditory reinforcer of a short burst of 800-Hz tone is also presented. Every 20 heart cycles, a new averaged response bar (a) is computed, and it becomes the criterion for comparison for the next 20 data samples. Graph (c) is a continuous record of the amplitude of each of these averaged 20 samples. Thus, the subject receives continuous information related to his or her progress during the session, as well as immediate reinforcement at each heart cycle. This type of display is designed to provide maximum multidimensional information about the success of any strategy devised by the subjects. It might also be useful to include information directly related to strategic success. Simple statements such as "You are not succeeding, change strategies," might improve performance and reduce frustration. The use of this information system has provided us with some interesting insights about the characteristics of the learning experience. Figures 4 and 5 show that, with minimal training (as little as one session), subjects can develop strategies that enable them to reach maximum response capabilities in a short period of time (about 30% of session time) in subsequent sessions. This indication of success is usually followed by a tendency to regress to baseline levels. Figure 4 shows the effect of hand temperature biofeedback (HTB) training on increasing finger temperature and finger pulse volume for a group of migraine headache patients (Elmore & Tursky, 1980). Notice the rapid learning in both measures in the early trials (each trial equals 200 heart cycles), followed by regression toward baseline levels in the subsequent trials. Figure 5 shows a similar training graph for two groups of normal subjects (Kluger, Jamner,

& Tursky, 1980), one trained to increase finger temperature, the other trained to increase finger pulse volume. The learning response on both measures for each group are shown in this figure. Similar patterns of rapid learning followed by a reduction in training effects are observed in all cases. Are these results an indication of a saturation effect in the system? Does it suggest that training sessions should be shortened in length and that frequent rest or distraction periods should be initiated to enhance the training process? These are questions that can only be answered by empirical research.

CONCLUSIONS

One of the aims of this chapter is to evaluate the "biofeedback" training program from an engineering viewpoint. The conclusion that can be drawn from this evaluation is that the present approach to biofeedback seems to be counterproductive. On

FIG. 4. Mean alteration in finger temperature (FT) (°C) and finger pulse volume (FPV) (percentage of change from baseline) across 10 trials (200 heart cycles per trial) for a group of migraine headache patients trained to increase hand temperature.

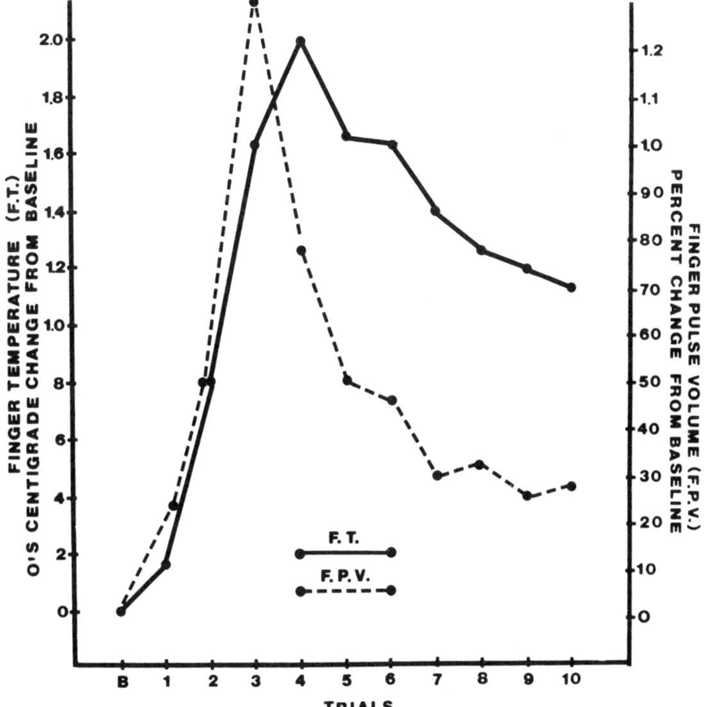

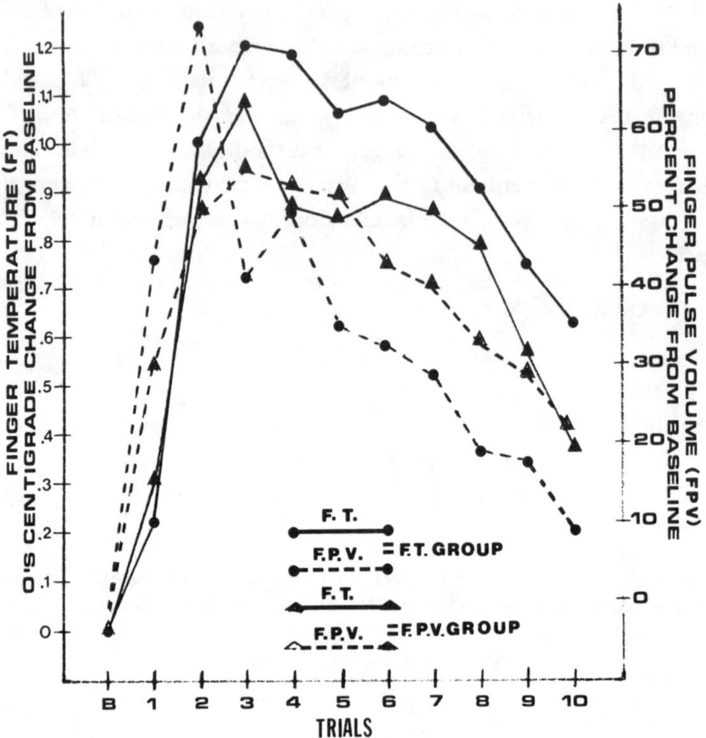

FIG. 5. Mean alteration in finger temperature (FT) and finger pulse volume (FPV) for two groups of normal subjects, one trained to increase finger temperature (FT group), and the other trained to increase finger pulse volume (FPV group).

the one hand, scholars are involved in a deep discussion of the theoretical issues that should explain the successes and failures of the biofeedback process. On the other hand, the clinical uses of this methodology are involved for the most part in a simplistic belief that the biofeedback system does work, and they are applying the process to all areas of biobehavioral complaints. These users' claim of success is based for the most part on their ability to use "biofeedback" as one tool in an arsenal of "treatments." They avoid getting bogged down in a need to justify their claimed successes by complex theoretical justifications. If my speculations about the nature of the biofeedback process are correct, it might be reasonable to discard the term "biofeedback" temporarily, since "feedback" does not seem to describe the process psychophysiologists are involved with. Terms like "physiological information processing" and "strategy development" may describe the process more accurately. Clinicians and researchers might return to the use of the term "physiological" or "biofeedback" when the engineers and biofeedback psychophysiologists resume their symbiotic relationship and evolve a safe and useful method to provide direct feedback into the afferent neural pathways that control each physiological system.

REFERENCES

Ax, A. F. Psychophysiologic methodology in an interdisciplinary psychiatric setting. *Psychophysiology Newsletter,* 1958, *4*(3), 8–23.

Ax, A. F. Electronic storage and computer analyses. In P. H. Venables & I. Martin (Eds.), *A manual of psychophysiological methods.* Amsterdam: North Holland, 1967.

Basmajian, J. V., Kulkula, C. G., Marayan, M. G., & Takebe, K. Biofeedback treatment of foot drop after stroke compared with standard rehabilitation technique: Effects on voluntary control and strength. *Archives of Physical Medicine and Rehabilitation,* 1975, *56,* 231–236.

Blanchard, E. B., & Young, L. D. Clinical applications of biofeedback training. *Archives of General Psychiatry,* 1974, *30,* 573–589.

Brener, J. A. A general model of voluntary control applied to the phenomena of learned cardiovascular change. In P. A. Obrist, A. H. Black, J. Brener, & L. V. DiCara (Eds.), *Cardiovascular psychophysiology.* Chicago: Aldine, 1974.

Brener, J. A. Sensory and perceptual determinants of voluntary visceral control. In G. E. Schwartz & J. Beatty (Eds.), *Biofeedback: Theory and research.* New York: Academic Press, 1977.

Brown, C. C. (Ed.). *Methods in psychophysiology.* Baltimore: Williams & Wilkins, 1967.

Brudny, J., Korein, J., Grynbaum, B. B., & Sachs-Frankel, G. Feedback therapy in patients with brain insult. *Scandinavian Journal of Rehabilitation Medicine,* 1977, *9,* 155–163.

Brudny, J., Korein, J., Levidow, L., Grynbaum, B., Lieberman, A., & Friedmann, L. Sensory feedback therapy as a modality of treatment in central nervous system disorders of voluntary movement. *Neurology,* 1974, *24,* 925–932.

Colgan, M. Effects of binary and proportional feedback on the bidirectional control of heart rate. *Psychophysiology,* 1977, *14,* 187–191.

Edelberg, R., & Burch, N. R. Skin resistance and galvanic skin response: Influence of surface variables and methodological implications. *Archives of General Psychiatry,* 1962, *7,* 163–169.

Elmore, A. M., & Tursky, B. The biofeedback hypothesis; an idea in search of a theory and a method. In A. A. Sugarman & R. E. Tarter (Eds.), *Expanding dimensions of consciousness.* New York: Springer, 1978.

Furedy, J., & Klajner, F. Imaginational Pavlovian conditioning of large-magnitude cardiac decelerations with tilt as US. *Psychophysiology,* 1978, *15,* 538–543.

Furedy, J., & Poulos, C. X. Heart rate decelerative Pavlovian conditioning with tilt as US. *Biological Psychology,* 1976, *4,* 93–106.

Garcia, J., & Koelling, R. A. Relation of cue to consequence in avoidance learning. *Psychonomic Science,* 1966, *5,* 121–122.

Kimmel, H. D. Instrumental conditioning of autonomically mediated behavior. *Psychological Bulletin,* 1967, *67,* 337–345.

Kleinman, K. M., Goldman, H., Snow, M. Y., & Korol, B. Relationship between essential hypertension and cognitive functioning. II: Effects of biofeedback training generalize to non-laboratory environment. *Psychophysiology,* 1977, *14,* 192–197.

Kluger, M., Jamner, L., & Tursky, B. *Learned control of finger temperature versus finger pulse volume using biofeedback.* Paper presented at the meeting of the Eastern Psychological Association, Hartford, Ct., 1980.

Kristt, G. A., & Engel, B. T. Learned control of blood pressure in patients with high blood pressure. *Circulation,* 1975, *51,* 370–378.

Lang, P. J., & Twentyman, C. T. Learning to control heart rate: Binary versus analogue feedback. *Psychophysiology,* 1974, *11,* 616–629.

Lykken, D. T. The GSR in the detection of guilt. *Journal of Applied Psychology*, 1959, *43*, 385–388.

Mackay, R. S. Telemetry and telestimulation. In C. C. Brown (Ed.), *Methods in psychophysiology*. Baltimore: Williams & Wilkins, 1967.

Miller, N. E., & Dworkin, B. R. Visceral learning: Recent difficulties with curarized rats and significant problems for human research. In P. A. Obrist, A. H. Black, J. Brener, & L. V. DiCara, (Eds.), *Cardiovascular psychophysiology*. Chicago: Aldine, 1974.

Mulholland, T. B. Biofeedback as scientific method. In G. Schwartz & J. Beatty (Eds.), *Biofeedback: Theory and research*. New York: Academic Press, 1977.

Noback, C. R. *The human nervous system*. New York: McGraw-Hill, 1967.

O'Connell, D. N., & Tursky, B. Silver–silver chloride sponge electrodes for skin potential recording. *American Journal of Psychology*, 1960, *63*, 302–304.

Schwartz, G. E. Clinical applications of biofeedback: Some theoretical issues. In D. Upper & D. S. Goodenough (Eds.), *Behavior modification with the individual patient: Proceedings of the Third Annual Brockton Symposium on Behavior Therapy*. Nutley, N.J.: Roche, 1972.

Schwartz, G. E. Toward a theory of voluntary control of response patterns in the cardiovascular system. In P. A. Obrist, A. H. Black, J. Brener, & L. V. DiCara (Eds.), *Cardiovascular psychophysiology*. Chicago: Aldine, 1974.

Schwartz, G. E. Biofeedback and patterning of autonomic and central processes: CNS–cardiovascular interactions. In G. E. Schwartz & J. Beatty (Eds.), *Biofeedback: Theory and research*. New York: Academic Press, 1977.

Schwartz, G. E. Behavioral medicine and systems theory: A new systhesis. *National Forum*, Winter 1980, pp. 25–30.

Shapiro, D., & Crider, A. Operant electrodermal conditioning under multiple schedules of reinforcement. *Psychophysiology*, 1967, *4*, 168–175.

Shapiro, D., Crider, A., & Tursky, B. Differentiation of an autonomic response through operant conditioning. *Psychonomic Science*, 1964, *1*, 147–148.

Shapiro, D., & Surwit, R. S. Learned control of physiological function and disease. In H. Leitenberg (Ed.), *Handbook of behavior modification and behavior therapy*. Englewood Cliffs, N.J.: Prentice-Hall, 1976.

Shaw, J. C. Quantification of biological signals using integration techniques. In P. H. Venables & I. Martin (Eds.), *A manual of psychophysiological methods*. Amsterdam: North Holland, 1967.

Shearn, D. Does the heart learn? *Psychological Bulletin*, 1961, *58*, 452–458.

Tursky, B. *The Harvard polygraph*. Unpublished manuscript, 1958.

Tursky, B. Integrators as measuring devices of bio-electric output. *Clinical Pharmacology and Therapeutics*, 1964, *5*, 887–892.

Tursky, B. Biofeedback research methodology: Need for an effective change. In R. Gatchel & K. Price (Eds.), *Clinical applications of biofeedback: Appraisal and status*. New York: Pergamon, 1979.

Tursky, B., Leiderman, P. H., & Shapiro, D. A system for recording and processing psychophysiological and behavioral data. In H. Zimmer (Ed.), *Computers in psychophysiology*. Springfield Ill.: Charles C Thomas, 1966.

Tursky, B., Shapiro, D., & Leiderman, P. H. Automatic data processing in psychophysiology: A system in operation. *Behavioral Science*, 1966, *11*, 64–70.

Venables, P. H., & Martin, I. (Eds.). *A manual of psychophysiological methods*. Amsterdam: North Holland, 1967.

Welford, N. T. The SETAR and its uses for recording physiological and behavioral data. *IRE Transactions of Biomedical Electronics*, 1962, *9*, 185–189.

Wolf, H. S. Telemetry of psychophysiological variables. In P. H. Venables & I. Martin (Eds.), *A manual of psychophysiological methods*. Amsterdam: North Holland, 1967.

Young, L. D., & Blanchard, E. B. Effects of auditory feedback of varying information content on the self-control of heart rate. *Journal of General Psychology*, 1974, *91*, 61–88.

Zimmer, H. (Ed.). *Computers in psychophysiology*. Springfield, Ill.: Charles C Thomas, 1966.

ROUND-TABLE DISCUSSION OF TURSKY

Joseph Brudny: I would like to strongly second the conclusion of Tursky's paper, because the acceptance of the methods that we are talking about in medicine is hampered by the word "biofeedback." When I started our work in the use of EMG for rehabilitation (see Chapter 10) nearly 10 years ago, we based our work on the physiological concept of feedback, which is the most important variable in learning. We based our concepts on the neurocybernetic or engineering concept where feedback is the reinsertion of a portion of the output into the system; and the problem we faced with brain-injured people is that their comparator is inoperative. They don't have information coming from the periphery, nor do they have output. By cognitively linking the output by means of visual information that can be meshed and compared with ideal performance, we reinstate the function of a comparator. And in this way, we feel, the recalibration of the system takes place.

Audience Question to Joseph Brudny: Could you illustrate how it would be possible to use that idea with, let's say, the more visceral responses?

Joseph Brudny: It will become apparent during my presentation that if you replace EMG by another physiological parameter, you could probably train the patient to improve upon his performance by giving him a visible target that represents a better performance and then narrowing the gap. I think it can be done for many areas.

Neal Miller: We all know that instrumental learning of skeletal responses is possible. We all know that instrumental learning of skeletal responses can influence visceral responses, at least certain of them. Now, the question is, is the direct instrumental learning of visceral responses possible or not? It is a scientific and a clinical question. In my opinion, that question has not been answered completely, although I think there's some pretty good suggestive evidence that it can be done; but it's certainly not proven.

I think that Tursky's point is that it's not just like reconnecting a feedback loop that's been disconnected in an amplifier, or replacing a thermostat in a house heating system. There's nothing magic in the feedback per se. The same feedback about heart rate can be used by the subject to either increase his heart rate or decrease his heart rate, according to the instructions. Now, substitute anything else for heart rate and you might get a larger or more reliable effect. Let's take muscle tension, in which the effect is quite clear. You could take a sound analog of EMG and tell him, "Now, we want you to make the tone sound faster," and he'll learn to do that very quickly. And so, just the EMG feedback by itself isn't going to do anything. It is not like soldering a loop. It's what the subject learns to do using the feedback that produces the effect.

Gary Schwartz: I find it, first of all, somewhat curious about people not liking the term "biofeedback," but feeling comfortable with the concept of "feedback" more generally, as well as, I think, "feedforward" in terms of differentiating current processes, since the term "feedback" is one that's very fundamentally used in biology in terms of biochemical mechanisms and physiological mechanisms. And it also lends itself to both biological and mathematical analysis. Our problem, I think, has been that we've not really learned the conceptual basis of what "feedback" and "control" mean. If we did, we would be less likely to come to the conclusion that, for example, just connecting the loop, without the subject trying to do anything, has no "control" effects. All of Mulholland's work [Mulholland, 1977] has been based on the idea that the way in which you connect the feedback, the biofeedback, this augmented feedback, has an effect on the stability and rhythmic processes, these "automatic, homeostatic controlling processes," without the subject "deliberately" trying to control it. Yes, you can instruct the subject to then move the feedback in a certain direction; but Mulholland would argue, as would I, that that's an added process on top of these others. You can think of it as parallel process loops, some of which may be feedforward and some of which may be feedback. If we began to look for control in more sophisticated ways, such as rhythmicity, such as stability, and so on, we might begin to discover relationships that until now we haven't observed.

Martin Orne: Excuse me, a point of information: Do you seriously believe that when you hook up that feedback loop and you have the subject looking at the display, there's no cognitive process which goes on in there that causes things to happen?

Gary Schwartz: Well, let me just give you some data. Of course it happens; the issue is whether or not that cognitive process is the "mechanism" to explain some of these autoregulatory effects. That's the issue. We have a paper in *Psychophysiology* [London & Schwartz, 1980] where we looked at that question. We found that whether or not you had tone-on or tone-off for learning to increase or decrease heart rate had effects on the amount of control that were not mediated in any obvious way by the person's cognitive interpretation of the stimulus and were directly related to whether or not the stimulus was contingent or not. We disentangled that by manipulating the presence or absence of different kinds of instructions as they interacted with the contingency and noncontingency of the feedback; and we assessed people's verbal reports. So, for example, you could find that tone-on feedback augments the ability for subjects to increase heart rate; tone-off feedback has a relatively inhibitory effect on the ability to raise heart rate, but that effect only occurs when the feedback is contingent. If the feedback is noncontingent, the instructions have their role, but the tone-on, tone-off becomes irrelevant. Whether it's yoked or true feedback, the subjects give the same self-reports with regard to their subjective impact of how much tone-on versus tone-off feedback helps one. But there are very different degrees of control as a function of the contingency as it interacts with the tone-on, tone-off process. Imbedded within instructed self-control is an interactive process that may be involving some of these lower loops.

This point is very important conceptually, that boon of awareness. Following directly from Jasper [Brener]'s theoretical orientation, if one were to, for example, simply instruct subjects to attend to particular physiological cues internally, without directed, focused attention, without any instruction to control the response—not increase, not decrease, just watch it—there should be some selective effects on the autoregulatory process to the extent that you have enhanced the subject's awareness of his system. Furthermore, if you were to augment the awareness by some "natural" feedback process such as taking the pulse, without any instruction to increase or decrease responses, or putting one's hand in front of one's nose to feel the air going in or out, that should have further effects—not on the mean per se, but on the stability and regularity of the system. You can then further influence responses by the imposed instructions to increase or decrease; and that's exactly what we have found the data to support. All I'm suggesting is that we not go to the either/or position, that it's all cognitive and we should think of it in terms of feedforward, or that it's all simply connective down the periphery. It may be much more complicated and involve combinations of processes; and I think, for me, it becomes helpful to learn more about the mathematics of control theories and different degrees of control and to look at stability, and so on, as a helpful way to uncover some of the effects.

Peter Lang: I was stimulated again by some things Gary [Schwartz] said. In a study we did long ago in the middle 1960s [Lang, Sroufe, & Hastings, 1967], we looked at two sets of yoked-control subjects in which the subjects were trying to restrict heart rate variability. They had particular targets. It was very much like a motor-skills task. We had one group that was told they were just tracking the stimulus, but they were in a contingency situation; and another group was, indeed, trying to restrict or aim at the target. And under those conditions, you got very significant but opposite results. In other words, relative to a control subject, the subjects who were trying to restrict and getting a contingency were successful. But the subjects who were simply in the loop were significantly more variable just as a function of being in the biofeedback loop.

John Furedy: It's always attractive to suggest that you're going to chuck a term which has caused a lot of conceptual confusion, but I think you have to be careful that rather than solving the problem, you're not just shelving it. It seems to me that in answering the question about how you would use this neurocybernetic or physiological information processing with the visceral system, you would have to establish that the provision of the target information in fact improved control. It looks as if that is true for the EMG preparations Dr. Brudny is working with. There's not much evidence that it's true for autonomic or visceral activities. We can call it *X*, if you like. Essentially, it's a biofeedback experiment. That is, does the provision of feedback improve control over the biological function? I don't think we're going to get away with simply saying this, and we've had a lot of confusion here. Let's talk about the *X* factor, or physiological information. Before I accept the notion that physiological information processing has occurred as a phenomenon, I have to be shown that giving the information about the physiological function has improved performance. Then we're back to the first question, which is the efficacy of this phenomenon.

Bernard Tursky: That's why I have addressed the notion of improving that phenomenon—that is, improving it by giving more information, if possible; by moving it in both directions, if necessary; and by understanding that it is not a simple procedure of simply reinforcing a certain particular response.

Robert Gatchel: I think, also, a more basic question is, and this is pointed out by the data Bernie [Tursky] presented, a saturation point in light of biofeedback studies. I think most of us have encountered that problem. It really points out, again, the need to look at some basic paradigms to be developed to maximize not only the attainment of a certain performance level, but also the maintenance of this performance level. And I think this is where operant-conditioning paradigms have been abandoned prematurely. I think they have been naively administered in biofeedback procedures; nobody has looked at ways of maximizing transfer to no-feedback conditions and things like salience of the reinforcer, which is very important. A lot of animal literature on that has shown it to have a great effect. In some of the pilot studies that we've been running, we've been able to sort of eliminate that saturation point and maintain performance at a higher level. So those basic questions are really important to know before we start going to the next step of mechanism, or they can be done simultaneously. The operant-conditioning paradigm might not explain biofeedback performance, but I think it will provide us with a technology to produce some significant performance effects. And once we have that effect reliably produced, then we can start looking at mechanisms; but we can't now because there are so many equivocal results.

Neal Miller: Of course, that's what you get in a lot of motor-skills learning, that the learning becomes less efficient. Towards the end of the session, you get poorer results. You can even have, with motor-skills learning, a series of curves later on that go up; you just get work decrements. But over the next day, they're better than during any previous day. That's a work decrement.

Audience Question to Robert Gatchel: Can you just briefly sketch how you develop reinforcement salience?

Robert Gatchel: Well, in order to develop salience of reinforcement, we have subjects earn tokens for performance with a 20-second sequence of heart rate samples. If they meet a certain criterion which we set, then a light comes on and they know that that will transfer to a token. At the end of the session, if they accumulate so many tokens, they can pick from a variety of reinforcements. It's not as though we give money or one type of reinforcement to all people. They can pick and choose after each session. I think it's more salient to do that. Then, also, we've relaxed a criterion if they don't meet it. Then, later, we make it a little bit more demanding. During the course of the training, we really monitor each 20-beat interval very precisely, rather than summarizing performance at the end of a session when you don't have that immediate pairing of the reinforcement.

John Furedy: Do you have noncontingent controls in those experiments?

Robert Gatchel: In the pilot studies that we've been running, we've been comparing that procedure to the standard continuous reinforcement that we've done in the past, just comparing that to our contingent fading. Then we also fade out the stimulus gradually. We eliminate 75% of the feedback stimulus.

John Furedy: I think, without the noncontingent controls, it's possible to interpret that data as a differential effect of instructional manipulation as a function of incentive motivation. It seems to me, it's critical, if you're going to study operant conditioning, to first of all establish whether you've got operant conditioning or whether you've got some instructional effects.

Audience Question to John Furedy: From the time of Ebbinghaus on, we have secured elaborate knowledge about how to change skeletal motor response. This is the kind of information you need. Do we now have to worry about whether it's contingent or noncontingent, what kind of a training schedule produces the larger visceral response?

John Furedy: Yes, we do; because, just like when 15 to 20 years ago the operant conditioners wanted to establish whether weak light was reinforcing for animals rather than just energizing, the first thing they had to do was to find out, was there a contingency effect? That's an important issue—just as in Pavlovian conditioning. I'm not interested in Pavlovian conditioning which gets a bigger effect with a bigger US if it has not been shown that it is the association of the CS with the US that is producing this bigger effect.

Gary Schwartz: We should recall, first of all, that this field greatly advanced, when, in fact, we included noncontingent controls and uncovered the phenomenon of contingency which was imbedded in the declining baselines and all kinds of other things, historically. And, secondly, often you can't uncover whether or not the effects are due to any kind of regulatory–conditioning effect without including a noncontingent group. You can misinterpret the data one way or another. So I think we should continue to think in terms of documenting a contingency element if we're going to talk about the "biofeedback" component.

Bernard Tursky: Bob [Gatchel] talked about this 20-beat interval, and we also have been working with 20-beat intervals. There's nothing magic about 20-beat intervals. The important thing, in engineering terms, is that you really are interested in the optimal input frequency and the optimal output frequency you can use for inserting and removing information from the system. We have some natural biological rhythms we can use. One might be breathing, a second might have to do with brain waves; but the ECG, the heart rate, lends itself, I think, best in terms of setting up that kind of input frequency in terms of how often you can inject your information into the system and how often you can take it out.

REFERENCES

Lang, P. J., Sroufe, A., & Hastings, J. E. Effects of feedback and instructional set on the control of cardiac-rate variability. *Journal of Experimental Psychology,* 1967, *75,* 425–453.

London, M. D., & Schwartz, G. E. The interaction of instruction components with cybernetic feedback effects in the voluntary control of human heart rate. *Psychophysiology,* 1980, *17,* 437–443.

Mulholland, T. B. Biofeedback method for locating the most controlled responses of EEG alpha to visual stimulation. In J. Beatty & H. Legewie (Eds.), *Biofeedback and behavior.* New York: Plenum, 1977.

COMMENTS ON THE CHAPTERS BY FUREDY AND RILEY AND BY TURSKY

THOMAS B. MULHOLLAND

COMMENTS ON THE CHAPTER BY FUREDY AND RILEY

In this difficult chapter, Furedy and Riley discuss a variety of issues: differential effects of feedback and reinforcement; the problem of defining a "response"; feedback as a US and as a CS; mediation; cognitive processes in relation to information processes; and the ambiguity of voluntary control. These are important issues, and the authors are to be commended for such an ambitious project. Yet, despite the importance of these issues, the chapter does not clarify them. Because of incessant jargon, idiosyncratic terminology, and spurious dichotomies, combined with a polemical tone and jumbled organization, readers do not explore the ocean of issues; they are cast adrift on it.

The first part of this chapter deals with the

Thomas B. Mulholland. Psychophysiology Laboratory, Edith Nourse Rogers Memorial Veterans Administration Hospital, Bedford, Massachusetts.

"response-learning" approach. The main ideas are as follows: (1) A response should be elicited reliably before any attempt is made to teach or train a subject to produce that response; (2) By properly identifying a US for a response, it can be reliably elicited; (3) A CS can be identified, which, after pairing with the US, will reliably elicit the response; (4) When the response to be trained is a visceral one, mediated by the ANS, two different procedures are used—the "informational-biofeedback" and "response-learning" approaches. Proper description of the response "topography" is important: For example, lengths of the temporal intervals between US, CS, UR, and CR are important parameters. With regard to acquisition, the temporal interval between an operant and its reinforcer is important.

These comments are quite reasonable and noncontroversial; yet they seem to be arbitrary and controversial because of the way idiosyncratic definitions are given, jargon is used, and spurious dichotomies are made. For instance, "fight or flight" is a "reflex"; a strategy that is an alternative to "environmental control" is "internal behavioral control"; "expensive computerized polygraphs" are, it seems, undesirable; "interstimulus intervals" are important, *rather than* "feedback information"; feedback is "propositional information"; a distinction is made between "propositional" and "response" processes; feedback is information, but a reinforcer is not.

These terms and statements must have meaning; the problem is that the authors do not make any attempt to explain them or to refer them to some consensual standard. Thus, the bewildering semantic decoration obscures the rather solid conceptual forms that are there.

The relation between feedback information and reinforcement *is* complicated. The authors cast the issue in terms of a dichotomy or polarity between temporal contiguity and amount of information *in the reinforcement*. The assumption is made that feedback information is reinforcing. This is acceptable in and of itself, but the authors seem unwilling to say that a reinforcer is feedback. Semantics are a problem here. For instance, "feedback" can be considered *any* information about the current status of a response that can be used by the learner for error correction. From this vantage, a food reinforcement for hunger provides information that the response that has occurred is selected from a class of responses that are followed by food. That information helps to reduce errors of food-getting behavior, that is, of making a response that does not get food. Also, in the theory of systems, "feedback information" refers to the current status of the controlled response. Thus, a time delay between the response and feedback to controlled must be considered a loss of information with regard to the current status. From this point of view, the temporal contingency of response and reinforcer is important because information depends upon that interval. Reinforcement is feedback, and useful feedback information decreases with time delay. The authors have identified an important parameter, however, and correctly asserts its importance. They outline an impressive series of experiments to test their hypotheses.

In the section on "Speculations," Furedy and Riley do define biofeedback in terms of its role in error correction. " 'Biofeedback' . . . [occurs] if and only if it is the contingent signal ('feedback') from a biological function that has led to [an] increase of control of that function" (p. 82). Unfortunately, they do not explain what an "increase of control" is or how it should be measured. This is important because if researchers could agree on a standard, quantitative definition of "control," it could be used to differentiate between information that was fed back but not used for error correction and information that was used for error correction. Thus, whether or not a configuration of apparatus and subject is one that provides error-correcting feedback or not could be decided. If control increases, error-correcting feedback is used by the system. Here Furedy and Riley have articulated an important issue.

The authors realize that, if information called "biofeedback" is not used or is not usable for error correction, it might detract from other processes used by subjects to control their responses. On this point, however, the authors take some shots at modern instrumentation that are not relevant. "Computerized polygraphic equipment" is criticized. It is "extremely expensive" and may give distracting information that can cause anxiety. It even seems that the term "computerized" becomes a perjorative one. But everyone knows that the *computerized* part of a polygraphic system is getting less and less expensive. At the same time, data acquisition and display capabilities are increasing without making many subjects anxious. The authors would not criticize trumpets because some players make sour notes with their trumpets, would they?

Later, a new (and, to me, confusing) dichotomy appears: "*either* operant conditioning *or* biofeedback" (p. 84; italics mine). Are they saying that biofeedback is never operant conditioning? By the way, it is confusing in biofeedback discussions to use the word "control" to refer to response processes and to refer to "control groups or conditions" to refer to experimental design. The fault here is not the authors', but it points up the need for a new term to refer to increases in the accuracy and precision of a response.

When the idea that information processing may be cognitive is presented, the genuine importance of that problem is obscured by confusing presentation. For example, they define cognitive as "that which can be experienced in propositional terms" (p. 91). Surely, this is a rather special meaning of the term "cognitive," and it is simply not helpful to discuss the problem of cognition and learning with such a specialized meaning. Moreover, the authors engage in a polemical attack (pp. 92–93) on the use and misuse of the term "cognitive" by "writers of textbooks on 'cognitive psychology' " (they don't tell us which writers or which textbooks), by computer scientists (they do tell us that humans differ from computers), and by "early Hullians" (whoever they were). Even "Platonic forms" take their knocks. At the end of the polemics, the authors provide a useful discussion of the role of messages in a communication system. They wisely use the term "messages" rather than the more general term "information." Soon, however, I am lost again when they introduce terms like "anxiety-ridden system" or "mediationally produced events". They do raise the readers' consciousness with the assertion that *messages* and *failure of messages* are paramount in the analysis of biofeedback systems.

At the end of this intense and dense paper, I was left with the feeling that an explanation of the idiosyncratic terminology over a few hours of coffee with the authors would have greatly enhanced my understanding of their paper.

COMMENTS ON THE CHAPTER BY TURSKY

The intention of this chapter, as expressed in the title, seems straightforward. It aims to document and illustrate the relationship between the general (and older) field of electrical or electronic engineering and the more specialized (and recent) field of biofeedback. Yet the paper falls short of its intention, because two very different "approaches" are presented, neither of which describes the current situation.

The first part of this chapter is a history of the relationship of electrical engineering and psychophysiology over the period from the 1950s to the early 1970s. Although the author correctly describes the many contributions of electrical engineering to the developing field of psychophysiology, especially in terms of instrumentation, the relevance of this history to that of modern biofeedback is questionable.

The second part attempts to draw from

electrical engineering a conceptual framework suitable for the abstract analysis and description of biofeedback systems. Unfortunately, such a conceptual framework is not to be found in electrical engineering, but in general systems theory and in the specialized fields of communication and control theory, that is, modern cybernetics.

The author seems very much aware of the deficiencies of his "approach" and states near the end of the chapter: "The conclusion that can be drawn from this evaluation is that the present approach to biofeedback seems to be counterproductive" (p. 123). If that conclusion had been stated at the beginning, perhaps this paper would have been a very different one.

In the mid-1960s, the role of the electrical engineer in electronic circuit design, prototyping, fabrication, and manufacture changed completely. Circuit design gave way to software development, prototyping to computer modeling, and manufacture of large instruments to that of microcircuits and to large-scale integration (LSI). By means of LSI and special software, a sophisticated, general-purpose "chip" can be dedicated to a single purpose; "genius" circuits can be assigned to "moronic" instrumentation functions. With microprocessors, a small, powerful computer can be dedicated to complex signal detection, processing, analysis, display, and storage of data. This profound advance in technology has made the relation between biofeedback and the technology of LSI and computers very different from the relation between electrical engineering and psychophysiology over the past 20 years.

There is still one area that requires large-component design (prototyping and fabrication of large components). This is the area of probes and transducers. But it can be expected that even probes and transducers will become miniaturized and functionally complex and programmable.

The second "approach" is a search for conceptual models drawn from electrical engineering to describe features of biofeedback systems. The vantage from which this approach is stated is definitely anachronistic. An analogy is drawn between biofeedback systems and simple electronic circuits based on a small number of specific physical components connected in a fixed three-dimensional configuration. This simple, restricted illustration is, as the author states, counterproductive. There is not enough conceptual complexity in that approach to do justice to a biofeedback system.

The proper reference model for biofeedback systems is that of adaptive control systems of the most complex type. Analogies between biological systems and adaptive control systems have been presented by many researchers and theorists. It can be admitted however, that the most elaborate cybernetic models are too simple in comparison with the human being considered as a "system." But they do provide a better basis for discussing salient characteristic features of biofeedback systems, because the conceptual content and descriptive vocabulary of adaptive control systems are far superior to those of older technologies.

A cybernetic model of adaptive control, even a simple one, does not refer to specific, physical, concrete components. Rather, the models refer to sources, transfer, and flow of information. Thus a cybernetic model is a configuration of functions that can describe sources, transfer, and flow of information. Such cybernetic ephemera can, of course, be located in a specific, physical, concrete form—namely, a machine, a computer, or a biosystem that actually does work or actually behaves.

A typical cybernetics system includes (1) a controller; (2) a controlled process; (3) a path for transfer of specific information (messages) from the controller to the controlled process; (4) transfer functions that describe the changes of the messages as they are transferred along the path; (5) a process of detecting and measuring the state of the controlled process; (6) a path for transferring messages that inform the controller of the state of the controlled process (these messages are "feedback"); (7) a process for combining or comparing the feedback message with the controller's message, which is sent to the controlled process; and (8) a process for transferring a new message that minimizes the difference between the feedback message and the controller's message. This difference is called "error," and the minimization of it is called "error correction." In the typical case, *feedback is only a means to an end*—its utility depends on how well it can facilitate the process of error detection and correction.

These categories, though too simple to describe any human biofeedback system completely, provide a useful framework. For instance, if the controlled processes is not adaptive or not following commands given to it, the "fault" may not be in the feedback and error-correction processes. The controller may be deficient; it may not accept feedback; it may issue commands that cannot be transferred or that are beyond the capabilities of the controlled process. In a biofeedback system, as in other cybernetic systems, deficiencies of feedback limit the possibilities for error detection and error reduction, so that the controlled process will be less controlled in comparison to the case in which feedback is intact.

Clearly, there can be many possible ways in which the regulation of a complex system can be degraded or improved. Some of these are not amenable to treatment by electronic biofeedback—for example, a controller that cannot correct errors because it sends garbled messages, or a defect in the forward path. The author indicates these complexities but cannot articulate them properly in the context of a model drawn from the theory of simple electrical circuits.

At this point, a further complexity can be added to the application of theories of adaptive control to a description of biofeedback systems. Biofeedback systems and some nonliving adaptive control systems are *intelligent,* capable of logical operations, able to create internal models of their relevant world and to use techniques to predict the future. Most existing nonliving adaptive control systems exhibit minimal intelligence; but even a minimal biofeedback system is very intelligent.

This feature is but one aspect of the complex, high-order adaptation processes that characterize a typical human. Such features as intelligence and symbolic language give a human biofeedback system many options for using or not using electronic biofeedback to increase regulation of a particular process. For instance, the author implies that a feedback display or stimulus may be processed as (1) an unconditioned stimulus, (2) a conditioned stimulus, (3) a sign, or (4) a symbol. From this point of view, the author is correct when he describes the many pitfalls and mistakes that are associated with a premature and even amateur application of biofeedback technology and equipment to the solution of human illness and disregulation. The enlargement of researchers' and clinicians' knowledge of these *cybernetic* systems, however, will facilitate rational applications of biofeedback in therapy.

REPLY TO MULHOLLAND[1]

DIANE M. RILEY AND JOHN J. FUREDY

We appreciate Mulholland's review of our work, and certainly agree with him that our chapter is "difficult" (p. 131), designed as it was to raise some complex issues to experts in the field, and addressed primarily to "the specialized group of contributors" (p. 75) to this volume. We do find it necessary to note, however, that a number of Mulholland's criticisms are, in our opinion, unjustified. A careful perusal of our paper would indicate a number of misreadings and misconceptions by Mulholland, some of which we would, for purposes of clarification, like to point out.

Concerning the concepts of feedback, information, and reinforcer, Mulholland attributes to us the views that "feedback is information but a reinforcer is not" (p. 132). This is obviously a rather implausible view, but, as perhaps is indicated by Mulholland's failure to reference it, it is nowhere asserted by us. In fact, we explicitly write of the reinforcer as information (e.g., p. 82), which is contrary to the notion of a "spurious dichotomy" (p. 132) attributed to us by Mulholland.

Another "spurious dichotomy" that Mulholland attributes to us is in his claim (p. 133) that on page 84 of our chapter we wrote of a process being *either* operant conditioning *or* biofeedback. This appears to be a misreading, since the cited claim does not appear at any point in the chapter. We would, indeed, oppose the claim because operant conditioning can be regarded as a form of biofeedback and vice versa, although this is not to say that the two are simply equatable. There may be important differences between the two, and as we argue in the chapter, assuming that biofeedback is always an instance of operant conditioning is to gloss over the central concern—that of whether the effects produced are really the result of contingent reinforcement (i.e., operant conditioning) or some other process (which is not operant conditioning).

To turn from misreadings to what seems to us to be misconceptions, we think that most will agree that the issues in the area of biofeedback are very complex. It is therefore of particular importance for the experts to agree on definitions of terms (or at least to agree upon where they disagree). It is only in this way that discussions between researchers can be meaningful collaborative interchanges leading to an increase in scientific understanding. Accordingly, we regret that our terms appear to Mulholland to be "idiosyncratic," and we would like to take this opportunity to clarify some of the most important ones. This sort of clarification may be useful for the more general reader, since the chapter itself was originally intended for a highly specialized audience. It is also the case, however, that communicating in the area of biofeedback is difficult even among the specialists. Biofeedback is very much an interdisciplinary area in which experts have come from

[1]Contrary to the format of the rest of this book, the response to our discussant's comments is presented as a separate reply rather than a revision—the comments were not received in time for the latter.

very diverse backgrounds. Moreover, the field itself has borrowed many terms from other areas and, unfortunately, has not always kept to a clear and consistent usage of these terms. Some clarification of our terminology is consequently in order.

Our use of the term "cognitive" to denote only propositional processes may appear idiosyncratic, but it is, in fact, in line with traditional epistemological usage, according to which only propositions can be known or cognized (e.g., Armstrong, 1973; Lacey, 1976). We are aware that, especially with the so-called paradigm shift to "cognitive" psychology (see, e.g., Segal & Lachman, 1972), the term "cognitive" has come to be so broadly used as to encompass *all* psychological activity. However, we think that such a broad use of the term "cognitive" will only cast readers adrift upon the ocean of issues (to use Mulholland's expression). By restricting the use of this term to a clearly specified case, we are able to call attention to an aspect of psychological functioning that would not otherwise achieve prominence and that, we assert, operates by radically different principles from those typically considered "cognitive."

Clarity is similarly critical when defining the term "biofeedback," which is a central concept in our chapter. Because of this, we devote part of one section (pp. 82–83) to this "terminological" issue. In this connection, Mulholland has expressed some difficulty in understanding our use of the expression "increase of control." We do not deal with the term "control" in any great detail, simply because our use of that word is in no way unusual. We use the term in the standard sense of regulation, or the ability to demonstrate regulation of the target response. Thus, if the target response is heart-rate deceleration (HRD), then it is quite easy to produce a "standard, quantitative definition of 'control' " (p. 132) by specifying the HRD in beats per minute. As indicated below, the issue of the sources of control is sometimes a difficult one, but the degree of control itself can be easily specified in a straightforward and quantitative manner.

On the other hand, the way in which Mulholland employs the term "feedback" is confusing to us because it is exceedingly broad, contrary to the kind of narrow definition offered in our chapter. Further, Mulholland's usage is not in keeping with traditional systems theory usage (e.g., Anliker, 1977; Tursky, Chapter 5); since feedback control systems as used in biofeedback are based upon the systems methodology, it would appear prudent to retain this original sense. Thus, to infer, as does Mulholland, that "If control increases, error-correcting feedback is used by the system" (p. 132–133) when speaking of biofeedback is to overgeneralize. According to the narrow sense of the term "biofeedback," as specified in our chapter, any increase in control must be shown to be the result of the response-contingent signal ("feedback") provided by the experimenter. It is not enough merely to show an increase in control, for some idea as to the *mechanism* of that increase is also needed. In other words, to assert validly that feedback is the mechanism of control, it must be shown that feedback is *necessary* for that increase in control. As pointed out by ourselves and by many others in this volume, however, it has not been unequivocally demonstrated that this response-contingent signal is, in fact, a requirement for the regulation of the target response. In the absence of such a demonstration, it cannot be concluded that "error-correcting feedback" is being used by all of the systems that demonstrate increased control during biofeedback training.

The issue of the necessity of feedback is a critical one, and Mulholland's apparent confusion regarding it is also evidenced by his criticism that we unjustifiably "malign" biofeedback because of its expense (p. 133). Our point, however, is that *any* expense is undesirable to the extent that the expense is *unnecessary* for producing the target behavior. Let us take Mulholland's example—the production of sweet trumpet-like sounds. We would most certainly not criticize the use of trumpets because some players produced sour sounds, but we *would* criticize the use of trumpets if it were the case that trumpets were not really necessary for the production of sweet trumpet-like sounds. Of course, trumpets are necessary for this, so the question does not normally arise. To continue with Mulholland's example, just as skills vary between trumpet players, so the efficacy of biofeedback may differ between subjects. Before considering individual differences in performance, however, it should be remembered that there is a preliminary question that, while answered for trumpets, has not been answered for biofeedback. That is, is the thing in question necessary for producing the target behavior at all? Unless it is shown that feedback is necessary, then any biofeedback equipment, no matter how inexpensive, is at best a waste of money, and may even be deleterious in its effects. Before leaping onto the technological bandwagon, it is perhaps wise to ensure that one will be riding on firm scientific ground.

In conclusion, we make no apology for the fact that our chapter demands careful reading. However, by considering the potential sources for misunderstanding raised by Mulholland, we hope to prevent needless confusion on the part of our readers. Communication in this field is often difficult, and even among experts criticism is often on an impressionistic–emotional level (e.g., "I *like* your data"; "Your *tone* is polemical") rather than on a rational–analytic one. Accordingly, our main purpose in this reply has been to promote the latter sort of communication by attempting to clarify some of the issues raised by Mulholland's comments. The difficulty of rational communication in the area of biofeedback makes it all the more important, in our view, to be prepared to define and redefine the key terms and to grapple with complex conceptual issues, rather than to adopt an easily readable but facile approach to the problems.

REFERENCES

Anliker, J. Biofeedback from the perspective of cybernetics and systems science. In J. Beatty & H. Legewie (Eds.), *Biofeedback and behavior.* New York: Plenum, 1977.

Armstrong, D. M. *Belief, truth and knowledge.* Cambridge: Cambridge University Press, 1973.

Lacey, A. R. *A dictionary of philosophy,* London: Routledge & Kegan Paul, 1976.

Segal, E. M., & Lachman, R. Complex behavior or higher mental process: Is there a paradigm shift? *American Psychologist,* 1972, *27,* 46–55.

III

CARDIOVASCULAR DISORDERS

SESSION I

FORMAL PRESENTATIONS

Interest in the potential of biofeedback as a treatment for cardiovascular disorders may be traced to Miller and DiCara's (Miller, 1969; DiCara, 1970) laboratory demonstrations of operant conditioning in the curarized rat. Although no longer replicable (Miller, 1969), these investigations reported exquisite stimulus control of heart rate, blood flow, and blood pressure. As noted in the individual papers, there have been other key studies that have spurred interest in individual disorders (i.e., Shapiro, Tursky, Gershon, & Stern, 1969, for hypertension; Weiss & Engel, 1971, for arrhythmia; and Sargent, Green, & Walters, 1973, for migraine headache). With the exception of biofeedback applications to Raynaud's disease, many studies of normal subjects preceded the studies of clinical populations. Although the mechanisms are interrelated, the first two papers in this section are concerned directly with cardiac response, while the latter two papers are concerned with vascular activity.

The chapters by Goldstein and by Cheatle and Weiss, covering hypertension and cardiac arrhythmias, respectively, concentrate particularly on the relevant studies in normal subjects. Each of these chapters considers issues in the diagnosis and pathophysiology of the disorder under consideration, in addition to evaluating the relative efficacy of biofeedback. Although Goldstein concludes that present evidence suggests that meditation or relaxation may be a convenient alternative to biofeedback, she notes a number of methodological issues involved in the conduct of many studies, such as inadequate diagnosis of patients and results confounded because of inadequate control or monitoring of external influences (such as stressful life events and/or changes in diet).

Cheatle and Weiss, whose thorough review contains many references to unpublished material not previously reported, conclude that future biofeedback trials in patients with arrhythmias should concentrate particularly on cases of sinus tachycardia and, to a lesser extent, on cases of premature ventricular contractions (PVCs). In sinus tachycardia, reduction of heart rate into the normal range is a relatively clear therapeutic goal. Drawing upon the extensive literature in normal populations, they suggest further studies of individual differences and motivational variables. The reader is referred to the round-table discussion following Chapter 4 for a further consideration of issues related to heart rate changes. It is the editors' impression that Furedy's response-learning technique may provide another approach to the control of arrhythmia.

Obrist's discussion of these papers emphasizes the problems involved in obtaining representative measures of blood pressure. In addition, he elaborates on the issue of individual differences in both hypertension and treatment response.

ROUND-TABLE DISCUSSION

The round-table discussion particularly considers issues raised by Goldstein's chapter on hypertension. (See the discussion following Chapter 4 for issues related to arrhythmias and heart rate.) Hypertension is due to heterogeneous factors, both physiological and psychological. The discussion examines this heterogeneity as it affects the selection of appropriate subgroups who might respond to behavioral approaches. When hypertension becomes fixed rather than variable, behavioral methods are unlikely to succeed. Behavioral approaches to hypertension are based upon an assumed interaction between the CNS and the cardiovascular system. Recent clinical and experimental studies suggest a greater degree of CNS influence on hypertension than had previously been assumed.

Much of the discussion concerns itself with methodological issues involved in the evaluation of blood pressure. Blood pressure, in fact, changes with each beat of the heart, and momentary phasic changes may be induced by psychological stimuli and subject to circadian variation. This variability in blood pressure introduces a degree of uncertainty regarding the validity of any sample readings as representative. This uncertainty concerning the individual variability of blood pressure readings may be confounded by the selection of subjects and by the evaluation of treatment response. It is interesting to note that here is a concern with precision of measurement among behavioral scientists that exceeds the concern usually encountered among cardiologists. It is the casual blood pressure reading obtained in the doctor's office that has been used in longitudinal studies of mortality rates.

Some new studies are briefly reported that shed light on the mechanisms whereby behavioral treatment packages, as reported by Patel (1977), may effect clinically significant reductions in blood pressure. The degree of involvement of the subject in the procedure may be more significant in obtaining reduction of blood pressure than the specific procedure used may be.

SESSION II

FORMAL PRESENTATIONS

In his selected review of the literature of biofeedback and migraine, Beatty contrasts the biofeedback literature's characteristic neglect of pathophysiology with the traditions of physical medicine and experimental physiology, where concern with pathophysiology is primary. A clear theme of this volume is that if biofeedback is to progress, it must deal more adequately with physiology in general and with pathophysiology in particular. Beatty's conclusion is that in the treatment of migraine headaches, there is no difference in efficacy between biofeedback and simple relaxation or placebo treatments.

Blanchard, in his formal discussion, raises two objections to Beatty's conclusion. Using an analytic procedure termed "meta-analysis" to examine data from comparative treatment studies, Blanchard finds that placebo effects are not as potent as either relaxation, biofeedback (EMG), or relaxation and biofeedback; and he therefore differentiates between placebo and relaxation effects. Blanchard also suggests that the methods of carotid pulse volume feedback may have more potential than that acknowledged by Beatty. Adams, Brantley, and Thompson (see Chapter 14) also note some potential for the pulse volume feedback technique. The differentiation of relaxation effects from EMG feedback is addressed by Adams and his colleagues as well. Since frontalis EMG does not generalize to other muscle groups (see Gatchel, Chapter 15), it is premature to consider relaxation as a final common pathway.

Surwit's review finds that, in the treatment of Raynaud's disease, patients typically report a 50% reduction of symptom frequency, and objective measures show increases in resting digital temperature of 3°–4°C. These findings are extremely significant in view of the inadequacy of surgical and medical approaches. However, again, comparative treatment studies argue against biofeedback as the *essential* technique in effecting results.

ROUND-TABLE DISCUSSION

In this round-table discussion, several points bearing on broad issues for biofeedback are raised. Because of the many interactive components that determine placebo effects, the magnitude of placebo effects varies between studies; within a single study, these effects may even mimic a learning curve (see Orne, Chapter 17). These characteristics of placebo effects may invalidate the meta-analytic method used by Blanchard to differentiate treatment and placebo effects in the treatment of migraine. An important distinction is made between biofeedback as a procedure and biofeedback as an effect whereby control of physiological response is achieved. Failure to make this differentiation in outcome studies may contribute to the low correlations obtained between clinical effects and physiological change. By greatly increasing the number of trials, learning of physiological control may be maximized.

The heterogeneity of migraine types may actually have implications for treatment that are frequently overlooked. Motivational variables determine discontinuation of successful self-control techniques among Raynaud's patients, and these are discussed. Pulse volume feedback has a potential for maximizing clinical results with migraine and Raynaud's patients. Tursky suggests that an advantage to the pulse volume method may be a physiologically determined relationship between this measure and temperature change. Pulse volume change may precede alterations in skin temperature and be more in phase with significant physiological processes.

The systems analysis approach recommended by Schwartz (pp. 60–65 and 127–129) as a guide to clinical trials proposes an interaction between specific treatments and the physiological and psychological heterogeneity of patients. The complexity of the model should not be misinterpreted as an excuse for not executing these studies, nor are these theories offered as a substitute for systematic data.

REFERENCES

DiCara, L. V. Learning in the autonomic nervous system. *Scientific American,* 1970, *222*(1), 30–39.

Miller, N. E. Learning of visceral and glandular responses. *Science,* 1969, *163,* 434–445.

Patel, C. Biofeedback-aided relaxation in the management of hypertension. *Biofeedback and Self-Regulation,* 1977, *2,* 1–41.

Sargent, J. D., Green, E. E., & Walters, E. D. Preliminary report on the use of autogenic feedback training in the treatment of migraine and tension headaches. *Psychosomatic Medicine,* 1973, *35,* 129–135.

Shapiro, D., Tursky, B., Gershon, E., & Stern, M. Effects of feedback and reinforcement on the control of human systolic blood pressure. *Science,* 1969, *163,* 588–590.

Weiss, T., & Engel, B. T. Operant conditioning of heart rate in patients with premature ventricular contractions. *Psychosomatic Medicine,* 1971, *33,* 301–321.

6 BIOFEEDBACK IN THE TREATMENT OF HYPERTENSION

IRIS BALSHAN GOLDSTEIN

INTRODUCTION

"Hypertension" is defined in terms of an elevation in blood pressure generally in excess of 160/95 mm Hg (WHO, 1959). According to Levy (1980), 35 million Americans have pressures at these levels. Pressures that range between 140/90 and 160/95 mm Hg define "borderline hypertension" and are present in about 25 million additional Americans. For approximately 90% of all hypertensive disorders, referred to as "essential," there is no known etiology. The remaining 10% have clearly definable causes, such as kidney dysfunction, cerebral disease, coarctation of the aorta, and other physiological malfunctions.

In 1977, 16,130 deaths resulted from hypertension and hypertensive heart disease. Hypertension also contributes to deaths due to congestive heart failure, coronary heart disease, stroke, and renal failure (Levy, 1980). It has been estimated that approximately 50% of all males die from causes that are somehow related to elevated blood pressure. In general, the higher the level of blood pressure, the greater the risk of complications developing in the patient and leading to death (Freis, 1974). For each increment of blood pressure above 100/60 mm Hg, there is a corresponding increase in death risk from a variety of disorders (Eyer, 1975).

The high incidence of hypertension and its associated complications underscore the importance of reducing blood pressure among hypertensives. Veterans Administration studies (1967, 1970) have demonstrated a significant reduction in mortality and morbidity rates when antihypertensive medication was used to lower blood pressure in patients with diastolic pressure in excess of 104 mm Hg. As a result of a recent drug study by the Hypertension Detection and Follow-Up Program Cooperative Group (1979), there is now support for effectiveness of drugs in patients with diastolic pressures between 90 and 105 mm Hg.

Although drugs play a vital role in the regulation of blood pressure, they do not exert adequate control in all patients and can lead to disturbing side effects.

Iris Balshan Goldstein. Department of Psychiatry, School of Medicine, The University of California at Los Angeles, Los Angeles, California.

There is also a problem with the hypertensive patient who will not comply with drug treatment. In such instances, behavioral methods may be utilized as an adjunct or possible alternative to drug treatment. According to Reeves and D. Shapiro (1978), "Behavioral treatments may expand the number of treated patients, aid in prevention, and help make patients more aware of responsibility for their health" (p. 121).

The purpose of the present chapter is to evaluate one particular behavioral treatment, biofeedback, and to determine its role in blood pressure control. In this context, the necessary criteria for a biofeedback study are discussed, and important research in this area is examined in light of these criteria. Finally, critical issues are considered in an attempt to determine appropriate avenues for biofeedback research to pursue in the future.

CRITERIA FOR A BIOFEEDBACK STUDY

In order to examine and evaluate the effects of biofeedback on hypertensives, it is important that certain controls be achieved in biofeedback research. As an aid in achieving these controls, the following criteria are suggested.

CAREFUL SELECTION AND DESCRIPTION OF POPULATION

In selecting patients for a hypertension study, researchers must be certain that the sample consists of individuals who do in fact have hypertensive disorders. Diagnosis should be verified by a medical examination and a medical history that includes such factors as duration of illness, medication and dosage level, and any other relevant disorders. Any tests necessary to determine whether the hypertension is essential in nature should also be included. In order to avoid the physiological complications of damage to secondary organ systems, many investigators confine their patient sample to essential hypertensives. Depending on the purposes of a study, a particular investigator may also wish to restrict the population studied to a particular age group, socioeconomic level, or racial group. In addition, in order to isolate the effects of biofeedback, it may be advisable to eliminate patients who are receiving other forms of therapy, such as psychotherapy or other behavioral treatments.

CONTROL OF MEDICATION EFFECTS

Patient medications must be carefully assessed at the onset as well as during the course of the study. For the sake of consistency, all patients should either be on or off drugs. If patients who are receiving medication are to be included with those who are not, they should be put in different groups or evaluated separately. Since it is sometimes virtually impossible to obtain sufficient numbers of drug-free patients, it may be advisable to limit the sample to patients taking a fairly common drug, such as diuretics, or at least to try to classify patients according to whether or not their medications are centrally acting. Furthermore, it is critical that drug dosage be stable. Patients should be maintained on drugs for some time prior to participating in the study, and dosage should not be changed during the experiment. In addition, each patient's drug compliance should be monitored. Finally, patients who are taking other kinds of medication that might influence blood pressure should not be included in the study.

CONTROL GROUPS MATCHED ON CRITICAL VARIABLES

The selection of appropriate control groups is critical in biofeedback studies of hypertensive patients. In selecting such groups, patients should be matched for age, sex, education, socioeconomic level, type of hypertensive disorder, duration of hypertension, and if possible, medications. Basically, controls are other hypertensive patients who are given some alternative treatment to biofeedback in order to evaluate the effectiveness of biofeedback in lowering blood pressure. If an investigator merely wishes to see if biofeedback will cause a reduction in blood pressure greater than the random pressure variations that occur over time, then a waiting-list control would be satisfactory. Enough, however, is known about placebo effects to make it apparent that increased attention alone can lead to a blood pressure reduction (Katkin & Goldband, 1979). It is important, therefore, to select a control group that (unlike a waiting-list control) receives attention equivalent in amount to that given the biofeedback treatment group. That is to say, experimental and control groups must be treated in a similar manner and must have equivalent contact with both the experimenter and the laboratory. In addition, in the eyes of the patients, expectancy of improvement must apply equally to all groups.

ADEQUATE BASELINE AND TREATMENT MEASURES OF BLOOD PRESSURE

Stable blood pressure measurements should be obtained prior to treatment (baseline measurements) as well as during the treatment procedures themselves. Such stability necessitates the recording of a number of consecutive blood pressure readings until the investigator is assured that adaptation has occurred. While there is no concurrence as to the number of recordings necessary to obtain stable values, investigators are aware of large intrasubject variability (Sokolow, Werdegar, Perloff, Cowan, & Brenenstuhl, 1970). Only with repeated measurements on several different occasions will enough blood pressure readings be obtained to permit the researcher to derive an approximation of the average blood pressure within a given time period for that patient.

ASSESSMENT OF TRANSFER AND MAINTENANCE OF TRAINING EFFECTS

In order to verify the effectiveness of a treatment in lowering blood pressure, investigators should assess its effects outside the training situation itself. While it is important to demonstrate that blood pressure can be controlled with biofeedback in the laboratory, concurrent pressure reductions in the patients' homes and even at work are more meaningful. Blanchard (1979) feels that the usefulness of a procedure lies in transferring laboratory-acquired responses to the patients' natural environments. In addition to assessing the effectiveness of the biofeedback procedure in a more natural setting, an attempt should be made to evaluate its effectiveness over time. That is, once biofeedback treatment has terminated, follow-up procedures should be instituted to test the duration of any blood pressure reductions that may have occurred.

With these criteria in mind, some of the major investigations of biofeedback techniques used with hypertensive patients are now discussed and evaluated. Because only a limited number of studies are cited, the reader is referred to the following for a more comprehensive review of the literature in this area: Agras and Jacob (1979); Blanchard (1979); Frumkin, Nathan, Prout, and Cohen (1978); Reeves and D. Shapiro (1978); Seer (1979); and A. P. Shapiro, Schwartz, Ferguson, Redmond, and Weiss (1977),

BIOFEEDBACK RESEARCH ON BLOOD PRESSURE CONTROL

BLOOD PRESSURE FEEDBACK

The utilization of biofeedback for blood pressure control is relatively new and dates back to the development of the ''constant-cuff'' technique by D. Shapiro, Tursky, Gershon, and Stern (1969). It has been adapted for use in most studies of blood pressure feedback, since it allows investigators to obtain a noninvasive measure of blood pressure with each heart beat and to feed this information back to subjects on a continuous basis. As utilized by D. Shapiro, the feedback and reward are contingent on either increases or decreases in systolic or diastolic blood pressure.

Investigations of Normotensives

Most of the early investigations of blood pressure control by D. Shapiro and his colleagues were done with normotensive subjects (Schwartz, 1972; Schwartz, D. Shapiro, & Tursky, 1971; D. Shapiro, Schwartz, & Tursky, 1972; D. Shapiro *et al.*, 1969). In all of these studies, a subject received visual and auditory binary (yes–no) feedback to indicate whether blood pressure was above or below an average set pressure. The subjects were not told to modify their blood pressure, only to make the feedback occur as often as possible. From these studies, it was found that normal subjects were able to modify their blood presure voluntarily, if only by small amounts. The largest changes were obtained for diastolic blood pressure, with subjects demonstrating increases of up to 25% and decreases of up to 15% of baseline values (D. Shapiro *et al.*, 1972).

With visual feedback only, Fey and Lindholm (1975) utilized a group given feedback for increases in systolic pressure; another given feedback for decreases in systolic pressure; and two control groups, one with random (noncontingent) feedback and the second with no feedback at all. With this carefully controlled study, only the "decrease" group exhibited significant blood pressure changes (mean decreases from baseline levels of approximately 5 mm Hg by the end of the session).

Of all the investigations with normal subjects Brener and Kleinman (1970) achieved the largest reductions obtained so far. By means of the finger-cuff method of following blood pressure, proportional feedback was given to one group of subjects. A control group was merely instructed to observe the feedback, but its meaning was not explained. After only 30 minutes of training, between-groups systolic differences were obtained of 20 to 30 mm Hg. Reeves and D. Shapiro (1978) felt that these large differences were the result of the finger-cuff technique and of instructing subjects about the meaning of the biofeedback display (unlike the procedure in D. Shapiro's studies).

The primary significance of the early work with normotensives was the demonstration that individuals can be trained to control their blood pressures. Furthermore, the development of the constant-cuff method provided a convenient means of obtaining continuous blood pressure feedback without arterial catheterization. Although blood pressure changes were comparatively small, it is important to remember that all of these subjects had relatively low pressures and that the experiments were conducted in a single session. These investigations are of value because they led to the establishment of procedures and techniques that could be applied to the study of hypertensives.

Investigations of Hypertensives

While more and more investigations of biofeedback with hypertensive patients are being conducted, only a few of the studies in this area are discussed here. The discussion will be centered around some of the better-designed studies, particularly those attempting to meet the aforementioned criteria. The first report of a controlled investigation of hypertensive patients was that of Benson, D. Shaprio, Tursky, and Schwartz (1971). After obtaining stable baseline blood pressures, the investigators gave patients biofeedback (constant-cuff method) and rewards for systolic reductions. Instead of there being a set number of training sessions, patients continued to come into the laboratory until five consecutive sessions had passed with no further reductions in blood pressure. The actual number of sessions ranged between 8 and 34. From baseline levels to levels at the end of training, five of the seven patients exhibited a mean decrease in systolic blood pressure of 16.5 mm Hg. This study had many unique features; however, since there was no control group it cannot be established for certain that the blood pressure reductions were a result of the biofeedback iteslf, and not of some other factors. Furthermore, there was no evaluation of transfer of training, either outside the laboratory or beyond the actual training period.

Kristt and Engel (1975) built in some fairly good procedures in their study of five essential hypertensives. After a 7-week period of having patients record their blood pressures at home, the investigators trained them in a shaping procedure to raise and lower their systolic blood pressures for 3 weeks (42 sessions). Not only were systolic pressures reduced significantly (18 mm Hg) from pretreatment levels, but patients learned to lower their diastolic blood pressure (8 mm Hg) as well. Moreover, learned control of blood pressure occurred both during training in the hospital and during a 3-month follow-up period, while patients continued to record pressures and practice a maneuver for lowering blood pressure at home. As in the prior study, the experimenters failed to utilize a control group.

Eight unmedicated essential hypertensives, with no control patients, were selected for participation in a biofeedback study by Kleinman, Goldman, Snow, and Korol (1977). They were given three weekly baseline sessions, followed by 9 weeks of biofeedback in which lights and tones were contingent upon decreases in systolic blood pressure. An important addition to this study was the recording of pressures by patients outside the laboratory five times a day. For these home and work measurements, significant reductions were exhibited in both systolic and diastolic pressures. In the laboratory, however, only diastolic reductions were significant, in spite of the fact that only systolic decreases were reinforced. Although blood pressure reductions continued for 4 months of follow-up, at this point in the study only three patients remained.

The fact that control groups can be utilized is shown by the research of Elder, Ruiz, Deabler, and Dillenkoffer (1973), in which hospitalized essential hypertensives were divided into three groups of six patients each: (1) a group kept in a no-feedback condition; (2) a group given intermittent feedback for reduction in diastolic blood pressure; and (3) a group given intermittent feedback coupled with contingent praise. Feedback by itself decreased blood pressures, but these reductions were not as large as those resulting from the combination of feedback and praise. While the presence of multiple control groups supported the conclusion that mere participation in a study was not enough to lower blood pressure, the study is complicated by the fact that there was only one baseline session. Although there were follow-ups, they lasted only 1 week.

Although only a few studies have been discussed here, Reeves and D. Shapiro (1978), in a more thorough review, have concluded that biofeedback does reduce blood pressure in patients with essential hypertension. Seer (1979) has questioned whether the decreases in pressure, although statistically significant, were clinically relevant and could persist over time. Moreover, the numbers of patients in these investigations were relatively small, and controls were not always adequate.

OTHER BIOFEEDBACK TECHNIQUES

Although most biofeedback research on hypertension has been done with blood pressure feedback, other techniques have been investigated also. Within the last few years a new procedure based on the use of pulse-wave velocity (PWV) feedback has been developed. PWV is the rate of propagation of a pressure pulse through the arteries and is dependent upon the size of the arteries and the distensibility of their walls. It has an advantage over standard blood pressure feedback, because it does not involve the use of an occluding cuff. While PWV may be measured by timing the interval between the arrival of a pulse at two different points along a given artery, pulse transit time (PTT) is more frequently recorded. Some investigators have measured the time elapsed between the left ventricular contraction (R wave of the ECG) and detection of the pulse in an extremity, and they have referred to this as PTT. Studies by Steptoe (1977) and Steptoe and Johnston (1976) have indicated that feedback adds to instructional control of PTT. While PWV and PTT offer an alternative to blood pressure feedback, more experimentation needs to be done before any conclusive results can be obtained. The assumption that changes in PWV are proportional to changes in mean arterial pressure, an assumption critical to its use in this area, has not been supported by Lane, Greenstadt, and D. Shapiro (1979), who found systolic blood pressure to be only moderately correlated with PTT.

Other forms of biofeedback utilized for blood pressure control have been based on the supposition that the more relaxed an individual is, the lower blood pressure will be. In order to achieve maximal relaxation, Moeller (1973) trained hypertensive patients in progressive relaxation combined with autogenic phrases, and also provided EMG feedback from the frontalis muscle. Patients who received 16 weeks of feedback and relaxation showed greater blood pressure reductions than did members of a control group who came into the laboratory for 4 weeks but received neither relaxation training nor feedback. While the treatment groups did not have the same amount of laboratory contact, the results suggested that EMG feedback and relaxation might be an effective means of reducing blood pressure in hypertensive patients. Varying the number of treatment sessions from one to two per week or having patients practice relaxation exercises at home did not have any effect on the results.

The most complete and interesting research on combined relaxation and biofeedback techniques is the work of Patel (see Patel, 1977, for a review). In her initial report, Patel (1973) combined feedback from a GSR device with a set of yoga exercises involving passive relaxation training and meditation. Assumedly, skin resistance increases would reflect sympathetic nervous system decreases, which would be expected during relaxation. In a sample of 20 hypertensive patients, not only were blood pressures reduced significantly, but drug requirements were reduced as well. A comparison with 20 hypertensive controls (Patel, 1975a), who reclined on a couch but were not given relaxation or biofeedback, indicated that increased information and the recording of blood pressure did not, by themselves, lead to blood pressure reductions in hypertensives.

In a well-controlled investigation, Patel and North (1975) assigned 34 hypertensive patients to one of two conditions. One group was taught relaxation with yoga and then given GSR and EMG feedback. Patients in the second condition were told to recline throughout all sessions with no specific instructions. Baseline recordings were taken on 3 separate days, followed by 12 treatment sessions over 6 weeks and a follow-up every 2 weeks for 3 months. While both groups exhibited blood pressure decreases, the group that received relaxation training exhibited significantly greater reductions (26.1 mm Hg systolic and 15.2 mm Hg diastolic). Although such blood pressure decreases are quite impressive, it is impossible to determine how much EMG and GSR biofeedback contributed to the lowering of pressures, because relaxation and biofeedback have always been combined in Patel's studies.

RELAXATION: AN ALTERNATIVE METHOD OF BLOOD PRESSURE CONTROL

The utilization of relaxation as a procedure for reducing blood pressure has been cited frequently in the literature. Although for years various techniques have existed for the purpose of altering states of consciousness, in recent times relaxation procedures have been associated with treatment for a variety of stress-related disorders. Most of the methods have developed from procedures such as "progressive relaxation" (Jacobson, 1939), "autogenic training" (Schultz & Luthe, 1969), and various forms of meditation. By means of mental and physical relaxation, these methods attempt to lower blood pressure. The fact that they have been successful has been confirmed in reviews by Agras and Jacob (1979); Frumkin *et al.* (1978); Jacob, Kraemer, and Agras (1977); and Tarler-Benlolo (1978). Seer (1979), in his review, has reported across-session reductions in relaxation studies ranging from 7 to 14 mm Hg for systolic blood pressure and 4 to 10 mm Hg for diastolic blood pressure. Furthermore, such reductions have frequently been maintained for several months. The results of a recent well-controlled investigation by Taylor, Farquhar, Nelson, and Agras (1977) indicated that the effects of a relaxation exercise (adapted from progressive relaxation) on blood pressure were greater than the effects attributable either to medical treatment alone, or to a nonspecific treatment introduced with apparent enthusiasm.

At this point in time, it is not clear if any one relaxation procedure is superior to any other in the regulation of blood pressure. Moreover, exactly what part of the relaxation procedure contributes to the lowering of blood pressure has not been established.

COMPARATIVE STUDIES OF RELAXATION AND BIOFEEDBACK

Since relaxation and biofeedback have both had some effect on the control of blood pressure, it is important to review investigations that have attempted to compare one method against the other. Only in this manner can it be determined which of the two methods has produced greater reductions in blood pressure. In such a study of 15 mild hypertensives, Shoemaker and Tasto (1975) compared progressive relaxation, noncontinuous proportional blood pressure feedback, and a no-treatment, waiting-list control. All patients underwent three baseline sessions and six 80-minute treatment sessions over a 2-week period. Only relaxation resulted in a significant lowering of systolic and diastolic blood pressure (6.8/7.6 mm Hg) throughout the course of treatment. There is reason to question whether biofeedback was given a fair chance, however, since it was presented once every 90 seconds and the display may have been difficult to interpret. Furthermore, initial blood pressures were quite low, and neither medication information nor follow-up data were presented.

Essential hypertensives, in an investigation by Friedman and Taub (1977), were assigned to one of four groups: (1) a group receiving blood pressure feedback; (2) a group receiving hypnosis; (3) a group receiving a hypnosis and biofeedback combination, and (4) a measurement-only comparison group. All patients received a baseline session and seven training sessions twice a week. At the time of the 1-month follow-up, the hypnosis-only and biofeedback-only groups exhibited significant reductions in blood pressure. Of all the procedures, however, the most impressive blood pressure declines were the result of hypnosis only. The authors suggested that having to attend to a biofeedback display may have detracted from the effects of hypnotic relaxation, and therefore may have resulted in the biofeedback–hypnosis group exhibiting very little blood pressure change. Further complications were the use of noncontinuous feedback, the use of only one baseline session, and the inclusion of both medicated and unmedicated patients. Finally, because of the nature of the study, group assignment was not random but was based on patient hypnotizability.

In a sample of borderline hypertensives, Surwit, D. Shapiro, and Good (1978) utilized three different procedures for reducing blood pressure: biofeedback for simultaneous reductions in heart rate and blood pressure (constant-cuff); biofeedback for reductions in integrated forearm and frontalis muscle tension; and a form of meditation relaxation based on Benson's "relaxation response." The study involved two baseline sessions, eight training sessions, and a 6-week follow-up, with half of the sample followed for a year. Although within-session reductions were noted in all three groups, the carry-over effects from one session to the next were not significant. In addition, there were no significant blood pressure differences between groups as a result of the treatments. The experimenters suggested that combining heart rate with blood pressure feedback may have been ineffective because the patients had low heart rates to begin with. Moreover, the insignificant blood pressure reductions may have been a result of the patients' initial low blood pressures.

One of the few comparative studies that showed positive effects of blood pressure feedback was done by Blanchard, Miller, Abel, Haynes, and Wicker (1979). Direct blood pressure biofeedback (systolic and diastolic) was compared with frontal EMG biofeedback and with a condition in which patients were simply told to relax. This study had the advantage of four baseline sessions. Although diastolic blood pressures were not affected, the systolic pressures of the patients in the blood pressure biofeedback group decreased significantly from baseline levels. Furthermore, the slight benefits of blood pressure feedback were maintained up to 4 months after treatment had ended. It should also be mentioned that there was a slight lag (4 to 5 seconds) in the blood pressure feedback, which may have resulted in some erroneous information being fed back to the patients.

When an investigator tries to draw conclusions from the comparative studies in this area, it becomes apparent that such studies, although basically sound, are not without their flaws and consequently present equivocal results. Problems exist because of methodology and/or because the initial pressures of the patients were too low for treatments to result in substantial blood pressure reductions. Without further research, it is impossible to conclude that any one behavioral method is superior to any others in the treatment of hypertension.

It may be that, rather than either one of the two techniques (biofeedback or relaxation) being superior to the other, a combination of strategies may result in the most effective blood pressure control. This is suggested by Fey and Lindholm's utilization (1978) of both blood pressure biofeedback and progressive relaxation with a sample of normotensives. Such a combined procedure resulted in significantly greater blood pressure reductions than did either progressive relaxation alone or a control relaxation procedure. Contrary to these results, Frankel, Patel, Horwitz, Friedewald, and Gaarder (1978) found that a combination of blood pressure feedback, EMG feedback, and verbal relaxation (autogenic training and progressive relaxation) was no more effective than sham biofeedback was. It is possible that a combination of so many techniques may have been too complicated, thereby arousing confusion in the patients. Evidently more research is necessary to determine whether a combination of biofeedback and relaxation is more effective than is either technique alone.

At this point in time, there are still a number of unresolved questions regarding the role of biofeedback in hypertension. It sometimes appears that the process of conducting research arouses more questions than it answers. In the next section of this paper, there is a discussion of some of the more cirtical questions and issues—and, it is hoped, some answers as well.

CRITICAL ISSUES

If no truly well-controlled clinical study of hypertension has been conducted in the area of biofeedback, as D. Shapiro and Surwit (1976) have claimed, it is not so much the fault of the experimenters as it is the nature of the problem. Such studies are frequently beset with a variety of problems, and even the most conscientious investigator cannot control for all of the myriad factors felt to be involved in blood pressure change. For example, it is not unusual to discover a sudden spurious blood pressure increase in a patient who has assumedly been successfully learning to control that pressure by means of biofeedback. Upon questioning the patient, the investigator may learn of the death of a family member, failure to take medication because of disturbing side effects, a sudden job loss, or a countless number of other factors. Much as it has been a formidable task for the experimenter to intervene in the psychotherapy process and to try to account for its success or failure, it appears to be similarly difficult to account for all of the variables involved in the success or failure of biofeedback with hypertensives. The complexity of this task, as well as some important issues in biofeedback research, is discussed here. In so doing, attempts are made, wherever possible, to resolve some of the more critical issues.

SAMPLE SIZE

A review of the literature indicates that the typical biofeedback study with hypertensives has been based on relatively small numbers of patients, usually between five and seven, in a single biofeedback condition (Blanchard, 1979). This is partially due to the time-consuming procedure involved in selecting uncomplicated essential hypertensives. Also, the requirements for a good biofeedback study necessitate an extensive number of baseline and training sessions. Since these requirements involve a considerable amount of both patients' and experimenters' time, practical matters severely limit the number of patients that can be seen within a given time span. Furthermore, any program that lasts more than a single session is likely to result in a patient loss. When the time period is expanded in order to obtain follow-up measures of a few months to a year, the patient loss is much greater. All of these factors contribute to the small number of patients in biofeedback studies.

Because blood pressure is such a variable measure to begin with, a large error term combined with small numbers of subjects often makes it difficult to obtain statistically significant results. The few patients who do not respond to treatment can have a tremendous influence on the group mean. Likewise, the reverse can occur and the overall effect of a given treatment can seem to be quite powerful, even though it is influenced primarily by extreme drops in pressure in only a few patients. Because of these problems, attempts should be made to accumulate data on larger numbers of patients, perhaps in much the same manner as in massive drug trials. Only with such large-scale studies can investigators achieve any meaningful results and generalize beyond their own samples of patients.

In the meantime, however, in the absence of large numbers of subjects, it is particularly important for experimenters to present their data in a manner that is as meaningful as possible. For example, although group means and standard deviations provide one type of information, the reader should also be informed about the relative progress or lack of progress of the individuals who make up these groups. In this manner, even if a statistical effect is not significant, the reader will know the exact number of patients who have reached some criterion level of blood pressure as a result of treatment.

INDIVIDUAL DIFFERENCES

Just as not all antihypertensive drugs are equally effective in lowering blood pressure in every hypertensive individual, there is no reason to assume that all behavioral techniques will result in automatic blood pressure reductions in anyone who is hypertensive. In fact, it is highly improbable that any single technique will be suitable for all hypertensives. Anyone who has conducted research in this area knows that some individuals respond to biofeedback with large blood pressure declines, whereas others show little or no change.

Even though such discrepancies exist, the problem of individual differences has only been infrequently discussed in the literature. In fact, the group model that is generally used assumes that if a given treatment is standardized across patients, such a treatment should affect all patients similarly. This issue has not been adequately dealt with, because so little is known about why individuals respond differentially to such treatments as biofeedback. Beyond the fact that biofeedback programs generally require that individuals be highly motivated to participate, there is a virtual lack of information regarding the characteristics of successful biofeedback subjects.

Future research should focus on seeking out those individuals who would benefit most from biofeedback treatment. Seer (1979) argues that single-case studies allow different modes of training to be suited to individual needs and would, therefore, be helpful in selecting appropriate treatment programs for hypertensive patients. While this is true, large-scale studies could also attempt to tease out those variables related to success in treatment.

In reviewing the hypertensive literature, Goldstein (1981) has concluded that, instead of there being a single personality pattern that is representative of hypertensives, there may be several subgroups, each displaying different behavior patterns. This has been suggested by the work of Esler, Julius, Zweifler, Randall, Harburg, Gardiner, and De Quattro (1977), who found high-renin essential hypertensives to differ both behaviorally and physiologically from normal-renin hypertensives. In view of these results, it would be of interest to determine whether any of these hypertensive subgroups respond differentially to various behavioral treatment programs.

STRESS

The majority of blood pressure investigations with hypertensives have focused on reducing blood pressure levels while patients have been resting. The utilization of biofeedback as a means of controlling blood pressure reactions to stress, however, is fairly unique, in spite of the well-known fact that patients with elevated blood pressures exhibit exaggerated pressor responses to a variety of stressful stimuli. Their pressor responses not only are greater in intensity than those of normals, but also take longer to return to baseline (Eyer, 1975; Gutmann & Benson, 1971; D. Shapiro & Goldstein, 1980). There is also evidence from animal research that blood pressure elevations become chronic when emotional stress is sustained (Eliot, 1977; Kagan &

Levi, 1974). The fact that blood pressure may not return to normal upon removal of the stressful stimulus implies not only that permanent impairment has occurred, but also that the problem of stress management is a significant one for hypertensives.

Patel (1975b) is one of the few investigators who has used behavioral methods to alter the hypertensive blood pressure response to stress. A combination of relaxation, meditation, and biofeedback (for GSR, EMG, and alpha waves in EEG) resulted in lower blood pressure during rest and in response to both exercise and cold pressor. Comparable drops in pressure were not observed in a control group given no specific treatment.

It has also been demonstrated that normal subjects can be taught with heart rate feedback to alter their heart rate in response to a cold pressor test (Victor, Mainardi, & D. Shapiro, 1978). From a study now being prepared by D. Shapiro and Greenberg (D. Shapiro & Greenberg, in preparation), it also appears that it is possible to train normotensives with blood pressure feedback to control their blood pressure response to a cold pressor test. This is clearly an area where research with hypertensives is needed. If it can be demonstrated that hypertensives can be trained to control their blood pressure responses to laboratory stressors, further attempts should be made to generalize these reactions to relevant situations in everyday life.

APPROPRIATE CONDITIONS FOR BIOFEEDBACK STUDIES

Because studies of biofeedback with hypertensives have been in progress for only about a decade, many of the crucial variables in these studies have not been clearly defined. Further research is needed to determine (1) the best variable to use for feedback (systolic or diastolic measures); (2) the most appropriate reinforcers; and (3) the number of treatment sessions necessary to produce a significant reduction in blood pressure.

Systolic or Diastolic Feedback?

It is not clear from the research in this area whether systolic measures, diastolic measures, or a combination of both measures of blood pressure should be utilized in studies of blood pressure feedback. It is even possible to utilize biofeedback not relating to blood pressure, as Patel (1977) has done, or to combine blood pressure with another variable, as Surwit *et al.* (1978) have done with heart rate.

Elder and his associates (Elder *et al.*, 1973) have suggested that experimenters use diastolic-contingent feedback, because diastolic blood pressure is more significant in the development of heart disease. Frumkin *et al.* (1978), arguing in a similar manner, claimed that diastolic pressure more closely reflects the level of peripheral vascular resistance. When Elder, Leftwich, and Wilkerson (1974) compared systolic with diastolic-contingent feedback, they found diastolic contingency to be the more effective method for controlling systolic and/or diastolic pressures.

In spite of these suggestions, some experimenters have utilized and achieved significant effects with systolic feedback. Kristt and Engel (1975) reported that training for decreases in systolic blood pressure resulted in both systolic and diastolic blood pressure reductions. Kleinman *et al.* (1977) obtained similar results with systolic feedback, but only diastolic decreases were significant. They felt that their results were due to the fact that both measures of pressure are correlated and that greater variability of systolic pressure, plus small sample size, precluded statistical significance. To complicate the issue further, Shannon, Goldman, and Lee (1978) have indicated that systolic and diastolic pressures can vary independently. In normal subjects trained to alter their systolic blood pressure, diastolic pressure often increased during systolic reductions.

All of these factors preclude the formation of any firm and consistent conclusions about the appropriate feedback contingent variable to use in feedback studies. Without further evidence it may be best to utilize the variable (systolic measure or diastolic measure) that appears to be more highly elevated in relation to the other in a given patient. D. Shapiro and Surwit (1979) have suggested that because systolic blood pressure is closely associated with morbidity and mortality rates in males over 45 years of age, systolic feedback should be utilized with male patients in this age group. In younger men, however, diastolic blood pressure would be more appropriate. On the other hand, morbidity and mortality in women of all ages is much more dependent on systolic blood pressure.

What Is the Best Reinforcer?

The presentation of blood pressure information to the patient is a critical variable in the reduction of blood pressure. Whether this information by itself is sufficient, or whether additional reinforcers are needed, has not been firmly established. Reinforcers may play a more important role in blood pressure control when normal subjects are being trained in biofeedback. For example, in addition to visual and auditory feedback, D. Shapiro *et al.* (1969) utilized slides of a nude from *Playboy* for changes in the desired direction. In another study of normal subjects, Fey and Lindholm (1975) combined visual feedback with brief verbal statements in the form of "good," "very good," or "excellent." Reinforcement was dependent upon how often the subject produced the desired response.

Elder *et al.* (1973) tested the effects of reinforcement on hypertensives by dividing subjects into the following three groups: (1) a control group receiving no feedback; (2) a group receiving a red light contingent on reductions in diastolic blood pressure; and (3) a group receiving verbal approval paired with the red light. Of the three conditions, the use of verbal approval and a light was most effective in producing a lowering of blood pressure between the third and the eighth sessions, whereas the red light alone did not show a significant effect until the seventh and eighth sessions.

Further studies like those of Elder *et al.* (1973) are necessary in order to determine how much reinforcement adds to the control of blood pressure. It is entirely possible that reinforcers may prove to be essential in lowering pressures in normotensives, but may have little or no effect in hypertensives. In our own research (Goldstein, Shapiro, Thananopavarn, & Sambhi, in press), although reinforcements have been utilized, it is apparent that reductions in pressure by themselves are highly reinforcing. A major concern of the majority of patients is a strong desire to be taken off all medications in order to rid themselves of disturbing side effects and of their dependency on the medication. Whether, even in a highly motivated individual, pressures can be reduced further by means of reinforcers remains at this point an empirical question.

How Many Treatment Sessions Are Needed?

A major question in this area has to do with the number of biofeedback sessions necessary to produce a significant reduction in blood pressure. It is now clear that the early single-session experiments were of insufficient duration to have had much effect on blood pressure. Although Surwit *et al.* (1978) suggested that their utilization of eight treatment sessions may not have been enough, no one knows what the critical number of sessions is. Because of limitations in cost and time, patients have usually come into the laboratory for a set number of sessions, varying between 5 and 20 (Blanchard, 1979).

Due to the apparent complexity of the learning process in biofeedback, several months of treatment may be necessary in order to train patients to control their pressure levels. Moreover, since patients do not all learn at the same rate, the critical number of sessions may vary with the individual. One patient may require 8 biofeedback sessions, whereas 20 sessions may be needed in the case of another. The model provided by Benson *et al.* (1971), which allows individuals to learn at their own rates, may be a good one to use in future studies.

DURATION OF EFFECTS

Investigators are generally concerned about the length of time that blood pressure will remain under control once the biofeedback training sessions have ended. Apparently the longer the duration of effects, the better the treatment. Does it follow, therefore, that biofeedback is ineffective if blood pressure becomes elevated again once treatment has terminated; and, if so, are investigators not expecting too much from biofeedback? After all, even the powerful effects of antihypertensive drugs do not persist if patients stop taking their medication.

Blanchard (1979) is of the opinion that a behavioral treatment such as biofeedback or relaxation must be regularly practiced for the effects to be maintained. Any discontinuation of practice at the end of treatment will consequently lead to a gradual return of elevated blood pressure. The superiority of relaxation techniques over biofeedback has been felt by some experimenters (e.g., Seer, 1979) to be due to the fact that patients can practice relaxation at home, whereas biofeedback training involves rather complex equipment that cannot be taken home. Kristt and Engel's use (1975) of the sphygmomanometer to maintain blood pressure control at home seems to have contributed to maintenance of reduced blood pressure once the laboratory sessions had ended. It would be extremely worthwhile for investigators in this area to construct some kind of biofeedback device, similar to Kristt and Engel's adaptation of the sphygmomanometer, that would be both portable and relatively inexpensive.

Until such a device is developed, the effects of biofeedback might be maintained by having patients monitor their home pressures both during training and in follow-up periods. The results of a study by Carnahan and Nugent (1975) suggest that patients can significantly lower their blood pressures merely by monitoring their pressures at home. Average drops in pressure were found to be about 10 mm Hg for both systolic and diastolic blood pressure.

A method that has not been considered in the literature and that might be used as a means of prolonging biofeedback effects involves the use of "booster" sessions. Once patients have completed biofeedback training, they could be requested to return to the laboratory for additional feedback sessions at periodic intervals. The actual time intervals necessary to maintain blood pressure control would have to be determined experimentally. Perhaps a combination of self-monitoring of pressures plus booster sessions would contribute maximally to prolonged maintenance of blood pressure control.

PLACEBO EFFECTS

In the process of performing clinical research, an investigator becomes aware of numerous factors that can influence the results of a study. While many of these factors can be controlled by the addition of multiple groups, it is usually impossible to control for everything in a single study. Many of these uncontrolled variables take the form of nonspecific effects—otherwise known as "placebo effects"—that are not part of a prescribed treatment or therapy but can strongly influence the outcome of a study.

A common placebo effect present in biofeedback studies arises because patients are suddenly given increased attention by a team of psychologists and physicians. Patients are now aware of being adequately cared for, and many of their anxieties and concerns are reduced. Moreover, with all this attention comes increased knowledge about hypertension. If patients are given sphygmomanometers to record their pressures outside the laboratory, daily blood pressure records provide them with a form of feedback, which informs them as to what activities lead to corresponding increases and decreases in blood pressure. Having confidence that a particular treatment will be effective can also influence the outcome of the treatment. This applies to the experimenters', as well as the patients', own belief systems. Finally, involving patients in a research program will probably have an effect on drug compliance. If patients have been receiving antihypertensive drugs, they will probably take their medication more consistently than they did before they were involved in the program.

An important question at this point in time is whether or not a placebo or nonspecific therapy will produce significant changes in blood pressure when such a treatment is introduced with as much enthusiasm as biofeedback or a new form of behavioral therapy generally is. The findings of Taylor *et al.* (1977) and Patel (1977) suggest that nonspecific therapy will add very little to the medical management of essential hypertension. On the other hand, a study by Goldring, Chasis, Schreiner, and Smith (1956) provide evidence of how effective a device can be when patients are convinced that it can produce a reduction in blood pressure. An electronic gadget with strange sparks and lights directed at different parts of a patient's body led to average blood pressure reductions of 27 mm Hg systolic and 18 mm Hg diastolic. The powerful effects of a placebo were also observed by Redmond, Gaylor, McDonald, and A. P. Shapiro (1974), who reported that verbal instructions to raise or lower blood pressure resulted in pressure and heart rate changes that were of a magnitude comparable to those reported in biofeedback studies. A comparable group given progressive relaxation showed no alteration of the blood pressure response.

The issue of placebo effects is complex and as yet unresolved. There are, however, indications that such nonspecific therapies have some effect on blood pressure control; attempts should be made, therefore, to incorporate them into the treatment of hypertension in order to make the effects of such treatment as powerful as possible.

MECHANISMS

After 10 years of conducting research on biofeedback with hypertensives, investigators are still unable to understand either the psychological or the physiological mechanisms involved. When patients trained in biofeedback procedures were asked to describe what they were doing to decrease their pressures, they were unable either to give an account of the process or to define the internal cues that indicated a reduction in pressure (Goldstein *et al.*, in press). In response to further questioning, patients reported that they tried a variety of strategies, such as altering their breathing, concentrating on pleasant thoughts, or relaxing. If there was a common thread that ran through all of the reports, it was an emphasis on some form of nonspecific relaxation. Schwartz (1973) feels that feedback enables the patient to learn to associate blood pressure changes with certain kinds of feelings, thoughts, situations, and actions. Somehow, without the patient being able to define what is involved, the learning process occurs.

Although it has not been definitely established, some investigators feel that biofeedback works through the same mechanisms as relaxation does by causing a diminution in general levels of physiological arousal (Taylor *et al.*, 1977). If this were true, then biofeedback would lower blood pressure by reducing the sympathetic responsiveness of the hypothalamus (see Patel, 1977). Experimenters who have investigated a number of physiological responses during biofeedback have indicated that the effects of blood pressure feedback are specific to the blood pressure system. Measures that have been used as indices of relaxation, such as brain alpha wave activity, breathing rate, and muscle tension, did not change during systolic blood pressure control periods in highly trained patients, even though blood pressure itself was affected (Kristt & Engel, 1975). Similarly, Goldstein *et al.* (in press) found that reductions in blood pressure as a result of biofeedback were unaccompanied by similar decreases in skin resistance, heart rate, respiration rate, or frontalis muscle tension.

Although the pathways involved in blood pressure control are known and have been described, it is not clear how biofeedback affects such pathways. A. P. Shapiro *et al.* (1977) have concluded that neither the peripheral nor central mechanisms involved in the self-regulation of blood pressure are currently known.

SUMMARY AND CONCLUSIONS

Because drugs do not always exert adequate control over blood pressure and may have disturbing side effects, the need for behavioral methods of blood pressure regulation has been emphasized. Biofeedback is suggested as one such method, and investigations utilizing biofeedback techniques have been evaluated. In general, individuals trained in biofeedback have learned to decrease their blood pressures, although the amount of the reduction varies from one study to the next.

One of the major problems with such studies has been a difficulty in adequately controlling significant variables. Patients have not always been carefully selected or adequately diagnosed, nor have their medications been continuously monitored. Where investigators have demonstrated significant blood pressure reductions as a result of biofeedback training, it is impossible to conclude without adequate control groups that such reductions were not due to factors other than the feedback itself. In addition, studies have often lacked sufficient numbers of blood pressure recordings during baseline and treatment sessions to ensure stability of pressures. Furthermore, very few investigators have assessed the degree to which blood pressure reductions have transferred to the patients' natural environments and the extent to which pressure reductions endured once treatment ended.

If the use of biofeedback as a treatment for hypertension is to continue, certain areas of investigation must be pursued. To begin with, the problem of individual differences should be investigated in order to detect those patients who would benefit most from biofeedback. Secondly, efforts should be concentrated on using biofeedback not only to lower hypertensives' resting responses, but to reduce their blood pressure reactions to stress as well. Future research programs should focus on answering questions about the appropriate variables to use for feedback, the most effective reinforcers, and the number of sessions necessary to control blood pressure adequately. Attempts should also be made to extend the effects of biofeedback treatment by experimenting with "booster" sessions after follow-up and by utilizing some type of home practice. Finally, experimenters should explore combined treatment techniques, such as relaxation coupled with biofeedback, in order to see whether the two treatments together can result in greater blood pressure control than can either technique alone.

At the present time, until more research is done, relaxation may offer a convenient alternative to biofeedback. The current literature indicates that, as a method of blood pressure control, relaxation is at least as effective as biofeedback. It offers the patient a technique that is easy to learn, can be practiced at home, and is much less costly than biofeedback.

ACKNOWLEDGMENT

This paper was supported by Research Grant HL19568, National Heart, Lung, and Blood Institute, National Institutes of Health.

REFERENCES

Agras, S., & Jacob, R. G. Hypertension. In O. F. Pomerleau & J. B. Brady (Eds.), *Behavioral medicine: Theory and practice*. Baltimore: Williams & Wilkins, 1979.

Benson, H., Shapiro, D., Tursky, B., & Schwartz, G. Decreased systolic blood pressure through operant conditioning techniques in patients with essential hypertension. *Science*, 1971, *173*, 740–742.

Blanchard, E. B. Biofeedback and the modification of cardiovascular dysfunctions. In R. J. Gatchel & K. P. Price (Eds.), *Clinical applications of biofeedback: Appraisal and status*. New York: Pergamon, 1979.

Blanchard, E. B., Miller, S. T., Abel, G. G., Haynes, M. R., & Wicker, R. Evaluation of biofeedback in the treatment of borderline essential hypertension. *Journal of Applied Behavior Analysis*, 1979, *121*, 99–109.

Brener, J., & Kleinman, R. A. Learned control of decreases in systolic blood pressure. *Nature*, 1970, *226*, 1063–1064.

Carnahan, J. E., & Nugent, C. A. The effects of self-monitoring by patients on the control of hypertension. *The American Journal of the Medical Sciences*, 1975, *269*(1), 69–73.

Elder, S. T., Leftwich, D. A., & Wilkerson, L. A. The role of systolic- versus diastolic-contingent feedback in blood pressure conditioning. *Psychological Record*, 1974, *24*, 171–176.

Elder, S. T., Ruiz, Z. R., Deabler, H. L., & Dillenkoffer, R. L. Instrumental conditioning of diastolic blood pressure in essential hypertensive patients. *Journal of Applied Behavior Analysis*, 1973, *6*, 377–383.

Eliot, R. Stress and cardiovascular disease. *European Journal of Cardiology*, 1977, *5*(2), 97–104.

Esler, M., Julius, S., Zweifler, A., Randall, O., Harburg, E., Gardiner, H., & De Quattro, V. Mild high-renin essential hypertension: Neurogenic human hypertension. *New England Journal of Medicine*, 1977, *296*, 405–411.

Eyer, J. Hypertension as a disease of modern society. *International Journal of Health Services*, 1975, *5*, 539–558.

Fey, S. G., & Lindholm, E. Systolic blood pressure and heart rate changes during three sessions involving biofeedback or no feedback. *Psychophysiology*, 1975, *12*, 513–519.

Fey, S. G., & Lindholm, E. Biofeedback and progressive relaxation: Effects on systolic and diastolic blood pressure and heart rate. *Psychophysiology*, 1978, *15*, 239–247.

Frankel, B. L., Patel, D. J., Horwitz, D., Friedewald, W. T., & Gaarder, K. R. Treatment of hypertension with biofeedback and relaxation techniques. *Psychosomatic Medicine*, 1978, *40*, 276–293.

Freis, E. D. The clinical spectrum of essential hypertension. *Archives of Internal Medicine*, 1974, *133*, 982–987.

Friedman, H., & Taub, H. A. The use of hypnosis and biofeedback procedures for essential hypertension. *The International Journal of Clinical and Experimental Hypnosis*, 1977, *25*, 335–347.

Frumkin, K., Nathan, R. J., Prout, M. F., & Cohen, M. C. Nonpharmacologic control of essential hypertension in man: A critical review of the experimental literature. *Psychosomatic Medicine*, 1978, *40*, 294–320.

Goldring, W., Chasis, H., Schreiner, G. E., & Smith, H. W. Reassurance in the management of benign hypertensive disease. *Circulation*, 1956, *14*, 260–264.

Goldstein, I. B. Assessment of hypertension. In L. A. Bradley & C. K. Prokop (Eds.), *Medical psychology: A new perspective*. New York: Academic Press, 1981.

Goldstein, I. B., Shapiro, D., Thananopavarn, C., & Sambhi, M. P. Comparison of drug and behavioral treatments of essential hypertension. *Health Psychology*, in press.

Gutmann, M. C., & Benson, H. Interaction of environmental factors and systemic arterial blood pressure: A review. *Medicine*, 1971, *50*, 543–553.

Hypertension Detection and Follow-Up Program Cooperative Group. Five-year findings of the Hypertension Detection and Follow-Up Program: I. Reduction in mortality of persons with high blood pressure, including mild hypertension. *Journal of the American Medical Association*, 1979, *242*, 2562–2571.

Jacob, R. G., Kraemer, H. C., & Agras, S. Relaxation therapy in the treatment of hypertension. *Archives of General Psychiatry*, 1977, *34*, 1417–1427.

Jacobson, E. Variation of blood pressure with skeletal muscle tension and relaxation. *Annals of Internal Medicine*, 1939, *12*, 1194–1212.

Kagan, A., & Levi, L. Health and environment—psychosocial stimuli: A review. *Social Science and Medicine*, 1974, *8*, 225–241.

Katkin, E. S., & Goldband, S. The placebo effect and biofeedback. In R. J. Gatchel & K. P. Price (Eds.), *Clinical applications of biofeedback: Appraisal & status*. New York: Pergamon, 1979.

Kleinman, K. M., Goldman, H., Snow, M. Y., & Korol, B. Relationship between essential hypertension and cognitive functioning: II. Effects of biofeedback training generalized to non-laboratory environment. *Psychophysiology*, 1977, *14*, 192–197.

Kristt, D. A., & Engel, B. T. Learned control of blood pressure in patients with high blood pressure. *Circulation,* 1975, *51,* 370–378.

Lane, J. D., Greenstadt, L., & Shapiro, D. *Pulse transit time and blood pressure: An intensive analysis.* Paper presented at the meeting of the Biofeedback Society of America, San Diego, February 1979.

Levy, R. I. Preventing the preventable. *American Pharmacy,* 1980, *20*(NS), 19–24.

Moeller, T. A. *Reduction of arterial blood pressure through relaxation training and correlates of personality in hypertensives.* Unpublished doctoral dissertation, Nova University, Fort Lauderdale, Florida, 1973,

Patel, C. Yoga and biofeedback in the management of hypertension. *Lancet,* 1973, *7837,* 1053–1055.

Patel, C. 12-month follow-up of yoga and biofeedback in the management of hypertension. *Lancet,* 1975, *7898,* 62–64. (a)

Patel, C. Yoga and biofeedback in the management of "stress," in hypertensive patients. *Clinical Science and Molecular Medicine,* 1975, *48*(Suppl.), 171–174. (b)

Patel, C. Biofeedback-aided relaxation in the management of hypertension. *Biofeedback and Self-Regulation,* 1977, *2,* 1–41.

Patel, C., & North, W. R. S. Randomized controlled trial of yoga and biofeedback in management of hypertension. *Lancet,* 1975, *7925,* 93–95.

Redmond, D. P., Gaylor, M. S., McDonald, R. H., & Shapiro, A. P. Blood pressure and heart rate response to verbal instructions and relaxation in hypertension. *Psychosomatic Medicine,* 1974, *36,* 285–297.

Reeves, J., & Shapiro, D. Biofeedback and relaxation in essential hypertension. *International Review of Applied Psychology,* 1978, *27,* 121–135.

Schultz, J. H., & Luthe, W. *Autogenic therapy: Autogenic methods* (Vol. 1). New York: Grune & Stratton, 1969.

Schwartz, G. E. Voluntary control of human cardiovascular integration and differentiation through feedback and reward. *Science,* 1972, *175,* 90–93.

Schwartz, G. E., & Shapiro, D. Biofeedback and essential hypertension: Current findings and theoretical concerns. *Seminars in Psychiatry,* 1973, *5,* 493–503.

Schwartz, G. E., Shapiro, D., & Tursky, B. Learned control of cardiovascular integration in man through operant conditioning. *Psychosomatic Medicine,* 1971, *33,* 57–62.

Seer, P. Psychological control of essential hypertension: Review of the literature and methodological critique. *Psychological Bulletin,* 1979, *86,* 1015–1043.

Shannon, B. J., Goldman, M. S., & Lee, R. M. Biofeedback training of blood pressure: A comparison of three feedback techniques. *Psychophysiology,* 1978, *15,* 53–59.

Shapiro, A. P., Schwartz, G. E., Ferguson, D. C. E., Redmond, D. P., & Weiss, S. M. Behavioral methods in the treatment of hypertension: A review of their clinical status. *Annals of Internal Medicine,* 1977, *86,* 626–636.

Shapiro, D., & Goldstein, I. B. Behavioral patterns as they relate to hypertension. In J. Rosenthal (Ed.), *Clinical pathophysiology of arterial hypertension.* New York: Springer, 1980.

Shapiro, D., & Greenberg, W. *Control of systolic blood pressure response to the cold pressor test by means of biofeedback training.* Manuscript in preparation.

Shapiro, D., Schwartz, G. E., & Tursky, B. Control of diastolic blood pressure in man by feedback and reinforcement. *Psychophysiology,* 1972, *9,* 296–304.

Shapiro, D., & Surwit, R. S. Learned control of physiological function and disease. In H. Leitenberg (Ed.), *Handbook of behavior modification and behavior therapy.* Englewood Cliffs, N.J.: Prentice-Hall, 1976.

Shapiro, D., & Surwit, R. S. Biofeedback. In O. F. Pomerlau & J. P. Brady (Eds.), *Behavioral medicine: Theory and practice.* Baltimore: Williams & Wilkins, 1979.

Shapiro, D., Tursky, B., Gershon, E., & Stern, M. Effects of feedback and reinforcement on the control of human systolic blood pressure. *Science,* 1969, *163,* 588–590.

Shoemaker, J. E., & Tasto, D. L. The effects of muscle relaxation on blood pressure of essential hypertensives. *Behaviour Research and Therapy,* 1975, *13,* 29–43.

Sokolow, M., Werdegar, D., Perloff, D. B., Cowan, R. M., & Brenenstuhl, H. Preliminary studies relating portably recorded blood pressure to daily life events, in patients with essential hypertension. *Bibliotheca Psychiatrica,* 1970, *144,* 164–189.

Steptoe, A. Voluntary blood pressure reductions measured with pulse transit time: Training conditions and reactions to mental work. *Psychophysiology,* 1977, *14,* 492–498.

Steptoe, A., & Johnston, D. The control of blood pressure using pulse wave velocity feedback. *Journal of Psychosomatic Research,* 1976, *20,* 417–424.

Surwit, R. S., Shapiro, D., & Good, M. I. A comparison of cardiovascular biofeedback, neuromuscular biofeedback, and meditation in the treatment of borderline essential hypertension. *Journal of Consulting and Clinical Psycholoyg,* 1978, *46,* 252–263.

Tarler-Benlolo, L. The role of relaxation in biofeedback training: A critical review of the literature. *Psychological Bulletin,* 1978, *85,* 727–755.

Taylor, C. B., Farquhar, J. W., Nelson, E., & Agras, S. Relaxation therapy and high blood pressure. *Archives of General Psychiatry,* 1977, *34,* 339–342.

Veterans Administration Cooperative Study Group on Antihypertensive Agents. Effects of treatment on morbidity in hypertension: I. Results in patients with diastolic blood pressure averaging 115 through 129 mm Hg. *Journal of the American Medical Association,* 1967, *202,* 1028–1034.

Veterans Administration Cooperative Study Group on Antihypertensive Agents. Effects of treatment on morbidity in hypertension: II. Results in patients with diastolic blood pressure averaging 90 through 114 mm Hg. *Journal of the American Medical Association,* 1970, *213,* 1143–1152.

Victor, R., Mainardi, J. A., & Shapiro, D. Effects of biofeedback and voluntary control procedures on heart rate and perception of pain during the cold pressor test. *Psychosomatic Medicine,* 1978, *40,* 216–225.

World Health Organization. *Hypertension and coronary heart disease: Classification and criteria for epidemiological studies* (WHO Technical Report Series No. 168). Geneva: Author, 1959.

7 BIOFEEDBACK IN HEART RATE CONTROL AND IN THE TREATMENT OF CARDIAC ARRHYTHMIAS

MARTIN D. CHEATLE AND THEODORE WEISS

Following Kimmel's demonstrations (1967) of operant-conditioning effects on the GSR, considerable attention was devoted to the possibility of voluntary control of human heart rate by means of biofeedback training. The typical training paradigm consisted of (1) allowing the subject access to exteroceptive feedback that conveys information about changes in heart rate (e.g., changes in tone pitch or meter needle deflection reflecting either increases or decreases in heart rate), and (2) giving in-

Martin D. Cheatle. Department of Psychiatry, University of Pennsylvania, Philadelphia, Pennsylvania.

Theodore Weiss. Department of Psychiatry and Biofeedback Unit, University of Pennsylvania, Philadelphia, Pennsylvania.

structions for the subject to change this feedback stimulus in some fashion (e.g., "Increase tone pitch" or "Move the needle to the left"). When the subject could consistently alter this feedback signal (i.e., heart rate) from a resting baseline level in the desired manner, this was taken as evidence that he or she could voluntarily control heart rate.

There is a large body of evidence that, by following this procedure, normal subjects can influence their heart rates (Blanchard & Young, 1973; Williamson & Blanchard, 1979a). These findings generated considerable enthusiasm for the notion that biofeedback techniques used effectively in heart rate control studies with normal subjects could be generalized for use in a clinical population—namely, patients with cardiac arrhythmias. However, research testing the efficacy of biofeedback in controlling clinically significant cardiac arrhythmias has been conflicting and in general not promising.

The major purposes of this chapter are threefold: (1) to provide a general review of the experimental literature on biofeedback-assisted heart rate control in normal subjects; (2) to review the attempts to use biofeedback in the treatment of a variety of cardiac arrhythmias (biofeedback is also compared to relaxation and to pharmacologic treatment of arrhythmias); and (3) to analyze, in the context of the biological constraints and mechanisms of the cardiovascular system, the shortcomings and possible future of biofeedback treatment for cardiac arrhythmias.

BIOFEEDBACK AND HEART RATE CONTROL: REVIEW OF STUDIES IN NORMAL SUBJECTS

Heart rate control has been one of the areas most extensively researched by biofeedback investigators. In this section, we provide a general overview of this research. A review of research on the important issue of mediation (Crider, Schwartz, & Schnidman, 1969) is not included. For a discussion of the possible role of somatic and cognitive mediators in heart rate control, the interested reader is referred to two exceptional articles by Blanchard and his associates (Blanchard & Young, 1973; Williamson & Blanchard, 1979a, 1979b).

In this section, a "significant" change in heart rate is defined as one that is statistically reliable. We agree with Engel (1974) that in studies of biofeedback and heart rate control with normal subjects, it is inappropriate to judge whether or not the magnitude of an observed heart rate change would be clinically significant. Here the term "clinically significant" is used only in reference to patients with medical disorders.

It is a well-documented fact that healthy subjects can learn to alter their heart rates significantly when given exteroceptive feedback of their cardiac activity. In the past 10 years, a number of studies have reported significant mean heart rate increases greater than 10 beats per minute (bpm) (e.g., Blanchard, Haynes, Young, & Scott, 1977; Blanchard, Young, Scott, & Haynes, 1974; Clemens & Shattock, 1979; Colgan, 1977; Davidson & Schwartz, 1976a; Gatchel, 1974; McCanne & Sandman, 1975a; Obrist, Galosy, Lawler, Gaebelein, Howard, & Shanks, 1975; etc.). Furthermore, in articles that reported individual data, there were examples of subjects who could significantly raise their heart rates greater than 15 bpm (e.g., Blanchard *et al.*, 1977; Scott, Blanchard, Edmunson, & Young, 1973; Scott, Peters, Gillespie, Blanchard, Edmunson, & Young, 1973; Wells, 1973), while others could increase theirs by more than 10 bpm (e.g., Headrick, Feather, & Wells, 1971; Scott, Blanchard, Edmunson, & Young, 1973; Stephens, Harris, & Brady, 1972). It has been noted (Williamson & Blanchard, 1979a), however, that there is a great deal of variability among subjects in the ability to accelerate heart rate. For example, Wells (1973) found that of nine subjects, six could raise their heart rates by at least 15 bpm, but the remaining three subjects could not increase theirs by more than 7 bpm.

In comparison to the numerous reports of subjects producing significantly large changes in heart rate as a result of learned cardiac rate acceleration training, positive results of biofeedback-assisted heart rate deceleration have not been as numerous or of the same magnitude. In their recent review, Williamson and Blanchard (1979a) discovered only five experiments that reported significant heart rate decreases of greater than 5 bpm (Bouchard & Granger, 1977; Colgan, 1977; Gatchel, 1976; Sirota, Schwartz, & Shapiro, 1974, 1976). In a recent unpublished study, McKinney, Geller, Gatchel, Barber, Bothner, and Phelps (1979) found significant heart rate decreases of more than 9 bpm. Of these studies, three (Bouchard & Granger, 1977; Gatchel, 1976; McKinney *et al.* 1979) compared heart rate deceleration over an experimental period to a preexperimental heart rate baseline. "Learned" heart rate deceleration was based on this comparison. However, Blankstein, Zimmerman, and Egner (1976) revealed evidence suggesting that using a preexperimental baseline as an index of learning fails to take account of habituating (i.e., falling) levels of cardiac rate and erroneously favors the finding of large decreases. Also, in one of the studies (Sirota, Schwartz, & Shapiro, 1974), the subjects were given only a brief, 5-minute preexperimental adaptation period. Therefore, the heart rate slowing reported in this study may be accounted for, at least to some degree, by the effect of the subject's inactivity during a 1-hour session. Thus, the cardiac deceleration observed across training trials in the majority of these studies may reflect a spontaneous change in heart rate resulting from adaptation, and not the acquisition of a learned cardiac response.

From this review, it is tempting to conclude that, whereas subjects given heart rate biofeedback can substantially increase their heart rates, the magnitude of learned heart rate deceleration is not as impressive. However, when commenting on the difference in magnitude of biofeedback-assisted cardiac acceleration and deceleration, the normal parameters of heart rate activity must be taken into account. The average heart rate of well-adapted subjects at rest is approximately 70 bpm. Heart rate decreases to a low of 50 to 55 bpm during sleep and increases to a high of 160 to 180 bpm during vigorous exercise (Brobeck, 1978). Thus, from a resting heart rate baseline of 70 bpm, the potential range of change for heart rate acceleration and deceleration is approximately 100 bpm and 15 bpm, respectively. In this perspective a learned heart rate increase of 15 bpm from a 70-bpm baseline is a 15% change in relation to the normal range of cardiac acceleration (i.e., 100 bpm). This is comparable to a learned heart rate deceleration of 2 to 3 bpm in relation to the normal range of heart rate deceleration (i.e., 15 bpm). Therefore, what appears to be a difference in magnitude between learned heart rate acceleration and deceleration in terms of absolute change may not be a difference in reality; the relative changes in heart rate allowed by the biological constraints of the cardiovascular system must be considered.

In summary, the weight of the evidence supports the contention that though there is individual variability, subjects who are given some form of cardiac biofeedback can learn to alter their heart rates significantly. The apparent discrepancy between the ability of subjects to increase and decrease their heart rates has led several theorists (e.g., Bell & Schwartz, 1975; Lang & Twentyman, 1974) to speculate that the mechanisms underlying learned heart rate acceleration and deceleration are different and therefore not amenable to the same training procedures. In fact, two strategies have been employed in an attempt to account both for this discrepancy and for the large amount of variability in the abilities of individual subjects to produce heart rate changes. These two approaches are reviewed in the following sections.

PARAMETRIC INVESTIGATIONS OF BIOFEEDBACK AND HEART RATE CONTROL

One approach that investigators have employed in attempting to account for the high degree of subject variability and to discover procedures to maximize voluntary heart rate deceleration has been to vary parameters of the biofeedback-training paradigm. Through these efforts, a number of parameters have been discovered to influence the acquisition of heart rate control. These are briefly reviewed here.

TYPE OF FEEDBACK

Two types of feedback have been employed in studies of biofeedback-assisted heart rate control, each of which provides different degrees of information concerning cardiac activity. With binary feedback, the subject is given dichotomous "yes–

no'' information about heart rate control. In other words, a criterion of successful heart rate change is established (e.g., 10% increase of heart rate above a pretreatment baseline level), and feedback consists of "Yes, this criterion has been met" or "No, it has not." In contrast, subjects given proportional feedback receive continuous beat-by-beat information about absolute levels of cardiac rate. Several studies comparing these two types of feedback found that, for increasing heart rate, the performance of subjects provided with proportional feedback was superior to subjects given binary feedback (Blanchard, Scott, Young, & Haynes, 1974; Colgan, 1977; Lang & Twentyman, 1974). One study that did not find an effect for feedback type (Young & Blanchard, 1974) used auditory feedback, in contrast to the studies that did find an effect of feedback, which used visual feedback. Whether or not differences in feedback sensory modality can account for this negative finding is not clear at this time.

With respect to lowering heart rate, there is also some evidence that proportional feedback is superior to binary feedback (Colgan, 1977). In general, it appears that the type of feedback used (proportional vs. binary) is a variable that influences heart rate control.

FEEDBACK FREQUENCY

Temporal aspects of the conditioning paradigm for heart rate control have been varied in several ways by investigators interested in testing a motor skills learning model of voluntary heart rate control (see Williamson & Blanchard, 1979b). In one study, Gatchel (1974) examined the effects of varied frequencies of feedback information on learning to increase and decrease heart rate by giving subjects proportional feedback after every beat, every 5 beats, or after every 10 beats. These feedback groups were compared to a tracking-task control group. Results revealed that, for increasing heart rate, the feedback groups were superior to the tracking-task control group, and that there was a significant linear trend across the feedback conditions. Subjects receiving beat-by-beat feedback were superior in increasing their heart rates to subjects in either the 5- or the 10-beat feedback groups, with the 5-beat group tending to be better than the 10-beat group. For heart rate deceleration, the feedback groups were significantly better than the tracking group, but there was no significant trend across feedback conditions.

In a second study, Haynes, Blanchard, and Young (1977) examined temporal aspects of heart rate biofeedback by distributing training sessions over varying time intervals. Subjects received four heart rate speeding trials, either all in one day, on 4 consecutive days, on every other day, or once every week for 4 weeks. All groups learned to increase heart rate, although there were no differences among the groups. Differences did arise, however, during a transfer trial (i.e., testing for heart rate control without feedback after feedback training). A week following training, subjects given a training trial once a week tended ($p < .10$) to do better in raising their heart rates than did subjects receiving a training session on 4 consecutive days.

In a final study, Williamson and Blanchard (1979c) explored the effects of delaying heart rate feedback on acquiring heart rate control. Subjects were given analogue heart rate feedback, either immediately or after delays of 1.4, 5, or 14 seconds. Williamson and Blanchard discovered that subjects receiving immediate feedback were able to increase or decrease their heart rates significantly, whereas a feedback delay of any duration disrupted subjects' ability to control heart rate.

These studies indicate that, in general, temporal aspects of the heart rate feedback process influence acquisition of learned heart rate control.

RESPONSE KNOWLEDGE

In a review of the early literature on human heart rate control, several methodological issues were discussed (Blanchard & Young, 1973). One of these issues was the question of whether it was important to inform subjects of the nature of the response they were attempting to control. Many early studies of biofeedback and heart rate control demonstrated significant changes in heart rate, even though subjects were unaware of the response to be controlled (e.g., Brener & Hothersall, 1966, 1967; Engel & Chism, 1967; Frazier, 1966; Levene, Engel, & Pearson, 1968). However, studies that directly examined the effects of subjects receiving knowledge of the response to be controlled discovered that specific response information enhanced control of both heart rate acceleration and deceleration (Bergman & Johnson, 1972; Blanchard, Scott, Young, & Edmunson, 1974; McCanne & Sandman, 1975a, 1976b). Thus, it appears that knowledge of the contingency between heart rate response and feedback facilitates the acquisition of heart rate control.

INCENTIVE

In the acquisition of any skill, reinforcement of the correct response is a critical component of the learning process (Mackintosh, 1975). In studies of human heart rate control, reinforcement typically consists of knowledge of the results of training (Blanchard & Young, 1973). While this might be reinforcing for a patient learning to gain control of a dysfunctional state, it may not be so for a healthy subject participating in a laboratory experiment. Several studies have examined whether the addition of a tangible reward (typically money) for successfully meeting a criterion of heart rate change would enhance heart rate control. Two studies used a within-subject design and compared a feedback-alone phase to a feedback-plus-incentive phase. Results of these studies indicated no clear difference between the use of monetary rewards and the knowledge of response for the acquisition of heart rate control (Blanchard, Young, Scott, & Haynes, 1974; Stephens, Harris, Brady, & Shaffer, 1975). However, in a third study (Lang & Twentyman, 1976), a between-group comparison of subjects receiving only feedback with subjects given only feedback in one phase and feedback plus monetary incentives in a second phase revealed that the added incentives facilitated heart rate speeding but not slowing during feedback sessions. During transfer trials without feedback, however, heart rate slowing was significantly enhanced by the addition of incentives, whereas heart rate speeding was not. Lang and Twentyman concluded that both heart rate speeding and slowing are enhanced by the addition of incentives, but that the effect is maximized at different points of training for the two tasks. In a final study (McCanne & Sandman, 1975b), subjects received three heart rate conditioning sessions employing only a monetary reinforcer and three sessions consisting of only visual feedback. Half the subjects received the trials with monetary reinforcement first, while the remaining subjects received the visual feedback trials first. The results indicated that subjects who received monetary reinforcement initially were better able to accelerate their heart rates than were subjects who received visual feedback trials initially. There was no difference between the groups during heart rate deceleration trials. Postexperimental interviews revealed that subjects who received monetary reinforcement first reported feeling more motivated to control their own physiological responses than did the subjects who received visual feedback first. Subjects in this latter condition reported that they felt initially discouraged by their lack of ability to control their responses, and that this discouragement persisted even when their correct responses were monetarily rewarded. These results suggest that an initial phase of monetary reinforcement may motivate subjects to do well at first, and that this enthusiasm may persist even when monetary reinforcement is no longer available. Perhaps, at this point in training, the act of performing well (i.e., positive response knowledge) becomes reinforcing in itself.

In summary, findings of the investigations examining the effect of supplementary tangible incentives on voluntary heart rate control are conflicting. Perhaps one way to maximize any effect that added incentives might have on heart rate control would be to allow subjects to select their own rewards. This could increase the saliency of the reinforcer, which has been demonstrated in the animal conditioning literature (Rescorla & Wagner, 1972) to facilitate learning of a task. McKinney *et al.* (1979) provide an example of this approach. In this study of heart rate deceleration, reinforcement consisted of points or tokens each time a criterion for slowing heart rate was met. At the end of training, these points could be exchanged for a variety of rewards (from records to money). Unfortunately, there were no comparison groups that received only feedback or feedback and a fixed type of reinforcer.

AMOUNT OF TRAINING

In laboratory studies of human and animal learning, learning, as indexed by performance, is strongly related to the amount of training. In an effort to increase the magnitude of effects in biofeedback-assisted heart rate control, many researchers extended the number of training trials. Although it is difficult to make comparisons across studies, in general it appears that there is no consistent advantage in extending the amount of training. For example, Davidson and Schwartz (1976a) reported that subjects given four 1-minute feedback trials significantly increased their heart rates on the average of 10.06 bpm. This was comparable to what Obrist *et al.* (1975) found when subjects with similar instructions (i.e., "Sit still and breathe normally") were administered 30 1-minute trials—an average increase of 10.4 bpm. These results are reported in terms of group means. However, studies that have reported individual data reveal that, for some subjects, extending training clearly enhances the magnitude of learned heart rate acceleration (Blanchard, Scott, Young, & Haynes, 1974; Colgan, 1977; Headrick *et al.* 1971; Wells, 1973). A striking example of the effect of extended training on an individual's performance is provided by Headrick *et al.* (1971), who gave 12 subjects 10 training trials of biofeedback-assisted heart rate control. At the end of training, subjects were able to increase their heart rates significantly (by an average of 3.40 bpm), but were unable to decrease their heart rates at all. One outstanding subject was capable of raising his heart rate as much as 35 bpm. A subject with below-average performance (a net increase of 3 bpm during the first five trials and a decrease of 1 bpm during the last five trials) was selected to receive extended training. After 34 additional training trials, he was capable of regularly increasing his heart rate by 5 to 10 bpm. On trial, 43 heart rate increases of as great as 44 bpm occurred, and these averaged 30 bpm for the duration of the trial. There was no effect of extended training on heart rate deceleration. Headrick *et al.* concluded that, for some individuals, the amount of training needed to produce effective heart rate control may be in the range of 50 to 100 1-minute trials. Thus, extended training appears to allow subjects who are slower in acquiring the response contingency between feedback and heart rate the opportunity to do so.

To summarize briefly, the strategy of varying training parameters has been successful in identifying critical variables that influence the acquisition of voluntary heart rate control. Much of the variability across subjects in the ability to increase heart rate can be accounted for by these variables. Varying the training parameters, however, has had little effect on enhancing voluntary heart rate deceleration. This reconfirms the hypothesis that the mechanisms underlying voluntary heart rate acceleration and deceleration are different and thus not influenced by the same factors: clearly, however, the biologically restricted range for heart rate deceleration must be taken into account in any theory of biofeedback and heart rate control.

INDIVIDUAL DIFFERENCES

The large intersubject variability in voluntary heart rate control studies suggests that the mechanisms that mediate learned heart rate changes are much more complex than researchers had originally thought. McCanne and Sandman (1976a) suggested that investigators interested in discovering optimal training procedures for heart rate control should be more sensitive to individual differences and, in fact, should incorporate these differences in theorizing about possible mechanisms that mediate learned heart rate changes. Many researchers have adopted this strategy and have attempted to uncover psychological and physiological factors that can account for individual differences.

PSYCHOLOGICAL FACTORS

One of the first psychological factors found to be related to voluntary heart rate control was Rotter's "locus of control of reinforcement" (Rotter, 1966). "Locus of control" is a personality construct governing the effects of reinforcement on preceding behaviors; briefly, these effects depend on whether individuals perceive the reinforcement as contingent on their behavior ("internal locus of control") or as independent of their behavior ("external locus of control").

Several studies have shown that locus of control, as measured in terms of Rotter's Internal–External (I-E) Locus of Control Scale, was correlated with the magnitude of voluntary heart rate change (Fotopolous, 1970; Ray, 1974; Ray & Lamb, 1974). Ray (1974) found that external control subjects were superior to internal control subjects in slowing heart rates, but that internal controls were significantly better in heart rate speeding. These promising results, however, have not been replicated by other investigators (Bell & Schwartz, 1975; Lang, 1975; Lang, Troyer, Twentyman, & Gatchel, 1975).

In an effort to discover other psychological variables that might be associated with voluntary heart rate changes, Stephens *et al.* (1975) trained subjects to increase and decrease their heart rates with cardiac feedback, and then correlated their results with psychological test scores from the Minnesota Multiphasic Personality Inventory (MMPI). They reported significant correlations between Barron's Es Scale ($r = +.32$ for speeding and $-.32$ for heart rate slowing), Welsh's Factor A ($r = -.44$ for speeding and $+.31$ for slowing), and changes in raising and lowering heart rate. The Es Scale is described as reflecting the subject's "ego strength," while Welsh's Factor A is related to numerous indices of anxiety.

In contrast to these results, Cox and McGuinness (1977) found that only subjects who measured high in anxiety on the IPAT Anxiety Scale could significantly increase their heart rates, whereas only subjects low in measured anxiety could significantly decrease their heart rates. These findings are directly opposite to the findings of Stephen *et al.* on heart rate control and anxiety. Furthermore, Lang *et al.* (1975) found no relationship between anxiety and heart rate changes. These conflicting results are difficult to interpret. The fact that the studies used different measures of anxiety may contribute to the contradictory results.

Other personality traits that have been found to be significantly correlated with heart rate control are impulsivity (Lang *et al.*, 1975), exhibitionism, deference, succorance, and aggressiveness (Pardine & Napoli, 1977).

In general, the attempts to correlate psychological traits and success in voluntary heart rate control have not been impressive. One inherent problem in this sort of research endeavor is that there is a great deal of skepticism about the reliability (as evidenced by the inconsistent results relating anxiety and heart rate control) and validity of the available psychological tests.

PHYSIOLOGICAL FACTORS

Weiss and Engel (1975) employed biofeedback training in an attempt to increase ventricular heart rate (VHR) in subjects with complete heart block. In complete heart block, the heart's atria and ventricles beat independently. The atria beat at 60 to 80 bpm, while the ventricles beat at a much lower rate of 30 to 45 bpm. Subjects were given feedback of their VHR and were requested to increase the rate above a control level. Although exercise and beta-adrenergic drugs increased VHR in all subjects, none of the subjects was able to increase VHR voluntarily. Since the nervous system only minimally affects the chronotropic action of the ventricles, Weiss and Engel proposed that the subjects' failure to learn VHR control may reflect the fact that appropriate innervation is necessary for learning heart rate control.

Several specific physiological variables also have been shown to be highly correlated with changes in heart rate during biofeedback training. These are briefly reviewed here.

Heart Rate Reactivity

Several researchers have observed that the magnitude of heart rate acceleration during biofeedback training can be predicted by the subject's prefeedback level of proficiency at heart rate control (Bell & Schwartz, 1975; Stephens *et al.*, 1975). Related to this finding is the observation that baseline heart rate variability is strongly correlated with subsequent feedback assisted heart rate control. Gatchel (1974) found that heart rate variability during an initial rest period was positively correlated with average speeding performance during feedback trials ($r > +.40$). Several groups (Lang *et al.*, 1975; Stephens *et al.*, 1975) reported similar findings for heart rate speeding, but also noted a significant relationship between heart rate variability and heart rate slowing (r's $> +.50$).

These findings suggest that heart rate variability (i.e., cardiac system lability) is one example of a predisposed biological factor that varies across subjects and influences the degree of learned heart rate control.

Electrodermal Lability

In a recent report, Katkin and Shapiro (1979) found that voluntary heart rate control varied as a function of individual differences in electrodermal lability. Specifically, on the basis of the baseline frequency of spontaneous conductance fluctuations, subjects were divided into "labile" and "stabile" groups. Results indicated that electrodermally stabile subjects produced significantly greater voluntary heart rate increases than did electrodermally labile subjects. There was no difference between groups in heart rate deceleration. This is another example of individual differences in physiological subject characteristics as important potential predictors of the effectiveness of biofeedback training.

Autonomic Perception

The relationship between autonomic awareness and heart rate control is another area that has recently received a great deal of attention. The notion is that heart rate control requires subjects to be able to perceive some aspect of their cardiac activity. Thus, the ability to control heart rate should vary according to the degree of awareness subjects have of this activity.

In testing this hypothesis, three different procedures have been employed to assess cardiac awareness. The most frequently used procedure has been the Autonomic Perception Questionnaire (APQ) developed by Mandler, Mandler, and Uviller (1958). The results of the studies using the APQ, however, have been conflicting. Three studies found a significant correlation between APQ scores and the ability of subjects to alter their heart rates (Bergman & Johnson, 1971; Blanchard, Young, & McLeod, 1972; Blankstein, 1975). Three other studies that assessed cardiac awareness by the APQ method, however, failed to replicate this effect (McCanne & Sandman, 1976b; McFarland, 1975; Whitehead, Drescher, Heiman, & Blackwell, 1977). Three studies employed a cardiac awareness questionnaire other than the APQ. These studies also found no difference in the magnitude of voluntary heart rate change between questionnaire-defined cardiac "aware" and "unaware" subjects (Lang *et al.*, 1975; Sirota *et al.*, 1974, 1976).

A more direct assessment of autonomic perception has involved subjects' attempts to discriminate between heart rate levels. Only two studies have employed this procedure. McFarland (1975) found that cardiac awareness was significantly related to subsequent heart rate control when awareness was defined in terms of a discrimination task. Whitehead *et al.* (1977), however, using a different discrimination task, failed to replicate McFarland's results.

A heart rate tracking task is a third procedure that has been used to measure autonomic awareness. Subjects are typically asked to track their heart rates by means of a button-pushing response. Autonomic awareness is defined in terms of successful tracking performance. Using this method, several investigators provided the most convincing evidence that ability to discriminate aspects of cardiac activity has functional implications for the acquisition of voluntary cardiac control (Kleinman & Brener, 1970; McFarland, 1975; McFarland & Campbell, 1975).

We agree with Carroll's conclusion (1977) that while results on the relationship between autonomic awareness and heart rate control are promising, more fundamental work needs to be completed on the assessment of cardiac perception.

Blood Pressure Regulation

Lott and Gatchel recently (1978) examined the possible influence of blood pressure homeostasis on voluntary heart rate control. They hypothesized that if voluntary heart rate changes are constrained by the blood pressure homeostatic system, then subjects who had poor blood pressure regulation would be less restricted and thus reveal greater heart rate changes than those with a well-regulated system. Using a cold pressor test, subjects were classified as "good" and "poor" regulators of blood pressure prior to bidirectional heart rate feedback training. Results indicated that high cold pressor reactors (poor regulators) produced significantly larger heart rate changes than did the low cold pressor reactors (good regulators). During training changes in stroke volume, calf blood flow, systolic and diastolic blood pressure, and respiration were recorded. Not only did poor and good regulators differ in the magnitude of heart rate change, they also demonstrated different response topographies when the records of these physiological responses accompanying heart rate changes were examined.

These results indicate that phasic blood pressure regulation influences the process of voluntary heart rate control. Also, the finding that different physiological response patterns were associated with the differing heart rate control performances of the two blood pressure regulation groups suggests that different mechanisms were employed by these groups to produce voluntary heart rate changes.

BIOFEEDBACK AND HEART RATE CONTROL: REVIEW OF STUDIES IN ARRHYTHMIC PATIENTS

In the normally beating human heart, the sinoatrial node initiates the cardiac impulse, discharging 60 to 100 times per minute. These impulses are conducted through the heart in a particular sequence, causing contraction of the cardiac chambers and the associated pumping of blood. A cardiac arrhythmia is an abnormality in either the site of impulse formation, the conduction sequence, the heart rate, or the rhythm with which the heart beats. The management of arrhythmias is considered an important medical problem, particularly in patients who also have coronary artery disease or cardiac failure, or in whom the arrhythmia itself gravely compromises cardiac functioning.

Almost all of the clinical applications of biofeedback-assisted cardiac control have been in the treatment of cardiac arrhythmias. Recently, Weiss (1977) reviewed the literature on biofeedback and cardiovascular dysfunctions. He found that small groups of patients with a variety of arrhythmias have benefited clinically from biofeedback training. Since this review, however, there have been few published reports on biofeedback-assisted control of cardiac arrhythmias. In fact, there has been less research on the use of biofeedback in arrhythmia management than on its use in other clinical areas (e.g., hypertension, Raynaud's disease, and migraine and tension headaches). We believe that there are two reasons for this dearth of research. First, cardiac arrhythmias tend to be viewed as a more serious problem than do the other clinical conditions that have been studied. Thus, patients with arrhythmias are likely to be treated with traditional pharmacological methods. Second, in general, the results of biofeedback studies with arrhythmia patients have been discouraging. Investigations with small numbers of patients typically have been unsuccessful in significantly modifying the arrhythmias; the studies often are not published, and the researchers have abandoned this area. The published and—when possible—the unpublished research that has been done is reviewed here.

PREMATURE VENTRICULAR CONTRACTIONS

Approximately 5% of the otherwise normal, healthy adult population, and up to 15% of in-hospital populations, show premature ventricular beats on electrocardiograms (Bellet, 1972). Biofeedback investigators have paid particular attention to premature beats that originate in the ventricles (premature ventricular contractions, or PVCs) for two reasons: their relationship to sudden death in certain patients (Gradman, Bell, & DeBusk, 1977) and the observation that these premature beats can be influenced by the central nervous system (Lown, Verrier, & Rabinowitz, 1977).

The most extensive published report in this area was a series of systematic case studies by Weiss and Engel (1971). Eight patients with well-documented and frequent PVCs received training in biofeedback-assisted heart rate control. By learning to control their heart rates voluntarily, these patients, it was hoped, would acquire a technique to decrease PVC frequency. Using a beat-by-beat digital feedback display, the authors trained patients to increase, decrease, and alternately increase and decrease heart rate. Next, most patients were instructed to reduce the amount of heart rate variability by keeping their heart rates within a specified range. An important aspect of this phase was that the feedback also gave the patients direct information about PVC frequency. To facilitate transfer of the task to the nonlaboratory environment, feedback was systematically faded out in the final phase of training, while the patients were slowing their heart rates or keeping them within a specified range. Results indicated that all patients showed some degree of heart rate control and that, at the end of training, five out of eight patients had reduced their PVC frequency. Initial follow-up studies indicated that, in four of these patients, the clinical benefit persisted after training. In fact, one patient was able to maintain a reduction in PVC frequency for over 21 months. A follow-up for 5 years or to the time of a patient's death showed clear clinical benefit in terms of persistently reduced PVC frequency for only the one patient noted above, a possible but equivocal PVC reduction in one patient, and no clear long-term benefit in four patients (Weiss & Baile, 1977). In two patients outcome was indeterminate, as new antiarrhythmic drugs were added to their regimen because multifocal PVCs were detected during the initial study's extensive monitoring.

An interesting individual difference was also observed in the Weiss and Engel study (1971). Pharmacological studies suggested that in one patient a decrease in beta-adrenergic activity to the heart was associated with PVC reduction, while in another patient PVC reduction was associated with an increase in efferent vagal tone. The heterogeneity of autonomic nervous system effects on PVCs indicates that there also may be individual differences in the physiological mechanisms that patients employ in controlling PVC frequency.

In the same laboratory, Engel and Bleecker (1974) replicated the main findings of this first study with another patient. During pretraining, this patient averaged 12 PVCs per minute. In the course of training, the frequency of PVCs declined to fewer than .5 PVCs per minute. During range training—when the patient received direct feedback of PVC frequency—she emitted no PVCs. Follow-up testing 9 months after training also revealed no evidence of PVCs. This improvement persisted for 18 months, at which time the patient developed intermittent atrial fibrillation, and her PVCs became more frequent. An effort to interrupt one episode of paroxysmal atrial fibrillation with several hours of heart rate biofeedback was unsuccessful

(Gottlieb & Engel, unpublished observation). At 2 years after the study, her fibrillation became fixed, and PVCs again became infrequent (Weiss & Baile, 1977).

In another laboratory (Pickering & Gorham, 1975), a 31-year-old woman with a ventricular parasystolic rhythm received heart rate biofeedback training. This patient's PVCs were not dependent, always being absent below a rate of 72 bpm and always present over a rate of 106 bpm. As a result of biofeedback training, the patient was able voluntarily to increase her heart rate by 25 bpm and decrease it by 1 to 2 bpm. Both voluntary heart rate speeding and exercise brought on PVCs, but as training progressed the threshold at which her PVCs typically occurred increased from 79 to 94 bpm. This change in threshold allowed the patient to engage in many nonstrenuous activities without having PVCs. This case study serves as another example of PVC management with heart rate biofeedback training, although the relevancy of daily treadmill exercise at the end of each session to the effects seen cannot be ruled out. In an extension of this work, Pickering and Miller (1977) found that two patients with high frequencies of PVCs and, at times, bigeminal rhythms learned to suppress their arrhythmias using a biofeedback heart rate control technique. Biofeedback aided one of the patients in controlling PVC frequency where a variety of antiarrhythmic drugs had failed. Only atropine was successful in suppressing the PVCs in this patient. A 2-month follow-up on the other patient revealed that he could still suppress PVCs approximately 50% of the time.

Since 1977 there have been no further published reports on biofeedback training for PVC management. However, in a recent unpublished study (Twentyman, 1980), two patients with PVCs were administered 20 1-hour sessions of biofeedback-assisted heart rate control. Over the 20 sessions, neither patient was able to decrease the frequency of PVCs consistently, and training was discontinued. Similar findings were made in a second unpublished report (Bergerman, 1980). One subject with PVCs as frequent as 15 per minute was given 27 2-minute sessions of biofeedback-assisted heart rate acceleration and deceleration training. Although the patient was able to suppress PVCs at times during training, by the end of it he could not exert any control over the arrhythmia. One major difference between this last study and the previous studies, which found positive effects of biofeedback on PVC suppression, is the amount of training the patient received. The patient received a total of 54 minutes of training. In the study by Weiss and Engel (1971), the amount of training received by subjects varied. In examining the individual data, Blanchard (1979) found that if the patient samples are divided into those receiving 47 or more training sessions and those receiving fewer than 47 sessions, there is a significant relationship between treatment length and treatment outcome (PVC reduction). Thus, the failure of the one patient in the unpublished report to suppress PVCs may reflect insufficient training, rather than a null effect of biofeedback training.

Consistent with this hypothesis is another unpublished report by Weiss and his associates (Weiss, Reichek, Greenspan, Kastor, & Schwartz, unpublished observation). A group of 12 PVC patients was given 24 16-minute sessions of heart rate biofeedback, including acceleration and deceleration training. No patient was able to produce a sustained reduction in PVC frequency.

In general, the results of these studies suggest that clinically significant changes in the frequency of PVCs can be achieved in some patients by training in biofeedback-assisted heart rate speeding and slowing. However, it seems clear that protracted training is necessary to achieve this effect.

TACHYARRHYTHMIAS

Patients with two types of tachyarrhythmia have been treated with biofeedback.

Sinus Tachycardia

Sinus tachycardia is an abnormally high cardiac rate (over 100 bpm) in which the rhythm is still controlled by the sinoatrial pacemaker. The occurrence of this arrhythmia is quite common. Four patients with sinus tachycardia have been successfully treated with biofeedback training in heart rate deceleration. One patient (Scott, Blanchard, Edmunson, & Young, 1973) was a 46-year-old man with a 20-year history of sinus tachycardia who had not been able to work because of this condition for 14 months prior to the study. During 43 trials with heart rate biofeedback, this patient was able to decrease his heart rate from a baseline level of 89 bpm to an average of 72 bpm during the last six trials. After training, his heart rate stabilized at 77 bpm. A 16-month informal follow-up revealed that this patient had obtained a job after having been out of work for 16 months as a result of the sinus tachycardia condition. Also, he was able to decrease his dosage of a minor tranquilizer from 40 mg per day to less than 10 mg per day. A second patient in the same study was a 50-year-old man who had a 26-year history of tachycardia and had been unemployed for 27 months prior to the study because of the tachycardia and feelings of anxiety. After 17 heart rate feedback trials, his heart rate declined from a resting baseline level of 96 bpm to an average of 82 bpm. By the end of the study, his heart rate stabilized at 78 bpm. No follow-up was described. A third patient (Engel & Bleecker, 1974) treated with biofeedback was a 53-year-old woman who had had sinus tachycardia for 4 years prior to the investigation. Over this 4-year period, her pulse rate never fell below 80 bpm, and it averaged 106 bpm during 50 different observations. Administration of barbiturates, digitalis, and small doses of quinidine and phenothiazine were not effective in controlling her condition. Over the course of 21 heart rate slowing sessions, her heart rate fell from an average of 86.3 bpm during early training to an average of 68.5 bpm during later sessions.

During training, independent measurements of her heart rate outside the laboratory by her own physician revealed an average of approximately 75 bpm. Also, her blood pressure dropped from 140/80 mm Hg before training to 115/75 mm Hg at the end of training. There was no follow-up reported.

A final case study (Weiss & Brady, 1978) was a 20-year-old woman with a 5-year history of sinus tachycardia and "skipped heart beats" (i.e., atrial premature contractions). Her only medication was 10 mg diazepam at bedtime for sleep. After four 1-hour adaptation sessions, she received 10 trial blocks of relaxation training (metronome-conditioned relaxation technique) and heart rate biofeedback training alternately in an ABAB design during 20 sessions. By the end of the first 20 training trials (10 relaxation and 10 biofeedback), the patient's heart rate declined from an adapted baseline level of 80 bpm to between 72 and 75 bpm at the end of the relaxation phase, and to under 70 bpm after biofeedback training. In the next block of relaxation training sessions, the patient's heart rate averaged 77 to 78 bpm, and during the last block of biofeedback sessions her heart rate was typically in the low 70s. There was no significant difference between relaxation and biofeedback training during the first 10 trials, but in the last 10 trials biofeedback produced significantly lower heart rates. After completing the laboratory phase of the study, the patient continued to practice the heart rate slowing technique to prevent or abort tachycardia episodes. She was able to control her tachycardia condition for over a year after the completion of training. She also reported that the frequency of premature atrial contractions, of which she was accurately aware, was reduced from an almost daily occurrence to occurrence only every few weeks.

Supraventricular Tachycardia

Two patients (Engel & Bleecker, 1974) with supraventricular tachycardia were successfully treated with heart rate biofeedback training. One patient was a 41-year-old man diagnosed as having paroxysmal atrial tachycardia 10 years prior to the study. At the time of the study, he was admitted to the hospital because his arrhythmia had led to exercise intolerance, paroxysmal nocturnal dyspnea, orthopnea, and evidence of mild congestive heart failure. His heart rate ranged from 130 to 140 bpm. In past hospitalizations, a variety of antiarrhythmic drugs had failed to ameliorate his condition. Over a 15-day period, the patient was administered 25 30-minute biofeedback heart rate slowing sessions. By the 15th day, his exercise tolerance had increased and his cardiogram had revealed a stable, normal sinus rhythm. The patient received five additional sessions 3 weeks after completing training. During two of these, his heart rate was approximately 60 bpm, while, at the time of the three other sessions, his rate varied from 120 to 160 bpm. During one session, he was able to convert an episode of supraventricular tachycardia with a rate of 156 bpm to a normal sinus rhythm of 66 bpm. During 5 months following training, his heart rate ranged from 60 to 75 bpm with no evidence of congestive heart failure.

A second patient was a 36-year-old woman with a history of paroxysmal atrial tachycardia and episodes of sinus tachycardia, and with a heart rate between 120 and 130 bpm. She was trained to slow, speed, and alternately slow and speed her heart. Following training, she was able to reduce the frequency of tachycardia episodes from approximately one per month prior to training to only one during the 6 months of follow-up. She reported that she was able to slow her heart voluntarily without medical intervention.

ATRIAL FIBRILLATION AND FLUTTER

Atrial fibrillation is the second most common arrhythmia after premature beats. It is one of the most important, because it is frequently associated with organic heart disease and heart failure. It differs from atrial flutter in that the atrial rate is lower in flutter—usually about 300 bpm. Also, in fibrillation, the P waves on the electrocardiogram—reflecting atrial electrical activity—are more erratic in form, and the ventricular response tends to be more irregular than in flutter. In a single group study (Bleecker & Engel, 1973a), six patients with atrial fibrillation were given biofeedback training in speeding and slowing VHR. VHR was designated as the target response because of its relationship to the clinical manifestations of atrial fibrillation. Results indicated that all patients were able to increase and decrease VHR significantly. Pharmacologic studies suggested that the learned control of VHR was mediated at the atrioventricular node by changes in efferent vagal tone to the heart. Since the primary goal of this study was not clinical, no information concerning clinical changes or follow-up was included.

In a clinical case study (Weiss & Brady, 1978), a 60-year-old man with a 5-year history of paroxysmal atrial fibrillation and flutter was first given relaxation training, which was later followed by heart rate biofeedback training. Near the end of the course of 18 relaxation training sessions, the patient's dosage of propranolol was tapered off and finally discontinued. During the 2 weeks after the discontinuation of his medication, the patient's arrhythmia recurred twice. Propranolol was reinstated, since this was a considerably higher frequency than he had previously experienced. Next, the patient was given a portable heart rate meter and requested to practice heart rate control at home twice a day. Also, over a 7-week period, he was given eight biofeedback-assisted heart rate control sessions in the laboratory. After the sixth session, the patient's dosage of propranolol was slowly reduced. During the following 2 weeks he had three episodes of atrial flutter. An attempt was made to interrupt the third episode using heart rate biofeedback. Although training was carried out for over 3 hours, the flutter persisted, and training had to be terminated. Thus, as with relaxation training, heart rate biofeedback was unsuccessful in ameliorating his arrhythmia. Two other patients with atrial fibrillation were studied incompletely because of poor adherence to the treatment regimen (Weiss & Brady, 1978). Neither patient benefited from relaxation or biofeedback training, but clearly lack of motivation to practice the techniques was a factor in this failure.

WOLFF-PARKINSON-WHITE SYNDROME

Wolff–Parkinson–White syndrome (WPW) is a preexcitation condition in which the atrial impulse bypasses the normal atrioventricular conduction pathway and activates the ventricular muscle earlier than it would if the impulse were conducted through the normal pathway. This conduction abnormality often is associated with paroxysmal tachycardia (Bellet, 1972).

Two patients with WPW syndrome attempted to control their arrhythmias with biofeedback training. One patient (Bleecker & Engel, 1973b) was a 29-year-old woman with a 10-year history of tachycardia treated with various antiarrhythmic drugs. During the last 3 years prior to the study, the presence of intermittent WPW syndrome, Type A, was detected. First, the patient was trained to slow, speed, and alternately slow and speed her heart rate. Next, she received a number of biofeedback sessions to control her atrioventricular conduction pathway. Control was made possible by selecting an electrocardiographic lead in which the major QRS complex —reflecting ventricular electrical activity—of WPW-conducted beats was of opposite polarity from that of normally conducted beats. Feedback consisted of signal detection equipment that was programmed to trigger a clicker selectively when detecting only normally conducted QRS complexes. During training, the patient was instructed to increase normal conduction (i.e., to increase the frequency of clicker sounds), then to increase WPW conduction (i.e., to decrease the frequency of clicker sounds), and finally to increase normal and WPW conduction alternately. In the final phase of training, the patient was instructed to increase normally conducted beats without feedback. Results indicated that the patient was able to modify successfully both heart rate and atrioventricular conduction during feedback training. She also was able to increase normal conduction during transfer trials (without feedback). Pharmacologic studies suggested that the mechanism by which she modified atrioventricular conduction was by changing vagal tone to the heart. Also, analyses of the patterns of heart rate changes and conduction changes revealed that the two responses were independent. In other words, her control of the conduction pathway was not mediated by her ability to control heart rate. The patient was still able to modify differentially her conduction pattern at the time of a 10-week follow-up test.

A second patient was a 31-year-old woman with WPW syndrome, Type B, diagnosed in infancy (Weiss & Brady, 1978). She had a history of paroxysmal supraventricular tachycardia since the age of 7, with episodes becoming more frequent during the 3 years prior to the study. Neither digoxin nor propranolol had been successful in controlling her condition. Initially, the patient was instructed in relaxation training, which over a 4-month period was not found to be effective in decreasing her dysrhythmia frequency. Next, she was given feedback training as described in the first case. While she was successful at increasing and decreasing her heart rate, she was generally unable to produce WPW-conducted beats. In the laboratory, except for one session, she always showed the normal conduction pattern. During several months of follow-up, she had less frequent episodes of dysrhythmia. On one occasion, she was able to terminate an episode of tachycardia by employing her technique for slowing heart rate. At 4 months following training, the patient reported one episode of tachycardia that required hospital treatment. She had attempted to terminate the episode by slowing her heart rate—which she had not practiced since training—but this was unsuccessful. At this point she began taking an antiarrhythmic drug, quinidine. In this case the patient did not benefit from either relaxation training or heart rate control training, although inadequate patient compliance may have contributed to the failure of these techniques.

BIOFEEDBACK AND CARDIAC ARRHYTHMIAS: AN EVALUATION

Recently, Blanchard (1979) suggested that at least seven different dimensions should be considered in evaluating the clinical applicability of biofeedback training. These include (1) the clinical importance of the changes observed; (2) the experimental design employed; (3) the extent of follow-up data; (4) the percentage of patients treated who improved significantly; (5) the amount of transfer of changes observed in the controlled laboratory situation to the patients' usual environments' (6) the replicability of results; and (7) a relationship between change in the biological response for which biofeedback was provided and change in the clinical symptom being treated (for example, change in frontalis EMG activity related to a patient's report of tension headaches). In evaluating the literature on biofeedback and cardiac arrhythmias, Blanchard concluded—we believe, correctly—that, although not extensive, the initial research in this area is promising, especially in patients with PVCs and sinus tachycardia. Case reports and single-subject experiments in both these areas have been successfully replicated; in particular, the work on treating PVCs by Weiss, Engel, and their associates has met many of Blanchard's evaluative criteria. These include good follow-up data (Weiss & Engel, 1971; Weiss & Baile, 1977), evidence of transfer of effects to a nonlaboratory environment (Weiss

& Engel, 1971), and independent replication (Pickering & Gorham, 1975; Pickering & Miller, 1977). Blanchard further noted that, while these initial reports are impressive, there is a need for "small-scale" group outcome studies in the future. For example, it would be desirable in evaluating biofeedback as an alternate or adjunct treatment to estimate what percentage of patients from a group with a particular arrhythmia improves with biofeedback training in comparison to the percentage from a similar group that did not receive training. Thus, future patients would be provided with information on the likelihood of improvement with biofeedback training.

While Blanchard's evaluative dimensions are clearly important, there are at least three other issues that should be addressed in analyzing the clinical efficacy of biofeedback. First, is the target response that biofeedback is intended to alter a clinically relevant variable? Second, does biofeedback provide a more effective treatment than relaxation training does? And, third, are there advantages in using biofeedback in the treatment of a clinical condition over using traditional therapies? These issues are briefly discussed here.

RESPONSE RELEVANCY

It is generally assumed that the response a treatment is aimed at altering is clinically relevant—that is, that eradicating or controlling the response is clinically beneficial to the patient. Tachycardia is clearly considered an abnormal condition. By definition, the critical response is heart rate, with the goal of treatment being to maintain it within the normal range. The relevant response in the treatment of PVCs, however, is not as well defined. Here the most important question is whether, in an otherwise asymptomatic patient, the presence of PVCs constitutes a significant risk factor for sudden cardiac death. The results of studies addressing this question have been contradictory. For instance, in one report (Kannel, Doyle, McNamara, Quickenton, & Gordon, 1975), the incidence of sudden death during a 16-year period in 4,000 men initially free of coronary heart disease was observed. The incidence of sudden death was not related to the presence of PVCs as recorded on routine ECGs. Significant prognostic indicators of sudden death were high blood pressure, evidence of left ventricular hypertrophy, obesity, and heavy cigarette consumption. In another study (Fisher & Tyroler, 1973), an 11-year follow-up with 1,214 male factory workers revealed that sudden cardiac death occurred in 60 subjects. The presence of PVCs on routine ECGs did not add to the prognostic significance of other ECG abnormalities. In contrast to these studies, Chiang, Perlman, Ostrander, and Epstein (1969) found that during a 6-year follow-up of 5,129 patients, the incidence of sudden death was 6.1% in the group with PVCs on routine ECG recordings and only 1.0% in patients without this arrhythmia—a significant difference. The presence of PVCs was also predictive of coronary heart disease, since 15.7% of the patients with PVCs had some form of coronary heart disease, whereas only 5% of patients without PVCs had coronary problems. In another study (Hinkle, Carver, & Stevens, 1969), 6-hour ambulatory ECG recordings of 283 subjects were collected. Of this sample, 62.2% revealed PVCs and complex ventricular arrhythmias. A significant correlation between the presence of 10 or more PVCs per 1,000 beats and the incidence of coronary-related death was found. In fact, the probability of death was 10 times greater in these patients than in those without ventricular ectopy. In a review of this literature, Moss and Akiyama (1974) concluded that the significance of PVCs as a prognostic indicator was directly related to the existence of underlying coronary disease. Thus, while the presence of PVCs may be significantly correlated with sudden death in a coronary population, those reviewers found no evidence that the arrhythmia raised the risk of sudden death in patients without heart disease. Furthermore, Lown (1979) has stated that the major inadequacy of PVCs as an indicator of risk for sudden cardiac death is that it is not known whether PVCs are the "trigger" for activity that leads to ventricular fibrillation and sudden death or an innocuous concomitant of the unstable heart.

Although it is not clear that the presence of PVCs increases the probability of sudden death, there is experimental evidence of a relationship between PVCs and reductions in coronary artery blood flow (Corday, Gold, DeVera, Williams, & Fields, 1959) and in cerebral blood flow (Corday & Irving, 1960). Thus it seems plausible that more frequent PVCs could cause angina or frank myocardial infarctions in the setting of coronary arteriosclerosis, or, in patients with cerebral vascular insufficiency, transient strokes or other neurologic problems, such as seizures, incontinence, tremor, or altered cognitive functioning (see, e.g., Corday, Rosenberg, & Weiner, 1956). This hypothesis does not appear to have been borne out in the work on sudden death discussed above. However, further systematic work comparing the occurrence of neurologic problems in patients with low versus patients with high PVC frequency needs to be done.

In the treatment of PVCs, the primary therapeutic goal is to decrease the frequency of this arrhythmia. Two problems have been discovered recently in regard to this goal. First, exercise stress testing is one of the major methods for detecting the prevalence of PVCs and coronary heart disease. Testing typically consists of intermittent monitoring of a patient during treadmill exercise. Antman, Graboys, and Lown (1979) discovered that the duration of monitoring influenced the estimated PVC prevalence. In a sample of 50 exercise tests, intermittent monitoring detected the presence of PVCs on 44% of the tests, whereas continuous monitoring detected PVCs on 62% of the tests—a statistically significant difference. In addition, there was a sixfold increase in the detection of complex and repetitive forms of PVCs with continuous monitoring over their detection with intermittent monitoring—also a significant change. This latter finding is important because there is evidence that only frequent advanced grades or complex forms enhance risk of sudden cardiac death in patients with coronary heart disease (Lown, 1979).

A second method of detecting PVCs is that of long-term Holter ECG monitoring in the ambulatory patient. Because of the spontaneous variations in the frequency of PVCs, Morganroth, Michelson, Horowitz, Josephson, Pearlman, and Dunkman (1978) evaluated three consecutive 24-hour ECG recordings in clinically stable patients with various cardiac problems and PVCs. Mean PVC frequency ranged from 37 to 1,801 per hour. The degree of spontaneous variation in PVC frequencies in individual patients from day to day was 23%; between 8-hour periods within a day, it was 29%; and from hour to hour, it was 37%. Morganroth and coworkers concluded that, to determine whether a reduction in PVC frequency was attributable to therapeutic intervention and not simply to spontaneous variation, researchers would have to document a change greater than 83% in frequency if only two 24-hour monitoring periods are compared, and a change greater than 65% if two 72-hour periods are compared. However, most studies rely either on intermittent monitoring or, at the most, on one 24-hour recording.

In summary, there is uncertainty about both the clinical value of treating patients with PVCs and the appropriate method and standards for measuring the effectiveness of a therapeutic intervention. More fundamental work needs to be done in both these areas.

BIOFEEDBACK VERSUS RELAXATION

A second issue that must be addressed in evaluating biofeedback for arrhythmias concerns its clinical effectiveness in relation to relaxation techniques, which are less expensive and less time-consuming. Preliminary data indicate that relaxation training is an effective technique for controlling PVCs. For instance, Benson, Alexander, and Feldman (1975) found that after 4 weeks of training in relaxation, 8 out of 11 patients showed some reduction in PVC frequency. While these findings are comparable to those found in biofeedback studies, at best they are only suggestive. As Weiss (1977) has noted, the only way to resolve this issue is by controlled comparisons of the two techniques in similar patient samples. Two studies thus far have employed this tactic. In one study (Weiss & Brady, 1978), three dysrhythmia patients described earlier—one with sinus tachycardia and premature atrial contractions, another with paroxysmal atrial flutter and fibrillation, and a third with WPW syndrome and supraventricular tachycardia—were administered both relaxation training and heart rate biofeedback. Biofeedback was found to be somewhat more effective in one of the three patients.

In a second study (Twentyman, Malloy, & Green, 1979), 40 college students with high heart rates (greater than 85 bpm at rest) were randomly assigned to one of four groups. One group served as a control, and subjects were asked to monitor a visual display of their heart rate but were given no instructions to decrease it. The remaining subjects were instructed to decrease their heart rates by utilizing either a relaxation technique, proportional feedback, or proportional feedback with criterion information. Results indicated that all training groups differed from the control group in ability to decrease heart rate, but did not differ from each other. It was concluded that biofeedback did not facilitate heart rate reduction better than a general relaxation technique did.

While work in this area is far from conclusive, it is very instructive along several dimensions. First, there is some evidence (Engel & Bleecker, 1974; Weiss & Brady, 1978; Weiss & Engel, 1971) that one advantage of biofeedback training is that it may allow patients the opportunity to develop optimal mental strategies for controlling their dysrhythmias through trial-and-error learning. Often the strategies are idiosyncratic (e.g., humming a lullaby, counting to oneself in a foreign language, etc.); this is in contrast to relaxation methods, which typically employ the same technique in all patients. There also is some experimental evidence (Davidson & Schwartz, 1976b) that subjects instructed to utilize a particular strategy in altering heart rate are less capable of raising their rates than are subjects given no specific strategy. Thus, there may be a trade-off between relaxation training, which offers an easily learned, inexpensive technique that works for many patients, and biofeedback, which over extended training may maximize the probability of an individual patient's acquiring a successful strategy for controlling the dysrhythmia.

A second area in which the effects of biofeedback and relaxation training diverge is that of the specificity of control. Biofeedback appears to produce more specific control of a given physiological variable, whereas relaxation techniques have a generalized effect (see, e.g., Kristt & Engel, 1975). Further research needs to be done to determine in which clinical conditions this effect of biofeedback would be an advantage over relaxation training. This issue is further discussed in the final section.

BIOFEEDBACK AS AN ALTERNATIVE TREATMENT

In evaluating any treatment, its effectiveness must be weighed against its possible risks. The generally accepted intervention in cardiac arrhythmias is antiarrhythmic drug therapy. Since PVCs usually are considered the most clinically significant arrhythmia, many investigators examining the efficacy of antiarrhythmic agents have studied PVC patients. In general, the results of these studies have been mixed. Myerburg, Conde, Sheps, Appel, Kiem, Sung, and Castellanos (1979) examined the long-term effects of two frequently used antiarrhythmic agents, procainamide and quinidine, for suppressing chronic ventricular arrhythmias in patients who had survived cardiac arrests. This patient population is particularly important, because it is at high risk for recurrent cardiac arrest and sudden death. Of the 16 patients treated with the antiarrhythmic drugs, eight survived longer than 12 months without a recurrent cardiac arrest (RCA) and eight had RCAs. Monthly 24-hour Holter recordings revealed that there were no significant differences between the frequency of PVCs in RCA patients and in patients who had not had RCAs. Furthermore, there was no relationship between therapeutic plasma levels of the drugs and the frequency of PVCs. In contrast, however, all RCA patients had subtherapeutic plasma levels, while six of the eight nonRCA patients consistently had therapeutic levels. Thus, adequate plasma levels of antiarrhythmic drugs may protect against RCAs, even though they fail to reduce PVC frequency.

In another study (Roland, Wilcox, Banks, Edwards, Fenton, & Hampton, 1979), patients with suspected myocardial infarction received either propranolol, atenolol (these being beta-adrenergic blocking agents), or a placebo. After 6 weeks of treatment, there was no difference in the incidence of arrhythmias between patients treated with propranolol or atenolol and those taking a placebo. In contrast to these findings, Woosley, Kornhauser, Smith, Reele, Higgins, Nies, Shand, and Oates (1979) reported that propranolol was effective in suppressing chronic high-frequency ventricular arrhythmias, especially ventricular tachycardia, in 24 out of 32 patients with no history of coronary disease. Here, the dosage of propranolol was increased until arrhythmia suppression was achieved or until a maximum dosage of 960 mg per day was reached. Only one-third of the patients responded to dosages under 160 mg per day, with 40% responding to between 200 and 640 mg per day. These results suggest that propranolol can effectively suppress ventricular arrhythmias if the appropriate dosage is administered.

While the clinical relevance of certain arrhythmias and the effectiveness of antiarrhythmic agents in suppressing these arrhythmias are not well understood, the side effects of drug therapy are. Many antiarrhythmic drugs are associated with a host of undesirable effects. For example, propranolol, which is representative of the beta-adrenergic blocking agents used as antiarrhythmic treatment, may cause or may worsen preexisting bradycardia, heart block, or cardiac failure (Winkle, Glant, & Harrison, 1975). There is also some evidence that one effect of propranolol therapy is a persistent reduction in glomerular filtration rate. This could be clinically significant, particularly in patients with preexisting renal insufficiency (Bauer & Brooks, 1979). Other side effects include fatigue, depression, nausea, diarrhea, hyperglycemia, and hyperosmolar coma (Winkle *et al.*, 1975). While not all antiarrhythmic drugs are as possibly problematic as propranolol, most effective ones are associated with undesired side effects or cannot be safely used in certain patient populations. The only deleterious effects of biofeedback are that it may not be effective in ameliorating certain types of arrhythmias or that the number of patients susceptible to the training may be limited. Thus, it seems conceivable that in certain arrhythmia patients biofeedback may provide a more advantageous treatment than the antiarrhythmic drugs currently available may.

SUMMARY AND CONCLUSIONS

In reviewing the literature on biofeedback-assisted heart rate control, it appears that normal subjects and patients with several arrhythmia conditions can learn to control cardiac functioning to some degree when provided with feedback of cardiac activity. In evaluating the "success" of such biofeedback training, however, investigators must employ different criteria when examining experimental results with normal subjects and when examining those from clinical studies. In studies with normal subjects, "success" is defined as the ability to alter a specific response at a statistically significant level. From our review, it appears that heart rate biofeedback training with normal subjects is indeed successful. In the application of these techniques to clinical populations, however, "success" is defined not only as a statistically significant change (especially a reduction) in the response, but also as the degree to which the magnitude of change and the response itself are clinically relevant. The initial attempts to control cardiac arrhythmias with biofeedback training have been encouraging, particularly in the cases of sinus tachycardia and, to a lesser extent, PVCs. In sinus tachycardia, the rapid heart rate is by definition a clinically significant condition, and the goal of treatment clearly is to bring heart rate into the normal range. Thus, the promising results with biofeedback treatment of this arrhythmia are clinically relevant. While there are some documented cases of patients significantly reducing the frequency of PVCs with biofeedback, there is some doubt about the clinical relevance of this response. Due to the spontaneous variation of PVC frequency, it has been difficult to specify what constitutes a clinically meaningful change in this condition. Also, and most importantly, it is not clearly established whether a high frequency of PVCs increases a patient's risk for sudden death or is simply a concomitant of a diseased heart that adds no risk in itself. Recent research suggests that the latter case is likelier. As mentioned earlier, PVCs can reduce coronary arterial and cerebral blood flow. There is suggestive evidence (Corday *et al.*, 1956) that those reductions may be clinically important. Thus, biofeedback training to reduce PVC frequency might be valuable in patients who also have angina or intermittent neurological symptoms. However, until more is understood about the clinical significance of PVCs, it seems that biofeedback research on arrhythmias would be more fruitfully devoted to cases of sinus tachycardia.

From the review of biofeedback studies of heart rate control in normal and arrhythmic subjects, several lines of research seem worth pursuing. It should be recalled that, with normal subjects, extensive research has focused on defining variables that influence learned heart rate control and individual differences in acquiring this control. Similar research carried out with arrhythmia patients could prove beneficial. For instance, one variable that was found to be possibly important in normal subjects was the incentive to learn heart rate control. While it seems that learning to control a dysrhythmic condition would be motivating in itself, this is not always the case. Weiss and Brady (1978) found that of five arrhythmia patients, three either did not adhere to the treatment regimen or dropped out of treatment completely. In several instances, monetary reward for achieving control of heart rate was found to be a motivating factor in normal subjects (Lang & Twentyman, 1976). Arrhythmia patients could be required to pay a pretreatment sum; part of this sum would be earned back by completing the treatment, with a bonus earned back by demonstrating successful control of the arrhythmia. This procedure has been effective in motivating patients to complete behavioral treatment for cigarette smoking (Chapman, Smith, & Layden, 1971) and problem drinking (Pomerleau, Pertschuk, Adkins, & Brady, 1978).

A second area of possible research is to search for individual differences predictive of success in controlling arrhythmias. With any clinical treatment, it is desirable to be able to differentiate between good and poor candidates. Knowledge of individual differences also provides the researcher with information about the possible mechanisms underlying the effectiveness of the treatment. Research with normal subjects has been particularly encouraging in this respect. Heart rate reactivity, electrodermal lability, and blood pressure regulation were all found to be predictive of subsequent success in controlling heart rate. Parallel studies of these discriminitive factors in arrhythmia patients could be informative.

ACKNOWLEDGMENT

Supported in part by National Institutes of Health Grant No. 5-Mo-1 RR 00040.

REFERENCES

Antman, E., Graboys, T. B., & Lown, B. Continuous monitoring for ventricular arrhythmias during exercise tests. *Journal of the American Medical Association,* 1979, *241,* 2802–2805.

Bauer, J. H., & Brooks, C. S. The long-term effect of propranolol therapy on renal function. *The American Journal of Medicine,* 1979, *66,* 405–410.

Bell, I. R., & Schwartz, G. E. Voluntary control and reactivity of human heart rate. *Psychophysiology,* 1975, *12,* 339–348.

Bellet, S. *Essentials of cardiac arrhythmias: Diagnosis and management.* Philadelphia: Saunders, 1972.

Benson, H., Alexander, S., & Feldman, C. L. Decreased premature ventricular contractions through use of the relaxation response in patients with stable ischemic heart disease. *Lancet,* 1975, *2,* 380–383.

Bergerman, A. L. Personal communication, 1980.

Bergman, J. S., & Johnson, H. J. The effects of instructional set and autonomic perception on cardiac control. *Psychophysiology,* 1971, *8,* 180–190.

Bergman, J. S., & Johnson, H. J. Sources of information which affect training and raising of heart rate. *Psychophysiology*, 1972, *9*, 30–39.

Blanchard, E. B. Biofeedback and the modification of cardiovascular dysfunctions. In R. J. Gatchel & P. Price (Eds.), *Clinical applications of biofeedback: Appraisal and status*. New York: Pergamon, 1979.

Blanchard, E. B., Haynes, M. R., Young, L. D., & Scott, R. W. The use of feedback training and a stimulus control procedure to obtain large magnitude increases in heart rate outside of the laboratory. *Biofeedback and Self-Regulation*, 1977, *2*, 81–92.

Blanchard, E. B., Scott, R. W., Young, L. D., & Edmunson, E. D. Effect of knowledge of response on the self-control of heart rate. *Psychophysiology*, 1974, *11*, 251–264.

Blanchard, E. B., Scott, R. W., Young, L. D., & Haynes, M. R. Differential effects of feedback and reinforcement in voluntary acceleration of human heart rate. *Perceptual and Motor Skills*, 1974, *38*, 683–691.

Blanchard, E. B., & Young, L. D. Self-control of cardiac functioning: A promise as yet unfulfilled. *Psychological Bulletin*, 1973, *79*, 145–163.

Blanchard, E. B., Young, L. D., & McLeod, P. Awareness of heart activity and self-control of heart rate. *Psychophysiology*, 1972, *9*, 63–68.

Blanchard, E. B., Young, L. D., Scott, R. W., & Haynes, M. R. Differential effects of feedback and reinforcement in voluntary acceleration of human heart rate. *Perceptual and Motor Skills*, 1974, *38*, 683–691.

Blankstein, K. R. Note on relation of autonomic perception to voluntary control of heart rate. *Perceptual and Motor Skills*, 1975, *40*, 533–534.

Blankstein, K. R., Zimmerman, J., & Egner, K. Within-subject control designs and voluntary bidirectional control of cardiac rate: Methodological comparison between pre-experimental and pretrial baselines. *Journal of General Psychology*, 1976, *95*, 161–175.

Bleecker, E. R., & Engel, B. T. Learned control of ventricular rate in patients with atrial fibrillation. *Psychosomatic Medicine*, 1973, *35*, 161–175. (a)

Bleecker, E. R., & Engel, B. T. Learned control of cardiac rate and cardiac conduction in the Wolff–Parkinson–White syndrome. *New England Journal of Medicine*, 1973, *288*, 560–562. (b)

Bouchard, M. A., & Granger, L. The role of instructions versus instructions plus feedback in voluntary heart rate slowing. *Psychophysiology*, 1977, *14*, 475–482.

Brener, J., & Hothersall, D. Heart rate control under conditions of augmented sensory feedback. *Psychophysiology*, 1966, *3*, 23–28.

Brener, J., & Hothersall, D. Paced respiration and heart rate control. *Psychophysiology*, 1967, *4*, 1–6.

Brobeck, J. R. (Ed.) *Best and Taylor's physiological basis of medical practice*. Baltimore: Williams & Wilkins, 1978.

Carroll, D. Cardiac perception and cardiac control: A review. *Biofeedback and Self-Regulation*, 1977, *2*, 349–369.

Chapman, R. F., Smith, J. W., & Layden, T. A. Elimination of cigarette smoking by punishment and self-management training. *Behaviour Research and Therapy*, 1971, *9*, 255–264.

Chiang, B. N., Perlman, L. V., Ostrander, L. D., Jr., & Epstein, F. H. Relationship of premature systoles to coronary heart disease and sudden death in the Tecumseh epidemiological study. *Annals of Internal Medicine*, 1969, *70*, 1159–1166.

Clemens, W. J., & Shattock, R. J. Voluntary heart rate control during static muscular effort. *Psychophysiology*, 1979, *16*, 327–332.

Colgan, M. Effects of binary and proportional feedback on bidirectional control of heart rate. *Psychophysiology*, 1977, *14*, 187–191.

Corday, E., Gold, H., DeVera, L. B., Williams, J. H., & Fields, J. Effect of the cardiac arrhythmias on the coronary circulation. *Annals of Internal Medicine*, 1959, *50*, 535–553.

Corday, E., & Irving, D. W. Effect of cardiac arrhythmias on the cerebral circulation. *American Journal of Cardiology*, 1960, *6*, 803–807.

Corday, E., Rosenberg, S. F., & Weiner, S. M. Cerebral vascular insufficiency: An explanation of the transient stroke. *Archives of Internal Medicine*, 1956, *98*, 683–690.

Cox, R. J., & McGuinness, D. The effect of chronic anxiety level upon self-control of heart rate. *Biological Psychology*, 1977, *5*, 7–14.

Crider, A. B., Schwartz, G. E., & Schnidman, S. On the criteria for instrumental autonomic conditioning: A reply to Katkin and Murray. *Psychological Bulletin*, 1969, *71*, 455–461.

Davidson, R. J., & Schwartz, G. E. Patterns of cerebral lateralization during cardiac biofeedback versus the self-regulation of emotion: Sex differences. *Psychophysiology*, 1976, *13*, 62–68.(a)

Davidson, R. J., & Schwartz, G. E. The psychobiology of relaxation and related states: A multi-process theory. In D. I. Mostofsky (Ed.), *Behavior control and the modification of physiological activity*. Englewood Cliffs, N.J.: Prentice-Hall, 1976.(b)

Engel, B. T. Comment on self-control of cardiac functioning: A promise as yet unfulfilled. *Psychological Bulletin*, 1974, *84*, 43.

Engel, B. T., & Bleecker, E. R. Application of operant conditioning techniques to the control of the cardiac arrhythmias. In P. A. Obrist, A. H. Black, J. Brener, & L. V. DiCara (Eds.), *Cardiovascular psychophysiology: Current issues in response mechanisms, biofeedback, and methodology*. Chicago: Aldine, 1974.

Engel, B. T., & Chism, R. Operant conditioning of heart rate speeding. *Psychophysiology*, 1967, *3*, 418–426.

Fisher, F. D., & Tyroler, H. A. Relationship between ventricular premature contractions on routine electrocardiography and subsequent sudden death from coronary heart disease. *Circulation*, 1973, *47*, 712–719.

Fotopolous, S. *Locus of control and the voluntary control of heart rate*. Paper presented at the meeting of the Biofeedback Research Society, New Orleans, 1970.

Frazier, T. W. Avoidance conditioning of heart rate in humans. *Psychophysiology*, 1966, *3*, 188–202.

Gatchel, R. J. Frequency of feedback and learned heart rate control. *Journal of Experimental Psychology*, 1974, *103*, 274–283.

Gatchel, R. J. The effect of voluntary heart rate deceleration on skin conductance level: An example of response fractionation. *Biological Psychology*, 1976, *4*, 241–248.

Gottlieb, S. H., & Engel, B. T. Unpublished observation.

Gradman, A. H., Bell, P. A., & DeBusk, R. F. Sudden death during ambulatory monitoring: Clinical and electrocardiographic correlations. Report of a case. *Circulation*, 1977, *55*, 210–211.

Haynes, M. R., Blanchard, E. B., & Young, L. D. The effects of the distribution of training on learning feedback-assisted cardiac acceleration. *Biofeedback and Self-Regulation*, 1977, *2*, 427–434.

Headrick, M. W., Feather, B. W., & Wells, D. T. Unidirectional and large magnitude heart rate changes with augmented sensory feedback. *Psychophysiology*, 1971, *8*, 132–142.

Hinkle, L. E., Carver, S. T., & Stevens, M. The frequency of asymptomatic disturbances of cardiac rhythm and conduction in middle-aged men. *American Journal of Cardiology*, 1969, *24*, 629–650.

Kannel, W. B., Doyle, J. T., McNamara, P. M., Quickenton, P., & Gordon, T. Precursors of sudden death with factors related to the incidence of sudden death. *Circulation*, 1975, *51*, 606–613.

Katkin, E. S., & Shapiro, D. Voluntary heart rate control as a function of individual differences in electrodermal lability. *Psychophysiology*, 1979, *16*, 402–404.

Kimmel, H. D. Instrumental conditioning of autonomically mediated behavior. *Psychological Bulletin*, 1967, *67*, 337–345.

Kleinman, R. A., & Brener, J. *The effects of training in heartbeat discrimination upon the subsequent development of learned heart rate control.* Unpublished manuscript, University of Tennessee, 1970.

Kristt, D. A., & Engel, B. T. Learned control of blood pressure in patients with high blood pressure. *Circulation*, 1975, *51*, 370–378.

Lang, P. J. Acquisition of heart rate control: Method, theory, and clinical implications. In D. C. Fowles (Ed.), *Clinical applications of psychophysiology*. New York: Columbia University Press, 1975.

Lang, P. J., Troyer, W. G., Twentyman, C. T., & Gatchel, R. J. Differential effects of heart rate modification training on college students, older males, and patients with ischemic heart disease. *Psychosomatic Medicine*, 1975, *37*, 429–446.

Lang, P. J., & Twentyman, C. T. Learning to control heart rate: Binary versus analogue feedback. *Psy-*

chophysiology, 1974, *11*, 616–629.

Lang, P. J., & Twentyman, C. T. Learning to control heart rate: Effects of varying incentive and criterion of success. *Psychophysiology*, 1976, *13*, 378–385.

Levene, H. I., Engel, B. T., & Pearson, J. A. Differential operant conditioning of heart rate. *Psychosomatic Medicine*, 1968, *30*, 837–845.

Lott, G. G., & Gatchel, R. J. A multi-response analysis of learned heart rate control. *Psychophysiology*, 1978, *15*, 576–581.

Lown, B. Sudden cardiac death—1978. *Circulation*, 1979, *60*, 1593–1599.

Lown, B., Verrier, R. L., & Rabinowitz, S. H. Neural and psychological mechanisms and the problem of sudden cardiac death. *American Journal of Cardiology*, 1977, *39*, 890–902.

Mackintosh, N. J. *The psychology of animal learning*. New York: Academic Press, 1975.

Mandler, G., Mandler, J. M., & Uviller, E. Autonomic feedback: The perception of autonomic activity. *Journal of Abnormal and Social Psychology*, 1958, *56*, 367–373.

McCanne, T. R., & Sandman, C. A. Determinants of human operant heart rate conditioning: A systematic investigation of several methodological issues. *Journal of Comparative and Physiological Psychology*, 1975, *88*, 609–618.(a)

McCanne, T. R., & Sandman, C. A. The impact of two different reinforcers on conditioned operant heart-rate acceleration and deceleration. *Biological Psychology*, 1975, *3*, 131–142.(b)

McCanne, T. R., & Sandman, C. A. Human operant heart rate conditioning: The importance of individual differences. *Psychological Bulletin*, 1976, *83*, 587–601.(a)

McCanne, T. R., & Sandman, C. A. Proprioceptive awareness, information about response–reinforcement contingencies and operant heart-rate control. *Physiological Psychology*, 1976, *4*, 369–375. (b)

McFarland, R. A. Heart rate perception and heart rate control. *Psychophysiology*, 1975, *12*, 402–405.

McFarland, R. A., & Campbell, C. Precise heart rate control and heart rate perception. *Perceptual and Motor Skills*, 1975, *41*, 730.

McKinney, M., Geller, D., Gatchel, R. J., Barber, G., Bothner, J., & Phelps, M. *The production and generalization of large magnitude heart rate deceleration by contingently-faded biofeedback*. Unpublished manuscript, University of Texas at Arlington, 1979.

Moss, A. J., & Akiyama, T. Prognostic importance of premature beats. *Cardiovascular Clinics*, 1974, *6*, 273–298.

Morganroth, J., Michelson, E., Horowitz, L., Josephson, M., Pearlman, A. S., & Dunkman, W. B. Limitations of routine long-term electrocardiographic monitoring to assess ventricular ectopic frequency. *Circulation*, 1978, *58*, 408–414.

Myerburg, R. J., Conde, C., Sheps, D. S., Appel, R. A., Kiem, I., Sung, R. J., & Castellanos, A. Antiarrhythmic drug therapy in survivors of prehospital cardiac arrest: Comparison of effects on chronic ventricular arrhythmias and recurrent cardiac arrests. *Circulation*, 1979, *59*, 855–863.

Obrist, P. A., Galosy, R. A., Lawler, J. E., Gaebelein, C. J., Howard, J. L., & Shanks, E. M. Operant conditioning of heart rate: Somatic correlates. *Psychophysiology*, 1975, *12*, 445–455.

Pardine, P., & Napoli, A. Personality correlates of successful biofeedback training. *Perceptual and Motor Skills*, 1977, *45*, 1099–1103.

Pickering, T., & Gorham, G. Learned heart rate controlled by a patient with a ventricular parasystolic rhythm. *Lancet*, 1975, *2*, 252–253.

Pickering, T., & Miller, N. E. Learned voluntary control of heart rate and rhythm in two subjects with premature ventricular contractions. *British Heart Journal*, 1977, *39*, 152–159.

Pomerleau, O., Pertschuk, M., Adkins, D., & Brady, L. P. A comparison of behavioral and traditional treatment for middle-income problem drinkers. *Journal of Behavioral Medicine*, 1978, *1*, 187–200.

Ray, W. J. The relationship of locus of control, self-report measures, and feedback to the voluntary control of heart rate. *Psychophysiology*, 1974, *11*, 527–534.

Ray, W. J., & Lamb, S. B. Locus of control and the voluntary control of heart rate. *Psychosomatic Medicine*, 1974, *36*, 180–182.

Rescorla, R. A., & Wagner, A. R. A theory of Pavlovian conditioning: Variations in the effectiveness of reinforcement and nonreinforcement. In A. H. Black & W. F. Prokasy (Eds.), *Classical conditioning* (Vol. 2, *Current research and theory*). New York: Appleton-Century-Crofts, 1972.

Roland, J. M., Wilcox, R. G., Banks, D. C., Edwards, B., Fenton, P. H., & Hampton, J. R. Effect of beta-blockers on arrhythmias during six weeks after suspected myocardial infarction. *British Heart Journal,* 1979, , 518–521.

Rotter, J. B. Generalized expectancies for internal versus external control of reinforcement. *Psychological Monographs,* 1966, *80,* 1–28.

Scott, R. W., Blanchard, E. B., Edmunson, E. D., & Young, L. D. A shaping procedure for heart-rate control in chronic tachycardia. *Perceptual and Motor Skills,* 1973, *37,* 327–338.

Scott, R. W., Peters, D. R., Gillespie, W. J., Blanchard, E. B., Edmunson, E. D., & Young, L. D. The use of shaping and reinforcement in the operant acceleration and deceleration of heart rate. *Behaviour Research and Therapy,* 1973, *11,* 179–185.

Sirota, A. D., Schwartz, G. E., & Shapiro, D. Voluntary control of human heart rate: Effect on reaction to aversive stimulation. *Journal of Abnormal Psychology,* 1974, *83,* 261–267.

Sirota, A. D., Schwartz, G. E., & Shapiro, D. Voluntary control of human heart rate: Effect on reaction to aversive stimulation. A replication and extension. *Journal of Abnormal Psychology,* 1976, *85,* 473–477.

Stephens, J. H., Harris, A. H., & Brady, J. V. Large magnitude heart rate changes in subjects instructed to change their heart rates and given exteroceptive feedback. *Psychophysiology,* 1972, *93,* 283–285.

Stephens, J. H., Harris, A. H., Brady, J. V., & Shaffer, J. W. Psychological and physiological variables associated with large magnitude voluntary heart rate changes. *Psychophysiology,* 1975, *12,* 381–387.

Twentyman, C. T. Personal communication, 1980.

Twentyman, C. T., Malloy, P. F., & Green, A. S. Instructed heart rate control in a high heart rate population. *Journal of Behavioral Medicine,* 1979, *2,* 251–261.

Weiss, T. Biofeedback training for cardiovascular dysfunctions. *Medical Clinics of North America,* 1977, *61,* 913–928.

Weiss, T., & Baile, W. F. *Heart rate biofeedback in patients with premature ventricular contractions: A follow-up.* Unpublished manuscript, University of Pennsylvania, 1977.

Weiss, T., & Brady, J. P. *Experience with biofeedback and relaxation training for cardiac arrhythmias.* Unpublished manuscript, University of Pennsylvania, 1978.

Weiss, T., & Engel, B. T. Operant conditioning of heart rate in patients with premature ventricular contractions. *Psychosomatic Medicine,* 1971, *33,* 301–321.

Weiss, T., & Engel, B. T. Evaluation of an intra-cardiac limit of learned heart rate control. *Psychophysiology,* 1975, *12,* 310.

Weiss, T., Reichek, N., Greenspan, A., Kastor, J., & Schwartz, P. J. Unpublished observation.

Wells, D. T. Large magnitude voluntary heart rate changes. *Psychophysiology,* 1973, *10,* 260–269.

Whitehead, W. E., Drescher, V. M., Heiman, P., & Blackwell, B. Relation of heart rate control to heart beat perception. *Biofeedback and Self-Control,* 1977, *2,* 371–392.

Williamson, D. A., & Blanchard, E. B. Heart rate and blood-pressure biofeedback: I. A review of the recent experimental literature. *Biofeedback and Self-Regulation,* 1979, *4,* 1–34.(a)

Williamson, D. A., & Blanchard, E. B. Heart rate and blood-pressure biofeedback: II. A review and integration of recent theoretical models. *Biofeedback and Self-Regulation,* 1979, *4,* 35–50.(b)

Williamson, D. A., & Blanchard, E. B. Effect of feedback delay upon learned heart rate control. *Psychophysiology,* 1979, *16,* 108–115.(c)

Winkle, R. A., Glant, S. A., & Harrison, D. C. Pharmacologic therapy of ventricular arrhythmias. *American Journal of Cardiology,* 1975, *36,* 629–650.

Woosley, R. L., Kornhauser, D., Smith, R., Reele, S., Higgins, S. B., Nies, A., Shand, D. G., & Oates, J. A. Suppression of chronic ventricular arrhythmias with propranolol. *Circulation,* 1979, *60,* 819–827.

Young, L. D., & Blanchard, E. B. Effects of auditory feedback of varying information content on the self-control of heart rate. *Journal of General Psychology,* 1974, *91,* 61–68.

COMMENTS ON THE CHAPTERS BY GOLDSTEIN AND BY CHEATLE AND WEISS

PAUL A. OBRIST

Both Chapter 6 and Chapter 7 present excellent critical reviews of the existing literature and many of the issues with which contemporary research should be concerned. My comments primarily concern still other issues, although I comment briefly on some raised in the chapters. My comments largely concern hypertension research, not only because I feel more competent in discussing this problem, but also because it has received greater experimental attention and the problems are more evident.

HYPERTENSION

I would like to address two fundamental issues that need to be underscored in any research utilizing behavioral procedures in the treatment and prevention of essential hypertension—issues to which I believe investigators pay inadequate attention. One is methodological, and it has two facets.

First, blood pressure can be quite labile both in normotensives and hypertensives and quite sensitive to rather subtle features of the social milieu. For example, when Bevan, Honour, and Stott (1969) made continuous direct recordings of blood pressure in four normotensives as they carried on their normal daily activities, they observed that systolic blood pressure values could vary up to 100 mm Hg across the course of a 24-hour period in the same individual. Other studies have shown an influence of the social milieu on resting or baseline blood pressure values in different ways. Medical students who were requested to come to a laboratory for a blood pressure determination without explanation and who lacked familiarity with the physical surroundings had an average resting value of 129/78 mm Hg (vs. 117/70 mm Hg in their student health records). On the other hand, those first invited to come to the laboratory for a tour and then given a blood pressure evaluation averaged 112/67 mm Hg (vs. 119/71 mm Hg in their student health records) (Ostfeld & Shekelle, 1967). My colleagues and I (Light & Obrist, 1980; Obrist, 1981; Obrist, Grignolo, Hastrup, Koepke, Langer, Light, McCubbin, & Pollak, in press) have seen an influence of both familiarity and expectation on baseline values in our "normotensive" young (18- to 20-year-old) study subjects. For the past several years, we have been obtaining two types of baselines. One is taken while subjects rest on their first visit to the laboratory and just before they are exposed to some procedures such as a shock-avoidance task. The second is obtained usually 1 to 2 weeks later, when the subjects come to the lab on two occasions to rest for 15 to 30 minutes. The subjects are explicitly informed that they will not be exposed to any

Paul A. Obrist. Department of Psychiatry, Division of Health Affairs, The School of Medicine, University of North Carolina at Chapel Hill, Chapel Hill, North Carolina.

other laboratory procedure. In two studies involving 138 subjects, the resting values for systolic blood pressure averaged 8 mm Hg higher on the stress day than on the no-stress days ($\bar{x}$ = 132 vs. 124 mm Hg), but the magnitude of the difference varied among subjects. A total of 21 subjects (15%) demonstrated an elevation of 20 mm Hg or more in systolic blood pressure while resting on the stress day as compared to their resting values on the no-stress day. On the other hand, 24 (17%) showed no difference between these resting conditions. It might be noted that these two extreme groups show comparable levels of systolic blood pressure on the follow-up or the no-stress baseline, indicating that the effects of the novelty of the situation and the anticipation of the procedures on the stress day baseline elevates the systolic blood pressure in the one subgroup but not the other. Thus, not only does the social milieu have an influence on resting values for systolic blood pressure, but it varies among individuals, being very appreciable in some and almost nonexistent in others.

The lability of blood pressure and its sensitivity to individuals' surroundings is not unique to normotensives but is evidenced by hypertensives as well. For example, Surwit and Shapiro (1977) recruited 24 individuals for a behavioral treatment study who, on the basis of their clinical records, would be considered at least borderline hypertensives. Prior to any treatment, they were given a physical exam and then 2 days of no-treatment baseline sessions, apparently to acclimate them to conditions. It was observed that the mean blood pressure from their clinical records was 156/94 mm Hg, and from the physical exam, 165/103 mm Hg. Such values are hypertensive by most criteria. However, by the beginning of the second baseline session, the mean blood pressure values had dropped to 142/87 mm Hg. By the end of the second baseline session, the subjects' systolic blood pressure averaged 134 mm Hg. Diastolic values were not reported, but such a systolic value indicates that half the subjects would no longer be considered hypertensive, using the 140 mm Hg value as a cutoff. Thus, in comparison with the data from their clinical records and the preexperimental physical exam, the decrease in the subjects' blood pressure was appreciable, but it must be considered to reflect almost exclusively an acclimatization effect.

An equally remarkable observation was made by Sokolow, Werdeger, Perloff, Cowan, and Brenenstuhl (1970), who observed that self-administered blood pressure readings taken by 124 hypertensives in the field were on the average lower than those taken in the clinic. The field values were obtained using a semiautomated portable blood pressure system, with readings taken approximately every 30 minutes over a 2-day period. Clinic values averaged 170/104 mm Hg, while field values averaged 156/94 mm Hg, with a number of individuals demonstrating average field values in the normotensive range (the number was never specified). These authors point out that this discrepancy between field and clinic values is all the more impressive because the clinic values were taken while the individuals rested, while the field values were taken during the course of ordinary daily activity.

Overall, these various observations raise some important questions. For example, how characteristic is a clinic's or a physician's blood pressure reading of any given individual's blood pressure under conditions of everyday life? Are our clinic hypertensives invariably hypertensive during their working hours? Should clinicians be treating people for hypertension, regardless of the method, when they rely only on a limited number of clinic values for diagnostic purposes without regard to how well the clinic values reflect nonclinic values? It might be replied that, with an appropriate acclimatization period, clinicians can ascertain whether a given subject's blood pressure level is unique to the novelty of the situation (as in the Surwit and Shapiro study), and thus can treat only those demonstrating little or no decrease in BP values over time. It might also be noted, in some studies evaluating behavioral treatment regimes, that an untreated control group is run and is reported to evidence little decrease in blood pressure upon repeated exposure to the circumstances. The studies by Patel (e.g., Patel, 1977) demonstrate this point. In any case, there is considerable evidence that clinicians cannot treat blood pressure as a more or less static event, and investigators need to make a greater effort to evaluate its inherent lability within a given individual, particularly in regard as to whether its more common values have been overestimated.

A second measurement problem also stems from the lability of blood pressure, but it represents the other side of the coin; namely, it is the question of whether blood pressure values obtained during successful behavioral treatment and follow-up *under*estimate the blood pressure values encountered in everyday events of life. This problem was suggested by the procedures used by Patel (Patel, 1977; Patel & North, 1975), who reported successful management of blood pressure in hypertensives through the use of biofeedback-aided relaxation and mediation that continued for up to 9 months after treatment. My concern is whether patients placed under any treatment regimen may develop a set (strategy) any time blood pressure is measured that facilitates its lowering. This is suggested by the procedures used in the Patel studies. Although some of the details are sketchy, it appears that in at least one study (Patel & North, 1975), patients undergoing active treatment were first presented information about hypertension, the treatment process, and so on; this was claimed to establish good rapport with the therapist. In the course of treatment, they were also shown their blood pressure records and given verbal encouragement. In the light of this atmosphere, it strikes me that once patients are led to understand the nature of hypertension, it would be quite reinforcing for them to learn strategies that would result in lower values at the time blood pressure is measured. In effect, such patients would be trained to maintain lower blood pressures during periods of measurement but not necessarily at other times, unless a similar set (strategy) could be maintained, which may or may not be possible. Obviously, we need to determine whether the lower blood pressure is characteristic of an individual's more common life experiences without making use of the procedure signaling the occurrence of a measurement. Measurement of blood pressure by occlusion of an appendage is one of the most discriminable procedures in use for the measurement of biological activity. I believe clinicians need to monitor cardiovascular changes by less obtrusive means, which is why measures like R-wave-to-pulse-wave transit time or pulse-wave-to-pulse-wave transit time (Obrist, Light, McCubbin, Hutcheson, & Hoffer, 1979) should be pursued.

Obtaining a more characteristic estimate of a given individual's levels of blood pressure and its lability presents a difficult methodology. Field studies are obviously called for. The study by Sokolow and colleagues (Sokolow *et al.*, 1970) represented an important first step in this direction. A problem faced with self-administered BP readings, besides the fact that a cuff (with its obvious cue value) is used, is that the investigator has no control over precisely when the individual takes a blood pressure reading. This was suggested as a problem by an initial study Light and I undertook about 3 years ago (see Light & Obrist, 1980). We had 38 young adult males take their own blood pressure outside the laboratory on 20 occasions over a 2-day period, using a portable self-inflating measurement system. The subjects were instructed to take readings at various times of the day except immediately following exercise. Prior to this, they had been involved in our laboratory procedures, where, among other things, we obtained both types of previously described baseline measures. To our surprise, the average field value was the same as the average baseline or resting values obtained on those 2 days when they did nothing but come to the laboratory and rest. This did not seem due to any error of measurement, since the field values across all 38 subjects were highly correlated ($r = +.79$) to the laboratory resting values. Our only explanation was that the subjects took their blood pressures usually when reasonably relaxed. This would not be surprising with some, since they verbalized concern about their blood pressures, and if denial mechanisms should be at work such individuals might resort to taking their pressure when feeling minimally stressed.

Work that we are just initiating in our laboratory will, we hope, get around these methodological problems. This concerns projects involving the assessment of myocardial and blood pressure reactivity under naturalistic field conditions in young adult humans. In order to insure that we sample blood pressure levels during both stressful and nonstressful occasions, we have developed a completely automated but portable cuff system that rapidly self-inflates from a battery-operated air pump, then slowly deflates. The pressure in the cuff and Korotkoff (K) sounds are recorded on a battery-operated tape recorder. Thus, the subject is unaware of the level of blood pressure at each occasion of measurement. The tape is decoded in the laboratory. Each blood pressure reading is programmed to occur at a fixed interval of time, and in excess of 100 readings can be taken over any period of measurement, such as a day. This system solves the problem of subject-initiated blood pressure readings, but it is still a cuff system, and we do not know whether the cue provided by cuff inflation will trigger a decrease or possibly even an increase in blood pressure. We hope to evaluate this problem by recording both heart rate and R-wave-to-pulse-wave transit time through the use of still another portable system. Since both events tend to covary inversely with the systolic blood pressure (Obrist *et al.*, 1979), we can determine whether there is any trend for the systolic blood pressure to be either higher or lower just before or after the cuff reading on the basis of whether heart rate or transit time consistently change in one direction or the other during inflation.

The second major issue to underscore is that it must continually be borne in mind that an elevated blood pressure is a symptom indicative of some derangement in the blood pressure control mechanisms. In principle, it is no different from an elevated body temperature. Neither are very informative, except that they indicate a derangement in bodily functions with potential pathological consequences. A fever does not tell either the type of infecting organism, the site of the infection, nor the way in which the infection was incurred. An elevated blood pressure neither specifies which of the many blood pressure control mechanisms may be involved nor reveals the means or events that trigger the breakdown in these mechanisms. There is an exception—namely, the secondary hypertensions where such factors as kidney disease are clearly indicated. But there are a clear minority. With primary or essential hypertension, the etiological picture remains undeciphered. My own guess is that when the truth is known (if ever), investigators will find that the etiological picture varies considerably among individuals or that, as Page (1977) has put it, "the causes are many. . . ." (p. 587). The relative importance of behavioral influences may also vary among individuals, being of greater significance in some than in others. The implication of this is that the effectiveness of behavioral intervention with hypertension, in the form either of treatment or of prevention, will vary equally. All this should warn investigators and clinicians that current behavioral treatment is risky, and it is not particularly surprising that success in treatment presents a very uncertain picture of the efficacy of the procedures used.

The problem with a symptomatic approach can perhaps be best illustrated by briefly reviewing some research and speculations concerning the delineation of blood pressure control mechanisms in essential hypertension (for a review, see Frolich, 1977; Julius,

1977b; Obrist, 1981; and Obrist *et al.*, in press). Borderline hypertension has been somewhat arbitrarily designated as blood pressure values ranging from 140 to 160 mm Hg systolic blood pressure and/or from 90 to 100 mm Hg diastolic blood pressure (Julius, 1977a). When borderline hypertension is observed in individuals who are less than 40 years of age, there is commonly involved an elevation of the cardiac output (CO) in the absence as yet of any increase in vascular resistance (Lund-Johansen, 1967; Safar, Weiss, Levenson, London, & Milliez, 1973). When it has been evaluated, the increase in the CO appears to be mediated by increased beta-adrenergic drive on the heart (Julius & Esler, 1976). That the elevated CO may be a precursor of a more established hypertension (i.e., 160/100 mm Hg or greater; Julius, 1977a) some time later in life, when the CO then is observed to be normal or even subnormal and the vascular resistance elevated, is suggested by two lines of evidence. First, borderline hypertension per se is somewhat predictive of established hypertension some 10 to 20 years later (Julius, 1977b). Second, in two longitudinal studies, scanning a period averaging 50 months in one case (Eich, Cuddy, Smulyan, & Lyons, 1969) and 10 years in another (Lund-Johansen, 1979), the initially elevated CO had decreased while the vascular resistance had increased by the time of follow-up—a picture more consistent with established hypertension, although the blood pressure itself had not noticeably increased. The basis of this shift in hemodynamics from a high CO to an elevated vascular resistance has been hypothesized to involve two mechanisms that could act in conjunction or independently. One involves autoregulatory (intrinsic or nonneurogenic) mechanisms (Coleman, Granger, & Guyton, 1971; Granger & Guyton, 1969), involving the microcirculation triggered by the excessive CO. In this case, the tissues are being overprofused in relation to metabolic requirements, which in time evokes a vasoconstriction that acts to bring tissue profusion to more metabolically appropriate levels. This acts to elevate vascular resistance but to reduce the CO, since venous return is lessened because of the damming up of blood in the arterial side of the circulatory tree. The net effect is to sustain or even to increase the elevated pressure. A second mechanism has been proposed by Folkow (Folkow, Hallback, Lundgren, Sivertsson, & Weiss, 1973). It involves structural changes in the arterioles brought about by an elevated pressure such that the vascular smooth muscles hypertrophy, and this in turn causes a narrowing of the resistive vessels and an elevated vascular resistance. It would act on the blood pressure and CO much as autoregulatory influences do, and, like the latter, is an intrinsic mechanism.

There is one other matter to discuss with respect to mechanisms—namely, renal influences on either the myocardium and the vasculature, or both (Brown, Fraser, Lever, Morton, Robertson, & Schalekamp, 1977; Guyton, 1977). The mechanism involved here is believed to involve the retention of sodium and water by means of tubular reabsorption. Perhaps the strongest argument that can be made for renal involvement is that an acute rise in the blood pressure would normally trigger an increase in sodium and water excretion, and hence a reduction first in plasma volume and then in the blood pressure. It is proposed that this does not happen in established hypertension because the kidney can no longer maintain sodium and water balance at normotensive levels. In effect, an elevated blood pressure is necessary to maintain the balance between intake and output because of this kidney abnormality. What is not clear in this scheme is how this kidney abnormality comes about in the first place, but it is quite conceivable that it could involve neural mechanisms. In such a case, renal influences in the etiological process could be acting in conjunction with the beta-adrenergic influences on the heart and influencing the myocardium and vasculature in a like manner (see Obrist *et al.*, in press, for a discussion of this issue). What is important to emphasize here is that Guyton (1977) and Brown *et al.* (1977) make a very compelling argument for renal involvement in the etiology of established essential hypertension—an argument that has gone largely ignored in behavioral biology, whether it be in research or in treatment. In summary, it can be proposed that one etiological route in the development of established essential hypertension begins with a neurogenic (beta-adrenergically) mediated elevation of the CO in which the blood pressure levels are only marginally elevated, but which over time evokes increases in the vascular resistance; this, in turn, acts to fix the blood pressure at even more elevated levels through intrinsic mechanisms. A second and possibly complementary route involves renal mechanisms that act to raise the blood pressure in order to maintain sodium balance.

While this scheme is quite speculative, it provides some working hypotheses with which to evaluate the role of behavioral factors in the etiological process (see Obrist, 1981; Obrist *et al.*, in press). For purposes of the present discussion, this scheme suggests several things that clinicians and investigators should keep in mind with regard to any behavioral intervention procedure with hypertension. Firstly, it indicates that the progressive nature of hypertension involves different blood pressure control mechanisms early in the disease process than it does later in the process. In turn, this suggests that if treatment begins with the blood pressure is only marginally elevated, clinicians should focus on reducing the CO (if elevated). Since heart rate can covary quite closely with the CO (Anderson, Yingling, & Sagawa, 1979; Langer, Obrist, & McCubbin, 1979), and since it is commonly reported to be elevated in borderline hypertension (Julius, 1977b), it would seem profitable to initiate regimes that reduce heart rate, possibly in conjunction with reductions in the systolic blood pressure. The latter is more apt to be elevated than is the diastolic blood pressure (see Safar *et al.*, 1973). In more established hypertension, it suggests that clinicians focus on reducing vascular resistance. This is difficult to assess, since the resistance is a derived value for which the CO must be known. However, the diastolic blood pressure, either measured with an automated pneumatic system or estimated from pulse-wave-to-pulse-wave transit time, probably provides the best estimate of vascular resistance when it cannot be derived more directly.

Secondly, this scheme offers some cautions. It suggests that neurogenic involvement, particularly with the myocardium, is more pronounced early in the etiology than it is at later stages in the disease process. Since any behavioral intervention technique should prove more effective when neurogenic involvement is maximal, behavioral intervention at this stage would be more effective than it would be when the hypertension is more established. This would particularly be the case if intrinsically mediated structural and autoregulatory changes have occurred. Furthermore, if established hypertension is serving to maintain sodium and water balance as a result of inefficient kidney function, it suggests that any effort to drop the blood pressure will probably prove ineffective unless the balance can be maintained, as with diuretics. These are probably very powerful renal mechanisms that would prohibit a drop in pressure if balance were to be compromised.

I do not wish to imply that this scheme is a proven fact. Further, I do not wish to imply that there are no other etiological routes. But this scheme at least gives us some guideposts to direct the planning of treatment procedures. To me, it is preferable to working with a symptom when we are essentially working blindly. Attempting to guide treatment procedures by this scheme may also help clinicians and investigators to evaluate its merit.

HEART RATE AND THE ARRHYTHMIAS

I was particularly glad to see the review of the treatment studies, the candid nature of the commentary, and the spelling out of the significant issues in treatment. It is a much-needed review, particularly in the light of the early Weiss and Engel studies (1971) and the attention they attracted. The only point I care to comment on extensively is the discussion of individual differences in the voluntary heart rate control studies in healthy individuals.

First, we (Obrist, 1981; Obrist *et al.*, in press) have observed with other behavioral paradigms appreciable stable individual differences in heart rate reactivity, using a variety of tasks. For example, one study involved 56 young (ages 18 to 20) adult college males exposed to the cold pressor, a pornographic movie, and a shock-avoidance task. We find that heart rate reactivity to one condition, such as the cold pressor, significantly correlates with heart rate reactivity to another condition, such as shock avoidance. The range of *r* values is from +.53 to +.58. However, this degress of stability was only observed when the baseline levels were the resting values obtained some 1 to 2 weeks following exposure to the experimental tasks described earlier in this discussion in regard to systolic blood pressure. If the basline session is the resting period when the subject first comes to the laboratory, just prior to exposure to the first task, these correlations are all nonsignificant. This is because some individuals during this initial baseline demonstrate appreciably elevated heart rates while others do not, thus causing an underestimation of reactivity in the more reactive individuals. I mention this because it is of considerable methodological importance for our studies as well as in biofeedback studies. This difference between baselines can be appreciable. In our one study (Obrist, 1981), it was 20 bpm or more in 12 of the 56 subjects, exceeding 30 bpm in 3 of them. These appreciable baseline differences, when encountered, are probably due to increased sympathetic tonus, since the follow-up baseline decreased to a level comparable to that observed with beta-adrenergic blockade—namely, 66 as opposed to 67 bpm (Obrist, Gaebelein, Teller, Langer, Grignolo, Light, & McCubbin, 1978).

In biofeedback studies where voluntary control is being attempted, I wonder whether reasonably appreciable decreases in heart rate could not be achieved in these individuals with the elevated baseline levels. Of course, one would have to control for acclimatization effects. Perhaps feedback would facilitate acclimatization. It should be noted that such baseline differences have been observed in a variety of circumstances—even in studies not using aversive stimulation, such as an unsignaled reaction time (RT) task involving self-competition and/or cohort competition (Light, 1981). This suggests that just the novelty or the challenge of the situation is sufficient to elevate baseline heart rates in some individuals.

We have not been able to identify the basis of these individual differences in heart rate reactivity, including the difference between baselines. We have tried without much success, as have several biofeedback studies, to see whether these heart rate effects relate to such psychometric devices as the Ego Strength Scale (Barron, 1956; Roessler, 1973) a version of the Type A-B Scale (Jenkins, 1976) and the Internal–External Locus of Control Scale (Rotter, 1966). The only behavior we have found to relate to reactivity is performance on an unsignaled RT task using a shock-avoidance paradigm, where the subjects with more reactive heart rates in one study (Light & Obrist, 1980) were significantly faster (241 vs. 267 msec, $p < .01$), and where the more reactive subjects in one other study (Obrist *et al.*, 1978) indicated in a postexperimental interview that they were both more engaged in the task and more stressed by it. But this would not explain why these subjects are also more reactive during pain, sexual arousal, or just a first visit to the lab. Currently, my own inclination is to view these individual differences as reflections of some biological predisposition. Yet I would not write off efforts attempting to seek behavioral correlates. It strikes me that our failure, as well as that of the biofeedback studies seeking to find relationships between behavioral traits and heart rate change, may reflect the fact that the selection of scales lacks any conceptual framework and that their choice is somewhat voguish. Perhaps, as Lazarus (1978) has suggested, investigators should pay closer attention to the way in which an individual appraises a situation and its significance, as well as the way in which the individual attempts to cope with the situation.

My remaining comments are quite brief. In the discussion of blood pressure homeostasis and heart rate control, it is indicated that subjects evidencing greater systolic blood pressure reaction to the cold pressor also produce greater heart rate increases during biofeedback training. I do not know how to interpret the result. It may reflect nothing more than the fact that better heart rate learners also demonstrate greater heart rate reactivity during the cold pressor. In turn, this reflects a greater increase in cardiac contractility and hence a more elevated systolic blood pressure. We have data suggestive of this possibility when we see heart rate and systolic blood pressure reactivity common to several circumstances. Whether this reflects an influence of blood pressure homeostatic mechanisms, such as the baroreceptors, is not certain.

The clinical data presented in the remainder of the paper is very valuable. I do have one question, however. Should a distinction be made between an effect mediated by decreased sympathetic drive and one mediated by increased vagal excitation? Are not the innervations synergistic in this context? I am confused as to why atropine should result in a decrease in PVC production when decreased sympathetic drive or increased vagal activity does so in still other patients.

The methodological problems faced with evaluating the prevalance of PVCs are quite important and are similar to those faced in hypertension research, where investigators are trying to assess the natural lability of blood pressure. I believe it all comes down to investing our energies in more long-term evaluative studies in which, among other things, reliable baselines can be obtained.

Finally, it was illuminating to learn that the significance of PVCs, even in individuals with sick hearts, is not clear. Do we know much about neural control of PVCs?

ACKNOWLEDGMENT

Research performed by the author was supported by Research Grant HL 18976, National Heart, Lung, and Blood Institute.

REFERENCES

Anderson, D. E., Yingling, J. E., & Sagawa, K. Minute to minute covariations in cardiovascular activity of conscious dogs. *American Journal of Physiology: Heart and Circulatory Physiology,* 1979, *5,* H434–H439.

Barron, F. An ego strength scale which predicts response to psychotherapy. In W. G. Dahlstrom & G. S. Welsh (Eds.), *Basic readings on the MMPI in psychology and medicine.* Minneapolis: University of Minnesota Press, 1956.

Bevan, A. T., Honour, A. J., & Stott, F. H. Direct arterial pressure recording in unrestricted man. *Clinical Science,* 1969, *36,* 329–344.

Brown, J. J., Fraser, R., Lever, A. F., Morton, J. J., Robertson, J. I. S., & Schalekamp, M. A. D. H. Mechanisms in hypertension: A personal view. In J. Genest, E. Koiw, & O. Kuchel (Eds.), *Hypertension: Physiopathology and treatment.* New York: McGraw-Hill, 1977.

Coleman, T. G., Granger, H. J., & Guyton, A. C. Whole body circulatory, autoregulation and hypertension. *Circulation Research,* 1971, *29* (Suppl. 2), II-76–II-86.

Eich, R. H., Cuddy, R. P., Smulyan, H., & Lyons, R. H. Hemodynamics in labile hypertension: A follow-up study. *Circulation,* 1966, *34,* 299–307.

Folkow, B. U. G., Hallback, M. I. L., Lundgren, Y. Sivertsson, R., & Weiss, L. Importance of adaptive changes in vascular design for establishment of primary hypertension, studied in man and in spontaneously hypertensive rats. *Circulation Research,* 1973, *32–33,* (Suppl. 1), I-2–I-16.

Frohlich, E. D. Hemodynamics of hypertension. In J. Genest, E. Koiw, & O. Kuchel (Eds.),

Hypertension: Physiopathology and treatment. New York: McGraw-Hill, 1977.

Granger, H. J., & Guyton, A. C. Autoregulation of the total systemic circulation following destruction of the central nervous system in the dog. *Circulation Research,* 1969, *25,* 379–388.

Guyton, A. C. Personal views on mechanisms of hypertension. In J. Genest, E. Koiw, & O. Kuchel (Eds.), *Hypertension: Physiopathology and treatment.* New York: McGraw-Hill, 1977.

Jenkins, C. D. Recent evidence supporting psychologic and social risk factors for coronary disease. *The New England Journal of Medicine,* 1976, *294,* 987–994; 1033–1038.

Julius, S. Classification of hypertension. In J. Genest, E. Koiw, & O. Kuchel (Eds.), *Hypertension: Physiopathology and treatment.* New York: McGraw-Hill, 1977.(a)

Julius, S. Borderline hypertension: Epidemiologic and clinical implications. In J. Genest, E. Koiw, & O. Kuchel (Eds.), *Hypertension: Physiopathology and treatment.* New York: McGraw-Hill, 1977.

Julius, S., & Esler, M. D. *The nervous system in arterial hypertension.* Springfield, Ill.: Charles C Thomas, 1976.

Langer, A. W., Obrist, P. A., & McCubbin, J. A. Hemodynamic and metabolic adjustments during exercise and shock avoidance in dogs. *American Journal of Physiology: Heart and Circulatory Physiology,* 1979, *5,* H225–H230.

Lazarus, R. S. A strategy for research on psychological and social factors in hypertension. *Journal of Human Stress,* 1978, *4,* 35–40.

Light, K. C. Cardiovascular responses to effortful coping: Implications for the role of stress in hypertension development. *Psychophysiology,* 1981, *18,* 216–225.

Light, K. C., and Obrist, P. A. Cardiovascular reactivity to behavioral stress in young males with normal and mildly elevated systolic pressures: A comparison of clinic, home and laboratory measures. *Hypertension,* 1980, *2,* 802–808.

Lund-Johansen, P. Hemodynamics in early essential hypertension. *Acta Medica Scadinavica,* 1967, Suppl. 182, 1–101.

Lund-Johansen, P. Spontaneous changes in central hemodynamics in essential hypertension: A 10-year follow-up study. In G. Onesti & G. R. Klimt (Eds.), *Hypertension: Determinants, complications and intervention.* New York: Grune & Stratton, 1979.

Obrist, P. A. *Cardiovascular psychophysiology: A perspective.* New York: Plenum, 1981.

Obrist, P. A., Gaebelein, C. J., Teller, E. S., Langer, A. W., Grignolo, A., Light, K. C., & McCubbin, J. A. The relationship among heart rate, carotid dp/dt and blood pressure in humans as a function of the type of stress. *Psychophysiology,* 1978, *15,* 102–115.

Obrist, P. A., Grignolo, A., Hastrup, J. L., Koepke, J. P., Langer, A. W., Light, K. C., McCubbin, J. A., & Pollak, M. H. Behavioral–cardiac interactions in hypertension. In D. Krantz, A. Baum, & J. E. Singer (Eds.), *Handbook of psychology and health* (Vol. 1, *Cardiovascular disorders).* Hillsdale, N.J.: Erlbaum, in press.

Obrist, P. A., Light, K. C., McCubbin, J. A., Hutcheson, J. S., & Hoffer, J. L. Pulse transit time: Relationship to blood pressure and myocardial performance. *Psychophysiology,* 1979, *16,* 292–301.

Ostfeld, A. M., & Shekelle, R. B. Psychological variables and blood pressure. In J. Stamler, R. Stamler, & T. N. Pullman (Eds.), *The epidemiology of hypertension.* New York: Grune & Stratton, 1967.

Page, I. H. Some regulatory mechanisms of renovascular and essential arterial hypertension. In J. Genest, E. Koiw, & O. Kuchel (Eds.), *Hypertension: Physiopathology and treatment.* New York: McGraw-Hill, 1977.

Patel, C. H. Biofeedback-aided relaxation and mediation in the management of hypertension. *Biofeedback and Self-Regulation,* 1977, *2,* 1–41.

Patel, C., & North, W. R. S. Randomised controlled trial of yoga and biofeedback in management of hypertension. *Lancet,* 1975, *2,* 93–95.

Roessler, R. Personality, psychophysiology and performance. *Psychophysiology,* 1973, *10,* 315–327.

Rotter, J. B. Generalized expectancies for internal versus external control of reinforcement. *Psychological Monographs,* 1966, *80,* 1–28.

Safar, M. E., Weiss, Y. A., Levenson, J. A., London, G. M., & Milliez, P. L. Hemodynamic study of 85 patients with borderline hypertension. *The American Journal of Cardiology,* 1973, *31,* 315–319.

Sokolow, M., Werdegar, D., Perloff, D. B.,

Cowan, R. M., & Brenenstuhl, H. Preliminary studies relating portably recorded blood pressure to daily life events in patients with essential hypertension. In M. Koster, H. Musaph, & P. Visser (Eds.), *Psychosomatics in essential hypertension (Bibliotheca Psychiatica No. 144)*. White Plains, N.Y.: Karger, 1970.

Surwit, R. S., & Shapiro, D. Biofeedback and meditation in the treatment of borderline hypertension. In J. Beatty & H. Legewie (Eds.), *Biofeedback and behavior.* New York: Plenum, 1977.

Weiss, T., & Engel, B. T. Operant conditioning of heart rate in patients with premature ventricular contractions. *Psychosomatic Medicine,* 1971, *33,* 301–321.

ROUND-TABLE DISCUSSION OF GOLDSTEIN, CHEATLE AND WEISS, AND OBRIST

Martin Orne: There's a very unfancy procedure which is still used clinically to this day. That is to take sleeping blood pressures or to do an amytol test where you give a grain of amytol every hour until the patient is out, and you see how much his hypertension drops. That is used as a criterion of how much give you've got in the system. It's a much easier way of assessing than assessing the kidney function directly, and what it does ask is "What's coming from the cortex that is causing the hypertension?" If you're going to ask "What can behavioral medicine do?," the question isn't just what the kidney does; it's more specifically "What does the cortex do?" I'm always puzzled why this is not a standard criterion in any behavioral medicine assessment, because you can be jolly well sure if you've got a fixed hypertension so that it's still high when the patient is asleep, there is nothing you're going to do for this guy with any behavioral techniques. Whereas, if it drops when he's asleep, there's a good reason to think that there's something you may be able to do.

Paul Obrist: In terms of blood pressure drops during sleep, you may have an increase in glomerular filtration rate. I don't know. The neural and humoral control of the kidneys are extremely complicated. An awful lot isn't known, as far as I know, in terms of the intact, conscious human. That's one of the directions in which we're moving, ourselves, right now.

Gary Schwartz: About the kidney and the CNS mechanisms: To the peripheral physiologist, the brain is very tiny and the complexity of the periphery is immense. Of course, to the neurophysiologist, the cardiovascular system is very tiny and the brain is very complicated. And we've got to get the levels of complexity back together again. Empirically, people are beginning to do that. There are some fascinating data coming out on the role of the CNS in the production of hypertension [Brody, Heywood, & Touw, 1980]. Using peripheral procedures of clamping the kidney, the classic Goldblatt clamp procedure, for producing a kidney-generated blood pressure increase turns out to require an intact CNS feedback loop to get the effects. If you ablate certain regions in the brain stem, also in the hypothalamus, you do not get high blood pressure mediated via the kidney.

Martin Orne: The brain stem and the hypothalamus don't go to sleep.

Gary Schwartz: That's right. I think we should begin to look more into cardiovascular–CNS interactions. They're finding afferent mechanisms now from the kidney back up to the brain, which is very curious.

Another point relates to some of the data that we've mentioned about personality predictors of success, particularly the hypochondriasis, which is very interesting. I was wondering whether you have any thoughts about why it is that individuals who report a lot of secondary symptoms and who would be experiencing some distress, I would think, or at least processing some sort of feedback from their bodies, are the ones who appear to be responding to—and, I guess, even remaining in—treatment.

Iris Goldstein: Basically, the hypochondriasis scale covers a variety of functions. It's not just because a person has high blood pressure; he has to score high on several things. The only thing that seems to be a link is that there is a certain amount of awareness about bodily processes, concern, maybe thinking about what's going on, that may relate to a drop in pressure.

Gary Schwartz: Have you looked at that with regard to renin or any of the other data?

Iris Goldstein: We've looked at our plasma renin data from beginning to end of treatment, and nothing's come out of it. Part of the problem is, almost all of the patients have normal renin levels.

David Shapiro: I just wanted to comment a little bit further on the issue of [blood pressure] methodology, which I think is very critical. There are portable systems that have been applied by various investigators, and we've been looking into that ourselves and plan to continue developing that technique. The relationship to the issue of stimulus control and blood pressure is something that is very interesting to me. I commented on that in my own paper [see Chapter 3]. In terms of the issue about interpreting the clinical results, first of all, it seems to me that usually the blood pressure taken during medical examinations is likely to be the highest measure. I think there's plenty of evidence on that already, and I think the work of Sokolow [Sokolow, Werdegar, Kain, & Hinman, 1966] has suggested that the measures taken outside the clinical-type measurements are probably more important with respect to the complications of hypertension. If Patel [1977] [see also Patel, 1973, 1975a, 1975b; Patel & North, 1975] has found reduced pressure during medical examinations and if the pressure is low on the outside, that would be interesting. In addition to that, I happened to see a study just yesterday in the library, I think it's Beiman [Beiman, Graham, & Ciminero, 1978], in which several case studies were done on patients who were studying relaxation techniques. First, the home blood pressure measurement was taken, and the pressures were reduced in the home but still were high in the medical examination. So they instituted a desensitization procedure and got the measurements lowered in the medical examination, also. Patel also had other kinds of techniques, such as cold pressor tests and treadmill tests, which showed positive results. So even though there's a lot of suspicion and difficulty with Patel, it's very hard to find flaws in the study.

Paul Obrist: Well, my concern there is that those pressures are not characteristic of the pressures of a good part of the rest of the day. Every time that cuff goes up, they are using some response strategy.

David Shapiro: But I'm suggesting that the other measurements they take at home, for example, are also percentages lower, so that would mean that she's getting an effect. I mean, it's likely to be lowered anyhow.

John Furedy: Paul [Obrist] was saying that he's using the field technique in order to reduce the problem that the patient knows that his blood pressure is being taken with a cuff. So the patient knows that his bood pressure is being taken, whether it's used in the field or he's in the physician's office. I don't see how this solves anything psychologically.

Paul Obrist: Well, we're going to try to solve it by simultaneously measuring pulse transit time and heart rate. If we find, for example, every time the cuff starts to inflate, his heart rate drops while pulse transit time increases, it would lead me to suspect that the pressure measurement we're getting with the cuff is not going to be characteristic of what the pressure was just before or after that, particularly if they bounce right back.

Richard Surwit: First of all, it's really of interest that the blood pressure recording which correlates best with mortality and morbidity is that casual reading the physician takes in his office. As sloppy as it is, that's the data that the insurance companies go by. It seems to be predictive. Secondly, in the work that David Shapiro and I did together on blood pressure [Surwit, Shapiro, & Good, 1978], we did look at blood pressure recorded automatically via remote controls, without another human being present, as compared to blood pressure taken moments later by the investigator. And there was always a reliable, at least 10 mm [Hg] difference, systolic and diastolic, between a pressure taken with a remote control system in an experimental chamber and the same pressure just moments later when the experimenter walks in with a sphygmomanometer and a stethoscope. There is an increase in the presence of the experimenter. This is reliable. The third thing I wanted to say is a comment about the Patel data. I know I made some remarks about it, too. My feeling is that we shouldn't see any magic here. Patel is actually getting an effect. Why can't anybody else get that effect? Why is it that that's the only study that has those large changes? I like to think that I have a little bit of clinical skill, both as a psychologist and also as a scientist, that I control my work carefully, and I don't understand why it is that nobody else around this table can get those results. I think that if they can be replicated, then whatever she's doing is a very useful design.

Paul Obrist: Those are exactly my thoughts. Why isn't everybody hopping on the bandwagon around here?

Martin Orne: This deviant study reminds me of a very famous insectologist. Once upon a time, he ran into an insect that he simply couldn't fit into his chart; and after trying for some time, he put it on the floor and stepped on it. This happens to be a pet horror of mine, and I think we need to have some care. The thing which I'd like to argue rather strongly and which we often run into in an emerging field is that somebody's coming up with findings which simply don't make sense to us, honest people at that. You try to replicate it and you can't. I think we often then need to go and look at what they, in fact, *do*. It turns out that many people don't know what they do, and they don't describe it properly simply because they don't know how. That doesn't mean that we can't learn from them. It may need a competent scientist to figure out what they're really doing, and there's a little detective job sometimes to be done; but there's much to be learned from it. I'd just like to propose that we be very careful in dismissing it.

Indeed, the findings you see—and this gets back to what we were saying this morning about Lourdes, the funny things that relaxation and the frequency of doing it are important—would suggest that a very convinced investigator who thinks he has a specific treatment and therefore communicates this is going to have significantly better results simply because he has a rationale which he believes in. Very few investigators are capable of compelling people to practice regularly when all they're doing is doing nothing as far as they're concerned, even though they know that's the specific treatment. I think you have tremendous problems because of this peculiar paradox as to what we feel comfortable in doing. As Dave Shapiro said earlier, even if relaxation and biofeedback work to the same extent, he'd feel more comfortable with biofeedback, meaning that he likes the explanations better; and that has an effect.

Gary Schwartz: I think part of the reason why Patel is getting much bigger effects than we're getting in all these studies is because she's doing, in real life, what I was talking about more this morning. I have treated six patients, over the past year, personally. I see them on a regular basis, using a variety of biofeedback and self-regulation procedures; and the effects that I get, on the average, approximate Patel's results. When we manipulate multiple aspects of the individual, there's a lot of personal rapport, a lot of patient education, a lot of motivation, and there's a lot of all kinds of stuff in there. Are we capitalizing the multiple processes? So, the issue is, to what extent we, when we isolate only one little ingredient under control conditions, eliminate a lot of sources of potential variance that are important clinically.

Richard Surwit: Do these patients have lower blood pressure when they go back to their physicians?

Gary Schwartz: Yes.

Theodore Weiss: Could you give us a couple of details on what are some of the manipulations you've done?

Gary Schwartz: They include self-monitoring and training in relaxation, which they practice at home using the cassette series. It also includes cognitive restructuring, where they learn to reinterpret certain kinds of cues, and some assertiveness training where individuals have communications problems, and so on. It's what a typical "behavioral medicine clinician" has in his armamentarium. But I just want to say that the basic components are "relaxation, self-monitoring," and decision making about life style.

Edward Blanchard: We attempted to replicate Patel's 1973 treatment package [Blanchard, Murphy, Haynes, & Abel, 1979] rather than the later one. This consists of 12 sessions, including a four-session baseline and twice-a-week sessions for an additional 4 weeks. Treatment consists of a package of meditation, skin resistance biofeedback, attention to breathing, and regular home practice. In the later report, she included EMG and other techniques, but we did not include these in our study. I'm not sure that it's possible to replicate the later mix of techniques, which included a whole kitchen sink full of stuff.

Our results were not bad. Trying to replicate her results, we obtained a reasonable general effect on diastolic pressure but no effect on systolic pressure. We did not find effects in both systolic and diastolic pressures, as Patel reported, but we did find almost the same reduction in diastolic pressures. At 3 months' follow-up, the reduction in diastolic pressure was maintained with no change, or actually a slight rise in systolic pressure.

Iris Goldstein: Did you do these separately?

Edward Blanchard: No. We tried to replicate the whole treatment package as described in 1973, but we did have a contrast treatment group. This group just came into the lab, relaxed regularly, and practiced doing that regularly. The contrast treatment group had the best results. We had people keeping track of how often they practiced. If you covary that out, that's where all the variance is. If your treatment has very few formal aspects to it other than telling people to relax regularly, and if they'll do it, then you get the treatment effects.

Henry Adams: I want to report another one of these odd experiments. We just completed a blood pressure study [Tollison & Adams, in press] with a 6-month follow-up. Essentially, what we did is, we used relaxation—both the Jacobson and progressive muscular relaxation—and EMG feedback. We also used GSR conditioning; we used a combination of both and a noncontingent feedback condition. Now interestingly enough, what we did is assess them in the lab and then sneak up on each of them at home or at work and take their blood pressure. The person doing this was blind to the treatment condition each subject was under. What we've found at the end of the study is that the EMG biofeedback and the combination of EMG and GSR really had even a larger effect, both on systolic and diastolic, than in Ed Blanchard's study, somewhere in the neighborhood of 7 or 8 [mm Hg] diastolic and 10 to 12 [mm Hg] systolic. The GSR, by the way, did not have this effect. It had some effect, but not as much, and the combination was about the same. The interesting effect, and this may be a fluke, is that over 3 months, and then at 6 months, the EMG [and] relaxation things faded. They tended to regress again towards the mean. But the group that got the GSR and the EMG maintained, and actually lowered, theirs a bit. Now these people were all on medication.

John Furedy: And the noncontingent group. What happend to that?

Henry Adams: No systematic change that we could count.

Martin Orne: How about the amount of practice with the procedure? When they had both, did you practice twice as much?

Henry Adams: They got the same amount of time—half GSR, half EMG. But if you looked at the learning curves, the acquisition of control with EMG and GSR, they look very confused the first five or six trials. And then when they caught on, they came up beautifully. But all the groups got essentially the same amount of treatment time. We also have them practicing at home and just check on them by telephone.

Martin Orne: One of the possibilities is the overlearning kind of phenomenon, which has been commented upon earlier. That's why the multimedia procedures tend to work better. It may be that you have this very specific example of that general effect.

Theodore Weiss: It sounds like there's a lot of evidence in the hypertension area that the main trick is to get the person engaged in whatever procedure you're going to do. There's a lot of data. Luborsky and Greer [unpublished manuscript] reviewed a lot of studies and found, similarly, [that] the technique wasn't so important, but the patient's persistance at doing it was critical in reducing blood pressure. I know Richard Surwit has some data about patients with Raynaud's disease, but I wonder if the whole issue isn't about a match between patient and type of behavioral therapy, as well as investigator and type of behavioral therapy. It seems to me we don't know anything much about that, and that's very important. I mean, that may be the crucial thing. Patients who come eager for biofeedback may do beautifully with biofeedback and badly with the relaxation response, and vice versa.

Paul Obrist: Let me emphasize a point I was trying to make. I'm not disputing Patel's work per se. The point I'm trying to make implies that with any type of treatment study, I will not believe that we have particularly good clinical success unless we're sure that the readings we're getting are representative of that individual's pressure during his waking hours and his interaction with the environment. It's a hairy methodology; I know it, but it's time we quit fooling around and get down to business and really ask questions about "What is the characteristic blood pressure of this person?" I had a physical a week,

4 weeks ago. I'm [called] mildly hypertensive by my internist. He says, "Well, with all your equipment over there, you'd better-check yourself a little bit more." He's aware that it might not be characteristic. They took 12 readings on me the other day, and I didn't have one above 130 [mm Hg] and one above 85 [mm Hg].

Richard Surwit: This is the reading, Paul, which correlates with morbidity and mortality, though.

Paul Obrist: That's disputable. According to Sokolow's studies [Sokolow, Werdegar, Perloff, Cowan, & Brenenstuhl, 1970], the pressures that stayed high in the field correlated with mortality; those that came down in the field didn't. The studies by the New Zealanders [Smirk, 1973], where they got that true basal pressure, also showed this. They acclimate the people to a hospital. Those whose pressure comes down have low mortality; those who stay up on their basal and "resting" pressures have high mortality.

Neal Miller: Those morbidity studies that you talk about were made by people who weren't trained. It's possible that if a person's trained to reduce his blood pressure so that he'll fake his score, then it would be quite different.

Bernard Tursky: I'd like to interject another line of thought into this discussion. We've heard now about Patel's work. We've heard also about other studies where blood pressure is being manipulated by biofeedback, but not by biofeedback on the blood pressure itself. In Andy Elmore's study on migraine headache patients [Elmore & Tursky, 1981], he found a very nice effect in giving them feedback for temporal pulse artery and for hand warming; but when I asked him to look at whether the people that reported the best results in terms of headache also produced the best results in terms of the feedback, it turned out there was no correlation. We have a couple of possible explanations for that; but it still doesn't take away from the point that if we're going to talk about Patel's work, or about anyone, and they're altering blood pressure by working in another system, they must report what happened in those systems and whether there is a correlation between learning in that system and learning in the blood pressure system.

Barry Sterman: Now I'm going to go in an entirely different direction, but this relates to what I heard in the heart rate data. There is a group in Little Rock, Arkansas [Pauly & Scheving, 1964; Scheving, Vedral, & Pauly, 1968], that have shown that if you give barbiturates to a diurnal animal at 8:00 in the morning, the dose just barely effective in producing anesthesia, given 12 hours later at 8:00 p.m., will kill that same animal. Now, this brings in a whole issue that I haven't heard mentioned here at all. It may be very important as a methodological issue—circadian and altradian rhythms and their impact on the kinds of studies that are going on. Is anybody looking at that?

Daniel Cox: There was one study presented at the Biofeedback Society of America about two years ago looking at temperature training values [Mercadal & Murphy, 1977].

Barry Sterman: Well, temperature is clearly very important. But how about arterial pressure and heart rate? I know that there are studies showing if you train at one time of the day, it might produce entirely different effects than at another. When you measure, this becomes very important.

Paul Obrist: We can't disentangle true rhythms from the various events that are going on around the person. You would need a "clinical research unit" where you control his environment and just let the patient relax for 24 hours. This is the problem. You've got to control the environment.

Theodore Weiss: To respond to Barry's question, Bernie Engel and I had a patient about whom we made an interesting observation. We were training this woman who had PVCs to control her heart rate. In the morning, she was pretty good at increasing her heart rate, generally. In the morning she could increase her heart rate, no PVCs; in the afternoon, she could increase her heart rate, lots of PVCs. This happened on 3 successive days. So, we had this saw-toothed curve, and we figured it had to be some kind of circadian rhythm. So it does seem to me that that's a very relevant issue.

REFERENCES

Beiman, I., Graham, L. E., & Ciminero, A. R. Setting generality of blood pressure reductions and the psychological treatment of reactive hypertension. *Journal of Behavioral Medicine,* 1978, *1,* 445–453.

Blanchard, E. B., Murphy, W. D., Haynes, M. R., & Abel, G. G. *A controlled comparison of four kinds of relaxation training in the treatment of hypertension.* Paper presented at the 13th Annual Convention of the Association for Advancement of Behavior Therapy, San Francisco, December 1979.

Brody, M. J., Haywood, J. R., & Touw, K. B. Neural mechanisms in hypertension. *Annual Review of Physiology,* 1980, *42,* 441–453.

Elmore, A. M., & Tursky, B. A comparison of two psychophysiological approaches to the treatment of migraine. *Headache,* 1981, *21,* 93–101.

Luborsky, L., & Greer, S. *Factors influencing psychophysiological effects of relaxation-inducing techniques—with special reference to blood pressure.* Unpublished manuscript.

Mercadal, D., & Murphy, P. *The contributions of biofeedback training and circadian rhythms in learning to relax.* Paper presented at the meeting of the Biofeedback Society of America, Orlando, Fla., 1977.

Patel, C. Yoga and biofeedback in the management of hypertension. *Lancet,* 1973, *7837,* 1053–1055.

Patel, C. 12-month follow-up of yoga and biofeedback in the management of hypertension. *Lancet,* 1975, *7898,* 62–64. (a)

Patel, C. Yoga and biofeedback in the management of "stress," in hypertensive patients. *Clinical Science and Molecular Medicine,* 1975, *48* (Suppl.), 171–174. (b)

Patel, C. Biofeedback-aided relaxation in the management of hypertension. *Biofeedback and Self-Regulation,* 1977, *2,* 1–41.

Patel, C., & North, W. R. S. Randomized controlled trial of yoga and biofeedback in management of hypertension. *Lancet,* 1975, *7925,* 93–95.

Pauly, J. E., & Scheving, L. E. Temporal variations in the susceptibility of white rats to phenobarbital sodium and tremorine. *International Journal of Neuropharmacology,* 1964, *3,* 651–658.

Scheving, L. E., Vedral, D. F., & Pauly, J. E. A circadian susceptibility rhythm in rats to phenobarbital sodium. *Anatomical Record,* 1968, *4,* 741–750.

Smirk, F. H. Causal, basal and supplemental blood pressures. In G. Onesti, K. E. Kim, & J. M. Meyer (Eds.), *Hypertension: Mechanisms and management.* New York: Grune & Stratton, 1973.

Sokolow, M., Werdegar, D., Kain, H. K., & Hinman, A. T., Relationship between level of blood pressure measured casually and by portable recorders and severity of complications in essential hypertension. *Circulation,* 1966, *34,* 279–288.

Sokolow, M., Werdegar, D., Perloff, D. B., Cowan, R. M., & Brenenstuhl, H. Preliminary studies relating portably recorded blood pressure to daily life events in patients with essential hypertension. In M. Koster, H. Musaph, & P. Visser (Eds.), *Psychosomatics in essential hypertension (Bibliotheca Psychiatica No. 144).* White Plains, N.Y.: S. Karger, 1970.

Surwit, R. S., Shapiro, D., & Good, M. I. A comparison of cardiovascular biofeedback, neuromuscular biofeedback, and meditation in the treatment of borderline essential hypertension. *Journal of Consulting and Clinical Psychology,* 1978, *46,* 252–263.

Tollison, C. D., & Adams, H. E. Biofeedback as an adjunct to pharmacological treatment of essential hypertension. *Psychosomatic Medicine,* in press.

8 BIOFEEDBACK IN THE TREATMENT OF MIGRAINE: SIMPLE RELAXATION OR SPECIFIC EFFECTS?

JACKSON BEATTY

Over the past decade, the clinical use of biofeedback procedures as a therapeutic intervention has become increasingly widespread. The rationale for biofeedback as therapy rests on the hypothesis that operant procedures may be employed to effect physiologically significant changes in ANS and CNS functions (Beatty & Legewie, 1977; Schwartz & Beatty, 1977). This approach to clinical treatment may be traced to several sources, all of which historically ignore the physiological question of mechanism with respect to either pathophysiology or therapeutics. First is the tendency of operant-learning theorists to concern themselves with the lawful control of behavior rather than with understanding the nature of the processes mediating that behavior (Skinner, 1938). A second, related heritage is that of behavior therapy. Again, traditionally, behavior therapy has been unconcerned by the mechanisms mediating behavioral change (Bandura, 1969). The third intellectual antecedent of biofeedback is systems theory, a branch of engineering that employs the concept of information feedback in understanding the behavior of many types of controlled processes (Riggs, 1970). In systems theory, at any particular level of analysis, systems are represented by components that display particular relations between their inputs and outputs, with the internal workings of each component being unspecified. Thus, it is not surprising to find that clinical biofeedback has not concerned itself with the question of pathophysiology or mechanism in effecting treatment, but rather has tended to treat the patient as a physiological or behavioral system with measurable parameters to be operantly modified.

This approach contrasts sharply with the intellectual tradition of experimental physiology or with the best examples of clinical medicine. There, the question of mechanism is dominant. The underlying physiological mechanism is important because very different pathophysiological processes can generate similar systemic

Jackson Beatty. Department of Psychology and Brain Research Institute, The University of California at Los Angeles, Los Angeles, California.

signs. Further, it is the nature of the underlying physiological process that determines which types of treatments should be employed. Finally, a knowledge of the underlying mechanism generates hypotheses concerning the ways in which the pathophysiological process may be circumvented or ameliorated.

In this chapter, the use of biofeedback in the treatment of clinical migraine is considered. I do not provide an exhaustive review of this literature, as several excellent reviews have been published recently. (See particularly Jessup, Neufeld, & Merskey, 1979; see also Adams, Feuerstein, & Fowler, 1980; Ray, Raczynski, Rogers, & Kimball, 1979; Yates, 1980.) Instead, I attempt to place the operant treatment of migraine in a physiological perspective: first, by describing the disorder and its precipitating causes; then by reviewing the essential features of migraine pathophysiology; and, finally, by considering the types of biofeedback interventions that might be hypothesized to have specific effectiveness. The present clinical literature is then evaluated from the perspective of the pathophysiological processes that give rise to migrainous headaches.

MIGRAINE: A DESCRIPTION OF THE DISORDER

"Migraine" is defined as a unilateral extracranial headache that often involves other symptoms (Dalessio, 1972). The pain is usually limited to the head, but gastrointestinal symptoms of nausea, vomiting, constipation, or diarrhea are common. Often the attack is accompanied by cold cyanosed extremities, facial pallor, sweating, and tremors. The temporal, frontal, or supraorbital vessels on the affected side are prominent and enlarged.

Migraine is a relatively common disorder, with an estimated incidence of 5% or more (Childes & Sweetnam, 1961; Lennox, 1941). Although migraine may be mixed with muscle tension headache in some patients, it frequently stands alone as a distinct pathophysiological condition.

In two-thirds of all patients, the headaches are strictly unilateral (Lance & Anthony, 1971), being bilateral in the remaining patients. In approximately one of five patients, the headache always affects the same side of the head (Selby & Lance, 1960). The incidence, intensity, and duration of these headaches varies widely both within and between migraine patients (or "migraineurs").

In classical migraine, the headache is preceded by focal neurological symptoms or auras, such as visual scotomas and illusions. These phenomena typically disappear for a short period before the onset of headache. In common migraine, focal neurological abnormalities are not noted.

In both types of migraine, the initial headache is characterized as a dull, pounding pain that becomes increasingly intense. As the headache develops, the pounding quality is replaced by a steady, intense pain that persists until the end of the attack. The duration of migraine headache may be brief, but it is more commonly measured in hours and, occasionally, in days. Sunrise-to-sunset headaches are not uncommon.

PRECIPITATING FACTORS

A variety of factors may precipitate a migrainous attack in susceptible patients (Dalessio, 1972; Lance, 1978). Both physical and emotional stress have been shown to induce migraine headache. An attack may be initiated by physical trauma to the head, by acute physiological stress, or by psychologically stressful events in the patient's life. In addition to such instances of clearly reactive migraine, sustained stress might be supposed to increase the incidence of headache in migraineurs. Physiological changes occurring in sleep may also provoke migraine, as the incidence of nocturnal headache that wakens the sleeper is rather high. Particular categories of foods and changes in dietary habits may precipitate an attack. But perhaps the most frequent precipitating factor in women is that of the hormonal changes that occur in the menstrual cycle. In approximately 60% of female patients, headaches are most common in the few days preceding or immediately following the menses. Finally, pharmacological agents that act to induce vasodilatation frequently trigger migraine, whereas vasoconstrictors are employed to abort an impending attack.

PATHOPHYSIOLOGY OF MIGRAINE

The clinical symptomatology of migraine may be related directly to the pathophysiological processes that give rise to the headache (Dalessio, 1972; Lance, 1978). Migraine is first and foremost a vascular phenomenon. In classical migraine, the aura warning of an attack reflects cerebral ischemia, particularly in the visual cortex, which receives blood in substantial part from the vertebral artery. However, migraine itself is a headache of the extracranial vasculature. Unlike the headache induced by histomine or alcoholic hangover, there is probably very little contribution of the intracranial vasculature to the head pain.

The importance of the extracranial arteries is evident for several reasons. First, simple examination reveals these vessels to be markedly distended only on the affected side of the head during the migraine attack. Second, pressure over these extracranial vessels directly reduces headache pain. Similarly, compression of the common carotid on the affected side both reduces the amplitude of pulsation in the extracranial vessels and reduces head pain. Third, Wolff (cited in Dalessio, 1972) has shown that the intensity of pulsatile pain and the amplitude of pulsation in the extracranial vessels are highly correlated throughout the migraine headache. Fourth, substances such as ergotamine tartrate that act to produce extracranial vasoconstriction specifically reduce or abort migraine headache. Fifth, the headache can be temporarily eliminated by spinning the migraineur in a centrifuge to drain blood from the head to the feet (Dalessio, 1972). Sixth, artificial distension of a superficial artery produces migraine-like head pain (Dalessio, 1972). Seventh, measurements of intracranial blood flow during migraine are inconsistent at best, being increased in some patients and decreased in others (Lance, 1978). These and similar lines of evidence indicate that the immediate cause of migraine headache pain is a loss of tone in the major extracranial vessels, leading to painful pulsatile distension.

It is in this early pulsatile phase of migraine headache that vasoconstrictor agents may act to abort the migraine attack. As the headache develops over a period of 1 to 2 hours, the distended vessels become rigid and tube-like. This results in a sterile edema in the muscular and adventitial structures of the artery wall. It is at this point that the quality of head pain changes from pulsatile to steady. From this point on, vasoconstrictors have no effect on migraine headache.

In all phases of the headache, a curious relation holds between the major affected extracranial arteries and the remainder of the peripheral vasculature. There is often intense peripheral vasoconstriction, leading to marked cooling of the extremities and cyanosis. A similar disparity appears to occur between the large- and small-caliber vessels in the affected hemicrania. The facial pallor characteristic of migraine attack may be explained by a reduction in superficial skin blood flow. This reduction is most marked on the affected side, with thermographically measured skin temperature being 1° to 2° C cooler on the side of the headache (Lance, 1978).

STANDARD TREATMENTS FOR MIGRAINE

It is useful to distinguish among at least three therapeutic approaches or types of treatment for migraine. The first of these attempts to remove or ameliorate the effects of various precipitating factors that act to trigger migraine in susceptible individuals. Psychological interventions play an important role here in reducing the severity of emotional stress on the patient. Relaxation therapies and stress-management techniques probably exert many of their beneficial effects in this prophylactic manner. It is important to note that such interventions are not specific for migraine and that choosing between differing methods of stress reduction does not depend upon the clinical symptomatology of the headache, but rather upon the nature of stresses in the patient's life. It is in this sense that relaxation therapies and stress-management techniques must be considered nonspecific interventions and must be evaluated in that context. Pharmacological treatments may also be nonspecific for migraine in this same sense. For example, the use of sedatives and tranquilizing agents in chronic migraineurs constitutes a nonspecific preventative therapy.

Conversely, some types of prophylactic procedures designed to counteract the effects of precipitating factors are specific for migraine headache. The modification of diet to eliminate migraine-inducing substances is one example of specific prophylaxis. Another is the appropriate selection of contraceptive methods for migrainous women, as many types of oral contraceptives intensify migraine headache.

A second approach to the treatment of migraine attempts to reduce an individual's susceptibility to vascular headache. Such therapeutic procedures may be highly specific for migraine, as when vasoconstrictive agents are administered chronically.

The third type of treatment, and perhaps the most interesting in the present context, is concerned with the treatment of an incipient or ongoing migraine episode. This is the type of intervention that has been proposed for most biofeedback procedures. As in the other types, both nonspecific and specific treatments are commonly employed. An example of a nonspecific treatment of a migraine attack is the use of analgesic agents. These, however, are not usually satisfactory. More useful are specific pharmacological substances that act to vasoconstrict the extracranial arteries to remove the source of migraine pain. Of these, ergotamine tartrate is the most widely used specific treatment for migraine. Ergotamine tartrate acts to produce vasoconstriction in the extracranial arteries without inducing significant changes in either the cerebral or the retinal circulation (Lance, 1978). In normal usage, ergotamine tartrate is administered by the most reliable direct route at the first signs of an impending migraine attack. The effect of the agent is to abort the headache before the extracranial arteries become rigid. These effects are so reliable that a positive response to ergotamine tartrate is considered diagnostic for migraine.

An overview of standard treatments for migraine is important in any consideration of the use of biofeedback for migraine, in that the standard treatments, with their own strengths and weaknesses, provide the benchmarks against which any new procedure must be judged. A new treatment must not only be better than no treatment (the usual control condition in biofeedback research); it must also be shown to be an improvement in some respect over alternative therapeutic procedures.

ASSESSING BIOFEEDBACK AS THERAPY: SOME ISSUES

Jessup *et al.* (1979), in their review of the literature on biofeedback therapy for headache, have provided an exhaustive and critical analysis of the state of the field. They are justifiably unimpressed with the evidence supporting the clinical use of biofeedback methods. They write: "The most challenging question that can be asked of current biofeedback research still remains the most basic: is there a phenomenon to explain?" (p. 226). Jessup *et al.*, like others reviewing this literature (Adams *et al.*, 1980; Ray *et al.*, 1979; Yates, 1980), find little evidence of biofeedback treatment effects that are not attributable to nonspecific effects.

Although the published literature is rather large, very little of it is relevant for critically evaluating the effects of biofeedback on migraine. It is not sufficient to establish that some percentage of patients improves when exposed to a biofeedback therapy; some percentage of patients improves when subjected to virtually any plausible therapeutic procedure. To establish that biofeedback exerts a beneficial effect that may be uniquely attributed to the treatment requires the use of controlled experimental designs. Unfortunately, very few rigorous experimental evaluations of biofeedback as a treatment for migraine have been attempted. Instead, case studies or group case studies are typically reported. Perhaps this relative absence of critical investigation reflects a deep suspicion as to the true power of the treatment.

In the remainder of this chapter, I evaluate these experimental studies. In contrast to the exhaustive reviews mentioned above, I restrict the present discussion by the following criteria. First, all individual and group case reports will be excluded, as they do not address the question of specific efficacy. Only experimental designs contrasting a biofeedback treatment either with other treatments or with control conditions will be considered. Second, the reports of the experiments must be published; dissertation abstracts and orally presented papers contain too little information for critical evaluation.

BIOFEEDBACK FOR MIGRAINE: HAND WARMING

The use of biofeedback methods to induce peripheral vasodilatation as a means of terminating an ongoing migraine headache was proposed by Sargent, Green, and Walters (1973). They reported that the idea "was suggested by the experience of a research subject who, during the spontaneous recovery from a migraine attack, demonstrated considerable flushing in her hands with an accompanying 10 ° F rise in two minutes" (p. 130–131). Using a combination of autogenic and biofeedback methods, the Menninger group has attempted to establish the use of hand warming in the treatment of migraine by using a series of case studies rather than an experimental evaluation.

How convincing are the experimental data that test the use of hand warming as a treatment for migraine headache? Using the criteria outlined above, there are only three experimental reports that are relevant. Taken together, they provide little evidence supporting the therapeutic use of feedback for hand warming in migraine.

First is the study of Andreychuk and Skriver (1975), which compared the effects of three treatments on a combined index of headache duration in hours and headache intensity in a group of 33 migraineurs. These subjects were also evaluated for hypnotic susceptibility. The biofeedback group received finger temperature feedback and instruction in autogenic relaxation. A second group received instructions in self-hypnosis and relaxation. A third group received relaxation instructions and feedback that attempted to induce an increase in occipital alpha-frequency EEG activity. All subjects received 10 training sessions at weekly intervals. A comparison of pretreatment and posttreatment headache scores revealed significant decreases in headache duration and intensity in each of the three groups, but indicated no significant differences among the groups. These data suggest that the biofeedback procedure contained no specific component of value in treating migraine. Also indicative of a nonspecific mechanism was the finding that the highly hypnotizable subjects tended to show more positive responses in all treatment groups.

In the second controlled study, Mullinix, Norton, Hack, and Fishman (1978) compared true and false feedback for digital skin temperature in 12 patients divided into two groups. Each subject was first given 6 training sessions within a 3-week period and then given three additional sessions in the 1st, 2nd, and 6th posttraining week. Subjects receiving accurate temperature feedback produced significantly greater increases in digital temperature during training. However, both groups showed similar improvements in headache symptomology following treatment: there was no significant difference in posttreatment headache between the groups. Furthermore, there was no correlation between the magnitude of hand warming and the percentage of improvement in headache symptoms. These data are also in accord with a nonspecific interpretation of the therapeutic effect.

The third study was reported by Blanchard, Theobald, Williamson, Silver, and Brown (1978), who tested a group of 30 migraine patients randomly assigned to one of three experimental conditions: temperature biofeedback with autogenic training; progressive relaxation; or waiting-list control. Blanchard *et al.* found that subjects in both the relaxation and the biofeedback conditions showed significant improvements on a variety of headache variables during the period of treatment. Subjects in both treatment groups improved significantly more than did the waiting-list controls in this phase of the experiment. The subjects in the waiting-list control group were then added to the two treatment groups. With this increase in sample size, the relaxation group showed a significantly greater improvement at the end of training than did the biofeedback group. In the 3-month follow-up period, there were no significant differences between the two treatment groups, as all patients tended to revert to their pretreatment headache levels.

Taken together, these three published experimental tests of hand-warming biofeedback as treatment for migraine suggest that the observed improved improvements in headache symptomology may be ascribed to nonspecific treatment effects. This interpretation is reinforced by the results of two additional experiments that attempted to assess the physiological mechanism by which biofeedback procedures may induce peripheral vasodilatation.

Price and Tursky (1976) tested 40 migraine patients and 40 normal controls under one of four experimental conditions in a single experimental session. The conditions were as follows: binary and analog feedback for increasing finger blood flow; yoked (false) feedback; a tape-recorded set of relaxation instructions; and a neutral tape describing techniques for growing avocados. Subjects in the neutral tape condition showed a significant decrease in digital blood volume over the experimental period. Subjects in all other groups tended to show nonsignificant increases in digital blood volume. The results of these experimental treatments did not differ significantly from one another. Measurements of temporal integral blood volume change were also obtained, which correlated with the corresponding digital measure at $r = +.66$ in the migraine population. This means that procedures that act to increase peripheral blood flow might also act to increase blood flow in the extracranial arteries—which is precisely the opposite of the specific vasomotor effect that is useful in treating migraine—if the peripheral treatment acted to increase digital blood flow. Such data argue against a specific effect of biofeedback procedures that attempt to increase peripheral vasodilatation to treat migraine headache.

Perhaps the most direct evidence concerning the mechanism by which feedback-induced hand warming is accomplished was provided by Sovak, Kunzel, Sternbach, and Dalessio (1978), who measured pulse volume in the supraorbital, superficial temporal, and digital arterial beds in 5 normal subjects and 10 migraine patients who were trained to increase finger temperature by a combination of feedback and relaxation methods. In the 5 normal subjects, digital vasodilation was accompanied by a significant temporal artery vasoconstriction, but no significant temporal pulse volume was observed in the 10 migraineurs. Of particular interest is the detailed hemodynamic analysis of these data. First, the utility of temperature feedback in specifically altering peripheral pulse volume may be questioned, as the delay between rapidly changing vasomotor responses and surface changes in skin temperature is quite long. The magnitude of this delay argues against the likelihood of the observed vasodilatation being an operantly acquired specific autonomic response. Second, Sovak *et al.* argue that the observed systemic redistribution of blood flow cannot account for the reported beneficial effects of hand-warming biofeedback on migraine. If that were the case, then migraine could be treated by inducing peripheral vasodilatation in response to placing the patient's hands in warm water. In fact, this is not an effective procedure. Third, Sovak *et al.* demonstrate that the only possible neural mechanism that could account for the total pattern of hemodynamic response (bradycardia and increased blood flow in both skin and muscle in the periphery) is a general decrease in sympathetic outflow. Furthermore, decreases in tonic sympathetic outflow are a known accompaniment of deep relaxation. These lines of reasoning lead to the conclusion that temperature feedback training may belong to the "same realm as general relaxation procedures, desensitization, hypnosis or autohypnosis" (Sovak *et al.*, 1978, p. 202). This view is in accord with the results of the systematic experimental investigations of hand-temperature feedback for migraine discussed above.

BIOFEEDBACK FOR MIGRAINE: EXTRACRANIAL VASOCONSTRICTION

An entirely different approach to the use of biofeedback for treatment of migraine involves direct measurement of pulse pressure amplitude in the large extracranial arteries. The theoretical rationale for using operant methods to induce extracranial vasoconstriction is straightforward: Since the single most effective pharmacological treatment for migraine, ergotamine tartrate, acts primarily to produce extracranial vasoconstriction and thereby to abort the headache, a behavioral intervention that produces similar vasomotor responses might also be therapeutic. In this sense, the use of feedback methods to produce decreases in pulse amplitude measured over the superficial temporal artery was proposed as a specific behavioral therapy for migraine by Friar and Beatty (1976). They reported the results of a controlled experimental test of the effects of pulse amplitude feedback on migraine.

Friar and Beatty selected a population of 19 young, otherwise healthy migraineurs whose history included a positive response to ergotamine tartrate. It was reasoned that the patients who did not respond favorably to a pharmacological vasoconstrictor would not be likely to benefit from learned vasoconstriction. The subjects were assigned to two groups; one was trained to reduce pulse volume of the temporal artery, and the other to reduce pulse volume in the arterial bed of the index finger. All subjects kept a headache log for 30 days before and after treatment. Each subject was given eight 1-hour training sessions and a ninth testing session in which the ability to regulate the vasomotor response without feedback was assessed. In all subjects, both temporal and digital pulse volume and temperature were recorded during each of the training and testing sessions. These procedures elicited measurable control of the target vasomotor response. Subjects in the control group (peripheral vasoconstriction) were able voluntarily to produce a 33% reduction in finger pulse amplitude when tested. No change in temporal pulse amplitude occurred in these subjects. Conversely, patients in the experimental group (the group that learned temporal vasoconstriction) were able voluntarily to produce a 20% reduction in temporal pulse amplitude, which was accompanied by a 30% reduction in finger pulse amplitude. These differences were all significant, as was the difference in temporal artery pulse amplitude between experimental and control subjects.

An analysis of the pretreatment and posttreatment headache data is suggestive of a specific therapeutic effect of the experimental treatment. Subjects in the control group reported a modest (14%) reduction in both total number of headaches and number of major migraine attacks (3 or more hours in duration). Neither reduction was statistically significant. Subjects in the experimental group showed larger mean reductions in both total incidence of headaches (36%; $p < .10$, one tailed) and incidence of major headache (44%; $p < .05$, one tailed). There was no reduction in mean rated headache intensity in either group. This is precisely the pattern of data that would be expected if the effect of the experimental treatment were specific. The primary result should be to abort migraine attacks in a manner analogous to the effects of ergotamine tartrate. The tendency toward fewer major headaches is in accord with this expectation. Furthermore, the intervention is not designed as an analgesic. Therefore, the failure to find a reduction in headache intensity is also in accord with a specific, nonplacebo mode of action. One would expect a placebo treatment to affect the intensity measure as a part of a generalized positive response to relaxing treatment.

Nonetheless, these data do not seem to foreshadow a new clinical treatment for migraine. First, the observed effects were rather small in magnitude, and prolonged follow-up data are not available. Thus, the clinical meaningfulness of the effect is open to serious question. Second, the measurement and training procedure employed by Friar and Beatty is technically difficult and complex. Although the measurement of pulse amplitude using pressure transducers is relatively straightforward, to insure that the data are not contaminated by mechanical movement artifacts requires sophisticated computer-based data processing techniques. In its present form, the technique is not easily exportable to a clinical setting.

SOME CONCLUSIONS

I am forced back to the question posed by Jessup *et al.* (1979): "Is there a phenomenon to explain?" There is, in my opinion, no convincing evidence even to suggest, let alone to establish, that biofeedback methods represent a reasonable therapeutic procedure for the treatment of migraine headache. Most of the published literature is not relevant for a critical evaluation of the effects of biofeedback procedures on migraine. The few experimental studies of the hand-warming procedures show no difference in efficacy between these treatments and simple relaxation interventions. Furthermore, detailed studies of the hemodynamic effects of hand-warming procedures suggest that any observed therapeutic effect cannot be attributed to specific effects on the pathophysiological processes, but rather are indicative of generalized relaxation. Finally, when feedback procedures are used to mimic the specific extracranial vasoconstrictive effects of ergotamine tartrate in the treatment of migraine, the magnitude of both the physiological changes and the therapeutic effects is too small to justify the use of this potentially specific intervention in a clinical setting.

While these data speak quite clearly against the continued use of biofeedback procedures in the treatment of migraine, they offer considerable hope for behavioral medicine more generally. The nonspecific effects of these treatments are often quite sizable, and they may be undertaken with no known detrimental side effects. Thus, it would appear a natural course of action for those interested in a behavioral approach to the treatment of migraine to concentrate their efforts on the development and refinement of the nonspecific relaxation therapies. As was mentioned earlier, these procedures should not be adapted to the specific properties of the disorder, but to the general physiological and psychological status of the patient. This, I believe, is the most significant approach that behavioral medicine might take in the clinical treatment of migraine headache.

REFERENCES

Adams, H. E., Feuerstein, M., & Fowler, J. L. Migraine headache: Review of parameters, etiology, and intervention. *Psychological Bulletin,* 1980, *87,* 217–237.

Andreychuk, T., & Skriver, C. Hypnosis and biofeedback in the treatment of migraine headache. *International Journal of Clinical and Experimental Hypnosis,* 1975, *23,* 172–183.

Bandura, A. *Principles of behavior modification.* New York: Holt, Rinehart & Winston, 1969.

Beatty, J., & Legewie, H. (Eds.). *Biofeedback and behavior.* New York: Plenum, 1977.

Blanchard, E. B., Theobald, D. E., Williamson, D. A., Silver, B. V., & Brown, D. A. Temperature biofeedback in the treatment of migraine headaches. *Archives of General Psychiatry,* 1978, *35,* 581–588.

Childes, A., & Sweetnam, M. Study of 104 cases of migraine. *British Journal of Industrial Medicine,* 1961, *18,* 243.

Dalessio, D. *Wolff's headache and other head pain* (3rd ed.). New York: Oxford University Press, 1972.

Frair, L. R., & Beatty, J. Migraine: Management by trained control of vasoconstriction. *Journal of Consulting and Clinical Psychology,* 1976, *44,* 46–53.

Jessup, B. A., Neufeld, R. W. J., & Merskey, H. Biofeedback therapy for headache and other pain: An evaluative review. *Pain,* 1979, *7,* 225–270.

Lance, J. W. *Mechanism and management of headache* (3rd ed.). London: Butterworths, 1978.

Lance, J. W., & Anthony, M. Thermographic studies of vascular headache. *Medical Journal of Australia,* 1971, *1,* 240.

Lennox, W. *Science and seizures.* New York: Harper, 1941.

Mullinix, J. M., Norton, B. J., Hack, S., & Fishman, M. A. Skin temperature feedback and migraine. *Headache,* 1978, *17,* 242–244.

Price, K. P., & Tursky, B. Vascular reactivity of migraineurs and non-migraineurs: A comparison of responses to self-control procedures. *Headache,* 1976, *16,* 210–217.

Ray, W. J., Raczynski, J. M., Rogers, T., & Kimball, W. H. *Evaluation of clinical biofeedback.* New York: Plenum, 1979.

Riggs, D. S. *Control theory and physiological feedback mechanisms.* Baltimore: Williams & Wilkins, 1970.

Sargent, J. D., Green, E. E., & Walters, E. D. Preliminary report on the use of autogenic feedback training in the treatment of migraine and tension headaches. *Psychosomatic Medicine,* 1973, *35,* 129–135.

Schwartz, G. E., & Beatty, J. (Eds.). *Biofeedback: Theory and research.* New York: Academic Press, 1977.

Selby, G., & Lance, J. W. Observations on 500 cases of migraine and allied vascular headache. *Journal of Neurology, Neurosurgery and Psychiatry,* 1960, *23,* 23.

Skinner, B. F. *The behavior of organisms.* New York: Appleton-Century, 1938.

Sovak, M., Kunzel, M., Sternbach, R. A., & Dalessio, D. J. Is volitional manipulation of hemodynamics a valid rationale for biofeedback therapy of migraine? *Headache,* 1978, *18,* 197–202.

Yates, A. J. *Biofeedback and the modification of behavior.* New York: Plenum, 1980.

9 BIOFEEDBACK AND THE BEHAVIORAL TREATMENT OF RAYNAUD'S DISEASE

RICHARD S. SURWIT

In the development of clinical biofeedback, the usual and logical course of events dictates that biofeedback be applied as a clinical treatment once it has been shown efficacious in controlling the particular physical response that relates to a particular disease. Thus, the Shapiro group (e.g., Shapiro & Schwartz, 1972) experimented extensively with blood pressure feedback before applying it to hypertension; operant control of EEG was widely investigated by Sterman and others before its application to the treatment of epilepsy; heart rate feedback was pioneered by Brener, Lang, and others before its application by Weiss and Engel to cardiac arrhythmias; and so on. The use of biofeedback in the treatment of Raynaud's disease did not develop in a similar fashion. Although there were several reports of the use of biofeedback to alter digital blood flow (e.g., Snyder & Noble, 1968) the majority of this literature was published after or during the extensive application of biofeedback to the treatment of Raynaud's disease.

Raynaud's disease, like essential hypertension, is a functional disorder of the cardiovascular system; that is, it involves no observable organic pathology in its idiopathic form. Its symptoms consist of intermittent bilateral vasospasms of the hands, feet, and (rarely) the face, which can be elicited by cold stimulation and/or emotional stress (Spittell, 1972). During an attack, the affected area classically exhibits a triphasic color change, first blanching, then turning cyanotic blue, and finally becoming bright red as the spasm is relieved and reactive hyperemia sets in. Severe manifestations of this disorder are not common, but it has been estimated (Lewis, 1949) that it affects approximately 20% of most young women in its mildest forms.

Richard S. Surwit. Department of Psychiatry, Duke University Medical Center, Durham, North Carolina.

Clinical Raynaud's disease is found to occur five times more often in women than in men (Spittell, 1972), the time of onset occurring in the first and second decades of life. A similar syndrome, known as Raynaud's phenomenon, is found to occur secondary to a variety of vascular diseases (Spittell, 1972). Raynaud's phenomenon is common in progressive systemic sclerosis, lupus erythematosus, thromboangiitis, obliterans, carpal tunnel syndrome, and so forth. However, the physiology of idiopathic Raynaud's disease is not well understood. While Raynaud himself (Raynaud, 1862) attributed the malady to sympathetic overreactivity, Sir Thomas Lewis maintained that the fault was primarily local (Lewis, 1949). This debate has not yet been resolved. Nevertheless, because the neural control of the peripheral vasculature is mediated entirely by the sympathetic nervous system, both Raynaud's disease and Raynaud's phenomenon make logical targets for the application of behavioral techniques.

CASE STUDIES

Shapiro and Schwartz (1972) conducted the first case study in which patients suffering from Raynaud's disease were trained to increase peripheral blood flow. In this study, two patients suffering from primary Raynaud's disease were provided with biofeedback of blood volume changes from a photoplethysmograph. Feedback of blood volume changes occurring in the finger was provided to one patient, while the other patient was given feedback of blood volume recorded from the great toe. The treatment was moderately successful for one patient, who reported a reduction in the severity of Raynaud's symptoms. Surwit (1973) reported the first systematic use of temperature feedback in the treatment of Raynaud's disease. The patient in this study was a 21-year-old female with severe vasospasms in both hands and feet. The patient had undergone cervical and lumbar sympathectomies, with remission of symptoms only in the lower extremities. Because she lived in Montreal, she was exposed to severe cold at least half of the year. The patient was initially trained in autogenic and progressive relaxation techniques and then provided with a series of 52 laboratory biofeedback sessions over a 9-month period. Results indicated that the patient's basal digital temperature rose from 23.3° to 26.6°C and that a concomitant decrease in the frequency of vasospastic attacks occurred over this time period. This patient continued to utilize these techniques and to report improvement in symptomatology up to 4 years following training.

Jacobson, Hackett, Surman, and Silverberg (1973) explored the utility of hypnosis in temperature feedback. In this case, the patient showed very little improvement during the hypnosis portion of training; however, when biofeedback training was introduced, and the patient was instructed to increase finger temperature in relation to that of the forehead, a marked reduction in the frequency of vasospasms was observed. This study is different from that previously reported by Surwit in that it placed much less emphasis on laboratory training and more on the patient's using self-control techniques at home.

Blanchard and Haynes (1975) have conducted the most systematic and controlled single-case study published to date. Changes in skin temperature and the frequency of vasospastic attacks were evaluated under three conditions: a no-treatment baseline; a self-control technique, in which the patient was asked to try to increase her hand temperature any way that she could; and biofeedback training to increase hand temperature in relation to that of the forehead. During the biofeedback sessions, the patient showed an ability to increase her hand temperature an average of 3.4 °F, whereas no consistent changes in temperature were noted under any other treatment condition. The authors also reported a gradual increase in basal finger temperature from 79 °F to 91 °F over the course of treatment. Reductions in the frequency of vasospastic attacks were achieved concurrent with temperature biofeedback training alone. These reductions were maintained up to 4 months' follow-up. Although control over skin temperature had deteriorated by 7 months after treatment, acquisition of the learned control was easily reinstated after five additional sessions. Thus, these results provide strong support for the utility of temperature feedback as opposed to autogenic training, hypnosis, or other relaxation procedures. Finally, Taub (1977) described training a patient with Raynaud's disease to increase hand temperature while the patient's body temperature was challenged by cold. The patient was fitted with a "cold suit" in which cold water could be rapidly circulated, exposing the patient's entire body to cold stress. Taub reports that this patient was actually able to increase hand temperature from 88 °F to 89.5 °F while the temperature of the cold suit was decreased from 80 °F to 60 °F. Unfortunately, no data are provided on the clinical changes observed in this patient.

In the past 4 years, a series of controlled-group outcome studies was performed in our laboratory. These studies attempted to identify the relative contribution of particular behavioral techniques in facilitating self-control of skin temperature in the treatment of Raynaud's disease. In the first study of the series (Surwit, Pilon, & Fenton, 1978), two major questions were addressed: What contribution does biofeedback make to a course of autogenic training in the control of hand temperature? And does autogenic training or biofeedback training need to be performed under laboratory conditions in order for patients to benefit?

A group of 30 female patients diagnosed as suffering from idiopathic Raynaud's disease was trained to control digital skin temperature, using either autogenic training or a combination of autogenic training and skin temperature feedback. Training was conducted either in a laboratory or in three group sessions supplemented by extensive home practice. The design of this study is presented in Fig. 1. All subjects were exposed to an initial cold stress procedure, in which they were seated in an experimental chamber while the ambient temperature was slowly dropped from 26 °C to 17 °C over 72 minutes. Skin temperature, heart rate, and pulse amplitudes were monitored during the temperature change. This procedure was given to half the subjects immediately before and immediately following a 4-week training sequence. The remaining half of the sample were exposed to an additional cold stress challenge prior to treatment as a control for possible habituation effects. The results of this study are illustrated in Fig. 2. All subjects, regardless of the condition in which they were trained, showed a significant improvement in their ability to maintain digital skin temperature, in relation both to the initial cold stress and to the second cold stress given to the half of the sample not immediately treated. Patients who served as a no-treatment control not only failed to show improvement during the second test, but actually deteriorated in performance. In addition to this objective finding, all treated patients reported significant reductions in the frequency of vasospastic attacks over the 4-week treatment period. No additional ben-

FIG. 1. Design of study. (From "Behavioral Treatment of Raynaud's Disease" by R. S. Surwit, R. N. Pilon, and C. H. Fenton, *Journal of Behavioral Medicine*, 1978, *1*, 323–335. Copyright 1978 by Plenum Press. Reprinted by permission.)

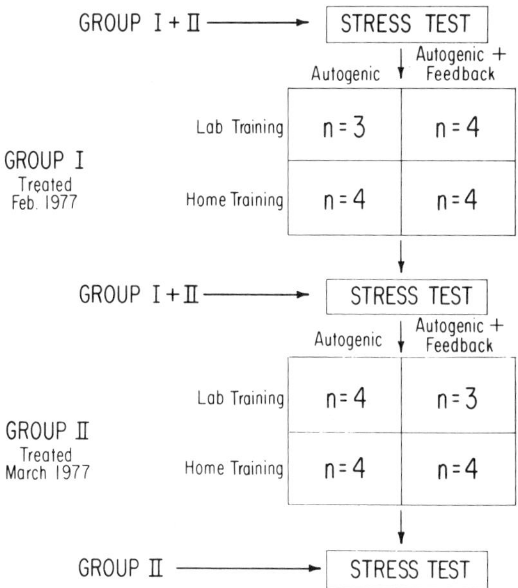

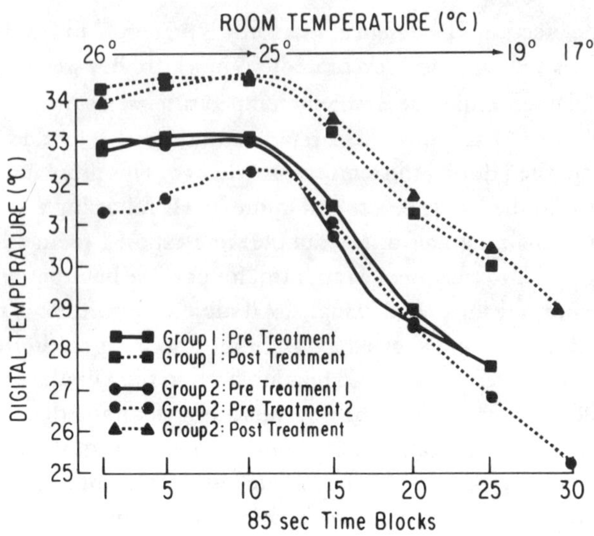

FIG. 2. Mean digital temperature during pretreatment and posttreatment stress tests. Recording of skin temperature was begun after a 10-minute stabilization period. (From "Behavioral Treatment of Raynaud's Disease" by R. S. Surwit, R. N. Pilon, and C. H. Fenton, *Journal of Behavioral Medicine*, 1978, *1*, 323–335. Copyright 1978 by Plenum Press. Reprinted by permission.)

efits could be observed for those subjects receiving skin temperature biofeedback or for those subjects whose training was conducted by the laboratory (see Fig. 3).

The second study of this series (Keefe, Surwit, & Pilon, 1980) served as a partial replication as well as an extension of the study just described. This second study attempted to provide a more rigorous test of home biofeedback training by having patients on home practice regimens use more sophisticated and sensitive temperature feedback equipment than had been used in the prior study. This study also compared the efficacy of autogenic training (which focuses specifically upon sensations of warmth and heaviness in the hands) to general relaxation training (which focuses upon reducing muscular tension generally throughout the body). In addition, this study used four laboratory cold stress challenges like those described in the previous study, given at the first week of a 4-week baseline and during the first, third, and fifth weeks of training. A total of 21 patients were randomly assigned to one of three treatment conditions. The first group received progressive muscle relaxation and home practice instructions; the second group received autogenic training and home practice instructions; and the third group received autogenic training and skin temperature feedback with autogenic instructions and portable skin temperature feedback equipment. The results confirmed those of the initial study in that all patients improved regardless of treatment (see Fig. 4). Data gathered from the cold stress procedures indicated that subjects improved gradually and significantly over the four cold stress challenges. This improvement was not felt to be a result of habituations, since the initial study had indicated that patients deteriorated in performance without training. The gradual improvement of the response to the cold stress procedure suggests that some learning process was taking place. As previously reported, all treated patients also experienced approximately a 40% reduction in the frequency of vasospastic attacks. This reduction in symptoms was obtained at the same time that a significant drop in ambient outdoor temperature was occurring.

In the final study (Keefe, Surwit, & Pilon, 1979) the maintenance of treatment gains was evaluated. Subjects were 19 patients who had undergone behavioral training in the initial study (Surwit *et al.*, 1978). Patients were asked to keep a daily log of frequency and severity of vasospastic attacks and to fill in a follow-up questionnaire dealing with their satisfaction with various elements in the treatment regimen. A year after initial treatment, patients were given an additional cold stress challenge. Thus, as before, both objective and subjective indices of symptom improvement were obtained. The results of the study are fascinating in that they appear on the

FIG. 3. Mean number of intensity of attacks per day reported by all subjects during the 4 weeks immediately preceding training and the 4 weeks of training. The reduction in the number of attacks across weeks of treatment was significant. (From "Behavioral Treatment of Raynaud's Disease" by R. S. Surwit, R. N. Pilon, and C. H. Fenton, *Journal of Behavioral Medicine,* 1978, *1,* 323–335. Copyright 1978 by Plenum Press. Reprinted by permission.)

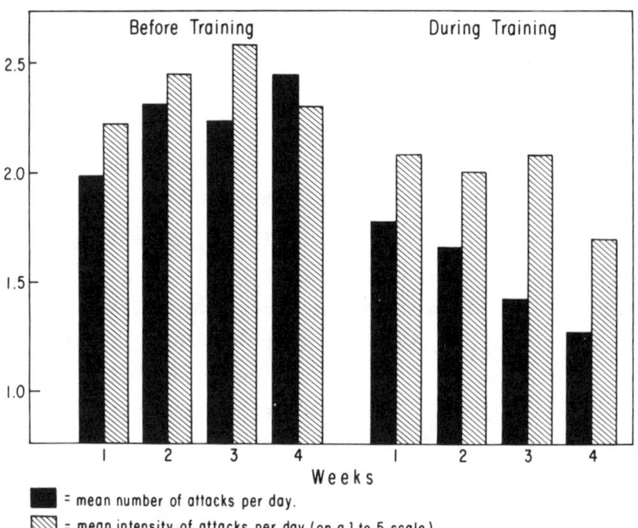

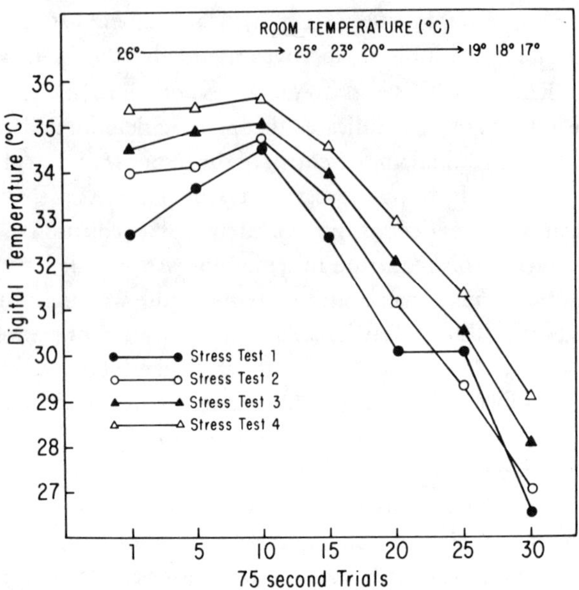

FIG. 4. Mean digital temperature during pretreatment stress tests (stress test 1) and posttreatment stress tests (stress tests 2–4). Recording of skin temperature was begun after a 10-minute stabilization period. (From "Biofeedback, Autogenic Training and Progressive Relaxation in the Treatment of Raynaud's Disease" by F. J. Keefe, R. S. Surwit, and R. N. Pilon, *Journal of Applied Behavior Analysis,* 1980, *13,* 3–11. Copyright 1980 by Society for the Experimental Analysis of Behavior. Reprinted by permission.)

surface to be contradictory. A year after treatment, patients reported an average of 1.2 vasospasms per day, compared to 1.3 attacks per day immediately following treatment 1 year earlier. However, the ability of patients to maintain digital temperature in the face of cold stress had significantly deteriorated and was virtually identical to their initial treatment performance (see Figs. 5 and 6). The contradiction implied by these two sets of data can be explained by examining data from the follow-up questionnaire administered to all patients. As can be seen in Fig. 5, most patients had stopped practicing the behavioral techniques they were taught during the spring months following their initial training. These patients had not returned to levels of practice comparable to those they were engaged in during the initial treatment. Thus, while response to performance during cold stress was seen as related to practice, the patients' subjective reports of improvement seem to be under the control of the other variables.

Another group of investigators has obtained similar results. Jacobson, Manschreck, and Silverberg (1979) gave 12 patients suffering from idiopathic Raynaud's disease 12 sessions of muscle relaxation training over a 6-week period. Half of the patients were also given auditory and visual skin temperature feedback during the

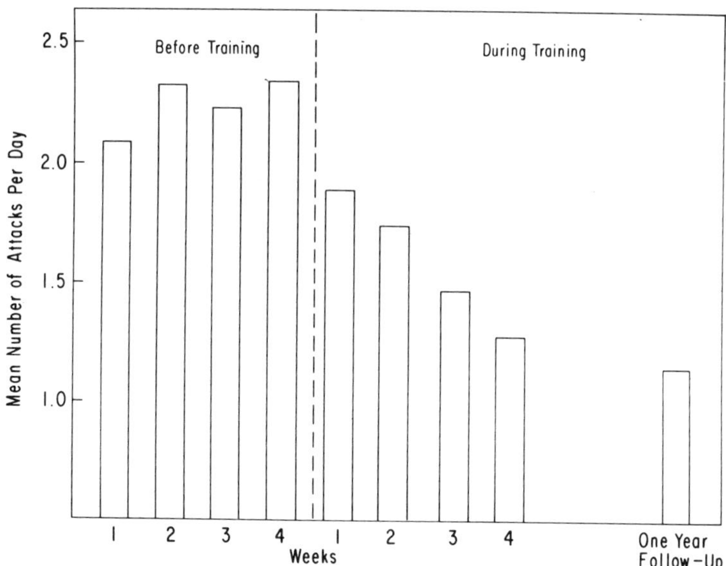

FIG. 5. Mean frequency of vasospastic attacks recorded during the 4 weeks before training, the 4 weeks during training, and the week of a 1-year follow-up. (From "A One Year Follow-Up of Raynaud's Patients Treated with Behavior Therapy Techniques" by F. J. Keefe, R. S. Surwit, and R. N. Pilon, *Journal of Behavioral Medicine,* 1979, *2,* 385–391. Copyright 1979 by Plenum Press. Reprinted by permission.)

FIG. 6. Mean digital temperature (°C) during could stress tests conducted before treatment, after treatment, and at a 1-year follow-up. (From "A One Year Follow-Up of Raynaud's Patients Treated with Behavior Therapy Techniques" by F. J. Keefe, R. S. Surwit, and R. N. Pilon, *Journal of Behavioral Medicine,* 1979, *2,* 385–391. Copyright 1979 by Plenum Press. Reprinted by permission.)

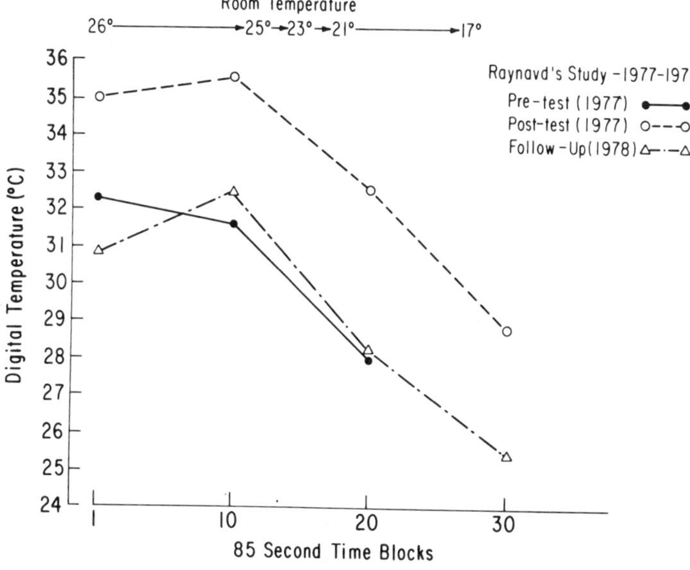

training sessions. Skin temperature during training, as well as patients' self-reports of improvement, were collected. Both groups showed significant increases in skin temperature during training, with larger skin temperature increases shown by the group not receiving feedback. All subjects rated themselves as moderately to markedly improved at 1 month, with seven subjects continuing to report improvement at 2 years. No data were collected on objective hand temperature changes at follow-up.

CONCLUSIONS

The review above allows the following conclusions to be drawn about the utility of biofeedback in the treatment of Raynaud's disease. First, it appears that biofeedback, especially when used with autogenic training or hypnosis, provides a reliable behavioral treatment for Raynaud's disease. Investigators have described both subjective reductions of symptomatology and objective indices of increased blood flow under conditions of cold stress subsequent to training. Typically, patients report up to 50% reduction in symptom frequency following training, with the increase of resting digital temperature approximately 3 to 4 °C. These results are impressive and parallel the best clinical effects of many medical as well as surgical interventions.

However, when we attempt to single biofeedback out of a general package of behavioral interventions, the peculiar contribution of biofeedback to therapy becomes more difficult to discern. In the three controlled-group outcome studies just reviewed, there is typically no difference in efficacy between relaxation techniques or relaxation techniques supplemented with biofeedback. One recent study coming from our laboratory at Duke University Medical Center does tend to point out a difference in therapeutic efficacy between biofeedback-assisted and nonbiofeedback-assisted relaxation procedures. Surwit and Fenton (1980) compared the performance of subjects during autogenic training both with and without skin temperature feedback. Eight subjects received eight sessions of feedback-assisted autogenic instructions, while eight subjects received eight sessions of autogenic training alone. Typically, all subjects showed a .3 °C rise from baseline temperature levels during the 5-minute interval when they were given autogenic instructions. Following the playing of the tapes, subjects were asked to recite the autogenic phrases to themselves over a 72-minute period. All subjects demonstrated a decrease in digital skin temperature over this period. However, those subjects receiving skin temperature feedback were able to maintain higher levels of digital temperature throughout the course of the session. Thus, while the autogenic instructions or suggestion were seen as responsible for initial changes in vasomotor tone, feedback did seem to be of some help in allowing subjects to maintain these changes.

Until recently, no study investigating the treatment of Raynaud's disease with skin temperature feedback used feedback to the exclusion of suggestion, autogenic training, or other relaxation procedures. However, Guglielmi (1979) recently conducted a group outcome study employing the double-blind design, in which both the subjects and the therapist were unaware as to whether subjects were getting skin temperature feedback, EMG feedback, or no-treatment control. While all patients showed a marked decrease in the number of vasospastic attacks, no significant differences were found among the three treatment groups on any of the clinical measures used to assess symptomatic relief. This study, in combination with the results previously presented, argues strongly against biofeedback being the essential ingredient in the therapeutic effects that are often attributed to it. Nevertheless, behavioral techniques appear to show strong promise as an effective means of controlling peripheral vascular disease. In the research reviewed here, the frequency of vasospasms was reduced an average of 50% in those patients receiving any type of relaxation treatment, including biofeedback. These results are impressive, particularly because of the lack of an adequate medical or surgical remedy (Spittell, 1972). Raynaud's disease may constitute one disorder for which behavioral treatments can be used as indicated.

ACKNOWLEDGMENT

Supported by Grant No. HL22547 from the National Heart, Lung, and Blood Institute and by Research Scientist Development Award No. MH 00303 to Richard S. Surwit.

REFERENCES

Blanchard, E. B., & Haynes, M. R. Biofeedback treatment of Raynaud's disease. *Journal of Behavior Therapy and Experimental Psychiatry*, 1975, *6*, 230–234.

Guglielmi, R. S. Personal communication, 1979.

Jacobson, A. M., Hackett, T. P., Surman, D. S., & Silverberg, E. L. Raynaud's phenomenon: Treatment with hypnotic and operant technique. *Journal of the American Medical Association*, 1973, 225, 739–740.

Jacobson, A. M., Manschreck, T. C., & Silverberg, E. Behavioral treatment for Raynaud's Disease: A comparative study with long-term follow-up. *American Journal of Psychiatry*, 1979, *136*, 844–846.

Keefe, F. J., Surwit, R. S., & Pilon, R. N. A one year follow-up of Raynaud's patients treated with behavior therapy techniques. *Journal of Behavioral Medicine*, 1979, *2*, 385–391.

Keefe, F. J., Surwit, R. S., & Pilon, R. N. Biofeedback, autogenic training and progressive relaxation in the treatment of Raynaud's disease. *Journal of Applied Behavioral Analysis*, 1980, *13*, 3–11.

Lewis, T. *Vascular disorders of the limbs: Described for practitioners and students.* London: Macmillan, 1949.

Raynaud, A. G. M. *De l'asphyxie locale et de la gangrène synchequie des extrémités.* Paris: Rignoux, 1862.

Shapiro, D., & Schwartz, G. E. Biofeedback and visceral training: Clinical applications. *Seminars in Psychiatry,* 1972, *4,* 171–184.

Snyder, C., & Noble, M. E. Operant conditioning of vasoconstriction. *Journal of Experimental Psychology,* 1968, *77,* 263–268.

Spittell, J. A., Jr. Raynaud's phenomenon and allied vasospastic conditions. In J. F. Fairbairn, J. L. Juergens, & John A. Spittell (Eds.), *Allen-Barker-Hines peripheral vascular diseases* (4th ed.). Philadelphia: Saunders, 1972.

Surwit, R. S. Raynaud's disease. In L. Birk (Ed.), *Biofeedback: Behavioral medicine.* New York: Grune & Stratton, 1973.

Surwit, R. S., & Fenton, C. H. Feedback and instructions in the control of digital temperatures. *Psychophysiology,* 1980, *17,* 129–132.

Surwit, R. S., Pilon, R. N., & Fenton, C. H. Behavioral treatment of Raynaud's disease. *Journal of Behavioral Medicine,* 1978, *1,* 323–335.

Taub, E. Self-regulation of human tissue temperature. In G. E. Schwartz & J. Beatty (Eds.), *Biofeedback: Theory and research.* New York: Academic Press, 1977.

COMMENTS ON THE CHAPTERS BY BEATTY AND BY SURWIT

EDWARD B. BLANCHARD

COMMENTS ON THE CHAPTER BY BEATTY

Although I would agree with many of Beatty's general conclusions about the state of the literature on the biofeedback treatment of migraine headache, I would take issue with one particular point—his equating the effects of relaxation training to nonspecific or placebo effects (p. 217).

In order to address this issue, several of my colleagues and I recently surveyed the literature on the psychological treatment of migraine headache with respect to treatment outcome, in order to examine relative efficacy of treatment through a relatively new analytic procedure known as "meta-analysis" (Glass, 1976; Smith & Glass, 1977). We compared the results from several psychological treatments of migraine headache to the reduction in headache obtainable by a pharmacologic, or true, placebo, in order to see whether these treatments contribute anything more than placebo effects.

A META-ANALYTIC VIEW OF BEHAVIORAL TREATMENT OF MIGRAINE HEADACHES

In meta-analysis, the results for the whole group of subjects given a particular treatment in a particular study becomes the unit of analysis. To be included in our analysis, a

Edward B. Blanchard. Department of Psychology, State University of New York at Albany, Albany, New York.

study had to present data on a group of at least five subjects, all of whom had been treated with the same procedure. Thus, single-group outcome and controlled-group outcome studies were used.

A "percentage of improvement" score was calculated for each of four possible dependent variables for each treatment condition in the studies included. We used the following formula:

$$\frac{\text{Baseline Value} - \text{End of Treatment Value}}{\text{Baseline Value}} \times 100 = \text{Percentage of Improvement}$$

The values entered in this equation were taken from tabular presentations of data, if available, or from interpolation from the graphical displays.

The four possible variables were, in order of preference, headache index, headache frequency, headache intensity, and headache duration. The headache index was a preferred measure, since it tends to combine intensity, duration and frequency, and is thus probably the most sensitive measure of change (Blanchard, Theobald, Williamson, Silver, & Brown, 1978). If data were unavailable to allow a calculation of the percentage of improvement on the first variable, we then sought values for frequency, intensity, or duration, in that order. In the event that no data were available on any of the four measures and that values were reported for the percentage of the total sample who were either much improved or improved, this value was used. Furthermore, if no values were available at the end of a treatment, then we used the value from the earliest follow-up data available, again with the same hierarchical choice of dependent variables when more than one was available. In so doing, we have attempted to be conservative by using the percentage of improvement in a headache parameter over an estimate for the overall population.

In order to generate a value for the degree of improvement obtainable by medication placebo in migraine headache, all of the double-blind, placebo-controlled drug trials with migraine headache that had been published in the previous decade and that we could find were surveyed. When sufficient data were available, a "degree of improvement" score was calculated from each study using either the above formula or the author's report of the percentage of the sample that was improved for the placebo condition.

For the purposes of this analysis, several different relaxation procedures were treated equivalently—passive, meditative forms of relaxation such as Benson's "relaxation response" (1975); abbreviated forms of Jacobson's "progressive relaxation" (1924); and variants of both.

In Table 1 are listed the studies of behavioral treatment of migraine headache with treatment conditions and degrees of improvement on the various dependent variables at the end of treatment and under two possible follow-up conditions: follow-up of 3 months or less, and follow-ups of more than 3 months.

In Table 2 are listed the "percentage of improvement" scores for groups of migraineurs given medication placebo from double-blind, placebo-controlled medication trials for migraine headache.

The values listed in Tables 1 and 2 were subjected to a one-way analysis of variance, in which the values for a whole group represented one datum. Four different treatments were compared: temperature biofeedback; temperature biofeedback with autogenic training; relaxation training; and medication placebo.

RESULTS

In Table 3 are presented the average degrees of improvement for each of the four treatment conditions. The analysis yielded a significant groups effect, $F = 5.90$, $df = 3,20$,

TABLE 1. Summary of Results from Treatment of Migraine Headache by Biofeedback and Relaxation

			Results (% Improvement)			
			End of Treatment		*3- to 6-Month Follow-Up*	
Authors	*Conditions*	*N*	*HA Index or Other Parameter*	*% Sample Improved*	*HA Index or Other Parameter*	*% Sample Improved*
Sargent, Green, & Walters (1972)	TBFD[a] + AT[a]	62	—	74	—	—
Sargent, Green, & Walters (1973)	TBFD + AT	19	—	63	—	—
Reading & Mohr (1976)	TBFD + AT	6	40	—	66	—
Mitch, McGrady, & Iannone (1976)	TBFD + AT	20	—	75	—	80
Fried, Lambert, & Sneed (1977)	TBFD + AT	5	—	60	—	—
Fahrion (1977)	TBFD + AT	21	—	—	—	71
Blanchard, Theobald, Williamson,	TBFD + AT	13	73	54	63	40
Silver, & Brown	Relax.[c]	13	81	85	45	56
(1978)	HA Monitor.	10	23	10	—	—
Turin & Johnson (1976)	TBFD	7	41	57	—	—
Mullinix, Norton, Hack, & Fishman	TBFD	6	21	63	—	—
(1978)	Control	5	8	—	—	—
Andreychuk &	TBFD	9	82	—	—	—
Skriver (1975)	Relax.	10	37	—	—	—
Largen, Mathew, Dobbins, Meyer, Sakai, & Clag-	TBFD	13	—	83	—	—
horn (1979)	Control	13	—	80	—	—
Lake, Raney, &	TBFD	66	32	—	32	—
Papsdorf (1979)	HA Monitor.	6	17	—	−4	—
Mitchell &	Relax.	7	—	—	26	—
Mitchell (1970)	No Trt.[d]	6	—	—	2	—
Hay & Madders (1979)	Relax.	98	—	70	—	—
Benson, Klemchuk, & Graham (1974)	Relax.	17	16	—	—	35
Warner & Lance (1975)	Relax.	14	—	—	—	83

[a]Thermal biofeedback.
[b]Autogenic training.
[c]Any form of relaxation training.
[d]No treatment.

TABLE 2. Effects of Medication Placebo on Migraine Headache ($\bar{x}$ = 16.5%)

Authors	*N*	*Percentage of Improvement from Placebo*
Lance, Anthony, & Sommerville (1970)	50	32
Waters (1970)	79	18
Weber & Reinmuth (1972)	19	11
Ludvigsson (1974)	28	25
Vardi, Robey, Streifler, Schwartz, Lindner, & Zor (1976)	8	0
Kallanranta, Hukkarainen, Hokkanen, & Tuovinen (1977)	50	13

p = .0047. Further individual comparisons showed that each of the treatment conditions yielded significantly more improvement than did medication placebo ($p \leq .05$). However, the t values for pairwise comparisons among the three treatment conditions were all nonsignificant.

Power Analysis

Because of the way the hypotheses are stated in statistical comparisons, the null hypothesis of "no difference among the conditions" either may be rejected or cannot be rejected. *Not being able to reject the null hypothesis, however, is not equivalent to accepting it.* To determine whether our calculated lack of difference among the three treatment conditions truly reflects no difference, we were obligated to perform a power analysis.

Following the procedures described by Keppel (1973), we calculated the power of the comparison of relaxation alone, temperature biofeedback alone, and temperature biofeedback combined with autogenic training. Setting the α level at .05, the observed power ($1 - \beta$) is .84. This means that β is equal to .16, or that there is only about one chance in six that, if differences truly existed between the three treatments, we would not have detected that difference.

Finally, it might be noted that a recent report by Attfield & Peck (1979) comparing abbreviated progressive relaxation training to thermal biofeedback in migraineurs also found no significant difference in headache reduction between the two treatments. (The manner of presentation precluded the inclusion of the results of this study in our analysis; no baseline or end-of-treatment values were given.)

TABLE 3. Average Percentage of Improvement in Migraine Headache Patients Treated by Biofeedback, Relaxation, or Medication Placebo

	Conditions			
	Thermal Biofeedback with Autogenic Training	*Thermal Biofeedback*	*Relaxation Training*	*Medication Placebo*
Average percentage of improvement	65.1	51.8	52.7	16.5
Number of studies	7	5	6	6
Total number of patients	146	41	159	234

OTHER BIOFEEDBACK TREATMENT OF MIGRAINE

As Beatty notes (p. 219), another biofeedback procedure for treating migraine headache has been described both in a study of his (Friar & Beatty, 1976), and a newer one (Bild & Adams, 1980).

Adams and his colleagues (see Adams, Feuerstein, & Fowler, 1980, for summary) presented a series of case reports on single-subject experiments in what they call "cephalic vasomotor training." Recently they reported a controlled-group outcome study (Bild & Adams, 1980) that compared their treatment procedure to frontal EMG biofeedback and to continued headache monitoring. Results showed that only the vasomotor biofeedback group had a significant reduction in headache frequency; however, there were no significant differences among the three groups on this measure at the 6-week follow-up. For headache duration, the cephalic vasomotor biofeedback condition led to significantly greater improvement after treatment than did the headache monitoring condition, but the improvement did not differ from that brought about by the frontal EMG biofeedback condition.

Unfortunately, since only two group studies were available utilizing this treatment, it was not possible to include it within our meta-analysis. It certainly seems promising and awaits further research.

DISCUSSION

From our meta-analytic approach to evaluating the efficacy of behavioral treatment of headache, it would seem that we can certainly conclude that behavioral treatment is more effective than medication placebo treatment is for migraine headache. In the treatment of migraine headache with relaxation or temperature biofeedback training, there is no difference among the three treatments, although there is a slight arithmetic advantage for the combination of temperature biofeedback and autogenic training.

The similarity of results leads to speculation, as voiced by Silver and Blanchard (1978), that there might be a final common pathway by which the treatments work—namely, relaxation. For migraine headache, Mathew (1979) has proposed a neurophysiological model to explain how relaxation is the final common factor in the treatment of migraine. Moreover, there is experimental evidence that temperature biofeedback leads to reduced sympathetic outflow (Sovak, Kunzel, Sternbach, & Dalessio, 1978), but does not lead to cerebrovascular changes as detected by regional cerebral blood flow techniques (Mathew, Largen, Dobbins, Meyer, Sakai, & Claghorn, 1980).

ACKNOWLEDGMENT

This research was supported in part by a grant from the National Institute of Neurological and Communicative Disorders and Stroke, NS-15235.

COMMENTS ON THE CHAPTER BY SURWIT

Surwit has provided a succinct review and summary of the published literature on the biofeedback and behavioral treatment of Raynaud's disease (which proves to be primarily a review of his own work). He has omitted a summary of one recent controlled comparison, that of Jacobson, Manschreck, and Silverberg (1979). These investigators compared the efficacy of abbreviated progressive muscle relaxation with and without temperature biofeedback. Very importantly, they obtained 2-year follow-up data on their patients.

The results are very similar in that there was equal improvement in both groups, both at 1 month after treatment and at 2 years. There was also a trend for the group *not receiving biofeedback* to show larger digital temperature increases than shown by those who received the thermal biofeedback. One other interesting point was the authors' note that for six of the seven best long-term responders, improvement was closely tied to continued practice of the relaxation exercises.

While I personally tend to agree with Surwit's conclusions about the role of biofeedback in the behavioral treatment of Raynaud's disease (he "argues strongly against biofeedback being the essential ingredient in the therapeutic effects. . . . "—p. 231), I would like to raise a question that is often posed to me by members of the Biofeedback Society of America (BSA): Did the patients in any of the studies receive adequate temperature biofeedback training? By this is usually meant, could the patients reliably produce a significant (probably 5 ° to 10 °F) increase in digital temperature very readily (probably within 3 to 5 minutes) without the assistance of feedback? Many within BSA would argue that only when patients can demonstrate this degree of thermal self-control can it be said that they have had an adequate trial of biofeedback training; furthermore, they would argue that it is inappropriate to compare patients inadequately trained in biofeedback to patients in other treatment conditions.

At one level, the position of BSA has some logical appeal. However, it is unclear how this position is ever to be tested scientifically.

Thus, I think we can safely conclude that the published literature does not support the advantage of fixed amounts of thermal biofeedback training over other treatment regimens of equal length using various relaxation training programs.

REFERENCES

Adams, H. E., Feuerstein, M., & Fowler, J. L. Migraine headache: Review of parameters, etiology, and intervention. *Psychological Bulletin,* 1980, *87,* 217–237.

Andreychuk, T., & Skriver, C. Hypnosis and biofeedback in the treatment of migraine headache. *International Journal of Clinical and Experimental Hypnosis,* 1975, *23,* 172–183.

Attfield, M., & Peck, D. F. Temperature self-regulation and relaxation with migraine patients and normals. *Behaviour Research and Therapy,* 1979, *17,* 591–595.

Benson, H. *The relaxation response.* New York: Morrow, 1975.

Benson, H., Klemchuk, H. P., & Graham, J. R. The usefulness of the relaxation response in the therapy of headache. *Headache,* 1974, *14,* 49–52.

Bild, R., & Adams, H. E. Modification of migraine headaches by cephalic blood volume pulse and EMG biofeedback. *Journal of Consulting and Clinical Psychology,* 1980, *48,* 51–57.

Blanchard, E. G., Theobald, D. E., Williamson, D. A., Silver, B. V., & Brown, D. A. Temperature biofeedback in the treatment of migraine headaches. *Archives of General Psychiatry,* 1978, *35,* 581–588.

Fahrion, S. L. Autogenic biofeedback treatment for migraine. *Mayo Clinic Proceedings,* 1977, *52,* 776–784.

Friar, L. R., & Beatty, J. Migraine: Management by trained control of vasoconstriction. *Journal of Consulting and Clinical Psychology,* 1976, *44,* 46–53.

Fried, F. E., Lambert, J., & Sneed, P. Treatment of tension and migraine headaches with biofeedback techniques. *Missouri Medicine,* 1977, *74,* 253–255.

Glass, G. V. Primary, secondary, and meta-analysis of research. *Educational Researcher,* 1976, *10,* 3–8.

Hay, K. M., & Madders, J. Migraine treated by relaxation therapy. *Journal of the Royal College of General Practitioners,* 1971, *21,* 644–649.

Jacobson, A. M., Manschreck, T. C., & Silverberg, E. Behavioral treatment for Raynaud's Disease: A comparative study with long-term follow-up. *American Journal of Psychiatry,* 1979, *136,* 844–846.

Jacobson, E. The technique of progressive relaxation. *Journal of Nervous and Mental Disease,* 1924, *60,* 568–578.

Kallanranta, T., Hukkarainen, H., Hokkanen,

E., & Touvinen, T. Clonidine in migraine prophylaxis. *Headache,* 1977, *17,* 169–172.

Keppel, G. *Designs and analysis: A researcher's handbook.* Englewood Cliffs, N.J.: Prentice-Hall, 1973.

Lake, A., Raney, J., & Papsdorf, J. D. Biofeedback and rational–emotive therapy in the management of migraine headache. *Journal of Applied Behavior Analysis,* 1979, *12,* 127–140.

Lance, J. W., Anthony, M., & Somerville, B. Comparative trials of serotonin antagonists in the management of migraine. *British Medical Journal,* 1970, *2,* 327–330.

Largen, J. W., Mathew, R. J., Dobbins, K., Meyer, J. S., Sakai, F., & Claghorn, J. L. The effect of direction of skin temperature self-regulation on migraine activity and regional cerebral blood flow. In *Proceedings of the Biofeedback Society of America: 10th Annual Meeting.* Denver: Biofeedback Society of America, 1979.

Ludvigsson, J. Propranolol used in prophylaxis of migraine in children. *Acta Neurologica Scandinavica,* 1974, *50,* 109–115.

Mathew, R. J. *A biochemical explanation for the biofeedback treatment of migraine.* Paper presented at the meeting of Texas Research Institute of the Mental Sciences, Houston, December 1, 1979.

Mathew, R. J., Largen, J. W., Dobbins, K., Meyer, J. S., Sakai, F. & Claghorn, J. L. Biofeedback control of skin temperature and cerebral blood flow in migraine. *Headache,* 1980, *20,* 19–28.

Mitch, P. S., McGrady, A., & Iannone, A. Autogenic feedback training in migraine: A treatment report. *Headache,* 1976, *15,* 267–270.

Mitchell, K. R., & Mitchell, D. M. Migraine: An exploratory treatment application of programmed behavior therapy techniques. *Journal of Psychosomatic Research,* 1971, *15,* 137–157.

Mullinix, J., Norton, B., Hack, S., & Fishman, M. Skin temperature biofeedback and migraine. *Headache,* 1978, *17,* 242–244.

Reading, C., & Mohr, P. D. Biofeedback control of migraine: A pilot study. *British Journal of Social and Clinical Psychology,* 1976, *15,* 429–433.

Sargent, J. D., Green, E. E., & Walters, E. D. Preliminary report on the use of autogenic feedback training in the treatment of migraine and tension headaches. *Psychosomatic Medicine,* 1973, *35,* 129–135.

Sargent, J. D., Green, E. E., & Walters, E. D. The use of autogenic feedback training in a pilot study of migraine and tension headaches. *Headache,* 1972, *12,* 120–125.

Silver, B. V., & Blanchard, E. B. Biofeedback and relaxation training in the treatment of psychophysiologic disorders: Or, are the machines really necessary? *Journal of Behavioral Medicine,* 1978, *1,* 217–239.

Smith, M. L., & Glass, G. V. Meta-analysis of psychotherapy outcome studies. *American Psychologist,* 1977, *32,* 752–760.

Sovak, M., Kunzel, M., Sternbach, R. A., & Dalessio, D. J. Is volitional manipulation of hemodynamics a valid rationale for biofeedback therapy of migraine? *Headache,* 1978, *18,* 197–202.

Turin, A., & Johnson, W. G. Biofeedback therapy for migraine headaches. *Archives of General Psychiatry,* 1976, *33,* 517–519.

Vardi, Y., Robey, I. M., Streifler, M., Schwartz, A., Lindner, H. R., & Zor, U. Migraine attacks: Alleviation by an inhibitor of prostaglandin synthesis and action. *Neurology,* 1976, *26,* 447–450.

Warner, G., & Lance, J. W. Relaxation therapy in migraine and chronic tension headache. *The Medical Journal of Australia,* 1975, *1,* 298–301.

Waters, W. E. Controlled clinical trial of ergotamine tartrate. *British Medical Journal,* 1970, *2,* 325–327.

Weber, R. B., & Reinmuth, O. The treatment of migraine with propranolol. *Neurology,* 1972, *22,* 366–369.

ROUND-TABLE DISCUSSION OF BEATTY, SURWIT, AND BLANCHARD

John Furedy: I'd like to question the logic of Ed Blanchard's comparative summary and analysis of migraine treatments. It assumes that placebo effects are something which are constant over time, space, and therapists. The best way I can express this disagreement is to quote from page 88 of our paper, where we discuss the best alternative treatment [BAT] control. We say that even with the best alternative treatment control, the more precisely specifiable, there would still be the problem that the biofeedback/best alternative treatment comparison would include the placebo benefits of biofeedback. These placebo effects are themselves not reliable, but vary over time and place as a function of society's awareness of and feelings toward biofeedback. The attitude of the therapist towards the treatment and the therapist–patient relationship are also factors which affect the nature of the placebo effects of biofeedback. I would say that even if Ed Blanchard had gotten a difference between the three groups—biofeedback, biofeedback with autogenic training, and relaxation—that would not have taught us anything, because that would be a placebo biofeedback effect. We would need, again, a noncontingent control or a specific control in this sort of system, where we could demonstrate one thing works as a function of the contingency whereas the other one doesn't.

Neal Miller: It has been argued that an effect that increases with a succession of trials or with a succession of days couldn't be a placebo effect. But this certainly is not true, because you can see administrations of placebo for antihypertensive drug tests that do improve for as much as 7 weeks. They keep getting a bigger and bigger effect. You can imagine, also, a possible mechanism for it. I don't know whether the patient knows about it; but certainly if he knows about it, and he finds he's getting better, that should have positive feedback for the placebo effect, so to speak. These increasing placebo effects may be seen in pharmacological studies using a pharmacological placebo. So, you know darn well it is either a placebo effect or a regression to the mean, which is never tested for in those studies.

Richard Surwit: I want to take exception to what Ed [Blanchard] said about feedback training. I think biofeedback is a procedure, not an effect. If you give a person the appropriate opportunity to learn using a feedback paradigm, then you have exposed him to biofeedback. Whether or not the feedback is efficacious in producing the effect it's supposed to is another question. There's a whole other literature on normals which is quite controversial, and the efficacy of feedback in controlling the skin temperature in normal subjects is open to question. In terms of the effect of feedback on this paradigm, what we found was that the entire effect of the feedback and autogenic training package occurred, when subjects were well trained, in the first 3 minutes of the autogenic training tape; and there was no vasodilatation that occurred subsequently. In the feedback-plus-autogenic-training condition, we got this increase; and then after the voice portion of the tape was over, which was after 5 minutes, we exposed the subjects to half an hour of feedback. You can see that feedback did help subjects maintain a higher skin temperature than subjects who did not have feedback. Both groups of subjects showed a gradual decrease in skin temperature over the next hour or so. The people who had feedback did show a significantly smaller reduction in temperature over that period of time; however, this difference was not clinically significant. Essentially, what it suggests to me is that possibly the feedback is helping subjects reinforce whatever they were doing with the autogenic training. It looks like biofeedback acts as a reinforcer here and that subjects who do not have it seem to be extinguishing more rapidly than subjects who do. But there is no differential clinical efficacy.

Martin Orne: I'd like to address the issue of whether or not you have a right to specify that a physiological response must be learned if you're going to use that response as a treatment. I think that this whole issue of defining treatment in terms of what you do to the patient, rather than what the patient learns, is a very serious problem. Now, in animal research, you solve the problem by doing pilot studies making certain that what you do to the organism is effective and it works, that it achieves the operant, etc. In humans you don't do that. So therefore, the alternative to doing that, and to doing extensive pilot studies, is to simply see whether it does work. Now, I think it is perfectly legitimate to insist, by the way, that people do learn the response if you're going to speak about the effects of hand warming, for example. It is also legitimate, then, to demand that people emphasize the negative, the *lack* of correlation between change in the physiological parameter and clinical effects, because that, then, becomes key data.

Jackson Beatty: Martin [Orne] raised a question as to why you should measure the effects of the degree of control of the physiological variable if the correlation with the therapeutic effect is 0. And the answer to that, of course, is that that is strong evidence that the effect is not specific.

Henry Adams: We should read more of Jasper Brener (see Chapter 2) as related to this business of control. The difference between controlling responses during biofeedback trials where you're getting the stimulus and voluntary control in the absence of the feedback signal is a very, very important distinction. Most of these studies with blood volume pulsations [BVPs], including my own, have shown very poor voluntary control. If that's the case, if they can't control on their own, why in hell do you expect them to change their migraine? You'd expect a very weak effect there. What we've found is when we go to 50, 60, 70 trials, where they can actually close down that blood volume pulse, we get much more potent clinical effects.

Bernard Tursky: The first point that I want to make is that there is another study to add to Surwit's review of biofeedback treatments of migraine, done by Elmore and myself as part of his dissertation [Elmore & Tursky, 1981]. We replicated Friar and Beatty's study [1976] and looked at a comparison between people treated with temporal artery pulse volume feedback and with hand-warming feedback. Both groups learned their task very well. They were able to master either the increase in temperature or the decrease in temporal artery pulse. I want to point out that when we're doing these kinds of studies, we try to be very careful that we do get our people to self-report in ways that are meaningful and in ways that can be quantified, not simply in terms of "it felt better." Our self-report measures are designed to meet the need for quantification. These measures were developed in my pain research. The procedure is to psychophysically scale a set of descriptors: one set of descriptors for intensity of pain, a second for the reactive or affective component of pain, and a third for quality of pain sensation. Our patients were asked to keep diaries for a month before they went into treatment and a month after they finished treatment. During that period of time, they kept accurate records of every pain episode. For each episode of pain, they selected a word from each of these three sets of words, which now had scaled values so that we were able to get information on intensity of pain, reactivity to pain, and quality of pain (e.g., throbbing, itching, dull) which could actually be quantified. We found that there was no difference between the two groups in terms of their self-report after treatment in intensity of pain; but the temporal artery pulse volume biofeedback group had a statistically significant reduction in their report of their reaction to pain, their reactivity scale. We also found that there was a significant difference between the two groups on two other measures. One measure was the amount of reduction in medication. The other was the frequency of headache. So we had three quantitative measures that showed an advantage to the pulse volume feedback group. It is indeed possible to quantify self-report.

Another point I'd like to make concerns the physiology and recording of skin temperature. My students [Marty Kluger, Larry Jamner, and Jim Papillo] have developed their own idea of what they should be looking at. They realized that hand temperature is controlled by other physiological variables such as blood volume, blood flow, and pulse volume, as well as thermal and psychological sweating. What if we looked at vascular alterations in the fingers instead of looking at temperature per se? What would we see? Figure 1 summarizes some pilot data [Kluger, Jamner, & Tursky, 1980] in which we simultaneously obtained recordings of finger temperature, finger pulse volume, and ECG at certain periods of time. If we look at the change in temperature, we can see that while temperature is changing and we're providing biofeedback information about temperature change, finger pulse volume has already been altered; there's a latency and a difference between these two measures. So, it's possible that during the time that we are reinforcing temperature change, we are missing an opportunity to reinforce another measure that has a faster response than the measure that we're interested in. Is it possible that we are not reinforcing the most effective variable?

Joel Lubar: I'm just going to make a comment in regard to Jackson Beatty's paper. I think that in discussing migraines, it's important to distinguish the different types of vascular headaches, and, perhaps, here there is some evidence that a differential treatment would work best with the different types. Just to make it simple, I'll use the classic migraine, where you have a prodromal symptom of vasoconstriction followed by hyperemia and vasodilatation. There, clearly, hand warming might be most appropriate during the vasoconstrictive phase, both because you have a warning and because you can use it preventatively. In the common migraine, however, if there's any kind of prodrome, it's very short; and sometimes there isn't any at all. It's as if there's a rapid biochemical trigger and there's instantaneous hyperemia, and the headache comes on suddenly. Maybe for that you can only work after the fact, either with ergotamine tartrate or with the pulsation, working with the temporal arteries. Then there are two other kinds that are very difficult to work with and that biofeedback clinics try to deal with. One of these is the menstrual migraine that occurs around the time of the menstrual cycle in females. It's usually the last migraine type of headache to drop out, and there doesn't seem to be any adequate behavioral treatment for that unless it's part of dysmenorrhea, in which case general relaxation sometimes helps. There's a type of nocturnal vascular headache that occurs in the early morning hours, perhaps associated with a trigger having to do with REM sleep; and the patient wakes up in agony and it's already too late to

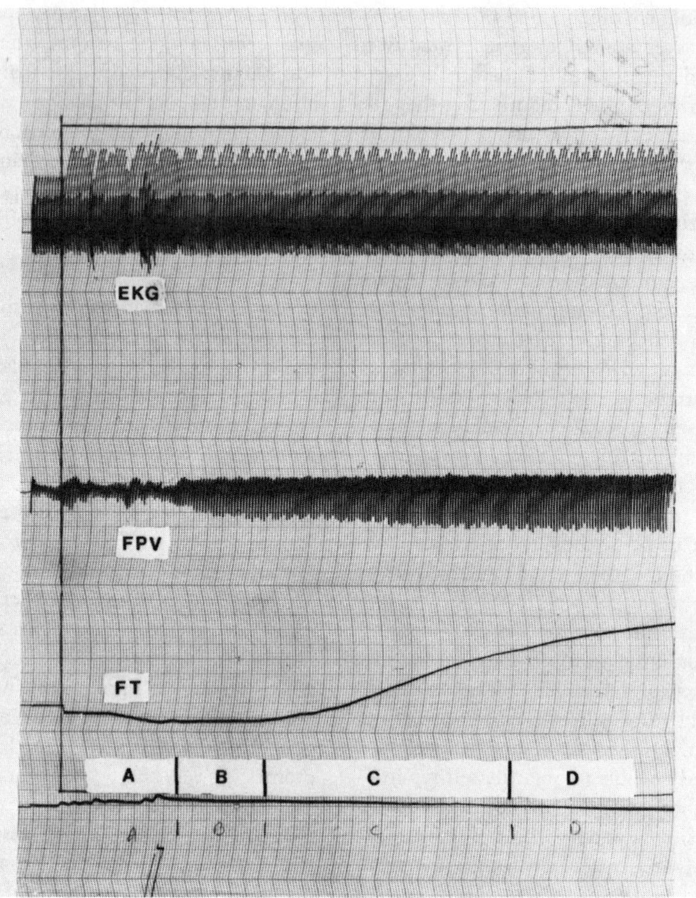

FIG. 1. Simultaneous recordings of ECG, finger pulse volume (FPV), and finger temperature (FT). (From *A Comparison of Peripheral Circulation Feedback Modalities* by M. Kluger, L. Jamner, and B. Tursky, Paper presented at a meeting of The Society for Psychophysiological Research, Vancouver, B.C., Canada, October 1980. Copyright 1980 by M. Kluger, L. Jamner, and B. Tursky. Reprinted by permission.)

do anything. It seems to me, there are no behavioral treatments or preventative treatments that you can use to try to control that. So I think when we talk about migraine and these studies that have been presented, which are very elegant, we ought to look at the different subtypes differentially.

John Lacey: You are proposing not only a subtype-specific intervention, but a time-bound intervention at particular times in the development of the symptoms.

Steven Wolf: I just wanted to get back to the point that Jackson [Beatty] and Joel [Lu- of the diagnosis as opposed to the specificity of the response. It may not hold or be justified in migraine, but I know that there are at least 50 different causes of stroke, each of which affects sensory motor enervation processes differently, and hence has a bearing on training strategies with feedback or any other treatment regimen. I know that there are at least seven forms of hypertension, and I would suggest that the mechanism underlying each of those is somewhat different; and therefore, we ought to think in terms of diversity of treatment approaches, according to the etiology. Perhaps one of the reasons why individuals aren't able to replicate [experiments] stems from the hidden differentials in the true diagnosis of the problem. I don't see that being addressed stringently enough in our critiques of existing literature. Let's not take away from the clinical realities, but I think if we're going to try to prove something works, specifically or nonspecifically, we have to be as unique and specific in identifying the diagnosis as well.

Barry Sterman: I would like to report on a study by Claghorn, Mathew, Largen, and Meyer (1981) which provides some impressive data. A group of migraine patients showed unilateral hypersensitivity in cerebral vascular changes. When antimigraine medications were given, these medications had unilateral effects that countered the hypersensitivity. They had no effects on normal subjects. That was then compared with thermal biofeedback and hand-warming biofeedback; and it was found that those treatments had no effect on cerebral circulation in normal subjects, but had unilateral therapeutic effects on these migraine patients in the same direction as the antimigraine medication. I thought that was a most dramatic demonstration of effect consistent with the disordered person and, in fact, specific to the hypersensitivity.

Audience Question to Barry Sterman: What are the controls?

Barry Sterman: He didn't have relaxation controls. He had hand-warming subjects.

Jackson Beatty: I agree that there are various different types of migraine, maybe less in terms of mechanism than percepitating causes; but the point of all that is, at least in my opinion, that there just is no phenomenon that is big enough and strong enough there to warrant the research effort that's needed to produce a differentiated treatment of the phenomenon. Now it may be that a particular type of migraine might be very reactive to such procedures, whereas other types aren't, but it doesn't look like that's so. It's not a matter of homing down on a phenomenon that's already strong. There just doesn't seem to be that much there.

Theodore Weiss: I have a lot of trouble understanding patients and their motivation. PVCs and hypertension are relatively occult diseases and you can say patients wouldn't be motivated. I'm very puzzled, though, by the Raynaud's patients, where this is a very uncomfortable problem that they have which was helped by your intervention and yet, a year later, they're not doing it. Does anyone have any insight about this?

Gary Schwartz: This is what we have to start looking at. Believe it or not, this is where some of the older "psychodynamic" and other literature becomes useful, as well as some of the personality literature. If you look at that literature, you find that a common characteristic of not all people, but at least fairly sizable proportion of people who have Raynaud's disease, hypertension, and all kinds of other things, show a "defensiveness." In fact, they even show "repression." Look at the data on hypertension as an example. When you look at anxiety scores, some studies report that hypertensive patients report higher anxiety than the control group. Others show no difference, and a number show lower anxiety scores than a random population. If you look at the reasons why, what differentiates those kinds of studies, you find the studies that typically find higher self-reports of anxiety in the hypertensives use hypertensives who were seen in a psychiatric situation. They were there for other problems and also happened to be hypertensive. But, if you truly randomize and you get people prior to the time that they know that they're hypertensive, you can find that typically there's a whole subset of people who report lower anxiety than the normal subject. Now the question is, is there really less anxiety, or is that indicative of the fact that some sort of denial, repression, or disattention mechanism exists? It's been seen in migraine. We have now been doing research trying to differentiate, among people who report low anxiety, the subjects who also report high defensiveness versus those who report low defensiveness. Danny Weinberger, Richard Davidson, and myself have published this paper in the *Journal of Abnormal Psychology* this past fall [Weinberger, Schwartz, & Davidson, 1979]. If you differentiate among people who report low anxiety, and you subdivide them into those who report high defensiveness and those who report low defensiveness, you find that people who report low defensiveness and low anxiety (which we call "true low anxiety") show autonomic and behavioral indices which are less than people who report high anxiety. The people who report low anxiety but are high defensives have anxiety scores that are even less than the low-anxious group, but physiologically and behaviorally they are equal, if not greater, in terms of their reactivity than the high-anxious subjects. Those are the individuals who denied the negative affect and symptoms. They're the most difficult problems with regard to motivation. I think we may want to think through the meaning of "self-report," because some people are going to report subjective decreases and be ignoring their peripheral physiology. Therefore, when you come back and you measure it again, you find out that they're not correctly processing the physiological information.

Audience Question to Gary Schwartz: Are you saying that the physiological problem is a mechanism for protection against any anxiety?

Gary Schwartz: That's one possibility. It may also, in fact, be disregulation out of disattention, so you get a hyperreactivity as a consequence of the ignoring. I don't think they're mutually exclusive processes, but nobody knows.

Richard Surwit: In addition to Gary [Schwartz]'s psychodynamic formulation, I think there were some other behavioral reasons why patients stopped practicing their control. One of the main reasons is that there is an aversive consequence of the practicing. They have to rearrange their schedule and change their life, which is very often more immediate than the pain of the disease, which comes episodically. The relief from the pain, even though it can be demonstrated over the period of a week or a month, is not immediate. So it is not a perfect reinforcement situation. And therefore, I think, behaviorally, you really can expect that to happen unless the therapist programs the therapy in such a way as to maximize those reinforcements as they occur in nature. Otherwise, they think it's natural for it to stop.

Daniel Cox: I'm wondering if Richard [Surwit] is looking at the right thing. When we did our Raynaud's study [Cox, 1979] and gave them cold challenges, there was no difference between giving people hand-temperature feedback and foot-temperature feedback. There was, however, a big difference during recovery after we took that cold stressor away. Those who had hand-temperature feedback in that hand recovered significantly quicker than those who received foot-temperature feedback. That argues to a specific therapeutic effect in thermal biofeedback, as does Taub's study [1977]. I'd like to make another comment about the lack of specificity of biofeedback with Raynaud's. Edward Taub's data argue very much to the contrary of what Richard [Surwit] was saying, suggesting that there is highly specific temperature control via biofeedback of digital skin temperature.

Jackson Beatty: In 1976, Linda Friar and I spent about 9 months trying to replicate Ed Taub's data, and we never could do it, which is the reason we ended up with our present study.

Martin Orne: It's very much a function of who the research assistant is who does it. Taub says that. He could not get it with one research assistant, while another research assistant got it, and it isn't fudged. It's just an entirely different role relationship that that gal has from other people.

Richard Surwit: First of all, it doesn't make any sense to me that one could obtain differences in temperature between points several centimeters apart on the surface of the hand. It doesn't make any sense, because the mechanisms, as far as we understand them, are just not that specific. They don't allow for that kind of specificity. Secondly, I have worked with skin-temperature feedback with normals for a long time; and not only did I get generalization at different points on one hand, but I got generalization between the hands, reliably, in many subjects. And I know that, in Neal Miller's lab, similar research is going on and similar difficulties have occurred.

Daniel Cox: Excuse me, but he got that specificity after about 26 or 30 training sessions.

Richard Surwit: I don't care how he got it. The fact is that, again, I wasn't able to get it; other people weren't able to get it. If it is a real phenomenon, I think we need to see it again.

Neal Miller: Did you give 20 or 30 training sessions? That's what I want to know.

Richard Surwit: In our research, we gave up to 11 training sessions; and in clinical work we've given much more than that. Again, we've never seen any type of specificity. Ed [Taub] was only claiming the general effect of feedback in terms of getting any vasal dilatation, not specific vasal dilatation depending upon the experimenter. The specific effect is something he talks about without making reference to any particular experimenter.

Martin Orne: It's the same study. I mean, this is part of the author's studies, and we lived through that with him. By the way, as far as other people looking at the specificity, he did take that to Framingham, and the people there did find that effect to be specific. So that it isn't just in his lab that specific effects were found.

Richard Surwit: For a long time, Wes Lynch and I thought that we were just incompetent because we couldn't replicate that and, indeed, maybe we are.

Martin Orne: No. I'm not saying you are. I do think, however, the issue of replication is a very tricky one; and the tendency in our field is to go ahead, read somebody's paper, and try to do what he says he did. If it doesn't come off right away, we assume that the guy is either a nudnik or a cheat. Now both are possibilities, I will grant you; and, in fact, we can all think of instances where this is so. I think that this is something which is always a problem. At the same time, I can tell you that in several instances, when you dig deeper, you find that there's some crucial thing which isn't clear. The attempted replication becomes possible only after you make your hegira to there and you really see what the guy's doing.

Richard Surwit: We went there and it still doesn't replicate. Well, even Ed [Taub] hasn't replicated it, has he?

Gary Schwartz: These two papers very nicely illustrate an important distinction we should keep in mind, and that is the use of biofeedback as a clinical research tool versus the use of biofeedback as "therapy." The potential specific effects that you can get vis-à-vis training become very useful for studying mechanisms of the disease process itself—pathogenesis and the like—because you can get selective control. The selective control interest becomes valuable if you want to study the relationship between controlling different parameters and its relationship to pain, and so on. All of that becomes very valuable in terms of basic research, basic research at the clinical level. But that does not mean that, therefore, we should apply that approach as the best possible way of using feedback or other behavioral procedures for treatment. So the issue of the specific effects f biofeedback is relevant to certain clinical research questions.

Martin Orne: Gary [Schwartz] made the point about the issue of specificity of treatment. It's kind of a research question, and we shouldn't get befuddled by the theory that, as good clinicians, we should go out and do the right thing by patients. I think we ought to keep reminding ourselves that the path of modern medicine has always been the search for specific treatment. Now, you go ahead and you treat without having a specific treatment because you haven't got it sometimes, but God help us if we stop looking for it.

Gary Schwartz: Oh, I didn't say we stop looking for it. I was just saying that it may be more complex because you deal with interactions. Most of this work is done in isolation; that was my point.

Martin Orne: However, I think it is not only appropriate, it is also essential that we concern ourselves with that issue in depth and neither drop it nor use the difficulties. I fear that your comments can be used as an excuse not to bother.

Gary Schwartz: I think some people could, but that was not my intent.

REFERENCES

Claghorn, J. L., Mathew, R. J., Largen, J. W., & Meyer, J. S. Directional effects of skin temperature self-regulation on regional cerebral blood flow in normal subjects and migraine patients. *American Journal of Psychiatry,* 1981, *138*(9), 1182–1187.

Cox, D. J. *A controlled investigation of the treatment efficacy and generalization of temperature biofeedback with primary idiopathic Raynaud's disease.* Paper presented at the 13th Annual Meeting of the Association for the Advancement of Behavior Therapy, San Francisco, December 1979.

Elmore, A. M., & Tursky, B. A comparison of two psychophysiological approaches to the treatment of migraine. *Headache,* 1981, *21,* 93–101.

Frair, L. R., & Beatty, J. Migraine: Management by trained control of vasoconstriction. *Journal of Consulting and Clinical Psychology,* 1976, *44,* 46–53.

Kluger, M., Jamner, L., & Tursky, B. *A comparison of peripheral circulation feedback modalities.* Paper presented at a meeting of the Society for Psychophysiological Research, Vancouver, B.C., Canada, October 1980.

Taub, E. Self-regulation of human tissue temperature. In G. E. Schwartz & J. Beatty (Eds.), *Biofeedback: Theory and research.* New York: Academic Press, 1977.

Weinberger, D. A., Schwartz, G. E., & Davidson, R. J. Low anxious, high anxious and repressive coping styles: Psychometric patterns and behavioral and physiological responses to stress. *Journal of Abnormal and Social Psychology,* 1979, *88*(4), 369–380.

IV

CENTRAL NERVOUS SYSTEM DISORDERS

SESSION I

FORMAL PRESENTATIONS

It has been widely acknowledged that the evidence for a specific, efficacious clinical effect of biofeedback is strongest in the area of rehabilitation medicine for the treatment of movement disorders resulting from peripheral nerve injury and stroke. In his chapter, Brudny not only reviews the findings of the extensive series of cases treated in his laboratory, but also provides a detailed description of his unique feedback system and the rationale for its development and application.

The formal discussion by Wolf, while acknowledging the unique contributions of a biofeedback approach to a program of rehabilitation, questions the advantages of using the extremely complex and sophisticated spatial–temporal patterns of muscle activity described by Brudny. Results from a smaller series of cases treated in Wolf's laboratory, using simpler feedback techniques, are comparable to those reported by Brudny. Wolf calls for greater standardization of quantified functional outcome measures. He also notes the importance of patient motivation in determining outcome and the need for further study of the interdependence of physiological and social–motivational variables in determining treatment results. Wolf cautions that there is no specific evidence that these changes in functioning seen with rehabilitation are due to changes in neuronal cytoarchitecture.

ROUND-TABLE DISCUSSION

The call for controlled studies sounded by Wolf is taken up and reinforced during the round-table discussion. There is also much interest expressed in examining the physiological basis for the development of these techniques, which may provide insights useful in other applications. The integrated electromyograph (iEMG) techniques discussed by Brudny are based upon an engineering analysis of motor control systems. The spatial–temporal characteristics of the feedback are thought to be compatible with the phase and amplitude of the biologically determined control systems. Visual feedback stimuli may be particularly potent in muscle retraining because of the evolutionarily determined biological linkage between visual and motor systems. The use of feedback compatible with the psychobiological mechanism may lead to a functional reorganization of brain activity by means of mechanisms of sensory substitution and functional plasticity of brain cells. Consistent with Jasper Brener's and Bernard Tursky's reexaminations of motor control systems (see Chapters 2 and 5), the data in motor rehabilitation suggest that although feedback plays a role in the acquisition of control, feedforward systems may be primary in the execution of acquired responses.

The significant role of motivational variables in determining clinical outcomes is also noted. Since motivational variables as well as information contained within the feedback signal contribute to motor rehabilitation, a multicenter, comparative treatment study may be necessary to facilitate the appropriate experimental controls for both the nature of the feedback signal and the motivational influences attributable to staff sophistication and expectations.

SESSION II

FORMAL PRESENTATIONS

Lubar's chapter comprises a report of a double-blind, cross-over study of sensorimotor rhythm biofeedback in a group of patients with intractable epilepsy. Although, as noted by Lubar, the study employed a small number of patients, it is notable for its control of a number of important variables. Particularly significant is the control for motor inhibition, which adds to the data indicating that immobility may be necessary but not sufficient for production of the sensorimotor rhythms. Other significant features of the study are a condition of reversal to alternative EEG frequencies and a noncontingent feedback trial. Although the subjects in the study were severely impaired, the training period was relatively short, and training was somewhat confounded by continuation of earlier effects beyond the cross-over of treatment, five of the eight subjects experienced seizure reductions.

Sterman presents an overview of the use of biofeedback in epilepsy that places Lubar's findings within the context of other studies. In his chapter, Sterman also reviews the physiological and anatomical structures subserving the sensorimotor rhythm and the evidence pertaining to the involvement of this mechanism in epilepsy. Briefly, this mechanism involves thalamocortical structures functioning as a "gating" mechanism that modulates somatosensory inputs and the control of corresponding motor responses. Several investigators using alternative electrode placements have found that their procedures result in seizure reductions of approximately 40%, while results from studies using optimal placement of electrodes report approximately 60% success. Since a transient seizure reduction of 30% in treatment-resistant epileptic patients may be obtained by a variety of nonspecific treatments, a comparison of treatments utilizing nonspecific methods with biofeedback treatments that use both optimal and alternative electrode placements may indicate the specificity of treatment effect.

ROUND-TABLE DISCUSSION

The application of sensorimotor rhythm biofeedback to the treatment of epilepsy has, from its beginnings, been based upon more fundamental research that has proposed a neurobiological mechanism to account for epilepsy. A proposed specific mechanism has enabled the research in this area to progress from studies first establishing general clinical efficacy to more controlled studies that have gone far to rule out alternative reasons for the efficacy of the procedure. Among the types of experimental evidence educed in support of specific efficacy are noncontingent controls, cross-over designs, alterations in electrode placement, and changes in contingent EEG frequencies. Data obtained from EEG sleep recordings show enhanced sensorimotor activity subsequent to treatment, which may represent normalization of brain waves. The increased sensorimotor EEG activity correlates with reduction of seizure activity and is compelling evidence of the specificity of the mechanism. Long-term follow-up studies are being planned.

In the round-table discussion, there is some clarification of the details of the physiological mechanism of the sensorimotor rhythm and its relationship to epilepsy. Questions are raised concerning alternative methods for influencing sensorimotor rhythms, such as sensory driving and voluntary immobilization. Although these alternatives cannot be entirely ruled out at present, there is some evidence suggesting that these approaches are not likely to be clinically useful.

10 BIOFEEDBACK IN CHRONIC NEUROLOGICAL CASES: THERAPEUTIC ELECTROMYOGRAPHY

JOSEPH BRUDNY

INTRODUCTION

Evidence accumulated over the past decade supports the notion that feedback of integrated electromyographic activity (iEMG), derived from attempted voluntary movement performed by chronically disabled neurological patients, facilitates the patient's ability to accomplish such acts in a more physiological manner (in contrast to a pathological or abnormal manner), and often results in functional restoration. Several reviews of this subject are contained in the literature (Blanchard & Epstein, 1977; Fernando & Basmajian, 1978; Inglis, Campbell, Donald, 1976; Keefe & Surwit, 1978). Though convincing, the evidence is not conclusive; it is perhaps best summarized in the following statement by Inglis *et al.* (1976): "Because the use of EMG biofeedback in neuromuscular rehabilitation looks so promising, and because so many aspects of its apparent success remain so obscure, well-controlled studies are essential in order to arrive at a rational therapy based on clear principles backed by secure data. There seems to be little doubt that psychologists should be able to make a significant contribution to this new development" (p. 319).

With all due respect to laboratory-oriented behavioral researchers, and in recognition of their contributions to the field, it must be emphasized that the phenomena of neurological rehabilitation are so complex and the problems so formid-

Joseph Brudny. Department of Rehabilitation Medicine, New York University Medical Center, Bellevue Hospital, New York, New York.

able that a multidisciplinary approach in which physicians play an integral part is a necessity. Without physicians, whose role, judgment, and input are essential for patients' welfare, this technique may remain experimental, restricted to the laboratory; it may never achieve widespread use in the clinic.

The reluctance, primarily on the part of physiatrists and neurologists, to utilize the therapeutic potential of EMG feedback is attributable to the fact that until recently (1) analytic and therapeutic equipment comparable to sophisticated laboratory computers usually employed by behavioral researchers was not available in clinics; (2) clinical studies regarding the efficacy of a particular retraining technique were hampered by the extreme difficulty of matching neurological patients; and (3) there existed a scarcity of discussion of mechanisms relating iEMG sensory feedback within the frameworks of motor control and cerebral plasticity.

I expect that recent advances in computer technology and analytical methods appropriate to individual patients, as referred to in this chapter, will provide some of the needed answers and will foster the clinician's ability to test or supervise testing of iEMG feedback effectively as a therapeutic modality. Such testing will, in my opinion, result in its routine application to treatment of neurologically disabled patients. From my perspective, nowhere is the need for innovation greater.

Neurological disorders of voluntary movement resulting from various brain insults constitute the leading cause of chronic disability and financial hardship in the United States today. Stroke, head trauma, cerebral palsy, and motor disorders related to cerebral imbalance of neurotransmitters—just to mention a few of the disorders in this group—are estimated to number approximately 5 million cases, with the annual cost of caring for these exceeding $20 billion per year, as illustrated in Table 1 (U.S. Dept. of HEW, 1976). The total cost of these disorders, including losses in productivity, income, tax revenues, and so forth, must be severalfold higher

TABLE 1. Estimated Numbers and Cost of Major Chronic Neurological Disorders[a]

Disability	*Cases*	*Annual Cost (Billions)*	*Remarks*
Cerebral palsy	750,000	$ 3.75	15,000 brain-damaged born each year
Epilepsy	2,000,000	$ 2	Some estimates as high as 4 million cases
Head injuries	3,000,000	$ 3	875,000 yearly with neurological deficits
Multiple sclerosis	250,000	$ 1.25	Additional 250,000 with related disorders
All neuromuscular disorders	1,000,000	$ 5	Estimate from Muscular Dystrophy Association
Parkinson's disease	500,000	$ 2.5	Incidence may be much higher
Spinal cord injuries	100,000	$ .5	5,000–10,000 new cases yearly
Stroke	2,500,000	$12.5	Yearly incidence 300,000–400,000

[a]From *Neurological and Communicative Disorders* (NIH Publication No. 77-152) by the U.S. Department of Health, Education, and Welfare. Washington, D.C.: U.S. Government Printing Office, 1976.

than this figure. Stroke is rapidly becoming the most common neurological disorder in the world. In contrast despite medical rehabilitation efforts over the past 30 years, the rate of functional recovery has remained notoriously low. While spontaneous recovery occurs fairly rapidly in a fortunate few, most patient suffer from chronic disability.

In human beings, learning or relearning motor skills is a sensorimotor task that is aided by immediate and pertinent feedback. This feedback reflects the patterns of movement and, by extension, the actual muscular events that control the movement. In patients with brain insult, there is often an inability to process incoming information from affected areas; hence, therapeutic compensation to provide sensory feedback is needed for the pertinent sensory information regarding movement. An attempt at such compensation is implicit in all conventional physical therapy approaches. However, such traditional techniques alone have yielded results that many clinicians and researchers consider suboptimal and controversial (Taft, Delagi, Wilkie, & Abramson, 1962).

This criticism was best summarized by Herman (1971), who stated: "Present day methods of observer-guidance of performance and of utilization of reflexive changes to restore function do not meet biological requirements for re-calibration" (p. xi). Arguing that recalibration or relearning of functions depends chiefly on information gained from sensory systems during active movement, Herman suggested the use of sensory electronic aids that provide continuous visual and/or auditory feedback of amplitude and rate of evolving movement. Such feedback, serving as guidance in response during retraining, has proven to be of help in motor recovery.

About the same time (i.e., about 1971), also critical of conventional therapies, I began to study the therapeutic efficacy of augmented iEMG sensory feedback in varying states of abnormal motor activity. Soon other faculty members of New York University Medical Center joined my study, which was conducted in Bellevue Hospital Center (Brudny, Grynbaum, & Korein, 1974). In 1973 an enlarged interdepartmental N.Y.U. Medical Center group was formed, with offices located in the ICD Rehabilitation and Research Center (Brudny, Korein, Levidow, Grynbaum, Lieberman, & Friedmann, 1974), to be known as Sensory Feedback Therapy Unit. Our therapeutic technique based on monitoring visual displays of iEMG during self-produced movement, combined with attempts to alter the abnormal iEMG responses in the muscles involved in movement, was termed "Sensory Feedback Therapy" (SFT) or "Therapeutic Electromyography." In designing this study, we were influenced by concepts drawn from psychology and from studies of motor development and motor skill acquisition (Bilodeau & Bilodeau, 1967; Connolly, 1970; Stelmach, 1976), brain plasticity (Bach-y-Rita, 1972; Luria, 1966; Stein, Rosen, & Butters, 1974), and operant conditioning (Catania, 1968; Skinner, 1938). The neurocybernetic concept and its postulation of signals as centrally processed during movement control have also influenced our approach (Anokhin, 1969;

Smith & Henry, 1967; Stark, 1968; Wiener, 1948). Finally, the pioneering work with neurologically disabled patients (Marinacci & Horande, 1960) and the work done previously with normal subjects in the area of motor control using EMG as a feedback source have provided encouragement and direction (Basmajian, 1967a; Hefferline, Bruno, & Davidowitz, 1970; Rubow & Smith, 1971a).

The work I refer to in this chapter has been conducted since 1971 in the affiliated institutions of Bellevue Hospital Center, the ICD Rehabilitation and Research Center, and the Institute of Rehabilitation Medicine/New York University Medical Center. The systems and methods developed during the course of this study, the results obtained, and some thoughts on the mechanisms involved are the subjects of this chapter.

EQUIPMENT

During the course of our research, a system known as the EMG Bioconditioner was developed, tested extensively, and recently made available commercially by Hyperion, Inc., a subsidiary of Cordis Corporation, Miami, Florida. This sytem permits detection, measurement, and display of EMG activity, and also contains augmented feedback capabilities used to train therapeutically desirable modifications of such EMG activity. The EMG Bioconditioner is a two-channel electromyographic device consisting of a microprocessor controller assembly and video monitor (see Fig. 1). Application of computer technology for the control and video display of EMG signals offers a sizable advance in terms of analysis and therapy. As for the analytic potential of the system, it provides for on-line, real-time computation of EMG and permits the measurement and recording of digitally integrated muscle potentials in units of microvolt-seconds on two channels simultaneously (Brudny, Weisinger, & Silverman, 1976). The concept of the microvolt-second is derived from computation of the raw EMG. The intensities of EMG that vary with time are made unidirectional by full wave rectification, and the resultant signals are digitally integrated over 100 milliseconds. Since the integral represents the area under the varying intensity waveform, and the electrical representation of the intensity in the muscle is in units of microvolts, the resultant unit of muscle activity is the microvolt-second. The recording of microvolt-seconds as an indication of altered muscle activity during movement provides a means of reflecting and verifying the status of motor control. The correctness and consistency of data recording provided by the microvolt-second unit has also been recognized and recommended by others (Winter, Rau, & Kadefors, 1979).

A digital-to-analog converter produces an analog signal from digital pulse for display on a video monitor and other peripherals. The data can be transferred to recording devices such as teletypes, polygraphs, tapes, discs, and printers, and can be

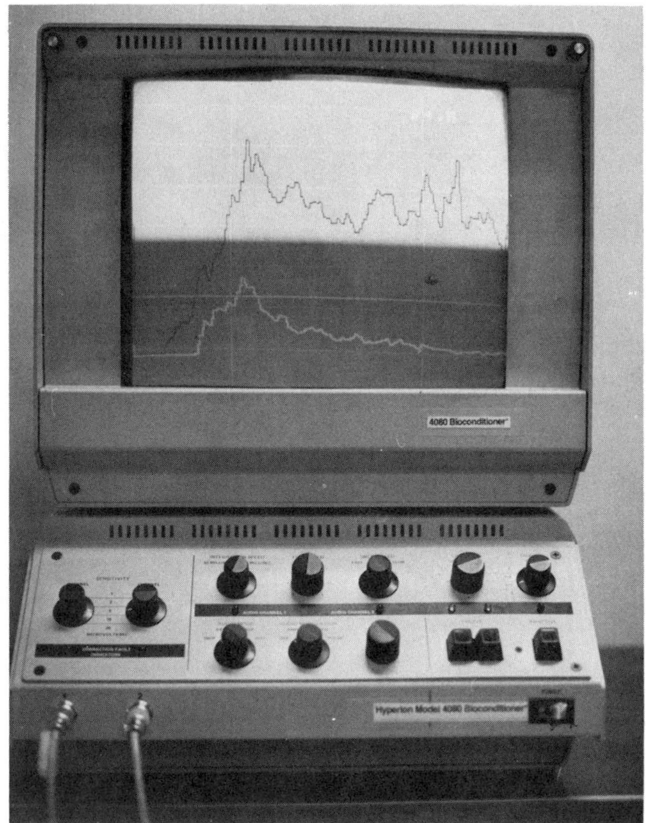

FIG. 1. The EMG Bioconditioner, a special-purpose, two-channel electromyograph for detection, measurement, and immediate display of iEMG activity. Third channel provides capability for setting therapeutic goals. Recorded EMG activity may be stored in the memory section and recalled as needed. The EMG activity is measured in microvolt-seconds. A raw EMG display is also provided.

also used for on-line computer processing. This system also has the capacity for storage of various discriminative traces derived from EMG recorded during movement, and it permits retrieval of these traces to serve as models for replication by the patient.

The therapeutic potential of this system is based on the generally recognized premise that, when transduced by surface electrodes and integrated digitally during short time periods, the EMG reflects adequately the ongoing muscle activity—that is, the muscle contraction (or its length) and the rate of changes of such contraction (DeVries, 1968; Gans & Noordergraaf, 1975). Controlled by a microprocessor, such iEMG appears instantaneously in the form of traces on a video monitor (see Fig. 2). The displacement of the trace line along the vertical axis reflects the magnitude of

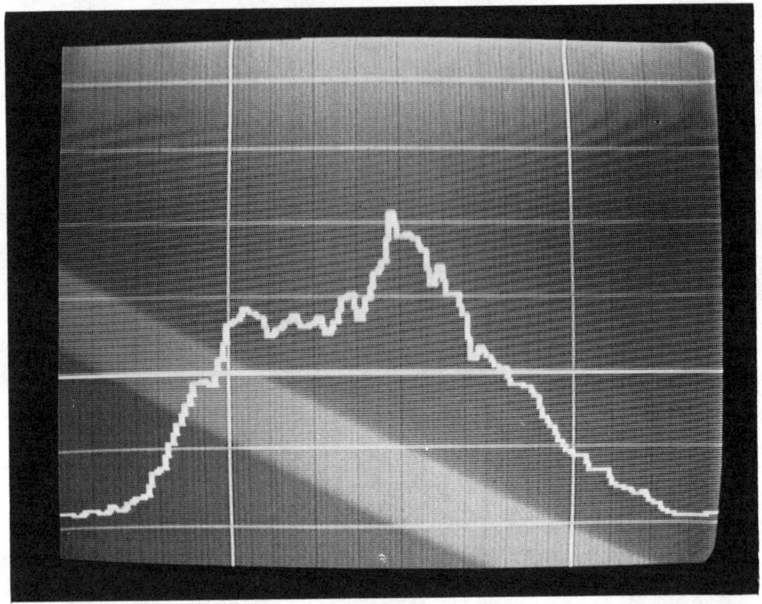

FIG. 2. Oscilloscopic trace reflecting the degree and rate of change of muscle activity (contraction and relaxation) during movement. Horizontal white line represents targeted level of iEMG amplitude to be matched or exceeded by the patient.

activity generated in the muscle, while the rate of change of such activity is reflected on the horizontal axis in the vertical displacement over time. Thus, this visual display reflects in a continuous manner the spatiotemporal events occurring in the monitored muscle during attempted or ongoing movement. Furthermore, such a display provides knowledge of the occurrence as well as the outcome of a patient's own response, instantaneously and while performance is still going on. Scheduling and presentation of auditory signals is used mainly as reinforcement for successful matching or approximating of the iEMG response to the model displays presented on the video screen.

ANALYTIC PROCEDURES

The analysis of a patient's iEMG response helps to establish specific training goals for that patient. In normal subjects, the patterns of iEMG generated in response to command or volition are quite constant and reproducible; they clearly reflect appropriate control of response activity within spatial and temporal dimensions. The coordinated nature of facilitation and inhibition of agonist and antagonist activities is also apparent. With such displays of iEMG, the monitored muscles truly "come alive," to paraphrase Basmajian (1967b), and their interplay becomes clearly expressed in visually organized form (see Fig. 3).

In contrast, the iEMG patterns derived from monitoring the muscles of a patient with spastic, paretic, or dyskinetic disorders of voluntary movement show typical abnormalities of response. The visual display readily confirms the clinical impression that while some movement can be initiated by the patient, the temporal and spatial iEMG parameters are not of a dimension appropriate to fostering functional control.

Paretic muscles show temporal delay in iEMG response and an inability to reach and sustain the steady levels of response needed for function. Muscles with clinically observed "excessive tone" (spasticity or spasmodic activity) demonstrate lack of temporal and spatial control, shown by an excessive and uncontrollable rise of levels of iEMG response as well as by inability to reduce such levels quickly, if at all.

When monitoring agonist and antagonist muscles simultaneously, a pattern of cocontraction is frequently seen (see Fig. 4). This pattern may completely restrict movement or prevent it from becoming functional as a result of excessive effort fol-

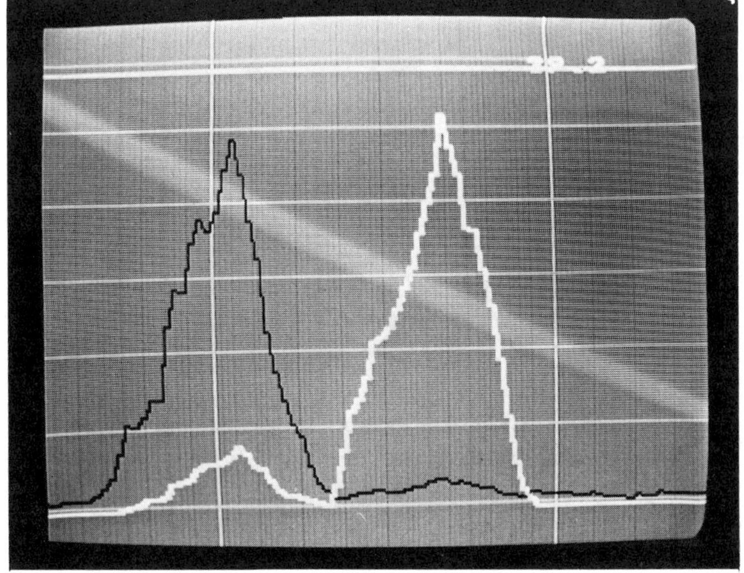

FIG. 3. Simultaneous monitoring of activity of agonist–antagonist muscles (biceps–triceps) during flexion and extension of the forearm. White trace represents activity of biceps muscle; black trace, activity of triceps muscle. Numbers in upper right-hand corner are microvolt-seconds of EMG activity. Values are updated every 100 milliseconds. This recording has been obtained from the unaffected upper limb.

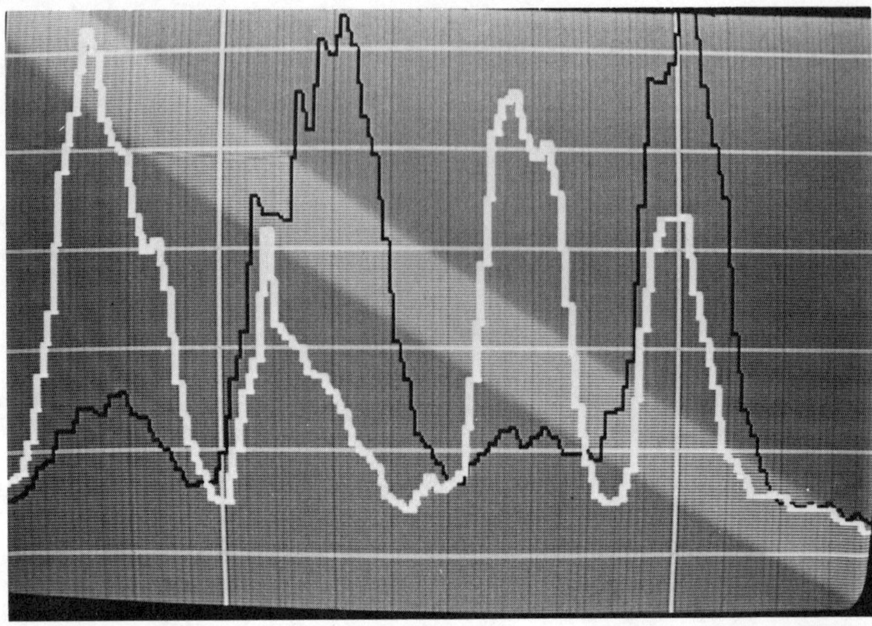

FIG. 4. Biceps and triceps muscles of hemiparetic arm being monitored during forearm flexion and extension. White trace represents activity of biceps muscle; black trace, activity of triceps muscle. Coactivation of biceps and triceps activity is present during forearm extension, with the spasticity of the biceps limiting function.

lowed by ensuing fatigability. The patient is usually unaware of the interfering factors and can rarely identify and / or suppress the undesired muscle activity. Overflow to other muscle groups occurring during excessive effort further complicates the attempt at movement.

TRAINING PROCEDURES

Following the clinical evaluation and analysis of abnormalities of iEMG response, treatment procedures are established for each patient individually. SFT involves focusing on events in individual primary movers and training the patient to alter volitionally any existing abnormal activity in muscles involved in the production of functional movement. Simultaneous monitoring and training of agonist and antagonist muscles form the cornerstone of treatment (Brudny, Korein, Grynbaum, Friedmann, Weinstein, Sachs-Frankel, & Belandres, 1976). While observing the visual displays reflecting the iEMG response to command or volition, the patient, with the therapist's guidance, has an opportunity to evaluate the otherwise covert and often inappropriate muscle activity. The patient can then attempt to bring the iEMG response closer to normal patterns while watching the video monitor on which performance and the models are simultaneously displayed. In this way, it becomes possible to determine immediately any existing gap between actual and intended performance. To bridge this gap, operant conditioning techniques developed for analysis and control of behaviors are included in the treatment package.

Coupling the auditory and visual capabilities of the EMG Bioconditioner produces a tone at appropriate points that can serve as a reinforcing event. This tone appears and remains in accordance with certain contingencies, thereby permitting the shaping of iEMG responses. In paretic muscles, increasingly greater iEMG responses, as well as extended ability to sustain such response levels, are often achieved as a result (see Fig. 5). In spastic or spasmodic muscles, reduction of excessive iEMG response produced by stretch, gravity pull, or movement is achieved and maintained following successive approximations to a desirable target level. This target, displayed as a horizontal threshold line, is progressively altered by the therapist toward more demanding and more functional levels of response.

Simultaneous monitoring of agonist and antagonist muscles on separate channels allows spasticity suppression training to be combined with paretic muscle strength-

FIG. 5. Intermediate stage of training patient in increased and sustained contraction of paretic triceps muscle. He has successfully increased contraction of triceps muscle, as evidenced by producing EMG amplitude sufficient to surpass targeted level (white horizontal trace), and has become able to sustain same for duration of sweep.

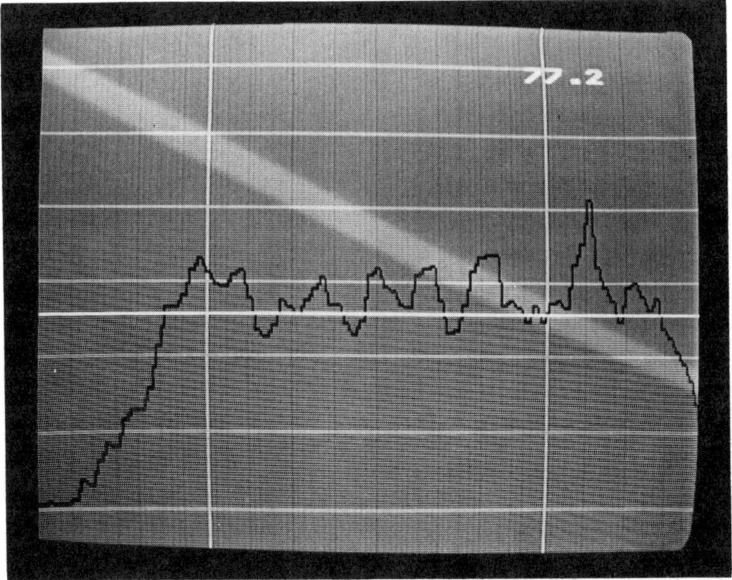

ening. In essence, such an avoidance training paradigm involves antagonist inhibition below a threshold level determined and set by the therapist during intended agonist activation (see Fig. 6).

Training is also carried out in more advanced stages by having the patient produce iEMG patterns with a hemiparetic extremity that match sample traces derived from similar movements in the unaffected limb, retrieved from computer memory, and displayed on the video screen (see Fig. 7). For such a performance to sample training paradigm, the Bioconditioner also provides an extensive repertoire of artificially designed variable traces (see Fig. 8). Selection of a model is made by the therapist, depending on the stage of the patient's response to training. When the response trace produced by the patients (the activity of the monitored muscle) approximates or matches the selected sample trace, a tone is produced by the instrument.

The frequency of training in our studies ranged from three to five times a week. The duration of each treatment was approximately 45 minutes. Between training sessions, patients were routinely given detailed instructions to carry out a program of repetitive daily self-administered exercises at home, with attention directed toward control of the primary movers that were trained in the clinic.

FIG. 6. Training suppression of spasticity in biceps (white trace) while triceps (black trace) is activated during elbow extension. Tone is emitted each time trace representing EMG level of biceps exceeds horizontal threshold line.

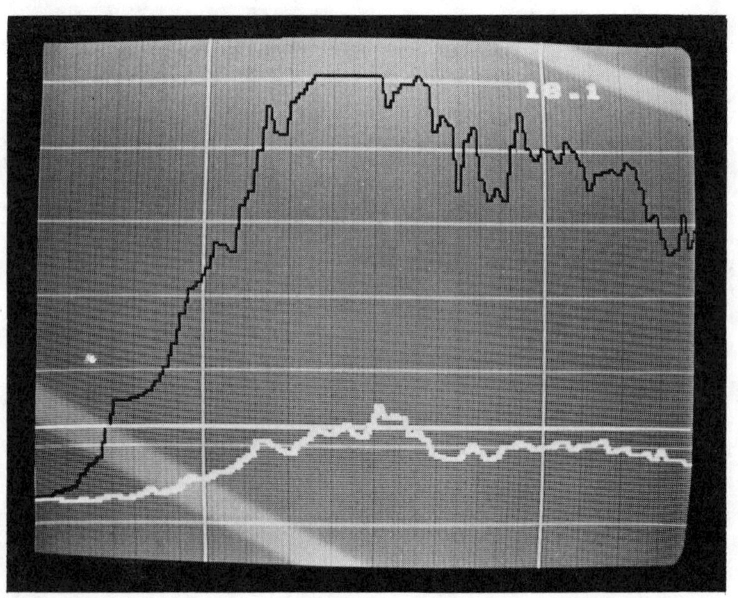

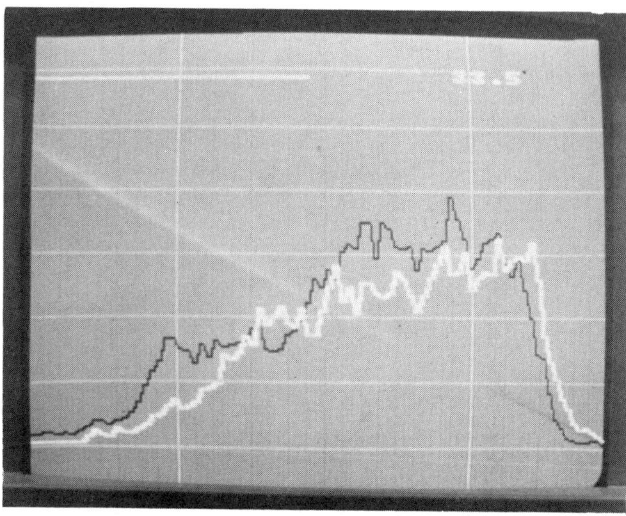

FIG. 7. White trace represents EMG pattern derived from movement in unaffected limb and retrieved from computer memory (wrist dorsiflexion and return to neutral position). When black trace produced by muscle activity monitored in affected limb approximates or matches sample, tone is produced, providing information on accuracy of patient's performance.

FIG. 8. White trace represents a variable-threshold trace, created artificially and displayed for any desired length of time. Black trace is produced by dorsiflexor muscle activity in the affected arm (wrist dorsiflexion and return to neutral position).

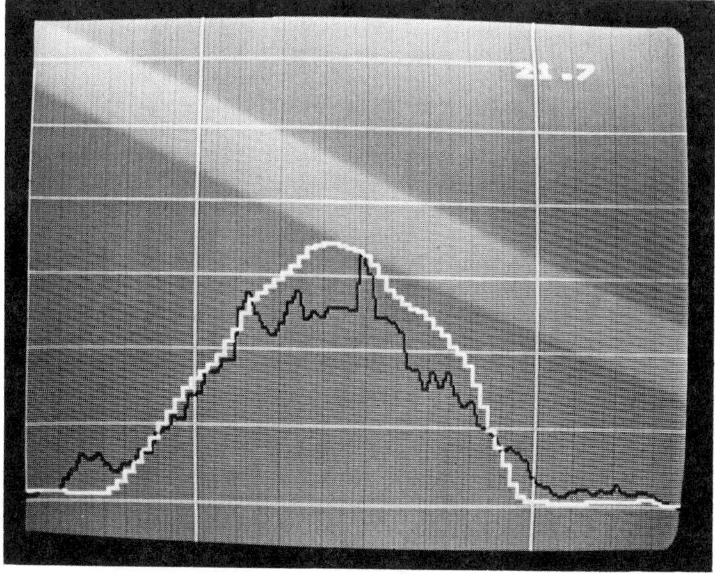

EVALUATION PROCEDURES

EMG measures were obtained early in our research in selected cases by means of recording microvolt-second values prior to treatment and during optimal performance following treatment. The systematic recording of microvolt-seconds as a means of verifying the status of motor control is more recently being included in single-subject methodology, as discussed later in the chapter.

In addition to EMG measures, results were evaluated in relation to changes in functional capacity, since our major concern was to improve the patients' functional status for activities of daily living. Functional capacity was evaluated collectively by three physicians at 4-week intervals. This evaluation allowed for the variations of initial severity levels. Grading scales were used to evaluate functional capacity and are presented in Table 2. The grading does not imply linear progression; the rationale underlying the functional evaluation scale is based on the concept of hierarchically ordered levels.

PATIENT POPULATION

Over 400 chronic neurological patients with a variety of clinical entities have been studied and treated by us. These have included small numbers of patients with spinal cord injuries as well as peripheral nerve injuries, and their response has been encouraging (Brudny, Lusskin, Campbell, Grynbaum, & Korein, 1979). The majority of patients had suffered brain insult and represented two groups: patients with hemi-

TABLE 2. Functional Grading of Results

Grading	*Hemiparesis*	*Focal Dystonia*
0	No change from initial status.	No response to feedback.
1+	Voluntary reduction of spasticity or increased strength (working against gravity).	Control with feedback only, but no carryover.
2+	Assistive capacity of the upper extremity without prehension (stabilizing, pushing, pulling, carrying, some bimanual activities due to shoulder and elbow control).	Meaningful changes in activities of daily living (ADL). Control lasting for days. Emotional stress and fatigue may cause temporary loss of control.
3+	Crude prehension for acquisition and release (time-consuming, especially release).	Major change in ADL. Lasting control for weeks and/or months. Rare episodes of involuntary movement rapidly attenuated.
4+	Skillful prehension.	

paretic–spastic syndromes, and patients with focal dystonic syndromes. The selection of these two groups was dictated by their notoriously low recovery rate despite a multitude of conventional therapies. All of the patients studied and treated by us had received conventional therapies until their progress had reached a point of diminishing returns. Some 62% of them had received their previous treatment in university-affiliated medical institutions. In addition, we were interested in testing a conceptually unified approach to the treatment of diverse clinical entities. A representative sample of each group is described in this chapter.

In treating hemiparetic patients, we concentrated our efforts primarily on the upper extremity, being aware that functional recovery is very low. Only 30% of hemiparetics recover function in an upper limb (Zenkel, Cobb, & Huskey, 1966), in contrast to 70% becoming ambulatory (Baker, Schwartz, & Ramseyer, 1968). A group of 70 patients, 12 to 78 years of age, with mean duration of illness being 2½ years, received a 9-month course of SFT for a nonfunctional upper extremity (Brudny, Korein, Grynbaum, Belandres, & Gianutsos, 1979). Table 3 describes this group in greater detail.

The selection of patients with focal dystonia became of particular interest to us early in the research (Brudny, Grynbaum, & Korein, 1974). The bizarre nature of focal dystonia, the occurrence of dyskinesias during certain actions, and their increased incidence during mental stress led to the belief that this disorder is psychogenic. Only recently has focal dystonic syndrome been classified as a neurological entity of similar pathophysiology to dystonia (Marsden, 1976). The abnormal motor activity in dystonia is considered to be related to a disturbance of the processing of incoming sensory signals in basal ganglia, with resulting excessive input being relayed to the motor cortex (Zeman, 1970). The underlying disturbance is biochemical in nature and is due to an existing imbalance in neuronal transmittal agents relating to the extrapyramidal system (Fahn, 1976). The agent most implicated is probably gamma-amino-butyric acid (GABA). Its main action is inhibitory in nature, both pre- and postsynaptically. The GABA-ergic system can be envisioned as setting the gain on the sensitivity of sensory receptors (Roberts, 1976).

With disturbed inhibition and processing of neuronal signals at sensory receptor sites in basal ganglia, certain thalamocortical feedback loops of the complex servosystem of voluntary movement transmit defective information causing excessive activity of the motor cortex, with the resulting manifestations of dystonic dyskinesias. Such being the case, the motor manifestations of dystonia imply malfunctioning sensory mechanisms. This entity seemed, therefore, to be an excellent model for our training, which we viewed as a form of sensory substitution mechanism. A group of 80 patients was treated and followed up to 4 years (Korein & Brudny, 1976). The results of a multitude of previous therapies (physical, medical, and surgical) were ineffective or moderately effective only. Data pertaining to this group are presented in Table 4.

TABLE 3. 70 Hemiparetic Patients

Median age at onset	49.5 years
Median duration of illness	5.0 years
Right hemiparesis present	38.5%
Left hemiparesis present	58.5%
Moderate to severe spasticity	80 %
Moderate to severe paresis	65 %
Various forms of dyskinesias	10 %
Somatosensory and proprioceptive abnormality	68 %
Nonambulatory	10 %
Infarction	65 %
Neoplasm, hemorrhage, embolism	11 %
Trauma	7 %

RESULTS

The hemiparetic patients who responded well to SFT demonstrated the ability to break up the pathological synergies present and were able to plan and execute patterned movement in a functional manner. Of the greatest significance seemed to be the knowledge of strategy to identify and suppress the undesirable motor activity. While most markedly increased speed and accuracy in executing the intended movement, their performance still rarely resembled the rapid, easily produced type of patterned movement characteristic of health. In the initial stages of retraining, arm and hand movement at times resembled those of an efficient myoelectric prosthetic arm (Brudny, Korein, Grynbaum, & Sachs-Frankel, 1977). At the same time, there was an evident need for planning the intended movement, and constant visual observation seemed to facilitate its execution. While some of the patients eventually became capable of carrying out the intended movement automatically, smoothly, accurately, and repeatedly, others showed a lasting need for awareness of and "attunement" to motor activity in the muscles. Whenever a patient succeeded in learning adequate motor control of a particular movement, "normalization" of iEMG

TABLE 4. 80 Patients with Focal Dystonia

Median age at onset	48 years
Median duration of illness	4.5 years
Predominant feature torticollis	86.2%
Other forms—orofacial, oromandibular, and single-extremity dyskinesias	13.8%
Positive family history	17.5%
Ethnic background—Caucasian	100 %
Various surgery—cryothalamectomy, nerve root and muscle section	10 %
Psychotherapy	56 %

response was always demonstrated in the primary movers responsible for this task. ("Normalization" can be defined as a progressive decrease of reflexive components of movement, with a simultaneous increase of its volitional, supraspinal components.) Such SFT-related progressive gains in control of sequential and simultaneous activity of biceps and triceps muscles can be clearly seen during flexion and extension of the forearm by a hemiparetic patients (Figs. 9, 10, and 11).

Using the established functional evaluation criteria and considering only gains of 2+ and 3+ as meaningful, 43 of the 70 described patients, or 61% of them, achieved such gains. The results of their treatment are presented in Table 5. A total of 21 of the patients who continued into Phase 2 were followed up for as long as 3 years, and all maintained the levels of functional movement achieved during therapy.

It is obvious from the above results that extended duration of treatment adds materially to the degree of functional recovery and allows more of these patients to attain prehension, which is the most skillful manipulative performance of the human arm. Recovery of motor function following brain insult may require a very prolonged period of time, and we have accordingly observed ongoing degrees of return of the skillful use of arm and hand in patients followed for over 4 years. In this light, extension of SFT beyond the boundaries of hospital and clinic and into a patient's home to overcome the fiscal constraints related to the duration of needed retraining seems to be a concept worthy of widespread test and implementation.

FIG. 9. A 54-year-old patient with 2 years' duration of right spastic hemiparesis. The attempt at extension of the forearm (black trace reflecting the activity of triceps muscle, white trace the activity of biceps muscle) is short-lasting and futile because of the biceps muscle spasticity causing cocontraction.

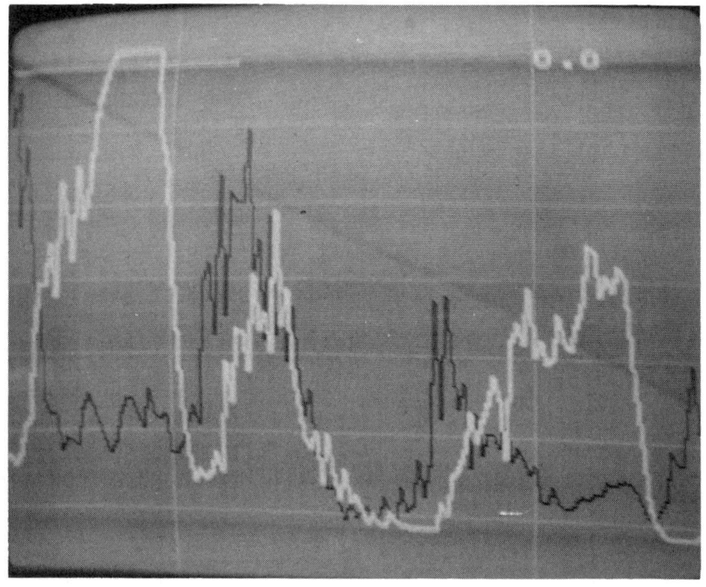

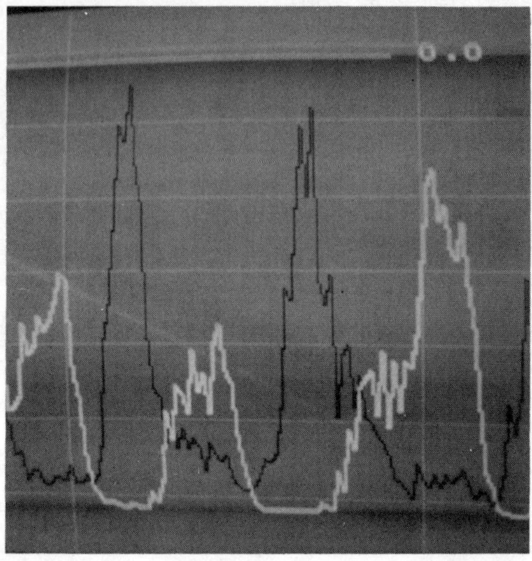

FIG. 10. The same patient after 4 weeks of SFT, the result of which is evident in voluntary suppression of the undesirable cocontraction of the biceps muscle.

FIG. 11. The same patient following 8 weeks of SFT. Flexion and extension of the forearm is carried out efficiently, fully, and without benefit of feedback. The ''normalization'' of iEMG response is quite evident in comparison with similar performance in an unaffected limb (Fig. 3).

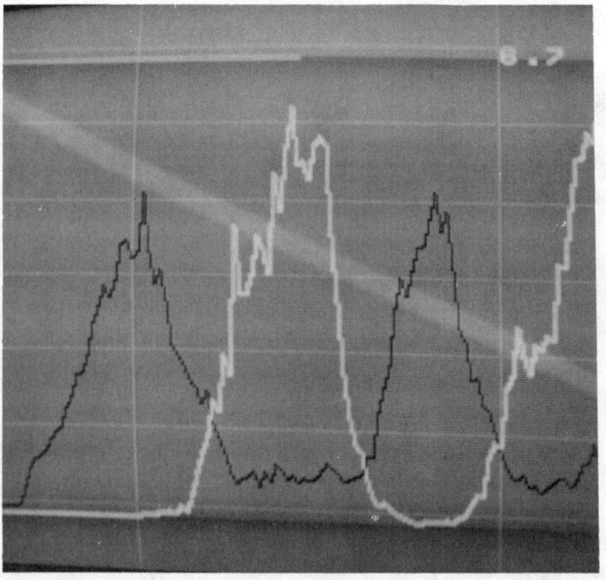

TABLE 5. Results of Treatment of 70 Hemiparetic Patients

Grading Scale Evaluation	*Number of Patients*	*% of Patients*
Phase 1—lasting 8 weeks		
Patients showing 0	9	12.9
Patients showing 1 +	24	34.3
Patients showing 2 +	26	37.1
Patients showing 3 +	11	15.7
Phase 2—lasting 24 weeks[a]		
Further gains from 1 + to 2 +	(*N* = 15) 6	40.0
Further gains from 2 + to 3 +	(*N* = 13) 7	53.8
Further gains from 3 + to 4 +	(*N* = 8) 7	87.5

[a]A total of 36 patients continued into Phase 2.

The patients with focal dystonic syndrome who responded to SFT learned to discriminate early the onset of spasmodic activity and were able to suppress such activity for varying time periods. In the initial phases of SFT, constant attention to variables of motor activity was obvious. Later on, the patients clearly demonstrated the automatic type of acquired control, being unaware of its mechanism. It is conceivable that while in SFT, some of these patients were also learning to discriminate and integrate other information derived from intact sensory modalities—for example, from receptors in skin, joints, and visual and vestibular systems—and were able to retain these patterns to aid motor performance following withdrawal of feedback.

Only patients who could control their movement disorders during activities of daily living for days (2 +) and weeks (3 +) were considered successes. When there was no change (0), or when the response to feedback was present only during training sessions (1 +), the patients were considered therapeutic failures. Of the described 80 patients treated, 34, or 44%, were classified as failures, and 45 patients, or 56%, were considered therapeutic successes. Along with learning control over previously spasmodic muscles, all these patients demonstrated significant changes in activities of daily living, including (in some) returning to work, driving a car, resuming social contacts, and so forth. Subsequently, after the follow-up of up to 4 years, regression occurred in 9 patients, while 36, or 45% of the original group, maintained their gains. We consider this a significant rate of improvement, in view of the long duration of their illness and their failure to respond to various forms of previous therapy.

The studies described represent summaries of work performed in a clinical setting over many years. Because of clinical pressures, ideal experimental conditions were not met or warranted. However, a collaborative study conducted by Gianutsos, Eberstein, Krasilowsky, and Goodgold (1979), employing the Bioconditioner for data gathering as well as for therapy, has provided rigorous experimental support of our results.

SINGLE-CASE METHODOLOGY

The study by Gianutsos *et al.*, which is still in progress, has very carefully documented iEMG responses in 30 hemiparetic individuals using single-case methodology (Gianutsos, 1980). This methodology, which has been successfully applied within a variety of experimental and clinical settings (Barlow & Hersen, 1973), was employed to assess the contribution of visually displayed EMG feedback to functional recovery in the hemiparetic upper extremity. Patients at the ICD Rehabilitation and Research Center, at Bellevue Hospital Center, and at the Institute of Rehabilitation Medicine/New York University Medical Center have been studied by such means.

Single-case experimental design methods offer many advantages to those engaged in research within a rehabilitation setting, particularly when hemiparetic patients are involved. The difficult if not impossible task of obtaining matched controls is avoided by employing such methods, since they are within-subject experimental designs where each subject serves as his or her own control. The latter feature also eliminates the need for withholding treatment from patients assigned to a control group.

The "multiple baseline across behaviors" design (Hersen & Barlow, 1976) has been employed. In this design, after a baseline has been established for all target activities, the introduction of EMG feedback is staggered, thereby allowing training effects to be dissociated from practice and recovery effects.

In a preliminary study (Gianutsos *et al.*, 1979), five hemiparetic patients in the chronic phase of recovery (.5, 1, 2, 3, and 4 years after the onset of cerebrovascular accident) participated. All had received traditional therapies and had reached the apparent limits of their progress in upper extremity function. They were assessed in each session for the following target activities: shoulder flexion (anterior deltoid–upper trapezius); elbow extension (triceps–biceps); and finger extension (digit extensors–digit flexors).

During the initial baseline phase (six to eight sessions), each patient attempted to execute the above target activities at the request of the therapist and without benefit of EMG feedback. During three subsequent phases, SFT was initiated successively for the three target activities, with the objective of increasing the amplitude of the agonist response while simultaneously reducing the amplitude of the antagonist response. Systematic measurement and training were continued as practical in a follow-through phase. The total number of sessions ranged from 42 to 54. In each session, the mean peak of iEMG for the six responses was calculated for each target activity (see Fig. 12). During data collection, no source of information about the EMG

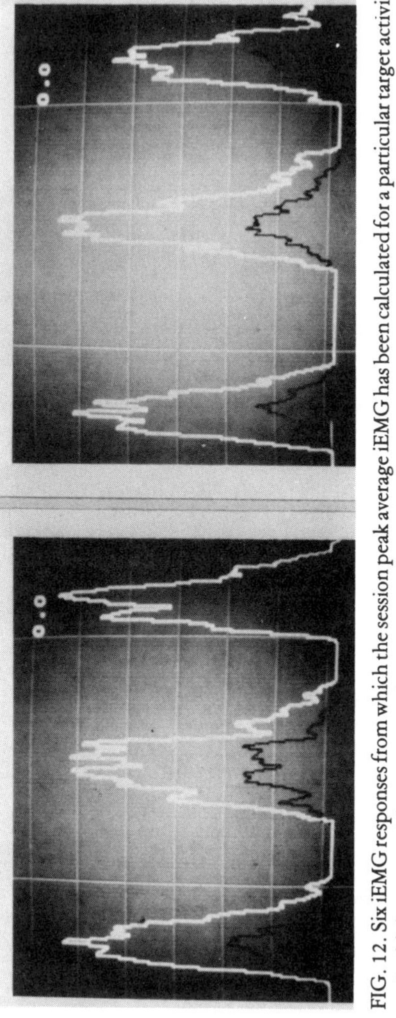

FIG. 12. Six iEMG responses from which the session peak average iEMG has been calculated for a particular target activity. In this instance, white represents the triceps activity and the black the biceps activity during elbow extension. During data collection, no source of information regarding the EMG response was made available to the patient. The patient is successfully suppressing the activity of the biceps muscle (the therapeutically desirable goal).

response was available to the patient. An exponential curve of predicted values for each target muscle was derived from data points obtained during the baseline phase.

All patients increased their ability to produce and modulate EMG activity in the hemiparetic upper extremity. Of the three target activities, elbow extension yielded the most impressive effects. These gains were reflected not only in increased iEMG response but in noticeable improvements in the range of motion. During shoulder flexion, all patients were able to reduce the synergistic pattern of elevated EMG activity of the upper trapezius in relation to the anterior deltoid, as well as to increase their active range of motion on this task. Finger extension proved the most difficult of the three tasks to accomplish. Nevertheless, three patients were able to accomplish finger extension and to increase the active range of finger motion. A typical result of this study is presented in Fig. 13, which contains the findings ob-

FIG. 13. Multiple baseline analysis of the effects of video-displayed EMG feedback on mean iEMG amplitude recorded from agonist–antagonist muscle pairs of the hemiparetic upper extremity. Introduction of the EMG feedback was staggered to different muscle pairs from the session indicated by the broken vertical lines. For each muscle group, data points on the left of this vertical line were obtained during the baseline phase, while those to its right were obtained during the feedback phase. The solid curves indicate a projected trend generated from baseline data points. Each session's data point represents the peak iEMG of six responses. The right column of graphs represents the differential score of the agonist–antagonist pair obtained by subtracting the iEMG values of each muscle in the middle column from its counterpart in the left column. Arrow orientation indicates the therapeutically desired direction of EMG change. (From "EMG Feedback in the Rehabilitation of Upper Extremity Function: Single Case Studies of Chronic Hemiplegics" by J. Gianutsos, A. Eberstein, G. Krasilowsky, and J. Goodgold, *International Neuropsychological Society Bulletin,* 1979.)

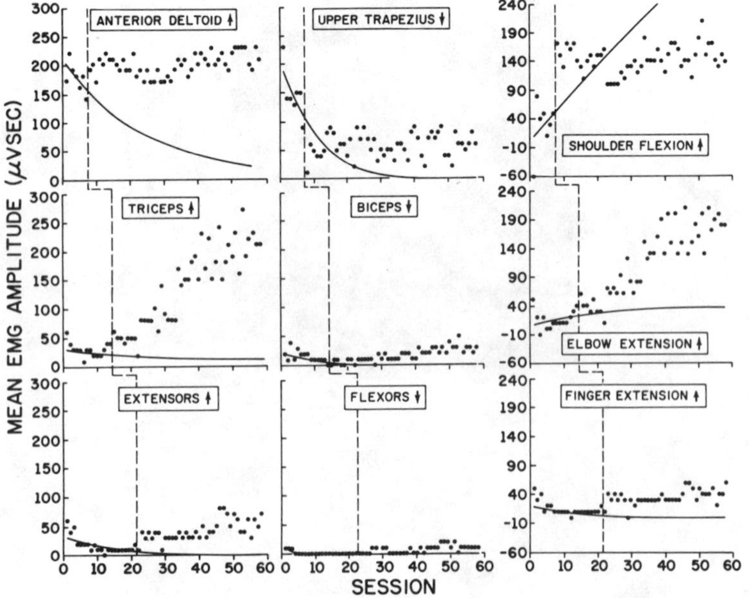

tained from a single-case study of a 73-year-old hemiparetic patient with 3 years' duration of illness who received SFT for his right upper limb. The analysis of the data indicates that introduction of feedback resulted in an immediate rise in the anterior deltoid–upper trapezius differential, that change was maintained throughout the remaining sessions, and that it allowed for shoulder flexion of 90°. In comparison to the projected trend, EMG feedback resulted in reversing the downward trend of the anterior deltoid muscle. As for elbow extension, it is obvious that the projected trend for decrease of triceps activity was reversed, allowing for 180° forearm extension. The cocontraction of both muscles, observed during baseline, was eliminated through restriction of biceps activity. Introduction of feedback resulted in immediate rise in iEMG levels in finger extensors, to such an extent that the patient was able to extend his fingers fully, despite relative and modest increase in iEMG levels in the finger flexors.

The results in this patient indicate that therapeutically desirable alterations of increase or inhibition of iEMG response in respective muscles were accomplished as the result of introducing feedback, in contrast to predicted trends established during the baseline phase. This was confirmed clinically in the follow-up period. Although the patient's hemiparetic right upper extremity served only as a gross assist prior to SFT, he was able following treatment to carry out manipulative, bimanual tasks, such as holding a fork while cutting food or tying apron strings.

COMMENT

On the basis of the clinical results obtained by the Sensory Feedback Therapy Unit with a large patient population, and confirmed on a smaller scale by well-documented controlled experimental evidence, the conclusion can be drawn that Therapeutic Electromyography allows clinicians to help patients transform abnormal movement patterns into more functional ones to a degree that conventional modes of therapy fail to achieve with chronic neurological patients.

Considering the different pathophysiology and pathoanatomy in the heterogeneous patient population reported on, a common mechanism contributing to functional recovery must be operational. This may perhaps explain our training efficacy in a variety of neuromotor disorders. The exact nature of this mechanism must remain a matter of speculation, and only hypothetical thinking on this subject can be offered. It is considered generally that facilitation of information transmission and processing fosters the functional reorganization of surviving neural tissue and aids in the restoration of voluntary movement (Rosner, 1974). It is this vital factor of information handling that seems to be a unique feature of the system and methods inherent in SFT, our technique that fosters a cognitive link between the generated iEMG response and a particular visual model. The ability to perform a "production to sample'' paradigm underlies the uniquely human capacity for language learning.

Hence, the concept of ''iEMG language'' suggests itself as it pertains to the patient's capacity to respond to visual information and, with its aid, to relearn more adequate motor control. It has been said of language that it gives purpose to sensation and action to movement (Penfield & Roberts, 1976). In this sense, to the patient unable to utilize sensory feedback from affected limbs and thus unable to learn the initial motor response, the visual patterns of the iEMG produced in response to command or volition can represent a modality substitute that reveals the muscular responses in understandable terms. Such ''visual language'' can, in turn, mediate the sensory motor integration within the CNS. The ''iEMG language'' is based on visually modeled traces that the patient attempts to replicate in training. For training to succeed, such replication requires the formation of precise spatiotemporal patterns of muscle activity. To form such patterns, patients must have the necessary residual neural substrate and thus the potential for increasing the supraspinal input and modulation of spinal cord mechanism involved in movement. While learning the components of movement is a necessary step in the recovery of movement, restoration of function is not accomplished until the ability to carry out those components in a coordinated manner is internalized and produced with minimal delay without the benefit of external feedback.

The terms of ''iEMG language'' are relevant, intelligible, accurate, simple, immediate, ongoing, and apparently capable of direct supraspinal access to the brain mechanisms concerned with motor performance; retention of such input is possible in time, as evidenced by the lasting ''normalization'' of iEMG response following the cessation of SFT.

At the stage at which ''memory of function'' has been internalized and ingrained, there may be no further need for feedback from the periphery, and the movement can be carried out in ''open-loop'' fashion. In this regard, it seems that the visual system plays a paramount role as a means of providing parallel information adequate to the repatterning of voluntary movements. The recall of the visual displays of iEMG was often reported by our patients as occurring during initiation and execution of the movement. Basmajian (1967a) reported that his subjects, when firing single motor units without benefit of feedback, were thinking about the feedback as they had seen and heard it previously. Luria (1963), using visual clues as external aids in his corrective afferent therapy of brain-injured patients, commented that these clues took root and became an internal representation of associated function.

The concept of ''iEMG language'' can be also expressed more conventionally in neurocybernetic terms as it pertains to transfer of information in the adaptive control system of the human brain. For its central motor programming and motor execution, such a system utilizes peripheral information from the muscles concerning the disposition of voluntary movement. While the muscle afferent information is not the only feedback loop, it is a most important one as far as movement is concerned, and it can suffice when joint and cutaneous afferents are not functional (Goodwin, McCloskey, & Mathews, 1972). The disruption or distortion of cerebral-level processing of muscle afferent feedback often may be overlooked clinically. The kinesthetic data, being mainly processed subcortically, rarely reach awareness, and there is no known test for estimating such deficit.

A grossly oversimplified "black box" analogue of CNS circuits related to motor control illustrates the significance of muscle afferent feedback (see Fig. 14).

It is assumed that, basing the decisions on information processing in sensory, associational, and motivational areas, the corticothalamic strategic command system initiates a learned movement. Subcortical structures, including the basal ganglia

FIG. 14. An aid in conceptualization of the interconnections and feedback loops of multiple servosystems involved in the initiation and execution of voluntary patterned movement and the therapeutic cortical input derived from visual displays of iEMG. The letters depict various afferent and efferent pathways subserving information transfer as it relates to motor control.

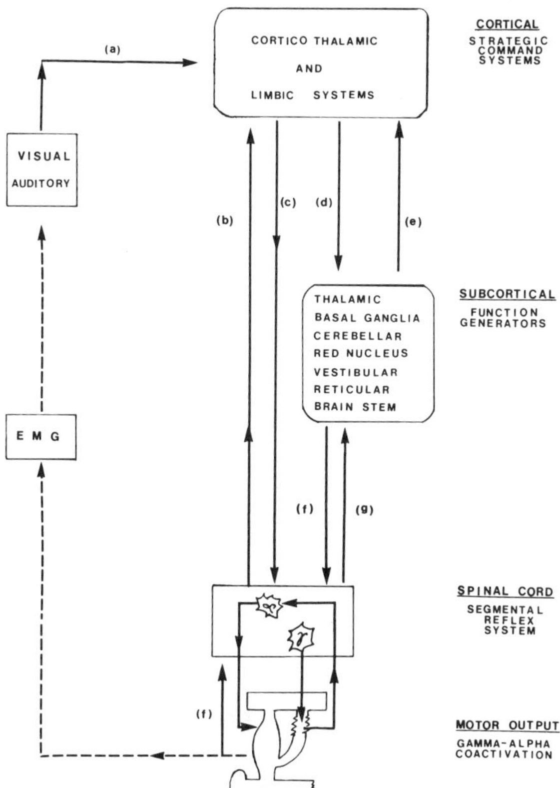

and the cerebellar complex, seem to serve as function generators for the outflow of spatio-temporal motor patterns. The basal ganglia are thought to serve as ramp generators for slow, smooth voluntary movements, and the cerebellar system is apparently preprogrammed for rapid, phasic movements (Kornhuber, 1974).

Information that is essential to peripheral organization of movement is provided by pyramidal, extrapyramidal, and subcortical inputs to the spinal cord's integrative mechanisms.

Motor output is accomplished by coactivation of intrafusal and extrafusal motor fibers or gamma–alpha linkage. The concept of so-called gamma leading or gamma ignition, for activation of the alpha motoneurons to initiate movement, has been reviewed by Granit (1970). More recent studies indicate that voluntary movement is initiated primarily by the supraspinal input to the alpha motoneurons (Kots, 1977), and that the actual role of alpha–gamma coactivation is to allow signaling from the muscle spindles concerning the length of the muscle and the rate of change during performance of a movement (Phillips, 1966). Such informational feedback is related in turn to the subcortical function generators and error detectors, and also in part to the sensory motor cortex, by means of cerebellar and thalamic relays. Similarly, the transcerebral servomechanism concept of Miles and Evarts (1979) views the gamma motoneuron discharge as afference copy needed for the error detection and error correction mechanisms of the brain.

It is evident from the foregoing that the integrity of motor planning and motor execution is dependent on cerebral-level processing of sufficient and pertinent informational feedback from muscle afferents. In this light, the external visual loop, derived from iEMG displays, assumes a special significance to the patient with brain insult, as it supplies quantifiable substitute information pertaining to the muscles' length and the rate of change in their length. For such substitute information to interact with the surviving parts of the disrupted nervous system, it must apparently present matching characteristics with the neural coding of the information on the intensity and rate of muscle contraction. It is this specific coded information on spatio-temporal changes in the muscles that may be incorporated into the neural circuits subserving voluntary movement, and thus may be retained. It is also conceivable that some patients, while responding to the external loop of information, are also able to discriminate and utilize again the previously only marginally perceived and processed kinesthetic feedback.

In support of such hypothetical reasoning, researchers may refer to the brain's adaptive response to functional demand, also known as "cerebral plasticity," which requires immediate and pertinent feedback information regarding the fulfillment of demand. If such demand is being repeatedly met, lasting functional changes are known to take place. This pertinent and needed information can be derived from a variety of sensory inputs. According to the concept of plasticity of the CNS as described by Bach-y-Rita (1972), one can envision perceptual mechanisms dealing with information supplied by receptors, conducted by pathways, and processed by central structures not previously concerned with the analysis of a particular modality of sensory information. The examples of clinically working sensory substitution mechanisms in patients deprived of vision, hearing, or sensation of touch are proof that these can be utilized therapeutically.

While investigators can assume that SFT enhances discrimination, transfer, processing, and utilization of pertinent information, this information in itself is not enough. The fact that only half of our patients responded adequately indicates that other factors must be related to therapeutic success. These can be identified as follows: (1) sufficiently preserved substrate of neural tissue both for central processing of information and for the signal outflow to the spinal motoneurons; (2) sufficient level of motivational drive enhancing the brain algorithms that constitute the basis of problem solving, pattern recognition, and learning of new motor programs (Napalkov, 1963); (3) awareness and attention essential to learning how to pattern the motions of individual muscles (the latter, according to Granit, 1972, is a capability that exists apart from that required in patterning the gross movements of the whole limb); and (4) operant conditioning, which, combined with EMG feedback, is apparently a powerful method for retraining patients with brain insult. Precise information on the pathways and central structures involved in operant conditioning is unknown. There is evidence that differing pathways may mediate such training and that feedforward mechanisms play a significant role in relearning voluntary movement (Goldberger, 1974). It is also assumed that, during operant conditioning, new and lasting connections may be formed between sensory and motor association areas. Such "associative learning" may be based to a considerable degree on perceptual images that act as triggers for motor action ("targeting reflexes") (Konorski, 1967). Finally, time is an essential factor. Because the time needed is often extensive, therapy beyond the clinic, in a patient's home with help from the family, is a concept whose introduction is overdue.

To sum up, a substantial foundation has been laid by many investigators, including the Sensory Feedback Therapy Unit to justify the widespread application and further exploration of the potential of Therapeutic Electromyography in the treatment of motor deficits in the neurologically disabled patient.

It is my belief that behavioral researchers and clinical investigators who have provided this foundation must now involve practicing, hospital-based physicians in a joint endeavor aimed at conclusively defining the benefits as well as the limitations of this modality. The credibility and efficacy of EMG feedback is ready for clinical tests beyond the confinement of the experimental laboratory, and preferably in university-affiliated medical institutions. Toward this end, the described systems and methods of analysis and therapy are offered as models.

ACKNOWLEDGMENTS

I wish to acknowledge: (*a*) the support received from the faculty of New York University Medical Center in the organization and operation of the Sensory Feedback Therapy Unit, in particular that of Drs. J. Ransohoff, C. Randt, H. Rusk, B. Grynbaum, and J. Goodgold; (*b*) the help and significant participation in the study by Drs. J. Korein, B. Grynbaum, P. Belandres, and J. Gianutsos, as well as the contributions of Drs. L. Friedmann, A. Lieberman, S. Weinstein, and J. Silverman; (*c*) the efforts of the staff involved in research and treatment aspects of this study: G. Sachs-Frankel, D. Fine, R. Messina, L. Levidow, and M. Weisinger; (*d*) the support received from ICD Rehabilitation and Research Center, in particular that from its president, J. Milbank; (*e*) the financial support given to this research by the following foundations: the J. M., the Achelis, the Bodman, the Surdna, the John Jay and Eliza Watson, the Arthur Davis, and the Downe.

REFERENCES

Anokhin, P. K. Cybernetics and the integrative activity of the brain. In M. Cole & I. Maltzman (Eds.), *Handbook of contemporary Soviet psychology*. New York: Basic Books, 1969.

Bach-y-Rita, P. *Brain mechanism in sensory substitution*. New York: Academic Press, 1972.

Baker, R. N., Schwartz, W. S., & Ramseyer, J. C. Prognosis among survivors of ischemic stroke. *Neurology*, 1968, *18*, 922–941.

Barlow, D. J., & Hersen, M. Single case experimental designs: Uses in applied clinical research. *Archives of General Psychiatry*, 1973, *29*, 319–325.

Basmajian, J. V. Methods of training the conscious control of motor units. *Archives of Physical Medicine and Rehabilitation*, 1967, *48*, 12–19. (a)

Basmajian, J. V. *Muscles alive*. Baltimore: Williams & Wilkins, 1967. (b)

Bilodeau, E. A., & Bilodeau, I. M. (Eds.). *Principles of skill acquisition*. New York: Academic Press, 1969.

Blanchard, E. B., & Epstein, L. H. The clinical usefulness of biofeedback. In M. Hersen, R. M. Eisler, & P. M. Miller (Eds.), *Progress in behavior modification*. New York: Academic Press, 1977.

Brudny, J., Grynbaum, B. B., & Korein, J. Spasmodic torticollis: Treatment by feedback display of the EMG. *Archives of Physical Medicine and Rehabilitation*, 1974, *55*, 403–408.

Brudny, J., Korein, J., Grynbaum, B. B., Belandres, P., & Gianutsos, J. Helping hemiparetics to help themselves: Sensory feedback therapy. *Journal of the American Medical Association*, 1979, *241*, 814–818.

Brudny, J., Korein, J., Grynbaum, B. B., Friedmann, L. W., Weinstein, S., Sachs-Frankel, G., & Belandres, P. EMG feedback therapy: Review of treatment of 114 patients. *Archives of Physical Medicine and Rehabilitation*, 1976, *57*, 55–61.

Brudny, J., Korein, J., Grynbaum, B. B., & Sachs-Frankel, G. Sensory feedback therapy in patients with brain insult. *Scandinavian Journal of Rehabilitation Medicine*, 1977, *9*, 155–163.

Brudny, J., Korein, J., Levidow, L., Grynbaum, B. B., Lieberman, A., & Friedmann, L. Sensory feedback therapy as a modality of treatment in central nervous system disorders of voluntary movement. *Neurology*, 1974, *24*, 925–932.

Brudny, J., Lusskin, R., Campbell, J. B., Grynbaum, B. B., & Korein, J. The role of sensory feedback of integrated EMG in the absence of proprioception. *Proceedings of the Fourth Congress of the International Society of Electrophysiological Kinesiology*, 1979.

Brudny, J., Weisinger, M., & Silverman, G. Single system for displaying EMG activity designed for therapy, documentation of results and analysis of research. In R. Foulds & R. Lund (Eds.), *1976 conference on systems and devices for the disabled*. Boston: Biomedical Engineering Center, 1976.

Catania, A. A. *Contemporary research in operant behavior.* Glenview, Ill.: Scott, Foresman, 1968.

Connolly, K. (Ed.). *Mechanisms of motor skill development.* New York: Academic Press, 1970.

DeVries, H. A. Efficiency of electrical activity as a physiological measure of the functional state of muscle tissue. *American Journal of Physical Medicine,* 1968, *47,* 10–22.

Fahn, S. Biochemistry of the basal ganglia. In R. Eldridge & S. Fahn (Eds.), *Advances in neurology* (Vol. 14, *Dystonia*). New York: Raven Press, 1976.

Fernando, C. K., & Basmajian, J. V. Biofeedback in physical medicine and rehabilitation. In J. Stoyva (Ed.), *Biofeedback and self-regulation* (Vol. 3). New York: Plenum, 1978.

Gans, B. M., & Noordergraaf, A. Voluntary skeletal muscles: A unifying theory on the relationship of their electrical and mechanical activities. *Archives of Physical Medicine and Rehabilitation,* 1975, *56,* 194–199.

Gianutsos, J. Personal communication, 1980.

Gianutsos, J., Eberstein, A., Krasilowsky, G., & Goodgold, J. EMG feedback in the rehabilitation of upper extremity function: Single case studies of chronic hemiplegics. *International Neuropsychological Society Bulletin,* 1979.

Goldberger, M. R. Recovery of movement after CNS lesions in monkeys. In D. G. Stein, J. J. Rosen, & N. Butters (Eds.), *Plasticity and recovery of function in the central nervous system.* New York: Academic Press, 1974.

Goodwin, G. M., McCloskey, D. I., & Mathews, P. B. L. The contribution of muscle afferents to kinesthetics shown by vibration induced illusions of movement and by the effect of paralyzing afferents. *Brain,* 1972, *95,* 705–748.

Granit, R. *Basis of motor control.* New York: Academic Press, 1970.

Granit, R. Constant errors in the execution and appreciation of movement. *Brain,* 1972, *95,* 649–660.

Hefferline, R. F., Bruno, L. J. J., & Davidowitz, J. E. Feedback control of covert behavior. In K. Connolly (Ed.), *Mechanisms of motor skill development.* New York: Academic Press, 1970.

Herman, R. *Neuromotor control systems—A study of physiological and theoretical concepts leading to therapeutic application* (Final report, 23P-551 15/3-03). Philadelphia: Temple University School of Medicine, December 1971.

Hersen, M., & Barlow, D. H. *Single case experimental designs: Strategies for studying behavior change.* New York: Pergamon, 1976.

Inglis, J., Campbell, G., & Donald, M. W. Electromyographic biofeedback and neuromuscular reeducation. *Canadian Journal of Behavioral Science,* 1976, *8,* 299–323.

Keefe, F. J., & Surwit, R. S. Electromyographic biofeedback: Behavioral treatment of neuromuscular disorders. *Journal of Behavioral Medicine,* 1978, *1,* 13–24.

Konorski, J. *The integrative activity of the brain.* Chicago: University of Chicago Press, 1967.

Korein, J., & Brudny, J. Integrated EMG feedback in the management of spasmodic torticollis and focal dystonia: a prospective study of 80 patients. In M. D. Yahr (Ed.), *The basal ganglia.* New York: Raven Press, 1976.

Kornhuber, H. H. Cerebral cortex, cerebellum and basal ganglia: An introduction to their motor functions. In F. O. Schmitt & F. G. Worden (Eds.), *The neurosciences: Third study program.* Cambridge, Mass.: MIT Press, 1974.

Kots, Y. M. *The organization of voluntary movement.* New York: Plenum, 1977.

Luria, A. R. *Restoration of function after brain injury.* New York: Pergamon, 1963.

Luria, A. R. *Higher cortical functions in man.* New York: Basic Books, 1966.

Marsden, C. D. The problem of adult-onset idiopathic torsion dystonia and other isolated dyskinesias in adult life. In R. Eldridge & S. Fahn (Eds.), *Advances in neurology* (Vol. 14, *Dystonia*). New York: Raven Press, 1976.

Marinacci, A. A., & Horande, M. Electromyogram in neuromuscular re-education. *Bulletin of the Los Angeles Neurological Society,* 1960, *25,* 57–71.

Miles, F. A., & Evarts, E. V. Concepts of motor organization. *Annual Review of Psychology,* 1979, *30,* 327–362.

Napalkov, A. V. Information process of the brain. In N. Wiener & J. P. Schade (Eds.), *Nerve, brain and memory models.* Amsterdam: Elsevier North Holland, 1963.

Penfield, W., & Roberts, L. *Speech and brain mechanisms.* New York: Atheneum, 1976.

Phillips, C. G. Changing concepts of the precentral motor area. In J. C. Eccles (Ed.), *Brain and conscious experience*. New York: Springer-Verlag, 1966.

Roberts, R. Some thoughts about GABA and the basal ganglia. In M. D. Yahr (Ed.), *The basal ganglia.* New York: Raven Press, 1976.

Rosner, B. S. Recovery of function and localization of function in historical perspective. In D. G. Stein, J. J. Rosen, & N. Butters (Eds.), *Plasticity and recovery of function in the central nervous system.* New York: Academic Press, 1974.

Rubow, R. T., & Smith, K. U. Feedback parameters of electromyographic learning. *American Journal of Physical Medicine,* 1971, *50,* 115–131.

Skinner, B. F. *The behavior of organisms.* New York: Appleton-Century-Crofts, 1938.

Smith, K. U., & Henry, J. P. Cybernetic foundations for rehabilitation. *American Journal of Physical Medicine,* 1967, *46,* 379–467.

Stark, L. *Neurological control systems: Studies in bioengineering.* New York: Plenum, 1968.

Stein, D. G., Rosen, J. J. and Butters, N. (Eds.). *Plasticity and recovery of function in the central nervous system.* New York: Academic Press, 1974.

Stelmach, G. E. (Ed.). *Motor control: Issues and trends.* New York: Academic Press, 1976.

Taft, L. T. Delagi, E. F., Wilkie, O. L., & Abramson, A. S. Critique of rehabilitative technics in treatment of cerebral palsy. *Archives of Physical Medicine and Rehabilitation,* 1962, *43,* 238–243.

U.S. Department of Health, Education, and Welfare. *Neurological and communicative disorders* (National Institutes of Health Publication No. 77-152). Washington, D.C.: U.S. Government Printing Office, 1976.

Wiener, N. *Cybernetics.* New York: Wiley, 1948.

Winter, D. A., Rau, G., & Kadefors, R. Units, terms and standards in the reporting of electromyographical research. *Proceedings of the Fourth Congress of the International Society of Electrophysiological Kinesiology,* 1979.

Zeman, W. Pathology of the torsion dystonias: Dystonia musculorum deformans. *Neurology,* 1970, *20,* 79–88.

Zenkel, H. T., Cobb, J. B., & Huskey, F. E. The rehabilitation of 500 stroke patients. *Journal of the American Geriatrics Society,* 1966, *14,* 1177–1184.

COMMENTS ON THE CHAPTER BY BRUDNY

STEVEN L. WOLF

When the progress achieved in the advancement of EMG biofeedback during the past decade is reviewed by practitioners of physical rehabilitation, little doubt exists concerning the significant contributions of Brudny and his colleagues at the New York University Medical Center. Both the quality and quantity of their work in developing training strategies and effecting positive outcomes among patients afflicted by stroke and dystonia have served as important landmarks from which clinicians can expand their methodologies and techniques for applying this modality. More than any other individual, Brudny has offered a unique body of information by virtue of the number of individu-

Steven L. Wolf. Departments of Rehabilitation Medicine, Anatomy, Surgery, and Community Health, and Biofeedback Research Programs, Emory University School of Medicine, Atlanta, Georgia.

als treated, the extent of follow-up data, and the solitary attempt at integrating basic and clinical neurophysiological findings to make comprehensible the modus operandi of this modality and its impact upon restorative function for neurological patients.

In the present context, Brudny has provided us with a model based upon the use of specific instrumentation, training techniques, and outcome analyses. As such, this model fulfills the ideal role for which it was intended; clinicians can accept its importance and emulate its ideals, or they can ponder its value and embellish its meaning. With the latter intent in mind, the following constructive commentary is submitted to supplement the excellent presentation provided by Brudny.

PERSONNEL

Any therapeutic intervention designed to improve sensorimotor integration among patients with neurological impairments requires a multidisciplinary approach. The potential value of SFT, while undoubtedly dependent upon well-controlled studies, must nonetheless by necessity compel many professionals to intervene to effect optimal patient progress. Thus, in physical rehabilitation, the psychosocial aspects of the patient's behavior must be dealt with (Fair, 1980). This component is often neglected in the rehabilitation process and calls for the involvement of behavioralists. However, with respect to applications of EMG, force, or positional feedback to improve motor function among patients with musculoskeletal or neuromuscular pathology, the clinician must have a firmly established foundation in anatomy, neurophysiology, and kinesiology to employ these modalities effectively. At present, the psychologist or psychophysiologist is not adequately trained to exercise these content areas optimally using EMG biofeedback.

On the other hand, most programs within the allied health professions now teach muscle biofeedback routinely, and this modality has become widespread in its usage. Whether techniques and equipment are utilized with prudence among such clinicians is still an open-ended question; that the physician should play a key role in overseeing the application of this modality is not. The painful reality of the matter is that most medical doctors will not take the time or expend the energy required to comprehend this treatment procedure. Furthermore, in cases of chronic neurological impairment, there is no question that this noninvasive application can cause little "harm" to the patient. Therefore, it would appear that feedback applications to patients with physical limitations are primarily relegated to allied health personnel, who, in turn, are directly responsible to the referring physician. Restoration of improved self-esteem, reduction in depression, and enhancement of motivation among such patients will, it is hoped, become more eminent interests among practitioners of behavioral medicine.

Certainly much of the commercial equipment available at the present time has some degree of sophistication and possesses the capabilities of providing quantified data. The interest in SFT among *any* member of the health care team is more easily related to time constraints and commitments than to questions of credibility concerning equipment, training strategies, or number of control studies.

EQUIPMENT

The EMG Bioconditioner developed by Brudny and his colleagues is indeed a unique piece of electronic instrumentation. More so than any other commercially available equipment, this instrument provides the patient with specific representations about the magnitude (spatial dimension) and time (temporal dimension) of ongoing EMG activity in clear pictorial terms. Within far less sophisticated constructs, most EMG biofeedback devices possessing meter displays with appropriate time constants for integration (and hence rate of "dial" movement control) provide a comparative option.

Unique aspects of the Brudny device, however, are the quantification schemes (microvolt-seconds) and the memory capabilities. In the latter case, the possibility of having the patient essentially "efferent copy" a known EMG pattern display is intriguing and ingenuous, since success in regularly performing these tasks must take into account both reduction in hyperactive muscle activity and increases in EMG responses among paralyzed or weakened muscle groups.

This single "copy" factor probably does more to create a meaningful "iEMG language" than any other aspect of the Bioconditioner. The effects of variable skin-electrode impedance or electrode placements on quantification of EMG and on reliability of measures over sessions is a problem confronted by all EMG biofeedback clinicians, no matter what instrumentation is employed. Furthermore, from an electrophysiological perspective, clinicians must make certain that when antagonist muscles are monitored simultaneously, volume-conducted EMG from the spastic group is not "picked up" by the other electrode pair. This occurrence is quite real and has been observed by clinicians at Emory University even when close-spaced surface electrodes are applied (Wolf, 1978).

The most relevant question to ask of the Brudny model is this: "Given the use of sophisticated machinery, are outcomes any more significant, especially with respect to cost-effectiveness, than other forms of EMG biofeedback?"

OUTCOME ASSESSMENTS

Brudny's data on outcomes for treatment of hemiparetic upper extremities with SFT are far more voluminous than that of most investigators. Extrapolation of information from Table 4 of his chapter, when analyzed numerically, suggests that many patients are seen for 9 months at three treatments per week, or approximately 109 sessions. A remarkable percentage of patients (61%) receive a grade of 2 + or 3 +, while the number of patients actually achieving full functional independence (4 +) is unclear. Using far less sophisticated instrumentation and relying upon quantification from less precise equipment than the Bioconditioner, our results (Wolf, Baker, & Kelly, 1979) for upper extremity outcomes are quite comparable to those of the Brudny group, although limited to a smaller sample size (N = 52). Outcomes for lower extremity feedback training for hemiparetics were even more favorable. Detailed follow-up data (Wolf, Baker, & Kelly, 1980) suggest that outcomes are not altered for at least 1 year following the conclusion of training sessions. Rarely did we find the need to approach 100 sessions, and generally our patients who were capable to achieving a 3 + to 4 + grade (on the Brudny scale) did so within 30 treatment sessions.

Therefore, it would appear that other training techniques using equipment with less capability for providing *unique* spatiotemporal information concerning performance may be as effective as Brudny's techniques at less cost and time. A difference in procedure, however, is the clear necessity to "break down" training strategies that use more conventional equipment, so that hemiplegic or spastic patients are first trained to relax spastic musculature and then trained to augment activity in the weakened antagonists (Kelly, Baker, & Wolf, 1979). Another alternative to modality-specific treatment effectiveness is the role of the clinician, who may be a more vital determinant in ultimate outcomes than has been hitherto thought. This notion is now being researched with respect to biofeedback applications (Basmajian, 1980).

Perhaps of primary significance has been a collective failure to standardize outcome assessments in terms of quantified functional measures. We have advocated using variants from the Kessler Institute Functional Ambulation Profile, and at present are using quantitative schema to assess upper extremity changes during feedback training (Wolf, 1980). If reimbursement for feedback services is to become a national issue (it already is a concern in many states), then quantified outcomes in terms that are clearly comprehensible to medical and lay personnel will become a necessity.

The clinical judgment scores presently used (Basmajian, Kukulka, Narayan, & Takebe, 1975; Brudny, Korein, Grynbaum, Belandres, & Gianutsos, 1979) to assess function are unacceptable. Clinicians must be able to relate function to neuromuscular measures quantitatively for the number of feedback sessions provided if a predictive index about the efficacy of this modality is to become established.

NEED FOR CONTROLLED STUDIES

The suggestion that well-controlled EMG biofeedback studies using the single-case design be employed with more frequency is a good one. The work by Gianutsos, cited by Brudny, utilizes training procedures similar to those used at Emory. In addition to the request for matched pairs (control–experimental) of patients with identical diagnosis (a notion often difficult to put into practice with precision), researchers must also develop means for examining the effect of patient–therapist interactions on biofeedback training outcomes.

Of equal importance is the need for quantitative studies that examine the effectiveness of muscle biofeedback training in isolation versus the effectiveness of training as an integral portion of a therapeutic exercise regimen. Such explorations are important because clinicians frequently implement feedback training during the execution of neuromuscular facilitory techniques. Whether this decision is prudent has yet to be determined.

MECHANISM

The development of "iEMG language" through precise establishment of spatiotemporal patterns using the Bioconditioner has two elements in common with training strategies that employ more conventional instrumentation. Both approaches attempt to teach patients to inhibit spasticity and to "internalize" the meaning of a visual representation of muscle activity. Both elements can only be successfully accomplished if the patient is capable of attaining satisfactory sensorimotor integration—that is, of making transition from audiovisual cues representing muscle behavior to self-reliance upon a "reappreciation" of proprioception. In this regard, iEMG language is probably a better vehicle by which to display muscle length changes and alterations in rate of muscle changes.

To effect sensorimotor integration of functional significance requires the activation of neural substrates (basal ganglia, cerebellum, and sensory and motor cortexes) in the manner so eloquently noted by Brudny. Whether this integration is dependent upon neuronal "plasticity" is uncertain. Invariably, subcortical systems are called into play to process sensory information in a manner previously unused or underused. These "alterations" in function among neuroanatomical entities should never be confused with the actual changes in neuronal cytoarchitecture studied so elaborately in animal models. To date, no evidence depicting, for example, physiological activity within reorganizing or regrowing neuronal structures within the CNS has been demonstrated.

Nonetheless, the factors identified by Brudny as related to therapeutic success are indeed accurate and relevant. Unquestionably, insufficient neural substrate or inadequate motivational drive (which in itself may be due to diminished neural substrate) are major deterrents to rehabilitation using any modality or technique. Often a patient's inattentive nature may coincide with lack of motivation and may impede rehabilitation.

In conclusion, I can only echo the words voiced so clearly by Brudny. Further investigation, in a controlled and scientifically acceptable manner, into the efficacy of muscle biofeedback or SFT is a necessity. A comprehensive multidisciplinary approach to the use of this modality can only increase its effectiveness. Further involvement of patients themselves and their family members outside the clinical environment will be required to make best use of the extensive time inherent in the rehabilitation process. While the credibility and efficacy of EMG feedback has, in many cases, already transcended the experimental laboratory, the quest for further information and knowledge about the ways in which patients adapt their nervous systems to make use of the instrumentation will be never-ending.

REFERENCES

Basmajian, J. V. Personal communication, 1980.

Basmajian, J. V., Kukulka, C. G., Narayan, M. G., & Takebe, K. Biofeedback treatment of foot-drop after stroke compared with standard rehabilitation technique: Effects on voluntary control and strength. *Archives of Physical Medicine and Rehabilitation*, 1975, *56*, 231–235.

Brudny, J., Korein, J., Grynbaum, B. B., Belandres, P. V., & Gianutsos, J. G. Helping hemiparetics to help themselves: Sensory feedback therapy. *Journal of the American Medical Association*, 1979, *241*, 814–818.

Fair, P. L. Biofeedback relaxation therapy in the treatment of spasticity and anxiety in CVA patients. *Emory University Regional Rehabilitation Research and Training Center: Anual Progress Report, 1979–1980.* Atlanta, Ga.: Emory University, 1980.

Kelly, J. L., Baker, M. P., & Wolf, S. L. Procedures for targeted EMG biofeedback training in the hemiplegic upper extremity. *Physical Therapy*, 1979, *59*, 1500–1507.

Wolf, S. L. Essential considerations in the use of muscle biofeedback. *Physical Therapy*, 1978, *58*, 25–31.

Wolf, S. L. Developing specific treatment strategies for muscle biofeedback in stroke patients. *Emory University Regional Rehabilitation Research and Training Center: Annual Progress Report, 1979–1980.* Atlanta, Ga.: Emory University, 1980.

Wolf, S. L., Baker, M. P., & Kelly, J. L. EMG biofeedback in stroke: Effect of patient characteristics. *Archives of Physical Medicine and Rehabilitation*, 1979, *60*, 96–102.

Wolf, S. L., Baker, M. P., & Kelly, J. L. EMG biofeedback in stroke: One year follow-up on the effects of patient characteristics. *Archives of Physical Medicine and Rehabilitation*, 1980, *61*, 351–355.

ROUND-TABLE DISCUSSION OF BRUDNY AND WOLF

John Lacey: Dr. Brudny, to what degree were your techniques guided by theory or by intuition?

Joseph Brudny: Dr. Lacey, there may have been an element of intuition or serendipity when devising the specifics of the signal used in our system; but when we set out to try to help Mother Nature, we felt that certain requirements must be met. In providing a feedback signal, we were testing the hypothesis that such a signal could substitute for the kinesthetic signal whose quantitative transmission and orderly processing may have been disrupted as the result of brain insult. The substitute signal, which enters the CNS through an intact sensory channel, was expected to have matching qualities in order to be recognized and decoded. To do so, we felt that the signal must be immediate, pertinent, and continuous. The most appropriate channel for transmission seemed to us to be the visual system. Connolly [Connolly & Jones, 1970] demonstrated that there is a mechanism of intersensory translation between visual and kinesthetic information on the basis of information held in a long-term integrated store. By analogy, the visual and kinesthetic inputs may be thought of as English and French dictionaries where, for each word in one language, there is a corresponding word in the other. The immediacy of signal delivery was stressed by many concerned with motor-control issues. I think that Bernstein [1967] was the first to formulate some basic principles of self-regulatory mechanisms and of the significance of feedback immediacy in the regulation of man's voluntary movement. Yates [1963a, 1963b] described experiments with delayed auditory feedback in subjects who were prevented from hearing their own voices. Under these conditions, speech became distorted and stammering. Karol Smith [Smith & Henry, 1967] demonstrated that, in tracking experiments, delayed visual feedback interfered with performance. The pertinency of our signal display to muscle activity is evident, as the provided information is related to magnitude and rate of change in muscle activity at any time during evolving movement [spatiotemporal factors].

John Lacey: Were you changing motor control from the central segmental spinal level to the progressive elicitation of supraspinal integration?

Joseph Brudny: We feel that in cases where we are successful in restoring degrees of voluntary motor function with corresponding "normalization" of iEMG response, as described in my presentation [see Chapter 10], it is obvious that we are dealing with an increase of voluntary components of supraspinal origin with a simultaneous decrease of reflexive, involuntary spinal-cord-level mechanisms.

There is a paradigm described by Evarts [Evarts & Granit, 1976; Evarts & Tanji, 1976] referring to reflex and intended responses, both in monkeys and humans. We intend to include such a paradigm in the study of patients who undergo retraining and who have regained functional movements to a great degree. We are going to measure the voluntary and involuntary components of their movements before and after Sensory Feedback Therapy.

John Lacey: So, this is probably one of the most significant advances that can be made. It illustrates that, in systems that are more easily accessible to our observations and which, in the developmental history of our species, have been subjected to voluntary control, we have a clear grasp of the fundamental mechanisms. Outside of the practical, clinical problems, this is probably the single most important reason for concentrating on EMG biofeedback. Not because we think we understand it, but because we have a better chance of eventually achieving an understanding. We have here a perfect example of a control system which can be treated in perhaps more precise terms than any other system in terms of engineering control systems theory. Have you introduced such things as correction against passive perturbations to get a better diagnostic handle? Obviously, here's an example where a proprioceptive input is not perforated in the control system. You get a beautiful dampening of the movement without overshoot, and so on. Now, if you introduce the passive perturbation of that, what kind of correction can the patient make?

Joseph Brudny: Until now, we haven't used this particular experimental approach; but, rather, we have relied on clinical evidence of altered motor control resulting from our retraining. We trained a number of stroke patients who suffered thalamic infarcts. The nature of such lesions leaves many with no ability to process and to integrate peripheral sensory input. Consequently, there is a lack of information that would guide them as to the adequacy of attempted movement. Such patients often show athetoid-like dyskinesias; by the way, approximately 10% of our patients showed one or another form of dyskinesia as a result of stroke. The degree of sensory loss in these patients is often so severe that one could safely attempt amputation of a forearm without need for anesthesia. We trained such patients for purposeful hand movements—like reaching out for this microphone, for example. In due time, they reduced the involuntary movements and were able to carry out the task well, especially when aided by visual guidance. We asked them to close their eyes, and they could still carry out the same movement equally well. They repeated such a performance 10 times and then opened their eyes and asked us, "Did I do it?" This phenomenon of carrying out a function without ability to discriminate is paralleling the studies in plasticity of the brain reported by Rosenzweig [1980] on training blind people in visual discrimination. Apparently the area adjacent to the visual cortex is capable of taking on some function in patients with cortical blindness. It was termed "blindsight." Such a subject does not perceive sight, but he is able to discriminate. He doesn't bump into objects when walking; he can even read newspapers, thus acting as if he had eyesight, although the perception of sight is very unclear. In our patients who ask, "Did I do it?" while carrying out the task perfectly well, a similar mechanism may be operational.

Barry Sterman: I wonder why, in light of the diagnostic problems that Steven Wolf mentioned (maybe I'm not aware of this), there hasn't been any experimental animal work in this area where precise lesions could be made and studies using feedback methods, which are easy to adapt to animals.

Joseph Brudny: I think that such studies have been performed. An extensive amount of work was carried out in the USSR by Konorski [1967], who induced experimental brain lesions in animals and accomplished restoration of function through operant-conditioning techniques. Liu and Chambers, and Yu [Liu & Chambers, 1971; Yu, 1976], have performed a lot of similar work in this country.

I would like to comment briefly on the concept of brain plasticity, which may not be appreciated by researchers who do not deal with motor control issues. Plasticity is certainly not due to regrowth of the neuronal connections. Plasticity is a basic, fundamental ability of the brain to respond to environmental demand. When the fulfillment of demand is confirmed by immediate feedback, the response may become learned and more permanent. This is in contrast to excitability of the brain, where no lasting changes are left. The plasticity issue has been discussed in depth by many researchers. For example, Evarts [1980] thinks that possibly other areas of the brain may take over function lost as a result of brain injury. He points to the concept of a "cortical neuron colony," by which he envisions adjacent cortical neurons taking over some function not previously carried out by them. He also considers the possibility that the cerebellum is capable of learning and [that] cerebellar control may be established to a degree that aids restoration of motor function. Hore and his colleagues [Hore, Meyer-Lohmann, & Brooks, 1977] studied the role of basal ganglia in motor control of movement. Cooling the basal ganglia of a monkey will cause a loss of voluntary movement of the arm. Yet, when provided with visual feedback reflecting the adequacy of intended movement on an oscilloscope, the monkey could perform the required task very well.

Others have also added credence to the notion that mechanisms of sensory substitution and plasticity are capable of functional reorganization of the brain. In this light, the concept of "iEMG language" becomes better understood. With the aid of such a "language," the patient who is not capable of normal subcortical processing of kinesthetic information from evolving movement can derive the necessary sensory information in a cognitive manner from iEMG displays. I think that the cognitive aspect of handling the immediate, pertinent, and continuous iEMG feedback is of considerable help in restoring greater degrees of motor control.

Daniel Cox: Bernie [Tursky] talked about microvolt-seconds. Some biofeedback companies talk about "peak-to-peak microvolt," and some talk about "root mean square." Is there any difference in terms of the functional nature of the feedback whether or not it represents different parameters of EMG?

Joseph Brudny: The microvolt-second is really a purely engineering computation approach. The intensity of EMG varies with time. It's bidirectional; by rectification we arrive at a unidirectional measure. Integrating over time, we are actually measuring the intensity under the varying curve. This unit as computed per second becomes a microvolt-second.

Bernard Tursky: It's a question of whether it's a circuit that will hold the value or whether the value will decay. If you simply use a passive capacitor to hold a charge and if there is less activity or no activity, then you have a decay or leak to ground. If you have additional dynamic circuitry, then you can hold the value; and there is no decay as a function of the circuit. Fluctuations are always unidirectional and a function of real alterations in EMG activity.

Steven Wolf: There are some people now who are capable of carrying out Evart's paradigm and the operant-conditioning model [Evarts, 1973, 1975]. Knowledge of what the timing relationships are between activity in motor cortical cells, cerebellum, basal ganglia, and EMG, both for active movements and for movements against perturbations, is now being examined after inducing lesions in those same animals. Shirley Sahrmann [Sahrmann, Clare, & Landau, 1979], for example, is asking the same question: How is the timing changed? And where is it changed? And what are the implications for that with respect to mechanism over time? If we subject the animal again to this operant paradigm, will the timing change back towards a normal correlation?

Barry Sterman: I think that studies like this one should evaluate very objectively and carefully the mechanisms of compensation. That's what we're talking about. I saw a show on TV the other day where this lady was born without arms and was walking through a market shopping with her feet. It was unbelievable. Now she learned this compensatory response. Again, I'm reminded of Ed Taub's disuse stuff [Taub & Berman, 1968]. If you could learn what the mechanisms for compensation are through careful control studies, you might be able to improve your efficiency.

Joseph Brudny: Just one more word. There is a body of evidence collected by Glees [1980], who studied patients with hemispherectomies performed for control of intractable epilepsy. He described a remarkable recovery of function following initial onset of hemiparesis, including functional, skillful, manipulative use of the hand in adults. Glees suggested the possibility that some of the pyramidal tract fibers that remain uncrossed may be the neural substrate mediating recovery, and that hemispheric involvement of the unaffected side may be potentiated by training. Such a mechanism of functional recovery can be considered as one that is truly a reflection of the plasticity of the CNS.

Gary Schwartz: I was curious about the consequences of "blindsight" that you mentioned. I had not heard of that before. There is other evidence suggesting that one can get processing of information in certain brain-damaged patients, discrimination of information without "awareness" [Weisenkrantz, Warrington, Sanders, & Marshall, 1974]. Patients with hemifield lesions in the occipital cortex, when given discrimination tests, can discriminate above chance; but when you ask what they saw, they report that they aren't seeing anything. Yet they can reliably discriminate, and they give the feeling that they sort of intuit it. The frontal cortex is still intact. They can process the information, and they don't have the occipital neurons to be able to organize the visual percept area. I wonder to what extent that phenomenon of information processing occurs a lot more often in the nervous system. The "conscious" component registering sensorally [*sic*] at the conscious level is only a small component of all the processing that's going on.

Jasper Brener: In our earlier discussion of the mechanisms underlying biofeedback training [see Chapter 2], we neglected to concentrate on the sorts of functions that are implicit in this work—namely, the function of exteroceptive feedback in recalibrating the interoceptive feedback that the body and the nervous system employ to regulate behavior. When one starts considering the interaction between how exteroceptive and interoceptive do interact, I think one can design and exploit the methods of exteroceptive feedback more adequately. I think this is well exemplified in Dr. Brudny's work. It seems, for example, in the work on adaptation to displacement prisms, that you have a very good model for understanding how calibration works and how one sensory modality may be calibrated by information in another sensory modality. There's a very interesting observation that is made by Kornheiser in his excellent review of this subject in 1976 [Kornheiser, 1976]. If the subject regulates a movement on the basis of one sensory modality, then the non-attended-to sensory modality is calibrated in terms of the attended-to sensory modality. If you are getting a patient to regulate a movement on the basis of visual information, then kinesthesia is calibrated in terms of this referent. One can then control which sensory modality is being calibrated in terms of which other sensory modality. The methods that we employ in biofeedback, where we give people terminal feedback rather than continuous feedback of their movements, will predispose the nervous system to recalibrate the wrong way, in the wrong direction. I think attention to this sort of literature might foster a better use of exteroceptive feedback as a means of reprogramming the motor control circuits that we are interested in.

Martin Orne: I guess I'm confused about why the sensory feedback works, and it's a kind of basic question that troubles me. As I understand it, the early work with rehabilitation provided new channels of information by putting the good hand on the biceps and asking the patient to relax this muscle.

Joseph Brudny: But that doesn't do much; it doesn't relax.

Martin Orne: That's the question I really have. I'd like to ask you to separate a number of things for me, conceptually, a little bit. Is it that you can get a much, much smaller response success to get the guy motivated to do something because the jump is too big normally? In other words, you can have small incremental steps so that you have many little success experiences; you therefore keep him working at it until he finally gets above threshold so you can actually see the movement. Now that's a possibility. Or is it more than that? Is it that you're really getting at a way of reorganizing things, which you're suggesting about the kind of equipment you're using, that may make a difference? Now, conceptually, I think it's a tremendously important distinction. Because, in one case, a good physiotherapist could do it without your biofeedback machine by keeping the guy motivated. Basmajian's technicians are more successful, I would interpret, as a function of their knowing it works [Basmajian, Kukulka, Narayan, & Takebe, 1975]; and so they therefore can keep at it, keep the guy motivated, and convince him that it's really going to work. They keep working until they get up to threshold, and that would mean that that's where the action is. The other possibility is that it's in the mechanism, itself, and I wish you would comment on that.

Joseph Brudny: We call it the "eureka" phenomenon. You are absolutely right. The moment the patient makes a minute voluntary adjustment to the paradigm of training, his effort is immediately identified; the immediacy is important. 50 msec is not much loss of time. Half a minute, by the time the therapist is touching the tendon and telling the patient he thinks there is a little trace of something, is too late. If the reinforcement is brought to his attention immediately, this effort can be ongoing and, step by step, brings him to greater achievement.

Martin Orne: If this is true, if you're right, then your system should not work if you introduce another—let's say, 500 msec—delay, which you can do electronically. Now it is my personal bet that your biofeedback equipment would work even if you introduce the delay.

Joseph Brudny: I think we don't have to guess. There have been many experiments with delay of sensory information, and it does defeat the purpose.

Richard Surwit: I want to make a quick comment relating to Basmajian's observation. The therapists that worked with EMG biofeedback and then went to work with patients without the machine were doing better than therapists who were not exposed to feedback devices. A year ago, Frank Keefe and I reviewed this literature [Keefe & Surwit, 1978], and it seemed to me that one of the problems of physical therapy in general, traditional physical therapy, is that the notion of shaping is not well understood by physical therapists. What biofeedback may be doing, in large part, is really training the therapist to shape the response. In fact, to make the point about the main issue of what Dr. Brudny said, I've had considerable experience with torticollis patients. I think I share Dr. Brudny's observation that a lot of them—or all of them, in fact—have these sensory deficits that they try to compensate for by touching themselves in odd ways. And I've been able to train several torticollis patients to straighten their heads without using biofeedback simply by shaping the prompt from the original position around towards the normal position, over a period of several months. So I think you might want to consider this, and this may be a really good area for some further research.

Daniel Cox: I wish to again raise the point of looking at using biofeedback for two types of patients. One type needs rehabilitation of gross physical damage, and the other type needs life style changes where the life style affects physiology. Has anybody experienced any difference in terms of stroke victims versus victims that have torticollis that have various significant psychosocial, etiological factors in terms of learning rehabilitation?

Steven Wolf: I don't think we've looked at enough of the psychosocial aspects of the continuum of care for these people. Motivation seemed to be a big factor; our people who didn't do well on progress notes as indicated by the therapist weren't well motivated. We thought it was a cop-out for a while until we began to realize, from a physiological point of view in respect to stroke, that there may be an organic component to account for lack of motivation as well as a psychological one.

Neal Miller: Well, what I wanted to say quite a ways back is that it is my observation if you close your eyes halfway and look at this whole area from a distance, [that] the most successes with biofeedback have been with organic cases like the ones we've just had—the fecal incontinence and some of the others. There's probably a very good reason for it, because there there is no motivation to do badly. If, however, a person is doing badly for psychological reasons, you have that problem to overcome. I think anybody would say that if someone has a motivation to do badly—say, he's collecting more insurance than he ever earned in his life—he's not going to be very good at this kind of treatment. I think these motivational factors are very important.

Steven Wolf: On the other hand, with respect to some central nervous system deficits, there are people who aren't motivated at all. That's a very important point. The correlation between the sensory reeducation and physical therapy, the two components, is definitely timing, the efficacy of time, and the precision of the information. To think that it's just the patient who gets that but not the therapist is naive. The therapist can use that information away from the immediacy of that patient, to work in other directions and on other problems.

Theodore Weiss: Dr. Brudny, would you comment about the status of results in biofeedback treatment of torticollis patients?

Joseph Brudny: Patients who learned to control the dyskinetic, dystonic movements usually carried out such control for long periods of time, for days or for weeks. Such patients were classified by us as clinical successes, although, except for a very few, they were never really free of occasional involuntary movements. What was different about these patients was that they did not allow the grotesque, psychologically and physically disabling dyskinesias to "take over." Rather than succumb, they were able to reinstate control quickly, apparently remembering the learned mechanisms needed for control.

If I may just add one more general observation: Many patients do recover from motor function brain insult, at times regardless of therapy. A case in point is actress Patricia Neal, who was rendered aphasic and hemiplegic and who, years later, recovered most of her motor function and speech as the result of nonprofessional attempts at therapy at home. If you had a chance to see her on television, you wouldn't be able to observe any abnormality in her actions. There are many so-called "unusual recovery" cases reported in the literature. Usually, such recovery is not expected by professionals; and it is the determined patient who doesn't give up and is able to return a year later, demonstrating to his physician functional use of previously hemiparetic limbs. These patients apparently have the necessary ability to discriminate even minute changes in the state of motor activity, to remember such changes, and to be able to develop a strategy for extending progressive control over these changes in the desired direction. I think that a close study of such unusual cases of recovery should be the combined effort of the behavioral researcher and the clinician. If we could identify the crucial elements involved, we could possibly apply a similar strategy in many other cases where recovery is lacking.

John Furedy: But we have talked about two methods of feedback. You can explain the electrical properties, and we can sit here and talk about different patient interactions. But we don't know which method of feedback is more efficacious for the learning of behavior until the same research institution takes those two methods; keeps the display constant so that, as far as the subject is concerned, he thinks that he's getting the same "treatment"; and sees which method is better. I think Steve Wolf raised the most relevant question: Given the use of sophisticated machinery, are the outcomes any more significant, especially with respect to cost-effectiveness, than other forms of EMG feedback? That is the right question to ask. But we cannot answer it by comparing across laboratories and across different types of displays. A group like Dr. Brudny's must present the display under two different feedback conditions with the double-blind technique, so the patient and the therapist think that they're administering the same sort of therapy, and then establish which feedback method is better.

REFERENCES

Basmajian, J. V., Kukulka, C. G., Narayan, M. G., & Takebe, K. Biofeedback treatment of foot-drop after stroke compared with standard rehabilitation technique: Effects on voluntary control and strength. *Archives of Physical Medicine and Rehabilitation,* 1975, *56,* 231–235.

Bernstein, N. *The co-ordination and regulation of movements.* New York: Pergamon, 1967.

Connolly, K., & Jones, B. Developmental study of afferent–reafferent integration. *British Journal of Psychology,* 1970, *61,* 259–266.

Evarts, E. V. Brain mechanisms in movement. *Scientific American,* 1973, *229,* 1–9.

Evarts, E. V. Changing concepts of central control of movement. *Canadian Journal of Physiology and Pharmacology,* 1975, *53,* 191–201.

Evarts, E. V. Brain control of movement: Possible mechanisms of functional reorganization. In P. Bach-y-Rita (Ed.), *Recovery of function: Theoretical considerations for brain injury rehabilitation.* Baltimore: University Park Press, 1980.

Evarts, E. V., & Granit, R. Relations of reflexes and intended movements. *Progress in Brain Research,* 1976, *44,* 1–14.

Evarts, E. V., & Tanji, J. Reflex and intended responses in motor cortex pyramidal tract neurons of monkeys. *Journal of Neurophysiology,* 1976, *39,* 1069–1080.

Glees, P. Functional cerebral reorganization following hemispherectomy in man and after small experimental lesions in primates. In P. Bach-y-Rita (Ed.), *Recovery of function: Theoretical considerations for brain injury rehabilitation.* Baltimore: University Park Press, 1980.

Hore, J., Meyer-Lohmann, J., & Brooks, V. B. Basal ganglia cooling disables learned arm movements in absence of visual guidance. *Science,* 1977, *195,* 584–586.

Keefe, F. J., & Surwit, R. S. Electromyographic biofeedback: Behavioral treatment of neuromuscular disorders. *Journal of Behavioral Medicine,* 1978, *1,* 13–24.

Konorski, J. *Integrative activity of the brain.* Chicago: University of Chicago Press, 1967.

Kornheiser, A. S. Adaptation to laterally displaced vision: A review. *Psychological Bulletin,* 1976, *83,* 783–816.

Liu, C. N., & Chambers, W. W. A study of cerebellar dyskinesia in the bilaterally deafferented forelimbs of the monkey. *Acta Neurobiologiae Experimentalis,* 1971, *31,* 263–289.

Rosenzweig, M. R. Animal models for effects of brain lesions and for rehabilitation. In P. Bach-y-Rita (Ed.), *Recovery of function: Theoretical considerations for brain injury rehabilitation.* Baltimore: University Park Press, 1980.

Sahrmann, S. A., Clare, M. H., & Landau, W. M. *Motor cortical unit activity related to several conditioned hind limb forces in the monkey.* Paper presented at the Ninth Annual Meeting of the Society for Neuroscience, Atlanta, 1979.

Smith, K. U., & Henry, J. P. Cybernetic foundations for rehabilitation. *American Journal of Physical Medicine,* 1967, *46,* 379–467.

Taub, E., & Berman, A. J. Movement and learning in the absence of sensory feedback. In S. J. Freeman (Ed.), *The neuropsychology of spatially oriented behavior.* Homewood, Ill.: Dorsey Press, 1968.

Weisenkrantz, L., Warrington, E. K., Sanders, M. E., & Marshall, J. Visual capacity in the hemianopic field following a restricted occipital ablation. *Brain,* 1974, *87,* 709–728.

Yates, A. J. Delayed auditory feedback. *Psychological Bulletin,* 1963, *60,* 213–232.

Yates, A. J. Recent empirical and theoretical approaches to the experimental manipulation of speech in normal subjects and stammerers. *Behaviour Research and Therapy*, 1963, *1*, 95–119. (b)

Yu, J. Functional recovery with and without training following brain damage in experimental animals: A review. *Archives of Physical Medicine and Rehabilitation*, 1976, *57*, 38–41.

11 EEG OPERANT CONDITIONING IN SEVERE EPILEPTICS: CONTROLLED MULTIDIMENSIONAL STUDIES

JOEL F. LUBAR

INTRODUCTION

In spite of comprehensive medical treatment, about 20% of the epileptic population remains very poorly controlled (Masland, 1976). Since 1972, a number of studies have indicated that operant conditioning of certain EEG components may be beneficial for reducing the number of seizures experienced by these patients (Finley, Smith, & Etherton, 1975; Lubar, 1977; Lubar & Bahler, 1976; Seifert & Lubar, 1975; Sterman & Friar, 1972; Sterman & Macdonald, 1978; Wyler, Lockard, Ward, & Finch, 1976; Wyler, Robbins, & Dodrill, 1979). These studies have employed a variety of operant conditioning (i.e., biofeedback) techniques for altering the EEG. Thus far, the most common technique has included the training of rhythmic activity of 12–16 Hz over the sensorimotor cortex (sensorimotor rhythm, or SMR, as designated by Wyrwicka & Sterman, 1968). Other approaches include increasing high-frequency activity (18 Hz) centering over the epileptogenic cortical foci (Wyler *et al.*, 1979); suppressing slow epileptiform activity (Cott, Pavlovski, & Black, 1979); simultaneously increasing 12–15 Hz activity and suppressing 4–8 Hz activity (Lubar & Bahler, 1976); or increasing 18–23 Hz activity and simultaneously suppressing 6–9 Hz activity (Sterman & Macdonald, 1978). Kuhlman and Kaplan (1979) have reported decreases in seizure rates following training of central mu rhythm (9–11 Hz). Additional techniques employing aversive forms of operant conditioning have

Joel F. Lubar. Department of Psychology, University of Tennessee, Knoxville, Tennessee.

been reviewed in detail by Mostofsky and Balaschak (1977). In summarizing these data, more than 150 patients have now been trained in a variety of laboratories in the United States, Canada, and Europe using these techniques. Success rates have varied from 43% (Wyler *et al.*, 1979) to greater than 60% (Sterman, Macdonald, & Stone, 1974; Lubar & Bahler, 1976).

Generally, current biofeedback-based techniques, though tedious and requiring months of training, are nonetheless encouraging for this refractory epileptic population. The possibility of decreasing the pharmacologically well-known toxic effects of antiepileptic medications, effects that are felt by many of these patients for their entire lives, is an important additional consideration. The study described in this chapter provides the first double-blind investigation for the use of operant conditioning in epilepsy. Eight epileptics, most retarded, and many with clear evidence of brain damage, were trained using three different schedules of feedback in an ABA cross-over design.

Participants were trained first to increase activity that previous research has indicated would help them achieve better seizure control; then to increase activity that should be deleterious; and then to increase again the initial beneficial activity. In addition, each subject was provided two periods of noncontingent EEG feedback (i.e., feedback controlled by electronic circuitry that bore no relationship to their ongoing EEG) in order to determine whether there were strong placebo or nonspecific factors operating. This study was multidimensional in that it included measures of seizure by type and intensity, periodic all-night sleep analyses, monitoring of anticonvulsant blood levels, and extensive neuropsychological testing. Behavioral measures and measures of performance were taken during training sessions to determine what other aspects of functioning may have been altered as a result of participation in this experimental treatment program. A shorter report on part of the current study recently has been published elsewhere (Lubar, Shabsin, Natelson, Holder, Whitsett, Pamplin, & Krulikowski, 1981).

METHODS

EXPERIMENTAL DESIGN

The study employed a double-blind design. For all phases of the study in which feedback was employed, technicians who did *not* know the experimental design were trained to prepare the patients by attaching their electrodes, taking them to the room where feedback was provided, and observing and tabulating specific categories of behavior observed through a one-way glass during the feedback training session. Feedback was administered by preprogrammed instrumentation that was set so that the technicians knew neither the type of feedback the patients were receiving nor the points at which feedback contingencies were changed over the 20-month duration of the study. Nor did the subjects know the specific design of the study during the time it was being done. The design is outlined in Table 1.

During the baseline period that followed initial interviews with each patient and discussion of the study with their referring physicians or neurologist, initial measures were obtained; these included a clinical EEG, a neurological examination, and measures of anticonvulsant levels. Prior to this period (October 1977), patients and their families (or teachers, in the case of children and adolescents) were trained to record seizures meticulously. During the 4-month baseline period, patients were

TABLE 1. Design of Study

	Group 1 (*N* = 3) *Patients:* *M. W., D. F., B. O.*	*Group 2* (*N* = 2) *Patients:* *V. T., A. K.*	*Group 3* (*N* = 3) *Patients:* *R. R., E. C., W. S.*
Baseline seizures Clinical EEG Neurological exam Blood levels—anti-convulsants	4 months	4 months	4 months
Noncontingent feedback	Noncontingent feedback, 2 months	Noncontingent feedback, 2 months	Noncontingent feedback, 2 months
Neuropsychological exams and Sleep EEG 1			
Contingent feedback training—first phase (A_1)	3 to 8 Hz suppression rewarded, 4 months	12 to 15 Hz presence rewarded 4 months	3 to 8 Hz suppression and 11 to 19 Hz presence rewarded, 4 months
Sleep EEG 2			
Contingent feedback reversal—second phase (B)	3 to 8 Hz presence rewarded, 2 months	3 to 8 Hz presence rewarded, 2 months	3 to 8 Hz presence and 11 to 19 Hz suppression rewarded, 2 months
Sleep EEG 3			
Contingent feedback training—third phase (A_2)	3 to 8 Hz suppression rewarded, 4 months	12 to 15 Hz presence rewarded, 4 months	3 to 8 Hz suppression and 11 to 19 Hz presence rewarded, 4 months
Neuropsychological exams and Sleep EEG 4			
Follow-up—noncontingent feedback drug changes	Noncontingent feedback, 4 months	Noncontingent feedback, 4 months	Noncontingent feedback, 4 months
Sleep EEG 5			

placed in the room where operant conditioning was to be later carried out. Their EEGs were recorded from central, frontal, and occipital EEG sites for spectral analysis using a fast Fourier transform (FFT). Abnormalities in the form of slow waves, spikes, polyspikes and waves, and so on, were readily apparent.

Following the baseline period, patients were provided with a 2-month period during which the EEG feedback was noncontingent. During this period, they observed feedback lights or heard feedback tones that bore no relation to their cortical EEG. They were, however, provided with a red light that was activated by excessive movement or muscle activity, and they were told to keep the red light off. This aspect of training was contingent primarily on non-EEG activity and provided an important control procedure to determine whether EMG training would have any specific effects.

During the A_1 contingent feedback training phase, the patients were subdivided into three groups, as shown in Table 1. Some were trained to suppress slow activity (3–8 Hz); others were trained to increase 12–15 Hz activity (SMR); and a third group (dual condition) was trained to increase 11–19 Hz activity and decrease 3–8 Hz activity simultaneously. All training was carried out over the central cortex for the hemisphere that exhibited the more abnormal EEG activity. During the 2-month reversal phase, B, patients in the first and second groups were trained to increase slow epileptiform activity, while the third group (dual condition) was trained to increase slow activity and suppress faster activity. The final feedback phase, A_2, reinstituted the contingencies of the A_1 phase,thus constituting the cross-over and completeing the ABA part of the study. A follow-up, phase during which anticonvulsants were changed, took place for 4 months following the A_2 phase. Spectral EEG changes during this phase will be analyzed and reported subsequently.

Before entering the study, Informed Consent was obtained for each of the patients.[1] The Informed Consent required that a contract be adhered to; the terms included regularly attending the sessions, recording seizures accurately, taking medication as prescribed, and undergoing anticonvulsant blood tests on a monthly basis. The participants were free to terminate participation at any time.

PATIENT SELECTION

Subjects were selected from a group of severely epileptic patients referred by area physicians. Patients with extensive psychiatric problems or substance abuse (e.g., alcoholism), young children or persons older than 60 years, and patients who

[1]The Informed Consent for this study was approved by both the Department of Psychology and the University-Wide Human Subjects Committee of the University of Tennessee, as well as the Professional Advisory Board of the Epilepsy Foundation of America. The studies reported in this paper conform to the Declaration of Helsinki.

were noncompliant regarding their anticonvulsants were rejected. After extensive interviews with approximately 15 patients or their parents or guardians, four males and four females were selected to participate. Their ages ranged from 11 to 50 (mean age 25). Other criteria for selection included a high incidence of seizures for a number of years, relatively refractory reactions to anticonvulsant medications, and a consistent distribution of seizures across time. A summary of the patients' EEGs, descriptions of seizures and neurological findings, and medications is shown in Table 2.

DEPENDENT MEASURES

A variety of dependent measures allowed monitoring of the subjects' progress during and following feedback training. The subjects and/or their families maintained diaries of seizure activity that provided daily accounts of seizure type and duration. With one exception, these diaries were begun at least 4 months prior to the noncontingent phase and were maintained throughout the study. In addition, monthly determinations of the level of anticonvulsants in the patients' blood were obtained by gas–liquid chromatography; these determinations allowed for the maintenance of anticonvulsant medications within therapeutic levels.

In addition to the keeping of seizure records and the determination of monthly anticonvulsant levels, a battery of neuropsychological tests, consisting of the Halstead–Reitan Battery and the Wechsler Adult Intelligence Scale (WAIS) or the Wechsler Intelligence Scale for Children—Revised (WISC-R), was administered once during the baseline phase and again following the A_2 phase.

During each feedback session, the activity was recorded for both the trained and the contralateral hemisphere from symmetrical sites located halfway between C_z–C_3 and C_3–T_3 and between C_z–C_4 and C_4–T_4. All electrode impedances were required to be less than 10k ohms. Instrumentation channels representing filter responses and inhibited activity were recorded on a multiple-channel polygraph. An example for two patients is shown in Fig. 1. Also during the baseline phase and following completion of the study, as well as following each of the training conditions (see Table 1), all-night sleep EEGs from multiple electrode sites were recorded for each subject. With the exception of data for one patient (M.W.), these data are to be published separately (Whitsett, Lubar, Holder, Pamplin, & Shabsin, in press).

COMPUTER ANALYSIS

Throughout all phases of the study, each of the patients' EEGs from the trained and contralateral sites was subjected to computer-assisted, real-time analysis. The system employed a 32K word, 16-bit Digital Equipment Corporation PDP 11-04

TABLE 2. Patient Seizure History and Anticonvulsant Medications

Patient and Sex	*W. S. (F)*	*D. F. (F)*	*V. T. (F)*	*R. R. (M)*
EEG findings	High-voltage, poorly organized activity. Generalized anterior and central dominant slow waves, 3 to 5 Hz.	High-voltage, poorly organized, mixed activity.	Suppression of normal 8 to 9 Hz alpha activity, right frontal and parietal regions.	Focal left temporal. Background 9 to 10 Hz alpha activity, most prominent in posterior regions. Spike and spike wave activity in left temporal region.
Diagnosis	Absences and myoclonic seizures. Mentally retarded.	Suspected temporal lesions. Dominant seizures tonic–clonic and partial complex. Also, tonic–clonic absences and akinetic seizures. Mentally retarded.	Focal seizures of partial complex type. Atrophied right parietal lobe. Mentally retarded.	Partial complex seizures. Mentally retarded.
Daily medications	Phenobarbital	Phenobarbital Primidone Carbamazapine	Phenobarbital Primidone Carbamazapine Dilantin Clonopin	Phenobarbital Primidone Carbamazapine
Disorder duration (years)	7	18	29	18
Age	11	20	32	23

Patient and Sex	*M. W. (M)*	*A. R. (M)*	*E. C. (M)*	*B. O. (F)*
EEG findings	Focal left temporal. 8 to 9 Hz background activity. Slow, low-voltage contoured and sharp waves.	Mild EEG slowing. 3 to 5 Hz activity centrally.	Generalized bilateral bursts of high-voltage spikes and slow waves. 8 Hz background activity. Isolated spikes in absence of wave complexes from frontal and parietal areas.	Moderately disorganized EEG with paroxysmal sharp waves, focal left temporal.
Diagnosis	Possible cyst left occipital area. Mentally retarded.	Atonic, tonic–clonic, and partial complex seizures. Normal intelligence.	Mixed seizures. Normal intelligence.	Partial complex seizures. Normal intelligence.
Daily medications	Phenobarbital Dilantin Clonopin	Phenobarbital Dilantin	Carbamazapine Tridione	Phenobarbital Primidone
Disorder duration (years)	19	28	7	39
Age	24	30	17	50

computer with 16 channels of A-to-D conversion. This system was used for data acquisition and analysis and peripheral device communication with an AED Corporation 6200 dual double-density floppy disk drive, a Houston Instruments Company DP-1 pen plotter, and a DECWRITER II. Software utilized included RT-11 monitor routines, Calcomp plotter routines, fast Fourier transforms (FFTs), and user–writer routines for data acquisition and output requirements specific to the present study.

An FFT analysis of each patient's EEG was conducted on line for each session. Grass preamplifiers (model P511H), with bandpasses between 1 Hz and 100 Hz and with rise-time constants of .3 msec, were used for initial processing of the EEG signal; the signal was then received by the computer, digitized, run through the FFT routines, and stored on disk. The sampling rate of the A-to-D conversion was 128 per second. Before being sampled, the signal was preprocessed by passing through a 60-Hz low-pass filter (Krohn–Hite, 24 db per octave). FFT epoch length consisted of four 4-second EEG segments averaged sequentially, giving a total epoch length of 16 seconds. All recording sessions during training consisted of 100 epochs. Computer analysis was performed on either the left or right hemisphere and alternated with each visit. Spectral plots, and power and percentage tables for each of eight frequency bands (0–3 Hz, 4–7 Hz, 6–9 Hz, 8–11 Hz, 12–15 Hz, 16–19 Hz, 20–23 Hz, 24–27 Hz), were obtained at the end of each session. These percentage and power tables were then stored on disks for cumulative analyses at the end of the study.

BEHAVIORAL INSTRUMENTATION

Visual and auditory feedback was provided by an instrumentation array so designed that neither patients nor technicians could distinguish between the variety of feedback formats available. Visual feedback was presented through a light display that informed the patient of the presence or absence of three separate target events. A circular green panel fluctuated in intensity as a direct or inverse analog of the target EEG amplitude and frequency described for each EEG feedback, training condition (see Table 1). In addition to the analog visual feedback, segments of a blue panel were programmed to light sequentially from left to right whenever the target EEG signal was maintained above threshold for a preset period of time. Both threshold level and time duration could be adjusted for purposes of shaping. That is, the feedback reinforcement stimuli were made easier to achieve at the beginning of training and were then made progressively more difficult as learning occurred. In this way, sessions with either very little or with almost continuous feedback were avoided, while those subjects who were increasing their skills had to meet progressively more difficult criteria in order to maintain a steady rate of feedback. Several

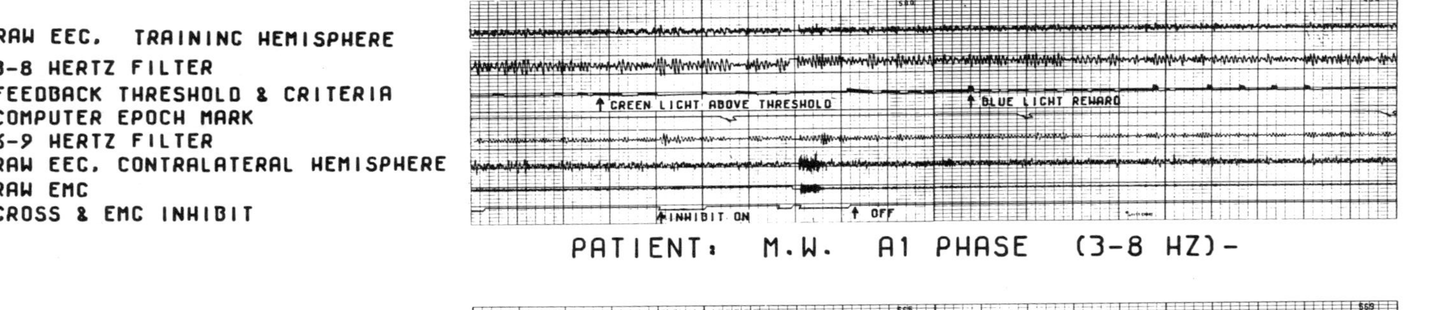

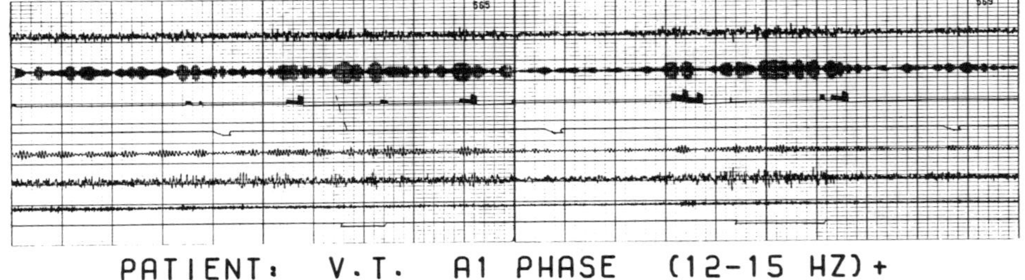

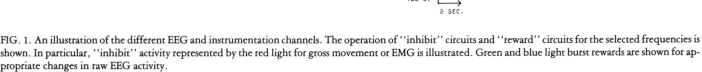

FIG. 1. An illustration of the different EEG and instrumentation channels. The operation of ''inhibit'' circuits and ''reward'' circuits for the selected frequencies is shown. In particular, ''inhibit'' activity represented by the red light for gross movement or EMG is illustrated. Green and blue light burst rewards are shown for appropriate changes in raw EEG activity.

analog and digital forms of auditory feedback could be made to coincide with these visual displays. A smaller red light indicating excessive amounts of muscle tension or high-amplitude EEG inhibited further reinforcement.

Feedback circuitry was activated through active bandpass filters (Frequency Devices Corporation) for the conditions shown in Table 1. Adjustable, level-sensitive Schmidt triggers, coupled with standard logic circuitry, provided the final interface to the visual and auditory feedback display.

In addition to providing feedback, information regarding a patient's performance during a session was recorded on a teletype. Raw data pertaining to session minute number, number of blue lights, number of seconds of EMG or high amplitude (red light), and seconds above threshold criteria (green light) were accumulated. Following the completion of each training minute, this information was transferred to a teletype and paper tape output.

BEHAVIORAL OBSERVATION FORMS

In addition to the training data just described, behavioral informatin was collected by the technician during each training session. Within 2-minute segments, the technician was instructed to record the following: (1) whether the patient appeared to be relaxed or tense; (2) whether the patient was focused on the feedback display or scanning the room; (3) whether the patient appeared to be alert or drowsy; and (4) what type of position changes (in any) had occurred. Position changes were additionally coded as to type (facial grimace, extremity, etc.). Finally, any occurrence of seizures was noted.

RESULTS

SEIZURES

Table 3 shows the percentage differences between successive conditions for each of the patients in the study, arranged by groups and contingencies. Five of the eight patients were improved in the A_1 condition, and five of the eight were improved in the A_2 condition. Also, four of the eight relapsed in the B (reversal) condition. The three patients (Group 1) who were trained first to suppress 3–8 Hz activity, then to increase this activity, and again to suppress it in the final A_2 condition followed the design better than patients in the other two groups. All three Group 1 patients (M. W., D. F., and B. O.) showed a decrease in seizure activity in the A_1 condition as compared with activity in the noncontingent phase, and two of them increased seizures when provided with feedback for increasing the slow activity (the

TABLE 3. Mean Seizure Rate for Baseline Phase and Percentage of Change in Seizures with Regard to Preceding Experimental Conditions for Each Phase of This Study

Group	*Mean Number of Seizures during Baseline*	*Percentage of Change from Each Preceding Condition*				*Mean Number of Seizures for A_2*	*Percentage of Change from Baseline to A_2*
		NC	*A_1*	*B*	*A_1*		
Group 1							
M. W.	19.1	+ 3.1[b]	−44.2[c]	+26.4	−68.3	4.4	−76.9
D. F.	9.0	+94.4	−56.6	−18.4	+ 3.2	6.4	−28.8
B. O.	15.4	+35.1	−51.0	+39.2	+26.8	18.0	+16.8
$\bar{x}$[a]	14.5	+33.1	−49.7	+18.75	−15.8	9.6	−33.8
Group 2							
V. T.	3.2	−25.0	+125	−25.9	−85.0	0.6	−81.3
A. K.	10.6	−36.8	+38.8	− 3.2	− 3.3	8.7	−17.9
$\bar{x}$[a]	6.9	−34.8	+62.2	−10.96	−27.7	4.75	−32.6
Group 3							
R. R.	2.8	−32.1	+63.2	+64.5	−27.5	3.7	+32.1
E. C.	15.1	− 8.6	− 2.9	+66.4	−26.9	16.3	+ 7.9
W. S.	60.0	− 4.8	−18.6	−37.4	+ 3.1	30.0	−50.0
$\bar{x}$[a]	26.0	− 6.5	−13.5	−10.5	−11.2	16.7	−37.2
Grand $\bar{x}$ all groups:		+ 1.45	−21.21	− 3.16	−15.53	10.33	−34.8

[a]Group means for Groups 1, 2, and 3 represent weighted means arising from unequal numbers of observations recorded for each of the individual conditions.

[b]+ = increased seizures.

[c]− = decreased seizures.

B condition). Only one of them (M. W.) showed a decrease again in the A_2 condition. Similar results have been reported by Sterman and Macdonald (1978) in a single-blind study involving a cross-over design. One interpretation of these results is that patients who were performing well in the A_1 phase and then performed poorly in the B phase may have continued to do so if they felt that they no longer had control over the feedback stimuli. For example, patient B. O. in our study and other patients in Sterman's study reported that they felt that they had lost control in the B phase, and they refused to work as diligently during the A_2 phase to try to regain this control. This was particularly a problem in a double-blind study, in which they could not be informed that contingencies of reinforcement had been altered. Nevertheless, at the end of A_2, all groups showed a 39.7% decrease in seizures as compared with their baseline levels.

Interestingly, the patients who did most poorly in terms of seizure control (Group 2) were provided first with 12–15 Hz (SMR) reinforcement. These patients showed an increase in seizures during the A_1 condition. However, patient A. K. complied less strictly with the requirements of the study than did any of the other patients. This individual often missed sessions or came to sessions late in the day. Concurrently, this patient showed few spectral changes. Nevertheless, both V. T. and A. K. did experience fewer seizures at the end of A_2 training, compared with their baseline levels. It should be emphasized that the very large changes shown in the A_1 and A_2 condition for patient V. T. were probably more a result of her low initial seizure rate than of the feedback. Also, her medical history indicated that some of her seizure behavior might be nonepileptic in origin.

The subjects receiving the dual condition (Group 3) had the most difficult task. In order to receive feedback in this condition, patients had to satisfy criteria that were the solution of a simultaneous equation. That is, they could obtain feedback by greatly increasing either 11–19 Hz activity and slightly decreasing 3–8 Hz activity, or by a slight increase in 11–19 Hz activity with a very large suppression of 3–8 Hz activity, as well as by a variety of other solutions. The contingencies for Group 3 most closely approximated a normalization of the epileptogenic EEG.

An important point is that during the noncontingent phase, which was designed to control for placebo effects, there were no spectral changes that correlated with the seizure changes. Changes in seizures were variable and showed no consistent pattern. Overall, this condition resulted in a 1.45% increase in seizures for all groups.

In addition to the results recorded in this table, the subjective reports of the patients and their families were also considered. Subjectively, six of the eight patients reported that they felt better and that they had achieved better seizure control as a result of participating in this research. Patient B. O. felt better at the end of the A_1 phase but did not believe that additional training improved her condition (in fact, it did not). Patient A. K. was noncompliant and was not convinced that this experience had helped him at all. Although he showed a decrease in A_2, it was too small to be clinically meaningful (−3.3%). Other positive changes noted were decreases in severity and duration of seizures (as reported by family members) for many of the patients during those periods in which they showed decreased numbers of seizures.

During the B phase of the study, several deleterious effects on the behavior of the patients were noted. One patient (E. C.) had to be withdrawn from this phase of the study 2 weeks early, and therefore only received 6 weeks of B training. During this period, E. C. experienced an increase in the duration and intensity of his tonic–clonic seizures, and his parents were quite concerned. Also, patient M. W. showed an increase in seizure intensity and duration, as well as an increase in antisocial behaviors. Patient W. S. experienced outbursts of anger and other negative behavior changes, in spite of a decrease in her seizures.

FEEDBACK CRITERIA CHANGES AND PERFORMANCE

Figure 2 shows, as an example, the results obtained for patient V. T. on learning measures during the training sessions. This patient was assigned to Group 2. Figure 2a shows the minimum microvolt values required for a burst (blue light) to occur. Figure 2b shows the length of time above which the predetermined microvolt

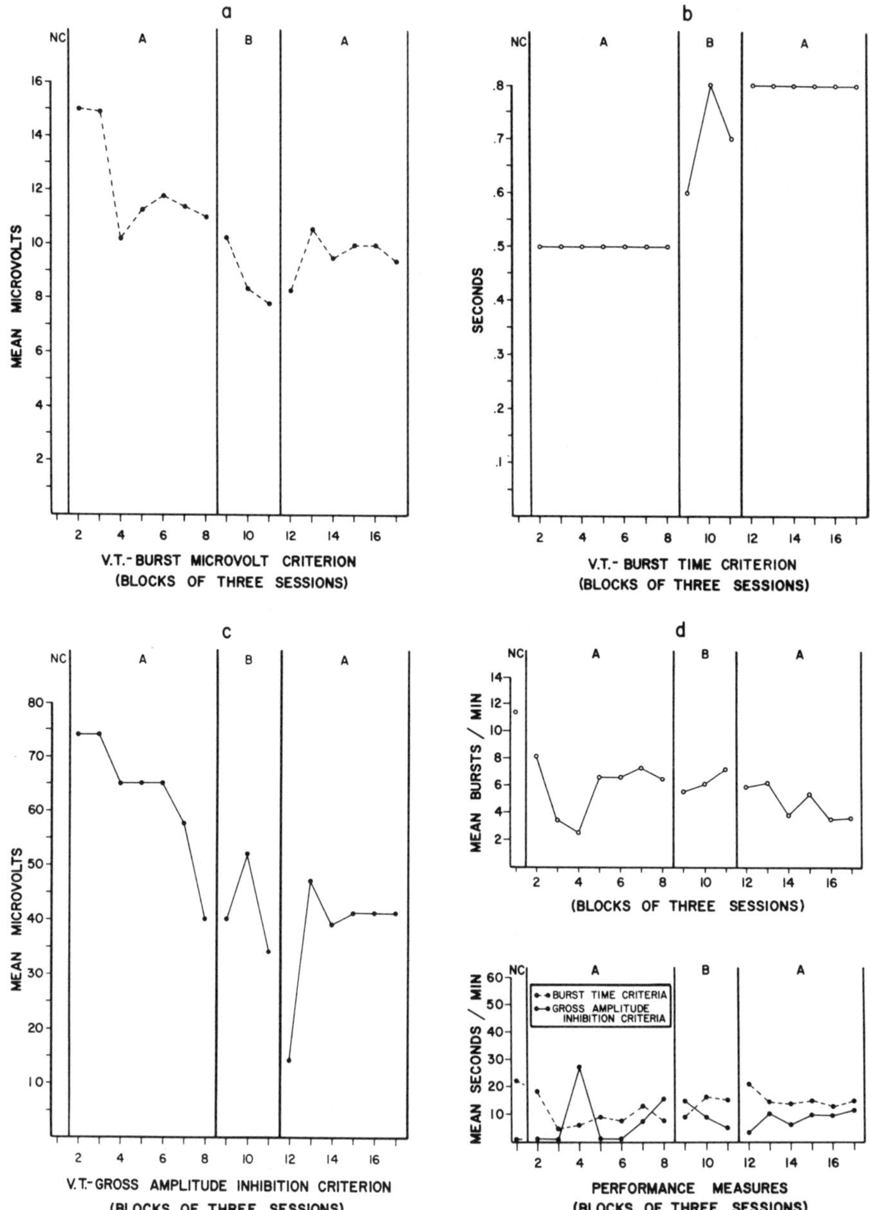

FIG. 2. Criteria settings for the "inhibit" light (red) and the "reward" lights (green and blue) are shown in Sections a, b, and c. Performance measures in d represent bursts obtained per minute and number of seconds per minute of green light reward, as well as the activity of the red inhibitory light, for patient V. T.

level must be maintained in order to receive a blue light or tone reward. The gross amplitude inhibition criterion plot (2c) shows changes in the setting of the inhibit level (red light). The performance plots shown in 2d display the mean number of bursts (blue lights) obtained per minute, the actual mean number of seconds per minute that feedback-contingent microvolt levels were exceeded (green light), and the mean number of seconds per minute that the inhibition criterion was exceeded (red light).

Learning would clearly be indicated by achieving successively more difficult criteria without showing decreases in the measures of performance. The difficulty of achieving a burst was most directly affected by the amplitude and duration of the target EEG. Inhibition time reduced the total time available for scoring bursts. For the particular patient shown (V. T.), evidence of learning is displayed in the following ways. There was a general increase in the burst time criterion between the A_1 and A_2 phases (2b). There was a general decrease in inhibition criteria, indicating perhaps a decrease in the amount of paroxysmal activity or gross body movement (2c). This was done without significantly increasing the number of seconds per minute for which gross inhibition occurred (2d). However, in achieving these gains, there was a sacrifice in the microvolt level (2a) that had to be obtained in order to achieve bursts. Some other patients in the study were also able to decrease gross inhibition levels, but at the expense of increasing the amount of time per minute that the red inhibition light was activated.

SPECTRAL ANALYSES

Spectral analyses were carried out for every patient for each session. Patterns of changes for these spectral analyses during the conditioning procedures were complex. Figure 3 presents an example for patient B. O. During the A_1 phase, while being reinforced for suppression of slow activity, this patient showed an increase in the percentage of power of higher-frequency activity for all frequency bands between 12–27 Hz. She also showed a corresponding decrease in power and, more clearly, a decrease in the percentage of activity for frequencies between 0–11 Hz, with the greatest change being a decrease in 0–3 Hz activity. This patient, then, appeared to show changes consistent with the training requirements. During the B phase, it can be seen that high frequencies leveled off and low-frequency activity began to increase, particularly in the scaled power measures. This patient showed a 39.2% increase in seizures over the previous decrease of 51% in the A_1 phase. However, in the A_2 phase, the pattern was more comples. This patient showed an increase in power of high frequency activity through Block 15. She also showed a continued decrease in very slow 0–3 Hz activity. The net effect of the changes in the A_2 phase was a sharp increase in total spectral power. It was also noted that during the period corresponding to the Block 15 power peak, this patient had experienced more seizures than at any other time in the study. This would tend to indicate that an overall increase in power, represented in all frequencies over the recorded site, was deleterious. During the A_2 phase, this patient either was unable to or did not follow the feedback contingencies. She also reported feeling no longer able to control her seizures and quite depressed.

Figure 4 shows the relationship between seizure activity and spectral analytic data for a patient trained initially to suppress slow activity (M. W.). This patient experienced a clear improvement in seizure control during the A_1 and A_2 phases, with a reversal during the B phase, that was reflected in an increase in the severity and duration of his seizures. With very few exceptions, this patient followed the training contingencies in terms of spectral analytic changes, both during training and as reflected in his sleep EEGs. He experienced better control of his partial complex seizures during the A_1 and A_2 phases of training than he did of his tonic–clonic seizures, which did show, however, smaller changes in the expected direction. Over the course of training, M. W. experienced an increase in spectral power and in percentage of power for frequencies between 16–23 Hz. He also experienced a decrease in percentage of power for frequencies between 0–7 Hz. The way in which these spectral changes occurred was reflected in an increase in both the power and the percentage of high-frequency activity but a relative decrease in the percentage of low-frequency activity without a concomitant decrease in power. Finally, there were no specific changes in individual frequency bands that clearly correlated with days in which seizure activity was very high or low for this individual. It appears that this patient's seizure reduction was more highly correlated with long-term EEG shifts.

Figure 5 shows changes in quantified power spectra obtained for the first 10-minute period of Stage 2 sleep for M. W. These analyses were performed after the baseline phase and after completion of the A_1, B, and A_2 phases of training. Significant decreases in 0–3 Hz and 4–7 Hz activity were found after A_1 and A_2 training. Significant increases in activity on these frequencies occurred after B reversal training, in relation to activity during A_1. In contrast, 12–15 Hz and 16–19 Hz activity increased after A_1 and A_2 training and decreased significantly after B reversal training, in relative to such activity during A_1. Changes in total all-night paroxysmal activity during all stages of sleep (1 through 4 and REM) followed the A_1, B, and A_2 contingencies for this subject as well, with more paroxysmal activity after B training and less after A_1 and A_2 training.

NEUROPSYCHOLOGICAL TESTS AND BEHAVIORAL OBSERVATIONS

The neuropsychological testing indicated little or no change for most of the patients. Only one patient (M. W.) showed a decrease in functioning on only one subtest of the battery (Finger Oscillation Test). Three of the patients showed improve-

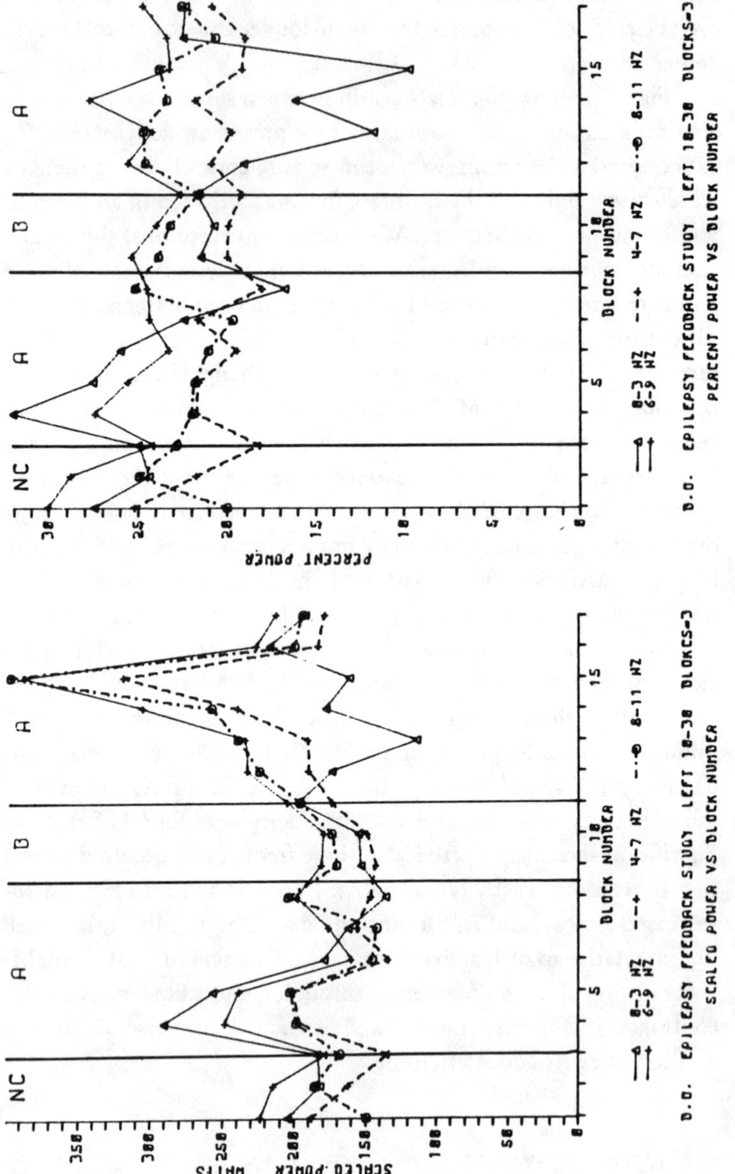
PERCENT POWER
NC
A
B
A
BLOCK NUMBER
0-3 HZ
6-9 HZ
4-7 HZ
8-11 HZ
D.D. EPILEPSY FEEDBACK STUDY LEFT 10-30 BLOCKS-3
PERCENT POWER VS BLOCK NUMBER
SCALED POWER WATTS
NC
A
B
A
BLOCK NUMBER
0-3 HZ
6-9 HZ
4-7 HZ
8-11 HZ
D.D. EPILEPSY FEEDBACK STUDY LEFT 10-30 BLOCKS-3
SCALED POWER VS BLOCK NUMBER

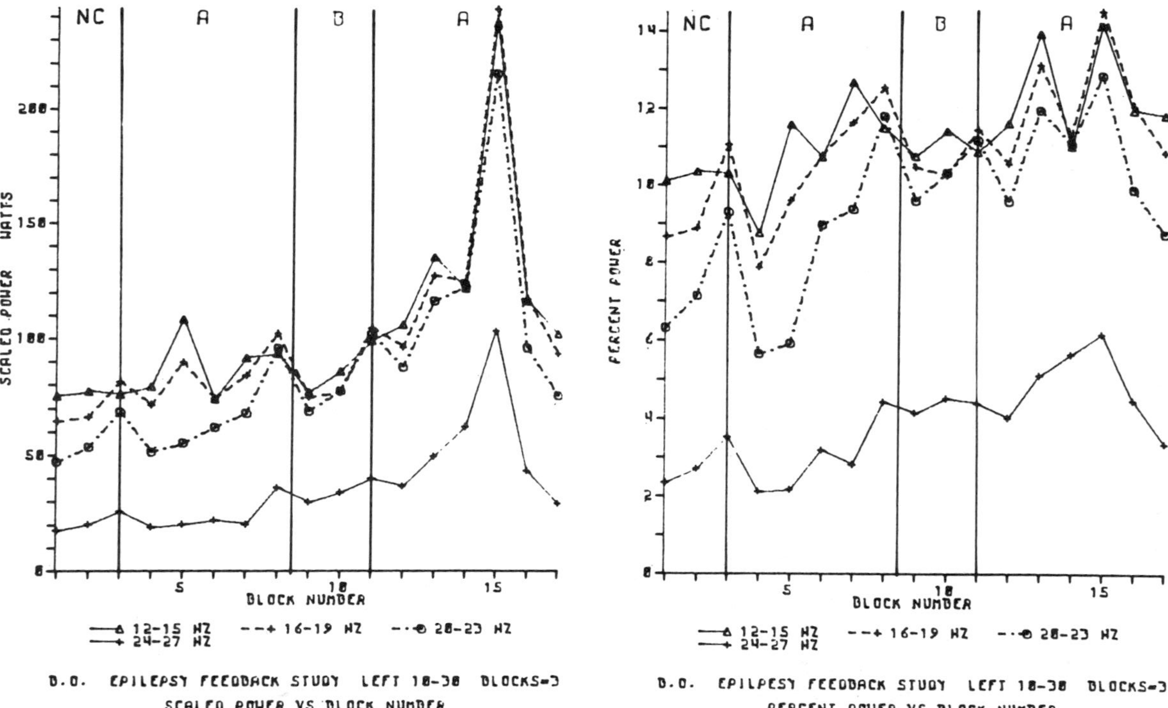

FIG. 3. Quantitative spectral changes for patient B. O. (Group 1) for Noncontingent, Contingent, and Reversal training phases. The upper figures represent changes in activity between 0–11 Hz; the lower figures between 12–27 Hz. Detailed explanations of specific changes are provided in the text.

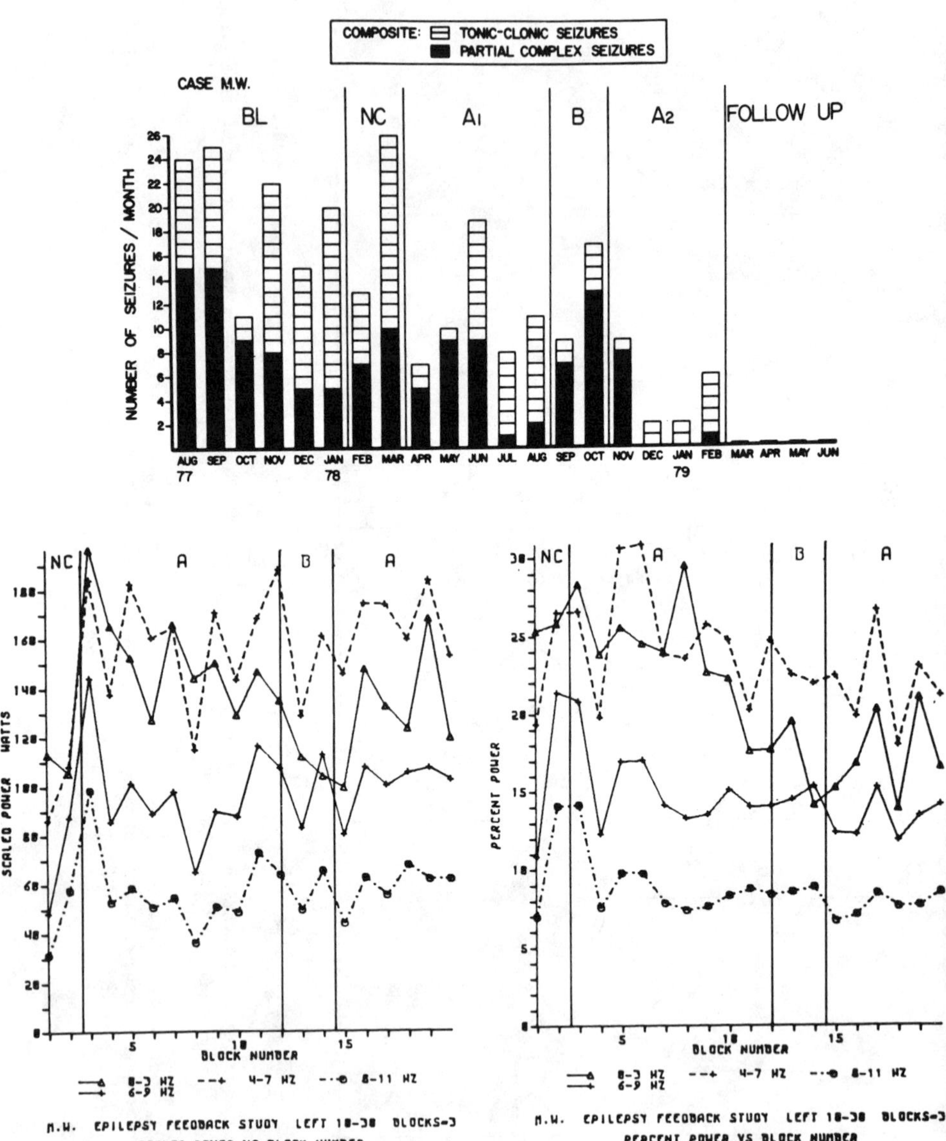

FIG. 4. EEG spectral changes and monthly seizures for patient M. W. (Group 1). The relationships between spectral changes and seizures for different phases of the study are presented in the text for this patient.

FIG. 4. (*continued*)

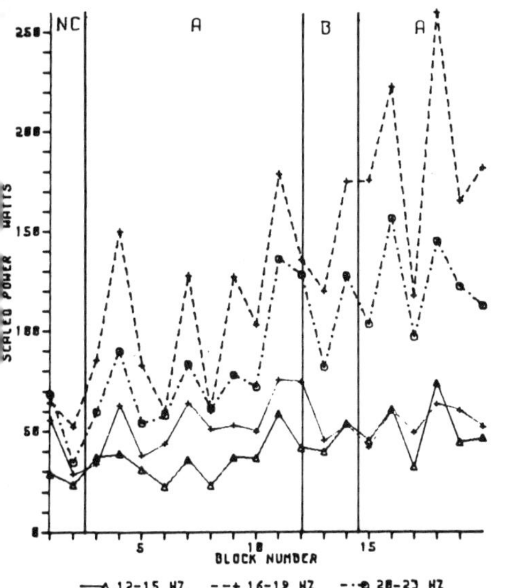

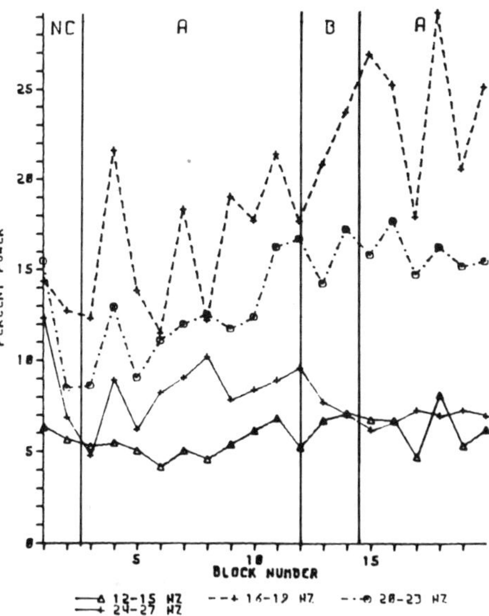

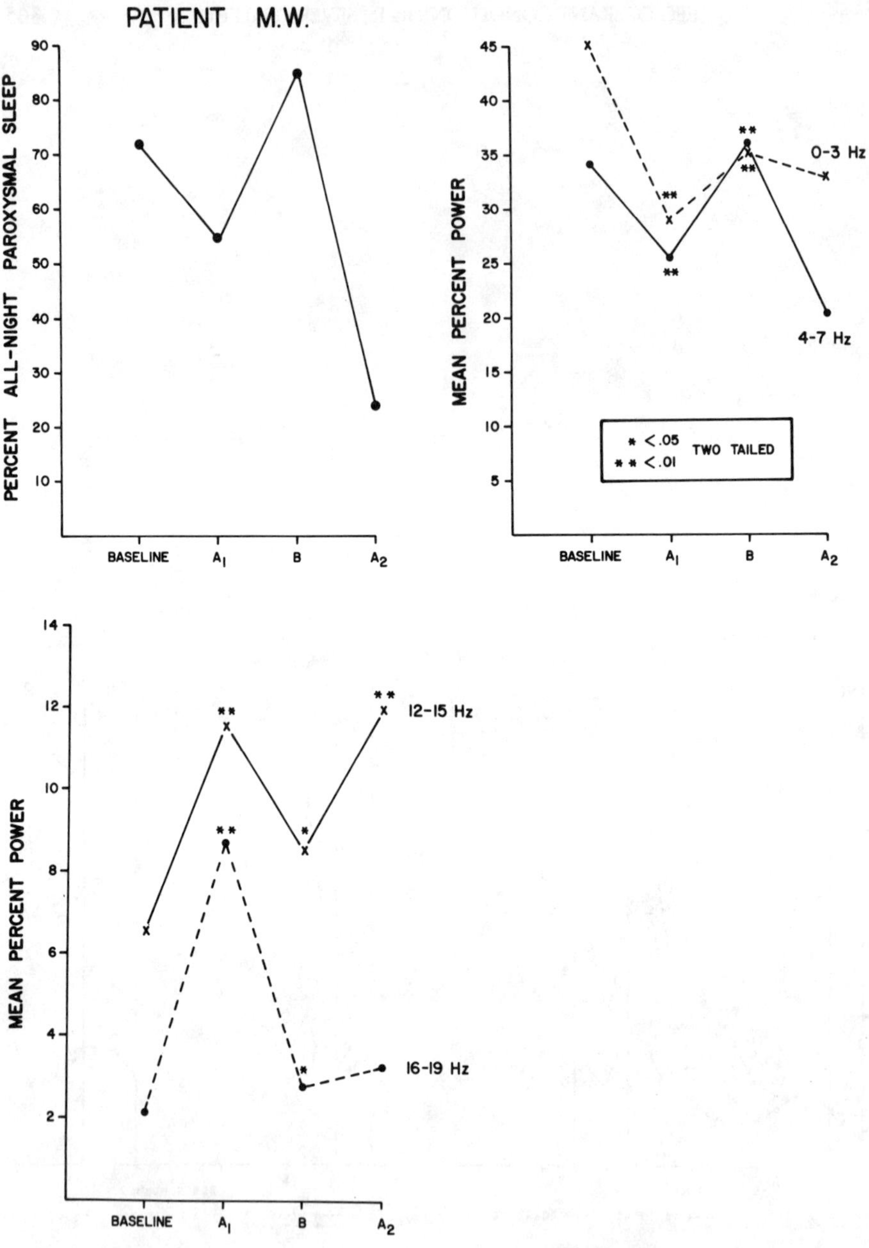

FIG. 5. Top Left Panel: Percentage of all-night sleep for patient M. W. (Group 1) during which paroxysmal activity occurred, measured at the completion of each training phase. Top Right Panel: Mean percentage based on fast Fourier spectral analysis for low-frequency activity. Bottom Panel: Mean percentage of power based on fast Fourier spectral analysis of higher-frequency activity. Note in particular decreased paroxysmal activity, decreased lower-frequency activity, and increased higher-frequency activity after A_1 and A_2 phases following training for suppression of 4–7 Hz activity. Also note the increased paroxysmal low-frequency activity and decreased higher-frequency activity following training for increased 4–7 Hz activity (Phase B).

ments on either gross motor or sensory portions of the Halstead–Reitan Battery, and one (R. R.) showed a significant increase in Full Scale IQ (from 48 to 54) as measured by the WAIS. These minimal changes concur with recent findings reported by Wyler *et al.* (1979), who found that operant conditioning of the EEG does not necessarily lead to clear changes in neuropsychological functioning. Most of the behaviors observed and recorded during training remained relatively stable throughout the course of this study, with these exceptions: Patient R. R. followed the ABA design for the category "relaxed–tense." In the A_1 and A_2 phases he was more relaxed (less tense) than in the B phase. Patient V. T. experienced more gross movement during the B phase. M. W. exhibited more tenseness during his reversal training in a pattern similar to that seen in R. R. (the ABA). These changes during the B phase for some patients might indicate that at some level they perhaps perceived a change and were reacting to it, although overtly they did not seem to be aware of a change in feedback conditions.

DISCUSSION

An important difference between this study and others published thus far is that the patients were given only 4 months for each of the A conditions. This provided them with relatively little time to alter their EEG, in comparison to the continuous 6-month or 2-year training programs that have been reported elsewhere (Finley, 1975; Lubar & Bahler, 1976). For this reason, it was not surprising that the degree of seizure reduction was less than that reported in these or other studies (e.g., Sterman *et al.*, 1974). Despite the difficulties imposed by the short training periods and the reversal phase, five of the eight subjects reduced the number of their seizures from baseline levels.

Although the present study, like many others cited, employed a small number of patients, one of its strong points is that it simultaneously takes into account many factors that have not been examined in combination in previous studies employing EEG biofeedback. For example, meticulous attention was directed toward training patients or their families to record and characterize different types of seizures. These records were collected monthly, and the data were not discussed with the patients. Another aspect of this study was the collection of neuropsychological data both before and after participation in the study.

In spite of the small number of patients, one conclusion that may be tentatively drawn is that the patients (Group 1) who received training for suppression of 3–8 Hz activity performed consistently best. In contrast, patients who were trained to reduce slow activity and increase fast activity (Group 3) did not perform as well as had been anticipated, although this group represented the model most closely approximating normalizing of the abnormal epileptic EEG. We now feel that feedback of this dual type may be too vague and too difficult to be effective in a clinical treatment employing feedback methods. This might explain why patients R. R. and E. C. performed best in the A_2 condition, as it may have taken them that long to learn what was necessary in order to receive feedback.

Although an ideal outcome would have been a clear ABA effect, in which an individual would show a decrease in seizures during the A_1 condition, an increase during the B condition, and a decrease during the A_2 condition, only two patients (E. C. in Group 3 and M. W. in Group 1) followed this paradigm. Other patients showed changes that followed parts of the design.

Two factors that must be considered in any evaluation of this study are the subjects' degree of impairment and the heterogeneity of seizure types. Most of the patients had a very high impairment index, as indicated by the Halstead–Reitan Battery (.85 or greater on a scale of 0 to 1). Five of the patients were mentally retarded. It is our impression that, had we been able to work with a more homogeneous population of patients matched for higher intelligence and type of seizures, even more consistent results might have been obtained. However, we did find that patient M. W., who was severely retarded (IQ = 49), learned the task best and showed the greatest seizure reduction.

The double-blind aspects of this study were maintained throughout its tenure. That is, at *no time* were patients told that the contingencies of feedback had been changed. Neither were the technicians responsible for working with the patients aware of which frequencies the patients were being trained for. Also, they were not shown the polygraph output, which was collected and stored from a remote monitor. The methods employed to shape each patient's learning during the contingent phase were an added strength of this study. To accomplish this shaping, thresholds were adjusted at each session to try to maintain an equal distribution of feedback (number of bursts) throughout the study. This was done so that patients would not be aware of the transitions from the noncontingent to the contingent phase or from the contingent to the reversal phase.

The findings that patients showed relatively little improvement during the noncontingent phase of the study and that some of them became worse are important. Overall, results for all groups indicated that a placebo effect probably was not significant and that the contingent EEG training was responsible for the improvement in their seizures. Also, during the noncontingent phase, contingent training (a placebo control) for EMG and movement was used.

In this study, we found that our previous notions concerning normalization of the EEG, either by increasing high-frequency activity (11–19 Hz) or by decreasing slow activity (3–8 Hz) for the EEG site employed for training, may not be the only conditions sufficient for amelioration of seizures. Instead, the EEG changes that correlated with decreased seizures were more complex. While some of our patients experienced more seizures when they were producing high-frequency activity, others did best when lower frequencies were being increased. The later finding was consistent with Kaplan's report (1975) that two of her patients showed a reduction in seizures when 6–12 Hz activity was reinforced. Furthermore, several of the patients in our study (except for B. O.) experienced an increase in overall spectral power, which correlated with an improvement in their seizures. It therefore appears that different types of EEG conditioning can be effective for managing different types of patients.

An important point that needs to be considered in both present and future studies is the relationship between changes in the cortical EEG and underlying subcortical processes. Such data, by necessity, must employ animal models. Studies with cats reported by Harper and Sterman (1972) have shown that there is an attenuation of the number of unit discharges in specific sensorimotor pathways during operant conditioning of 12–16 Hz activity over the sensorimotor cortex. Other work from their laboratory (Howe & Sterman, 1972; Wyrwicka & Sterman, 1968) demonstrated changes in the firing rate of unit activity in both the brain stem and the thalamic structures modulating efferent activity of the sensorimotor cortex during operant conditioning. This correlated with their report that in order to obtain rewards for producing 12–16 Hz activity, cats had to remain motionless (i.e., experience sensorimotor inhibition). These combined findings further strengthen the concept that there is a neuropsychological and perhaps a neurochemical basis for the mediation of feedback-learned changes in the EEG that correlates with decreased seizure activity.

The overall results of our study, viewed in conjunction with the large number of studies that have been published in this area, appear encouraging. It seems appropriate that wide-scale clinical trials be initiated to determine whether EEG feedback conditioning can become a valuable adjunct in the treatment of epilepsy.

ACKNOWLEDGMENTS

I wish to acknowledge the dedication of time, energy, and technical abilities of my graduate students and colleagues: Harry S. Shabsin, Gary S. Holder, Stan F. Whitsett, William E. Pamplin III, and Don I. Krulikowski. I wish especially to acknowledge Stephen E. Natelson, MD, who provided considerable direction to the plan and implementation of this program. Without the combined help of these people, of many technicians who implemented the double-blind design of the project, and of the patients and their families who participated, this program could have never been undertaken. I also acknowledge the help of Ms. Teri Albanese, who has typed this manuscript for publication.

The research reported here was supported by grants from the Epilepsy Foundation of America to myself and by the Physicians Medical Education and Research Foundation.

REFERENCES

Cott, A., Pavlovski, R. P., & Black, A. H. Reducing epileptic seizures through operant conditioning of central nervous system activity: Procedural variables. *Science,* 1979, *203,* 73–75.

Finley, W. W. *Seven weeks noncontingent feedback after one year of SMR biofeedback treatment in a severe epileptic: Follow-up study.* Paper presented at a meeting of the Biofeedback Research

Society, Monterey, California, 1975.

Finley, W. W., Smith, H. A., & Etherton, M. D. Reduction of seizures and normalization of the EEG in a severe epileptic following sensorimotor biofeedback training: Preliminary study. *Biological Psychology,* 1975, *2,* 189–203.

Harper, R. M., & Sterman, M. B. Subcortical unit activity during a conditioned 12–14 Hz sensorimotor EEG rhythm in the cat. *Federation Proceedings,* 1972, *31,* 404.

Howe, R. C., & Sterman, M. B. Cortical–subcortical EEG correlates of suppressed motor behavior during sleep and waking in the cat. *Electroencephalography and Clinical Neurophysiology,* 1972, *32,* 681–695.

Kaplan, B. J. Biofeedback in epileptics: Equivocal relationship of reinforced EEG frequency to seizure reduction. *Epilepsia,* 1975, *16,* 477–485.

Kuhlman, W. N., & Kaplan, B. J. Clinical applications of EEG feedback training. In R. J. Gatchel & K. P. Price (Eds.), *Clinical applications of biofeedback: Appraisal & status.* New York: Pergamon, 1979.

Lubar, J. F. Electroencephalographic biofeedback methodology and the management of epilepsy. *Pavlovian Journal,* 1977, *12,* 147–185.

Lubar, J. F., & Bahler, W. W. Behavioral management of epileptic seizures following EEG biofeedback training of the sensorimotor rhythm. *Biofeedback and Self-Regulation,* 1976, *1,* 77–104.

Lubar, J. F., Shabsin, H. S., Natelson, S. E., Holder, G. S., Whitsett, S. F., Pamplin, W. E., & Krulikowski, D. I. EEG operant conditioning in intractable epileptics. *Archives of Neurology,* 1981, *38,* 700–704.

Masland, R. L. *Epidemidogy and basic statistics on the epilepsies: Where are we?* Paper presented at the Fifth National Conference on the Epilepsies, Washington, D.C., 1976.

Mostofsky, D. I., & Balaschak, B. A. Psychobiological control of seizures. *Psychological Bulletin,* 1977, *34*(4), 123–750.

Seifert, A. R., & Lubar, J. F. Reduction of epileptic seizures through EEG biofeedback training. *Biological Psychology,* 1975, *3,* 81–109.

Sterman, M. B., & Friar, L. Suppression of seizures in an epileptic following sensorimotor EEG feedback training. *Electroencephalography and Clinical Neurophysiology,* 1972, *33,* 89–95.

Sterman, M. B., & Macdonald, L. R. Effects of central cortical EEG feedback training on incidence of poorly controlled seizures. *Epilepsia,* 1978, *19,* 207–222.

Sterman, M. B., Macdonald, L. R., & Stone, R. K. Biofeedback training of the sensorimotor electroencephalographic rhythm in man: Effects on epilepsy. *Epilepsia,* 1974, *15,* 395–416.

Whitsett, S. F., Lubar, J. F., Holder, G. S., Pamplin, W. E., & Shabsin, H. S. A double-blind investigation of the relationship between seizure activity and the sleep EEG following EEG biofeedback training. *Biofeedback and Self-Regulation,* in press.

Wyler, A. R., Lockard, J. S., Ward, A. A., Jr., & Finch, C. A. Conditioned EEG desynchronization and seizure occurrence in patients. *Electroencephalography and Clinical Neurophysiology,* 1976, *41,* 501–512.

Wyler, A. R., Robbins, C. A., & Dodrill, C. B. EEG operant conditioning for control of epilepsy. *Epilepsia,* 1979, *20,* 279–286.

Wywricka, W., & Sterman, M. B. Instrumental conditioning of sensorimotor cortex EEG spindles in the waking cat. *Physiology & Behavior,* 1968, *31,* 703–707.

12 EEG BIOFEEDBACK IN THE TREATMENT OF EPILEPSY: AN OVERVIEW CIRCA 1980

M. BARRY STERMAN

A number of issues relevant to the study of EEG biofeedback in the treatment of epilepsy have been raised in this volume generally and in Lubar's chapter in particular. I would like to discuss these both from an historical perspective and within the context of recent work in my laboratory. Fortunately, the amount of data that has now been generated in this area of biofeedback research allows for a comprehensive review and the opportunity to clarify some important questions.

REPLICATION

First, the issue of replication must be considered. Because of findings from our earlier animal studies, my colleagues and I adopted some methodologic conventions when we first turned our attention to the application of EEG feedback training in epileptics (Sterman, Macdonald, & Stone, 1974). Among these was an attempt to place signal detection electrodes in humans at sites homologous to those mapped in cats for optimal recording of the 12–14 Hz sensorimotor rhythm (SMR). We and others have described a primary focus of this activity over the left lateral somatosensory cortex in the cat (Howe & Sterman, 1972; Rougeul, Letalle, & Corvisier, 1972). Accordingly, electrodes were placed mediolaterally over the left somatosensory area at sites 10% and 30% lateral to vertex, between T_3–C_3 and C_3–C_z, respectively, according to the international 10–20 system (Fig. 1). In addition, we had hypothesized that suppression of abnormal slow frequencies might contribute to a facilitation of the desired intermediate frequency, and had therefore included a negative feedback component for frequencies below 10 Hz in our detection-and-reward system. Final-

M. Barry Sterman. Research Service, Veterans Administration Medical Center, Sepulveda, California; Departments of Anatomy and Psychiatry, The University of California at Los Angeles, Los Angeles, California.

ly, we decided that the occurrence of high-voltage spike and slow-wave activity in epileptics, and the possibility of movement artifacts in the high-impedance recordings obtained from surface electrodes, would require the addition of high-voltage transient "inhibit" circuits, which we incorporated into both the logic circuitry and feedback display of our system.

As can be seen in Fig. 1 and Table 1, with the exception of the studies of Finley and his colleagues (Finley, Smith, & Etherton, 1975; Finley, 1976), Lubar and Bahler (1976), and Ellertsen and Kløve (1976), who actually adhered to these conventions, many others found it necessary or desirable to make changes. Despite this fact, however, these authors often claimed to be testing our 1974 conclusions. Kaplan (1975), for example, described her study as an effort to replicate our work, yet virtually every aspect of her investigation was different, including electrode placements, signal detection methods, and reward criteria.

FIG. 1. Summary of bipolar recording electrode placements and reward criteria described in comprehensive publications applying EEG biofeedback training to the treatment of epilepsy. "High-voltage transient inhibit" refers to amplitude detection circuits that prevent reward for high-voltage events (50–100 μV) such as abnormal spikes and slow waves or movement artifact.

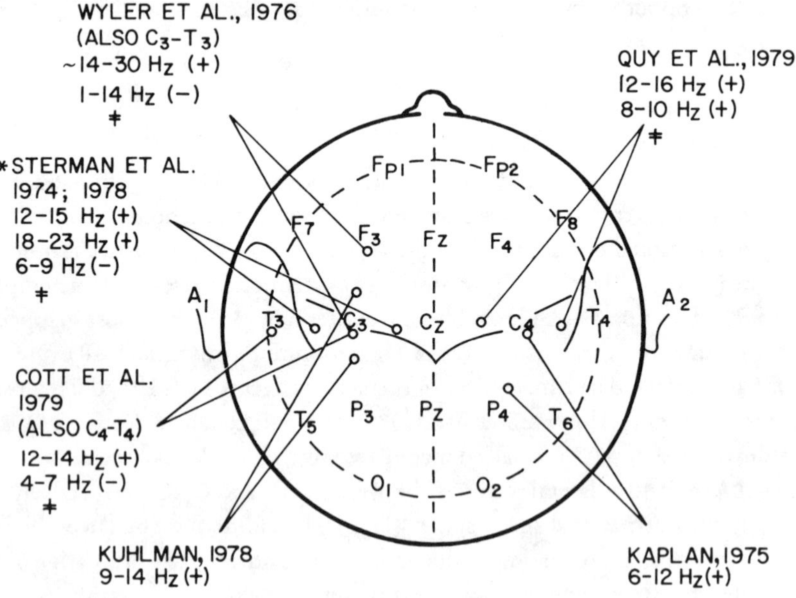

Adversity, however, often leads to progress. Thus, because of these deviations, the question of electrode placements has to some extent been resolved. Investigations using electrodes placed over the somatosensory or more generally over the sensorimotor cortex have reported significant seizure reductions in at least 60% of the patients studied, while others using alternative electrode sites have noted poorer results. It should be kept in mind that among the poorly controlled, highly epileptic patients who have served as subjects in all of these studies, transient seizure reduction is typically observed in some 30% regardless of the manipulation employed, as long as it is new or produces a change in the life situation. Thus, while a 60%-plus response rate can be taken very seriously, the 40% and 41% rates of reduction reported by Kaplan (1975) for training over the central parietal cortex and by Wyler, Robbins, and Dodrill (1979) for training over variable sites of focal discharge (see Table 1), respectively, are less convincing. Moreover, in an attempt to apply such training over the occipital cortex, Kuhlman (1980) obtained significant seizure reduction in only one of three patients studied. It can be tentatively concluded, therefore, that some degree of localization over the sensorimotor cortex is required for optimal therapeutic efficacy with this procedure.

ESTABLISHMENT OF JUSTIFICATION FOR BIOFEEDBACK TREATMENT

Several other conclusions also arise from a consideration of the overview provided in Table 1. Certainly it is clear that the uncontrolled studies that characterized this literature in the early and mid-1970s have been replaced by increasingly sophisticated and comprehensive designs. As others have suggested in the present volume, the appropriate objective of investigation when a new idea is being explored is to determine whether or not there is sufficient justification for the larger investment in time and energy required for a properly controlled study. This justification was indeed established for the use of biofeedback with epileptics by 1976. Since that time, a number of important alternative explanations for the therapeutic results obtained have been put to rest. Interestingly, throughout this evaluation, the percentage of patients showing significant therapeutic response (with the exceptions mentioned above) has remained relatively consistent at approximately 60% to 80%.

Wyler (Wyler, Lockard, Ward, & Finch, 1976) was the first to show that noncontingent feedback under identical training conditions was ineffective in altering seizure rates. This was confirmed later by Kuhlman (1978) and by Sterman and Lantz (1981) (data presented in Table 1), who used yoked-control methods, as well as by Lubar in the present volume, who used random feedback with contingent movement suppression. In fact, the most interesting contributions to this literature that Lubar's chapter in this book provides relate to this and to his reward for 3–8 Hz

TABLE 1. Summary of Central Cortical EEG Feedback Training Studies in Epileptics Indicating Selected Parameters for Comparison (Complete to May 1980)

Investigator(s)	*Frequency Rewarded*	*Number of Patients*	*Number Showing Seizure Reduction*	*Design and Approximate Duration of Training*	
Sterman & Friar (1972)	11–13 Hz (+)	1	1	Single-case	3 mo.
Sterman, Macdonald, & Stone (1974)	12–14 Hz (+) < 10 (−) EMG + Spks[a] (−)	4	4	Group Pre–post[b]	6–18 mo.
Finley, Smith, & Etherton (1975) and Finley (1976)	11–13 Hz (+) < 10 (−) EMG + Spks (−)	2	2	Two single-case	10–22 mo.
Seifert & Lubar (1975) and Lubar & Bahler (1976)	12–14 Hz (+) 4–7 Hz (−) EMG + Spks (−)	8	7	Group Pre–post	6–9 mo.
Kaplan (1975)	12–14 Hz (+) 6–12 Hz (+)	2 3	0 2	Group Pre–post	3–4 mo. 5–6 mo.
Wyler, Lockard, Ward, & Finch (1976)	14–30 Hz (+) (variable) < 14 Hz (−)	5	4	ABA (variable)	1.5–6 mo.
Kuhlman (1978)	9–14 Hz (+)	5	3	AB	1–2 mo.
Sterman & Macdonald (1978)	12–15 Hz (+) 18–23 Hz (+) 6–9 HZ (−) EMG + Spks (−)	8	7	ABAB (counter-balanced)	12 mo.
Cott, Pavloski, & Black (1979)	12–14 Hz (+) 4–7 Hz (−) EMG + Spks (−)	7	6	Baseline in lab Train	1 mo. 6 mo.

Wyler, Robbins, & Dodrill (1979)	18 Hz (+) EMG + Spks (−)	22	9	Baseline EMG Train Focal Train	1–2 wks. 3–6 wks.
Lubar (1980)	Noncont with EMG (−) 3–8 Hz (−) 12–15 Hz (+) 11–19 Hz (+)/ 3–8 Hz (−) 3–8 Hz (+)	8	5	Baseline, Non-cont/ EMG (−) ABA	1 mo. 19 mo.
Sterman & Lantz (1981)	10–15 Hz (+) 1–5 Hz (−) 20–25 Hz (−)	15	13	Baseline Seiz Tab Noncont Contingent	6 wks. 6 wks. 6 wks.
Totals (independent)		90	63 (70%)		

[a]Spikes.

[b]Comparison of pre- and posttraining measures.

activity. Previously, Wyler (Wyler *et al.*, 1976) had reported preliminary evidence showing that the suppression of EMG activity alone had no effect on seizure rates. These various findings, together with others to be reviewed here, make it extremely unlikely that the reduction of seizures documented with central cortical EEG feedback training results from movement suppression or from other nonspecific factors associated with arousal or the training situation.

A second primary contribution provided by Lubar's chapter derives from the boldness shown in rewarding low-frequency activity in his epileptic patients. In an earlier study, using a contingency-reversal paradigm (Sterman & Macdonald, 1978), we had been reluctant to facilitate these low frequencies for fear of worsening the patients' condition. Accordingly, we choose to use the 6–9 Hz band for cross-over training as a compromise. However, Lubar proceeded to explore this area after obtaining appropriate approval for this test as well as close medical supervision. The outcome was as predicted: two of the three patients provided with this training deteriorated rapidly and had to be withdrawn prior to the date specified by the design. Thus, it is clear that facilitation of abnormal EEG patterns can produce exacerbation of seizure disorders. This is an important conclusion since it indicates that these methods can effectively alter the pathological substrate.

The fact that suppression of these same frequencies proved to be an effective training strategy for seizure reduction is in agreement with the findings of Cott, Pavloski, and Black (1979) and does not detract from the importance of changes in intermediate, rhythmic frequencies. Using power-spectral analysis, Lubar found that central cortical EEG activity in these patients during both training and slow-wave sleep showed a decrease in abnormal low-frequency activity *together with* an increase in 12–15 Hz activity, even when this frequency band was not specifically reinforced. During sleep, changes in 16–19 Hz activity partially paralleled those seen at 12–15 Hz. This finding is in complete agreement with recent observations (discussed below) from Sterman and Shouse (1980), and it stresses the importance of evaluating the total dynamics of EEG change resulting from feedback training. Unfortunately, Cott *et al.* (1979) failed to do this and, as a result, drew some rather myopic conclusions.

In an earlier paper (Sterman & Macdonald, 1978), we reported significant seizure reductions in patients from two training groups. One group was trained for successive 3-month blocks in an ABA design. In the A_1 phase, reward for 12–15 Hz sensorimotor cortical activity was provided only in the absence of concurrent 6–9 Hz activity; these contingencies were then reversed (B), followed by a reversal again to the original contingencies (A_2). A second group underwent identical training but with alternating reward for the combination of 18–23 Hz and 6–9 Hz, instead. After initial laboratory training, this design was initiated with portable equipment and training was carried on in the home except for laboratory recordings at 2-week intervals. In essence, this was a totally blind study, since the patients knew nothing of our contingency changes and their training was achieved at home without contact with any of our staff.

When reported seizure rates were evaluated, subjects in the first group showed a contingency-specific seizure response; positive reinforcement for 12–15 Hz, followed by seizure reductions and reversed contingencies (6–9 Hz [+] and 12–15 Hz [–]), resulted in a return to baseline seizure rates. To our surprise, however, patients in the second group showed an immediate and progressive seizure reduction that was unaffected by contingency reversals. On the surface it would appear that these responses were quite discrepant, despite the fact that both groups showed overall seizure reductions averaging approximately 60%.

The subsequent analysis of other data collected in this study (Sterman & Shouse, 1980) contributed significantly to the interpretation of these results. Figure 2 provides a summary of these measures for the subgroup rewarded with frequency combinations of 12–15 Hz and 6–9 Hz. Training performance was evaluated in terms of the change in reward rates from the beginning to the end of each training phase of the study (Fig. 2, top graph). Values greater than 1 indicated increase response rates, while numbers less than 1 showed a response decrement. Significant increases in response rates were obtained for this group over training in each of the three phases of the study. Transitions between training phases were accompanied by a decrement in performance.

Data from power-spectral analysis of samples of slow-wave sleep taken from all-night sleep recordings at the end of each training phase indicated significant changes in four frequency bands over the sensorimotor cortex (Fig. 2, second graph). Following three months of training in the A_1 condition (12–15 Hz [+], 6–9 Hz [–]), power in the 12–15 Hz band was increased significantly during slow-wave sleep. A similar trend was noted in the 8–11 Hz band, while power at 0–3 Hz and 20–23 Hz was slightly reduced. Following training in the B condition (contingencies reversed), an opposite pattern of spectral density distribution was obtained, with values once again comparable to baseline characteristics. With reversal to the A_2 condition, both the 12–15 Hz and 8–11 Hz bands again showed increased power, the latter reaching significance. The low- and high-frequency bands were again somewhat attenuated.

It is clear from the third graph in Fig. 2 that these and other changes cannot be attributed to altered compliance with medicational instructions, as indicated by corresponding blood levels of anticonvulsant drugs. Individual values are shown over the period of study for phenytoin in three patients (solid lines) and primidone in the fourth (dashed line). Three of the patients showed drug levels within established therapeutic range throughout the study, with two indicating a slight decline during the B condition. Reported seizure rates in these patients were the focus of our earlier report (Sterman & Macdonald, 1978). Mean changes from baseline seizure rates over the training sequence in this study are shown in the bottom graph of

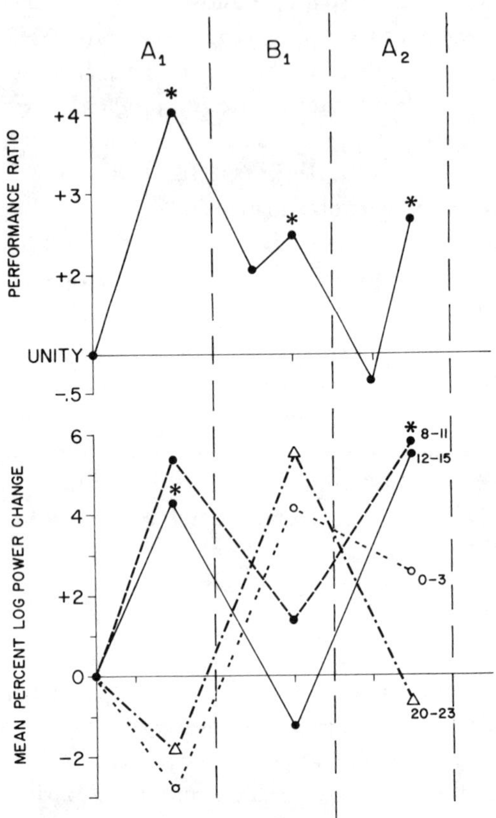

FIG. 2. Composite of four response parameters measured in this study in relation to the ABA design employed for patients in subgroup I. The top graph shows performance ratios derived from reward values at the beginning and end of each training phase, as well as across contingency reversals. Equivalence between values is designated as "unity," while improved performance on the contingency imposed is indicated by values greater than 1. Response acquisition was demonstrated in each of the three training phases. The second graph presents corresponding changes in power-spectral density during NREM sleep for four selected frequency bands (see text). Reciprocal changes among the various bands are apparent. The third graph shows blood levels of phenytoin measured prior to training and at the end of each training phase in three patients (solid line), and corresponding data for primidone in the fourth (dashed line).

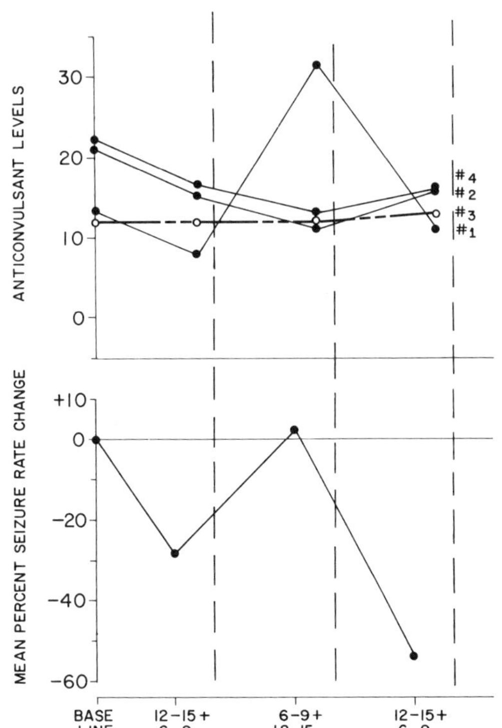

No systematic group changes were observed (see text for details). The bottom graph summarizes seizure rate change for these patients from a previous report (Sterman & Macdonald, 1978). Seizure reductions in this subgroup were only documented during periods of positive reinforcement for 12–15 Hz activity. Statistically significant changes from baseline levels in data from the present study (top three graphs) are indicated by asterisks ($p < .05$). (From "Quantitative Analysis of Training, Sleep EEG and Clinical Response to EEG Operant Conditioning in Epileptics" by M. B. Sterman and M. N. Shouse, *Electroencephalography and Clinical Neurophysiology*, 1980, *49*, 558–576. Copyright 1980 by *Electroencephalography and Clinical Neurophysiology*. Reprinted by permission.)

Fig. 2. Two of the four patients in this group showed significant seizure reductions during the A_1 training condition, and all four showed marked reductions again (three of them statistically significant) during the A_2 condition.

In order to evaluate further the relationship between observed changes in power-spectral densities and seizure rates, correlation coefficients were calculated between these parameters over the various phases of study (see Table 2). Seizure incidence was correlated negatively with activity in the 12–15 Hz band and the 8–11 Hz band and positively with activity in the 20–23 Hz band. Correlation with other frequency bands was negligible.

Data for the four patients provided with feedback reward for alternating combinations of 18–23 Hz and 6–9 Hz bands were similarly evaluated. In this group, performance during training in the A_1 condition (18–23 Hz [+], 6–9 Hz [–]) tended to increase over training but did not change significantly. Performance at the beginning of the B condition (6–9 Hz [+], 18–23 Hz [–]) was attenuated but then increased significantly over the course of training. Response rates were reduced again with contingency reversal in the A_2 condition. Performance during this later phase of training showed no significant improvement. Changes in power-spectral density distributions during sleep in this group were different from those in Subgroup I. During the A_1 condition, power in the 0–3 Hz band showed a trend toward decline, which was sustained and extended over the course of training. Power in the 8–11 Hz band showed a somewhat reciprocal increase, while power at 12–15 Hz was slightly increased in the A_1 and B conditions and then showed a sharper increment

TABLE 2. Pearson Product–Moment Correlations between Spectral Densities in Six Frequency Bands and Seizure Rates across the Three Training Phases of the ABA Design Described in the Text

Frequency Band (Hz)	*Correlation: EEG Frequency versus Seizure Rate*	
	Subgroup I (12–15 Hz)	*Subgroup II (18–23 Hz)*
0–3	.27	.99*
4–7	.26	.75
8–11	–.93*	–.90*
12–15	–.96*	–.33
16–19	–.24	–.20
20–23	.82	.97*

Note. Data are shown for two training subgroups of epileptic patients identified by the different high-frequency bands reinforced during training.

*p = <.05

in the A_2 period. Conversely, power at 20–23 Hz increased slightly in the A_1 phase and then declined progressively thereafter. Accordingly, by the end of training in this group, power in the 8–11 Hz and 12–15 Hz bands was increased, while power in the 0–3 Hz and 20–23 Hz bands were reduced. These results are similar to those obtained by Lubar in the preceding chapter. Only three of the patients in our second group used anticonvulsant drugs during participation in this study. Phenytoin levels in two of these patients were initially within therapeutic limits but showed a gradual decline over the period of study. A third patient had very low levels of phenytoin (3–5 μg/ml), which showed little change over time. Corresponding reported seizure rates declined significantly during the A_1 condition in three of the four subjects in this group. This reduction was increased during the B condition and became significant in all four patients. After contingency reversal to the A_2 condition, three of these subjects achieved their lowest seizure rates, while a fourth reported a slight increase in seizures. In this group, seizure incidence was again correlated *negatively* with power at 8–11 Hz (Table 2); however, the correlation with 12–15 Hz activity was not significant in this case because of individual variability in response. In addition, seizure rate was correlated *positively* with power in the 0–3 Hz and 20–23 Hz bands.

A further analysis of these data was achieved by considering findings during the training phase associated with the greatest seizure reduction for each individual. A similar strategy was adopted by Sterman and Macdonald (1978), in order to tabulate the training contingencies and training phases most related to seizure reductions. Seizure rates and medication changes, as well as training compliance (derived from a strip chart recorder in the portable home training unit) and performance values during maximum therapeutic effect, are provided for individuals in Table 3. Seizure rates were 66.79% lower than rate during pretraining baselines in the eight subjects. In five patients, improvements in seizure rates at these points in the study were also evident in independent clinical EEG reports. Six patients showed maximum seizure reduction in the final training condition (A_2), one during the initial condition (A_1), and one during the intermediate condition (B). Thus, the greatest therapeutic benefit occurred during periods of reward for 12–15 Hz or 18–23 Hz frequency bands in seven of eight patients. Home training compliance was relatively high, averaging 75.87% during the condition associated with maximum therapeutic effect. This was reflected in performance ratios as well, which averaged 1.96, or virtually twice the baseline performance rate. Drug levels, on the other hand, were not correlated systematically with changes in seizure incidence. In fact, phenytoin levels showed a mean reduction of 28.20% from pretraining levels, and three subjects had levels below the therapeutic range.

Combined spectral values for the two samples were analyzed to determine whether characteristic power-spectral density changes accompanied seizure reductions, and to compare findings in this regard from sensorimotor and parietal–oc-

TABLE 3. Training and Clinical Characteristics of Subjects in Both EEG Feedback Subgroups during Study Period Associated with Maximum Therapeutic Benefit

Subjects	*Training Phase*	*Percentage of Compliance*	*Performance Ratio*	*Change in Phenytoin Levels (%)*	*Percentage of Change in Seizure Rates*
Subgroup I					
1	A_1	75.0	6.17	−15.38	−100
2	A_2	77.8	1.38	−27.14	− 74
3	A_2	91.7	1.68	+ 8.33[a]	− 39
4	A_2	75.0	2.43	−27.27	− 19
Group $\bar{x}$	—	79.9	2.92	−15.36	− 58
Subgroup II					
1	A_2	88.9	.50	+33.3	− 78
2	A_2	61.1	2.16	—	−100
3	A_2	50.0	1.20	−72.73	− 53
4	B	87.5	1.14	−60.00	− 36
Group $\bar{x}$	—	71.9	1.25	−33.14	− 66.79

Note. From "Quantitative Analysis of Training, Sleep EEG and Clinical Response to EEG Operant Conditioning in Epileptics" by M. B. Sterman and M. N. Shouse, *Electroencephalography and Clinical Neurophysiology,* 1980, *49,* 558–576. Copyright 1980 by *Electroencephalography and Clinical Neurophysiology.* Reprinted by permission.
[a]Primidone in this subject.

cipital bipolar recording sites. Accordingly, changes in spectral densities between baseline sleep recordings and recordings obtained after training periods associated with maximum seizure reduction were calculated for each patient. These data are displayed in terms of mean percentage of change for each frequency band in Fig. 3. During periods of maximal clinical improvement, EEG changes in sensorimotor recordings showed reduced power in the 0–3 Hz and 20–23 Hz bands and increased power in the 4–7 Hz, 8–11 Hz, and 12–15 Hz bands. Only the increased power at 8–11 Hz ($p < .05$) and 12–15 Hz ($p < .05$), however, were statistically significant. These findings are in agreement with the outcomes of the correlation studies carried out within each subgroup in suggesting that seizure reduction was accompanied by decreased power in low- and high-frequency bands and by increased power at intermediate EEG frequencies. Minimal and nonsignificant changes were found in corresponding data recorded from the parietal–occipital cortex.

Having documented a characteristic pattern of change in the sleep EEG that was associated with seizure reduction, it seemed appropriate to evaluate pretreatment differences in these same measures between this epileptic population and nonepileptic controls as well. To this end, an expanded epileptic group (10 patients) was recruited and compared to 10 age-and-sex-matched nonepileptic subjects as controls. This comparison involved a quantitative evaluation of EEG power-spectral distributions in these groups, using identical 10-minute samples drawn from slow-wave sleep at the beginning, middle, and end of the night. The details of this study are presented elsewhere (Sterman, 1981). For present purposes, it is important to note that the epileptic group differed significantly from the control group in a pattern essentially opposite to that characterizing the changes obtained after therapeutic EEG feedback training. Figure 4 shows the profile of baseline differences in sleep EEG power-spectral densities between epileptic and nonepileptic groups. It can be seen that the epileptic patients differed statistically as a group from controls by showing increased power at 0–3 Hz and 4–7 Hz, decreased power at 12–15 Hz, and a second trend toward increased power at 20–23 Hz. Once again, these differences were greater over the sensorimotor cortex than over the parietal–occipital cortex, suggesting that these effects may be primarily localized to the sensorimotor cortex. From these findings, we concluded that this population of epilep-

FIG. 3. Mean percentage of change from baseline levels of EEG power-spectral densities in six frequency bands during NREM sleep. Data from the sensorimotor and the parietal–occipital cortex were each combined for all eight subjects during the experimental condition associated with maximum therapeutic effect. A suppression of low (0–3 Hz) and high (20–23 Hz) frequencies and a facilitation of intermediate (8–15 Hz) frequencies over the sensorimotor cortex accompanied optimal therapeutic response. In contrast, no change occurred in parietal–occipital recordings. Data designated as C_3–T_3 actually derive from central cortical recordings described in text. (From "Quantitative Analysis of Training, Sleep EEG and Clinical Response to EEG Operant Conditioning in Epileptics" by M. B. Sterman and M. N. Shouse, *Electroencephalography and Clinical Neurophysiology,* 1980,*49,* 558–576. Copyright 1980 by *Electroencephalography and Clinical Neurophysiology*. Reprinted by permission.)

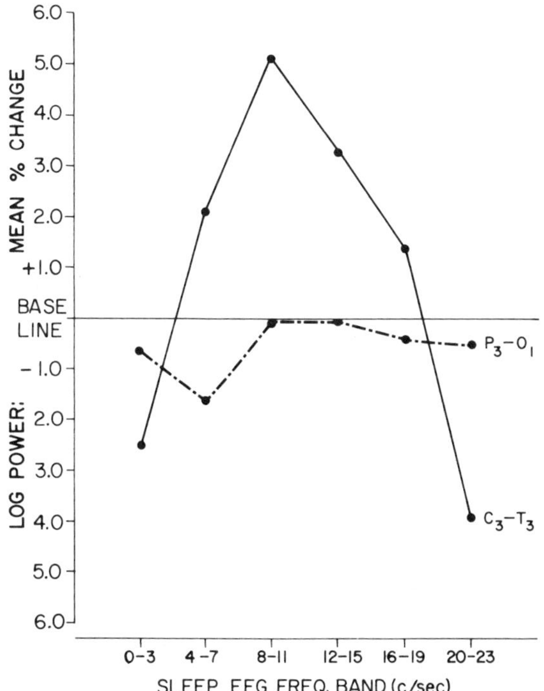

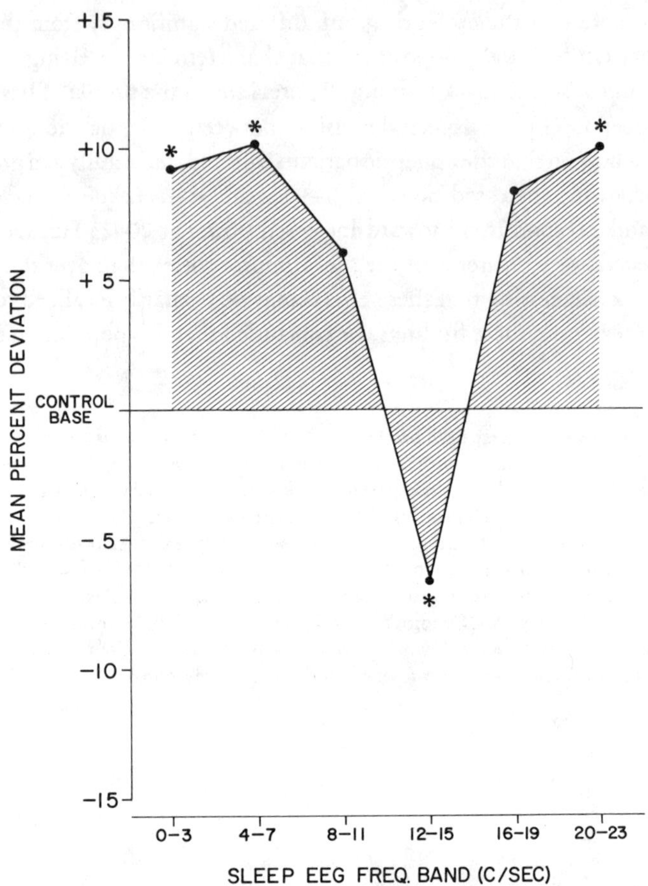

FIG. 4. Mean power-spectral density distribution of EEG activity recorded from the left rolandic (sensorimotor) cortex in 10 epileptic subjects during slow-wave sleep is compared here with identical data obtained from a group of matched nonepileptic subjects. Data are combined from three 10-minute samples obtained at the beginning, middle, and end of the night and are expressed as percentages of deviation of the epileptic group from the nonepileptic group. Asterisks indicate statistically significant deviation ($p < .05$) in the direction shown on ordinate.

tics may share certain deficits in comparison with normal subjects, despite their more obvious characteristic of heterogeneity.

FURTHER REFINEMENTS

On the basis of this interpretation, the most recent study of EEG biofeedback effects on poorly controlled epileptics in my laboratory has incorporated several new strategies. First, it was assumed that the therapeutic effects of EEG feedback training are mediated by a normalization of disordered neural substrates underlying the disturbance of EEG patterns that characterizes this group. Accordingly, reward strategy is directed to a reduction of abnormal low and high frequencies in the sensorimotor cortex and a facilitation of intermediate, rhythmic frequency bands. In brief, this objective was incorporated into a reward system resembling a hockey game, with progress of the puck (a moving amber lamp) toward the goal dependent on the criterion production of 10–15 Hz EEG activity. The goal is defended by three red lamps activated, respectively, by criterion 1–5 Hz activity, 20–25 Hz activity, and the occurrence of high-voltage transients (50 + μV). Reward, in terms of a cumulative digital score over a four-quarter "game" period, is thus dependent on facilitation of intermediate frequencies in the absence of low and high frequencies and of high-voltage transients.

Secondly, our therapeutic objectives were clarified; it was realized that the goal is not to "treat" these patients but to obtain a rapid assessment of the effects on seizure rates of specific experimental manipulations. Accordingly, this study employed three 30-minute training sessions per week over a sequence of 6-week periods. Three different experimental groups were established. All subjects were required to have at least a 3-year history of frequent complex–partial or generalized seizures with motor symptomatology, and to have failed to achieve control with anticonvulsant medications. All were also required to have had at least a 2-month accurate tabulation of seizures prior to participation. After baseline measures of sleep and anticonvulsant blood level, one group of patients merely continued tabulating seizures for a 6-week period, but with special logs and instructions that we provided. Afterwards, they were given 6 weeks of contingent training and 4 weeks of gradual withdrawal from training; they were then followed closely for an additional 6-week period. A second group began feedback training immediately but with noncontingent reward. For these patients, the signals activating the feedback device were derived from tape recordings of contingent training sessions from matched subjects in a third group. This group thus constituted a noncontingent, yoked control. After 6 weeks of this condition, they were shifted to contingent reward (without their knowledge) and completed the sequence outlined above for the first group. The third group, as noted, received contingent reward initially and continued through this same sequence. Anticonvulsant drug regimens were kept constant and monitored throughout the study.

Reported seizure incidence from 15 patients (5 in each group) observed during the first year of this study are presented in Table 4. These data are self-explanatory and indicate that (1) controlled tabulation tended to produce an increased detection of seizures; (2) noncontingent reinforcement resulted in no change in the rates of seizures from baseline rates; and (3) contingent reinforcement was followed by seizure reductions in 13 of the 15 patients, with an overall mean reduction of approximately 60%. Moreover, therapeutic effects tended to be sustained during withdrawal and follow-up periods. The least impressive overall results obtained

TABLE 4. Reported Seizure Rates per Week in Three Groups of Poorly Controlled Epileptic Patients

Subject		*Baseline*	*Control Tabulation*	*Noncontingent Training*	*Contingent Training*	*Training / Withdrawal*	*Follow-Up*
W. A.		7.0	13.3	—	4.7	1.7	2.0
M. S.		4.0	8.3	—	1.7	0	0
S. W.		2.7	4.3	—	4.3	4.7	2.7
W. T.		1.3	1.0	—	.67	1.7	2.0
J. E.		1.0	1.0	—	.30	0	.67
	$\bar{x}$	(3.2)	(5.6)		(2.3)	(1.6)	(1.5)
M. R.		21.4	—	38.0	19.2	—	—
J. M.		19.7	—	13.3	8.7	—	—
R. B.		6.0	—	3.7	2.0	1.7	3.0
D. R.		5.3	—	4.3	2.3	3.7	—
J. W.		2.7	—	2.7	3.0	1.0	2.3
	$\bar{x}$	(11.0)		(12.4)	(7.0)	(6.9)[a]	(7.4)[a]
P. R.		8.0	—	—	4.3	2.3	2.7
A. C.		3.3	—	—	.67	.67	1.0
S. A.		3.0	—	—	2.0	3.0	1.7
R. A.		1.7	—	—	0	0	0
W. G.		1.0	—	—	1.3	.67	1.7
	$\bar{x}$	(3.4)			(1.6)	(1.3)	(1.4)
	$\bar{x}$	5.87	5.6	12.4	2.40	3.27[a]	3.42[a]
Percentage of change			+75.0	+12.72	−59.12	−44.29	−41.74

Note. Data are based on mean rates during the last 3 weeks of indicated baseline and experimental conditions.
[a]Missing data replaced by values of preceding treatment.

were from the noncontingent group, and three subjects in this group were the only patients studied who failed to comply with instructions for reporting data (see the missing seizure rate data). It is possible that the frustration associated with noncontingent training may jeopardize potential gains once contingent reinforcement is provided. It should also be noted that three of the 15 patients (20%) demonstrated virtually total seizure control during and after contingent training. One of these individuals has been seizure-free for over a year, and the other two have sustained excellent control for 3 months or more. Interestingly, somewhat similar outcome percentages were reported for this type of patient population following temporal lobectomy (Engel & Crandall, 1980), with the exception of the fact that some patients were left in worse condition after surgery than before.

CONCLUSIONS

Considering all of the findings reviewed here, the picture with regard to the application of EEG biofeedback in the treatment of epilepsy is most encouraging. However, an effect without an explanation is unsatisfactory. In reality, this has never been a problem, since studies in my laboratory have been guided by a model for underlying mechanism that has gradually evolved from animal experiments. This model is summarized in Fig. 5 and has been elaborated in detail elsewhere (Sterman & Bowersox, in press). The anatomical organization of the afferent somatosensory pathway and some elements of the efferent motor system are presented in diagrammatic form. The electrophysiological responses indicated at various levels of this organization are based on documented findings and have been observed in relation to the patterns of rhythmic EEG activity over the sensorimotor cortex, shown at the top. Both the rhythm associated with attentive immobility in the waking state, which is focused over the somatosensory cortex (SI) and termed the SMR (right), and

FIG. 5. Simplified diagram of thalamic gate mechanism and associated sensorimotor afferent and efferent pathways to the somatosensory cortex (SI) and from the motor cortex (MCx). Shown also are representations of actual electrophysiological findings from studies in cats. Rhythmic 12–15 Hz activity in the form of SMR (top right) and sleep spindles (top left) is accompanied on the sensory side of reduced somatic afferent (SA) discharge, a shift to rhythmic activity in ventrobasal somatosensory transmission neurons (VPL, VL), and increased discharge in cells presumed to mediate recurrent inhibition (RI), leading to rhythmic thalamic and consequently cortical electrical patterns. Corresponding characteristics of motor response include a suppression of unit activity in the red nucleus (RN), attenuated monosynaptic reflex activity (not shown), and a reduction of both tonic and phasic motor activity. (From "Sensorimotor Functional Gate Mechanism" by M. B. Sterman and S. S. Bowersox, *Sleep*, in press. Reprinted by permission.)

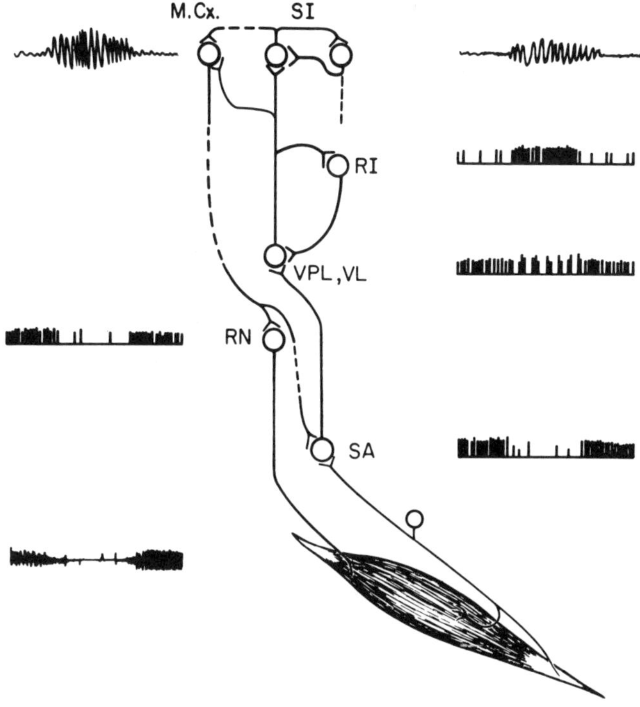

the characteristic sleep spindle (left), which is also associated with immobility but more localized to the motor cortex (MCx), are attributed to gated thalamocortical discharge resulting from a negative feedback loop involving recurrent inhibitory neurons (RI) acting on ventrobasal thalamic elements (VPL, VL). This organization was originally determined by the work of Adrian (1941) and Andersen and Sears (1964) and has been comprehensively reviewed in works by Andersen and Andersson (1968); Purpura (1974); Scheibel (in press); and Steriade, Wyzinski, and Apostol (1972). It is the established basis for the origin of rhythmic EEG patterns in sensorimotor cortex (Creutzfeldt, 1974).

The concept of a thalamic pacemaker related to distinctive EEG patterns allows for evaluation of an important sensorimotor regulatory function through reference to these EEG patterns. The primary element of our model considers this thalamocortical organization as a "gate" mechanism regulating both afferent and efferent aspects of sensorimotor activity. Work in my laboratory and by others has found that the closing of this gate (i.e., the presence of these rhythmic sensorimotor patterns) is associated with an attenuation of both somatosensory (Bowersox & Sterman, in press; Harper & Sterman, 1972; Hongo, Kubota, & Shimazu, 1963; Howe & Sterman, 1973; Shouse & Sterman, 1979) and related motor (Babb & Chase, 1974; Chase & Harper, 1971; Harper & Sterman, 1972; Wyrwicka & Sterman, 1968) discharge. Thus, the integrity of this gate mechanism appears to be essential for the filtering of incoming somatosensory signals and the control of corresponding motor responses. Damage to this gate (i.e., reduced or disordered rhythmic patterns) could presumably reflect aberrant input–output characteristics, one manifestation of which could be the development of seizures.

A more comprehensive discussion of the evidence in support of this model and its implications for seizure pathology is beyond the scope of this chapter. Suffice it to say that, in animal studies, manipulations that close this gate (i.e., release intrinsic rhythmic activity or prevent abnormal cortical activation) protect against seizures induced by drugs or by amygdala kindling (Bowersox & Sterman, in press; Shouse & Sterman, 1979; Sterman & Kovalesky, 1979; Sterman & Shouse, 1981). These findings are in complete agreement with our documentation of attenuated or disturbed sensorimotor rhythmic patterns in epileptics and provide a basis for understanding the therapeutic effects of the EEG feedback procedures reviewed here. If, indeed, thalamocortical gating circuits are disturbed in epilepsy, then regardless of the morphologic or neurochemical basis of this disturbance, any procedure that tends to restore regulated function can be therapeutic. It is already known that a variety of drugs that facilitate these sensorimotor rhythmic patterns can achieve this objective (Johnson, Hanson, & Bickford, 1976; Kaplan, 1977). Findings in the area of EEG biofeedback suggest that appropriate behavioral methods can be equally effective, at least in relation to seizures involving sensorimotor functions.

REFERENCES

Adrian, E. D. Afferent discharges to the cerebral cortex from peripheral sense organs. *Journal of Physiology, London*, 1941, *100*, 159–191.

Andersen, P., & Andersson, S. A. *Physiological basis of the alpha rhythm*. New York: Appleton-Century-Crofts, 1968.

Andersen, P., & Sears, T. A. The role of inhibition in the phasing of spontaneous thalamocortical discharge. *Journal of Physiology, London*, 1964, *173*, 459–480.

Babb, M. I., & Chase, M. H. Masseteric and digastric reflex activity during conditioned sensorimotor rhythm. *Electroencephalography and Clinical Neurophysiology*, 1974, *36*, 357–365.

Bowersox, S. S., & Sterman, M. B. Changes in sensorimotor sleep spindle activity and seizure susceptibility following somatosensory deafferentation. *Experimental Neurology*, in press.

Chase, M. H., & Harper, R. M. Somatomotor and visceromotor correlates of operantly conditioned 12–14 c/sec sensorimotor cortical activity. *Electroencephalography and Clinical Neurophysiology*, 1971, *31*, 85–92.

Cott, A., Pavloski, R. P., & Black, A. H. Reducing epileptic seizures through operant conditioning of central nervous system activity: Procedural variables. *Science*, 1979, *203*, 73–75.

Creutzfeldt, O. D. The neuronal generation of the EEG. In A. Remond (Ed.), *Handbook of electroencephalography and clinical neurophysiology* (Part C, Vol. 2, Sec. 4). Amsterdam: Elsevier North Holland, 1974.

Ellertsen, B., & Kløve, H. Clinical application of biofeedback training in epilepsy. *Scandinavian Journal of Behavior Therapy*, 1976, *5*, 133–144.

Engel, J. P., & Crandall, P. Personal communication, 1980.

Finley, W. W. Effects of sham feedback following successful SMR training in an epileptic: Follow-up study. *Biofeedback and Self-Regulation*, 1976, *1*, 227–236.

Finley, W. W., Smith, H. A., & Etherton, M. D. Reduction of seizures and normalization of the EEG in a severe epileptic following sensorimotor biofeedback training: Preliminary study. *Biological Psychology*, 1975, *2*, 189–203.

Harper, R. M., & Sterman, M. B. Subcortical unit activity during a conditioned 12–14 Hz sensorimotor EEG rhythm in the cat. *Federation Proceedings*, 1972, *31*, 404.

Hongo, T. K., Kubota, K., & Shimazu, H. EEG spindle and depression of gamma motor activity. *Journal of Neurophysiology*, 1963, *26*, 568–580.

Howe, R. C., & Sterman, M. B. Cortical–subcortical EEG correlates of suppressed motor behavior during sleep and waking in the cat. *Electroencephalography and Clinical Neurophysiology*, 1972, *32*, 681–695.

Howe, R. C., & Sterman, M. B. Somatosensory system evoked potentials during waking behavior and sleep in the cat. *Electroencephalography and Clinical Neurophysiology*, 1973, *34*, 605–618.

Johnson, L. C., Hanson, K., & Bickford, R. G. Effect of Flurazepam on sleep spindles and K-complexes. *Electroencephalography and Clinical Neurophysiology*, 1976, *40*, 67–77.

Kaplan, B. J. Biofeedback in epileptics: Equivocal relationship of reinforced EEG frequency to seizure reduction. *Epilepsia*, 1975, *16*, 477–485.

Kaplan, B. J. Phenobarbital and phenytoin effects on somatosensory evoked potentials and spontaneous EEG in normal cat brain. *Epilepsia*, 1977, *18(3)*, 397–403.

Kuhlman, W. N. EEG feedback training of epileptic patients: Clinical and electroencephalographic analysis. *Electroencephalography and Clinical Neurophysiology*, 1978, *45*, 699–710.

Kuhlman, W. N. Personal communication, 1980.

Lubar, J. F., & Bahler, W. W. Behavioral management of epileptic seizures following biofeedback training of the sensorimotor rhythm. *Biofeedback and Self-Regulation*, 1976, *1*, 77–104.

Purpura, D. P. Intracellular studies of thalamic synaptic mechanisms in evoked synchronization and desynchronization of electrocortical activity. In O. Petre-Quadens & J. D. Schlag (Eds.), *Basic sleep mechanisms.* New York: Academic Press, 1974.

Quy, R. J., Hutt, S. J., & Forrest, S. Sensorimotor rhythm feedback training and epilepsy: Some methodological and conceptual issues. *Biological Psychology,* 1979, *9,* 129–149.

Rougeul, A., Letalle, A., & Corvisier, J. Activité rythmique du cortex somesthésique primaire en relation avec l'immobilité chez le chat libre éveille. *Electroencephalography and Clinical Neurophysiology,* 1972, *33,* 23–39.

Scheibel, A. B. The brain stem reticular core and sensory function. In I. Darian-Smith (Ed.), *Handbook of physiology.* Washington, D.C.: American Physiological Association, in press.

Seifert, A. R., & Lubar, J. F. Reduction of epileptic seizures through EEG biofeedback training. *Biological Psychology,* 1975, *3,* 81–109.

Shouse, M. N., & Sterman, M. B. Changes in seizure susceptibility, sleep time, and sleep spindles following thalamic and cerebellar lesions. *Electroencephalography and Clinical Neurophysiology,* 1979, *46,* 1–12.

Steriade, M., Wyzinski, P., & Apostol, V. Corticofugal projections governing rhythmic thalamic activity. In T. L. Frigyesi, E. Rinvik, & M. D. Yahr (Eds.), *Corticothalamic projections and sensorimotor activities.* New York: Raven Press, 1972.

Sterman, M. B. Power-spectral analysis of EEG characteristics during sleep in epileptics. *Epilepsia,* 1981, *22,* 95–106.

Sterman, M. B., & Bowersox, S. S. Sensorimotor EEG rhythmic activity: A functional gate mechanism. *Sleep,* in press.

Sterman, M. B., & Friar, L. R. Suppression of seizures in an epileptic following sensorimotor EEG feedback training. *Electroencephalography and Clinical Neurophysiology,* 1972, *33,* 89–95.

Sterman, M. B., & Kovalesky, R. A. Anticonvulsant effects of restraint and pyridoxine on hydrazine seizures in the monkey. *Experimental Neurology,* 1979, *65,* 78–86.

Sterman, M. B., & Lantz, D. Effects of sensorimotor EEG normalization feedback training on seizure rate in poorly controlled epileptics. *Epilepsia,* 1981, *22,* 246. (Abstract)

Sterman, M. B., & Macdonald, L. R. Effects of central cortical EEG feedback training on incidence of poorly controlled seizures. *Epilepsia,* 1978, *19,* 207–222.

Sterman, M. B., Macdonald, L. R., & Stone, R. K. Biofeedback training of the sensorimotor EEG rhythm in man: Effects on epilepsy. *Epilepsia,* 1974, *15,* 395–416.

Sterman, M. B., & Shouse, M. N. Quantitative analysis of training, sleep EEG and clinical response to EEG operant conditioning in epileptics. *Electroencephalography and Clinical Neurophysiology,* 1980, *49,* 558–576.

Sterman, M. B., & Shouse, M. N. Kindling and sleep: A new direction in the search for mechanism. In J. Wada (Ed.), *Kindling two.* New York: Raven Press, 1981.

Wyler, A. R., Lockard, J. S., Ward, A. A., & Finch, C. A. Conditioned EEG desynchronization and seizure occurrence in patients. *Electroencephalography and Clinical Neurophysiology,* 1976, *41,* 501–512.

Wyler, A. R., Robbins, C. A., & Dodrill, C. B. EEG operant conditioning for control of epilepsy. *Epilepsia,* 1979, *20,* 279–286.

Wyrwicka, W., & Sterman, M. B. Instrumental conditioning of sensorimotor cortex EEG spindles in the waking cat. *Physiology and Behavior,* 1968, *3,* 703–707.

ROUND-TABLE DISCUSSION OF LUBAR AND STERMAN

Audience Question to Barry Sterman: Barry, you recorded from the sensorimotor cortex, regardless of the locus of the seizures?

Barry Sterman: Yes, because of our model of epilepsy. Somatosensory and cutaneous and proprioceptive afferents go through the three-neuron arch of the somatosensory system, with a gate mechanism established at the thalamic level. It is a well-established fact that the activity coming from the lateral thalamus, ventrobasal thalamus, and the sensorimotor cortex is gated by censor or filter mechanisms that function as a negative feedback loop. These data show that whenever you see the sensorimotor rhythm or a sleep spindle, you're seeing that gate closed. That is the way we think about it, as an open–close gate. Now the epileptic, we think, has a broken gate. It's jammed partially open. How can this gate be manipulated? By training them to close it, which we think we're doing with the biofeedback training. That's one way that we can try to correct the broken gate, as it were, in the epileptic. However, there are other things. You can lesion the afferent pathways, because this is an intrinsic mechanism; and if you withdraw the coded discharge of the somatosensory system, it will close by itself. So, in our animal research, we've made lesions in dentate nucleus; we've made medial–miscus lesions; we've made dorsal column lesions. All of them increase this activity, and all of them raise threshold procedures. Another thing we've done with monkeys is simply restrain them, using leather straps to hold their wrists and arms so that they're immobile. They're already in a restraint chair, and that is just as therapeutic as perodoxine for hydrozine seizures. You can get exactly the same effects with restraint, which, indeed, does close that gate. So, theoretically, another therapy might be to have a little closet; and when epileptics have their aura, they jump in it and close the door. That, of course, is not going to work. If you can train them to do that through meditation or something, it should be effective; and I think it would be perfectly reasonable to demonstrate why it's effective.

Joel Lubar: I just wanted to say something about mechanism. Barry, you still believe pretty strongly that the sensorimotor rhythm is related to sleep spindle, that they are pretty much the same mechanism, right? One thing has always bothered me with that. Why is it that you see Stage 2 sleep spindles all over the brain, but you only see SMR at a very restricted area of the motor cortex and you never pick it up anywhere else? What happens during waking to shut off the rest of the mechanism?

Barry Sterman: Traditionally, the findings in electroencephalography have been that this sigma rhythm, the sleep spindle, tends to be focused to sensorimotor cortex. Now that doesn't mean that you can't pick it up with other leads, but it is generally accepted that it's generated in the central motor cortex.

Joel Lubar: But when you do multiple recordings, you see it all over the place.

Barry Sterman: I think that's a function of how you record it. It may be that every system that is organized in this manner has the potential for generating that rhythmic frequency—the auditory system and the visual system, as well as the somatosensory system. But the dominant focus of sleep spindles is central cortex.

John Lacey: You use the word "broken" gate. Do the hinges need oiling or is the gate destroyed? That's an important question. Are we dealing with a substitute mechanism or some mechanism that reinstates the functionality of this gate in the system?

Barry Sterman: Well, we have some ideas about what's going on. An interesting thing happens during quiet sleep and in an immobile but not-too-aroused waking animal. When this gate closes, you see 12–15 or 8–11 Hz activity. When that animal or person enters rapid-eye-movement [REM] sleep, which is a condition of disinhibited cortical neuronal activity, there is a hyperexcitable cortex. Unit studies show this very clearly. The thalamic mechanism changes its frequency to a theta kind of pattern, and it's really very interesting. What you see over and over again in these epileptic patients is this 4–7–8 Hz activity. Sometimes you talk to them and you look at their EEG, and you can't believe they're responding, because their brain activity is sine-wave 7 Hz. I used to think it was due to drugs, but it's not. If you put hydrazine on normal cortex like a somatosensory cortex, it becomes hyperexcitable. Normal rhythmic activity is changed to paroxysmal discharge and increased theta activity. We think that two things might be happening in epilepsy. You have a population of hyperexcitable cortical neurons, which, in turn, because of the hyperexcitability, are changing the characteristics of this gate and allowing additional aberrant discharge to pass through this protective mechanism to further kindle those cortical neurons [Sterman & Shouse, 1980].

John Lacey: Is the existence of the gate inferred, or did you see it with microelectrodes?

Barry Sterman: You know how neurophysiologists are. A whole generation of neurophysiologists have fought over what the actual interneuron is, but that it exists nobody doubts.

John Lacey: Would you know Winston's work with dentate gyrus, where the gate is demonstratively shown?

Barry Sterman: Well, Scheibel's most recent study [in press], and I agree with it, shows that the nucleus reticularus of the thalamus seems to receive colaterals from a ventral basal projection to the somatosensory cortex that mediate this gate mechanism, but Purpura [1974] and others have been fighting over this for years. Concerning the mechanism involved in epilepsy, there is another interesting fact. When you stimulate the amygdala every day, you kindle seizures; that's called the "kindle seizure model." Everyone thinks that's a limbic function. All you've got to do is make a lesion that blocks that information from getting through this gate, and you can prevent kindling.

Bernard Tursky: Have there been any attempts to drive these frequencies, both in animal and in human studies?

Barry Sterman: The only study I know that's done that is Peter Towler's laboratory at Baylor. Peter has been very interested in cerebellar stimulation. There was this whole period where cerebellar stimulators were being planned. He showed that in Rhesus monkeys, the kind of stimulation that was effective in walking seizures was driving 15-Hz rhythmic activity in central motor cortex.

John Furedy: Why isn't there interest in the concept of driving, rather than sort of sitting back and waiting for the appearance of the rhythm?

Barry Sterman: It could be that dorsal column stimulators used for pain are achieving the same thing, because their gate mechanisms could have an effect on perception of pain, too. That's another area that we would like to look at.

John Furedy: It's significant that there hasn't been as much interest in the concept of driving, which may be more efficacious—or, at least, it might start the process off which you may later want to condition.

Barry Sterman: Well, it's very complicated in that there are really two spindle mechanisms, two rhythmic mechanisms. One is a specific sensory system mechanism that is produced when you create what we call the augmenting-response type driving in animal studies; the other is a nonspecifically mediated mechanism, which is the recruiting response. They use different pathways, and it would be an interesting thing to do.

John Lacey: But when you drive, you're producing harmonics and subharmonics in ways that are not natural.

Barry Sterman: It might be better to stimulate caudate, which will trigger sleep spindles.

Bernard Tursky: Are there any selection criteria for patients which may maximize results?

Barry Sterman: In our new study, we do select. Before, we took anybody that could walk in the door. Now we have age criteria. We don't want really young or really old patients with degenerative-type disorders. We require, because of our model, that they have a documented deficit in sleep spindles before they can be accepted into our study. So we get our baseline sleep recordings before we make our final decision. If that patient doesn't have the abnormality that we functionally believe we're treating, since it's based on our animal work in the mechanism approach, we won't run him.

Edward Blanchard: Once you get this change in brain activity, does it stay, or do you have to do booster sessions?

Barry Sterman: We have a problem in this kind of research. It's not a drug. We can't administer it simply. It's a big investment of time and money to keep track of these patients. So, in essence, we bring a patient in, we do our thing, and we send him off into the sunset. Then a neurologist says, "Well his seizures came back," and I say, "What would happen if you took the drugs away?" For certain patients, when we get them completely under control, we have them come in once a month for booster sessions. That seems to hold, but that whole area needs exploration.

Edward Blanchard: How about the home trackers in your earlier study?

Barry Sterman: Right now they're too expensive to give out. But they worked in the study, so they should work in the field.

Joel Lubar: We're trying to do a maintenance program, also, where they come in as infrequently as every 2 months. I have one fellow who's down 95% of the seizures. This is 4 years after he started and he comes in just periodically. We're also at the point now where we're just about getting vocational rehabilitation to send patients to us and pay for their treatments, with long-term follow-up.

Neal Miller: If you were mass-producing these advanced electronic devices, what's your estimate of what one of these home devices would cost?

Barry Sterman: Oh, I think, it could be brought down into the couple-of-hundred-dollars range.

Martin Orne: Why not have the person come to the laboratory or to an office to use that gadget, because essentially it can be taught; and you can simply schedule the gadget with a physical therapist? The cost could be minimal.

Joel Lubar: We're going to set one of those up in the child rehabilitation center in our area. That's exactly what they're going to be doing on an outpatient basis.

Gary Schwartz: Do you think any of this can be done nonelectronically? There has been work on "behavioral approaches" to seizure control without utilizing direct recording of EEG activity. You've shown very elegant specificity effects and are really getting at the mechanism that you're interested in. It's beautiful. One still wants to ask the question whether there are ways of producing the same effects given the same mechanisms without direct feedback of EEG.

Martin Orne: As in the animal studies mentioned, restraint results in seizure reduction. One ought to be able to condition the nonmovement response without restraints.

Barry Sterman: Well, that's why a few other studies, such as Lubar's [Chapter 11], and Wyler's and others [Wyler, Robbins, & Dodrill, 1979] have shown that just suppression of movement in epileptic patients has no effect; so while quiescence, suppression of movement, is necessary, it is not sufficient.

Martin Orne: But it is sufficient in the monkey if he can't move?

Barry Sterman: No, but we've recorded his EEG; and when he gets into that state and holds it, he produces this "closed gate" state.

Martin Orne: Why can't a human learn or be instructed to learn that kind of a response which causes an EEG response?

Barry Sterman: Well, because the quiescence isn't sufficient.

Gary Schwartz: Is the EMG flaccid in the primate or is it actually being held and stabilized?

Barry Sterman: EMG goes down but not to 0. The limbs become somewhat limp but not completely limp.

Martin Orne: Is that related to what is called animal hypnosis?

Barry Sterman: Some people think so.

Gary Schwartz: One of the possibilities is that this biofeedback orientation will, in the future, demonstrate phenomena and provide ways of getting at mechanisms which will then allow us to learn what the best strategies are for producing those desired effects without going through this initial process. At that point, biofeedback will be seen more clearly as a clinical research tool and may not necessarily be required in order to produce clinically desirable outcomes. Of course, for some individuals under some conditions, we will need it. Certainly, diagnostically, you will be able to assess whether or not a given behavioral intervention does reinstate this individual. You might want to be able to record the EEG and see whether or not the restraint is leading to the effect. But once you've got that, you have instituted a comprehensive biobehavioral-feedback process and are then able to get rid of the equipment.

Barry Sterman: Perhaps.

REFERENCES

Purpura, D. P. Intracellular studies of thalamic synaptic mechanisms in evoked synchronization and desynchronization of electrocortical activity. In O. Petre-Quadens & J. D. Schlag (Eds.), *Basic sleep mechanisms.* New York: Academic Press, 1974.

Scheibel, A. B. The brain stem reticular core and sensory function. In I. Darian-Smith (Ed.), *Handbook of physiology.* Washington, D.C.: American Physiological Association, in press.

Sterman, M. B., & Shouse, M. M. Kindling and and sleep: A new direction in the search for mechanisms. In J. Wada (Ed.), *Kindling 1980.* Raven Press: New York, 1980.

Wyler, A. R., Robbins, C. A., & Dodrill, C. B. EEG operant conditioning for control of epilepsy. *Epilepsia,* 1979, *20,* 279–286.

V

STRESS AND ANXIETY

SESSION I

FORMAL PRESENTATIONS

Interest in using biofeedback techniques to induce anxiety- or stress-free states has been one of the dominant themes within the biofeedback literature. The breadth of the stress and anxiety constructs, and the accompanying ubiquity of disorders in which these factors have been implicated as having etiological significance, may in large part account for the widespread clinical use of biofeedback techniques. This area of inquiry brings into sharp focus several methodological issues: problems of classification, measurement, use of subjective criteria and verbal report, and placebo effects.

Most of the clinical work currently being carried out with tension headache assumes that the experienced headache pain is a consequence of tension in the frontalis muscles and that biofeedback is effective because it serves to relax that muscle group. Cox and Hobbs introduce their review of the literature on the biofeedback treatment of tension headache with a description of the interrelated muscle groups of the head and neck. Later in their chapter, they analyze the mechanism involved in the etiology and therapy of tension headache.

Contrary to the assumptions of many clinicians, biofeedback-mediated acquisition of direct organ control may not be the mechanism of symptom relief. Cox and Hobbs' analysis suggests, rather, that relief from tension headache subsequent to biofeedback treatment is due to a greater awareness of subtle physiological responses that eventuate in cognitive reappraisal or a change in life style. It may be worth noting that this statement regarding mechanisms of biofeedback effects can readily be generalized to a variety of psychophysiological responses and to disorders other than tension headache. This model assigns to awareness and cognitive processes a central position in the therapeutic process, which is characteristic of the broad interpretation of "biofeedback" effects. Direct organ control may accompany increased bodily awareness but is not the primary objective of treatment, as it is in the narrower definition of "biofeedback." Ultimately, in this paradigm, a reduction in headache is the consequence of a change in overt behavior or in cognitive interpretations of the environment.

The complexity of the muscles of the head and neck, the ambiguity surrounding the degree and focus of their role in muscle tension headache, and the potential involvement of complex cognitive processes in determining "tension headaches," in our view, are persuasive reasons for discontinuation of studies testing the efficacy of narrowly defined biofeedback on tension headache and for directing efforts toward more analytic studies.

In their chapter, Adams, Brantley, and Thompson discuss unsolved methodological issues that they feel currently frustrate all efforts to determine treatment efficacy. Primary among these are inadequate classification criteria and inadequate specification of and testing for what is actually learned during biofeedback treatment.

ROUND-TABLE DISCUSSION

In this round-table discussion, there is little support for the conclusion reached by Cox and Hobbs that EMG biofeedback is a specific, efficacious treatment for tension headache. Particularly damaging to this thesis is the failure to find statistically significant relationships between treatment-induced changes in frontal EMG responses and reported changes in headache. However, the findings that, subsequent to biofeedback training, "tension headache" patients report reductions in headache remain. Until there are further refinements in the differential diagnosis of tension headaches and a more precise understanding of the physiology of tension headache, it will remain difficult to differentiate the specific clinical effects of any behavioral approach to treatment.

The round-table discussion continues the examination of the methodological issues of classification and measurement of headache initiated by Adams, Brantley, and Thompson. Several suggestions for improving differential diagnosis of headache are discussed. Among them are methods for obtaining greater precision in the reporting of pain; the multidimensional approach to evaluation of headache, including physiological, performance, and self-report criteria; and a more precise determination of the physiology of the headache process.

SESSION II

FORMAL PRESENTATION

One of the reference studies that initially fostered enormous interest in the clinical use of biofeedback methods was that of Kamiya (1969), which suggested that accompanying enhancement of EEG alpha waves was an experiential state marked by the absence of anxiety. Although subsequent studies (Orne & Wilson, 1977; Plotkin, 1977) have not borne out these initial findings regarding the clinical utility of alpha biofeedback, interest in the use of biofeedback to reduce anxiety persists.

It is widely acknowledged that EMG is the most frequently used biofeedback technique for the treatment of anxiety. Gatchel begins his chapter by briefly tracing the developments that led to interest in this use of EMG biofeedback. He notes a number of methodological issues (i.e., state vs. trait anxiety, individual differences, and the role of placebo factors) that often have not been adequately considered in evaluative research in this area. Gatchel's review of the clinical studies of effectiveness of EMG on anxiety reduction includes both clinical case studies and control-group studies. Based upon his review, Gatchel finds that "[alternative clinical approaches], such as progressive relaxation training, are at least equally effective" (Chapter 15, pp. 392–393). Collectively, however, these methods, when used in isolation, have limited clinical effectiveness; and Gatchel suggests that a more broad-based, multimodal psychotherapy that deals with the complex interactions between individuals and the environment is a more reasonable approach to anxiety.

ROUND-TABLE DISCUSSION

The treatment of a disorder and the ability to evaluate the effectiveness of that treatment rely heavily on the degree of accuracy in specifying and measuring the entity in question. Although convention has rendered the term "anxiety" acceptable, consensus upon appropriate techniques of measurement remains elusive. It is appropriate, then, that the round-table discussion devotes considerable time to the problem of defining "anxiety." Several alternative approaches to the definition and measurement of anxiety are discussed. The measurement of anxiety has been frustrated by a failure to find hypothesized correlations between alternative measures. Physiological, performance, and verbal-report measures are not significantly correlated, either within or between response domains. Alternative suggestions for improved definitions are offered. Briefly summarized, these suggestions vary from recommendations for selecting a single-response dimension as a defining criterion to consideration of patterns of physiological, behavioral, and emotional experience in response to varied stimuli.

When the discussion turns to an examination of the data of comparative treatment studies, a number of other methodological issues are raised. Are the number of learning trials traditionally used in biofeedback-versus-meditation comparisons sufficient to allow the full potential of biofeedback to be realized, or is there a natural competition between trying to lower autonomic responses and attending to the external biofeedback signal? To what degree can findings in normal populations be generalized to clinical populations? Are there individual differences in physiology or in psychological variables relating to aptitude for attentional deployment that may predict differential treatment response? Since comparative treatment studies indicate equal anxiety reduction for a number of techniques, do they all have their effect via a common, nonspecific mechanism, or "placebo"? And, therefore, can treatment be maximized by developing an understanding of these mechanisms?

It has been established that direct exposure to the feared object is an effective treatment for the specific fears of phobia. Similarly, treatment of anxiety ought to consider the nature of individuals' transactions with their particular environments. Although EMG biofeedback treatment for anxiety may effect symptom reduction, it does not operate by the proposed mechanism, nor is it more potent than alternative, simpler techniques.

REFERENCES

Kamiya, J. Operant control of the EEG alpha rhythm and some of its reported effects on consciousness. In C. T. Tart (Ed.), *Altered states of consciousness: A book of readings.* New York: Wiley, 1969.

Orne, M., & Wilson, S. Alpha, biofeedback and arousal/activation. In J. Beatty & H. Legewie (Eds.), *Biofeedback and behavior.* New York: Plenum, 1977.

Plotkin, W. B. Social psychology of experiential states. In J. Beatty & H. Legewie (Eds.), *Biofeedback and behavior.* New York: Plenum, 1977.

13 BIOFEEDBACK AS A TREATMENT FOR TENSION HEADACHES

DANIEL J. COX AND WILLIAM HOBBS

HISTORY AND OVERVIEW

Headache is the most common bodily complaint (Adams, 1977; Philips, 1977) in contemporary texts, and the variety called "tension headache" makes up the largest proportion in today's clinical population. Yet Osler's *The Principles and Practice of Medicine* (1892/1978), while discussing migraine in some detail, does not even mention the tension variety. Chronic head pain is only discussed as a manifestation of various disorders, such as cerebral tumors and metabolic disturbances. Indeed, in this 1892 volume, chronic pain as a problem in itself is not considered. Less than a century later, there are chapters and entire textbooks on the subject of chronic pain. Entire clinics and careers are devoted to the problem, and this development has surely affected the way in which people perceive headache.

The increase in the complaint of chronic pain among the population over these 80 years may be due to the development of treatment-oriented physicians, the delivery of health care to nearly all of the population, and the concept that chronic disabling illness is a compensable condition, along with the more time-honored concept of the role of sickness as a legitimation of unfulfilled responsibilities. As is true of any other behavior, pain can be considered as an operant; if followed by reinforcers, it can be expected to increase in frequency. To look at it on another level, the concept of symptoms as tactics in human relationships helps to explain pain behaviors within the family system (Spradlin & Porterfield, 1979).

Clinicians may think that the term "tension" used to describe these headaches has been borrowed from the physical sciences to describe the psychophysiological

Daniel J. Cox and William Hobbs. Behavioral Medicine Center and Department of Behavioral Medicine and Psychiatry, University of Virginia Medical Center, Charlottesville, Virginia.

process that is the subject of this paper, but the first use of the term in English was as "the condition, in any part of the body, of being stretched or strained; a sensation indicating or suggesting this; a feeling of tightness" (*The Compact Edition of the Oxford English Dictionary*, 1971).

DESCRIPTION

Since the complaint of the patient with tension headache falls within the broad category of "pain" or "discomfort," and must remain intrinsically subjective, how can clinicians use patient report to provide valid diagnostic criteria for this dysfunction? It is chronic head pain or discomfort that brings the patient to the clinician, and the differential diagnosis of chronic pain syndromes is difficult, regardless of the location of the pain.

Apart from structural considerations, other hypothesized etiologies for chronic pain include the psychoanalytic concept that the pain is a manifestation of a defense mechanism called "conversion" (Abse, 1974); such a pain serves to symbolize in veiled fashion an underlying, unconscious conflict, as well as to reduce the anxiety attendant upon the conflict's incomplete repression. This same process may serve to elaborate a pain already present from some structural disorder, a process called "conversion elaboration." The operant and interpersonal consequences of this process may lead to reinforcement of the pain behavior, and if reinforced the pain may continue, even if the underlying structural disorder and/or the underlying conflict are removed. The anxiety reduction described above is often called "primary gain"; its operant and interpersonal consequences are called "secondary gain."

The ideas of conversion and primary gain are well established, but they have proved difficult to apply to the problem of chronic pain (Fordyce & Brockway, 1979). They also lead to treatment modalities, such as insight-oriented psychotherapy, that have not been shown to be effective for chronic pain patients. It is also important to distinguish here between the hysterical personality and conversion syndromes. Not all people who meet the *Diagnostic and Statistical Manual of Mental Disorders* (DSM-III) (American Psychiatric Association, 1980) criteria for "hysterical personality" are found to exhibit conversion phenomena, even of the more classic variety, such as paralysis or anesthesia. Many people with this personality type go through their entire lives without evidence of conversion. Also, an hysterical type of personality organization is not necessary in order for conversion syndromes to appear.

Most chronic pain is axial in location, rather than appendicular, and prominent sites for its residence include the abdomen, the chest, and the lower back, as well as the chronic head pain with which this chapter is concerned. A significant number of tension headache sufferers describe their pain as chronic and unremitting in nature, rather than as the purely episodic pain characteristic of migraine headache as described earlier in this chapter. Clinicians may find similarities among people suffering from the varieties of chronic unremitting pain, whether it be from head, back, chest, or abdomen, that would not characterize the suffering of migraine patients. That tension headache sufferers do experience intermittent exacerbations of their pain, often using descriptive terms reminiscent of migrainous attacks, is an indication of the similarities that may exist between the mechanisms of these two types of headache.

Tension headache, while demonstrating considerable clinical heterogeneity, is generally described as being continuous or nonthrobbing in nature and having a dull or aching quality, as well as creating sensations of pressure or tightness. It is bilateral and occipitofrontal, often more specifically along the bony nuchal ridge where lies the insertion of the mass of suboccipital muscles whose function is to hold the head in its upright position (Adams, 1977). Pain may extend farther down the back of the neck to the trapezius muscle on either side. From this continuous base, the pain may spread to involve the frontal regions and the vertex of the cranium during periods of exacerbation. It is these latter periods of exacerbation that may be identified by the patient as occurring during periods of increased stress. Some patients with tension headache report a unilateral, throbbing headache more characteristic of migraine during these periods of exacerbation. Others describe isolated frontal pain unrelated to any suboccipital discomfort.

The first organized attempt to define and describe varieties of headache was the report of the Ad Hoc Committee on Classification of Headache (1962), a group of physicians appointed by the American Medical Association. Among 16 headache varieties, tension headache was described as follows:

> Ache or sensation of tightness, pressure, or constriction widely varied in intensity, frequency, and duration, sometimes long-lasting, and commonly suboccipital. It is associated with sustained contraction of skeletal muscles in the absence of permanent structural change, usually as part of the individual's reaction during life stress. (p. 718)

This kind of definition, understood in its historical context, is typical of definitions of medical illness by physicians at that time. A disorder was described by using a "classic" example or case, but the conceptual limits or boundaries of disorders were not well defined. Clinical medicine is slowly moving toward more operational definitions of the disorders it treats, as exemplified by criteria for the diagnosis of various connective tissue disorders such as systemic lupus erythematosis, and by the operational criteria for psychiatric disorders in the DSM-III (American Psychiatric Association, 1980). This same approach, however, has not yet been applied by physicians to headache. The lack of precision of the Ad Hoc Committee's description, and its underlying assumptions, have been described by Philips (1978).

Muscle relaxants, such as the minor tranquilizers diazepam (Valium) and chlordiazepoxide (Librium), are generally considered only marginally effective in the long-term treatment of tension headache. However, this may be largely related to other actions of these drugs. First, most if not all skeletal muscle relaxants also exert tranquilizing effects on behavior, including relative blockade of EEG arousal from brain-stem stimulation and reduced suppressive effects of punishments (Goodman & Gilman, 1975), probably through actions at the level of limbic system structures. All of these medications create both tolerance and withdrawal symptoms in persons taking them, and it is this addictive potential that contributes to their marginal effectiveness in long-term treatment of tension headache. Withdrawal from these agents, after dosages of as little as 40 mg per day and durations of as little as a few months, can be expressed in headache, even in previously headache-free individuals. Anecdotal clinical reports do indicate that, in subjects with tension headache, a dose of these medications effectively reduces both pain and anxiety for a period of several hours; whether this effectiveness lies in the muscle-relaxing or tranquilizing effects is unclear, however.

FUNCTIONAL ANATOMY

On the basis of observations made during head surgery with patients remaining awake, the following structures have been found to be sensitive to mechanical stimulation (Adams, 1977):

1. Skin; subcutaneous tissue, muscles, and arteries; and periosteum of skull.
2. Delicate structures of eye, ear, and nasal cavities.
3. Intracranial venous sinuses and their tributary veins.
4. Parts of the dura at the base of the brain and the arteries within the dura and piarachnoid.
5. The trigeminal, glossopharyngeal, vagus, and first three cervical nerves.

The bony skull, most of the meninges, and the brain tissue itself lack sensitivity, but mechanical stimulation of the above-listed structures was felt almost entirely as pain (Adams, 1977).

Mechanisms of cranial pain include the following:

1. Distension, traction, and dilatation of the intracranial or extracranial arteries.
2. Traction or displacement of large intracranial veins or the dural envelope in which they lie.
3. Compression, traction, or inflammation of sensory cranial and spinal nerves.
4. Voluntary and involuntary spasm and possible interstitial inflammation and trauma of cranial and cervical musculature.
5. Raised intracranial pressure.

Woodburne's *Essentials of Human Anatomy* (1965) considers that both the frontalis and occipitalis are really two bellies of a single muscle, the epicranius, and that these two bellies directly connect with one another by means of the galea aponeurotica—a strong membranous sheet of connective tissue underlying the scalp, the fibers of which are oriented longitudinally with respect to the head rather than transversely. The major resting stresses on this sheet are also longitudinal rather than transverse. While the occipital belly of this muscle attaches along the nuchal crest of the occipital bone, no similar bony attachment exists for the frontalis belly. It attaches instead to the skin of the eyebrows and the root of the nose, where its fibers intermingle with muscles surrounding the eyes. The action of the frontalis portion of the epicranius is to raise the eyebrows, a behavior of perhaps more communicational than mechanical or supportive significance.

The muscles of the suboccipital area, which include the trapezius and a large group of short, thick muscles often referred to as the deep cervical muscles, comprise a volume of huge proportions in comparison with that of the frontalis belly. These muscles hold and brace the head in an upright position, while also providing some rotational movement. One or more of these deep cervical muscles may, by chronically increased tension on its insertion site, lead to chronic neck and suboccipital pain, but this still contributes only a small amount to the total amount of EMG activity recorded from surface electrodes overlying this region. The issues of vasomotor tone and buildup of metabolic products, such as lactic acid, remain to be addressed.

When more operational definitions of tension headache have been attempted, the region of psychophysiological measurement has been most commonly the area of the forehead overlying the frontalis muscle, probably because of the ease of application of electrodes to this area. But as a site for monitoring and feedback signals, the frontalis differs in several respects from other muscles about the head and shoulders. First, while the complex and bulky array of suboccipital musculature has as its function the physical support of the head during the waking hours, no similar mechanical function can be assigned to the frontalis. Indeed, movement of this muscle in humans probably has more to do with facial expression, and so with the communication of feeling states, than with any mechanical function. In this respect, the frontalis muscle is more like the platysma, that thin sheath of muscle embedded in the skin and subcutaneous tissue of the face and neck, the movement of which is also intimately related to emotional expression. The movements of other muscles about the head and shoulders can convey feeling states, of course, but they also have other, more mechanical functions. This may have relevance to the psychological and communicational aspects of suboccipital versus frontal headaches.

Second, the frontalis, a relatively thin muscle, overlies the bony skull, while the suboccipital group overlies the deeper structures of the neck, vertebral column, and skull. Since a population of muscles is recorded in the latter case, investigators cannot be sure which muscles are contributing most to the electrophysiological signal—a problem not encountered to the same degree in the region of the frontalis. A single deeper suboccipital muscle, such as the splenius capitis, might have a high resting level of electrical activity; yet this electrical activity difference may be lost in the group measurement that which surface electrodes give us.

Third, a result of the relative bulk and depth of the muscle bellies of the suboccipital group is that the surface electrodes are at varying distances from these muscles and muscle spindles within muscles—a condition present only to a much milder degree when measuring the frontalis.

When tension is viewed more as a form of communication, or as an operant, perhaps the use of the frontalis is more understandable (Philips, 1977).

INSTRUMENTATION

The electrical activity accompanying voluntary muscular contraction consists of repetitive wave forms called "muscle action potentials" (MAPs). The individual motor units that produce MAPs discharge from 8 to 40 times per second. The electrical signal recorded from the skin is the summation of MAPs from a large number of cells. This signal has a frequency spectrum that is rather sharply peaked, with, for instance, nearly half of the activity of the biceps muscle being concentrated in the 37–75 Hz range (Hayes, 1960)—a frequency that is commonly rejected or filtered out in the design of the amplifiers of many biofeedback instruments. The EMGs arising from voluntary activity are generally very complex wave forms made up of bursts of polyphasic pulses (Gottlieb & Agarwal, 1970). Little is known about the frequency spectrum of EMG activity arising from the muscles of the head and neck in people who have tension headaches, compared to those of people without head pain, and it cannot yet be assumed that there are no significant differences.

Grossman and Weiner (1966) state that while the significant frequency spectrum of the MAPs extends from 20 Hz to 8–10 kHz, "the greater part of the electrical activity is found in a narrower range at the lower end of the spectrum" (p. 80).

The Report of the Committee on EMG Instrumentation considers that the recording system should have a frequency response flat within 3 db between 2 Hz and 10 kHz (Guld, Rosenfalck, & Willison, 1970). Narrower ranges distort the MAP wave forms. The tendency to restrict the bandpass of amplifiers to the 100–200 Hz range is perhaps premature.

CLINICAL RESEARCH LITERATURE

This section reviews crucial treatment research literature involving tension headaches and biofeedback. It addresses the following questions: (1) Does biofeedback work? (2) How does biofeedback work? (3) What are the successful and the unsuccessful applications? (4) What are the limitations? (5) What is its relative efficacy?

(6) What is the duration of the treatment effect? Though blood volume pulse feedback (Feurstein, Adams, & Beiman, 1976), EEG feedback (McKenzie, Ehrisman, Montgomery, & Barnes, 1974), and thermal biofeedback (Sargent, Green, & Walters, 1973) have been used with tension headaches, this review is restricted to craniocervical EMG feedback. This is done because only the EMG feedback literature contains controlled-group studies.

It must be pointed out that all of the available studies deal with very small samples (six to nine patients per group); have not addressed the variability of treatment responsiveness; have typically used frontalis or frontal[1] electrode placements, regardless of location and nature of pain; and have not used double-blind procedures.

DOES BIOFEEDBACK WORK?

Research efforts to date, using Fisherian statistics, have assessed the effectiveness of biofeedback in terms of absolute and relative pretreatment to posttreatment group changes[2] across various parameters of headache activity. These indices of headache activity include intensity, duration, frequency, a headache composite of all three factors, and headache medication. Such an approach tells little about outcome variability or patient characteristics that covary with outcome. Consequently, clinicians are left to assess whether biofeedback works on the basis of group mean symptom reduction. Unfortunately, this tells clinicians little about whether biofeedback will help a given patient.

In asking whether biofeedback "works," we are concerned with external validity; consequently, this section will be restricted to controlled-group studies using medically documented tension headache patients. The question is not whether biofeedback is better than other interventions, but whether it is better than a nonactive treatment.

Budzynski, Stoyva, Adler, and Mullaney (1973) compared contingent EMG frontal feedback with a noncontingent feedback and a no-treatment control after 8 weeks of biweekly training sessions. The two feedback groups were given nonspecific instructions to relax at home. After treatment, using a composite headache index, four of six frontal feedback subjects showed significant improvement; the remaining two reported not practicing relaxation regularly. One of the six noncontingent

[1]The standard placement of disk surface EMG electrodes over the frontalis muscle, when using a wide band pass such as 90 to 1000 Hz, records skeletal-muscular activity for the general cranial–cervical region and not just the frontalis muscle. Consequently, the term "frontal" is used in this section, rather than "frontalis."

[2]The only exception to this was the report of Budzynski, Stoyva, Adler, and Mullaney (1973), which analyzed the regression curves for each patient as well as group means.

feedback subjects and none of the no-treatment subjects showed a significant headache reduction. Six of eight of the controls who were subsequently given the active treatment package showed marked headache improvement. Decrements in the composite headache score were paralleled by reductions in headache medication usage.

Similarly, Haynes, Griffin, Mooney, and Parise (1975) compared six sessions of frontal EMG feedback with no-treatment controls, using seven headache-prone college students per group. Only group mean data is available. They demonstrated that feedback significantly reduced headache frequency and composite headache scores, in comparison with the no-treatment control.

Cox, Freundlich, and Meyer (1975) randomly assigned 27 medically documented tension headache patients to either frontal feedback, progressive relaxation training, or medication placebo groups for eight biweekly sessions. Eight, four, and two of the feedback, progressive relaxation training, and placebo subjects, respectively, demonstrated at least 50% reduction of the composite headache index. Similar reductions occurred in headache frequency and in the duration and use of headache medication.

Philips (1977) compared five subjects receiving EMG frontal or temporalis feedback with four subjects receiving pseudofeedback for 12 biweekly sessions. There was no posttreatment difference between groups on headache frequency. Subjects receiving EMG feedback demonstrated significantly greater reduction in headache intensity following treatment and significantly less medication usage at the 8-week follow-up.

Cram (1978) compared two groups of subjects, given EMG feedback with instructions either to *lower* or to *maintain* frontal skeletal muscle activity, with two control groups that either meditated on a noncontingent tone or simply charted headache activity. Pretreatment, treatment, and posttreatment periods were each 3 weeks in length. A group of 10 undergraduate students served as biofeedback trainers. Only the two EMG groups showed significant pretreatment to posttreatment reduction of headache composite scores, though there was no between-group difference in reduction of headache frequency. Medication usage was not monitored. Treatment success, as defined by 40% to 100% reduction of composite headache scores, was observed after treatment in six, three, three, and four patients, respectively in the groups practicing EMG lowering, EMG awareness training, meditation, and headache charting.

Holroyd and Andrasik (1980a) compared EMG frontal feedback to an equally credible pseudotherapy of meditation and to a symptom-monitoring control group after seven biweekly treatment sessions. Subjects in the study were 27 female and 4 male introductory psychology students. An 80% reduction of a composite headache score was reported by 88%, 22%, and 27% of the feedback, pseudotherapy, and control group subjects.

On the basis of this review, it is clear that EMG biofeedback training leads to significant headache relief in medically diagnosed chronic tension headache patients. The therapeutic effect is superior to no treatment, noncontingent feedback or pseudofeedback, medication placebo, meditation on an auditory tone, or simple headache charting. This therapeutic effect appears in approximately 75% of biofeedback participants. It must be pointed out, however, that EMG feedback typically exists in the context of home relaxation practice, therapist contact, feedback of EMG changes to the therapist, and headache charting.

HOW DOES BIOFEEDBACK WORK?

It is much easier to say that EMG biofeedback works than to say *how* it works. Initial theory implicated tension headaches with excessive and persistent cranial–cervical skeletal muscle activity. If such EMG activity could be recognized and controlled with biofeedback training, it followed that tension headaches should be controlled with such training procedures.

This was initially supported by Budzynski *et al.* (1973), who reported that for biofeedback subjects, in-session EMG correlated + .90 with reduction of out-of-session headache activity, while correlating – .05 for pseudofeedback subjects. However, subsequent findings have not supported this simple relationship. Cox *et al.* (1975) found a correlation of + .42 between pretreatment to posttreatment EMG change and headache change, suggesting that reduction in EMG accounted for only 17% of headache reduction variance. Epstein, Abel, Collins, Parker, and Cinciripini (1978) demonstrated EMG biofeedback effective in reducing headache in three of six subjects. In five of six subjects, however, EMG activity was not correlated with headache activity. They concluded, "In-session changes of EMG may not be sufficient to reduce headache reports" (p. 45). Similarly, Philips (1977) and Bakal and Kaganov (1977) found poor concordance between headache activity and EMG.

From another perspective, Cram (1978) found that EMG feedback-awareness training produced no changes in EMG activity while significantly *reducing* headache activity to a degree equivalent to that of the EMG relaxation group, which did demonstrate significant EMG reduction. The most striking finding discounting the "in-session EMG reduction/out-of-session headache reduction" hypothesis was that of Andrasik and Holroyd (1979). Three groups of 10 patients each were taught either to *lower* frontal EMG, to *increase* frontal EMG, or to lower forearm EMG while *maintaining* a constant frontal EMG. Across the seven treatment sessions, frontal EMG went in the intended direction, but all groups showed significant and equal reduction of headache activity (79%, 61%, and 74%, respectively).

Though EMG feedback is an effective, active therapeutic agent, it must be concluded that its effectiveness is not mediated through the instruction to lower in-session skeletal-muscular tension per se. If tension headaches are conceptualized as the end product of a chain of events (see Table 1), then it becomes clear that EMG control by means of biofeedback training focuses on only the last element in the headache chain.

It is quite possible that EMG frontal biofeedback training serves, rather, to increase the patients *awareness* of physiological dysregulation occurring in the chain. In doing this, awareness of physiological shifts becomes a discriminant stimulus, allowing a new feedback loop that permits the patient to identify triggering stimuli and mediating cognitive–behavioral reactions that initiate such ANS dysregulation. This awareness could then promote earlier and more effective avoidance of or coping with the triggering and mediating events. Patients frequently report such a process (Epstein *et al.*, 1978; Reeves, 1976).

This speculation is supported by the fact that all studies providing contingent feedback have demonstrated similar and significant results. In contrast, those patients exposed to noncontingent feedback, or to information that does not allow patients more accurate information of their internal state, have not demonstrated equivalent therapeutic gains.

This hypothesis, that the effective agent of EMG feedback is its ability to train patients' identification of the headache chain that may lead to alternate coping strategies, is indirectly supported by some nonbiofeedback literature. Holroyd and Andrasik (1978) have demonstrated that teaching patients to be aware of cognitive headache chains and to initiate subsequent behaviors and cognitions incompatible with the perpetuation of such chains is effective in reducing tension headaches, while having no effect on frontal EMG. Also, Cram (1978) reported that three "headache charting" subjects showed significant improvement in headache activity, reportedly because charting allowed them to recognize and change those events that culminated in headaches. Finally, long-term follow-up data indicate that approximately 50% of tension headache patients who receive EMG feedback maintain their gains (Diamond, Medina, Diamond-Falk, & DeVeno, 1979), while 88% of patients who have received feedback plus training in additional coping strategies are similarly improved (Adler & Adler, 1976).

SUCCESSFUL AND UNSUCCESSFUL APPLICATIONS?

Currently, there are no documented patient characteristics known to predict successful or unsuccessful applications of EMG biofeedback with tension headaches. There are two post hoc findings suggesting that individuals with excessively elevated initial frontalis EMG readings do more poorly with EMG feedback (Bruhn, Olesen, & Melgaard, 1979; Epstein *et al.*, 1978). However, Cram (1978) reported a tendency for subjects who were less muscularly responsive to experimental stressors and who also had higher resting frontal EMGs to do better with feedback.

There is some evidence that therapist variables are significantly influential in

TABLE 1. Understanding of Migraine and Muscle-Contraction Headache Mechanisms: Headache Model

Sequential Headache Factors					
Triggering strain →	Individual predisposing factors (genetic and learned) →	Stress response: Initiation of headache mechanisms →	Symptom →	Triggering strain →	Environmental response
Physical: Noise Trauma Allergies	*Physical:* (Unstable ANS) Response stereotype of increased muscle tension and cranial–cervical vasoconstriction	*Physical:* ↑ Muscle contraction and vasoconstriction (tension) ↑ Intracranial vasoconstriction (migraine)	*Physical:* Sustained muscle contraction and anoxia (tension); cranial vasodilatation, vascular inflammation, local chemical discharge, muscle tension (migraine)	*Physical:* Accumulation of lactic acid and anoxia (tension; chemical dysregulation (migraine)	Positive or negative reinforcement: punishment and/or frustration of either self-help or "sick" role behavior
Psychological: Conflict Frustration Anger Depression Guilt	*Psychological:* Cognitive and emotional hyperactivity to perceived threats; low pain threshold	*Psychological:* Rumination over perceived threat to homeostasis by strain and pending headache	*Psychological:* Pain experienced	*Psychological:* Distress over pain, disruption of function, irritability	

the clinical efficacy of biofeedback. Taub (1977) reported data from a prospective study indicating that the peripheral vasodilatation response of thermal biofeedback is more quickly and thoroughly learned with sympathetic and supportive biofeedback trainers than it is with cold, distant trainers. Cox, Klee, and Meyer (1977) reported that female therapists produced greater frontal EMG reductions than did male therapists in women receiving relaxation training for dysmenorrhea. In a retrospective analysis of multiple variables associated with biofeedback treatment of 120 headache patients, Greenspan (1979) reported that the single variable that accounted for the greatest amount of outcome variance was the therapist's personality. Supportive, understanding therapists produce greater improvements.

Such therapist facotrs have never been prospectively investigated in EMG feedback with tension headaches. However, this factor may have played a large role in the literature previously cited, due to the great variability of the therapists used. For example, Cram (1978) used undergraduate students as therapists; Adler and Adler (1976) used a male psychiatrist and a female psychologist; Holroyd and Andrasik (1978) used research assistants for biofeedback therapists, while the authors functioned as therapists for the cognitive therapies; Diamond *et al.* (1979) primarily relied on nurses as therapists.

There is some evidence suggesting that EMG biofeedback combined with verbal whole-body relaxation exercises is superior to EMG feedback alone. Chesney and Shelton (1976) demonstrated that such a combined treatment approach significantly influenced headache severity, while neither procedure in isolation had such an effect. Sime, DeGood, and Noble (in press) documented a differential effect of EMG feedback and progressive relaxation training (PRT); while PRT allowed more accurate awareness of craniocervical muscle tension, biofeedback produced a faster EMG recovery from stress.

Repeatedly, post hoc analysis has shown that continued practice of relaxation exercises following treatment is associated with maintenance of therapeutic gains. However, it is unclear whether effective headache relief encourages continued practice or whether continued practice encourages maintenance in the therapeutic effect.

WHAT ARE THE LIMITATIONS?

The therapy literature suggests that EMG biofeedback is inappropriate or insufficient for some tension headache patients, as techniques currently exist. Part of the variable treatment effect may be a reflection of inaccurate diagnoses that attribute tension headaches to excessive skeletal muscle tension instead of to such actual causes as depression, allergies, referred pain from a cervical malady, a simple reflection of environmental consequences (positive and negative reinforcement) that maintain the headache complaint, or a conversion symptom.

Like many therapeutic procedures, biofeedback is limited by the patient's compliance in acquisition and application of the skills taught in biofeedback. This is illustrated by Budzynski *et al.*'s two treatment failures (1973). To date, issues of compliance with either acquisition or application have not been addressed from an empirical basis.

Given an appropriate diagnosis and a motivated patient, there also is the possibility that the typical biofeedback experience of 2 hours a week is grossly outweighed by the overwhelming triggering life stresses with which the patient must contend. The quality and quantity of patients' life stresses and their capacity to cope effectively with them have a major limiting factor on treatment efficacy of EMG biofeedback. The role of such factors is implicitly acknowledged in the study by Cram (1978), who selected out from participation four individuals who had significant psychological problems as indicated by the MMPI and the clinical interview. The actual influence of such factors has yet to be addressed.

As discussed earlier, the typical EMG biofeedback unit monitors muscle activity greater than 90 Hz, while the frequency spectrum for some skeletal muscles is significantly below this level. Consequently, EMG biofeedback may not be feeding back the most relevant information.

WHAT IS BIOFEEDBACK'S RELATIVE EFFICACY?

Biofeedback has been compared to verbal progressive relaxation training exercises, cognitive behavior therapy, and standard medical treatment. Repeatedly, EMG frontal biofeedback has been found to produce mean group reductions of headache activity similar to those achieved through progressive relaxation training (Cox *et al.*, 1975; Haynes *et al.*, 1975). In contrast, Chesney and Shelton (1976) reported progressive relaxation training with or without EMG biofeedback to be superior to biofeedback alone. Again, such studies use far too gross a procedure to address the real question adequately. Clinical experience suggests that the most appropriate question is "For this particular patient, does EMG feedback work best, does progressive relaxation training work best, or are both treatments indicated?" Pilot data (Cox *et al.,* 1977) suggest that individuals with an external locus of control on the Norwickie–Strickland scale do better with the highly structured progressive relaxation training procedures of Bernstein and Borkovec (1973), while internally controlled subjects do better with standard biofeedback.

In a relatively biased study, Holroyd, Andrasik, and Westbrook (1977) demonstrated the superiority of cognitive behavior therapy to EMG biofeedback. The biasing factor was that the authors conducted the cognitive therapy, while biofeedback was relegated to the research assistants. Subsequent research (Holroyd & Andrasik, 1978), however, suggests that general headache discussion groups were equally effective as a training procedure for skill in cognitive coping.

Bruhn *et al.* (1979) have been the only investigators to evaluate the relative effectiveness of EMG biofeedback and standard pharmacological treatment with chronic tension headaches. They found feedback superior in reducing headache activity and medication usage, with 7 of 13 biofeedback patients and only 1 of 10 pharmacologically treated patients experiencing 50% to 100% reduction of a headache composite score. However, this should not be surprising, since, by the very definition of the patient sample—"chronic headache patients"—there was a bias to select past medication failures.

WHAT IS THE DURABILITY OF THE TREATMENT EFFECT?

Prospective studies have conducted follow-ups at points ranging from 1 to 18 months after treatment, while two retrospective clinical surveys have followed up patients for as much as 5 years.

The difference between the pseudofeedback and real frontal feedback groups of Philips (1977) was reportedly being maintained at 6 to 8 weeks.

Headache composite scores and drug intake were unchanged from posttreatment assessment to 3 months' follow-up in the Bruhn *et al.* study (1979).

At 4 months' follow-up, Cox *et al.* (1975) reported that 88%, 88%, and 44% of the patients contacted in the biofeedback, progressive relaxation training, and medication placebo groups, respectively, maintained their treatment gains. This is in contrast to 89%, 44%, and 22% such improvements after treatment.

Cram (1978) reported that the number of subjects reporting 40% to 100% headache reduction after treatment versus those maintaining it at 6 months' follow-up came to six of eight versus three of seven for biofeedback relaxation subjects; three of eight versus three of five for biofeedback awareness training subjects; three of eight versus four of seven for the meditating group; and four of eight versus two of three for the subjects in the headache charting condition.

The longest prospective follow-up was reported by Budzynski *et al.* (1973). At 18-month follow-up, four of the six feedback patients were contacted, while the remaining two had moved out of state. Three of the follow-up patients, who were initially "successful" patients after treatment, continued to have markedly diminished headache complaints. The one post-treatment failure reported modest gains at follow-up.

Holroyd and Andrasik (1980b) contacted 8 of 10 patients previously treated with biofeedback for tension headache (Holroyd *et al.*, 1977). The four patients who had experienced at least 50% reduction of headache activity after treatment reported a maintenance of this therapeutic effect at 2-year follow-up. Results at 2-year follow-up correlated +.54 with pretreatment headache severity and +.92 with posttreatment headache improvement.

The two retrospective clinical studies were conducted by Adler and Adler

(1976) and Diamond *et al.*, (1979). Adler and Adler (1976) reported on a retrospective study of 19 tension headache patients whose EMG biofeedback treatment had terminated between 3⅓ to 5 years previously. They concluded, "The results at follow-up were similar to those recorded in the chart at the end of treatment. The success rate (75–100% remission) for tension headache patients was 88%" (p. 190). In conjunction with biofeedback, 75% of their patients received concurrent psychotherapy because "It became apparent that for continued improvement it was essential that treatment focus on all aspects of the patient and his headaches, including social, psychological and physical context" (p. 190).

In a 3- to 5-year retrospective follow-up questionnaire survey of 19 chronic tension headache patients who had previously been refractory to all forms of pharmacological therapy, 75% reported that a combined program of EMG and thermal biofeedback "helped" (Diamond *et al.*, 1979). When asked whether the improvement was transitory or permanent, it appears that 100% of those reporting improvement reported the improvement to be permanent.

All of the previously cited studies suffer from the common problem of attrition. For example, in Cram's follow-up (1978), only three of the original eight "headache charting" subjects were secured, and in the Budzynski *et al.* study (1973), only 66% of the biofeedback-treated subjects were evaluated at the 18-month follow-up. It is impossible to tell whether or not those individuals cooperating with a follow-up reflect a sampling bias that either favors or tarnishes the evaluation of biofeedback training. It is important that future systematic research on therapeutic maintenance effects secure a high percentage of treated patients at follow-up to diminish the possibility of such selection bias.

It is clear that for the vast majority of tension headache patients successfully treated with EMG biofeedback, therapeutic gains are maintained over an extended period of time. Data exist indicating that removal of the headache complaints has positive spinoff effects in terms of reducing ancillary somatic complaints (Cox *et al.*, 1975) and improving personality profiles on the MMPI (Budzynski *et al.*, 1973; Cram, 1978). There is no evidence of any form of symptom substitution. However, there have been no systematic prospective studies explicitly testing the issue of symptom substitution (Cox & Hobbs, 1980).

FOCUS AND ISSUES FOR FUTURE RESEARCH

As this review indicates, there is little that can be concluded from existing data, other than that EMG frontal biofeedback is more effective than placebos are in the treatment of tension headaches. There are several major areas that require extensive exploration, including (1) pathophysiology of the headache complaint; (2) patient characteristics that interact with biofeedback and influence its effectiveness; (3) the relative cost-effectiveness of alternative and adjunctive treatment procedures; (4) and the positive and negative (symptom-substitution) long-term effects of biofeedback.

PATHOPHYSIOLOGY

One significant contribution of biofeedback has been its clarification of the poor relationship between the amount of EMG activity as typically measured and the amount of subjective distress. As Philips (1978) and Gannon, Haynes, Safranek, and Hamilton (in press) have pointed out, though excessive cranial–cervical EMG activity and vasoconstriction are implicated in tension headache, the exact nature of their involvement is unclear. Future research needs to divide patients into homogeneous groups according to the subjective complaint at *headache initiation*. This would involve clustering patients whose headaches begin frontally, suboccipitally, or occipitally. Measurements taken from the various muscles (frontalis, temporalis, occipitalis) and vascular sites (superficial temporal, posterior auricular, supratrochlear) should be conducted during various conditions (relaxation, physical stress, psychological stress) when the patient is headache-free and *throughout* the course of a headache. Such EMG analyses should involve spectral analyses from multiple sites that assess the specific EMG characteristics differentiating no headache, early headache, and continued headache conditions. Likewise, monitoring of such vascular functions as pulse rate, blood volume pulse, and pulse amplitude should be monitored from various sites to understand their complementary contributions to tension headaches. Concurrent to physical monitoring, assessment of the quality and quantity of the subjective distress should be conducted within and across patients. A better understanding of the physical process and its relationship to subjective distress will allow a clearer focus for future biofeedback procedures.

PATIENT CHARACTERISTICS

Despite great variability in responsiveness to EMG biofeedback, there has been no successful clarification of the relevant patient variables that contribute to this. There have been suggestions that individuals with markedly elevated or depressed frontal EMGs, and those whose EMG is excessively labile to stress, are less favorable biofeedback candidates. It has also been implied that individuals under excessive environmental stress and/or who have poor general psychological adjustment either respond poorly or demonstrate minimal therapeutic maintenance. Primary depression that predates the headache history (i.e., depression that is not secondary to the chronic headache) has been suggested either to interfere with the acquisition

TABLE 2. Advantages and Disadvantages of Pharmacological and Behavioral Treatment Strategies for Headaches

Pharmacological Treatment		*Behavioral Treatment*	
Advantages	*Disadvantages*	*Advantages*	*Disadvantages*
1. Minimal physician time	1. Physical side effects	1. No known negative physical side effects	1. Major time investment by health professional
2. Minimal patient time	2. *Dependence*	2. Sense of control	2. Major patient investment
3. Minimal life disruption	3. *Abuse*	3. Nonabusive	3. Resistance to "psychological" treatment
4. Moderately effective	4. Compliance	4. Eventual independence of health providers	
	5. Intolerance	5. Possible use of technicians	
	6. Resistance to drug therapy	6. Generalized health benefits (e.g., better sleep, fewer medications, etc.)	
	7. Long-term maintenance	7. Applicable in all situations (i.e., not dependent on availability of prescriptions)	
	8. Availability of pills		

of EMG control or to produce headaches that do not primarily originate in muscle contraction. Recent retrospective questionnaire data by Diamond *et al.* (1979) have suggested that older individuals, males, and patients who were previously habituated to medications do more poorly at follow-up than their counterparts do. Environmental contingencies have long been implicated in the maintenance of pain behavior and have been incorporated in some headache treatment literature (Yen & McIntire, 1971).

However, biofeedback researchers have ignored these potent factors. In future research, it will be crucial to document these factors on a large group of homogeneous headache patients and to prospectively identify the relationships of such factors to treatment outcome.

RELATIVE COST-EFFECTIVENESS

It is obvious that in the short run, it is much easier, less disruptive, more inexpensive, and less time-demanding to take a pill for headache relief than it is to undergo EMG biofeedback training and subsequent integration of the newly learned skills into the life style. Whether or not concurrent utilization of such techniques is complementary or competitive is not clear. Also, the long-term benefits in relation to subsequent medical expenses, lost work time, general effectiveness, psychological effects, medical side effects, compliance, intolerance, abuse, and so forth, are unclear. Szajnberg and Diamond (1980) have speculated that biofeedback-produced symptomatic relief of migraine patients results in disruption of psychological homeostasis that restabilizes with the formation of new symptoms. Table 2 presents some potential positive and negative factors associated with biofeedback and pharmacological approaches. The short- and long-term costs and benefits of biofeedback and more traditional therapeutic interventions deserve serious future consideration.

REFERENCES

Abse, D. W. Hysterical conversion and dissociative syndromes and the hysterical character. In S. Arieti & E. B. Brody (Eds.), *American handbook of psychiatry* (2nd ed.). New York: Basic Books, 1974.

Adams, R. D. Headache. In G. W. Thorn, R. D. Adams, E. Braunwald, K. J. Isselbacher, & R. G. Petersdorf (Eds.), *Principles of internal medicine* (8th ed.). New York: McGraw-Hill, 1977.

Ad Hoc Committee on Classification of Headache. Classification of headache. *Journal of the American Medical Association,* 1962, *179,* 127–128.

Adler, C. S., & Adler, S. M. Biofeedback–psychotherapy for the treatment of headaches: A 5–6 year follow-up. *Headache,* 1976, *16,* 189–191.

American Psychiatric Association. *Diagnostic and statistical manual of mental disorders* (3rd ed.). Washington, D.C.: Author, 1980.

Andrasik, F., & Holroyd, K. *A test of the specific effects in the biofeedback treatment of tension headache.* Paper presented at the 13th annual meeting of the Association for the Advancement of Behavior Therapy, San Francisco, December 1979.

Bakal, D. A., & Kaganov, J. A. Muscle contraction and migraine headache: Psychophysiological comparison. *Headache,* 1977, *17,* 208–215.

Bernstein, D., & Borkovec, T. *Progressive relaxation training.* Champaign, Ill.: Research Press, 1973.

Bruhn, P., Olesen, J., & Melgaard, B. Controlled trial of EMG feedback in muscle contraction headache. *Annals of Neurology,* 1979, *6,* 34–36.

Budzynski, T. H., Stoyva, J. M., Adler, C. S., & Mullaney, D. J. EMG biofeedback and tension headache: A controlled outcome study. *Seminars in Psychiatry,* 1973, *5,* 397–410.

Chesney, M. S., & Shelton, J. L. A comparison of muscle relaxation and electromyograph biofeedback treatments for muscle contraction headache. *Journal of Behavioral Therapy and Experimental Psychiatry,* 1976, *7,* 221–225.

The Compact Edition of the Oxford English Dictionary. Glasgow: Oxford University Press, 1971.

Cox, D. J., Freundlich, A., & Meyer, R. G. Differential effectiveness of electromyograph feedback, verbal relaxation instructions and medication placebo with tension headaches. *Journal of Consulting and Clinical Psychology,* 1975, *43,* 892–898.

Cox, D. J., & Hobbs, W. Scientific critique of "Biofeedback, migraine headaches and new symptom formation." *Headache,* 1980, *20,* 282–283.

Cox, D. J., Klee, O. S., & Meyer, R. G. Predictive variables in EMG responsiveness to EMG feedback and verbal relaxation training. *Proceedings of the Second Meeting of the American Association for the Advancement of Tension Control,* 1977, *2,* 151–159.

Cram, J. R. EMG biofeedback and the treatment of tension headaches: A systematic analysis of treatment components. *Proceedings of the Biofeedback Society of America, Ninth Annual Meeting,* 1978, *9,* 49–51.

Diamond, S., Medina, J., Diamond-Falk, J., & DeVeno, T. The value of biofeedback in the treatment of chronic headache: A five-year retrospective study. *Headache,* 1979, *19,* 90–96.

Epstein, L. H., Abel, G. G., Collins, F., Parker, L., & Cinciripini, P. M. The relationship between frontalis muscle activity and self-reports of headache pain. *Behaviour Research and Therapy,* 1978, *16,* 153–160.

Feurstein, M., Adams, H. E., & Beiman, I. Cephalic vasomotor electromyographic feedback in the treatment of combined muscle contraction and migraine headaches in a geriatric case. *Headache,* 1976, *16,* 232–237.

Fordyce, W. E., & Brockway, J. A. Chronic pain and its management. In J. D. Jeffers (Ed.), *Psychiatry in general medical practice.* New York: McGraw-Hill, 1979.

Gannon, L. R., Haynes, S. N., Safranek, R., & Hamilton, J. A psychophysiological investigation of muscle contraction and tension headaches. *Journal of Psychosomatic Research,* in press.

Goodman, L. S., & Gilman, A. (Eds.). *The pharmacological basis of therapeutics* (5th ed.). New York: Macmillan, 1975.

Gottlieb, G. S., & Agarwal, G. C. Filtering of electromyographic signals. *American Journal of Physical Medicine,* 1970, *49,*(2), 142–146.

Greenspan, K. Biological feedback: Some conceptual bridges with analytically oriented psychotherapy. *Psychiatric Opinion,* 1979, *16*(7), 17–18, 20.

Grossman, W. I., & Weiner, H. Some factors affecting the reliability of surface electromyography. *Psychosomatic Medicine,* 1966, *28,* 78–83.

Guld, C., Rosenfalck, A., & Willison, R. G. Report of the committee on EMG instrumentation. *Electroencephalography and Clinical Neurophysiology,* 1970, *28,* 399–413.

Hayes, K. J. Wave analyses to tissue noise and muscle action potentials. *Journal of Applied Physiology,* 1960, *15,* 749–752.

Haynes, S. N., Griffin, P., Mooney, D. & Parise, M. Electromyographic biofeedback and relaxation instructions in the treatment of muscle contraction headache. *Behavior Therapy,* 1975, *6,* 672–678.

Holroyd, K. A., & Andrasik, F. Coping and the self-control of chronic tension headache. *Journal of Consulting and Clinical Psychology,* 1978, *46,* 1036–1045.

Holroyd, K. A., & Andrasik, F. A comparison of EMG biofeedback and a credible pseudotherapy in treating tension headache. *Journal of Behavioral Medicine,* 1980, *3,* 29–39.

Holroyd, K. A., & Andrasik, F. *Do the effects of cognitive therapy endure: A 2-year follow-up of tension headache sufferers treated with cognitive therapy or biofeedback.* Paper presented at the meeting of the Association for the Advancement of Behavior Therapy, New York, November 1980. (b)

Holroyd, K. A., Andrasik, F., & Westbrook, T. Cognitive control of tension headache. *Cognitive Therapy and Research,* 1977, *1*(2), 121–133.

McKenzie, R., Ehrisman, W., Montgomery, P., & Barnes, R. The treatment of headache by means of electroencephalographic biofeedback. *Headache,* 1974, *13,* 164–172.

Osler, W. *The principles and practice of medicine.* Birmingham, Ala.: The Classics of Medicine Library, 1978. (Originally published, 1892.)

Philips, C. Tension headache: Theoretical problems. *Behaviour Research and Therapy,* 1978, *16,* 249–261.

Philips, C. The modification of tension headache pain using EMG biofeedback. *Behaviour Research and Therapy,* 1977, *15,* 119–129.

Reeves, J. L. EMG-biofeedback reduction of tension headache: A cognitive skills-training approach. *Biofeedback and Self-Regulation,* 1976, *1,* 217–225.

Sargent, J. D., Green, E. E., & Walters, E. D. Preliminary report on the use of autogenic feedback training in the treatment of migraine and tension headaches. *Psychosomatic Medicine,* 1973, *35,* 129–135.

Sime, W. E., DeGood, D. E., & Noble, B. J. Effect of relaxation training upon accuracy of and recovery from a tension production task. *Biofeedback and Self-Regulation,* in press.

Spradlin, W. W., & Porterfield, P. B. *Human biosociology.* New York: Springer-Verlag, 1979.

Szajnberg, N., & Diamond, S. Biofeedback, migraine headache and new symptom formation. *Headache,* 1980, *20,* 29–31.

Taub, E. Self-regulation of human tissue temperature. In G. E. Schwartz & J. Beatty (Eds.), *Biofeedback: Theory and research.* New York: Academic Press, 1977.

Woodburne, R. T. *Essentials of human anatomy* (3rd ed.). New York: Oxford University Press, 1965.

Yen, S., & McIntire, R. W. Operant therapy for constant headache complaints: A simple response-cost approach. *Psychological Reports,* 1971, *28,* 267–270.

14 BIOFEEDBACK AND HEADACHE: METHODOLOGICAL ISSUES

HENRY E. ADAMS, PHILLIP J. BRANTLEY, AND KEVIN THOMPSON

The chapters in this volume addressing the efficacy of biofeedback treatment of headache, like other reviews in the psychological literature (Adams, Feuerstein, & Fowler, 1980; Beatty & Haynes, 1978; Blanchard, Ahles, & Shaw, 1979; Turk, Meichenbaum, & Berman, 1979), attempt to assimilate the findings of numerous studies in the area. Rather than commenting directly on the present articles, we believe that a more productive approach is to address some of the methodological issues involved in the evaluation of biofeedback treatment for head pain. Among the group at the University of Georgia laboratory, we have arrived at the conclusions that attempts to determine the efficacy of biofeedback with headaches, on the basis of the present literature, are premature. In this chapter, we attempt to justify this conclusion.

CLASSIFICATION OF HEADACHE

Investigators in the field of biofeedback and headache apparently have not profited from a difficult lesson learned by investigators in other areas of applied research (e.g., schizophrenia; see Pope & Lipinski, 1978). A fundamental tenet of scientific research may be summarized by the following brief statement: The necessary precursors to the *investigation* of a phenomenon are "*description, classification,* and *measurement*" of the phenomenon (italics ours) (Cattell, 1946). A scheme for description and classification of headache was proposed almost 20 years ago by the Ad

Henry E. Adams and Kevin Thompson. Department of Psychology, University of Georgia, Athens, Georgia.

Philip J. Brantley. Department of Psychology, Louisiana State University, Baton Rouge, Louisiana.

Hoc Committee on Classification of Headache (Friedman, 1962). If only head pain without a structural basis is considered, there are four major categories. The following descriptions are taken from the scheme proposed by the Ad Hoc Committee (Friedman, 1962).

1. *Vascular headaches of migraine type*—recurrent attacks of headache widely varied in intensity, frequency, and duration. The attacks are commonly unilateral in onset; are usually associated with anorexia and sometimes with nausea and vomiting; occasionally are preceded by or associated with conspicuous sensory, motor, or mood disturbances; and are often familial. This disorder is commonly assumed to be due to a cephalic vasomotor disorder.

2. *Muscle-contraction headache*—ache or sensation of tightness, pressure, or constriction, widely varied in intensity, frequency, and duration; sometimes long-lasting; and commonly suboccipital. It is associated with sustained contraction of skeletal muscles in the absence of permanent structural change, usually as part of an individual's reaction during life stress. Note that a defining characteristic of this disorder is "sustained contraction of skeletal muscles."

3. *Combined headache: vascular and muscle-contraction*—combinations of vascular headache of the migraine type and muscle-contraction headache prominently coexisting in an attack. Perhaps a more meaningful and more frequently used criterion is that the two types of head pain may also occur independently in the same person.

4. *Headache of delusional, conversion, or hypochondriacal states*—headaches in which the major clinical disorder is a delusional or a conversion reaction, and a peripheral pain mechanism is nonexistent. Closely allied are the hypochondriacal reactions in which the peripheral disturbances relevant to headache are minimal. Note that the defining characteristic of this type of head pain is "a lack of peripheral pain mechanism." Four our purposes, we refer to this type as "psychogenic head pain."

Proceeding from this classification scheme, the next step would be to devise measurement procedures that would allow clinicians and researchers to sort headaches into these types. These criteria should include subjective, behavioral, and physiological measures that would allow for differentiation among the categories. A brief example of this tripartite assessment procedure used in our laboratory is provided in Table 1. (For further detailed descriptions, see Sturgis, Brantley, & Adams, 1981.)

Considering the classification scheme offered by the Ad Hoc Committee (Friedman, 1962) and the suggestion of criteria for headache type shown in Table 1, a review of the biofeedback and headache literature reveals some interesting points:

1. Not a single case of psychogenic head pain has been reported in the biofeedback and psychological literature since the publication of the Ad Hoc Committee's diagnostic and classification scheme. There has been one study that has controlled

TABLE 1. Tripartite Assessment of Head Pain

	Assessment Procedure		
Headache Type	*Subjective*	*Behavioral*	*Physiological*
Migraine	1. Usually unilateral onset 2. Prodromes 3. Nausea 4. Pulsating, throbbing pain	1. Emergency room treatment 2. Bed rest required 3. Avoidance of sound and light 4. Vomiting and other signs of ANS distress	1. Cephalic vascular lability in headache and nonheadache states 2. Response to vasoconstrictive and potent analgesic or sedative drugs
Muscle-contraction	1. Dull, aching headband or neck pain 2. Pain attacks less severe; soreness of scalp and neck muscles	1. Only rarely requires cessation of ongoing activities or bed rest 2. Pain elicited in stressful situations	1. Elevated muscle tension in facial and neck areas during headache episode and/or nonheadache states 2. Often responsive to mild analgesics
Conversion	1. Pain report typically not fitting pattern of migraine or muscle-contraction 2. Iatrogenic effects	1. Presence of secondary gain (reinforcement) 2. Presence of an initial precipitating event	1. Lack of physiological basis for pain (e.g., no elevated EMG or vasomotor disorders)
Combined	1. Characteristics of both muscle-contraction and migraine, either coexisting in same attack or occurring in separate attacks	1. Disability a function of type of headache	1. Physiology may vary as a function of type of pain 2. When both types exist in same attack, physiological changes may involve vascular and musculoskeletal components

for these cases. This is rather amazing, since a high percentage of other types of pain (e.g., back pain) described in the pain literature is assumed to be psychogenic in nature, with no physiologic pain mechanism evident (Fordyce, 1976).

2. By *definition,* muscle-contraction headaches involve elevated muscle tension in the cephalic or neck region, either in the headache and/or nonheadache condition. However, a large number of cases described as "muscle-contraction" and used to evaluate treatment strategies do not exhibit this characteristic, as shown in Table 2.

3. In spite of the fact that these types of head pain vary substantially in subjective, behavioral, and physiological characteristics, the major criterion for classification has been the investigator's or the physician's judgment based on the patient's self-report. Not a single study has been conducted to determine rater agreement or other reliability estimates of these judgments. An extended discussion and docu-

TABLE 2. Basal EMG Levels in Muscle-Contraction and Combined Headache Studies

EMG Levels (in microvolts)	*Number of Studies (N = 31)*
Not reported	18
0–7.5	5
7.5–10	4
10	4

mentation of these methodological problems has been conducted in another article, reviewing the headache literature for various subject selection criteria and classification procedures (Thompson, Turkat, & Adams, 1980). A summary of these findings is presented in Table 3.

It is obvious, given the preceding discussion, that headache populations have varied substantially across investigations. The only major subject selection control seems to be the elimination of individuals exhibiting migrainous symptomatology, and these procedures have been inadequately reported. This state of affairs has led to suggestions by Bakal (1979) that headaches differ only in severity of symptoms, as well as to claims by Haynes (1979) that preintervention assessment of muscle-contraction headache is unnecessary. One is reminded of the hundreds of useless studies of schizophrenia when diagnosis was determined by psychiatrist opinion or hospital admission, a situation properly evaluated by Pope and Lipinsky (1978).

The major point is this: It does not matter how sophisticated and controlled the research design and procedures are if there is an inadequate description and classification of the target populations. Until an adequate classification is formulated, no useful information, either about etiology, about mechanisms of pain, or about treatment outcome, can be generated.

TABLE 3. Descriptions of Diagnostic Criteria Reported in Headache Treatment Studies

Type of Description	*Number of Studies (N = 50)*
No diagnostic criteria reported	27
Nonspecific criteria[a]	12
Specific criteria[b]	11

[a]Denotes vague descriptive criteria (e.g., "general tension headache syndrome").

[b]Denotes specific listing of criteria (e.g., unilateral onset, etc.).

WHAT CONSTITUTES BIOFEEDBACK THERAPY?

Unlike many other forms of psychological intervention, biofeedback therapy easily lends itself to the study of process variables as well as outcome effects. In fact, the evaluation of outcome in biofeedback therapy represents a somewhat meaningless exercise in the absence of a thorough examination of process variables. The process in biofeedback, simply stated, involves learning. Through the use of external feedback, an individual acquires control of a targeted physiological system, thus producing a desired change in a pathological condition. If, however, it has not been demonstrated that an individual has learned a desired response, it would seem a bit premature to evaluate the impact of the biofeedback procedure on the pathological condition.

The evaluation of process or learning in biofeedback must be determined by two distinct indices, which are related but not identical. In the first case, it has to be demonstrated that an individual can change his or her behavior from baseline with the aid of external feedback. This we arbitrarily label as "biofeedback control." Interestingly enough, while this variable has been evaluated in a number of studies, many investigations have apparently ignored the issue of biofeedback control. The second, and probably the more crucial, evaluation of whether learning has occurred concerns "voluntary control" of the targeted response. This measure of learning was described by Brener (1974) as the ability of an individual to control a targeted response, on command, without the aid of external feedback. Unfortunately, few studies in the biofeedback literature on head pain have employed a *voluntary*-control procedure (see Table 4). In those that have, the procedures have varied dramatically. For instance, some investigators have used a procedure whereby the subject is instructed to perform a desired response after the completion of feedback trials (Blanchard *et al.*, 1979; Epstein & Abel, 1977). Others have used a final session subsequent to feedback sessions as a measure of voluntary control (Budzynski, Stoyva, Adler, & Mullaney, 1973; Friar & Beatty, 1976).

TABLE 4. Incidence of Voluntary-Control Procedures in Biofeedback Studies of Headache

Voluntary-Control Procedures	*Number of Studies (N = 34)*
No voluntary-control procedures used	13
No data to show acquisition of voluntary control	10
Subjective report of acquisition of voluntary control	4
Objective data reported in article for various procedures of voluntary control	7

It is our contention that the only appropriate method for evaluating voluntary control involves testing the subject at the beginning of each feedback session. After a baseline has been established, the subject is instructed to modify the appropriate response system without the aid of external feedback. This approach, unlike those previously mentioned, allows for an assessment of the acquisition of voluntary control uncontaminated by external feedback trials. (Unfortunately, this voluntary-control design has been used in only three of the 34 biofeedback studies for headache.) This procedure has an additional advantage in that once a subject begins to show voluntary control, he or she can begin practicing the procedure at home. Home practice is certainly not an uncommon procedure in the biofeedback literature, in spite of the fact that it is probably meaningless to recommend home practice for patients before evaluating their ability to perform the response voluntarily. Our review of the literature suggests that only two studies have recommended home practice *after* demonstration of acquired voluntary control (Gainer, 1978; Sturgis, Tollison, & Adams, 1978).

Since we are dealing with the phenomenon of learning, we might make a point concerning the acquisition of these responses. More information is needed on the nature of learning with visceral and autonomic responses. For example, how many sessions are required for learning to occur? Will biphasic or bidirectional feedback improve the rate of learning? Are there carry-over effects from one biofeedback procedure to another? Should discrimination training of the targeted response precede attempts to teach control of the response? (We have evidence that *prior* discrimination training for cephalic vasoconstriction or dilation facilitates acquisition of the blood volume pulse response.)

It is our position that, once we have a better understanding of the parameters of learning in a particular response system (e.g., vasomotor, muscular), then we are in a better position to evaluate the effects of that learning on a particular dysfunctional response system.

EMG BIOFEEDBACK, RELAXATION, AND PLACEBO AS METHODS OF ELIMINATING MUSCLE-CONTRACTION HEADACHES

Turning from an analysis of the target population to a discussion of treatment procedures, we find ourselves unable to concur with Cox and Hobbs' hint (Chapter 13) that biofeedback may be the treatment of choice for tension headache. However, we experience even more difficulty with Blanchard's premature suggestion that relaxation may be "the final common pathway" for the biofeedback treatment of psychophysiological disorders (Blanchard & Ahles, 1979; Silver & Blanchard, 1978). A necessary first step in the evaluation of biofeedback as a treatment intervention is to define the type of biofeedback and the procedures used for comparison. We illustrate this point with EMG feedback, relaxation training, and placebo.

Relaxation training is a technique designed to induce *complete generalized* body relaxation and a state of low arousal *directly*. This may result in decreases in muscular activity, heart rate, skin conductance, respiration, and other autonomic responses (Paul, 1969; Schandler & Grings, 1976). Frontalis feedback, or other specific EMG feedback, is designed to reduce muscle tension *directly* in a *specific* muscle group. This procedure may or may not generalize to adjacent muscle sites or across response systems (Stoyva, 1979; Gatchel, Chapter 15). The placebo effect is probably caused by the patient's belief in or expectance of positive outcome of treatment intervention. This expectance is influenced by a number of factors, but two are of major importance: the credibility of treatment procedures and the credibility of the therapist. The major effect of placebo would seem to be a *general* state of lowered arousal and increased relaxation. Thus, placebo may be an indirect way of producing the relaxation response. In summary, all three procedures directly or indirectly promote relaxation in either specific and/or general response systems of the ANS.

Turning to the literature on muscle-contraction headache, we have noted several problems with the evaluation of EMG biofeedback as a treatment procedure. For example, if pain is due to tonic and/or phasic elevation of the cephalic or neck regions, it would seem that specific feedback for relaxation of the involved muscle groups would be most effective. However, if there is no elevated muscle activity in these regions, or if muscle tension is generalized, then a clinician could not expect the effects of specific EMG biofeedback training to be greater than that produced by some type of relaxation training or possibly placebo. In fact, recent evidence suggests that frontalis EMG decreases do *not* generalize to adjacent muscle groups (Fridlund, Fowler, & Pritchard, 1980). These considerations have not been evaluated in the headache literature, with the possible exception of Epstein and Abel (1977), who utilized elevated EMG as a criterion for inclusion in a biofeedback treatment group. To add further to the confusion, no study had controlled for the *credibility* of treatment strategies. In order to evaluate the effects of placebo as opposed to those of other treatment procedures, groups must be measured and equated on this important variable. For example, some studies have utilized technicians to run biofeedback groups, while employing trained therapists for cognitive treatments (as noted by Cox & Hobbs, Chapter 13).

MIGRAINE HEADACHES AND BIOFEEDBACK

In regard to the effect of temperature biofeedback, relaxation training, EMG biofeedback, and the placebo effect on migraine, we are in agreement with Beatty's conclusion in Chapter 8. However, several points should be made about the use of blood volume pulse (BVP) feedback with migraine. Unlike temperature training, it is possible that if BVP feedback has any effects on migraine activity, the effects are direct rather than indirect. A number of studies have demonstrated that changes in the cephalic vasomotor response are not highly related to temperature in the periphery (Largen, Mathew, Dobbins, Meyer, & Claghorn, 1978) or to other indices of lowered arousal (Sturgis *et al.*, 1978). Consequently, any effects of BVP feedback cannot be attributed to a relaxation response produced by a generalized relaxation effect. Consistent with Beatty's position in this book, a review of uncontrolled and controlled single-case designs as well as the two controlled studies in the literature has consistently shown a significant effect of BVP on migraine activity. While it can be argued that this effect is small, there is still the possibility that additional research exploring the more effective utilization of this type of approach may result in useful treatment techniques. Compared with other procedures used with other disorders in the biofeedback literature, the BVP research has been characterized by an extremely small number of trials (averaging less than 15 sessions in most applications), in spite of the fact that voluntary control of vasoconstriction is difficult to learn. For example, if one looks at the number of training sessions used by the researchers in control of epileptic seizures through biofeedback (close to 100 sessions), it is fairly safe to say that researchers have not adequately explored learned vasoconstriction in migraine populations.

In the University of Georgia laboratory, we have been looking at cases of clinical failure after 15 BVP training sessions and have found a number of subjects with as many as 50 to 60 sessions. With these cases of very severe and long-standing migraine (20 to 30 years), we have consistently obtained marked reduction or elimination of head pain. In all these cases, success was due to the individuals' acquisition of extremely effective voluntary control of the vasomotor response. Again, the point is that clinicians need to know about the conditions of learning that will produce a highly effective method for training voluntary control in a short period of time. With a well-learned response, it is then possible to determine whether acquisition of this response results in a change of pain activity. Further, appropriate clinical applications of BVP training require only a polygraph, a Schmitt trigger, an audio generator, and a few connections.

CONCLUSIONS

The current chapter has addressed critical methodological issues in the area of headache research. In order to determine whether a treatment technique is effective with any physical or psychological disorder, several prerequisites must be considered:

1. There must be a clear description and definition of the disorder. Criteria for identifying and measuring the disorder must be clearly specified and

utilized. The reliability and validity of these criteria must be established.

2. The mechanism of the disorder should be known in order to investigate etiological factors and intervention procedures.

3. The nature and parameters of the intervention technique must be clearly specified, where it is dose–response curves with chemotherapy or rate of acquisition of the target response with biofeedback.

4. After these prerequisites have been met, then well-controlled outcome studies can be conducted.

It is difficult to escape the conclusion that few if any of these prerequisites have been met, or even considered, in the biofeedback and headache literature to date.

REFERENCES

Adams, H. E., Feuerstein, M., & Fowler, J. L. The migraine headache: A review of parameters, theories, and interventions. *Psychological Bulletin,* 1980, *87,* 217–237.

Bakal, D. A. Headache. In R. A. Woody (Ed.), *Encyclopedia of clinical assessment.* San Francisco: Jossey-Bass, 1979.

Beatty, E. T., & Haynes, S. W. Behavioral intervention with muscle-contraction headache: A review. *Psychosomatic Medicine,* 1979, *41,* 165–180.

Blanchard, E. B., & Ahles, T. A. Behavioral treatment of psychophysiological disorders. *Behavior Modification,* 1979, *3,* 518–549.

Blanchard, E. B., Ahles, T. A., & Shaw, E. R. Behavioral treatment of headaches. In M. Hersen, R. M. Eisler, & P. M. Miller (Eds.), *Progress in behavior modification.* New York: Academic Press, 1979.

Brener, J. A general model of self-control applied to the phenomena of learned cardiovascular change. In P. P. Obrist, A. H. Black, & L. V. DiCara (Eds.), *Cardiovascular psychophysiology.* Chicago: Aldine, 1974.

Budzynski, T. H., Stoyva, J. M., Adler, C. S., & Mullaney, D. J. EMG biofeedback and tension headache: A controlled outcome study. *Psychosomatic Medicine,* 1973, *35,* 484–486.

Cattell, R. B. *Description and measurement of personality.* New York: World, 1946.

Epstein, L. H., & Abel, G. G. An analysis of biofeedback training effects for tension headache patients. *Behavior Therapy,* 1977, *8,* 37–47.

Feuerstein, M., & Adams, H. E. Cephalic vasomotor feedback in the modification of migraine headache. *Biofeedback and Self-Regulation,* 1977, *2,* 241–254.

Feuerstein, M., Adams, H. E., & Beiman, I. Cephalic vasomotor and electromyographic feedback in the treatment of combined muscle contraction and migraine headaches in a geriatric case. *Headache,* 1976, *16,* 232–237.

Fordyce, W. *Behavioral methods for chronic pain and illness.* St. Louis: C. V. Mosby, 1976.

Friar, L. R., & Beatty, J. Migraine: Management by trained control of vasoconstriction. *Journal of Consulting and Clinical Psychology,* 1976, *44,* 46–53.

Friedman, A. P. Ad hoc committee on classification of headache. *Journal of the American Medical Association,* 1962, *179,* 717–718.

Friedman, A. P. Characteristics of tension headache: A profile of 1,420 cases. *Psychosomatics,* 1979, *20,* 451–461.

Fridlund, A. J., Fowler, S. C., & Pritchard, D. A. Striate muscle tensional patterning in frontalis EMG biofeedback. *Psychophysiology,* 1980, *17,* 47–55.

Gainer, J. C. Temperature discrimination training in the biofeedback treatment of migraine headache. *Journal of Behavior Therapy and Experimental Psychiatry,* 1978, *9,* 185–188.

Haynes, S. N. Behavioral variance, individual differences, and trait theory in a behavioral construct system: A reappraisal. *Behavioral Assessment,* 1979, *1,* 41–50.

Largen, J. W., Mathew, R. J., Dobbins, D., Meyer, J. S., & Claghorn, J. L. Skin temperature self-regulation and noninvasive regional cerebral blood flow. *Headache*, 1978, *18*, 203–210.

Paul, G. L. Physiological effects of relaxation training and hypnotic suggestions. *Journal of Abnormal Psychology*, 1969, *74*, 425–437.

Philips, C. Tension headache: Theoretical problems. *Behaviour Research and Therapy*, 1978, *16*, 249–261.

Pope, H. G., & Lipinski, J. F. Diagnosis in schizophrenia and manic–depressive illness. *Archives of General Psychiatry*, 1978, *35*, 811–828.

Schandler, S. L., & Grings, W. W. An examination of methods for producing relaxation during short-term laboratory sessions. *Behaviour Research and Therapy*, 1976, *14*, 419–426.

Silver, B. V., & Blanchard, E. B. Biofeedback and relaxation training in the treatment of psychophysiological disorders: Or are the machines really necessary? *Journal of Behavioral Medicine*, 1978, *1*, 217–239.

Stoyva, J. M. Some unresolved issues in the generalization of muscle relaxation. In N. Birbaumer & H. D. Kimmel (Eds.), *Biofeedback and self-regulation*. Hillsdale, N.J.: Erlbaum, 1979.

Sturgis, E. T., Adams, H. E., & Brantley, P. J. The parameters, etiology and treatment of migraine headaches. In S. N. Haynes & L. R. Gannon (Eds.), *Psychosomatic disorders: A psychophysiological approach to treatment and etiology*. New York: Praeger, 1981.

Sturgis, E. T., Tollison, C. D., & Adams, H. E. Modification of combined migraine–muscle contraction headaches using BVP and EMG feedback. *Journal of Applied Behavior Analysis*, 1978, *11*, 215–223.

Turk, D. C., Meichenbaum, D. H., & Berman, W. H. Application of biofeedback for the regulation of pain: A critical review. *Psychological Bulletin*, 1979, *86*, 1322–1338.

Thompson, J. K., Turkat, I. D., & Adams, H. E. *Assessment and classification of headache*. Unpublished manuscript, 1980. (Available from the authors.)

ROUND-TABLE DISCUSSION OF COX AND HOBBS AND ADAMS, BRANTLEY, AND THOMPSON

Jackson Beatty: As you were reviewing the muscle tension headache studies, I came to two conclusions: (1) There is what I would regard as an exceptionally high success rate, between 75% and 100%; and (2) these rates are equivalent to those produced by other therapies, such as psychotherapy and simple relaxation therapy. Is that true?

Daniel Cox: About two-thirds of the chronic headache victims experience 75% to 100% reduction. There is a substantial therapeutic effect.

Jackson Beatty: These effects are so potent that I'm surprised there's such a thing as a chronic headache victim left.

Gary Schwartz: What is the usual percent improvement on placebo medication?

Daniel Cox: Thirty-six percent improved.

Gary Schwartz: Thirty-six percent? So it was almost double in the biofeedback studies? I would like to report my experiences with a case which has a bearing on the long-term effects of behavioral treatment. You sometimes put people into a dilemma when you train them in self-control methods, and this was really brought home to me this year by a patient I saw in a research clinic. He was a second-year medical student at Yale who was successfully practicing relaxation and cognitive restructuring for his headaches. Frequency of headache was decreasing, but it was really bad when he studied, particularly when he was studying pathophysiology and anatomy. As you know, these are tremendously difficult subjects which require intense concentration and may result in much corrugating in the frontal region. We brought him to the laboratory and hooked him up to the EMG equipment while he practiced studying. Listening to the feedback, he found that he could reduce his EMG to quite low levels and his headaches would disappear. But he had to slow the speed and the rate with which he was trying to cram in this information in order to maintain those low levels.

Martin Orne: Better he should have his headaches.

Gary Schwartz: That's what he ultimately chose. He decided he would rather take Valium. Many people in life have this play-off between maintaining or reducing relevant systems compared to alterations in their environment, and this is going to have, I think, obvious bearing with regard to "long-term effectiveness" of biofeedback.

John Furedy: I want to take issue both with Dr. Cox and with the discussant[s] [Henry Adams, Phillip Brantley, and Kevin Thompson]. The message of Dr. Cox's paper seems very clearly to be that we now know that biofeedback works and the next issue to get on to is that of mechanisms. However, on page 346 of his chapter, he indicates that the therapeutic effect of biofeedback is superior to no treatment, to noncontingent [feedback] or pseudofeedback, etc. Yet, aside from how you view the literature in general, I think that's grossly inconsistent with what he says on page 345. On page 345, the sentence[s] talking about Philips' study [1977], [it is stated that] there is no posttreatment difference between groups on headache frequency. It seems to me that sentence as a summary and also as a general characterization is inaccurate. I agree with Dr. Adams. I don't think we do know whether biofeedback is effective, and it isn't time to get on to the mechanisms yet. However, I think that his requirements, though necessary, are not sufficient. In particular, the notion of saying that you've established a biofeedback effect once you have voluntary control is not sufficient, because that too can be a simple instructional effect which has nothing to do with the feedback of the information required. In our study of heart rate [Riley & Furedy, 1979, 1981]—which is, of course, a different situation—when we asked subjects to decrease or increase their heart rate on instructions, we found a gradual learning effect over sessions. So you have a gradual learning effect of the voluntary response. We obtained this potentially clinically significant, hard-to-get decelerative heart beat, but there was no biofeedback effect because there was no difference at all between the groups who received contingent feedback about their heart rate and those who received inaccurate information. You've got all the marks of learning here—a gradual increase over trials and a relatively large desirable response—but it is not a *biofeedback* effect.

Martin Orne: I was bothered earlier on by Dr. Cox's statement that biofeedback would document that tension headache is not due to tension. I believe the data cited for that are the low correlations between the clinical results of biofeedback and the effect of training on learning how to relax; whereas I believe that the data upon which the clinical assumption is based show that tension headache is related to muscle tension.

Daniel Cox: The most recent literature using current electromyographic techniques among tension headache patients has found no difference between periods of headache and headache-free periods as measured at the frontalis, trapezius, and temporalis sites. Now, within that group, there are individuals that do demonstrate marked elevations in EMG; but as a group, that has not been found.

Edward Blanchard: The Epstein and Abel paper [1977] shows almost a zero-order correlation between report of pain sensation and EMG level measured in a session.

Henry Adams: If you look at that paper by Epstein, (1) there was no correlation reported; but (2) when you use the data presented in his table to calculate the correlation yourself, you find that there's a fairly substantial correlation of approximately +.6.

Richard Surwit: Were any studies that report correlations between EMG and headache pain concerned with the relationship between trapezius activity and headache, because the trapezius is the relevant muscle body in muscle-contraction headaches, not the frontalis? Has anybody looked at that?

Daniel Cox: Several people have. I think Philips [1977] demonstrated that that was the most responsive musculature and that that musculature was one which differentiated tension headache victims from normals.

Richard Surwit: Is there any information on the correlation between changes in trapezius tension?

Joel Lubar: I find that training the trapezius is much more effective than frontalis; I don't find there's any particular relationship with frontalis.

Richard Surwit: Does anybody have data on the relationship between trapezius levels and pain, or doesn't that exist?

Daniel Cox: Philips [1977] reported that, too, and there was no relationship.

Jackson Beatty: I think that the lack of the relationship between muscle tension and tension headache may be due to the fact that the correlation is taken on two different kinds of patients; and that correlation is going to be darned near zero if you put together psychogenic headache and muscle tension headache, because you're going to have one population of patients who report head pain but who have very, very low muscle tension.

Joel Lubar: I have a question of clarification for Dr. Cox. You said that although there was no overall difference in muscle tension between the patients that have headaches and those that do not, there was a great deal of variability, and some of them had very high tension levels. The first question is how they differed in terms of other factors, personality or otherwise; and secondly, do biofeedback or some of the other self-control techniques work better for that group where the tension is high initially than for the group who are normotensive?

Daniel Cox: The research on individual differences tends to get a little thin. In terms of elevated EMG, two studies [Bruhn, Olesen, & Melgaard, 1979; Epstein, Abel, Collins, Parker, & Cinciripini, 1978] have found that extremely elevated EMG at pretreatment predicts poor treatment responses, and that's with frontalis EMG biofeedback.

Gary Schwartz: There is some recent work being reported by Qualls and Sheehan [1979], who did a number of studies based on individual differences in the measure of "absorption level," which correlates highly—about +.25, which is relatively high in that literature—with hypnotic susceptibility. These studies examined frontal EMG response to meditation procedures versus biofeedback procedures for lowering EMG levels. At least in the first session or two, subjects with high scores on absorption do better with meditation than with biofeedback; and you get the reverse effect for low absorbers.

In other words, people who become involved in the imaginal processes and can just lose themselves do better in reducing EMG by simply ignoring the feedback and getting into their meditation than they do by attending externally to the feedback, at least initially. Low absorbers, however—people who have a difficult time attending to internal cues and their own imaginal processing—do better while attending to external stimuli. This may relate, also, to some important individual differences in self-regulation of muscle tension in headache patients.

Robert Gatchel: Today we've talked about tension headaches, and yesterday vascular headaches. Where does the mixed type fit in, and has there been enough effort to sufficiently make a differentiation between the two types of headache?

Daniel Cox: Bakal and Kaganov's article [1977] looked at neurologically diagnosed muscle-contraction and neurologically diagnosed migraine headaches. They looked at location, type of pain, and symptoms. The only things that were unique in migraine patients were responsiveness to ergotamines and nausea and vomiting. Tension headache patients had parietal, unilateral throbbing pain, while migraine patients also had frontal, bilateral, steady aching pain.

Robert Gatchel: What is the relative breakdown in terms of percentage? I always come across confusing statistics in terms of percentage of mixed versus vascular versus tension. I hear everything from 20% to 80% mixed.

Edward Blanchard: We have a series of about 80 consecutive chronic headache people coming in for pretreatment. It's about 50% tension, 20% pure migraine, 20% mixed, and 10% cluster.

Steven Wolf: Ed, does that say that no patients are the psychogenic patients in anxiety?

Edward Blanchard: Well, I'm lumping what he calls psychogenic headache under tension headache, and probably mistakenly so.

Henry Adams: We've done some studies with one particular type of combined headache, the Sturgis study that was reported in JABA [Journal of Applied Behavior Analysis; Sturgis, Tollison, & Adams, 1978]. We've used a multiple baseline, first with BVP feedback and then with EMG feedback, and have shown that the BVP feedback will knock out the migraines but won't touch the tension, and the reverse. But there are some cases where the migraine patients report that it starts with muscle tension. Not all of them, but some 10% or 20% would tell you that during the development of migraine, they begin to feel muscle tightness.

Richard Surwit: Lance, the Australian neurologist, has an excellent book out called *Mechanism and Management of Headache*, third edition, published by Butterworths [Lance, 1978]; and it's a fabulous review of the pathophysiology of and treatment approaches to headache, including behavioral treatments. He says, by the way, that from his point of view, relaxation training with or without biofeedback is the treatment of choice for muscle-contraction headache, for whatever it's worth. I think you'll find your figures as to incidence in that book. Also, Lance points out that a muscle-contraction headache may very well be partially ischemic. He claims that it may be necessary for ischemia and muscle tension to occur simultaneously; and we all know that that is an excellent way of producing pain. In fact, this could be the reason why the classic migraine starts out as a muscle pain in the back of the neck, because that's part of the vasoconstrictor, ischemia phase, which gives way to the active hyperemic phase.

Bernard Tursky: That's a very interesting point from the standpoint of being able to report pain, because ischemic pain is pure pain intensity. There is very little affect that goes with ischemic pain, so that there might be a teasing out of differences between the migraine and the tension headache using psychophysical methods.

Martin Orne: The trouble is that the migraine headache is the one which the neurologist tries to define. Histamine response is a criterion which is used and which is reasonably objective and accurate. However, everything else tends to get put into "tension headache," and "tension" is not defined. In fact, for most neurologists, it doesn't really mean "muscle tension"; it means "tension" in a generic sense. You know, Excedrin headaches go into the same category. It is necessary to identify and separate the components before we can make any real sense of the data. Maybe then we'd find that there is some sense in the biofeedback therapy concerning those who respond. That is yet to be documented. I think that the data are very compelling that any specific treatment which is accepted as specific treatment by the patient, if not by the therapist, tends to work. One of the most difficult problems regarding the determination of specific efficacy is whether core placebo treatments in biofeedback are inactive placebo treatments. Also, if there are characteristics of the placebo that allow the patients to break the blind conditions, the "placebo" may be inadequate or limited as an experimental control. I am reminded of the first Thorazine placebo study I was involved in. We compared Thorazine and placebo on the ward. Obviously, none of the doctors and none of the nurses knew which pill was placebo and which was Thorazine. I was nasty enough to ask patients, and every patient knew whether he was on drug or placebo.

Peter Lang: In terms of the classification of headache patients, I wonder if it isn't similar to the sort of problem that we have in research with fear and anxiety. We may be confusing the classification system with a theoretical mechanism, and then confounding discussion of treatment effects as reflected in the data with changes in the theoretical mechanism; or are we talking about some difference in a response level? To some extent, behavioral modification has been using a three-system analysis for fear, and I think the same kind of three-system analysis may apply to the analysis of pain. What defines an affect like fear, and in part what defines pain, is the verbal report. Now that can be very complex and analyzed in complex ways. One component of pain or fear may be manifest as a performance or behavioral deficit. In the case of fear, that may be evaluated by avoidance behavior. In the case of headache, there may be performance consequences of headache that are independent of when the person says it. Another axis is physiology. One of the things you find in fear and anxiety is that verbal report, behavioral response, and physiological response don't necessarily correlate. They move in different ways, but there are patterns and they're to be understood. Bernie Tursky's psychophysical methods may also be used to refine verbal reports of pain. You might then be able to differentiate several types of headaches. We must establish a data base for headache which goes beyond the verbal report "I've got a headache!"

REFERENCES

Bakal, D. A., & Kaganov, J. A. Muscle contraction and migraine headache: Psychophysiological comparison. *Headache,* 1977, *17,* 208–215.

Bruhn, P., Olesen, J., & Melgaard, B. Controlled trial of EMG feedback in muscle contraction headaches. *Annals of Neurology,* 1979, *6,* 34–36.

Epstein, L. H., & Abel, G. G. An analysis of biofeedback training effects for tension headache patients. *Behavior Therapy,* 1977, *8,* 37–47.

Epstein, L. H., Abel, G. G. Collins, F., Parker, L.,

& Cinciripini, P. M. The relationship between frontalis muscle activity and self-reports of headache pain. *Behaviour Research and Therapy*, 1978, *16*, 153–160.

Lance, J. W. *Mechanism and management of headache* (3rd ed.). London: Butterworths, 1978.

Philips, C. The modification of tension headache pain using EMG biofeedback. *Behaviour Research and Therapy*, 1977, *5*, 119–129.

Qualls, P. J., & Sheehan, P. W. Capacity for absorption and relaxation during electromyograph biofeedback and no-feedback conditions. *Journal of Abnormal Psychology*, 1979, *88*, 652–662.

Riley, D. M., & Furedy, J. J. Instructional and contingency manipulations in the conditioning of human phasic heart rate change using a discrete-trials procedure. *Psychophysiology*, 1979, *16*, 192. (Abstract)

Riley, D. M., & Furedy, J. J. Effects of instructions and contingency of reinforcement on the operant conditioning of human phasic heart-rate change. *Psychophysiology*, 1981, *18*, 75–81.

Sturgis, E. T., Tollison, C. D., & Adams, H. E. Modification of combined migraine–muscle contraction headaches using BVP and EMG feedback. *Journal of Applied Behavior Analysis*, 1978, *11*, 215–223.

15 EMG BIOFEEDBACK IN ANXIETY REDUCTION

ROBERT J. GATCHEL

As I have noted elsewhere (Gatchel, 1979), one of the important potential applications that attracted many clinical researchers to the field of biofeedback was the possible use of learned control of physiological responses as a means of treating anxiety. Over the years, various treatment techniques were developed with the major goal of reducing the physiological underpinnings of anxiety. Many of these approaches were formulated on the basis of theoretical accounts of anxiety that suggested the importance of physiological responsivity in fear behavior (a discussion of these theoretical accounts can be found in Gatchel, 1980). In treatments such as progressive relaxation therapy (Jacobson, 1938), systematic desensitization (Wolpe, 1958), and autogenic training (Schultz & Luthe, 1959), the primary aim is the production of a low state of physiological arousal that competes against the anxiety response and accompanying elevated arousal level. Biofeedback was viewed by many as possibly providing a more direct method of modifying the physiological component of this aversive emotional state.

Robert J. Gatchel. Department of Psychiatry, University of Texas Health Sciences Center, Dallas, Texas.

The possibility of employing EMG biofeedback procedures for the induction of generalized muscular relaxation that could compete against anxiety was first suggested by Budzynski and Stoyva (1969). These authors anecdotally reported that when individuals successfully reduced tension levels in the frontalis muscle, there was a generalized relaxation effect produced in other skeletal muscles in the body. Also, there was an accompanying subjective feeling of relaxation and calmness. Stoyva and Budzynski (1974) subsequently called this procedure "cultivated low-arousal training," and claimed that reductions in autonomic measures also accompanied the decreased tension in the frontalis. Studies such as that of Smith (1973) also started to appear in the scientific literature, suggesting a relationship between resting frontalis EMG levels and the anxiety levels of subjects. Thus, even though there were also a number of studies not showing a significant relationship between EMG levels and anxiety (e.g., Balshan, 1962; Shipman, Oken, & Heath, 1970), single-site EMG biofeedback training was viewed as possibly providing an effective means for reducing the tension and anxiety level of individuals.

In this chapter, I review the numerous studies that have evaluated the treatment efficacy of EMG biofeedback methods in alleviating anxiety. However, before reviewing this research, the following issues are briefly discussed: (1) problems associated with the definition and measurement of anxiety; (2) the importance of differentiating between "situational" or "state" anxiety and "general" or "trait" anxiety; (3) the importance of taking into account individual differences in response to biofeedback treatment; and (4) the potentially significant role of placebo factors in biofeedback treatment. These are important issues that have significant implications for the design, analysis, and interpretation of results of biofeedback treatment studies. The EMG biofeedback investigations that are subsequently reviewed vary in their attempts to deal with these issues adequately.

THE DEFINITION AND MEASUREMENT OF ANXIETY

Before embarking on a discussion of whether EMG biofeedback is effective in reducing anxiety, an important prerequisite is agreement upon just what anxiety is and how to go about measuring it. Although most people have a subjective feeling of what anxiety is, there is unfortunately no universally accepted definition of this aversive emotional state. Indeed, this is reflected in the fact that there are no fewer than 120 procedures available that are purported to measure anxiety (Cattell & Scheier, 1961). As Lang (1978) has indicated, "It is curious that a phenomenon so widely remarked and considered fundamental to psychopathology should be so resistant to precise definition" (p. 143).

As we are all aware, "anxiety" is a construct that is inferred in order to account for some form of behavior. It is usually viewed as a mediator or unobservable inferred construct that accounts for some observable behavior, such as task performance differences between individuals. Of course, if a construct such as "anxiety" is used to explain some form of behavior, it is imperative that a precise operational definition be developed and that objective and quantifiable measures of that construct be employed.

An increasing number of clinical researchers interested in the study of anxiety operationally define it as a complex of responses consisting of three broad components of behavior: (1) subjective or self-report measures; (2) physiological responding; and (3) overt motor behavior, such as trembling or stuttering. However, what makes the study and measurement of anxiety so difficult is that researchers cannot always assume that these three broad behavioral component measures will be highly correlated with one another. A person may verbally report that he or she is not anxious, but yet may be observed trembling and stuttering, and displaying a greatly accelerated heart rate. It is therefore very important to evaluate all three components in specific situations whenever possible, with the expectation that there may well be some complex interaction among components. Moreover, the nature of these interactions may differ from one type of anxiety-producing situation to the next.

Within the physiological component, there may also be low correlations among various measures (Lacey, 1967). For example, in a biofeedback study that is reviewed later in this chapter, Gatchel, Korman, Weis, Smith, and Clarke (1978) demonstrated that an EMG biofeedback group was able to maintain a learned low level of frontal EMG activity during a stress induction procedure. This low level of EMG activity, though, did not generalize to other physiological measures. Both heart rate and skin conductance levels increased, and these increases coincided with the subjects' self-reports of anxiety. Similar findings for such "fractionation" of physiological responding during stress were reported in an EMG biofeedback study conducted by McGowan, Haynes, and Wilson (1979).

This fractionation of physiological responding expresses itself not only across physiological response systems, but also within a system. Within the somatic system, there is no unequivocal evidence that feedback-induced muscle tension reduction at a single site, such as the frontalis, will have a generalized effect on other muscle sites (e.g., Alexander & Dimmick-Smith, 1979; Fridlund, Fowler, & Pritchard, 1980).[1] As is emphasized throughout the present chapter, EMG reduction at a single site, such as the forehead, cannot be automatically assumed to be a measure of the general relaxation state of an individual.

[1]The term "frontalis EMG" has been used by investigators in the majority of studies to be reviewed in this paper. The proper term, however, is the two frontalis *muscles* or "frontales" because one electrode was placed over each frontalis muscle in these studies. Also, it should be realized that muscle groups adjacent to the frontales are also involved in this EMG measure.

One must also keep in mind that many physiological measures of anxiety are also indices of other arousal states. A greatly accelerated heart rate, for example, is associated with anxiety not only, but also with such positive emotional states as sexual arousal. However, if an individual reports that he or she is anxious and tense, displays a greatly elevated heart rate, and is observed to be trembling and sweating, then an observer would be on relatively solid ground in inferring the presence of anxiety in that person.

Finally, as I have pointed out previously (Gatchel, 1979) concerning the assessment and treatment of anxiety,

> Proponents of social learning/behavioral approaches have been most vocal in emphasizing the importance of clearly specifying stimulus conditions and then assessing how they modulate response system interactions when dealing with a maladaptive behavior such as anxiety. . . . This approach has increasingly been demonstrated to be both practical and heuristic in its emphasis upon an individual's behavior in specific situations. . . . An anxiety treatment procedure can then be developed to modify an individual's maladaptive response pattern to a specific stress situation. Treatment success is able to be subsequently assessed in terms of the amount of desirable changes in the specific target behaviors which occur before and after therapy. Such an approach emphasizes the integration of assessment and treatment. Assessment is a vital procedure used in order to clearly define the focal problem behavior and, also, to allow quantifiable interpretation of therapy results. (p. 150)

As becomes apparent, the EMG biofeedback studies I review vary greatly in the precision of this assessment–treatment process.

STATE ANXIETY VERSUS TRAIT ANXIETY

Directly related to the above approach emphasizing the direct assessment of an individual's behavior in specific situations is the traditional distinction made between "situational" or "state" anxiety and "general" or "trait" anxiety. Providing only limited biofeedback training over a short period of time cannot be expected to produce an overall reduction in general trait anxiety. This would most likely require many months and even years of treatment. This limited training, though, might be capable of having some momentary impact on an aversive situation, since the individual would now possess a self-control skill that he or she could actively employ to compete against the momentary situational or state anxiety. Clinicians and researchers must be careful not to become too grandiose in expecting global reductions in trait anxiety levels of such persons in studies providing only a limited amount of biofeedback training. As may be seen in the studies to be reviewed, some researchers are guilty of this grandiosity.

INDIVIDUAL DIFFERENCES IN RESPONSE TO BIOFEEDBACK TREATMENT

To date, there has been no systematic research on individual differences in response to biofeedback treatment. As I note later, the majority of studies to be reviewed in this chapter are between-group designs in which EMG biofeedback is employed across all subjects without independently determining whether EMG, as well as the specific site from which it was recorded, was a major component of anxiety for a particular individual. Also, it is important to determine whether that individual can learn to exert a significant degree of control over the specific target physiological response.

Individual differences in physiological responding have been well documented (Lacey, 1967). It therefore appears essential to take into account these individual differences in psychophysiological patterns of responding in deciding upon the target physiological behavior around which to tailor the biofeedback treatment. A specific site used in EMG biofeedback may not be effective for all subjects, but only for those who can learn to control EMG voluntarily, and for whom EMG is a dominant component of the anxiety response. For other individuals, some other physiological response or combination of responses may be dominant. For still other people, a particular physiological component of anxiety may not be dominant at all. Rather, the cognitive component may be more important. In such cases, some type of cognitive behavior therapy would have to be employed. Indeed, the concept of tailoring treatment to each individual client is not novel to the field of behavior therapy (e.g., Goldfried & Davison, 1976). Such "tailoring" is required for biofeedback treatment, with the expectation that biofeedback will not be clinically useful for all clients. Such "tailoring" has not been employed in past research assessing the clinical effectiveness of EMG biofeedback in reducing anxiety.

THE ROLE OF PLACEBO FACTORS IN BIOFEEDBACK TREATMENT

A great amount of publicity and exaggerated accounts of "cure-all" biofeedback techniques regularly appear in the news media. This publicity and enthusiasm for biofeedback technology may have as much to do with its therapeutic success as the treatment itself, because of the expectancy or demand for improvement associated with it. Indeed, biofeedback has been referred to as "the ultimate placebo" (Stroebel & Glueck, 1973). Only recently, have studies such as those by my colleagues and myself (Gatchel, Hatch, Maynard, Turns, & Taunton-Blackwood, 1979; Gatchel, Hatch, Watson, Smith, & Gaas, 1977; Gatchel & Proctor, 1976) been conducted to demonstrate carefully the important role that placebo factors play in biofeedback programs directed at the reduction of fear and anxiety. A great deal more of such controlled research is sorely needed in the area of EMG biofeedback. In passing, it should be noted that even if placebo factors are eventually found to be the major active ingredient in biofeedback treatment, such a revelation would not detract from its therapeutic effectiveness, *as long as clinicians realize this* so that they can best choose the appropriate treatment for their patients. Psychiatry and medicine have had a long history of employing placebo effects, and have continued to rely upon them (Shapiro, 1971). Indeed, there is a long-accepted maxim in medicine: "Treat many patients with new remedies while they still have the power to heal" (Shapiro, 1971, p. 442).

CLINICAL APPLICATIONS OF EMG BIOFEEDBACK

There is currently a paucity of systematic, well-controlled research that has adequately assessed the effectiveness of EMG biofeedback in the treatment of anxiety. I here review clinical case studies and controlled-group studies that have been conducted to date in which anxious patients were evaluated. In reviewing these studies, it should be kept in mind that a necessary requirement of them is a demonstration that subjects learn to control their EMG with biofeedback training. The failure to find such evidence for a learning effect would invalidate the efficacy of EMG biofeedback for the particular anxiety-related problem being examined. Finally, it should be noted that I do not review the numerous reports of EMG biofeedback and anxiety presented at scientific meetings and conventions for which only summary abstracts are available. Not enough information is available in such abstracts to allow a careful evaluation of method and results.

CLINICAL CASE STUDIES

Individual case studies that involve uncontrolled observations without attempts at objective measurement have basically no formal scientific value in the assessment of therapeutic outcome. Without some form of measurement, the evaluation of change remains purely on the subjective, inferential level. If a researcher introduces some form of assessment at pretreatment and posttreatment phases, there will be at least some basis for evaluation of change in even the individual case study. However, this still does not allow a precise delineation of cause–effect relationships in treatment outcome, because of the absence of control over important factors (such as therapist contact, placebo–expectancy effects, etc.) that may play an equally significant role in affecting changes in the patient's behavior. In passing, it should be noted that Barlow, Blanchard, Hayes, and Epstein (1977) have reviewed some basic procedures for the use of single-case experimental designs in clinical biofeedback evaluation research.

When there is a combination of case studies into a single-group design, there is an increase in one's confidence in the reliability of a clinical result because of the presence of a number of replications. All the problems associated with the single-case study method, however, are equally true for the single-group design.

Presently, there are a number of single-case studies and single-group studies evaluating the clinical effectiveness of EMG biofeedback in the treatment of anxious patients. Table 1 summarizes this work. These studies should only be viewed as suggestive of potential clinical effectiveness, and not as scientifically valid and conclusive demonstrations.

In one of the earliest case studies reported, Wickramasekera (1972) used EMG biofeedback-assisted muscle relaxation training as an adjunct to systematic desensitization in the treatment of test anxiety. Two initial relaxation training sessions were administered to a female client, using EMG biofeedback of frontales muscle activity. The client then visualized the hierarchical scenes to herself, and was instructed to terminate visualizing the scenes whenever the EMG biofeedback signal reached a predetermined high level. This treatment method was found to be successful in eliminating anxiety and allowing the client to pass an examination that she had avoided taking many times in the past because of her high anxiety. Delk (1977) also reported a case study, using a similar procedure, in the successful treatment of a 25-year-old woman with an obsessive–phobic–depressive syndrome. In addition, Budzynski and Stoyva (1973) have reported the successful use of EMG biofeedback as an adjunctive procedure in behavior therapy techniques for eliminating anxiety. However, no specific details of their procedure were reported.

In the first single-group study assessing the clinical effectiveness of EMG biofeedback training in reducing anxiety, Raskin, Johnson, and Rondestvedt (1973) examined the effects of daily deep muscle relaxation, achieved through frontales EMG biofeedback training, on the symptoms of 10 chronically anxious patients. All 10 of these patients reported that their anxiety symptoms significantly disrupted their daily lives. Therapist ratings of anxiety, insomnia, and tension headaches were assessed for 8 weeks prior to the training, during the period of feedback training, and during the 8 weeks of daily relaxation practice. On the basis of these ratings, it was determined that the biofeedback intervention had beneficial therapeutic effects on the anxiety of 4 of the 10 patients. One of these patients reported a dramatic decrease in all of his anxiety symptoms, while the other three learned to employ the relaxation method to lessen previously intolerable situational anxiety.

Leboeuf (1977) evaluated the effect of EMG biofeedback on state anxiety levels of anxious introverts and extroverts. State anxiety was assessed by the use of the state anxiety scale of Spielberger's State–Trait Anxiety Inventory, administered immediately before and after the final training sessions. Results indicated that both groups learned to relax their muscles adequately, assessed on the basis of changes from beginning to end of training sessions. The interesting finding of this study was that only introverts reported a significant decrease in state anxiety. Some of the anxious extroverts actually reacted adversely to the technique. These results point to the potential importance of at least one individual difference—introversion–extroversion—in predicting response to treatment.

Acosta, Yamamoto, and Wilcox (1978) assessed the effects of frontales EMG biofeedback on tension reduction in schizophrenic, neurotic, and tension headache outpatients. Analyses of EMG levels across training sessions revealed a significant learning effect for all three patient groups. There were no significant differences among the three groups. Unfortunately, no assessment was made of the effect of this training on the experiential states and symptomatology displayed by these patients.

Finally, Reeves and Mealiea (1975) used EMG-assisted relaxation in the treatment of three cases of flight phobia. Successful treatment results were reported with this procedure.

One of the major problems with the above studies is that most of them used systematic desensitization or relaxation procedures along with EMG biofeedback training. These former two procedures have been shown to produce significant therapeutic improvement of anxiety-related disorders in their own right. Thus, these studies do not answer the important question of whether EMG biofeedback adds anything significant to these basic procedures. Some of the controlled-group studies that are reviewed next have addressed this question.

CONTROLLED-GROUP STUDIES

A "true experiment" of treatment effectiveness involves administering treatment to one group of patients, while an equivalent group either does not receive treatment or receives some other form of therapy. Both groups are assessed before and after the treatment procedure. In employing such an experimental design, there is a possibility that cause–effect relationships can be statistically isolated. Such experiments, though, can still vary greatly in the precision and power associated with isolating such relationships, depending upon the characteristics of the experimental design utilized. For example, without including appropriate types of control groups to control for factors such as placebo–expectancy or the amount of therapist contact, which could have some important impact on anxiety, it may be impossible to isolate a clear, unconfounded cause–effect relationship. There are a wide variety of experimental designs that can be used in treatment evaluation research. Campbell and Stanley (1970) have provided an excellent review of many such designs.

TABLE 1. Case Studies and Single-Group Studies of EMG Biofeedback in Anxiety Reduction

Study	*Number and Types of Subjects*	*Type of Treatment*	*Treatment Duration*	*How Anxiety Measured*	*Results*
Reeves & Mealiea (1975)	3 flight-phobic patients	Frontales EMG biofeedback-assisted, cue-controlled relaxation and systematic desensitization	S_1 = 18 sessions S_2 = 19 sessions S_3 = 21 sessions	Posttreatment self-report of therapy effectiveness	All *S*s showed a reduction in EMG levels over training sessions; all *S*s reported subsequent ability to fly without major discomfort
Delk (1977)	1 patient with obsessive–phobic–depressive syndrome	Frontales EMG biofeedback-assisted systematic desensitization	10 sessions	Pretreatment and posttreatment assessment of frequency and intensity of depressive and obsessive–phobic thoughts associated with 13 common events in patient's life	Significant decrease for both frequency and intensity of obsessive–phobic–depressive thoughts
Leboeuf (1977)	16 anxious introverts and 16 anxious extroverts	1 session of extensor EMG biofeedback and 4 sessions of frontales EMG biofeedback	5 sessions	Pretreatment and posttreatment administration of State–Trait Anxiety Scale	Both introverts and extroverts showed significant reductions in EMG levels; introverts demonstrated a significant decrease in state anxiety; extroverts did not
Acosta, Yamamoto, & Wilcox (1978)	5 neurotics, 6 schizophrenics, and 3 ten-	Frontales EMG biofeedback	10 sessions	Not assessed	Significant decrease in EMG levels across

	sion headache patients, all complaining of chronic tension				training sessions for all patient types
Wickramasekera (1972)	1 highly test-anxious patient	Frontales EMG biofeedback-assisted systematic desensitization	Not clearly specified (at least 13 sessions)	Posttreatment self-report of therapy effectiveness	Patient learned to decrease EMG level over sessions; treatment found successful in eliminating anxiety and allowing patient to pass an examination she had avoided taking many times in the past because of high anxiety
Raskin, Johnson, & Rondestvedt (1973)	10 chronically anxious patients	Frontales EMG biofeedback-assisted muscle relaxation	Variable, with average training period of 6 weeks (five sessions per week)	10-point anxiety rating scale at beginning and end of each session; therapist ratings of anxiety, insomnia, and tension headaches before, during, and after treatment; patient ratings on 65-item mood checklist of anxiety	All patients learned to reduce EMG levels (by 1/2 to 1/8 of their initial values); no significant correlations between EMG scores and anxiety ratings within sessions; 4 out of 10 patients were rated as showing improvement in dealing with anxiety (based on the therapist and patient ratings)

Table 2 summarizes the various controlled-group studies that have evaluated the effectiveness of EMG biofeedback in reducing anxiety. A review of these studies makes it evident that they vary greatly in the adequacy of their experimental designs, and thus in the resultant ability to isolate treatment outcome effects clearly.

In the first controlled-group study of EMG biofeedback effectiveness in reducing anxiety, Townsend, House, and Addario (1975) employed chronically anxious patients who were matched in pairs on a combination of resting frontales EMG, state–trait anxiety, and total mood disturbance scores. They were assigned to one of two treatments: EMG biofeedback-mediated relaxation, or a short-term, structured group psychotherapy experience dealing specifically with anxiety. Initially, there were 15 patients assigned to each of the groups, but because of a variety of attrition factors, only 10 subjects in the biofeedback group and 8 in the group therapy condition completed the full treatment program. Evaluation of changes from the time of pretreatment assessment to periods during and after treatment indicated significant decreases in EMG levels, mood disturbances as measured by the Profile of Mood States, trait anxiety, and (to a lesser extent) state anxiety in the biofeedback group. No such decreases occurred in the comparison group-therapy condition.

Nigl and Jackson (1979) evaluated the effectiveness of EMG biofeedback training in the treatment of two groups of psychiatric patients—psychoneurotics and schizophrenics—and normal subjects. Here again, however, in addition to biofeedback, all subjects received training in muscle relaxation. Results indicated that all three groups reduced their levels of muscle tension. Moreover, the two patient groups had significantly lower ratings of pathological symptomatology and abnormal behavior after treatment. Also, these two groups of patients had a shorter length of hospitalization than did patients who received standard psychiatric treatment but no biofeedback training.

Page and Schaub (1978) divided 32 male alcoholics into two groups on the basis of their MMPI profiles: A group of those who were determined to be tense and anxious, and a more heterogeneous sample of personality types. Compared to subjects in a control group who merely listened to taped music and had their EMG monitored, those anxious patients receiving muscle relaxation training and EMG biofeedback demonstrated greater levels of relaxation. All patients showed a significant increase over time in the direction of improved mood states, as measured on the Profile of Mood States.

The results of the above three studies suggest the potential effectiveness of EMG biofeedback. However, the individual contribution of the deep muscle relaxation training provided to the biofeedback procedure cannot be separately assessed. Also, no attempts were made to control for possible placebo effects.

In another EMG biofeedback study, which did make such a separate assessment of the relative contribution of relaxation training, Canter, Kondo, and Knott (1975) directly compared the effectiveness of frontales EMG biofeedback to that of traditional Jacobson progressive muscle relaxation training in treating psychiatric patients diagnosed as anxiety neurotics. One-half of these patients reported having acute episodes associated with their condition, while the remaining half were typically more chronically anxious, without acute panic episodes. Results indicated that both the EMG biofeedback and relaxation training produced significant reductions in frontales tension levels. The biofeedback group, though, was found to be generally more effective in producing greater reductions in muscle activity, with a coincident greater relief in anxiety symptoms for a larger number of patients. These results suggest that EMG biofeedback training produces some therapeutic improvement above and beyond that produced by traditional progressive muscle relaxation training. However, the investigators report that the sample sizes were too small for a reliable determination of the statistical significance of the differences between groups.

A number of other studies have *not* found greater effectiveness of EMG biofeedback over progressive muscle relaxation. In one such study, Miller, Murphy, and Miller (1978) assessed the effects of frontales EMG biofeedback and progressive relaxation on the anxiety reactions of patients having recurrent negative reactions to dental treatment. Subjects were assigned to one of three treatments: EMG biofeedback, progressive relaxation training, or a control self-relaxation procedure. Results indicated greater decreases in EMG levels and in a number of self-report anxiety measures in the biofeedback and relaxation groups, as compared with the control self-relaxation group. There were no significant differences between the biofeedback and progressive relaxation groups.

In another study, Beiman, Israel, and Johnson (1978) employed subjects selected from respondents to local newspaper ads that solicited tense people to participate in a psychological study to alleviate their anxiety. Subjects were randomly assigned to one of four training conditions: live progressive relaxation, taped progressive relaxation, self-relaxation, or EMG biofeedback. In this study, besides EMG level, skin conductance and heart rate were also recorded, along with self-reported anxiety. Results indicated that across all measures, live progressive relaxation was superior to the other three procedures. Thus, this study demonstrates the superiority of live progressive relaxation training over biofeedback. The fact that the other relaxation procedures were not found superior indicates that the manner in which relaxation is administered makes a significant difference. This suggests that in comparative studies, care must be taken to administer relaxation training in the same careful therapeutic manner as that which is usually associated with the administration of EMG biofeedback.

Taken as a whole, the above studies do not support the contention that EMG biofeedback alone is any more effective than is simple progressive relaxation training in reducing anxiety. It is clear that both procedures can produce equally positive results. However, as Tarler-Benlolo (1978) has pointed out in a review of the litera-

TABLE 2. Controlled-Group Studies of EMG Biofeedback in Anxiety Reduction

Study	*Number and Types of Subjects*	*Type of Treatment*	*Treatment Duration*	*How Anxiety Measured*	*Results*
Canter, Kondo, & Knott (1975)	28 psychiatric patients diagnosed as anxiety neurotics	1. Frontales EMG biofeedback (14 *S*s) 2. Jacobson progressive relaxation training (14 *S*s)	10–25 sessions (determined by length of stay in hospital for inpatients, or indication by patient or therapist that no more sessions were needed for outpatients); inpatients = 3–4 sessions per week; outpatients = 6 sessions during first 10 days, then sessions at 1-week intervals	Posttreatment assessment of change in patient self-rating of anxiety, and independent ratings by their primary therapists of major anxiety symptoms	Both groups showed a decrease in EMG levels, but Group 1 demonstrated greater reductions than did Group 2; 85.7% of biofeedback subjects and 50% of relaxation subjects reported improvement; 66.7% of biofeedback subjects and 33.3% of relaxation subjects were reported improved by therapists
Townsend, House, & Addario (1975)	18 chronically anxious patients	1. Frontales EMG biofeedback-assisted relaxation (10 *S*s) 2. Group psychotherapy (8 *S*s)	*Biofeedback:* 9 20-minute training sessions over 2 weeks; 1/2 hour relaxation each day for 4 weeks *Psychotherapy:* 16 sessions	Pretreatment and posttreatment assessment of trait anxiety and state anxiety (measured by the State–Trait Anxiety Scale) and mood disturbance (measured by Profile of Mood States)	Significant decrease in EMG levels, mood disturbances, trait anxiety, and (to a lesser extent) state anxiety in the biofeedback group; no such changes in the psychotherapy group
Garrett & Silver (1976)	9 highly test-anxious college students	1. Frontales EMG biofeedback (10 *S*s) 2. Alpha biofeedback (10 *S*s) 3. Combined EMG and alpha biofeedback (9 *S*s) 4. Relaxation (10 *S*s) 5. No-training control (10 *S*s)	10 sessions for Groups 1–4	Pretreatment and posttreatment assessment on a Test Anxiety Questionnaire	EMG group decreased mean tension level 49.6% (combined group, 41.37%, relaxation group, 41.37%); alpha group increased mean level 33.2% (combined group, 44.9%, relaxation group, 18.4%); significant decrease in test

						anxiety for Groups 1–3 but not for Groups 4 and 5; no significant differences among groups for changes in grade-point average during the semester
Jessup & Neufeld (1977)	20 hospitalized psychiatric patients (predominately depressed)	1. Frontales EMG biofeedback (5 *Ss*) 2. Noncontingent EMG biofeedback (5 *Ss*) 3. Unaided self-relaxation (5 *Ss*) 4. Autogenic phrases (5 *Ss*)	4 sessions		Administration of Nowlis Mood Adjective Check List (MACL) before and during training sessions	No differences in EMG reduction between Groups 1 and 2; MACL anxiety scores decreased in only the noncontingent and autogenic groups; heart rate decreased in only the noncontingent group; no other reductions in dependent measures
Lavallée, Lamontagne, Pinard, Annable, & Tétreault (1977)	40 patients with free-floating anxiety	1. Frontales EMG biofeedback and diazepam (10 *Ss*) 2. Frontales EMG biofeedback and diazepam placebo (10 *Ss*) 3. Self-relaxation control and diazepam (10 *Ss*) 4. Self-relaxation control diazepam placebo (10 *Ss*)	8 sessions		Administration of Hamilton Anxiety Scale, Institute of Personality and Anxiety Testing Anxiety Scale, and deBonis Trait–State Anxiety Scale before treatment, after treatment, and at 1-, 3-, and 6-month follow-ups	Groups 1, 2, and 3 reduced muscle tension during treatment; reductions maintained by Groups 1 and 2 at 1-month follow-up; no difference between groups at 3- or 6-month follow-ups; Groups 1, 2, and 3 significantly reduced anxiety scores on all measures after treatment and at 1-month follow-up; only Groups 1 and 2 maintained reductions at 3 months; reductions were not maintained significantly at 6 months

(continued)

TABLE 2. *(continued)*

Study	*Number and Types of Subjects*	*Type of Treatment*	*Treatment Duration*	*How Anxiety Measured*	*Results*
Beiman, Israel, & Johnson (1978)	40 *Ss* who responded to a newspaper ad soliciting tense people to participate in a study to alleviate their tension	1. Live progressive relaxation (10 *Ss*) 2. Taped progressive relaxation (10 *Ss*) 3. Self-relaxation (10 *Ss*) 4. Frontales EMG biofeedback (10 *Ss*)	5 training sessions, 1 self-control session	Pretreatment and posttreatment assessment on the Trait Scale of the State–Trait Anxiety Inventory and the Multiple Affect Adjective Checklist (MAACL)	During self-control session, all subjects showed a decrease in EMG levels; all groups reported reductions in anxiety on the Trait Scale and MACL, with no differential change across groups; live relaxation was superior to all other treatments in producing decreases in spontaneous GSR
Counts, Hollandsworth, & Alcorn (1978)	40 highly test-anxious students	1. Frontales EMG-assisted, cue-controlled relaxation (10 *Ss*) 2. Cue-controlled relaxation (10 *Ss*) 3. Attention–placebo relaxation (10 *Ss*) 4. No-treatment control (10 *Ss*)	6 training sessions	Pretreatment and posttreatment assessment on Test Anxiety Scale, State–Trait Anxiety Inventory, and the Otis–Lennon Mental Ability Test (a measure of test-taking performance)	No results reported for EMG level reductions; cue-controlled relaxation alone was more effective in increasing test performance than the other treatment groups were; Groups 1, 2, and 3 showed greater decreases in test anxiety and state anxiety than the no-treatment control did; no differences among the three treatment groups

Gatchel, Korman, Weis, Smith, & Clarke (1978)	12 students who reported great difficulty managing everyday stress and anxiety, who were interested in learning a method for coping with it	1. Relaxation and frontales EMG biofeedback (6 *S*s) 2. False frontales EMG biofeedback (6 *S*s)	*Group 1:* 1 session of relaxation training, 2 sessions of biofeedback training *Group 2:* 1 adaptation session in which tones were administered, followed by 2 sessions of false biofeedback training	Pretreatment and posttreatment assessment of anxiety produced by mental arithmetic and threat-of-shock conditions (5-point self-report rating scale)	Significant reductions in EMG by Group 1 but not Group 2 during posttreatment stress task; no differences between groups on self-report anxiety measure
Kappes & Michaud (1978)	12 highly test-anxious students	Reverse design *Group 1:* Contingent frontales EMG biofeedback, followed by noncontingent biofeedback (6 *S*s) *Group 2:* Noncontingent frontales EMG biofeedback, followed by contingent biofeedback (6 *S*s)	5 sessions of contingent biofeedback and 5 sessions of noncontingent biofeedback	Pretreatment and posttreatment administration of the Suinn Test Anxiety Behavior Scale (STABS) and the Manifest Anxiety Scale (MAS)	Group 1 demonstrated significant lowering of EMG levels; Group 2 did not; no difference in MAS scores during contingent and noncontingent biofeedback sessions; STABS scores showed a significant decrease for both types of feedback in Group 2 and a greater decrease in contingent session in Group 1

(continued)

TABLE 2. *(continued)*

Study	*Number and Types of Subjects*	*Type of Treatment*	*Treatment Duration*	*How Anxiety Measured*	*Results*
Miller, Murphy, & Miller (1978)	21 dental patients having recurrent negative reactions to dental treatment	1. Frontales EMG biofeedback (7 *Ss*) 2. Progressive relaxation (7 *Ss*) 3. Self-relaxation control (7 *Ss*)	10 training sessions	Pretreatment and posttreatment assessment, during dental appointment, on the Corah Dental Anxiety Scale and the State–Trait Anxiety Inventory	Greater decrease in EMG levels by Groups 1 and 2 than by Group 3; no differences between Groups 1 and 2; all groups showed significant decrease in Corah Dental Anxiety scores and state anxiety and scores of Groups 1 and 2 were significantly lower than scores of Group 3; all groups showed significant decrease in trait anxiety, no differences among groups
Page & Schaub (1978)	32 alcoholics, half of whom were tense and anxious as determined by their MMPI profiles, and half of whom were a more heterogeneous sample of personality types	1. Progressive relaxation and frontales EMG biofeedback (8 anxious and 8 heterogeneous *Ss*) 2. Taped music and EMG monitoring (8 anxious and 8 heterogeneous *Ss*)	14 sessions	Administration of Profile of Mood States (POMS) during sessions 1, 5, 10, and 14	Group 1 *Ss* demonstrated significantly lower EMG levels that did Group 2 *Ss*; both groups reported reduced tension–anxiety over training, no group differences
Nigl & Jackson (1979)	10 psychoneurotics; 10 acute schizophrenics; 20 randomly selected patients with similar diagnoses as the above; 10 normals	1. Initial relaxation training followed by 6 sessions of frontales and extensor biofeedback (placement randomized for each session	6 training sessions for Group 1; number of sessions for Group 2 not known	Pretreatment and posttreatment administration of the MMPI, Ward Behavior Inventory (WBI), and Psychiatric Behavior Rating Scale (PBRS) for the	The two patient samples and normals in Group 1 reduced their EMG levels; significantly more improvement of pathological behavior assessed by WBI and PBRS for

		across subjects) (10 psychoneurotics, 10 acute schizophrenics)		psychiatric patients in Group 1; posttreatment administration of WBI and PBRS for Group 2	patients in Group 1 than in Group 2
Raskin, Bali, & Peeke (1980)	31 subjects satisfying the DSM-II criteria for diagnosis of anxiety neurosis and having their symptoms for 1 year or more	1. Frontales EMG biofeedback (11 *Ss*) 2. Muscle relaxation training (10 *Ss*) 3. Transcendental meditation (10 *Ss*)	18 sessions	Pretreatment, posttreatment, and later follow-up assessments of the following: trait anxiety as measured by the Taylor Manifest Anxiety Scale; state anxiety measured by the Current Mood Checklist; situational anxiety measured on 4-point scales; anxiety symptoms measured on 4-point scales; sleep disturbance and social ratings of maladjustment as assessed by the Structured and Scaled Interview to Assess Maladjustment	40% of the subjects demonstrated a clinically significant decrease in anxiety; there were no significant differences among the three groups in terms of effectiveness

ture on the role of relaxation in biofeedback training, it is currently impossible to determine the relative effectiveness of biofeedback and relaxation techniques because of a lack of standardization of the two procedures. Additional studies are needed to evaluate the relative effectiveness of these two procedures more systematically, both alone and in combination, in the treatment of fear and anxiety.

There have also been some EMG biofeedback studies that have examined the impact of placebo factors in reducing anxiety. In one such study, Garrett and Silver (1976) assessed the comparative effectiveness of EMG biofeedback training, alpha biofeedback, a combination of EMG and alpha biofeedback training, self-relaxation training designed to control for placebo effects, and a no-contact group in reducing test anxiety in highly test-anxious subjects. Test anxiety was measured on a questionnaire before and after training. Results demonstrated that the three biofeedback groups showed a decrease in test anxiety, while the self-relaxation and no-contact control groups did not. The three biofeedback groups were found to be equally effective in reducing anxiety. There were, however, *no* differences found among the five groups for improvement in academic performance during the year.

One problem with the above study was the possibility of low credibility being associated with the self-relaxation condition. Subjects in this group were merely given instructions to relax, blank the mind, and relax the muscles (these were the same instructions given to the biofeedback groups). The perceived credibility and therapeutic impact of such a placebo procedure can be seriously questioned.

Another investigation compared the relative effectiveness of EMG-assisted cue-controlled relaxation (while relaxing, focusing attention on breathing and saying the word "relax" with each exhalation); relaxation alone; and an attention–placebo relaxation procedure, in which subjects listened to a tape consisting of soothing music that they were told would produce relaxation. In this study, conducted by Counts, Hollandsworth, and Alcorn (1978), college undergraduates scoring in the upper third of a self-report of test anxiety were evaluated. Results demonstrated that cue-controlled relaxation alone was more effective in increasing the test performance of these test-anxious subjects than was either of the other procedures. The relaxation and combined relaxation–biofeedback procedures produced a greater decrease in self-reported anxiety than did the attention–placebo group. Again, it can be seriously questioned whether the perceived credibility of this placebo condition was equal to that of the other groups. However, the placebo group did demonstrate a significant decrease in the subjective measure of anxiety when compared to a no-treatment control group; this indicates that self-report measures of anxiety are susceptible to placebo effects.

There have been a number of other studies demonstrating the impact of placebo factors. Jessup and Neufeld (1977) reported some preliminary results of a study that evaluated the effectiveness of four techniques—frontales EMG biofeedback, noncontingent biofeedback, unaided self-relaxation, and autogenic phrases—in helping hospitalized psychiatric patients to relax. The noncontingent biofeedback training consisted of tape-recorded tones characteristic of those produced by biofeedback subjects who were able to relax successfully. These subjects were instructed simply to listen to the tape and "let the tone relax you." A host of physiological measures, as well as the Nowlis Mood Adjective Check List (MACL), were assessed before and during the daily training sessions. Results demonstrated that heart rate and MACL anxiety scores decreased significantly in subjects receiving the noncontingent biofeedback. However, except for a decrease in MACL anxiety scores for autogenic-phrase group subjects, the three treatment procedures did not significantly affect any of the dependent measures. This lack of therapeutic impact of the three treatments, all of which are usually found to produce some degree of relaxation, may have been due to the limited amount of training employed (only four sessions). Moreover, for the type of patient group used (predominantly depressed), a relaxation response may not have been an appropriate behavior upon which to focus treatment. Nevertheless, the fact that the noncontingent biofeedback group produced the greatest amount of relaxation behavior indicates the significant impact that nonspecific placebo-type procedures can have in the alleviation of anxiety.

Kappes and Michaud (1978) employed subjects who were selected on the basis of high test-anxiety scores. A reverse design was used, in which half of the subjects received five sessions of contingent EMG biofeedback followed by five sessions of noncontingent biofeedback; the other half received the reverse order. Results demonstrated no difference in manifest anxiety levels during contingent and noncontingent sessions. Also, Suinn Test Anxiety Behavior Scale scores showed a significant decrease for both types of feedback in the contingent–noncontingent order group. Again, therefore, noncontingent biofeedback can have a significant impact on anxiety level.

Similar results to the above were also found in the earlier-discussed experiment conducted by Gatchel *et al.* (1978). In this study, college students who experienced great difficulty in managing everyday anxiety and stress were employed. Findings indicated that there were no differences in anxiety reduction between the contingent EMG biofeedback and the false EMB biofeedback groups when subjects were exposed to laboratory stressors (a mental arithmetic task and a threat-of-shock procedure).

Finally, the only study in the literature to compare EMG biofeedback and drug effectiveness in reducing anxiety was conducted by Lavallée, Lamontagne, Pinard, Annable, and Tétreault (1977). This interesting experiment compared the effectiveness of frontales EMG biofeedback and diazepam, administered either separately or in combination, in the treatment of patients with chronic free-floating anxiety. Four treatments were employed in this study: (1) EMG biofeedback plus diazepam, (2) EMG biofeedback plus diazepam placebo, (3) diazepam alone, and (4) control self-relaxation plus diazepam placebo. The drug dosage was 5 mg of diazepam or placebo administered three times a day. The patients in this investigation had experienced chronic anxiety for at least 6 months, characterized by persistent and recurrent states of apprehension or nonspecific fear accompanied by physiological signs of arousal, such as tachycardia, palpitations, tremors, or dizziness.

Results of this study demonstrated that during treatment, the effects of EMG biofeedback plus diazepam were additive in reducing muscle tension levels. Overall, Groups 1, 2, and 3 were more effective than the placebo group was in reducing muscle tension level. During a 1-month follow-up, only the two biofeedback groups (Groups 1 and 2) continued to show a reduction in EMG. However, during 3- and 6-month follow-ups, there were no differences among the four groups.

Assessment of the anxiety measures yielded some rather interesting results. Groups 1, 2, and 3 demonstrated a significant reduction in anxiety after treatment and also at the 1-month follow-up; however, only the group receiving biofeedback alone (Group 2) maintained this significant reduction at the 3-month follow-up. At the 6-month follow-up, all the significant reductions had disappeared. Thus, the results of EMG training and diazepam administration were short-lived. The investigators pointed out, however, that some follow-up booster sessions may have helped maintain improvement. This possibility will need to be examined in future research.

An unexpected finding of this study was that, during follow-up evaluations, the mean anxiety level for patients in the placebo condition (Group 4) was lower than their levels during the pretreatment assessment period had been. The authors interpreted this unexpected finding as a possible result of the fact that the patients in this group reported significantly more regular and frequent home practice of relaxation than members of the other treatment groups did. Even though these patients were not instructed in a specific relaxation procedure, their regular practice with self-relaxation may have led them to develop an effective method on their own. Of course, this is only speculation that will require independent validation. The results, nevertheless, do again show the significant potential role that placebo factors can play in reducing anxiety. Future evaluation studies of biofeedback treatment will need to control carefully for their influence.

SUMMARY AND CONCLUSIONS

I have reviewed a variety of case studies and controlled-group studies that have assessed the effectiveness of EMG biofeedback in reducing anxiety. What, then, is the verdict on EMG biofeedback? A number of these studies have indicated that this procedure may be clinically effective with patients suffering primarily from anxiety. However, as a whole, the research conducted to date suggests that more easily administered and cost-efficient methods, such as progressive relaxation training, are at least equally effective. It is clear that the strong claims for the superior therapeutic efficacy of EMG biofeedback have been quite exaggerated and premature.

In a series of four experiments employing normal college students, Lang and his colleagues have come to basically the same conclusion regarding the equal effectiveness of other methods in producing relaxation (Cuthbert, Kristeller, Simons, Hodes, & Lang, 1980). These investigators found that Benson's secularized mediation training (Beary & Benson, 1974; Benson, Rosner, Marzetta, & Kleinchuk, 1974) generally produced greater relaxation (as reflected by heart rate, skin conductance, and verbal self-report data) than did heart rate biofeedback training. Heart rate biofeedback, in turn, was similar to frontales EMG biofeedback in its effects. Benson suggests that relaxation is a very generalized response that is most effectively produced by altering the subject's cognitive state. Subjects are encouraged to ignore the environment and to make the mind blank and free of thoughts through a silent verbal ritual (such as saying the word "one" repetitively with each respiratory cycle). Obviously, such a procedure would be preferred over biofeedback, because it requires no costly instrumentation. Zaichkowsky and Kamen (1978) have also found no difference between frontales EMG biofeedback training and the Benson meditation technique in reducing muscle tension level.

In a recent study, Raskin, Bali, and Peeke (1980) compared the relative effectiveness of EMG biofeedback, transcendental meditation, and muscle relaxation training in the treatment of chronic anxiety. Subjects employed in this study satisfied DSM-II criteria for the diagnosis of anxiety neuroses and had had their symptoms for 1 year or more. The investigation consisted of a 6-week baseline period, 6 weeks of treatment (three sessions per week), a 6-week posttreatment observation period, and a later follow-up. Trait anxiety, state anxiety, situational anxiety, anxiety symptoms, sleep disturbance, and social ratings of maladaptive behavior were obtained during these periods. Results indicated that 40% of the subjects displayed a clinically significant decrease in their anxiety. There were no significant differences among the three treatment procedures in terms of effectiveness. These results, therefore, again highlight the fact that more easily administered and cost-efficient methods are as effective as EMG biofeedback in the treatment of anxiety. Moreover, the fact that only 40% of the subjects demonstrated a decrease in anxiety argues that these relaxation-type therapies may have only a limited place in the treatment of chronic anxiety.

Another interesting finding of this study was the fact that there was very little relationship found between frontales EMG levels and anxiety. During the baseline period, the treatment period, and posttreatment periods, there were no statistically significant correlations found between the various measures of anxiety and EMG scores. Thus, one of the original assumptions underlying the use of EMG biofeedback—that there is a direct relationship between frontales EMG level and anxiety level of subjects—was not verified by these results.

As I have also pointed out in this chapter, an important factor associated with biofeedback that can significantly contribute to its therapeutic impact is the placebo effect. A number of studies reviewed have demonstrated the importance of placebo factors in EMG biofeedback, especially as reflected in the self-report component. As mentioned earlier in this chapter, placebo factors have been shown to contribute significantly to anxiety reduction in the heart rate biofeedback studies conducted by my colleagues and myself. They also appear to play an important role in EMG studies. Future EMG biofeedback investigations will need to take them into account more carefully in order to isolate their specific contributions to therapeutic improvement. (A number of placebo-control procedures to employ in biofeedback studies have recently been delineated by Katkin & Goldband, 1979.) One possible advantage of biofeedback procedures over more easily administered methods, such as relaxation and meditation, may be the stronger impact of such placebo factors. Since anxiety is especially responsive to placebo effects (Shapiro, 1971), it will be of great interest in future investigations of biofeedback and anxiety reduction to attempt to maximize placebo impact across all treatment procedures, and then to evaluate relative therapeutic effectiveness. Under such conditions, biofeedback may yield greater improvement.

Another issue that needs to be systematically investigated in future studies is the effect of individual differences in response to biofeedback. The assumption that a standard type of biofeedback, such as frontales EMG biofeedback, can be used with all individuals for anxiety reduction is naive at best. For the field of clinical biofeedback to progress, it will be vital to assess individual differences in the behavioral concomitants of emotional states such as anxiety. In response to the same stressor, different individuals will demonstrate different behavioral topographies. Administering a certain type of biofeedback training to the same target response in *all persons*, for example, in order to allow them to relax more effectively and to cope with the physiological component of anxiety, may not be maximally effective for all these individuals. An approach is needed that tailors the biofeedback training to the target physiological response(s) most involved in a person's anxiety reaction. Another procedure might also then be needed to deal with "cognitive" components (e.g., negative self-verbalizations) of the anxiety response. Such "tailoring" will be a necessary accompaniment of the full realization that biofeedback may not be clinically useful for all patients. Various nomothetic factors may also be uncovered that will help suggest which individuals will physiologically respond best to biofeedback, and which to other procedures such as relaxation.

Finally, an important point related to the above, and one that is often lost sight of, is the fact that biofeedback alone does not offer a simplistic solution to anxiety reduction in the great majority of cases. Skilled clinical intervention is usually required to discover what role anxiety plays in an individual's life and how best to help that person cope and interact with his or her environment. Indeed, Lazarus (1977) has placed biofeedback within the context of psychotherapy in general. He has noted, "First, we cannot in our thinking isolate the somatic disturbances and their self-regulation in biofeedback from the larger context of the person's adaptive commerce with his environment. Second, this adaptive commerce is constantly being mediated by social and psychological processes" (p. 73). Future research will need to take this into account and be sure to assess and treat anxiety carefully in specific situational contexts.

ACKNOWLEDGMENT

The writing of this paper was supported in part by a grant to the author from the National Heart, Lung, and Blood Institute (Grant No. NIH HL 21426-01).

REFERENCES

Acosta, F. X., Yamamoto, J., & Wilcox, S. A. Application of electromyographic biofeedback to the relaxation training of schizophrenic, neurotic, and tension headache patients. *Journal of Consulting and Clinical Psychology,* 1978, *46,* 383–384.

Alexander, A. B., & Dimmick-Smith, D. Clinical applications of EMG biofeedback. In R. J. Gatchel & K. P. Price (Eds.), *Clinical applications of biofeedback: Appraisal and status.* New York: Pergamon, 1979.

Balshan, I. D. Muscle tension and personality in women. *Archives of General Psychiatry,* 1962, *7,* 436–448.

Barlow, D. H., Blanchard, E. B., Hayes, S. C., & Epstein, L. H. Single-case designs and clinical biofeedback experimentation. *Biofeedback and Self-Regulation,* 1977, *2,* 221–239.

Beary, J. F., & Benson, H. A simple psychophysiologic technique which elicits the hypometabolic changes of the relaxation response. *Psychosomatic Medicine,* 1974, *36,* 115–120.

Beiman, I., Israel, E., & Johnson, S. A. During-training and posttraining effects of live and taped extended progressive relaxation, self-relaxation, and electromyogram biofeedback. *Journal of Consulting and Clinical Psychology,* 1978, *46,* 314–321.

Benson, H., Rosner, B. A., Marzetta, B. R., & Kleinchuk, H. P. Decreased blood pressure in borderline hypertensive subjects who practice meditation. *Journal of Chronic Disease,* 1974, *27,* 163–169.

Budzynski, T. H., & Stoyva, J. M. An instrument for producing deep muscle relaxation by means of analog information feedback. *Journal of Applied Behavior Analysis,* 1969, *2,* 231–237.

Budzynski, T. H., & Stoyva, J. M. Biofeedback techniques in behavior therapy. In N. Birbaumer (Ed.), *The mastery of anxiety: Contribution of neuropsychiatry to anxiety research.* Munich: Verlag Urban & Schwarzenberg, 1973.

Campbell, D. T., & Stanley, J. C. *Experimental and quasi-experimental designs for research.* Chicago: Rand-McNally, 1970.

Canter, A., Kondo, C. Y., & Knott, J. R. A comparison of EMG feedback and progressive muscle relaxation training in anxiety neurosis. *British Journal of Psychiatry,* 1975, *127,* 470–477.

Cattell, R. B., & Scheier, I. H. *The meaning and measurement of neuroticism and anxiety.* New York: Ronald Press, 1961.

Counts, D. K., Hollandsworth, J. G., Jr., & Alcorn, J. D. Use of electromyographic biofeedback and cue-controlled relaxation in the treatment of test anxiety. *Journal of Consulting and Clinical Psychology,* 1978, *46,* 990–996.

Cuthbert, B., Kristeller, J., Simons, R., Hodes, R., & Lang, P. J. *Strategies of arousal control: Motivation, meditation, and biofeedback.* Manuscript submitted for publication, 1980.

Delk, J. L. Use of EMG biofeedback in behavioral treatment of an obsessive–phobic–depressive syndrome. *Diseases of the Nervous System,* 1977, *38,* 938–939.

Fridlund, A. J., Fowler, S. C., & Pritchard, D. A. Striate muscle tensional patterning in frontales EMG biofeedback. *Psychophysiology,* 1980, *17,* 47–55.

Garrett, B. L., and Silver, M. P. The use of EMG and alpha biofeedback to relieve test anxiety in college students. In I. Wickramasekera (Ed.), *Biofeedback, behavior therapy and hypnosis: Potentiating the verbal control of behavior for clinicians.* Chicago: Nelson-Hall, 1976.

Gatchel, R. J. Biofeedback and the modification of fear and anxiety. In R. J. Gatchel & K. P. Price (Eds.), *Clinical application of biofeedback: Appraisal and status.* Elmsford, N.Y.: Pergamon, 1979.

Gatchel, R. J. Perceived control: A review and evaluation of therapeutic implications. In A. Baum, J. Singer, & S. Valins (Eds.), *Advances in environmental psychology.* Hillsdale, N.J.: Erlbaum, 1980.

Gatchel, R. J., Hatch, J. P., Maynard, A., Turns, R., & Taunton-Blackwood, A. Comparative effectiveness of heart rate biofeedback, false biofeedback, and systematic desensitization in reducing speech anxiety: Short- and long-term effectiveness. *Journal of Consulting and Clinical Psychology,* 1979, *47,* 620–622.

Gatchel, R. J., Hatch, J. P., Watson, P. J., Smith, D., & Gaas, E. Comparative effectiveness of voluntary heart rate control and muscular relaxation as active coping skills for reducing speech anxiety. *Journal of Consulting and Clinical Psychology,* 1977, *45,* 1093–1100.

Gatchel, R. J., Korman, M., Weis, C. B., Smith, D., & Clarke, L. A multiple-response evaluation of EMG biofeedback performance during training and stress-induction conditions. *Psychophysiology,* 1978, *15,* 253–258.

Gatchel, R. J., & Proctor, J. D. Effectiveness of voluntary heart rate control in reducing speech anxiety. *Journal of Consulting and Clinical Psychology,* 1976, *44,* 381–398.

Goldfried, M. R., & Davison, G. C. *Clinical behavior therapy.* New York: Holt, Rinehart & Winston, 1976.

Jacobson, E. *Progressive relaxation.* Chicago: University of Chicago Press, 1938.

Jessup, B. A., & Neufeld, R. W. J. Effects of biofeedback and "autogenic relaxation" techniques on physiological and subjective responses in psychiatric patients: A preliminary analysis. *Behavior Therapy,* 1977, *8,* 160–167.

Kappes, B., Michaud, J. Contingent versus noncontingent EMG feedback and hand temperature in relation to anxiety and locus of control. *Biofeedback and Self-Regulation,* 1978, *3,* 51–60.

Katkin, E. S., & Goldband, S. The placebo effect and biofeedback. In R. J. Gatchel & K. P. Price (Eds.), *Clinical applications of biofeedback: Appraisal and status.* New York: Pergamon, 1979.

Lacey, J. I. Somatic response patterning and stress: Some revisions of activation theory. In M. H. Appley & R. Trumbull (Eds.), *Psychological stress.* New York: McGraw-Hill, 1967.

Lang, P. J. Anxiety: Toward a psychophysiological definition. In H. S. Akiskal & W. L. Webb (Eds.), *Psychiatric diagnosis: Exploration of biological criteria.* New York: Spectrum, 1978.

Lavallée, Y., Lamontagne, Y., Pinard, G., Annable, L., & Tétreault, L. Effects of EMG feedback, diazepam, and their combinations on chronic anxiety. *Journal of Psychosomatic Research,* 1977, *21,* 65–71.

Lazarus, R. S. A cognitive analysis of biofeedback control. In G. E. Schwartz & J. Beatty (Eds.), *Biofeedback: Theory and research.* New York: Academic Press, 1977.

Leboeuf, A. The effects of EMG feedback training on state anxiety in introverts and extroverts. *Journal of Clinical Psychology,* 1977, *33,* 251–253.

McGowan, W. T., Haynes, S. N., & Wilson, C. C. Frontal electromyographic feedback: Stress attenuation and generalization. *Biofeedback and Self-Regulation,* 1979, *4,* 323–336.

Miller, M. P., Murphy, P. J., & Miller, T. P. Comparison of electromyographic feedback and progressive relaxation training in treating circumscribed anxiety stress reactions. *Journal of Consulting and Clinical Psychology,* 1978, *46,* 1291–1298.

Nigl, A. J., & Jackson, B. Electromyograph biofeedback as an adjunct to standard psychiatric treatment.

Journal of Clinical Psychiatry, 1979, *40*, 433–436.
Page, R. D., & Schaub, L. H. EMG biofeedback applicability for differing personality types. *Journal of Clinical Psychology*, 1978, *34*, 1014–1020.
Raskin, M., Bali, L. R., & Peeke, H. V. Muscle relaxation and transcendental meditation: A controlled evaluation of efficacy in the treatment of chronic anxiety. *Archives of General Psychiatry*, 1980, *37*, 93–97.
Raskin, M., Johnson, G., & Rondestvedt, J. W. Chronic anxiety treated by feedback-induced muscle relaxation: A pilot study. *Archives of General Psychiatry*, 1973, *28*, 263–267.
Reeves, J. L., & Mealiea, W. L. Biofeedback-assisted cue-controlled relaxation for the treatment of flight phobias. *Journal of Behavior Therapy and Experimental Psychiatry*, 1975, *6*, 105–109.
Schultz, J. H., & Luthe, W. *Autogenic training: A psycho-physiologic approach in psychotherapy*. New York: Grune & Stratton, 1959.
Shapiro, A. K. Placebo effects in medicine, psychotherapy, and psychoanalysis. In A. E. Bergin & S. L. Garfield (Eds.), *Handbook of psychotherapy and behavior change*. New York: Wiley, 1971.
Shipman, W. G., Oken, D., & Heath, H. A. Muscle tension and effort at self-control during anxiety. *Archives of General Psychiatry*, 1970, *23*, 359–368.
Smith, R. P. Frontalis muscle tension and personality. *Psychophysiology*, 1973, *10*, 311–312.
Stoyva, J. M., & Budzynski, T. H. Cultivated low arousal—An anti-stress response? In L. V. DiCara (Ed.), *Recent advances in limbic and autonomic nervous system research*. New York: Plenum, 1974.
Stroebel, C. F., & Glueck, B. C. Biofeedback treatment in medicine and psychiatry: An ultimate placebo? *Seminars in Psychiatry*, 1973, *5*, 379–393.
Tarler-Benlolo, L. The role of relaxation in biofeedback training: A critical review of the literature. *Psychological Bulletin*, 1978, *85*, 727–755.
Townsend, R. E., House, J. F., & Addario, D. A comparison of EMG feedback and progressive muscle relaxation training in anxiety neuroses. *American Journal of Psychiatry*, 1975, *132*, 598–601.
Wickramasekera, I. Instructions and EMG feedback in systematic desensitization: A case report. *Behavior Therapy*, 1972, *3*, 460–465.
Wolpe, J. *Psychotherapy by reciprocal inhibition*. Stanford, Calif.: Stanford University Press, 1958.
Zaichkowsky, L. K., & Kamen, R. Biofeedback and meditation: Effects on muscle tension and locus of control. *Perceptual and Motor Skills*, 1978, *46*, 955–958.

COMMENTS ON THE CHAPTER BY GATCHEL

PETER J. LANG

Gatchel has provided the field with an excellent review. The current literature does not suggest that muscle potential feedback training is either an efficient or an especially effective treatment for clinical anxiety. The purpose of this discussion is not to dispute this conclusion, but rather to underline several points on which the argument rests: (1) Laboratory experiments do not support the view that biofeedback is either a unique or especially effective method for arousal reduction. (2) Variables such as instructional set, motivation, and quality of the interpersonal context (i.e., variables usually lumped under the

Peter J. Lang. Department of Psychology, University of Wisconsin, Madison, Wisconsin.

rubric "placebo") are at least as powerful as biofeedback in effecting changes in a patient's physiology. (3) The evaluation of biofeedback effectiveness (or that of any therapy) requires that the target affect be assessed in terms of its verbal report aspects, overt behavior, and physiological pattern. This has rarely been accomplished in biofeedback therapy outcome research. (4) Affective states such as anxiety represent transactions between the organism and the environment. It is unlikely that treatment methods focusing exclusively on the patient's response and neglecting completely the stimulus context that occasions affective behavior will be effective in the treatment of anxiety.

BIOFEEDBACK AS A METHOD OF AROUSAL REDUCTION

Research both in our laboratory (University of Wisconsin) and elsewhere, using heart rate biofeedback, has clearly demonstrated that instructed heart rate acceleration is modulated by feedback variables. Thus, greater acceleration can be shown with incentives than without, with more frequent information about organ activity than with less frequent information, and with repeated training sessions. None of these variables have been similarly effective in modifying cardiac deceleration. In a recent series of experiments, Cuthbert, Kristeller, Hodes, and Lang (1981) examined a number of alternative training strategies to see if any could be shown to be more effective than heart rate biofeedback in directly prompting palpable cardiac deceleration and in reducing other common physiological estimates of activation. Significantly for the present discussion, our first experiment compared heart rate biofeedback with frontalis muscle biofeedback, and also compared both treatments with a nonfeedback control task. Over several training sessions, the two feedback methods generated the same modest reductions in heart rate and muscle activity. Subjects using both methods achieved significantly greater reductions during feedback than did subjects performing the control task. However, when all three groups were compared during instructed arousal reduction, in the absence of either a feedback or a control display, there was no difference between groups in either cardiac rate or muscle tension.

In subsequent experiments, biofeedback was compared with the meditation exercise developed by Wallace and Benson (1972). In no case was biofeedback superior to control tasks in effecting arousal reduction, and it was more than once significantly inferior to meditation in reducing heart rate. These results certainly do not encourage confidence in a biofeedback-based therapy for anxiety. While it is true that they were accomplished with normal and not with anxious subjects, and that more trials or sessions could have produced a different effect, the findings do argue that biofeedback is not a specifically potent method for reducing levels of visceral activity. Thus, assuming that this is the role of biofeedback within a therapy for anxiety, it appears to be, at the least, not a very cost-efficient method for accomplishing this goal.

THE ROLE OF "PLACEBO" VARIABLES IN EFFECTING CHANGE

In the course of studying the relative effectiveness of meditation and biofeedback strategies in producing arousal reduction, we have determined that factors such as the subject–experimenter relationship and "knowledge of results" exert a profound influence on outcome measures (Cuthbert *et al.*, 1981). In fact, their power appears to be sufficient either to markedly enhance or to completely eliminate significant differences between strategies. Furthermore, these variables interact in ways that are not completely obvious. Thus, we found in an initial experiment that meditation was clearly more effective than biofeedback was in reducing heart rate and generating other psychophysiological evidence of arousal reduction. However, in a subsequent experiment, this difference was not replicated. Examination of the two experimental protocols revealed that the relationship between experimenter and subject has been (inadvertently) quite different in the two assays of the phenomenon. The first experimenter had been warm, and encouraging, responsive, had made frequent inquiries about performance, and had been personally reactive to the subject. Experimenters in the second study, following the good research practice of consistency of instruction, were inadvertently more formal, more distant, and less individually responsive and supportive than the experimenter in the first examination of the problem had been. The hypothesis that this difference in psychosocial relationships prompted the difference in outcome was tested in the next experiment. The result was consistent with the hypothesis: Under the same conditions of performance information used in the previous two studies, meditators in the socially positive, high-involvement subject–experimenter condition generated greater heart rate reduction than did similarly treated biofeedback subjects. Under low-involvement conditions, no difference between training methods was observed. Thus, the experiment emphasized the important role of human relationships in moderating the technology of arousal reduction.

The part of the experiment described above was carried out under conditions in which, in addition to biofeedback or meditation instructions, subjects received information about overall performance after each practice period. In the final study of this series, this "knowledge of results" variable was also manipulated, so that some subjects were not given this information. The effect of this manipulation on heart rate reduction was also profound, and it interacted with the relationship variable to produce a new effect on training method. Now, the effect of high psychosocial involvement was the opposite of what we had previously observed. When "knowledge of results" was not provided, the meditators did best under low-involvement conditions! In fact, the best and most consistent arousal reduction produced by any group, in any of these experiments, was observed in *low-involvement* meditators who *were not given regular information* about their performance.

The implications of these results are several. Clearly, future comparisons of relaxation methods will need to control for the subject–experimenter (or patient–therapist) relationship. This is particularly difficult when we consider that there is no way to calibrate this variable against an absolute standard. The enterprise is further complicated by the fact that relationship variables appear to be changed (or even reversed in effect), depending on the performance information provided to subjects during the task.

Cuthbert *et al.* (1981) have considered meditation instructions to be a method of reducing cognitive load, tending to block the cardiovascular and somatic muscle outflow that is associated with "mental work." In contrast, the usual biofeedback paradigm requires continuous analysis and processing of external and internal signals, and thus it may be expected to increase heart rate and muscle tension (in competition with the specific task goals). On this basis, we predicted superior arousal reduction with meditation. Our data encourage such an interpretation. Indeed, it was the group provided with the least information and the least motivational stimulation that was best able to produce a psychophysiology of relaxation.

THE IMPORTANCE OF FULL ASSESSMENT OF THE AFFECTIVE RESPONSE

The research just described did not utilize anxious subjects, and it is not certain that similar results would be obtained with this population. Furthermore, it is important to consider that the goal of anxiety reduction may not be precisely the same as that of producing a physiology characterized by low organ activity. "Anxiety" has been described as a complex response construct, indexed by activity in three behavioral systems (Lang, 1968, 1971, 1978): (1) verbal report and expression; (2) patterns of physiological activation; (3) behavioral acts (performance deficits, avoidance, and the like). It is a common finding that these systems often show low concordance and do not change in a synchronous way with treatment (Rachman & Hodgson, 1974). For example, physiological arousal is in no sense pathognomonic of clinical anxiety. Sympathetic activation is certainly a component of joy, anger, productive work, sexual performance, and many other states or actions—none of which necessarially prompt a clinical diagnosis of anxiety. It is possible that the focus on reducing physiological arousal, to the neglect of behavioral acts and verbal report measures, is misplaced.

The purpose of treatment should perhaps be stated not as a task of generating states of physiological inactivity, but one of producing an efficient psychophysiology for the task at hand. In this model, "anxiety" is defined as a performance deficit, in which verbal and physiological behavior inconsistent with optimal performance provide a converging definition of the anxious state. If anxiety is viewed in this way, the role of biofeedback is less straightforward. It is not obvious that high-density information about organ systems should be introduced into the behavioral context that prompts anxious behavior. For example, it might function as a distractor or as a mechanism of cognitive avoidance. It is not clear that distraction would facilitate an anxiety-laden social performance (such as speaking before an unfamiliar group). In this case, the individual's efforts may be best bent to the primary rather than to an ancillary task. On the other hand, information about patterns of physiology can be useful to the therapist (and even at times to the patient) in planning treatment, monitoring the effects of various interventions, and assessing both optimal task characteristics and success of performance.

THE IMPORTANCE OF STIMULUS CONTEXT AND CONCEPTUAL PROCESSING

In describing the complexity of the anxiety response, we have already been forced to consider stimulus context. Nevertheless, few investigators studying biofeedback have approached response modification in terms of a target setting. The effort has most often been to try to teach a generalized response (relaxation or lowered physiological arousal) that would either lead to persisting change in tonic levels, as is hoped for by some investigators training for reductions in blood pressure, or would become a technique to be utilized intentionally by the subject in any context that prompted distress. However, work in psychopathology suggests that most fear and anxiety responses are context-specific, and, furthermore, that stimulus and response information are conceptually bound together in the brain's programs of behavior.

Recently, investigators have begun to examine the effects of biofeedback training conducted in the specific context of the target stressor (e.g., Sirota, Schwartz, & Shapiro, 1976). However, it is possible that this dual task strategy has significant limitations. As we have already noted, biofeedback has its own complex task demands. Integrating biofeedback into the conceptual context of the stressor strikes me as a potentially inordinate load for the processing system, or at the least, one not likely to promote efficiency in the primary environmental transaction.

The above analysis has prompted me to turn my own research more towards an examination of the conceptual behavior of subjects as it integrates the affective stimulus setting, context-specific overt behavior, *and* covert physiologies (Lang, 1977, 1979; Lang, Kozak, Miller, Levin, & McLean, 1980). It is worth noting here that the most effective single treatment for pathological fear (i.e., phobia) is repeated, massed "exposure" to the phobic object (Marks, 1977). In this approach, the emphasis is clearly on the stimulus and not on the training of a new physiological response. However, physiological responding does change. Furthermore, for some subjects the entire process may be accomplished through imagery, in which the subjects are instructed to visualize the stimulus context *and* their psychophysiolgocial response. Under these circumstances, it is the progressive alteration of a conceptual process that leads to fear reduction.

Our recent research indicates that there are broad individual differences in ability to invoke imagery that controls the visceral and somatic physiologies. However, this capacity can be to some extent trained and brought under the control of external commands and self-instruction. Furthermore, patterns of physiological response in the imagery of such trained subjects appear to parallel patterns observed in the objective stress context. There are even preliminary data suggesting that the evocation of such conceptual structures (i.e., images) that include the relevant physiology is an important condition of change in fear behavior (e.g., Lang, Melamed, & Hart, 1970).

CONCLUSION

In summary, the biofeedback paradigm as it has come to be formalized in research may not prove to be a cost-efficient relaxation technique or a powerful therapeutic vehicle. However, clinicians and researchers have greatly advanced understanding of many problems of instructed visceral control. I have mentioned here the effects of organ display processing and knowledge of results, as well as the importance of target stress and psychosocial context. It not seems that research must broaden its approach. Investigators should not continue to consider the subject's (or patient's) physiology as something that may be trained independently of its natural constraints or its functional role in affective behavior. My own inclination is to consider the control of peripheral physiology in the context of the brain's information-processing function. Higher-order conceptual behavior mediates relationships between stimulus context and physiological events in emotion. It is this process that increasingly merits researchers' and clinicians' attention as they seek to understand and treat anxiety.

REFERENCES

Cuthbert, B., Kristeller, J., Hodes, R., & Lang, P. J. Strategies of arousal control: Biofeedback, meditation, and motivation. *Journal of Experimental Psychology: General,* 1981, *110*(4).

Lang, P. J. Fear reduction and fear behavior: Problems in treating a construct. In J. M. Schlien (Ed.), *Research in psychotherapy* (Vol. 3). Washington, D.C.: American Psychological Association, 1968.

Lang, P. J. The application of psychophysiological methods to the study of psychotherapy and behavior modification. In A. E. Bergin & S. L. Garfield (Eds.), *Handbook of psychotherapy and behavior change.* New York: Wiley, 1971.

Lang, P. J. Anxiety: Toward a psychophysiological definition. In H. S. Akiskal & W. L. Webb (Eds.), *Psychiatric diagnosis: Exploration of biological predictors.* New York: Spectrum, 1978.

Lang, P. J. A bio-informational theory of emotional imagery. *Psychophysiology,* 1979, *16,* 495–512

Lang, P. J., Kozak, M. J., Miller, G. A., Levin, D. N., & McLean, A., Jr. Emotional imagery: Conceptual structure and pattern of somatovisceral response. *Psychophysiology,* 1980, *17*(2), 172–192.

Lang, P. J., Melamed, B. G., & Hart, J. D. A psychophysiological analysis of fear modification using an automated desensitization procedure. *Journal of Abnormal Psychology,* 1970, *76,* 220–234.

Marks, I. M. Clinical studies of phobic obsessive–compulsive and allied disorders. In W. S. Agras (Ed.), *Behavior therapy in clinical psychiatry*. Boston: Little, Brown, 1977.
Rachman, S., & Hodgson, R. I. Synchrony and desynchrony in fear and avoidance. *Behaviour Research and Therapy*, 1974, *12*, 311–318.
Sirota, A. D., Schwartz, G. E., & Shapiro, D. Voluntary control of human heart rate: Effect on reaction to aversive stimulation. A replication and extension. *Journal of Abnormal Psychology*, 1976, *85*, 473–477.
Wallace, R. K., & Benson, H. The physiology of meditation. *Scientific American*, 1972, *226*, 85–90.

ROUND-TABLE DISCUSSION OF GATCHEL AND LANG

Barry Sterman: I should think that this would be a well-developed area, but there really are a lack of measurement criteria for anxiety. I can't believe that some technique can't be evolved to deal with this. We can't take out the adrenal cortex and measure, but maybe we can weigh their underwear or whatever. Isn't there something?

Martin Orne: That's very extreme anxiety.

Barry Sterman: How about 17-ketosteroid? Do that sort of urinalysis to see if you get some objective measure of physiological response that correlates with anxiety, much as counting boluses does when you're studying a rat.

John Furedy: But the bolus count is a very simple and valid measure becuase you don't have to ask rats about their other feelings. Humans, unfortunately, have a number of responses that you can measure, and those measures don't necessarily correlate. I doubt that bolus counts, for example, are very well correlated with blood pressure increases in rats, except nobody's measured that.

Peter Lang: Well, the point is that those measures will not necessarily correlate with somebody's verbal report. An individual may say he's got all kinds of trouble—that he's in the age of anxiety, or that he's got an identity crisis—but the reported anxiety may be almost totally linguistic and may not appear in physiological responses or behavior. You can say that's not what you mean by anxiety, but you won't get a lot of people agreeing with you. Another person may appear smooth and cool and report, "I'm not anxious." Indeed, he may show no performance deficits, but his guts may be torn apart. Other individuals may have performance deficits and not have the other components of anxiety. In other words, these are all profiles which are probably meaningful and should be understood.

Barry Sterman: There is no question that there are such people. But you have to make a decision on this information. I have seen a person who was writhing and agitated but who had a perfect alpha rhythm. There is a similar problem in sleep research in defining the problem of insomnia. There are people who complain that they can't sleep but who immediately fall asleep when being recorded in the sleep laboratory. Are they really insomniac? Well, Bill Dement [Carskadon, Dement, Mitler, Guilleminault, Zarcone, &

Spiegel, 1976] has dealt with this, and he calls such patients pseudoinsomniacs. After the recording is made, he reviews the sleep record with that patient and he says, "Look, you slept great!" Subjectively, they're insomniacs; physiologically, they slept.

Audience Comment: But they go away and they're still insomniacs.

Barry Sterman: No, they're not. That's the point. He has found that a high percentage of them do not complain any more. He reports that just pointing out to them that they slept fine is a therapy.[1]

Bernard Tursky: There are psychophysical scaling techniques that can be used to scale anxiety and information related to anxiety. In the Political Science Department [of SUNY at Stony Brook], we have demonstrated that we can psychophysically scale and validate such concepts as degree of support for a cause and attitudes about various political concepts. These concepts are at least as confusing as anxiety. Using techniques developed by Stevens [1975] and augmented in our own laboratory, we give individuals an opportunity to generate interval data that express their attitude about any political concept. The measures used are numerical estimation, line length and tone intensity. The procedure is simple. In the case of anxiety, we would first ask the individual to produce a response that expresses a moderate amount of anxiety. We would then ask him to produce a response indicating the amount of anxiety caused by various stimuli or by the present situation. The use of more than one response measure makes it possible to cross-modally validate the responses. We have been extremely successful in demonstrating the effectiveness of this technique [Lodge & Tursky, 1980; Tursky, Lodge, & Reeder, 1979]. If you want to go one step further, you can also record psychophysiological measures and thus parcel out any bias related to social desirability.

Peter Lang: There are linguistic conventions and you can get at them that way, but that's different from psychophysics, which has an objective referent. I think we're dealing with a linguistic convention.

Paul Obrist: About 22 years ago, my friend John Lacey said something to me to the effect that you can't measure a psychological statement or concept with physiology. I kind of vaguely believed him, but I didn't take him too seriously because of Malmo's work on activation at the time [1959]. But what I question here is the use of heart rate or any of these indices as measures of an anxious state. This issue was really driven home by some data that we have [Obrist, Gaebelein, Teller, Langer, Grignolo, Light, & McCubbin, 1978]. We see these phenomenal individual differences in heart rate reactivity. In a homogeneous group of young college males with a very standardized task, you can see some individuals increase heart rates by 50 or 60 beats, while there are others whose heart rates do not change one iota. These differences appear across tasks. Now with some tasks, these typical responses become more apparent, such as with threat of shock, pain, cold pressor, sexual arousal, and competitive games. There's absolutely no way you can make the case that these differences have anything to do with anxiety, motivation, or any other psychological concept, as far as I'm concerned. I just think we ought to get this cleared. Anxiety is a behavioral concept. Let's leave it at that.

Robert Gatchel: In terms of biological indicators, there's a recent study which indicates that there are significant differences between public speaking anxiety and a physical exercise task in terms of relative amounts of epinephrine and norepinephrine in plasma [Dimsdale & Moss, 1980]. The speech anx-

[1]Editors' note: The Sleep Disorders Clinic and Laboratory at Stanford actually has quite limited experience in using this technique in cases of "pseudoinsomniacs" (Mitler, 1980).

iety is associated with greater amounts of epinephrine and physical exercise with more norepinephrine, which suggests differential contributions of SNS [sympathetic nervous system] activity versus that of the adrenal medulla. So, there is some possibility that physiologically we can find differences among activation-type situations.

Gary Schwartz: Research on anxiety is probably the crudest of all of the research areas and is as myopic in its research field as in the kinds of medical fields that tend to look at a particular disorder. There's a huge literature on people and anxiety. There's another literature for depression. There's a certain literature about hostility. The investigators in the hostility literature only assess hostility and don't ask patients whether they are depressed or anxious. In the anxiety literature, you almost never see a cross-reference to depression, even though we know that the correlation between anxiety and depression scales is typically +.6 or +.7. The literature are somewhat overlapping, although they are treated as if they were different. What I suggest—and we have data on this now—is that we start looking at patterns of self-report in the same way that we look at patterns across physiological systems, that is, across different emotions. When we do that, things pop out. You will find, for example, that some people report high anxiety and high frustration; others report high anxiety and low frustration to the same stimulus conditions. These emotional response patterns differ with regard to their patterns of physiological response to the same situation. I'm suggesting that as we consider assessing multiple psychological parameters, we also look at patterns of affective conditions, because some things which currently appear obscure and confusing may become better understood. I want to suggest that we consider asking people—subjects and patients—to evaluate patterns of affective experience under different situations. We now have subjects complete a self-report scale we call HSAFAD, which stands for happiness, sadness, anger, fear, anxiety, and depression [Schwartz, 1981]. People rate the *blends* of emotions that they experience in different life situations. We obtain both subjective and, if we can, more objective indices of physiological activity for various situations. The first time I did this clinically was with a cellist who was complaining of pain and cold hands under stress. She said when she was anxious, her hands got cold, and it interfered with her cello playing; and could I give her biofeedback so she could warm her hands and play the cello better? But when we assessed her patterns of self-report, her hand temperature, and her sweat gland activity, we found sometimes she had cold hands that were dry; sometimes she had wet hands that were warm; and sometimes she had cold hands that were also wet. When we looked at these patterns of self-reported emotion and of sweating and coldness, we found that her initial hypothesis was wrong. The data, as she collected them over the approximately 2 weeks of monitoring in these various situations, were that the coldness was associated with frustration and anger for her, and the sweating was associated more with fear. In situations where she was *both* frustrated and anxious, she showed coldness and sweating. When we started therapy, we dealt with the frustration components in certain situations and anxiety components in other situations. We then began to see relative shifts in the patterns of self-report. I'm not saying that this is a panacea. If anything, it makes life more complicated, because we must then begin to look at patterns of physiological activity as well as patterns of affective experience.

Neal Miller: I would just like to challenge the fact that there's enough training in these comparisons of biofeedback with meditative techniques. To be a little unfair, it would be like saying we're studying the effectiveness of different ways of teaching people to play the violin. What we've done in biofeedback is comparable to three sessions of instruction, each of which involved a total of 15 minutes of exposure to the violin. From that we've concluded that it's probably better just to let the child scrape the violin than to try to instruct him.

Peter Lang: It's clear to me that the information-processing demand by the feedback task interferes with most of these efforts.

Barry Sterman: Yes, in three sessions, but not in 30.

Martin Orne: Then it's up to someone to show the data that with 30 sessions there are greater effects for biofeedback. Peter Lang has shown us data that with three sessions, the effects are greater in the meditation subjects. Now, instead of saying that this research is wrong, let the proponents of biofeedback do the work and document its advantages.

Robert Gatchel: I think you need to be careful in generalizing that effects with normal subjects under nonstressful training situations are similar to those results that would occur if you were treating a highly anxious person in a stressful situation. We can't jump to the conclusion that meditation would work best with high-anxious people exposed to stressful situations. We need to be very careful of that.

Barry Sterman: Claghorn, Mathew, Largen, and Meyer (1981) reported that in normal subjects, hand warming produced no changes in cerebral vascular distributions; but in migraine subjects, both therapeutic drugs and hand warming produced the same kinds of changes. The disregulated system responded differently from the normal system. You certainly have to find out what is normal. When you want to evaluate the utility of biofeedback in treating sick people, you have to do it in more than three trials. It certainly took the sick people more than three sessions to learn to be sick.

Peter Lang: These weren't sick people. The data were from a controlled normative study. Biofeedback is a field that was built on one-session experiments, although it probably shouldn't have been.

Barry Sterman: No, it was shot down on one-session experiments.

Peter Lang: The data from these experiments using three and four sessions are perfectly consonant with Bob Gatchel's review of the literature. In other words, carefully controlled experiments in a laboratory with normals are completely consistent with what's showing clinically—sometimes with longer trials, sometimes not. In biofeedback clinics, many people are treated with six to eight trials.

Barry Sterman: It doesn't make any sense.

Peter Lang: If you're not even measuring to see where your effects are, it seems to me incumbent on the person who says that 500 trials later it's going to be there to provide the data. I know when I get tired. If somebody can be encouraged by the data to the point that he wants to run those 500 trials, I'd be happy to see those data. I don't know about your area, but in this particular area it's not there.

Barry Sterman: Did you ever see a child learn to walk? It's a torturous process. The point is that his motivation is to get up there and be part of what's going on. I just hope we don't oversimplify.

Peter Lang: Meditators who are willing to persist for 3 years are a special population. No one but the most dedicated autonomic athlete will sit there and see if he can do the running heart rate change a little better than somebody else after 50 or 60 trials. When you don't have indications at the beginning that frontalis EMG biofeedback helps anybody in the clinic, and when research indicates that you don't even get as much reduction in physiological measures as you do with passive, cognitive techniques, it doesn't seem to me you ought to be really encouraged.

Joel Lubar: I don't find anything perplexing or paradoxical about the fact that the heart rate change was the largest in the meditation group as compared with the heart rate group. I would suspect that if you looked at the meditation group, you would find that their skin conductance has decreased, their peripheral blood flow has increased, their EMG at certain points has decreased, and perhaps their EEG frequencies have decreased. In other words, a simple-minded way of looking at this is to say they're showing a parasympathetically dominant shift. All these groups do, more or less. There are some differences in pattern, but I think people who get heart rate feedback tend to show greater alterations in respiration, so you can get significantly different respiration patterns. The point I'm trying to make is that heart rate conditioning is an active process. People may be competing with the device. While they're trying to reduce their heart rate using biofeedback, they're competing with the machine. They may get angry, and their heart rate may go up but certainly not down. Everyone knows that passive concentration techniques, whether meditation or autogenic training, always give better results than specific feedback for any of these physiological responses.

Peter Lang: I'm glad everybody knew; I just wish I knew why all these people were being given EMG feedback.

Gary Schwartz: There are individual differences in response to different kinds of interventions. Just because two interventions, let's say heart rate biofeedback versus meditation, lead to the same overall effect does not imply that they operate in the same individuals. If anything, from Peter [Lang]'s data you get suggestions that although the treatments of meditation and heart rate biofeedback are superficially the same in terms of mean heart rate decrease, they vary in two important ways that have been repeatedly documented. One is that with heart rate biofeedback, you get respiratory irregularities, and with meditation you don't. There's some sort of phenomenon going on there. Secondly, with heart rate biofeedback, you get a relationship between the amount of heart rate decrease and resting level, whereas with meditation you do not. I want to suggest that we keep open to the idea that these different "behavioral" procedures may operate by different biobehavioral mechanisms and that may be differentially active in different individuals. The self-selection issues may be very important in determining treatment response. . . . Steven Warrenburg [Pagano & Warrenburg, in press] tried to validate whether or not meditation led to "more right hemispheric functioning," or to a shift from left to right, as in various cognitive tasks. He also evaluated the finding of a previous retrospective study which indicated that long-term meditators were higher in "absorption." "Absorption" is a personality or psychological characteristic that correlates with hypnotic susceptability and the ability to become involved in imaginary inner mental processes. He studied long- and short-term meditators and followed these groups longitudinally. He not only found that absorption was correlated with a relative right hemispheric effect, as indicated by cognitive test performance, but he also found evidence for a self-selection process. That is, the people who were higher absorbers tended to stay with the meditation procedure, and they were also the ones who happened to have this right hemispheric effect on the cognitive task. So, we have to look at the self-selection issue and [determine] how it matches with the particular therapeutic strategy used.

Joel Lubar: It is necessary to understand this bugaboo of placebo effect and not to treat it as if it were some ephemeral, magic thing. When patients chart their symptoms, there is usually an immediate reduction of 15% to 30% in most symptoms. If we were able to measure a variety of physiological systems during this time of charting, I am certain that we would find that the coping mechanisms they use are psychophysiological. The charting doesn't make the symptoms magically disappear. Expectancy is not just a cognitive thing; it's a psychophysiological phenomenon. This is not a placebo effect in the usual sense, but a specific effect. It is just a matter of patients experimenting with ways to bring about the desired effect.

Robert Gatchel: The terms "placebo" and "placebo effects" should not be viewed in a negative way. Of course, in clinical settings, you want to maximize the placebo effect of your treatment. That will maximize your treatment. You need to know the relative contribution of placebo effects, but nobody does that kind of research.

John Furedy: But surely it must bother those people who have been told through this new biofeedback method whereby we provide information to the subject about a particular biological function in which he is not normally aware, we can produce an increase in control. Now you're telling us, "Don't worry about that, because by using these placebo effects whereby we put in all these cognitions, maybe they can do even better." Certainly these cognitions have physiological effects, but who knows what the basis is? You are saying, "Well, so what?"

Joel Lubar: No, I'm not saying that. I'm saying if you do these measurements and you find out which components are responsible for the effects, maybe then you can go back and you can train subjects to enhance those components even more and bring them under really elegant control, thereby getting a really strong effect.

John Furedy: What effect are you talking about? What I'm suggesting is that in the cases where you don't have proper controls, there is no demonstrated biofeedback effect to talk about. I think that the effects you're talking about are changes in psychophysiological functions as a function of stimulation. Well, those effects go on all the time. We all know that, psychophysiologically, we're changing all the time as a function of the stimulus condition. It's too broad a concept.

Joel Lubar: No, I'm talking about the effects seen and the reasons for them when we find that people tend to get better when they're told about a new treatment or are brought into something new; when patients improve when they just have to chart their symptoms during a baseline before any treatment's applied. I think we can ferret out why this happens. It's not magic.

Neal Miller: He's saying we should analyze the placebo effect and study the placebo effect. You might learn something from that study. Surely you don't disagree with that?

John Furedy: I want to suggest very strongly that we should *not* study placebo effects. I do want to argue against the notion of studying placebo effects because, as I said in my chapter [see Chapter 4], the placebo effects themselves are not reliable; they vary over time and place, as a function of society's awareness and between therapists and subjects. I think we've got enough problems studying biological events without going out of this situation and into a completely wild and woolly beyond. Let's leave that to a hundred years later. Let's work out, first of all, the procedures about which we *can* talk, such as biofeedback and anxiety. Let's not study placebo effects; it would be unprofitable.

Jasper Brener: But it seems to me you just specified the five or six determinants of placebo effects.

Martin Orne: The things which we believe are determinants of placebo effects.

Peter Lang: One man's placebo is another man's treatment.

Martin Orne: I won't rise to the bait now, because I will address these issues in my summary [see Chapter 17].

Joel Lubar: I hope you will address that, Martin, because I think that we really have to hash it out. I will make a comment about Peter Lang's suggestion that the best way to desensitize somebody is to put them right into the situation. That bothers me very much. I would much rather treat phobic or anxious patients by measuring autonomic reactivity in various systems, evaluating their physiological responses, and trying to train them to control that reactivity which is potentially disease-producing. In other words, develop a coping mechanism first, then expose them gradually to the situation. I'm sure that you're going to kill a lot of people if you just put them into the situation for which they're most phobic. I can imagine somebody with an airplane phobia being put in the airplane and dropping dead of a heart attack.

Peter Lang: The current treatment of choice is what's called "exposure." Basically, what that involves is getting the person, as quickly as possible, next to the phobic context or the phobic object. For the person with an obsessive-compulsive ritual, response prevention is the treatment. This is the most effective treatment around.

Richard Surwit: First of all, if I'm correct, most of that research comes from Britain.

Peter Lang: There are studies in this country, mainly Edna Foa's group, for example [Foa & Steketee, 1979]; and there's a large series at Temple . . . [and one] . . . in Sweden, as well [Ohman, 1979].

Richard Surwit: As a clinician, Peter, I think that I would not dispute the efficacy of taking a patient and putting him in the phobic situation without any coping mechanisms or prior training, but you wouldn't have a large clientele for very long. Your referral sources would dry up overnight.

Edward Blanchard: About 15% of people refuse to enter treatment when you describe the treatment. You lose about another 15% who drop out during treatment. Then, in the remaining 70%, you do very, very well. You do not lose that many people.

Peter Lang: It doesn't mean that the therapist is hostile or a forbidding figure, or that he doesn't encourage or reinforce the client; but the whole idea is to keep the patient on top of it. It needs to be done for long periods; that is, you can sensitize him if he gets a quick exposure and then anxiety reduction is achieved by avoidance of the stimuli. So, you've got to hold him in there. It's a dramatically different treatment. One of the things that's amused me is to see, when clinical psychologists and psychiatrists get exposed to this to begin with, that it requires a style of treatment so different from what they've been doing in the past. There's no 50-minute hour here. You've got to have a team that's willing to stick with the patient until they get the job done. Of course, you may cure him in 2 days.

John Lacey: Is it a marathon session?

Peter Lang: Not necessarily, but you must keep the client in the phobic situation until you get some anxiety reduction.

Henry Adams: I have helped to run those initial compulsive hand-washer subjects with Vic Meyer and Levy [1973]. Essentially, what the treatment consists of, and the patient is agreeing to, is to allow you to prevent him from washing. The first couple of days the patient is really very emotional. You've got to watch him 24 hours a day and, except for a brief wash, you never allow any washing. A cure rate of approximately 95% is achieved in a period of 10 days. It's a very effective technique.

Richard Surwit: It's been shown that the effective ingredient of systematic desensitization is exposure. But when exposure is in a slow and graded fashion, with relaxation training, you make the patient more comfortable during the experience. I think, for that reason, systematic desensitization is always going to be preferable in many situations.

Henry Adams: You were talking about anxiety that was elicited by a specific situation, but there's another type of anxiety where you cannot specify exactly why the patient is anxious, why he continues to be anxious, why he has all the autonomic arousal, and why he has panic states. We don't really have any effective treatment for these patients. I wonder how the research with specific anxiety applies to those kinds of cases of free-floating and pervasive anxiety.

Peter Lang: I think that's a very serious problem, but I doubt that it will be helped by ignoring the stimuli, the context, and the environment in which those events are occasioned. I doubt that one can train into a subject habits of "emotional control," however you define that, that can suddenly activate in any stress situation that comes down the road. That's part of the problem. We have to backtrack and consider the transactions of the organism with the environment. You can't just say, "I'm going to train up these marvelous responses."

Richard Surwit: It seems to me that what we're concluding is that, for anxiety, biofeedback doesn't make any sense because there is no one specific physiological response that we can target and train, and that other behavioral techniques, such as exposure, do make more sense. Up until now, biofeedback methods have yet to be proven effective.

REFERENCES

Carskadon, M. A., Dement, W. C., Mitler, M. M., Guilleminault, C., Zarcone, V. P., & Spiegel, R. Self-reports versus sleep laboratory findings in 122 drug-free subjects with complaints of chronic insomnia. *American Journal of Psychiatry,* 1976, *133,* 1382–1388.

Claghorn, J. L., Mathew, R. J., Largen, J. W., & Meyer, J. S. Directional effects of skin temperature self-regulation on regional cerebral blood flow in normal subjects and migraine patients. *American Journal of Psychiatry,* 1981, *138*(9), 1182–1187.

Dimsdale, J. E., & Moss, J. Plasma catecholamines in stress and exercise. *Journal of the American Medical Association,* 1980, *243,* 340–342.

Foa, E. B., & Steketee, G. S. Obsessive–compulsives: Conceptual issues and treatment interventions. In M. Hersen, R. M. Eisler, & P. M. Miller (Eds.), *Progress in behavior modification.* New York: Academic Press, 1979.

Gatchel, R. J., Hatch, J. P., Watson, P. J., Smith, D., & Gaas, E. Comparative effectiveness of voluntary heart rate control and muscle relaxation training as active coping skills for reducing speech anxiety. *Journal of Consulting and Clinical Psychology,* 1977, *45,* 1093–1100.

Lodge, M., & Tursky, B. Comparisons between category and magnitude scaling of political opinion employing SRC/CPS items. *American Political Science Review,* 1980, *73,* 50–66.

Malmo, R. B. Activation: A neuropsychological dimension. *Psychological Review,* 1959, *66,* 367–386.

Meyer, V., & Levy, R. Modification of behavior in obsessive–compulsive disorders. In H. E. Adams & I. P. Unikel (Eds.), *Issues and trends in behavior therapy.* Springfield, Ill.: Charles C Thomas, 1973.

Mitler, M. M. Personal communication, 1980.

Obrist, P. A., Gaebelein, C. J., Teller, E. S., Langer, A. W., Grignolo, A., Light, K. C., & McCubbin, J. A. The relationship among heart rate, carotid dp/dt and blood pressure in humans as a function of the type of stress. *Psychophysiology,* 1978, *15,* 102–115.

Ohman, A. Fear relevance, autonomic conditioning, and phobias: A laboratory model. In S. Bates, W. S. Dockens, K. Götestam, L. Melin, & P. O. Sjöden (Eds.), *Trends in behavior therapy*. New York: Academic Press, 1979.

Pagano, R., & Warrenburg, S. Transcendental meditation: In search of a unique or dramatic effect. In R. Davidson, G. E. Schwartz, & D. Shapiro (Eds.), *Consciousness and self-regulation*. New York: Plenum, in press.

Schwartz, G. E. Psychophysiological patterning and emotion revisited: A systems perspective. In C. Izard (Ed.), *Measuring emotion in infants and children*. Cambridge, England: Cambridge University Press, 1981.

Stevens, S. S. *Psychophysics: Introduction to its perceptual, neural and social prospects*. New York: Wiley, 1975.

Tursky, B., Lodge, M., & Reeder, R. Psychophysical and psychophysiological evaluation of the direction, intensity and meaning of race-related stimuli. *Psychophysiology*, 1979, *16*, 452–462.

VI

SUMMARY COMMITTEE'S REPORTS

16 REGULATORY PHYSIOLOGY AND BIOFEEDBACK

JOHN I. LACEY

INTRODUCTION

Bernard Tursky and Leonard White, knowing that I have no personal experience with biofeedback, have asked me to serve only as a ''scholarly commentator'' for this book. I now find it difficult to meet this responsibility, because this volume has covered an extraordinarily large number of topics, sometimes in great detail. Points of concern have ranged from considerations of acute renal shutdown to the multiple ways of assessing anxiety; from advanced methods of statistical inference to the adverse effects of psycholinguistic labeling conventions. The book has even touched on the vast topic of general systems theory as applied to psychology and physiology. I would rapidly exceed limits of time and personal competence were I to attempt an orderly survey and integration of even a small sample of these topics.

Several questions, however, have been raised repeatedly, either explicitly or implicitly. I should like to rephrase some of these questions, and to suggest some directions that might be taken in attempting a theoretical and empirical resolution of the troubling problems these questions present.

Two chapters in particular—those by Tursky (Chapter 5) and Brener (Chapter 2)—have had a major effect on my own thinking about this volume, for between them they have touched on almost all the major theoretical problems. These excellent chapters, then, are my point of departure, and the discussion that follows may

John I. Lacey. Section of Behavioral Physiology, Fels Research Institute, School of Medicine, Wright State University, Yellow Springs, Ohio.

be viewed as variations on some of the themes they have introduced. Tursky's chapter is entitled "An Engineering Approach to Biofeedback"; my remarks can be entitled "A Psychophysiologist's Approach to the Engineering Approach to Regulatory Physiology, with Applications to Biofeedback."

Tursky calls our attention to the all-important fact that the nervous system possesses many negative feedback loops. In control engineering, such loops have been subjected to sophisticated mathematical and experimental analyses, and are well understood and widely used devices. Moreover, the control system principles derived from such analyses have been applied to the study of a number of classical physiological problems such as cardiovascular control, temperature control, glucose regulation, and regulation of water exchange, as well as many others. (The classic references are Escobar, 1964; Grodins, 1963; Milhorn, 1966; and Yamamoto & Brobeck, 1965.) The evolution of this vital field is continuing today, as can be seen in current journals of physiology.

While this approach to problems of integrative biology by the route of control system theory has resulted in many important contributions to physiology, many authors have noted that physiological control systems are vastly more complex than technological control systems. The conceptual leap from hardware devices to the nervous system does not require only an isomorphic translation, a simple replacement of a hardware component by a chunk of neural tissue, or a description of processes of neural transmission. In considering a lack of isomorphism, as well as the existence of some easily applicable *analogies* between hardware and the nervous system, investigators will find the beginnings of principles that may have a major impact on biofeedback theory, and, indeed, on general psychophysiological theory.

HOMEOSTASIS: THE TRADITIONAL VIEW

I start, as does Tursky, with the sensor, which must exist both in hardware devices and in the nervous system as a basic and indispensable component of a control system. The body is internally organized to sense physiologically important signals, such as blood glucose levels, blood pressure levels, and core temperature. (This is a very restricted listing of the many variables that are internally sensed.) These signals, however, must be transduced into codes "understood by" the nervous system. Blood pressure levels, for example, are decoded into pulse frequencies and temporal patterns of pulses by the baroreceptor nerves. In the case of inborn physiological sensors and transducers, the signal codes naturally are appropriate for decoding by the nervous system, and naturally are routed to appropriate areas of the nervous system. In biofeedback, the reinforcing signal does not automatically produce a transduced neural code appropriate to the desired corrective effects. This may be one reason for the necessity for prolonged learning!

The decoded signal initiates the corrective processes that implement the ultimate "purpose" of the negative feedback loops. These multiple corrective processes result, more or less successfully, in the restoration of a physiological variable to some relatively stable value after an induced perturbation.

The detailed study of the nature and physical substrate of these homeostatic processes reveals several principles of theoretical and practical importance for the student and practitioner of biofeedback. While my own experimental studies deal with cardiovascular control processes, I recently have become intrigued by the problem of temperature regulation, for some of the most useful insights into the applicability of control systems theory to psychophysiology are emerging from studies in this area. It is fortunate that thermal regulation also is a prominent subject in the biofeedback venture. In my discussion, I shamelessly borrow from recent writings by Satinoff. Her papers, both experimental and theoretical, can serve as an illuminating and authoritative introduction to this area. (See, in particular, Satinoff, 1978.) My discussion is vastly oversimplified, but, I hope, will not have serious inaccuracies.

Consider a rat in a cold environment. The effect of this adverse environment, in the absence of corrective actions, would be to lower the core temperature, with catastrophic consequences for the animal. The list of corrective actions is familiar: Heat production is increased by shivering; heat loss is decreased by surface vasoconstriction; and appropriate goal-directed behaviors emerge, such as huddling in a nest of paper created by the rat from nearby materials. In the face of an elevated environmental temperature, another and contrary set of corrective actions appears. The animal sprawls immobile in a characteristic posture, which decreases heat porduction; and heat loss is increased by panting and cutaneous vasodilation. The thermosensitive neuronal circuits in the hypothalamus that mediate these corrective actions have been mapped in considerable detail. They can be manipulated rather precisely by selective local heating and cooling and by selective lesions. Here we have a clear example of a complex negative feedback loop that seems to result in an integrated adaptive pattern of skeletal motor, vasomotor, and complex behavioral responses. Whenever physiological control systems are studied,the same characteristics emerge: spatially and temporally *patterned* responses, *integrated* to produce *multiple* corrective and adaptive actions. These are the classical attributes of homeostatic processes.

DISSOCIATION OF RESPONSES

Such a traditional description of homeostasis, however, raises almost insuperable difficulties for psychophysiology in general and for biofeedback in particular. The fundamental problem is how such hard-wired circuitry permits *dissociation* of the component parts of the seemingly integrated adaptive pattern. The clinical and experimental reality is that such dissociation does occur. This volume, for example, repeatedly has given evidence that single responses, considered classically to be only components of an integrated adaptive response pattern, can be selectively elicited and selectively modified. Miller's paralyzed patient, who had severe crippling orthostatic hypotension, first responded to operant conditioning with "integrated" blood pressure and heart rate responses, but with prolonged training the blood pressure response alone was selectively modified and became selectively controllable.

Modern neurophysiological and psychophysiological experiments yield many instances of such apparent *dis*association. Moreover, a theoretical framework is emerging that enables investigators to begin to understand the neural mechanisms of this process and to grapple in meaningful ways with such vast problems as the definition of the "self-regulating dynamic organism." It also enables investigators to raise meaningful objections to assertions that variable A (say, total body oxygen consumption) is inevitably and tightly "biologically coupled" to variable B (say, heart rate).

The starting point for this theoretical framework is the modifiable "set point" of a hardware feedback loop. Household thermostats provide a familiar example. If the thermostat setting is changed from 72 °F to 68 °F, the set point is changed. Now, if the room temperature falls below 68 °F, the furnace will produce more heat in order to restore the desired temperature, whereas previously the corrective action would have occurred as soon as the temperature fell below 72 °F. To effect this new response, a single set point has been changed, and thereby a single and fixed network of wires, motors, and solenoids has been influenced.

If the physiological thermoregulatory feedback loop behaved like this household thermoregulatory loop, then there should be a single set of thermosensitive neurons, a single neuronal circuit to effect changes (or at least multiple circuits that always work together), and a single, albeit modifiable, set point. The physiological system does not satisfy any of these conditions. Detailed mapping of the thermosensitive neurons in the hypothalamus, and the ability to heat or cool or lesion specific portions of the circuitry selectively, has made possible a series of critical experiments, the results of which show that the various components of the thermoregulatory process are separable, and have separate set points. How has this come about? What are the more general implications?

EVOLUTIONARY COADAPTATION

An appealing theoretical interpretation has been made that most, if not all, thermoregulatory reflexes have evolved out of systems that were originally used for other "purposes." The peripheral vasomotor system first served as a supplemental respiratory organ in amphibia. In reptiles, it became a heat collector and dispenser. Only in the endotherms did it become an essential part of the temperature-regulating mechanism. These evolutionary changes, it is proposed, did not involve successive restructuring of the underlying components into a single coordinated mechanism.

The components remain demonstrably separable, with for example, separable set points. The emerging principle is that of "evolutionary coadaptation." A mechanism that has evolved for one "purpose" can be incorporated into a mechanism with a different adaptive value in an entirely different system.

Whatever the ultimate merits of this evolutionary theory, it provides at least a preliminary basis for understanding a clearly demonstrable fact: the same physical structures and the same physiological processes may indeed serve different adaptive needs. We do not need sophisticated laboratory investigations to demonstrate this fact. The cricket communicates with other members of the species by producing sounds by friction of the hind legs, normally devoted to locomotion. Humans communicate by producing sounds by control of the passage of air over the vocal cords. But it should be noted that humans have not developed a separate airway to control sound. This commonplace fact needs emphasis. One of the most vital needs of human beings is to execute with ease and skill the complex and intricate processes of external respiration, in order to promote the purposes of internal respiration. We must breathe in and out so that gas exchange can occur properly inside our bodies. Oxygen must be taken in and used; carbon dioxide must be eliminated. Yet humans are so constructed that part of the mechanism serving this fundamental process is used also in speech and song. External respiration came about earlier in evolution than speech did. Part of the mechanism of respiration was incorporated into a mechanism with a different adaptive value in an entirely different system, to repeat an earlier phrase in this chapter. Shifts in vasomotor tone and regional shifts in blood flow are essential and prominent processes in thermal regulation. But these same processes are essential and prominent processes in cardiovascular regulation, and their role (in exercise, for example) is here somewhat different.

Such coadaptation is achieved at a cost. If the same structure and process can serve different goal-directed behaviors (using "behavior" in its widest sense to include covert physiological processes), then some additional neurophysiological apparatus has to be developed to mediate competition between possibly contradictory uses of that structure, and to establish a priority scheme, just as computers must guard against bus competition and must be able to resolve simultaneously occurring interrupts on the basis of preassigned priorities. Airway utilization for speech cannot be permitted to compete successfully, for an indefinitely long time period, with airway utilization for gas exchange. A singer can sustain middle C only for a finite time before the more fundamental respiratory need *must* take over.

RESOLUTION OF COMPETITION BETWEEN DEMANDS

In thinking about the implications of this commonplace example of the resolution of competition between two contrary demands on the same body structure, the investigator becomes aware of a gaping hole in psychophysiological theory. Researchers have only a small body of data and a limited theoretical structure to facilitate their understanding of how the nervous system resolves such competition. In my opinion, this should be made a central theoretical concern in biofeedback. This is because biofeedback training not only often seems to set up a competition between a learned demand and an already existent and more ''fundamental'' demand, but moreover, attempts to produce a reassignment of biological priorities, so that the learned demand wins. This is exemplified by training a patient with Raynaud's disease to produce cutaneous vasodilation on cue, despite environmental temperatures that normally would produce vasoconstriction.

Indeed, a prime basis for often-expressed (but a priori) doubts of the clinical efficacy of biofeedback is the notion that there are fundamental priorities built into the nervous system that cannot be reassigned. This criticism has surfaced in this volume in another way, by the assertion that there are universal, ''biologically inevitable'' associations between specific demands and specific physiological accompaniments. Brener, for example, in his extraordinarily rich and scholarly paper, asserts such an association between skeletal motor activity and heart rate, an association produced by the need for increased oxygen intake during locomotion or exercise, for example. This is an appealing and apparently defensible claim because of the large body of data in the field of exercise physiology that shows nicely linear relationships among work load, oxygen consumption, and heart rate; and also because of Brener's own elegant and extensive psychophysiological studies. If such an assertion is true, then some of the claims of practitioners of biofeedback necessarily must be suspect. Investigators can draw up their own lists of phenomena, at least alleged to have been found in biofeedback studies, that seem to challenge such strict, ''biological coupling.'' Heading such a list would be the emergence of specificity of response—of ultimate dissociation between physiological responses that appear together early in training, so that finally only the target response is modified.

Is there *any* physiological basis for expecting such dissociation, which, in terms of the theoretical structure I am attempting to sketch, is an example of a reassignment of biological priorities? A claim for universality in science is disprovable by a single negative example. Fortunately, there are several negative examples in cardiovascular physiology, and even an understanding in at least one instance of the underlying mechanism. I turn first to a study that dramatically shows decoupling of heart rate from rather vigorous skeletal motor activity.

An increase in heart rate undoubtedly is an important component of the total bodily response to exercise, or even of preparation for exercise, for there is a high biological priority assigned to providing oxygen for internal consumption. It is extremely easy to study this phenomenon in the laboratory by using graded amounts of exercise, either dynamic (e.g., on a bicycle ergometer) or isometric (e.g., sustained handgrip on a spring-loaded device). Fortunately, it is also easy to provide a demand for decreased heart rate by invoking the so-called ''diving reflex.'' In aquatic vertebrates, a dramatic and sustained bradycardia is invoked upon diving. This bradycardia is accompanied by apnea, peripheral vasoconstriction, and a fall in cardiac output. It is widely considered to be an oxygen-conserving reflex. In man, the same responses can be elicited by apnea in combination with stimulation of cold receptors on the face by immersion of the face alone in water. The apnea alone is not as effective in producing bradycardia as is its combination with cold wetness. The question may now be asked: What are the results of simultaneously demanding of the heart an exercise-induced tachycardia and a diving-reflex-induced bradycardia? Precisely this question was asked by Bergman, Campbell, and Wildenthal (1972). When the dive reflex was elicited simultaneously with moderate dynamic exercise, the oxygen-conserving response totally supplanted the oxygen-consuming response. Heart rate fell to the same levels during "dives" executed during exercise as during "dives" executed from a resting baseline condition. When the dive reflex was elicited simultaneously with isometric exercise, there was an intermediate result. Neither of the two contradictory demands totally won over the other. The heart rate fell between the values elicited in response to each demand taken alone. These results show (1) a complete decoupling of heart rate from the dynamic exercise demands, using work loads up to 600 kilopound meters (KPM) per minute; (2) a higher "biological priority" in humans for oxygen conservation than for oxygen consumption, under the conditions of the experiment; and (3) a compromise resolution between conflicting demands, rather than an all-or-nothing resolution, for isometric exercise.

It should be emphasized at this point that exercise physiology itself provides a prime example of the plasticity of the organism in reassigning biological priorities. Consider that one of the most often-cited examples of homeostatically imposed response patterning is that heart rate and blood pressure are inversely related, particularly in a relatively relaxed state. As blood pressure increases, heart rate decreases, presumably to maintain a stable cardiac output. This reflex is easily elicited, and it is often demonstrated in elementary physiology by graded injection of norepinephrine or kindred agents. The graded pressor responses so produced "inevitably" produce graded bradycardias. This powerful reflex effect disappears when the baroreceptor nerves are sectioned. Yet during exercise, or even in anticipation of exercise, or even in such behavioral tasks as mental arithmetic or withstanding pain, heart rate and blood pressure increase at the same time. The reflexively controlled inverse relationship disappears. It is as though the baroreceptor nerves had been functionally sectioned. What accounts for this obliteration of a seemingly fundamental feedback process?

POSSIBLE MECHANISMS FOR DISSOCIATION

Several mechanisms for this obliteration have been demonstrated. The first is that the *sensitivity* of the sensor itself may be dynamically changed. This comes about in the following way. The so-called "baroreceptors" are more accurately described as "stretch receptors." They are stimulated by the pressure-induced deformation of the thinned portions of the arterial wall in which they reside. But the degree of stretch depends on the stiffness of this arterial wall, and this stiffness, or degree of elasticity, is itself physiologically regulated, possibly by adrenergic processes (Peterson, 1962; Reis & Fuxe, 1968). Hence a given blood pressure change, being variably effective in deforming the arterial wall (because of elasticity changes), is also variably effective in initiating a bradycardia.

This may be only a physiological way of varying the set point of the circuit that produces a decrease in heart rate when blood pressure increases. Underlying this process, however, is another level of neurophysiological complexity, one not easily made analogous to simple hardware devices, and one that implies more complex processes than simple modifications of set points. This is that the baroreceptor reflex is not mediated simply by independent and isolated circuits in the brain stem. Indeed, the baroreceptor reflex can be either potentiated or diminished by many suprabulbar structures, such as the cerebellum, hypothalamus, and various components of the limbic lobe (Gebber & Snyder, 1970; Hockman, Talesnik, & Livingston, 1969; Moruzzi, 1940; Reis & Cuenod, 1964, 1965). In the case of hypothalamic stimulation (Gebber & Snyder, 1970), it was concluded that the results were not to be attributed simply to increased adrenergic activity, but to a specific suprabulbar inhibition of cardiac vagal activity. The "fine tuning" of homeostatic processes to which Miller refers almost certainly must involve learned modifications of the complex interrelationships of such controlling pathways. Neurophysiology is replete with examples of multiple pathways and with rerouting of impulse traffic along these pathways.

INFLUENCE OF VARIABLES ON REMOTE PROCESSES

The nervous system is so organized that homeostatic mechanisms do not exist as segregated and neatly boxed entities. As I have already indicated, one process can influence another, and multiple processes may require access to the same bodily structure, sometimes in contradictory ways. It is even more important for behavioral science, however, that sensors involved in homeostasis may simultaneously send messages to physiologically and anatomically remote structures, and hence influence a much wider variety of processes than would be anticipated by a limited focus on what variable (say, cardiac output) is being controlled. Another way of saying this is that a *controlled* variable in one feedback process simultaneously becomes a *controlling* variable for another. The best known example—indeed, perhaps the only one—is that blood pressure, by means of the baroreceptive sensor, influences a surprisingly large number of seemingly alien variables. In the first comprehensive review of reflexive control of cardiovascular activity, an entire and seminal chapter was devoted to "Baroreceptor Reflexes Other than Circulatory" (Heymans & Neil, 1958). The list is extraordinary: Baroreceptors influence respiration, bronchomotor tone, the gastrointestinal tract, the bladder, the pupil, striated muscles, and the electroencephalogram. The EEG and motor effects are particularly noteworthy for behavioral scientists. In both cases, blood pressure increases result in inhibition. Miller's illustration of the somnolence produced in a cat when blood pressure was markedly increased by the injection of phenylephrine replicates in a sense the demonstration by Koch in 1932 (cited by Heymans & Neil, p. 98) of relaxation and sleep in a dog produced by mechanically increasing pressure in the isolated carotid sinus (an area richly endowed with blood-pressure-sensing receptors). The effect on somatic activity is a very direct one, as recently demonstrated by Coleridge, Coleridge, and Rosenthal (1976), who, on the basis of single-cell studies, concluded: "Evidence has been accumulating for more than 40 years to support the notion that stimulation of carotid sinus baroreceptors exerts widespread and prolonged inhibitory effects on the nervous system. . . . It is now clear that these effects involve single neurons of the motor cortex" (p. 645). (Indeed, it is this aspect of the remote role of cardiovascular feedback that forms one basis for the studies in my own laboratory at Fels Research Institute of the relationship of short-lived cardiac responses to sensorimotor integration.)

Another behaviorally significant demonstration of the apparently remote effects of feedback processes, based again on modern neurophysiological techniques, is provided in a recent paper by Gahery and Vigier (1974). These authors found that stimulation of the complex of feedback fibers (i.e., visceral afferent fibers) in the vago-aortic trunk profoundly depressed the response of single cells in the cuneate nucleus, either upon natural stimulation of the skin surface or upon electrical stimulation of the radial nerve. Hence, blood pressure changes can influence such fundamental sensory modalities as touch and kinesthesis. Gahery and Vigier concluded that "the inhibitory effects . . . suggest that vago-aortic afferents are ***not limited to a vegetative role*** [my italics] but may also be involved in a variety of physiological regulations" (p. 246). This sort of process could be another basis for that part of Dworkin's hypothesis (reviewed in Miller's keynote address; see Chapter 1) that blood pressure increase can diminish the effects of aversive stimulation.

But what sort of process is it? It seems that there may be direct interference with neural transmission across the synapse. There are several ways by which synaptic transmission can be influenced. One of the most important mechanisms is presynaptic inhibition. This is not the place to review this powerful and ubiquitous mechanism. Let it suffice to say that the CNS can reach back even to the level of the first synapse in a receptive chain to block transmission of a nervous impulse. Indeed, Gahery and Vigier (1974) showed that presynaptic inhibition was the mechanism underlying their results.

Hence, the nervous system can gate inputs. If the gate is open, the impulse traffic can proceed; if the gate is closed, traffic is stopped. A series of such gates, operating in different temporal patterns, can route traffic along diverse paths. Just such gating and rerouting has been demonstrated by Winson and Abzug (1977, 1978a, 1978b) with implanted electrodes in a well-defined synaptic chain in the hippocampus. The titles and the contents of each of the cited papers emphasize that neuronal transmission varies with behavioral state. The states studied were grossly defined: REM sleep, quiet alertness, slow-wave sleep. As techniques improve, it is almost certain, in my opinion, that smaller variations in behavioral state will be shown to influence such gating and rerouting processes. In the meantime, it should be noted that the title of one of the papers by Winson and Abzug (1978b) succinctly provides an operational definition of the "self-regulating organism": "Neuronal Transmission through Hippocampal Pathways [Is] Dependent on Behavior."

CONCLUSION

I conclude this discussion of homeostasis with a summary of the messages it is meant to convey. The title of this volume is *Clinical Biofeedback: Efficacy and Mechanisms.* I have chosen to discuss primarily the nature of underlying mechanisms. I have emphasized the banal but often-ignored fact that the organism is enormously plastic and has many complexly interacting mechanisms. Given appropriate circumstances, tightly coupled variables become uncoupled; given appropriate circumstances, the sign of the correlation between cooperating variable may be reversed; given appropriate circumstances, one variable may have direct consequences on almost inconceivably remote processes; given appropriate circumstances, one component of a commonly integrated pattern of response may be singled out for selective elicitation and modification. The job of the psychophysiologist is to understand the appropriate circumstances for each of these challenges to the concept of hard-wired universality of relationship. Systems theory, and control theory in particular—sophisticated and useful as they are—need extensive modification before they can be applied precisely to such topics as we have considered in this volume.

There has been much discussion and controversy in this volume concerning the question of whether biofeedback has any specific effects not attainable by other, easier techniques (such as progressive relaxation), or more mysteriously (by undefined mechanisms of the placebo effect). I think that here I must agree with the broad perspective of Neal Miller: In the long run, this is not the major question. The major question is this: How do any of these techniques produce their effects, even if these effects are small or temporary? And, for me at least, the major basic problem is to understand the underlying neurophysiological processes so that, in the end, such knowledge will sharpen our questions and the techniques we use to get answers.

REFERENCES

Bergman, S. A., Jr., Campbell, J. K., & Wildenthal, K. "Diving reflex" in man: Its relation to isometric and dynamic exercise. *Journal of Applied Physiology*, 1972, *33*, 27–31.

Coleridge, H. M., Coleridge, J. C. G., & Rosenthal, F. Prolonged inactivation of cortical pyramidal tract neurones in cat by distention of the carotid sinus. *Journal of Physiology (London)*, 1976, *256*, 635–649.

Escobar, A. (Ed.). *Feedback systems controlling nervous activity*. Mexico City: Sociedad Mexicana de Ciencias Fisológicas, A. C., 1964.

Gahery, Y., & Vigier, D. Inhibitory effects in the cuneate nucleus produced by vago-aortic afferent fibers. *Brain Research*, 1974, *75*, 241–246.

Gebber, G. L., & Snyder, D. W. Hypothalamic control of baroreceptor reflexes. *American Journal of Physiology*, 1970, *218*, 124–131.

Grodins, F. S. *Control theory and biological systems*. New York: Columbia University Press, 1963.

Heymans, C., & Neil, E. *Reflexogenic areas of the cardiovascular system*. Boston: Little, Brown, 1958.

Hockman, C. H., Talesnik, J., & Livingston, K. E. Central nervous system modulation of baroreceptor reflexes. *American Journal of Physiology*, 1969, *217*, 1681–1689.

Milhorn, H. T. *The application of control theory to physiological systems*. Philadelphia: Saunders, 1966.

Moruzzi, G. Paleocerebellar inhibition of vasomotor and respiratory carotid sinus reflexes. *Journal of Neurophysiology*, 1940, *3*, 20–32.

Peterson, L. H. The mechanical properties of the blood vessels and hypertension. In J. H. Cort, V. Fencl, Z. Hejl, & J. Jirka (Eds.), *The pathogenesis of essential hypertension*. Prague: State Medical Publishing House, 1962.

Reis, D. J., & Cuenod, M. Tonic influence of rostral brain structures on pressure regulatory mechanisms in the cat. *Science*, 1964, *145*, 64–65.

Reis, D. J., & Cuenod, M. Central neural regulation of carotid baroreceptor reflexes in the cat. *American Journal of Physiology*, 1965, *209*, 1267–1277.

Reis, D. J., & Fuxe, K. Adrenergic innervation of the carotid sinus. *American Journal of Physiology*, *1968*, *215*, 1054–1057.

Satinoff, E. Neural organization and evolution of thermal regulation in mammals. *Science*, 1978, *201*, 16–22.

Winson, J., & Abzug, C. Gating of neuronal transmission in the hippocampus: Efficacy of transmission varies with behavioral state. *Science*, 1977, *196*, 1223–1225.

Winson, J., & Abzug, C. Dependence upon behavior of neuronal transmission from perforant pathway through entorhinal cortex. *Brain Research*, 1978, *147*, 422–427. (a)

Winson, J., & Abzug, C. Neuronal transmission through hippocampal pathways dependent on behavior. *Journal of Neurophysiology*, 1978, *41*, 716–732. (b)

Yamamoto, W. S., & Brobeck, J. R. (Eds.). *Physiological controls and regulations*. Philadelphia: Saunders, 1965.

17 PERSPECTIVES IN BIOFEEDBACK: TEN YEARS AGO, TODAY, AND . . .

MARTIN T. ORNE

It is an exceedingly difficult task to discuss meaningfully a considerable number of highly diverse chapters, and as these chapters are incisive and some of them deal with their topics in a definitive fashion, it becomes presumptuous even to try to deal with them in a summary manner. Fortunately, each section has had individual discussions; further, Miller's keynote address not only serves to introduce the chapters that follow, but can also be reread fruitfully as the discussion. Both John Lacey and I felt we should address some of the more overall issues that emerge from this volume and are reflected in the field in general. In particular, it seems worthwhile to look at how we got to be here. This volume grew out of a research symposium on clinical biofeedback. Many of us were at a conference some years ago (October 20–22, 1969) in Santa Monica, California, where the term "biofeedback" became institutionalized.

ORIGINS OF THE TERM "BIOFEEDBACK"

At this conference, there were discussions about whether the phenomenon was to be called "operant conditioning," "self-regulation," or "biofeedback." Each of these terms focused on different aspects, and each had vocal proponents among the 142 individuals who attended the organizational meeting.

A strong contingent of scientists argued for using the concept of "operant conditioning," since much of the technology relevant to biofeedback has been derived from the technology used in operant conditioning. Further, the work of Miller (1969) and DiCara (DiCara & Miller, 1968) had shown that dramatic visceral changes

Martin T. Orne. Department of Psychiatry, University of Pennsylvania, Philadelphia, Pennsylvania; Unit for Experimental Psychiatry, The Institute of Pennsylvania Hospital, Philadelphia, Pennsylvania.

could be brought about with operant techniques, even in curarized animals. Similarly, the early work of D. Shapiro, Tursky, and Schwartz (1970) with blood pressure, and that of D. Shapiro, Crider, and Tursky (1964) with the electrodermal response, was presented within the operant-conditioning paradigm. This was equally true for the work of Engel (1972) in treating arrhythmias, and for Kamiya's research (1969) with alpha feedback training. Thus, there were a number of distinguished investigators, some of who had worked with animals and others who had worked with humans, who felt that "operant conditioning of visceral responses" was the appropriate terminology and would lead future investigators to think about the phenomenon in the proper fashion.

A number of participants, however, felt that the most important aspect of the new technologies was that they helped individuals to learn how to control bodily functions that were previously viewed as automatic or reflexive in nature. These participants objected to the term "operant conditioning" because it had overtones suggesting that individuals were somehow passive; whereas it was obvious that whatever mechanisms of learning were involved in gaining control over such parameters as blood pressure, heart rate, or brain waves also involved the individual's active participation and ultimately resulted in these individuals gaining increased mastery over themselves. Particularly since the mechanisms over which the individuals would seek to gain control were generally involved with reestablishing an appropriate homeostasis, the concept of "self-regulation" seemed to emphasize what, to many participants of the meeting, was the key factor.

Finally, yet another group argued that the notion of "feedback," already well established in engineering and neurophysiology, was the process central to learning control over involuntary physiological processes. The proponents of this view recognized that motivation was important, but cogently argued that, in the operant conditioning of human subjects at least, it was impossible to present the reinforcer without simultaneously presenting information. Since the motivation of an individual with frightening cardiac symptoms to control these symptoms is likely to be greater than any motivation created by some trivial monetary reward, it seemed best to speak about the effect of information on gaining control. Though such a situation could be conceptualized in operant terms without much difficulty (by acknowledging that the motivation to control the cardiac symptoms made certain information reinforcing), the majority of the participants were eager to adopt a term that lacked the psychological overtones of passivity associated with "conditioning."

It is also true that the studies that began carefully to address the relative importance of information as opposed to motivational factors for the process of acquiring control over physiological functions remained to be done; in part, this issue is only now being addressed in a basic way in some work such as that discussed by Brener (see Chapter 2). Further, the kinds of processes studied under the rubric of "biofeedback" typically involve a preexisting ability of the individual to assert volitional control in one direction with a lack of such an ability in the other. For example, in the presence of light, it is very easy to block alpha; but it requires some training to learn to ignore the visual inputs and to generate alpha freely. Again, it is relatively easy for individuals to produce electrodermal responses on demand, whereas it is more difficult to block the production of electrodermal responses. Consequently, the usual operant-research strategy of comparing the ability to increase and decrease a response could easily be misleading in what has become known as biofeedback research. For a variety of reasons, then, the term "biofeedback" was deemed desirable. Since it was a new term, it did not have any previous associations to contend with; it sounded both novel and exciting, and it implied not only a new area of research, but perhaps even a new era of research.

BIOFEEDBACK THEN AND NOW: DIFFERENCES IN CONCERNS

It is difficult to imagine how recently the term "biofeedback" came to denote a field of investigation. It is worthwhile, however, to remember the excitement and enthusiasm that characterized the Santa Monica meeting only a little over 10 years ago, largely due to the expectation of the participants that they were helping to usher in a new area of research and clinical application. The emerging field of biofeedback was unusual in that it brought together psychologists, physiologists, engineers, neurobiologists, physicians, psychophysiologists, and enthusiastic laymen; all of these people shared the hope that man could learn to self-regulate not only blood pressure, heart rate, or brain waves, but also levels of activation and states of anxiety, as well as the hope that it would be possible ultimately to replace many of the drugs in current usage, including the ubiquitous tranquilizers, simply by training people to self-regulate. These did not seem far-out hopes, not only because we were meeting in California, but because it really looked as though there were data to suggest that rapid learning of psychophysiological self-control, aided by appropriate electronic devices, was a plausible eventuality.

The meeting out of which this volume grew was quite different. The organizers carefully selected participants to represent the major areas of work in biofeedback over the past several years, including a number of people who were at that first meeting. Much basic work has been done in the field since then. Perhaps almost as interesting as the issues that are discussed in this volume are some of the issues that are conspicuously absent.

At the Santa Monica meeting, perhaps over half of the attendees were there because of an interest in alpha feedback training, a phenomenon that seemed to provide a bridge between Eastern traditions of meditative discipline and Western know-how. Great enthusiasm was engendered by the publication in such august scientific journals as *Time, Life,* and *Newsweek* of promises of instant *samadi*, which would allow people to gain in a few sessions benefits of meditation that would normally take a lifetime to acquire. Much of that promise appears to have been illusory, and it is interesting to note that no one in this volume discusses the clinical application of alpha feedback training.

Equally striking is the difference between the scientific issues that preoccupied basic science participants 10 years ago and those prominent today. The burning question then was that of whether operant conditioning of physiological parameters was directly possible, or whether some form of mediation inevitably occurred. While the reasons for discrepancies between early and later empirical findings in this area have yet to be clarified, the issue as such is no longer a vital one for the understanding of clinical biofeedback. Strikingly, the two major factors that led to the organization of the Biofeedback Research Society—the work by DiCara and Miller (1968) showing huge physiological effects with the operant conditioning of curarized animals, which provided the emerging field with much-needed scientific stature, and the work on alpha feedback training, which was widely accepted as having been shown to have salutary effects on psychological states—no longer form a significant basis for today's studies of biofeedback. Indeed, even the very concept of "biofeedback," which seemed so intuitively sensible, has been effectively challenged by Bernard Tursky's elegant discussion (see Chapter 5). While I believe that Tursky is undoubtedly right in his conceptual critique, the concept of "biofeedback" is likely to be with us for a long time to come. The research that has been prompted by the notion of "biofeedback" can stand on its own; and if some of the data that originally piqued our interest turned out to be different from what was once anticipated, investigators have learned enough that is new and worthwhile to justify continuing concern with these matters.

Having commented upon the appropriate absence of a discussion of alpha feedback training in the context of a symposium on clinical biofeedback, it is difficult to leave the topic without pointing out that even here some key issues have yet to be resolved. Paskewitz and I (Paskewitz & Orne, 1973) reported that feedback training to increase alpha density is easily achieved in the presence of light, but very difficult (if not impossible) to demonstrate with dark-adapted subjects in a totally dark environment. Further, contrary to our expectations, dark-adapted subjects exposed to the threat of shock and even exposed to actual electric shock failed to show a drop in alpha density, though they gave clear evidence of increased arousal behaviorally, by retrospective inquiry, and by dramatic increases in heart rate and spontaneous electrodermal responses (Orne & Paskewitz, 1974).

Though these findings clearly document that alpha density changes need not accompany changes in level of arousal, further analysis of these data demonstrates that while most subjects showed no changes in alpha density in response to shock or threat of shock, some subjects showed *decreases* in alpha density (in line with the generally accepted view), while some subjects showed an *increase* in alpha density associated with increased heart rate and spontaneous galvanic skin responses. In fact, the highest increment in alpha density (observed in a totally darkened room) was associated with intense arousal in a subject whose response to increased arousal is sharply increased alpha density. The observation that there are individual differences in alpha dynamics in relation to arousal is congruent with observations by Travis, Kondo, and Knott (1975) and others. (For a detailed discussion of these issues, see Orne & Wilson, 1978.)

I am trying to suggest that while alpha feedback training is unlikely to be a particularly useful clinical procedure, for selected subjects it could potentially be highly effective, while for some other selected subjects, training to decrease alpha might have the desired relaxing consequence. These comments are not intended to tout alpha feedback training; rather, since some of our work has been instrumental in suggesting the lack of a physiological mechanism that would justify the widespread use of alpha feedback training, they are intended to point out that even here the data are not all in. There may yet be a potentially useful phenomenon in this area, provided the basic mechanism can be elucidated and the rational application based on an understanding of the underlying processes.

MECHANISMS: SPECIFIC VERSUS NONSPECIFIC EFFECTS

As scientists, one would like to first understand the basic mechanism underlying any technique that is to be applied clinically. There is no substitute for such an understanding. The remarkable effectiveness of modern medicine owes much to such a systematic scientific approach. Traditional medicine has, however, also been an empirical art. A great many drugs were used centuries before their pharmacological mechanisms were fully appreciated. While it is considered essential today that any therapeutic approach provide a reasonable rationale for its effectiveness, there is often a wide gap between that rationale and clinical application. Behavior therapy, for example, justifies its existence by asserting that its procedures are related to findings of laboratory research. However, as London (1972) has pointed out, the link is often tenuous and even nonexistent, though the assertion has important heuristic value. Similarly, the rationale for biofeedback is sufficiently plausible and well-accepted to provide an umbrella for a wide range of therapeutic maneuvers that seem to be effective.

Since in many instances the systematic documentation of the mechanisms by which presumed effects occur is lacking, it becomes a central question to ask whether the therapeutic effects are specific or nonspecific effects. What do we mean by a "specific effect?" This has been incisively discussed by Jasper Brener from a conceptual point of view (see Chapter 2), and has been touched upon by others as well.

While, from a theoretical viewpoint, it is very important wheher or not biofeedback makes it possible for individuals to learn control over visceral or quasivisceral responses in a way that they could not do otherwise, this does not distinguish between whether such learning takes place primarily by way of an efferent or an afferent stimuli, or whether it is fed forward or fed backward. Further, from the point of view of application at least, the pathway is far less of an issue than the question of whether it is a specific effect.

I would like to distinguish here between important conceptual scientific questions such as, "Are we really dealing with feedback effects?" or "How is the effect mediated?" which are not key problems relating to the application of the phenomenon, and the question of whether there is a specific effect, which *is* central to clinical application. I believe that these types of issues tend to be confounded, and I intend to focus here on the issue of specificity.

When asking the question, "What is a nonspecific factor, as opposed to a specific factor?" one of the major problems is that what is nonspecific today becomes specific tomorrow. In other words, what is nonspecific relates very much to the present state of ignorance, and the task of medical science has always been to make whatever is known into more and more specific knowledge. To take a well-known example, the discovery of digitalis was made by a witch who picked foxglove at the new moon and mixed it with bats' wings and similar good things, which resulted in a concoction that effectively treated dropsy. Dropsy was believed at the time to be an illness, and was only later recognized as a symptom, now called edema. Of course, the concoction only effectively treated edema resulting from cardiac causes. There was the problem, however, of the specific as opposed to the nonspecific component of that concoction. It took some time to learn that it was not essential that foxglove be picked at the new moon; neither were the bats' wings necessary; and after many years of work, scientists now know that there is a specific effect of digitalis, which is contained in foxglove. It appears an easy question to resolve, but at the time that people had this concoction and asked, "Does it work?" they had to ask first, "Is the effect of this concoction specific or nonspecific?"

The first thing to establish is whether there is a specific effect of the concoction *in its totality*—bats' wings and all—and to do that, investigators must have an appropriate kind of control for the concoction as a whole. For example, early researchers might have tried to determine whether an equally foul-smelling concoction presented by the same witch is as effective. It might have turned out that it was important that the witch did not know which concoction she was giving the patient, and so on. Only after it was shown that there is a real effect on dropsy specific to this concoction could it have made sense to begin the analytical work to take this mixture apart and determine whether the new moon was important, whether the bats' wings were important, and whether the old woman with her convictions was needed or whether a doctor might be just as effective. These kinds of questions are secondary to having first established whether there is a specific effect worthy of inquiry.

It appears to me that many of the problems of researchers reside in both undercontrol and overcontrol. In other words, control procedures are often applied too soon, before it has been established that a "concoction" works as a totality. The first question must be whether there is a phenomenon worth investigating. Only then does it become sensible to engage in ever more careful control procedures, to dissect and analyze the aspects of the total procedure in which the phenomenon resides. Consequently, what is specific and nonspecific depends upon where investigators are in this sequence of research. In the early stage, they ask, "Is there a specific effect due to the totality of the concoction?" *Later on*, they ask: "Is there a specific effect due to the bats' wings?" "Is there a specific effect due to the foxglove being picked at the new moon?" "Is there a specific effect due to the kind of person who gives the concoction?" and so on. Much disagreement can be avoided if researchers are careful not to confuse the issue of where they are in a line of investigation with what they are trying to do.

The basic question of whether there is a specific effect due to the overall procedure has yet to be answered for much of the biofeedback literature. For example, in the biofeedback of epilepsy, it was first essential to show that there is a specific phenomenon that is *not* simply an attention variable, that is *not* simply a matter of being nice to these people whom everybody ignores as "crocks"—in other words, to show that something *is* happening that is a specific effect above and beyond the general nonspecific effects. To answer this deceptively simply question is often an exceedingly difficult and complex problem. However, until this is done, it is often difficult to justify going on to dissect the process itself and to see what is there that accounts for the specific effect. Until the mechanism is understood, no one has a true understanding of the phenomenon. At the same time, it is appropriate, given the present stage of development of biofeedback, to establish first that there is a specific effect. Sterman's research (see Chapter 12) has gone far to show such an effect and is now appropriately exploring the specific mechanisms involved.

THE ISSUE OF CONTROLS: CONTROLLING FOR PLACEBO EFFECTS

Much of the discussion of those of us oriented toward doing basic laboratory research must appropriately focus on mechanisms. Those of us who are more directly concerned with the application often feel that while they ultimately need to study mechanisms and that this is *the* appropriate way of going about it, it is first necessary to establish that the phenomena are real. How does an investigator go about that? It seems appropriate here to address the question of what constitutes an appropriate control. This question has been raised in several of the papers, and I do not intend to review the matter in a generic sense here, except to point out that an appropriate control can never be specified unless researchers have a theory that they seek to test.

There is no such thing as specifying an appropriate control in the abstract. A control becomes possible only after investigators are willing to specify, for the moment at least, what they consider to be the active ingredient they are studying. Unless such an active ingredient is specified, they cannot control for it; by the same token, as soon as they specify the active ingredient to be investigated, they implicitly specify what constitutes some of the meaningful controls.

In this context, I intend to talk about the placebo controls, because they happen to be an area of my particular interest. A very interesting comment has been made on how to compare the effect of biofeedback on headache with that of a placebo control (see Cox & Hobbs, Chapter 13); the effect of biofeedback on headache was compared with the effect of a placebo (in this case, a pill without an active ingredient) in a controlled study of headache. On the face of it, this is a very interesting and sensible control. Unfortunately, it ignores what a placebo is intended to do. In psychopharmacology, particularly, a placebo is intended to be a control that conveniently embodies all aspects of pill-taking behavior, with the patient's expectancies and beliefs and the physician's attitudes. This seems to be conveniently and easily done by giving an identical pill without an active ingredient.

It should be emphasized, however, that the effects of drugs as such are almost never studied. There are some studies—very few—such as that by Lyerly, Ross, Krugman, and Clyde (1964), in which amphetamines and barbiturates respectively were slipped into subjects' orange juice without their knowledge; they were then asked to rate how they felt. The investigators also gave these subjects the same drugs as pills without indicating what they were. It turned out that the effects were quite different when subjects knowingly took a drug from what they were when the subjects had ingested the drug without their knowledge. The mood changes were considerably larger when associated with pill-taking behavior, probably because they could now attribute them to a pill and acknowledge them comfortably.

Normally, the effect of a pill containing an active pharmacological ingredient is compared with that of a pill without an active pharmacological ingredient (placebo). Note that investigators do not study the pharmacological ingredient as such; they only study the effect of taking a pill with or without it. Another way of putting it is that a drug effect includes the placebo effect plus an active pharmacological effect. It is worth keeping in mind that any treatment procedure has placebo components which have powerful effects on their own.

The placebo, then, is a way of attempting to control for the totality of the nonpharmacological effects associated with receiving drug therapy. It is this concept that has generalized to the notion of the placebo effect of psychotherapy, as, indeed, there are profound placebo effects of psychotherapy (A. P. Shapiro, 1959). Similarly, there are placebo effects of biofeedback. Any time a treatment receives a great deal of publicity, and particularly if it involves elaborate equipment, investigators can anticipate profound placebo effects.

When researchers begin to examine placebo effects with care, it becomes clear that if a therapist knows which patient is receiving the active drug and which is receiving the placebo, a larger effect with the active ingredient almost invariably results. There is a simple reason for that. Doctors giving a new pill generally expect some effect, and they also are typically quite concerned about patients' reactions. If a patient comes to a doctor and says, "Doctor, I have a ringing in my ears," and the individual is on the active drug, the physician will say, "Well now, come, I want to examine you." After a thorough physical, the doctor is likely to say, "Here's my home number. Call me if anything strange happens." On the other hand, if the patient who is on placebo comes in saying exactly the same thing, the physician pats this patient on the back and says, "Don't worry, my friend. It will go away." Clearly, these people are treated radically differently, and it is therefore not surprising that it is important for therapists to be blind as to whether they are giving drug or placebo.

As an example, I recall the first clinical trials of Marsilid. You may remember this was the first effective, widely used antidepressant, an MAO-inhibitor that was eventually taken off the market because of liver complications associated with its use. In the original drug trials, two patients came down with glomerulonephritis. They were, of course, immediately taken off drugs. It was only much later that it was learned that both of these patients happened to be on placebo. (If, by chance, both of those patients had been on the drug, it might never have been released.)

I participated in the discussion of a placebo biofeedback experiment that is discussed elsewhere in this volume (see the round-table discussion of Cox & Hobbs and Adams, Brantley, & Thompson), where I asked, "Did you know which individuals were receiving the active ingredient?" The reason I asked was because the patient who showed side effects was on the active treatment and therapy was, of course, discontinued. I would have preferred that the principal investigator hadn't known which patients were receiving the active treatment, because he might then also have discontinued treatment of one or two people on the placebo therapy who were complaining of side effects; this virtually never happens as long as the responsible physician knows that the patient is on placebo. It is for this reason that not only the therapist who is in contact with the patient, but also the physician who has overall medical responsibility, must be blind. Indeed, it can be argued that especially that individual must be blind, because he or she is going to make the decision as to whether a patient needs a little reassurance and can continue, or whether that patient should be taken off the experimental therapy. It is crucial that a physician not know whether the patient is or is not on placebo at that point, because differential treatment vitiates the entire double-blind procedure.

Another issue I take up briefly in the same discussion is that it is not uncommon for technicians to be blind but for the patient not to be blind. In one of the first studies comparing Thorazine to placebo, the medical staff, nurses, and attendants were carefully kept blind. However, when I asked some patients whether they were getting drugs, they had no difficulty telling me whether they were or were not, because those on drug had a dry mouth, and patients do talk to each other. As one patient aptly pointed out, "I may be crazy, but I am not dumb."

How the patient may be kept blind in a placebo study on biofeedback is a huge problem. For example, the control most typically used is a yoked control; that is, one subject is run with biofeedback, and a second subject, who is "yoked" to the first subject, receives the feedback *signal* that has been displayed for the first subject instead of being given feedback; thus the amount of "reinforcement" given to these two subjects is matched. In the same fashion, each subject is paired or yoked to another, one receiving true feedback and the other receiving false feedback. In our early alpha studies, we found that even though subjects could not increase alpha density in a dark room, they were aware (typically within 10 minutes of trials) of when they were not receiving accurate feedback. They felt that there was something different. They couldn't spell it out, but they knew that something was wrong and they responded differently. There is little question that a simple yoked control is not appropriate with virtually any of the biofeedback procedures, because it is an inactive placebo control. It is closely analogous to the realization of the patient who is getting a placebo and doesn't have a dry mouth that he or she is not getting the active drug. If subjects get a hint that they are not getting feedback, then they will simply not respond.

The notion of what constitutes an adequate control in such a situation is a very tricky point. By the way, Lubar (see Chapter 11) has added a very interesting and very useful and appropriate aspect in his procedure by including a spot that remains responsive to muscle control. That is an excellent way of creating an active placebo. It is one of the very few studies I know of that has used a procedure analogous to an active placebo with biofeedback.

There are some other ways of attempting to create an active placebo in biofeedback research. One of them is to start out by giving subjects actual biofeedback and letting them experiment with it, and then gradually to degrade the signal until eventually they are presented with the same information that had been given to yoked controls. The problem here is that, as I mentioned earlier, the physiological response to biofeedback training is rarely symmetrical. That is, subjects typically only need to learn control in one direction; they inherently have control in the other direction. For example, with alpha feedback training, subjects could always block alpha with fairly good success, simply by attempting to see, even in a dark room. Again, with EMG feedback, subjects can always increase muscle tension; the training is needed to teach them to decrease muscle tension, and so on. Since subjects have volitional control in one direction, it is an easy matter for them to determine whether they have any control, simply by trying to block alpha or to increase muscle tension. Therefore, if researchers gradually degrade the signal, they are always faced with the possibility that subjects may at any time decide to test their control and thus may readily find out that it is nonexistent.

An alternative that I find ingenious was used in a study by Otis, McCormick, and Lukas (1974). Employing EMG feedback, they set up contingencies in a way that when subjects tensed their muscles, they obtained correct feedback; but when they relaxed, they obtained random feedback. In this fashion, the subjects had control—that is, the unilateral kind of control that people always have and don't need to learn—but they could be given false yoked feedback for relaxation as long as the circuit was arranged to override the yoked control and give correct feedback for tensing muscles when a certain EMG level was exceeded.

The control employed by Otis *et al.* is a potentially useful approach to creating a viable, active placebo for feedback training. The subject does have control over one direction of change, but it is not the direction that matters. I would hope that this ingenious and useful solution to some of the problems of control associated with biofeedback will be more widely used.[1]

Not only is it necessary for a placebo to be active in order to provide similar expectancies for the treatment and control groups; it is also important to consider the expectancies of the therapist in assessing the effects of a placebo. It is not merely that the therapist must be blind as to which patient is receiving an active treatment; it is important to know something about the therapist's beliefs concerning the active treatment.

Consider, for example, Blanchard's report earlier in this volume that, with migraine, placebo typically had a 16.5% effectiveness (see Blanchard, Table 2, "Comments on the Chapters by Beatty and by Surwit"). There is a tendency to take an observation of this kind, derived from one study, and to use it as a rule of thumb for an estimate of nonspecific effects in other treatment contexts of the same condition. A secondary analysis, carried out by Fred Evans in our laboratory, shows the difficulties with such an approach. He reviewed a whole series of placebo studies (Evans, 1974) that treated the placebo as if it were a new analgesic drug. He pointed out:

> The efficacy of an unknown analgesic can be determined by comparing it with a strong analgesic, such as morphine, and perhaps to a weaker analgesic, such as aspirin. What could be called the index of drug efficiency can be expressed as the ratio: Reduction in pain with unknown active drug/Reduction in pain with known analgesic. For example, comparing a mild analgesic such as codeine with morphine would yield a relative low index, indicating it is less effective than morphine. Comparing codeine with aspirin would presumably yield an index greater than 1.00, indicating that codeine is more effective than aspirin. (p. 294)

[1]Editors' note: An alternative methodology for insuring double-blind procedures with yoked subjects has also been noted earlier by D. Shapiro (Cohen, Graham, Fotopoulos, & Cook, 1977; see Chapter 3).

Using this index, he then compared the effectiveness of placebo with a strong and a mild analgesic. He observed that the index of placebo efficiency compared to a standard dose of aspirin was .54, indicating that placebo is 54% as effective as aspirin (averaging 10 studies). If placebo is a relatively weak drug compared to aspirin, what could be expected of its efficiency when compared to a standard dose of morphine? Surprisingly, contrary to expectation, the index of efficiency was *not* much lower; rather, it turned out to be .56 compared to morphine. The same drug (placebo) now suddenly seems quite powerful, having some 56% of the effectiveness of morphine. When Evans compared placebo with Darvon, it again showed an efficiency index of .56. In each instance, placebo was compared blind to a different drug, but its actual capacity to relieve pain was far greater when it was being compared to morphine than when it was being compared to aspirin. Thus, the efficiency index turned out to be identical when placebo was compared against a powerful, a mild, or a moderate analgesic.

The analysis by Evans elegantly demonstrates that the effectiveness of a placebo varies with physicians' expectations about the effectiveness of the drug they are administering. The relative effectiveness is essentially identical, regardless of whether it is being compared to a powerful or a weak analgesic. This means that the strength of the placebo effect is a function of the physicians' expectations concerning the strength of the therapeutic effect of the active drug with which it is being compared. To speak of a fixed magnitude of a placebo effect ignores this little-known but startling attribute of placebos.

Though troubling at first, these observations actually make a great deal of sense. Since the placebo effect assesses the totality of nonspecific factors, the expectations of therapists and those around them about therapeutic outcome should either maximize or minimize the nonspecific components. Unfortunately, this also means that the notion of somehow simply measuring the magnitude of placebo effects in the abstract is unlikely to be helpful; instead, the placebo component must be assessed in the specific therapeutic context in which the presumed active treatment is being given.

One additional point concerning placebo effects is worth considering. Typically, investigators think of these effects only in terms of positive therapeutic consequences. However, just as the expectations of therapists and patients concerning a positive outcome may help to bring about such a result, so negative expectations by therapist and patient may serve to interfere with specific therapeutic effects. In a classic study by Lasagna, Tetreault, and Fallis (1962), it was found that the 14% of patients who had reacted positively to each of several placebo administrations showed mean pain relief of 95% to morphine. On the other hand, from among the 21% of patients who had failed to respond to placebo, the administration of morphine resulted in only 54% of pain relief. It seems reasonable to view their results as showing that, just as positive nonspecific factors may serve to potentiate therapeutic effects, negative nonspecific factors may counteract them. It is impressive that these effects can be powerful enough to interfere with the analgesic effects of morphine; and it should also be kept in mind that in addition to patient and therapist expectancies prior to treatment, the manner in which a treatment is carried out, the apparent competence of therapists and their technicians, the appropriateness of the setting, and a myriad of related factors may serve to create a profound nonspecific therapeutic effect under an appropriate set of circumstances. By the same token, however, the same kind of nonspecific factors may also serve to defeat a specific therapeutic effect. Some confusing findings concerning the clinical application of biofeedback are very likely to be related to these issues.

Much of the discussion in this volume has focused on the problems of control of nonspecific factors, which are typically subsumed under the catch phrase of "placebo effects." The need for studies to control for these factors relates to the present level of knowledge in the field of biofeedback. As knowledge increases, it becomes possible to specify more and more factors that initially were lumped together under the rubric of nonspecific effects. In some areas of medicine, as, for example, in the assessment of antibiotics, there is relatively little need for placebo controls. Enough is known so that dose–response curves and comparisons with other active drugs generally suffice. The better investigators are able to specify the relevant factors, the smaller and less important the area of nonspecific factors becomes. It is for this reason that today's nonspecific factors may tomorrow become identified as a series of specific factors.

The nonspecific effects of psychotherapy provide an example of this kind. There is little doubt that psychotherapy has placebo components. However, some components that are considered placebo effects may in fact be quite specific. While no study is yet available, I would like to share some observations still in progress. A phenomenon that seems particularly intriguing is the "honeymoon" of psychotherapy, which is generally thought of as a combination of transference and placebo effect. However, it is well known that troubled individuals who are given an appointment for some 2 weeks after the time at which they seek help generally become much calmer during this time; when they are seen and a therapist explores the recent past, they report having felt better since the appointment was made.

At first sight, this may be interpreted as an obvious placebo effect, since no treatment has taken place. On further examination, however, it turns out that a number of important reality changes have taken place in such patients' lives since they not only made the decision to seek help, but made an appointment with a therapist. When these patients are asked, "Tell me, with whom did you discuss going into psychotherapy?" it turns out that they have typically discussed it with spouses and other significant others, who know that the patient has obtained an appointment to see a therapist; and while the relationship may have been very tenuous and the spouse quite angry with the patient, the knowledge that the patient is going to seek treatment significantly alters the spouse's behavior. Typically, a spouse is relieved that a patient is seeking help and that there is a prospect for change; equally, the spouse will worry about what the patient will say to the therapist, and it is characteristically important to the spouse that he or she is presented as a good, desirable person. Consequently, the way the patient is treated will have changed during the time preceding the first visit. Assume for the moment that such an effect is common and real. It is clearly due to psychotherapy. It is clearly not a function of the specific treatment by the therapist; and in that sense, it is a nonspecific effect. By the same token, this effect can be identified, isolated, and measured; thus, it becomes a specific effect that can be taken into account in its own right.

This example illustrates that, when analyzed, something that looks to all the world like a nonspecific effect is likely to have a number of very specific, identifiable components. As long as these specific components are not understood, it is necessary to use a broad placebo control; but once a phenomenon has been established, investigators can begin to focus on and acquire a better understanding of many of the specific components that were initially subsumed under the general rubric of "placebo effects." As investigators are able to do this, they gain specific control over them.

SPECIFIC EFFECTS OF BIOFEEDBACK

I now want to say a few words about biofeedback in the context of this discussion. It is clear that some specific effects due to biofeedback have been documented. However, they are far more limited than had once been thought. It is made clear in this volume, for example, that in the treatment of neuromuscular disorders, stroke, and the whole area of rehabilitation, biofeedback technologies may be extremely useful in what appear to be specific ways. The treatment of epilepsy by means of biofeedback also appears to be a specific effect. While it has not been talked about much, the work on fecal incontinence also appears to be in the category of a specific effect. On the other hand, biofeedback therapy of hypertension is a more complex matter. Some level of learned volitional control over blood pressure within a relatively brief time can be readily shown. However, the magnitude of that effect, except under very special circumstances, tends to be quite trivial from a clinical point of view. Biofeedback has achieved some clinical results in this area, but when these are compared with results of such therapies as relaxation training, the latter are as significant as the former.

While biofeedback at one time was thought of as a very specific intervention, it has become increasingly clear that biofeedback therapy in actual practice, particularly as applied to stress-related disorders, involves changes of a kind that biofeedback as such is a relatively minor, though potentially effective, adjunctive treatment. However, it is not *the* treatment. Rather, as has been discussed in this volume, treatment for these disorders involves changes in life style; and biofeedback may help both the patient and the therapist obtain some useful information to help bring about the necessary changes.

In a variety of studies, the therapeutic effect of biofeedback has been compared to that of relaxation therapy, self-hypnosis, or meditation; typically, there has been little difference among them. In thinking about the failure to find differences among these various approaches, investigators must not forget that the findings were that each of these techniques showed considerable therapeutic effect. Rather than focusing on the lack of differences in a negative sense, it may be appropriate to ask why relaxation training and related techniques have been overlooked for many years, at least in this country. From my point of view at least, one of the major contributions that biofeedback has made is to reawaken our interest in the importance of a number of potentially significant therapeutic tools. Though the overall results are similar with these various procedures, it does not seem likely that each of these techniques is equally effective with the same individual. Perhaps it is time research was directed at determining which therapeutic approach is most effective for which kind of patient under what circumstances.

Looking back on the development of biofeedback, it appears that the technique is a specific treatment only in a very few instances; on the other hand, in the most common uses of biofeedback today—in stress-related disturbances, as an adjunct to various forms of psychotherapy, and even as a technique of self-exploration—there is little doubt that therapists are dealing with a myriad of factors, of which the appropriate use of electronic aids plays a relatively minor role. Nonetheless, the potential for measuring change can provide an important source of information to both therapist and patient; and as the therapeutic community develops more sophistication vis-à-vis biofeedback, relaxation training, and related techniques, investigators may anticipate that these methods will ultimately be incorporated into both behaviorally and psychotherapeutically-oriented treatment programs in an effective and integrated manner.

REFERENCES

DiCara, L. V., & Miller, N. E. Instrumental learning of vasomotor responses by rats: Learning to respond differentially in the two ears. *Science,* 1968, *159,* 1485–1486.

Engel, B. T. Operant conditioning of cardiac function: A status report. *Psychophysiology,* 1972, *9,* 161–177.

Evans, F. J. The placebo response in pain reduction. In J. J. Bonica (Ed.), *Advances in neurology* (Vol. 4, *Pain*). New York: Raven Press, 1974.

Kamiya, J. Operant control of the EEG alpha rhythm and some of its reported effects on consciousness. In C. T. Tart (Ed.), *Altered states of consciousness: A book of readings.* New York: Wiley, 1969.

Lasagna, L., Tetreault, L., & Fallis, N. E. Analgesic drugs and experimental ischemic pain. *Federal Proceedings,* 1962, *21,* 326.

London, P. The end of ideology in behavior modification. *American Psychologist,* 1972, *27,* 913–920.

Lyerly, S., Ross, S., Krugman, A., & Clyde, D. Drugs and placebos: The effects of instructions upon performance and mood under amphetamine sulphate and chloral hydrate. *Journal of Abnormal and Social Psychology,* 1964, *68,* 321–327.

Miller, N. E. Learning of visceral and glandular responses. *Science,* 1969, *163,* 434–445.

Orne, M. T., & Paskewitz, D. A. Aversive situational effects on alpha feedback training. *Science,* 1974, *186,* 458–460.

Orne, M. T., & Wilson, S. K. On the nature of alpha feedback training. In G. E. Schwartz & D. Shapiro (Eds.), *Consciousness and self-regulation: Advances in research and theory* (Vol. 2). New York: Plenum, 1978.

Otis, L. S., McCormick, N. L., & Lukas, J. S. Voluntary control of tension headaches. *Proceedings of the Biofeedback Research Society: Fifth Annual Meeting,* 1974.

Paskewitz, D. A., & Orne, M. T. Visual effects on alpha feedback training. *Science,* 1973, *181,* 360–363.

Shapiro, A. K. The placebo effect in the history of medical treatment: Implications for psychiatry. *American Journal of Psychiatry,* 1959, *116,* 73–78.

Shapiro, D., Crider, A. B., & Tursky, B. Differentiation of an autonomic response through operant reinforcement. *Psychonomic Science,* 1964, *1,* 147–148.

Shapiro, D., Tursky, B., & Schwartz, G. E. Differentiation of heart rate and systolic blood pressure in man by operant conditioning. *Psychosomatic Medicine,* 1970, *32,* 417–423.

Travis, T. A., Kondo, C. Y., & Knott, J. R. Subjective aspects of alpha enhancement. *British Journal of Psychiatry,* 1975, *127,* 122–126.

VII

CONCLUSION

18 WHERE ARE WE . . . WHERE ARE WE GOING?

LEONARD WHITE AND BERNARD TURSKY

Differentiation of clinical potential from the demonstrated efficacy of biofeedback has been a major objective of this book. Although it was anticipated that a single summary statement would be an improbable outcome because of the diversity of clinical applications, we did not anticipate the degree of heterogeneity of issues that have emerged in this volume. In this chapter, we attempt to differentiate particular issues within the field of biofeedback, which has too often been viewed as a unitary enterprise.

SUMMARY OF CONCLUSIONS AND RECOMMENDATIONS

Table 1 contains a summary of the conclusions and recommendations for further study set forth in the course of this volume for each of the disorders discussed, based upon the conclusions and percentages of the reviewers and discussants and the consulted transcripts of the round-table discussions.

It is apparent that the data in support of specific efficacy of biofeedback are currently strongest for sensorimotor rhythm feedback for epilepsy and EMG feedback for neuromuscular rehabilitation, both CNS functions. Concerning cardiac arrhythmias, the data are particularly encouraging in the treatment of sinus tachycardia and, to a

Leonard White. Long Island Research Institute and Department of Psychiatry and Behavioral Science, School of Medicine, State University of New York at Stony Brook, Stony Brook, New York.

Bernard Tursky. Laboratory for Behavioral Research and Department of Political Science, State University of New York at Stony Brook, Stony Brook, New York.

lesser extent, in the treatment of PVCs. In Raynaud's disease, the results of behavioral intervention are particularly impressive in the absence of effective medical or surgical treatments, but there appears to be no difference between biofeedback and simple relaxation methods. For migraine headaches, biofeedback of hand temperature produces significant improvement but is not more efficacious than relaxation or placebo effects. Hemodynamic studies of the hand-warming procedure suggest that changes are due to reduction of sympathetic activity. Feedback of information related to temporal pulse amplitude may reduce the incidence and intensity of migraine by mimicking the vasoconstriction of the temporal artery produced by ergotamine compounds. Present data, however, are marginal, and further study of individual differences and treatment parameters is recommended. Evaluation of the treatment of tension headache and of generalized anxiety is particularly problematic because of methodological issues of classification and measurement. The assumed relationship between frontalis muscle tension and clinical symptoms, which provides the rationale for a narrowly defined biofeedback approach to these symptoms, is not corroborated by systematic studies. Although biofeedback therapy may effect significant reductions in clinical symptoms, relaxation and placebo may be as efficacious in these usually imprecisely defined disorders. Measurement profiles of psychological and physiological variables may be helpful in subclassification of these heterogeneous populations and for prescriptive selection of treatment alternatives.

FUTURE STUDIES

In reviewing in Table 1, we are struck by the degree to which simple relaxation and/or placebo have significant clinical effects, as well as by the degree of imprecision associated with the use of these terms.

In pharmacology, "placebo" designates all the variables uncontrolled for in a study and excludes only the additional effects of the pharmacological agent. Placebo may include spontaneous remission of symptoms, as well as changes mediated by reassurance and other processes of social influence. Indeed, it includes all those things not controlled for or specified by the pharmacologist. The term "placebo" may be best understood by behavioral practitioners as referring to "unspecified" effects as contrasted with "specified" effects. In the biobehavioral sciences, the "specified" effect is due to something other than a direct pharmacological effect. The primary point is that this kind of distinction forces an investigator to specify a component as the effective ingredient and is a precondition for a test of that hypothesis.

One of the problems attendant upon the use of relaxation as a specific procedure in behavioral medicine is the differentiation of specific relaxation from placebo. Throughout this volume, there appears to be confusion over the terms "relaxation"

TABLE 1. Summary of Conclusions and Recommendations, Listed by Disorder

Disorder	*Results of Biofeedback*	*Behavioral Treatment Results*	*Comments*	*Needed Research*
Hypertension	Individuals with essential hypertension trained in blood pressure biofeedback have learned to decrease blood pressure. Amount of reduction varies among studies.	Until more research is done, it appears that relaxation may offer a convenient alternative to biofeedback.	Blood pressure biofeedback has specific effects without corresponding changes in alpha brain waves, respiration, muscle tension, skin resistance, heart rate, or frontalis muscle tension. A treatment package including a variety of behavioral methods may be effective to the degree that the individual is engaged in and committed to the procedure.	Patient selection; blood pressure measurement; transfer to natural environment; individual differences; effective reinforcer; number of sessions.
Cardiac arrhythmia	Biofeedback training using heart rate yields particularly encouraging results in sinus tachycardia and, to a lesser extent, with PVCs.	—	In normal subjects, a proportional heart rate feedback display is superior to a binary system. Temporal delay of feedback disrupts ability to learn control.	Motivational variables; individual differences; predictors of differences.

Migraine	Significant improvement with hand-warming techniques.	Effects of hand-warming biofeedback not significantly different from those of relaxation or placebo controls. Although statistical "meta-analysis" of the literature suggests that biofeedback and relaxation alone or in combination are more efficacious than medication placebo is, this analysis may be biased because of the variability of placebo response with time, place, and person.	Pattern of hemodynamics during hand warming, including bradycardia and increased blood flow in periphery, suggests a general decrease in sympathetic outflow (i.e., relaxation effect).	
	Extracranial vasoconstriction by means of temporal pulse amplitude resulted in 36% reduction in incidence of all headaches and 44% reduction in incidence of major headaches.	In comparison with control groups, pattern of response to temporal pulse feedback suggests specific effects.	Although Beatty notes small advantages to temporal pulse feedback, in light of the technical difficulties involved in implementing this procedure and the marginal data presently available, he appears cautious.	Elmore and Tursky, Adams, Brantley, and Thompson, and Blanchard offer comments in support of continued study of these procedures. Some parameters to explore are number of trials, individual differences in acquisition of control, and differentiation of headache types.

(continued)

TABLE 1. *(continued)*

Disorder	*Results of Biofeedback*	*Behavioral Treatment Results*	*Comments*	*Needed Research*
Raynaud's disease	Skin temperature biofeedback provides reliable treatment, particularly in conjunction with relaxation.	No differences between relaxation and biofeedback treatments. 60% reduction in symptom frequency; 3–4 °C increase in resting digital temperature.	The results of behavioral interventions for relief of symptoms are impressive in the face of no effective alternative medical or surgical treatment.	Maintenance of treatment effects; individual differences.
Rehabilitation of voluntary movement in neurological cases	Sensory Feedback Therapy (SFT) using integrated EMG activity (iEMG). In hemiparetic treatment-resistant patients, 61% achieved success in controlling movement disorders during daily activities, with gains tending to be maintained during follow-up. In treatment-resistant patients with dystonia, a 56% success rate was achieved initially and retained in 45% of cases.	—	One of the most substantiated clinical uses of biofeedback. Wolf contends that training techniques using less sophisticated EMG biofeedback and not involving "unique [SFT] spatial–temporal information" may be as effective at less cost and time.	Intercenter comparative study recommended. Introduction of home-based programs; evaluation of motivational variables; more precise and reliable methods for defining movement disorders and functional gain.
Epilepsy	Feedback of sensorimotor rhythm (SMR) EEG (12 to 15 Hz) resulted in seizure reduction in 63% to 70% of patients with intractable epilepsy.	Approximately 30% response for placebo procedures.	Studies have gone far to eliminate alternative explanations (e.g., relaxation, placebo). Particularly impressive have been the findings of alterations in power-spectral analyses of sleep EEGs, which correspond to symptom reductions.	Home-based treatment programs; consideration of the total dynamics of change in EEG activity; role of motor inhibition in SMR; maintenance of treatment; patient selection based upon EEG criteria.

Tension headache	Feedback of frontalis EMG, usually combined with home charting, therapist contact, and home relaxation, resulted in therapeutic effect in 75% of patients.	Adams, Brantley, Thompson, and panel do not agree with Cox and Hobbs, who suggest biofeedback as treatment of choice. Placebo and other controls are judged inadequate, largely because there were either single-blind or readily differentiated treatments.	There is much discussion of problems related to diagnosis and the failure to find correlations between measured EMG levels and headache, either diagnostically or during treatment. Although treatment is delivered within the context of an operant paradigm, interpretation of treatment is offered in terms of change in life style, mediated by increased awareness of physiological responses.	Refined diagnostic procedures that particularly redefine the syndrome of "tension headache" in terms of specific psychological and physiological components.
Anxiety	Frontalis EMG biofeedback effects symptom reduction in a significant number of cases of "anxiety."	Studies do not support the contention that biofeedback alone is any more effective than simple progressive relaxation training alone. Lang notes that for specific phobias, exposure has proven to be treatment of choice.	Behavioral treatment of anxiety may have to proceed in the context of the individual's transactions with the environment, in which patterns of task performance, physiological activity, and cognition are taken into account.	A unitary physiological arousal model upon which much of area is based is probably false. Measurement of generalized anxiety is surprisingly elusive. Interrelationships between physiological, behavioral, and self-report methods of evaluation need to be understood.

and "placebo." When subjected to critical analysis, the data on relaxation effects do not seem to substantiate readily the claim of specific effects relative to sitting quietly in a room with minimal stimulation (Smith, 1975, 1976; West, 1980). Davidson and Schwartz (1976) have suggested that "relaxation" itself is a multidimensional condition having active, passive, cognitive, and physiological components; other authors (Luiselli, Marholin, Steinman, & Steinman, 1979) have noted that, in the literatureure, "relaxation" refers to a family of procedures, and the immediate consequences of those procedures are rarely specified. Although it appears that, with some ingenuity, it is possible to design a double-blind, controlled study of biofeedback (Cohen, Graham, Fotopoulos, & Cook, 1977), the specific effects of relaxation as a procedure have defied experimental test because adequate control groups have not been defined.

The interdependence between a theory of a mechanism of action and a demonstration of specific efficacy has been amply illustrated throughout this volume. The diversity of opinion encountered regarding a presumed mechanism of action has been elicited not only because of the unique properties and constraints of individual physiological systems, but also because of varying definitions of the term "biofeedback" itself. An examination of these interrelated issues may be important not only to the understanding of clinical biofeedback, but also to their application in the more recently established field of behavioral medicine as it seeks to be *bold* in the development of behavioral methods for the diagnosis and treatment of diverse medical disorders but *cautious* in what it claims (Schwartz & Weiss, 1977).

DEFINITION OF "BIOFEEDBACK"

In Chapter 17, Martin Orne, who attended the California Conference in 1969, recalled the controversy experienced there in deciding the name for this emerging area of study. The major alternatives proposed were "biofeedback" and "self-regulation." Although the term "biofeedback" has tended to predominate as a generic term, the linkage of the terms continues within the title of the journal *Biofeedback and Self-Regulation*. Frequently, the choice of a name for an area of study not only is a question of semantics, but also involves theoretical assumptions concerning the nature of the phenomenon. The issue of terms and their accompanying paradigms reemerges during the first round-table discussion of this volume in the form of defining "biofeedback."

The two poles of the definition of "biofeedback" may be characterized as the "broad" and "narrow" definitions. The narrow definition of "biofeedback" derives, in large part, from the paradigm of operant conditioning of autonomic responses (Miller, 1969; DiCara, 1970), which provided a major impetus for scientific interest in the biofeedback enterprise. Within this paradigm as it is presented in the animal literature, a discrete feedback signal is presented subsequent to the occurrence of a desired response. If the feedback signal leads to a satisfactory state within the organism, the probability of recurrence of the response is increased. The basic operant relationship is an S-R arc in which the temporal contiguity between the stimulus and the response is the only determining factor. This approach is abiological and acognitive.

The conceptual leap and procedural changes involved in the transformation of this laboratory model of operant conditioning to clinical biofeedback have been traced by Tursky (1979). When operant procedures were initially applied to uninformed human subjects, the results proved to be statistically significant but clinically unimportant, and subsequent studies actively instructed the subjects in the process of altering their responses. The dominant models for biofeedback increasingly concerned intraorganismic biological and cognitive processes of the following form: S → $\boxed{\text{O}}$ → R. With these developments in theory, the definition of "biofeedback" is broadened.

The broader definition of "biofeedback" allows that the biofeedback procedure may not necessarily lead to direct control of organ functioning, but that changes in physiological responses and related emotional responses may be the consequences of changes in life style, which may be fostered by a greater awareness of the psychophysiological consequences of alternative response styles. In practice, biofeedback may be only one technique within a multimodal treatment package. In this broader definition, biofeedback becomes merged with behavioral medicine's approach to altering medical disorders. The individual's conscious cognitive processes are presumed major vehicles for effecting change, and the specific contribution of high-density feedback to this process may be of marginal importance.

In order to consider these multifaceted consequences of a particular definition of biofeedback, it will be instructive to examine the several alternative paradigms used within the biofeedback literature, which are too often intertwined and muddled. The network of meanings contained in the paradigms has consequences that are usually only implied and rarely explicitly contrasted with alternative examples.

ALTERNATIVE PARADIGMS FOR PRODUCTION OF SPECIFIC BIOFEEDBACK EFFECTS

The major derivative theories are represented in this volume. A listing of these alternative theories is presented in Table 2, which also includes additional factors that may affect clinical results.

Although there is overlap in the formulations of several of the theories, each

TABLE 2. Paradigms Used in Clinical Biofeedback

1. Operant conditioning
2. Response learning
3. Bioengineering
4. Response discrimination/control
5. Motor learning/rehabilitation
6. Systems disregulation
7. Multimodal therapy/life style change
8. Relaxation therapy
9. Instructional effects
10. Placebo
    a. Changing sensory inputs
    b. Belief/faith
    c. Spontaneous processes/natural history
    d. Interpersonal influences

presents a unique perspective and is validated by supporting data from either clinical or experimental studies. A synthesis of thes perspectives that would ultimately address the mind–body problem remains a task for the future.

The ordering of the items in the list approximates a corresponding change in the breadth of the implied definition of "biofeedback" in each item; the movement is from narrow to broad definitions. The first-listed paradigms are primarily concerned with noncognitive or biologically determined modes of information processing, but cognitive processes become increasingly important in the later-listed paradigms.

An experimental paradigm contains an implicit guide for future research. Although, as exemplified in the chapters and commentaries by Brener, Schwartz, Tursky, Furedy and Riley, and Mulholland, there are alternatives to a simple operant paradigm for specific biofeedback effects, these paradigms have been exploited relatively rarely in the search for specific biofeedback effects. These paradigms or theories direct attention not only to the biological and psychological constraints operating during the biofeedback experiment, but also to psychobiological potential and flexibility.

One of the manifestations of the attempt to bridge the cognitive–physiological dichotomy that emerges in this volume is the notion of the biological meaning of the feedback signal. This concept appears in a number of presentations. In the combined classical and operant procedures described by Riley and Furedy, the classical procedures are used to lend stimulus value to the feedback signal. Tursky's use of the concept of selective associability recognizes the biologically determined meaning of particular stimuli. Brudny acknowledges that the use of visual feedback may be particularly potent in muscle rehabilitation because of the evolutionarily determined relationship between visual and motor systems.

The systems disregulation theory (Schwartz, 1980), perhaps more than any other behavioral medicine approach, aspires to bridge the cognitive–biological dichotomy characteristic of much of the theory-building concerned with biofeedback.

The fundamental concepts of general systems theory are (1) interaction among the component units of the system, and (2) the emergence of properties in which the interaction of the components yields a quantitative or qualitative difference not characteristic of any subset of the total system.

Within the context of biofeedback, this approach may lead investigators to search for that combination of factors (i.e., psychosocial, motivational, and physiological), involved in a disease process within an individual and possibly amenable to intervention, either using an approach of direct organ control or, alternatively, seeking to develop that unique combination of treatment approaches that yields clinical results in a given disorder. In either case, the systems approach requires the development of factorial and/or multivariate research designs in order to identify these interactive effects. Although it is conceptually elegant to discuss the possibility of interactive processes, it is much more difficult to demonstrate the efficacy of a multidimensional treatment package.

There is, however, merit to the recommendation of multivariate and factorial designs. A factorial study of patients in rehabilitation that includes measures of patients' physiological and motivational status, as well as characteristics of the feedback display, might lead to an understanding of the interaction of factors; such an understanding, in turn, may eventuate in more effective prescriptive treatment.

The often-repeated recommendation for studies on individual differences heard during this conference may best be carried out, we believe, within a multivariate design in which there is subclassification of the patient group. Anxiety and pain syndromes may be particularly amenable to multifactorial analyses, which have the potential for examining the interdependence of physiological, motivational, and psychosocial influences upon the clinical course of symptoms.

REFERENCES

Cohen, H. D., Graham, C., Fotopoulos, S. S., & Cook, M. R. A double-blind methodology for biofeedback research. *Psychophysiology,* 1977, *14,* 603–608.

Davidson, R. J., & Schwartz, G. The psychobiology of relaxation and related states: A multi-process theory. In D. Mostofsky (Ed.), *Behavior control and modification of physiological activity.* Englewood Cliffs, N.J.: Prentice-Hall, 1976.

DiCara, L. V. Learning in the autonomic nervous system. *Scientific American,* 1970, *222,* 30–39.

Luiselli, J. K., Marholin, D., Steinman, D. L., & Steinman, W. M. Assessing the effects of relaxation training. *Behavior Therapy,* 1979, *10,* 663–668.

Miller, N. E. Learning of visceral and glandular responses. *Science,* 1969, *163,* 434–445.

Schwartz, G. E. Behavioral medicine and systems theory: A new synthesis. *National Forum,* Winter 1980, pp. 25–30.

Schwartz, G. E., & Weiss, S. M. *Yale conference on behavioral medicine* [DHEW Publication No. (NIH) 78-1424]. Washington, D.C.: U.S. Department of Health, Education and Welfare, 1977.

Smith, J. C. Meditation as psychotherapy: A review of the literature. *Psychological Bulletin,* 1975, *82,* 558–564.

Smith, J. C. Psychotherapeutic effects of transcendental meditation with controls for expectation of relief and daily sitting. *Journal of Consulting and Clinical Psychology,* 1976, *44,* 630–637.

Tursky, B. Biofeedback research methodology: Need for effective change. In R. Gatchel & K. Price (Eds.), *Clinical application of biofeedback: Appraisal and status.* New York: Plenum, 1979.

West, M. Meditation and the EEG. *Psychological Medicine,* 1980, *10,* 369–375.

AUTHOR INDEX

SUBJECT INDEX